Personal Financial

Management

Second edition

Nico Swart

JUTΛ

Personal Financial Management
First published in 1996
Second edition 2002
Reprinted 2004
Reprinted February 2006
Reprinted March 2007
Reprinted September 2007
Reprinted April 2009

Copyright © Juta & Co. Ltd, 2002
PO Box 24309
Lansdowne 7779

ISBN 978 07021 5514 7

Editing and proofreading: Laurie Rose-Innes
Design and typesetting: Orchard Publishing
Cover design: Orchard Publishing
Indexing: Ethné Clarke

Printed and bound by Mega Digital, Cape Town

The Publisher has made every effort to obtain permission for and acknowledge the use of copyright material. Should any infringement have occurred, please contact the Publisher and every effort will be made to rectify omissions or errors in the event of a reprint or new edition.

Preface

This book, the second edition of *Personal financial management*, is still the only South African academic publication dealing with the field of personal finances. Because of their scope, chapters on 'Productivity planning' and 'Self-management' have had to be omitted. Nevertheless, this book provides the best available structure for, and comprehensive overview of, the field of personal finances.

Chapters on 'Starting a business: entrepreneurship', 'Buying an existing business', and 'Buying a franchise' have been included in the companion volume to this book by Nico Swart 2002. *Starting and buying your own business or a franchise*. Cape Town: Juta. Readers are advised to read/study these books together.

Despite closed doors, monopolies, bureaucracies and very high cost, this pioneering work on personal financial planning has borne fruit. After a decade of perseverance, the field has been established as an undergraduate and postgraduate academic subject.

This book deals with the best life skill any individual could have, namely the financial life skill. It should be included in all degree or diploma courses, even if only as an optional subject. No one should be without this knowledge.

To be able to do personal financial planning, knowledge of a number of personal financial planning areas is essential. Every one of these planning areas is important and comprises factors that can have far-reaching positive or negative financial implications for the individual. For the purposes of this book, the following planning areas are distinguished:
- career planning;
- income tax planning;
- estate planning;
- investment planning;
- protection planning;
- credit planning;
- health care planning;
- retirement planning; and
- emigration planning.

All these important planning areas must be taken into account during the personal financial planning process. By doing so, the individual will be able to take informed, personal financial decisions, because as many factors as possible will have been considered during the decision-making process. Ensure that you realise the extent to which each of these planning areas can influence your own financial future, as well as your financial independence after retirement.

The concept 'personal financial planning' is nothing new, especially in the times in which we are presently living. Research reveals that, in South Africa, less than one out of every ten individuals is financially independent on retirement. Such statistics are indicative of the fact that most people do not know what personal financial planning entails or how to undertake such planning.

Consequently, it is the purpose of this book to identify and, where possible, quantify the numerous factors that can influence a person's finances either positively or negatively.

Personal financial management is a field of study that affects all people. Persons with knowledge of basic money matters can take responsibility for their own financial future themselves. These skills can also be transferred to their children and, thus, ensure that they have a positive financial future. There are more job opportunities for people with this knowledge, be it as employee or as successful entrepreneur and businessperson. Business success is hereby increased.

The South African challenge

The financial empowerment of the South African population is a key challenge facing South Africa. Currently, the South African educational system does not cater for the structured and targeted education and training of school children, students and adults in managing their personal financial matters. This leads to a financially uneducated community that has no insight into its financial affairs. However, early financial education would have made a difference to these people.

Furthermore, the planning of personal financial matters does not exist at all in certain target groups (these include certain culture groups, the unemployed, the youth, retrenched and retired workers and people in rural areas). As such, these people do not know how to deal with money matters, with a resultant negative impact on the micro enterprise, the economy and the personal financial situation of millions of people in this country. This way of living has become obsolete in a global community that regards finances as a key factor in creating a prosperous livelihood for all citizens, leading to an enhanced quality of life for all. The poverty spiral becomes a negative cycle from which these groups struggle to escape. This results in rising crime, violence, theft, corruption and protest action, which create related economic problems. The cost is high in terms of wasted resources, lost production and loss of confidence in the future of the country.

South Africa needs educational strategies that are focused on developing its human capacity, that is the development of skills, attitudes and behaviours that are necessary to survive and prosper as a country, and which individuals need to exhibit in the multiple roles they play as community members, family members, learners, workers, consumers and global citizens. The National Skills Development Strategy has as its objective an integrated skills development system that will enable South Africa to achieve improved competency levels, and which promotes social development and economic growth through a focus on education, training and employment services. Business enterprises need to support the national initiatives by introducing structured and targeted education and training (learning) programmes that will help develop the nation's human capacity. Human capacity needs to be developed within the four core domains of productive and purposeful human interaction that lie at the heart of human capacity, namely: family life, livelihood, civic affairs and environmental stewardship. Business enterprises can make a tremendous contribution to solving the needs of individuals in the area of personal financial planning, education and training. Business enterprises are currently unaware of the important role they can play in developing human capacity and facilitating the wealth of individuals, as far as the provision of structured and targeted education and training (learning) programmes is concerned.

Learning programmes must incorporate a learning science that teaches people how to participate as global and responsible citizens. These learning programmes should provide learners with potential productive interactions in which they can engage and that allow them to contribute to the development of their nation, communities and families. Participation opportunities span the course of a person's life cycle and vary accordingly. They include the opportunity to gain a good education, secure a livelihood, influence political or civic affairs, promote family development and protect the environment. Among other things, such opportunities also encompass the chance to partake in recreation, cultural events and entrepreneurial behaviour.

Furthermore, learning programmes should be flexible, accessible and customised to the specific needs of the targeted learner audience. They should take cognisance of the specific learning preferences of the audience, with due consideration to their cultural background and level of education. The learning programmes should inspire a willingness and deep motivation for adopting the values and attitudes required to bring about the desired behaviours. In addition, the learning programmes should empower the learners with the necessary self-management skills to sustain the newly acquired values, attitudes and behaviours.

Nico Swart
July 2002

About the author

Nico Swart, South Africa's Mr. Personal Financial Management, is subject head of Personal Financial Management and Real Estate at the University of South Africa. He has a passion for community service, has written many informative study guides on financial matters, co-authored several books, published hundreds of articles, participated in more than 100 radio talks and has also appeared on television. Nico is the author of 18 books on personal finances, including *Personal financial management, Basic financial life skills, How to plan your money matters after school and university, Investing your package: All you need to know* and *Starting or buying your own business or a franchise.*

He is the academic father of the education and training of employees in personal financial planning. In 1993 he completed a doctorate research

proposal and delivered national and international papers in this regard. Nico has conducted extensive research on personal financial planning models in South Africa, and has received numerous awards, such as annual merit awards, the Researcher of the Year Award and the Principal's Prize.

He is currently writing a series of books aimed at uplifting and educating people in financial matters, in order to contribute to the economic and social development of the South African population. Nico has a business background, has provided financial advice to millions of people and has contributed to the development of one of the world's leading personal financial planning models with patent rights (since 1997) in the USA, Canada, United Kingdom and Australia for a period of 20 years.

Contents

CHAPTER 1

PERSONAL FINANCIAL PLANNING

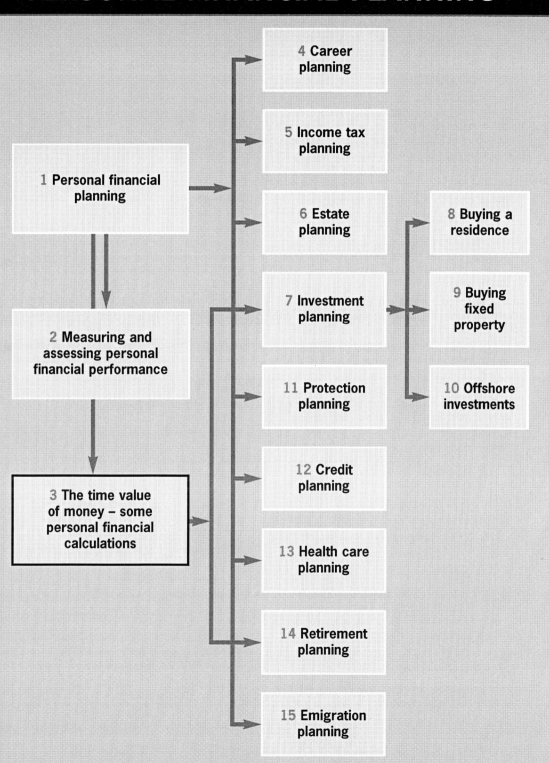

1.1 LEARNING OUTCOMES

After studying this chapter, you will be able to:
- Explain the importance of personal financial planning.
- Recognise your position in the financial planning cycle.
- Identify the different steps in the personal financial planning process.
- Explain the advantages of personal financial planning.
- Recognise the different personal financial planning areas.

1.2 INTRODUCTION

As a result of constant change, all people are continually confronted with new circumstances and situations for which they require answers. Uncertainty, and its result, stress, may well be the most common 'illness' of our time. In the case of an individual, this uncertainty eventually culminates in a lack of trust in his or her financial position and future. Because all people consist of body and soul, it is almost impossible for humans to envisage a happy future without adequate sustenance.

Not that life revolves around money, or an abundance thereof, but unfortunately the existence of all people is inescapably linked to money, whether we like it or not. Receiving a salary because we are presently employed is one thing – the efficient management and planning thereof is something else entirely, because a prerequisite is a knowledge of personal financial management. This knowledge is the most important life skill any person can have, as should become clear from a study of this book.

Although it is almost impossible to provide concepts and answers regarding all aspects of personal finance in any single book, the most important aspects are addressed and illustrated in this one.

The main secret of personal financial management and planning is to be aware of the many factors that may influence your personal financial situation positively or negatively at the present time or in the future.

- Study the many factors mentioned in this book.
- Be aware of your present financial situation – needs and financial risks.
- Determine your immediate, short-, medium- and long-term goals.

Plan your financial future, in other words what you are going to do to get from where you are now to where you want to be in the future. This will be different for every individual.

The second secret is to know what is meant by the term 'personal financial planning'.

- What is meant by personal financial planning?
- What different personal financial planning areas constitute personal financial planning?

If all people were to know and understand these two secrets, they would also understand that the timely financial planning required would eliminate many current and future financial uncertainties. After gathering information on these secrets, an individual can then consult an expert in a particular field of personal money matters. This means the 'right' questions can be asked, so as to get the 'right' answers in the light of your personal financial situation and planning.

In my view, the greatest uncertainties in the minds of South Africans (and I assume the same holds good for other countries) are created by the following three factors:
- constantly changing legislation (in all areas of money matters – just think about income tax, estate duty and capital gains tax);
- the development of hundreds of new financial and insurance products; and
- the introduction and presentation of these two factors in and by the media:
  - to inform and warn the public, on the one hand, and
  - as part of the marketing strategies of financial institutions, insurance companies and brokers (particularly those with great influence in the media) to attract investments from the public, on the other.

What is the greatest mistake the public makes regarding personal financial management and planning? The answer is quite simple. People confuse personal financial planning with investment planning. As you will notice later, personal financial planning consists of a number of different planning areas. Investment planning is only one of the various areas of personal financial planning. A lack of knowledge as to what personal financial planning entails is the major cause of this confusion.

What is the biggest mistake brokers make? Brokers want to and need to earn commission from investments in order to make a living. Products are therefore often marketed with inadequate emphasis, in many cases, on personal financial planning for the individual (potential investor).

All of us constantly strive to satisfy our needs and improve our economic welfare. Research on the financial independence of people in South Africa has shown, however, that success in the quest for economic welfare and independence is less common that we might expect: only one out of ten people is financially independent after retirement (Goldman 1983:8). Personal financial planning, which is so often neglected, can make a difference. The personal financial results we achieve are not a matter of luck – they depend on the efforts of the individual (Block *et al.* 1998:3): 'Luck comes when preparedness and opportunity get together.'

In the absence of personal financial planning, people's financial positions during and particularly in the last quarter of their lives frequently are not as they would have hoped. Amling & Droms (1986:3) point out that financial independence does not necessarily suggest great wealth, but rather that the individual has made optimum use of his or her income, irrespective of the level of that income. A higher level of income allows people to achieve financial independence at an earlier stage. Personal financial planning is becoming increasingly complex, for the following reasons, amongst others:

- changing economic conditions;
- the changing political climate;
- inflation (the declining purchasing power of money);
- the large number of financial institutions;
- advertisements in the media;
- a multitude of financial instruments and products; and
- conflicting financial advice.

Although we are, therefore, faced with circumstances beyond our control, we have means and instruments at our disposal to adapt to circumstances. These means and instruments can be used in a personal financial plan. This plan may vary from elementary (limited financial means) to extensive planning (for example, when someone has a large estate).

1.3 CONCEPTUAL FRAMEWORK

Effectively applying an individual's or household's resources is a prerequisite for efficient personal financial management and planning. The same can be said for the application of the resources of a business or a whole country. Every individual, household, business or country has only limited resources, but these resources must be applied to satisfy unlimited needs. This is only possible if there is efficient personal financial management, business management and national management.

This is why management training in and expertise regarding money matters plays such a crucial role in the lives of individuals, households, businesses and the country as a whole. The two diagrams below illustrate the role that the required training (i.e. knowledge and the application thereof) plays.

Exactly the same can be said about managing an individual's or household's money matters.

DIAGRAM 1.1 The influence of management training on a country
(Source: Swart & Coetzee 2000:150)

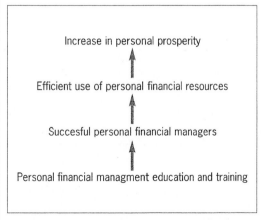

DIAGRAM 1.2 The influence of management training on an individual's money matters
(Source: Swart & Coetzee 2000:150)

Therefore, knowledge of personal financial management enables each individual and household to make better and more informed choices about the application of limited resources to reach financial goals. In the case of a household, these resources consist, amongst others, of assets, skills, trained persons, knowledge, money, equipment and entrepreneurial spirit (also a skill).

The financial function of an enterprise comprises the flow of funds to and from the enterprise. It, therefore, consists of the acquisition of funds (the financial decision) and the employment of funds (the investment decision) in order to achieve the primary objective of the enterprise, namely:

- *Maximum prosperity for the owners of the enterprise over the long term.* In an enterprise, the person responsible for the financial function is the financial manager. The financial manager must remain informed of all variables that may affect the enterprise. In this way he or she will be in a position to make those vital financial decisions that will contribute towards attaining the primary objective of the enterprise.

So we may ask what the financial function of a household would be. What applies to an enterprise also applies to a household. In a household, the financial function comprises the flow of funds to and from the household. Funds have to be acquired and employed in order to achieve the primary objective of the household, namely:

- *To attain financial independence after retirement.* In a household, the financial manager is that person who manages and looks after the household's financial affairs. This person takes the lead when it comes to making financial decisions that will affect that household. Financial decisions can only be effective if the person concerned knows exactly what factors affect the household's financial affairs.

1.3.1 Management

It should be clear by now that the money matters of all households should be managed. However, management is a process (the management process) that consists of the following elements:

- planning (what to do);
- organising (how to do it);
- leading (to keep the job moving); and
- controlling (comparing results with plans).

We will now briefly discuss each of these elements.

Planning
Planning gives direction to the individual's or the household's finances. It also reduces risk and uncertainty and helps to avoid crisis management. Crisis management means you only pay attention to a financial matter when an out-of-hand situation occurs. Planning involves goal-setting and the development of plans to attain these goals. Goals should be measurable and attainable. Different plans ought to be evaluated in order to choose the best plan to attain each goal. If the best plan is too expensive, another plan should be chosen. When you plan, you look at and consider your financial strong and weak points as well as the financial opportunities and threats in your environment.

Organising
When you have set your financial goals and objectives and know how you are going to attain them, you start with the organising process. Organising involves the allocation of resources in order to execute the plans, the clarification of authority and responsibility and the division of work between household members.

Leading
The person who manages the household's money matters must also take the lead in financial matters. The members of a household must voluntarily follow this person's decisions on personal finances. The financial manager or leader should at all times try to ensure good relations amongst family members where money matters are concerned. If there is conflict, this must be resolved and managed through sound communication.

Controlling
Managing also includes the controlling of the resources of the household. Controlling involves a comparison between the goals and the actual performance (results) of the individual or household. During the controlling process you should concentrate on serious deviations only.

The elements of the management process (planning, organising, leading and controlling) are applicable to each of the different personal financial planning areas (see Section 1.8).

Financial decisions are becoming increasingly complex because of the future demands of the economy. Medical progress has meant that people tend to live much longer (up to 20 years longer) than in the past, with the result that their financial resources can more easily become exhausted. On the other hand, diseases have increased to such an extent that people have to make sure that they have sufficient funds to cope with serious operations, disability and lengthy illness leading to job loss (for example, medical care necessitated by dreaded diseases).

The world economy is collapsing and famine occurs even in First World countries. Famine has increased among retired people and there is no solution to the economic collapse in Third World countries and the thousands of people who die of hunger every day. Whereas in the past family members were able to care for each other, this is no longer possible. It is up to each family unit to ensure that it is in a position to meet its own future financial needs.

As we can see, financial planning is becoming vitally important to each and every household. So what is financial planning? Mittra (1990:5) defines it as follows:

Personal financial planning is the organisation of an individual's financial and personal data for the purpose of developing a strategic plan to constructively manage income, assets and liabilities to meet near- and long-term goals and objectives.

According to Botha (1985:2), personal financial planning means that objectives, desires and needs are expressed in rands and cents in terms of the individual's perceptions, and are manifested in existing and future provisions, also expressed in rands and cents. Consequently, it is possible to determine to what extent shortfalls (inadequate provision for the person's needs) or surpluses (excessive provision for the person's needs) may arise at present or in the future.

Of course, it is very difficult or even impossible to do any planning if you do not have a job and income. Getting a job (as part of career planning), in order to earn an income, is therefore a prerequisite for further planning.

In South Africa, millions of poor people have no knowledge of money matters. Those who do have a job, may have no credit record, and can therefore not gain access to financing for other needs. This is why a new micro-lending industry (as distinct from former 'loan sharks') has come into existence. This industry is controlled by the Micro Finance Regulatory Council, and in January 2001 encompassed about five million micro-borrowers.

For our purposes, the money skills wheel in Diagram 1.3 may be used to explain personal financial planning in South Africa.

The wheel consists of six areas that include the following: basic planning, budgeting, debt/financing, retirement, investments and starting a new business. Say we divide the country into three groups or classes: the poor, the middle class and the rich. Furthermore, we have to accept that there will be those who do plan or simply act like members of another class.

We may define personal financial planning as follows:
Personal financial planning involves the determination of immediate, short-, medium- and long-term goals by means of a personal financial planning process based on your own identified lifestyle, phase(s) of the life cycle, risks and needs in all the various personal financial planning areas in order to be able to retire with financial independence.

Firstly, the poor class, representing the masses, will aim their planning mainly at basic planning, budgeting and debt/financing. The lives of these countless millions mainly revolve around credit planning and financing planning for their livelihoods. This is the main reason why so many 'loan sharks' could, until recently, lend money to the poor at ridiculously high interest rates (for example, up to 500% per year). The real problem is that these people have no credit record or, particularly, any knowledge of money matters.

Secondly, the middle class should include all six areas in their planning, and even enter new planning areas, for example emigration planning.

Thirdly, the rich class will place far greater emphasis on investment planning, their own businesses and particularly lifestyle investments.

However, you should never simply accept that the middle and rich classes have adequate knowledge regarding money matters, especially not what is meant by personal financial planning.

Personal financial planning has to do with your life and your money matters, and not:
- what your neighbours are doing;
- what somebody is doing overseas; or
- what the world's richest people have done (even though this sounds very interesting if quoted somewhere – we may as well learn from them, in particular about the value of hard work and focus).

Yes, personal financial planning is unique for every individual and household, because it depends on your own risk profile, risks, needs and financial goals. Somebody else's investment may be the wrong type of investment for you. Read more about this in Section 1.6.

1.4 THE FINANCIAL PLANNING CYCLE

Planning requires anticipating both known and unknown future events. Such events have a bearing on an individual's present position in the financial

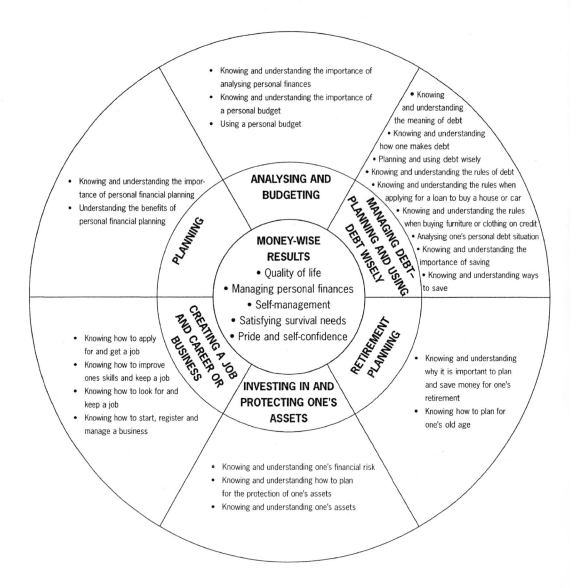

DIAGRAM 1.3: Money skills wheel
(Source: Swart & Coetzee 2000:52)

planning cycle. Table 1.1 illustrates the financial planning cycle.

From Table 1.1 it is apparent that our financial priorities change as we move through the planning cycle. Within the same cycle, people's priorities and preferences will change according to their current individual circumstances. Similarly, individuals' planning and priorities will differ in accordance with the different levels at which they find themselves in terms of Maslow's hierarchy of human needs. This hierarchy is represented in Figure 1.1.

As our needs at a specific level (for example, level 1) are met, we are motivated to meet those at the next level (level 2). The attainment of the higher levels becomes the driving force and so personal financial planning should be directed at higher levels.

Figure 1.2 illustrates a similar structure, which is based on accepted principles of financial planning, where the meeting of needs rises from level one to level four.

TABLE 1.1 **The financial planning cycle (life cycle)**
(Source: Amling & Droms 1986:6)

CYCLE	Formative years	High school, tertiary study years	Career-working years	Period after retirement
PRIORITIES		• Career planning • Budget • Saving	• Budget • Housing • Saving • Investments • Credit control • Income tax • Retirement planning • Estate planning • Insurance	• Budget • Investment management • Estate planning

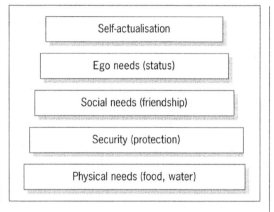

FIGURE 1.1 **Maslow's hierarchy of human needs**
(Source: Goldman 1983:16)

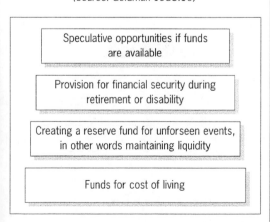

FIGURE 1.2 **Progressive satisfaction**
(Source: Goldman 1983:16)

Figure 1.3 further illustrates this viewpoint by describing the needs structure in monetary terms.

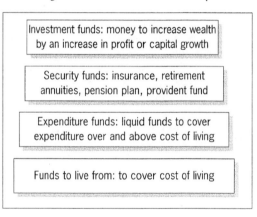

FIGURE 1.3 **Progressive satisfaction (monetary terms)**
(Source: Goldman 1983:16)

1.5 YOUR OWN PERSONAL FINANCIAL PLANNING

Perhaps the most important aspect of personal financial planning is to remember that you are engaged in personal financial planning for yourself and your household. It is, therefore, a prerequisite firstly to determine where you and your family fit into the following 'picture':
• you/your phase(s) in the human life cycle;
• age;

Personal financial planning | 7

- gender;
- marital status
  - unmarried
  - cohabiting
  - married (or planning to marry)
  - divorced (or planning to separate/divorce)
  - widower/widow;
- religious orientation;
- gay/lesbian;
- fortune hunter (through marriage, divorce, multiple divorces);
- standard of living;
- lifestyle;
- inheritances already received;
- a package taken;
- current financial situation;
- current investments;
- whether you wish to emigrate;
- household's life skills;
- unemployed;
- employee;
- employer/own business (local or overseas);
- both employee and employer;
- your political viewpoints;
- risk profile (do you avoid risk or do you like risk);
- individual and household risks;
- individual and household needs;
- where in South Africa you recently immigrated to;
- personal health (or family member with a chronic or life-threatening illness);
- physically or mentally disabled family members;
- number of dependants;
- number of family members who earn a living;
- unrehabilitated insolvent;
- your antenuptial contract (married in community of property, with antenuptial contract excluding accrual or with antenuptial contract including accrual);
- criminals in the household and/or amongst in-laws;
- previous sequestration and/or liquidation;
- current legislation regarding the whole field of personal finances (for example capital gains tax);
- spouse's estate being administered;
- parent(s) with child(ren);
- already retired;
- I/we had a child late in life; and
- maintenance obligations due to divorce settlement.

You must then determine which of the situations above apply to yourself and your household, and do your personal financial planning accordingly. Remember that the various family members should do their own personal financial planning, but should also know where they fit into the planning for the whole household. The picture for every individual family member is, therefore, added to that for the combined household.

Next we will briefly look at more illustrations of the human life cycle. Note where your family members fit into the cycle, and adapt your planning accordingly. Have another look at Table 1.1 and decide for yourself which priorities/planning activities are required for every member of the family and the household.

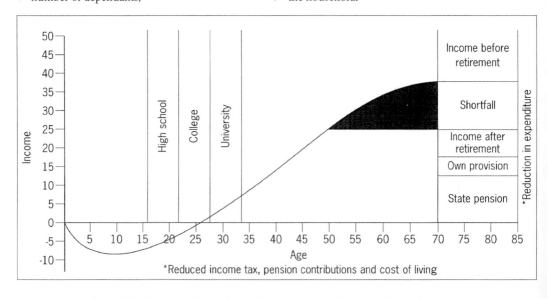

FIGURE 1.4 **Human life cycle and the shortfall of income after retirement**
(*Source: Adapted from Amling & Droms 1986:506*)

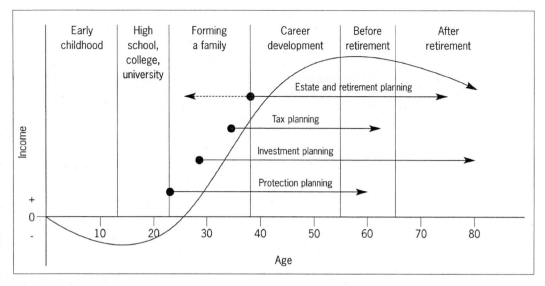

FIGURE 1.5 The personal financial planning cycle over a person's lifetime
(Source: Adapted from Gitman & Joehnk 1987:12)

1.5.1 An example of personal financial planning for women

Women today must be able to stand on their own feet financially. They must become actively involved in their own, as well as their household's personal financial planning. The days when women could stand on the sidelines and leave money matters to the men are gone for good.

The financial needs of women have changed considerably in recent years – or is this merely being noticed for the first time nowadays? Traditionally the man was responsible for the household's money matters, regardless of whether one out of 100 knew anything about money matters or not. Until recently, women accepted this state of affairs.

Numerous factors brought women to the realisation that they have a financial life with financial independence. Prominent among these factors has been the information explosion (in the media) and the many financial products that have been brought to their attention.

Women have unique needs because their careers are often interrupted, for example by pregnancy or illness, such as breast cancer. Just as any individual's financial needs differ, so women's financial needs differ in accordance with the following situations: working as employee; working as employer (own business); unemployed; unmarried with/without children; married with/without children; divorced; living together; or successive marriages.

The phase of the human life cycle in which every woman finds herself will also determine the planning that has to be done, namely: youthful years (20–30);

family years (30–40); career years (40–50); pre-retirement years (50–60); retirement years (55+).

With due consideration of the specific phase of life and marital status of every woman, the following aspects of money matters should receive special attention, namely: the budget (an administrative system, income and expenditure, as well as conflict); tax; estate; investment; protection; and retirement planning. Now let us take a brief look at the basic financial planning that a woman should do in each of these planning areas to ensure that she, too, can retire financially independent, with or without the financial assistance of a man/her husband.

Empower yourself

Before you can plan, you must know what is at stake and how the planning process works. Every woman must empower herself in the area of personal finance by obtaining as much information about it as possible. It is advisable to buy books written by specialists. If women are serious about money matters they can purchase a book on personal financial management (which will cover most aspects of personal finances).

A budget

Every women should draw up a budget, whether for herself or for her partner. A married woman, or one who is living with a partner must, therefore, help to draw up a household budget. Inputs must be made and she must know what each family member's role is in drawing up and interpreting the budget (how much may you spend/receive?). Financial conflict, a major reason for divorce, can thus be reduced or avoided.

However, a prerequisite for planning and a budget is an efficient system of household records in which all documentary evidence of income, expenses, agreements, guarantees, investments (including policy documents) and loans (including mortgages) are kept. Place the various documents in files according to your own record system. This is important for your budget, income tax purposes and drawing up your annual financial statements.

Your financial risks and needs

It is important to know what risks you as a woman are subject to. You must also know that these risks necessarily determine your financial needs in the immediate, short-, medium- and long-term. Furthermore, these needs (risks) differ: they are constant (food, clothing, accommodation), increasing (cost of living), decreasing (mortgage to be paid), fluctuating (emergency situations in a household), permanent (estate duty or provision for retirement), temporary (a child at university or a bank loan to be repaid) or future (debt after your death). It is, therefore, simply logical that no two women will plan the same, and that various actions and financial products will have to be used to meet these needs.

Let us briefly look at your risks (and possible provisions):

- loss of income as a result of
  - death (a life policy, group insurance)
  - illness (medical insurance)
  - disability (disability insurance);
- loss of property as a result of
  - death/fire (home, self, short-term insurance, mortgage – life policy)
  - car (short-term insurance)
  - household contents (short-term insurance);
- personal liability as a result of
  - home-ownership (accidentally injuring your neighbour – short-term insurance)
  - car-ownership (injuring a pedestrian with your car – short-term insurance)
  - malpractices (guilty of something regarded as a malpractice by the law – insurance that covers legal liability);
- business risks (business insurance);
- estate duty (life policy or trust with donations and loans);
- estate administration costs (any investment);
- retirement (long-term investments with capital growth);
- estate planning (will and/or trust);
- too much debt accumulated in pursuit of desires (use debt to satisfy desires and to acquire assets with capital growth);

- inflation (investments with capital growth; also adjust insurance policies for inflation);
- income tax (use legitimate tax avoidance if possible);
- constantly changing legislation (be informed and consult a broker who is well-informed);
- interest rate risk (interest rates may decline while you are dependent on an income derived from interest for your survival – invest, e.g. for a fixed two-year term);
- market risk (overseas markets may change and cause a decline in local share and unit trust prices);
- business risk (e.g. the business in which you invested is very vulnerable to a recession);
- financial risk (e.g. you finance 95% of your business with debt – interest costs that make your instalment very high);
- exchange risk (investors who invest internationally are exposed to this risk, as well as persons who operate an import-export business);
- national risk (e.g. investments in politically unstable countries); and
- health risk (do health planning as a prerequisite for retirement planning).

Self-insurance is dangerous

Do not try to practice self-insurance by creating (alone or with friends) some emergency fund or other. This is too risky. Rather pay your short-term insurance premiums.

As a woman you should pay special attention to financial needs that may arise from death, disability and retirement. A broker can help you to combine provisions for these needs.

Your financial goals

Before goals, in other words where you want to go (point B), can be determined, you first have to know exactly where you are (point A – your financial situation). A prerequisite for any planning is knowledge of such things as the following: family particulars such as names; ages; marital status; conjugal assets disposition; financial statements; fixed assets; movable assets; cash; other investments such as life insurance policies (obtain a summary from all institutions with which you have contracted policies); death and disability benefits; pension benefits; group benefits; expected inheritances; and current and potential sources of income.

Make sure that you know your risk profile (the amount of risk you are prepared to assume and for what return on what kind of investment), and that you are clear about your political and economic views concerning the country.

Now your current financial situation must be compared with your identified financial needs. The financial needs, for which you have yet to make short- and long-term provision, now become your short-, medium- and long-term goals.

You will notice that immediate goals precede the setting and achievement of short-, medium- and long-term goals.

Immediate goals (settle all debts):
- study debt;
- bank overdraft;
- credit card;
- clothing and other accounts;
- loan to family member;
- car; and
- home loan.

Short-term goals:
- study fund for children;
- start a new career to provide additional income for living expenses; and
- open an offshore South African bank account for each child.

Medium-term goals:
- create an investment for each child as a deposit on their own house;
- start an investment portfolio for each child;
- buy a second property from the proceeds of a second job;
- establish a trust for each child; and
- have a knee operation during second career.

Long-term goals:
- supplement retirement provision (your package);
- retire at age 60 (or 55);
- travel for two months of the year; and
- buy a holiday home.

Determine your own short-, medium- and long-term goals.

As you can see from the following planning process, goals can only be achieved if the household budget can accommodate them. The planning process is shown in Diagram 1.4.

Analyse your existing financial situation
This first step in the process is to do a situation analysis concerning the individual's or household's assets, liabilities and unique financial situation. The income and balance statements serve as aids here.

Set short-, medium- and long-term goals
Every individual or household should set goals for these three time horizons. The goals must also be

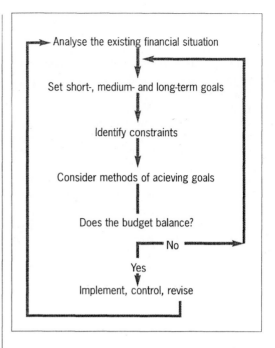

DIAGRAM 1.4 The planning process

arranged in order of priority. This gives direction to the process, while at the same time norms are set for the measurement of results.

Identify your limitations
There are always external influences, beyond a person's control, that have to be taken into account in personal financial planning. These factors can be restrictive, or they may even be completely in conflict with personal goals. Examples of such factors are tax, untimely death, retirement, illness, property risks and liability risks.

Consider methods of meeting goals
The methods that can be used to achieve goals and aims, and also to minimise the identified constraints, must be carefully considered. Examples of such methods are the reduction of spending, securing credit, risk avoidance, loss prevention and control, different kinds of insurance, retirement annuities and other investments.

Does your budget balance?
It is critically important to have a budget that balances, which means that income must be equal to expenditure plus savings. A surplus or deficit indicates that the planning process requires further attention.

Implement, control and revise
If a short-term goal is to open a savings account for a child, it stands to reason that to achieve this goal,

you should visit a financial institution and open an account. Plans should be controlled and constantly adapted as circumstances change (marriage, death, a baby, divorce, receiving an inheritance, for example).

Are you an employee?

Remember that you can only earn as much as a particular occupation in a particular kind of business (e.g. computers) allows in a particular area (rural, urban, growth area). You must start investing for retirement from your very first cheque/salary, notably in a life insurance policy (a must for everybody because it can accommodate 90% of your financial risks/needs), unit trusts for capital growth, a retirement annuity to save money on income tax, and an offshore investment. Ask your employer to structure your remuneration package so that you pay as little income tax as possible.

Make sure that you join your employer's pension or provident fund as well as the medical aid fund of your employer. Also inform yourself of the benefits provided by your group insurance scheme (death and disability cover). Make sure that you include trauma insurance and AIDS cover in your life insurance policy. Invest in a home of your own as soon as possible.

Exercise financial discipline while you still have an income. Develop yourself at all times with a view to career planning and keep an up to date *curriculum vitae* (CV) handy.

Younger women should adopt a fairly risk-laden investment strategy, while middle-aged women should have a balanced investment portfolio that is less exposed to risk, and women who have retired, or are approaching retirement, must invest very conservatively (low risk).

Ensure that your will is valid and up to date and find out whether you need a trust for minor children, assets or offshore investments.

Are you unemployed?

Do not loose heart. Use your updated CV and consult as many friends, acquaintances and former colleagues as possible. Accept any 'ethical' work. Remember, the challenge in the short-term is to find employment while the long-term challenge is to keep your job in order to make investments for your retirement.

Are you an employer?

Employers particularly make use of retirement annuities and additional capital-growth investments for retirement planning purposes (failing a pension or provident fund). Women with a business of their own often have to conclude purchase-and-sale agreements in the case of joint ownership by several people (e.g. partnerships). By this means, each partner arranges for the other partner(s) to buy out his or her share in the event of his or her death. The amount of money needed to buy such a share is acquired by such measures as taking out partnership insurance on the lives of the partners. There are different forms of this type of insurance. Similarly, key-person insurance must be contracted where your business has such a person. In the event of such a person's death, the proceeds of the life insurance policy (taken out on the key person's life) can then be used to obtain the services of another person who can take the place of the deceased.

The same kind of personal financial planning is done as for an employee. Remember, the business derives an income, expenditures are deducted and a profit/loss arises. A salary is paid from profits, just as it is in the case of an employee, and the same financial planning follows.

Unmarried?

Unmarried women's planning is simpler than that of women who are married or divorced, or who have been married several times, because in these cases there are more often children to consider. Conflict about money matters is absent in the case of unmarried women, who are therefore in full control, provided they exercise financial discipline with a view to retirement. Decide for yourself what financial risks you are exposed to and how you are going to utilise your money over a lifetime. No estate duty would be payable if you were to bequeath your possessions to a charitable (or church) organisation after your death, which would allow you to maintain a higher standard of living because you do not have to make provision for estate duty. A trust can also be used. Attend to the drafting of an antenuptial contract (ANC) if you are going to marry.

Married?

Even though money matters may 'look the same' for all women, further problems arise where your household's planning is concerned. The money matters and views of two people now have to be reconciled. Marriages frequently disintegrate because of money. The severe constraints hampering a marriage in or out of community of property with inclusion of the accrual system, is a further cause of conflict in the household. Your marital goods dispensation will determine for the rest of your life how you may buy assets, whether you need your marriage partner's signature (consent) if you want to dispose of your own assets, whether you may change investments without consent, whether you can take out a bond on the communal home for such purposes as furthering your career (your spouse may refuse to add his signature to the bond application), whether you may buy or sell assets, how your own or your joint assets will pass by inheritance, and the extent to which you can do estate planning (to mention but a few).

So how does conflict about money matters arise? Some of the reasons are: marrying without any knowledge of money matters; attitudes and views of spouses-to-be concerning money matters are not discussed before the wedding (the reasons for and content of their ANC included); spouses want to remain in control of their own funds; spending habits (e.g. overspending or parsimony/conservatism) are carried over from parental homes (rightly or wrongly) into the marriages; stress or depression in households causes overspending in an effort to fill gaps or make up for a sense of deficiency in individuals, which often leads to a debt crisis; one spouse only wants to invest (for retirement), while the other only spends (to enjoy life now); the one who has more possessions at the outset thinks he or she, therefore, automatically knows more about money and has to control the household's affairs; the choice of specific investments as well as reinvestments; the choice between a car or a house, or between cars; different attitudes towards risk; different financial goals; natural differences between men and women; spouses fail to discuss their financial needs; and the individual spouses do not keep funds for themselves in order to make their own financial investments and serve their own particular needs and goals.

Children make further demands on your planning. From their birth you must ensure that the necessary investments (for capital growth) are made to serve such needs as a matric farewell function, tertiary studies, a wedding or two, a deposit on a car for children, and so on. Study costs currently amount to thousands of rands, and a life insurance policy should be taken out for each child, or an investment can be made in unit trusts. If such provision is not made, unemployed children (after leaving school or after tertiary study) will derail their parents' household budget and there will be no funds to provide for their parents' retirement. Teach your children about money matters, otherwise they are going to exert a negative influence on your financial future. Empower young people in the area of personal finances and buy the necessary books for them – it is in your own interest.

Divorced/single parent?

Change your will immediately after a divorce to suit your new situation and needs (or leave it as it was if you still want to help your former spouse). Note that children are always entitled to life support from the estate of a deceased spouse. If you are also unemployed, you are entitled to apply under the Maintenance of Surviving Spouses Act 27 of 1990 for life support from the estate. Remember spouses can also bequeath group benefits to non-family (e.g. a friend) to utilise together with their children in the event of their death. Create a trust by way of your will to make provision for your minor children in the event of your death.

Homemaker?

If you are a homemaker who does not contribute to a retirement fund, you must make sure that you are familiar with the details of your antenuptial contract so that you can be informed about its financial implications for yourself and your marriage partner. Pay special attention to your retirement provision and to what extent you will be able to survive in the event of your spouse's retirement, death or disability. Look at the rules of your spouse's retirement fund(s) and at the stipulations concerning death and disability that are applicable to annuities. Make sure that you will receive benefits from annuities even after the death of your spouse, in other words, up to and including your own death.

Are you living with someone?

There are many potential pitfalls awaiting you if you live with someone and you have not drawn up a cohabitation agreement. Such an agreement must clear up such matters as the following: how income will be applied; how investments will be made; in whose name(s) investments will be made; how expenses will be incurred and from what account(s); in whose name the dwelling will be rented/purchased (who signs the lease or purchase agreement); how assets and investments will be divided if the relationship is terminated; how debt obligations will be met; what will happen in the case of the death of one or both of the parties; and how the estate will pass to heirs (by way of your joint will drawn up to your mutual benefit).

Successive marriages (instant families)

Actually, we should call this section 'successive opportunities for conflict', which is what such marriages are. There are more granddads, grannies, dads, moms, kids, stepchildren and stepmothers involved, as well as all these parties' financial matters, all of which impact directly or indirectly on your planning.

Gain clarity about your current financial situation, in other words, what do you own, owe and earn. Determine the same for the other party (spouse). It is particularly important that existing financial commitments are openly declared so that you know exactly which child is entitled to a financial benefit or asset, and when. Make sure, therefore, that you know whether a former marriage partner is entitled to the pension of your spouse on his death. Otherwise, you may be under the mistaken impression that you are going to receive the pension benefits in question. The contents of earlier settlements concerning assets are therefore important, as well as the extent to which financial commitments have already been met or are yet to be met (find out when exactly).

Keep your own assets, investments, income and commitments as separate from those of your new spouse as you can. Make sure that at the end of the day you do not have to meet financial obligations on behalf of someone else and then lose your last possessions (investments) as well.

You must, therefore, protect your *status quo* in your ANC with your new spouse.

A succession of marriages requires a better understanding of planning, just as it requires more understanding about marriage. A step-family often has to cope with a lowered standard of living, because existing income has to be shared by more people. Remember that support for dependants has to be accommodated in the household budget.

Pay attention to your joint will and remember bequests to all the children concerned. The spouses may also draw up separate wills. Remember, however, that your joint will must be consistent with your ANC.

Invest in your health
A healthy woman can work harder and better (has more energy) and can earn more than a woman whose health is less sound. Consequently, more investments can be made for personal goals and retirement. Invest in your health, therefore, by eating and drinking right, exercising, not smoking and lowering your stress levels in every respect. Remember, women generally live longer than men – so plan thoroughly.

Your broker
Choose a broker or brokers with expertise required to help you with your planning. Consult an attorney to attend to legal matters and concerns.

Emigration
Like offshore investments, emigration calls for a great deal of homework. First consult your bank manager and then the Reserve Bank for more information.

Your domestic help
You must take the initiative and help your domestic servant with an investment in a policy or unit trusts as provision for retirement. Perhaps you can even

take out a funeral policy for him or her. Remember the service contract you have with him or her.

Conclusion
Every woman should become involved with her own personal financial planning in order to ensure that she will be able to retire financially independent. Knowledge of personal finances has become a prerequisite for every woman's financial future and survival, besides which it is probably the best skill a woman can possess.

Start planning your money matters today.

1.6 THE PERSONAL FINANCIAL PLANNING PROCESS

Even though individual needs differ, the same steps in the personal financial planning process can be followed. Gitman & Joehnk (1984:186) divide this planning process into three activities:
- analysing your present situation;
- setting financial objectives; and
- preparing a budget for the achievement of objectives.

The first activity shows us where we are at the present moment, the second where we would like to be, and the third shows us the way or method of getting there. This planning process can be briefly explained as follows.

1.6.1 Gathering information and preparing personal financial statements

Information needs to be gathered about the following, amongst others: details of the family, such as names, ages, marital status, matrimonial arrangements, gender and health; income statement; balance sheet, which clearly indicates the present construction of the estate, such as fixed property, current assets, personal property, equities, rights, cash, investments and liabilities, insurance portfolio with a summary of immediate cover, claim values, death benefits, disability benefits, annuities, provident funds, group insurance, pension benefits, employee benefits and anticipated inheritance. The potential earning ability of persons in the household, as well as any other potential source of income, must be included here.

Besides the aspects mentioned above, information must be gathered on the person's liquidity preferences, attitude towards risk or security (his or her risk profile), political views and views about the country's economic prospects. Everybody should be able to determine their present financial position and views in respect of the above, since all further decisions or plans will be based on these aspects.

The next step in the planning process is to prepare a personal income statement and a balance sheet. A specialist in this field could be called in to assist with drawing up these statements if you are unable to do it yourself. A personal income statement indicates the financial activities that took place over a specific period and includes income, expenditure and contributions towards savings and/or investments. A personal balance sheet indicates your welfare (or wealth), which is reflected in the way in which assets are funded and not by the number of assets owned.

The link between income statements and balance sheets is the amount of equity capital. Equity capital is calculated by deducting total liabilities from total assets. Any positive contribution towards savings or investments (irrespective of how the contribution is employed) will lead to an increase in wealth (equity capital). Similarly, a negative contribution leads to a decline in wealth.

1.6.2 Identification of objectives and needs

1.6.2.1 Evaluation and persons involved

Before a person can decide what he or she wishes to achieve, he or she must consider what is important to him or her. Someone who wishes to achieve success will have to work smarter and harder and do without holidays (occasionally). Others may have a more balanced approach. Block *et al.* (1988:5) recommend that married people should involve the entire family in setting objectives.

1.6.2.2 Linking objectives to time

The formulation of objectives is a statement by a person of the prospects for his or her financial future. Planning, therefore, centres on objectives and how to achieve them. Objectives should be linked to specific time horizons. The reason for the last-mentioned statement is that most objectives can be achieved by using more than one method. In Table 1.2, financial objectives of a student are set out in terms of specified time horizons.

Immediate or short-term objectives: Short-term objectives are aspired to in the early stage of the life cycle and must be very specific (Table 1.2). Funds for such objectives are generated from current income and/or savings or investment plans. Alternatively, funds may be borrowed, or a hire-purchase or lease agreement may be concluded.

Medium-term objectives: Medium-term objectives usually occur during the working years and stretch over the largest part of the life cycle. The achievement of objectives during this stage is a prerequisite for the achievement of objectives in the long term. Spending patterns could be adjusted to provide for needs over the medium term.

Long-term objectives: These objectives provide the greatest flexibility during planning. Retirement planning is usually the most important planning component of the last stage of the life cycle.

People of all ages will have short-, medium- and long-term objectives. The example of a student's objectives is not an explanation of the concepts short-, medium- and long-term, but an illustration of an applied case.

TABLE 1.2 **Time considerations for financial objectives (life cycle)**
(*Source: Block et al. 1988:7*)

Short-term	Medium-term	Long-term
• Complete studies • Positive balance in cheque account • Get holiday job • Buy second-hand motor car • Repay loan • Take out minimum insurance cover	• Find full-time employment or start own business • Buy a house • Take out comprehensive insurance cover • Start a fund for children's education • Begin investment programme • Begin contributions to programme for retirement	• Gather Rx • Retire at age x • Travel x months of the year

1.6.2.3 Listing of priorities

Objectives must be listed in order of importance. A distinction must be made between urgent (immediate) and important needs. It may be urgent to get a telephone at home, but it is more important to draw up your own valid will. Higher priority must be given to important needs, because of the negative financial implications of not being able to meet those needs.

1.6.3 Identification of constraints

There are always external influences or constraints that have to be taken into consideration in personal financial planning. These are factors that may restrict or even be entirely in conflict with the personal objectives and needs that have been identified. Examples of such factors are income tax, untimely death, retirement, illness and liability risks.

1.6.4 Comparison of current situation with identified needs

Information regarding a person's current situation shows what planning has been done to date. A comparison between the current situation and all identified needs indicates which needs have already been provided for, and which needs still have to be provided for. In other words, the needs that have not been provided for should receive attention.

Goldman (1983:49) points out that needs with a low priority may already have been met. The priority list may indicate needs with a high priority that have not been met and which would require more funds than needs with a lower priority. In that case, consideration

should be given to replacing needs with a lower priority with needs with a higher priority. This would mean that more funds would be available for needs with a higher priority, since those with a lower priority would have been set aside.

1.6.5 Analysis of investment opportunities

Before any decisions are made to meet certain needs, an analysis of existing investment opportunities is necessary. It is essential to examine the purpose of each investment alternative, as well as the advantages and disadvantages involved in each. For example, although savings may earn relatively low interest if invested in a fixed deposit for six months, this would nevertheless provide more liquidity than a fixed investment over a ten-year term.

1.6.6 Development of the plan

During this phase, a person must decide which investment will provide for which need. In Table 1.3, certain risks are listed, as well as an investment plan for each risk. Needs are expressed in terms of the risks involved in the occurrence of certain events. Insurance options to counteract these events, or provide for such risks, are listed opposite each risk. In order to develop a plan, a person must choose (in the case of life insurance) an insurance company and decide on the specific amount required for life cover, and the monthly premium he or she can afford (on the basis of his or her personal budget).

TABLE 1.3 Exposure to risks
(Source: Amling & Droms 1986:237)

Type of risk	Insurance
1. Personal risks	
(a) Loss of income – untimely death	Life insurance
(b) Loss of income – disability	Disability insurance
(c) Loss of income – illness or injury	Medical fund
2. Property risks	
(a) Theft of or damage to vehicle	Vehicle insurance
(b) Loss of or damage to home and/or contents	Homeowner's insurance
(c) Loss of or damage to personal property	Personal property insurance
3. Liability risks	
(a) Liability resulting from homeownership	Homeowner's insurance
(b) Liability resulting from vehicle ownership	Vehicle insurance
(c) Liability resulting from negligence or malpractice	Comprehensive liability insurance/Malpractice insurance

1.6.7 Balancing the budget

It is of cardinal importance that the budget should balance, in other words that income should be equal to expenditure plus savings. A surplus or a shortfall indicates that the plan requires further attention.

1.6.8 Implementation of the plan

During this phase, a specific insurance policy could be taken out, for example an endowment policy for retirement purposes. Perhaps money could be placed in an investment account. If necessary, professional advice may be sought. It is important to note that no plan can be implemented if there are not sufficient funds.

1.6.9 Periodic revision of the plan

As with any other plan, a financial plan cannot be expected to remain the perfect plan. Periodic revision is necessary in order to provide for changing needs and circumstances. It is recommended that the plan be revised once a year. Significant changes will require changes in the financial plan.

Goldman (1983:168) gives the example of starting a business as a significant change in a person's needs. Besides requiring capital, a person who has resigned from his or her job to start a business would also no longer belong to a pension fund, group life insurance and medical scheme. It would be necessary to consider providing for his or her changed needs as soon as possible (if financially feasible) by means of a financial plan. Diagram 1.4 on p.11 sets out the personal financial planning process.

1.7 THE ADVANTAGES OF PERSONAL FINANCIAL PLANNING

The advantages of personal financial planning are as follows:
- Many individuals and households find out more about their current financial situation for the first time.
- Financial needs are identified.
- Household risks are identified.
- Reasons for cash flow problems (usually as a result of over-spending – most households spend R1 000 to R3 000 more than they think) are identified.
- There is budgeting regarding expenses and investments to reach immediate, short-, medium- and long-term goals.
- Financial crises are identified well in time.
- You take responsibility for your own financial future.

- The influence of new legislation on a household's money matters is understood more readily, even though it may be accepted with difficulty.
- The uncertainty surrounding retirement planning is removed.
- It becomes possible to retire with financial independence.
- Provision is made for the maintenance of a particular standard of living before and after retirement.
- Households (and individuals) know where they are heading and can continue with a purposeful life, because they know how to get to where they want to be.
- The entire household is involved in the budget process and learns more about money matters.
- Children learn about money matters from an early age, and about the necessity of saving.
- All the family members learn the most important life skill, namely the financial life skill.
- Children are able to stand on their own feet much earlier, which enables them to function independently of their parents as far as finances are concerned.
- Thanks to the latter, there is less pressure on the parents' household budget from an earlier stage, so that they can make more of their own investments with a view to retirement.

1.8 PERSONAL FINANCIAL PLANNING AREAS

Decisions have to be made on all matters relating to your personal financial position. Various areas are involved in the planning process, for which plans with predetermined objectives must be made. If any of these planning areas is disregarded, this could have far-reaching financial implications. For that reason, it is necessary to be familiar with the contents of each area, particularly in view of obtaining financial independence after retirement. The following personal financial planning areas are distinguished:
- career planning;
- project planning;
- family planning;
- income tax planning;
- estate planning;
- investment planning;
- protection planning;
- credit planning;
- productivity planning;
- health care planning;
- retirement planning;
- emigration planning; and
- business planning (see Swart 2002).

These planning areas are interdependent. An estate planning decision, for example, affects income tax and retirement planning to a large extent. The same can be said of an investment decision. The different planning areas (except for project and family planning) are discussed in later chapters.

The planning process includes all these planning areas. All personal financial decisions form part of the overall planning process, since ultimately they all have to be accommodated in the domestic budget.

1.9 SUMMARY

Personal financial planning is a broad concept that includes various personal financial planning areas. Personal financial planning occurs only by means of a personal financial planning process. At this stage it should be clear that this planning is unique for every individual and household, because it is based on individual and household financial situations. Individual and household resources must be obtained and applied in such a way as to satisfy needs and reach goals after retirement.

Knowledge of money matters is a prerequisite for efficient personal financial management and planning. All individuals and households must be aware of the many factors that could positively or negatively influence their financial position now and in the future. By now you should also realise that personal financial planning involves much more than simply making investments. A thorough knowledge of personal finance enables every individual to make informed choices regarding his or her financial future. Planning takes you from where you are at present to where you would like to be – in other words towards your future goals.

Do your own planning with the help of experts, but make sure that mass hysteria (the things the masses do on the grounds of what they read in the media) does not confuse you. Adapt your planning where necessary, but stick to sound financial principles. You can do all manner of things in order to retire with financial independence. You do not have to do what others are doing.

Personal financial planning should start the day you receive your first salary cheque (or wage). Therefore, begin planning today, and ensure your financial future.

1.10 SELF-ASSESSMENT

- Discuss the different steps in the personal financial planning process.
- Explain the importance, and list the advantages, of personal financial planning.

BIBLIOGRAPHY

Amling, F. & Droms, W.G. 1986. *Personal financial management.* 2nd edn. Homewood: Irwin.

Block, S.B., Peavy, J.W. & Thornton, J.H. 1988. *Personal financial management.* New York: Harper & Row.

Botha, G.J. 1985. *'n Bespreking van positiewe teoretiese modelle en die ex-ante waardebepaling van die verwagte opbrengskoerse by verskeie beleggingsalternatiewe.* (M.B.A. script, Postgraduate Management School. Pretoria: University of Pretoria.)

Gitman, L.J. & Joehnk, M.D. 1984. *Fundamentals of investing.* 2nd edn. New York: Harper & Row.

Goldman, P.L. 1983. *A wealth optimisation model for personal financial decisions.* (M.B.A. script, Faculty of Business Administration. Johannesburg: University of the Witwatersrand.)

Mittra, S. 1990. *Practicing financial planning.* Englewood Cliffs: Prentice-Hall.

Swart, N.J. 2002. *Starting or buying your own business or a franchise.* Cape Town: Juta.

Swart, N.J. 1999. *Investing your package: All you need to know.* Pretoria: Unisa.

Swart, N.J. & Coetzee, M. 2000(a). *My money matters: Education and training manual.* Johannesburg: Creda.

Swart, N.J. & Coetzee, M. 2000(b). *My money matters: Six golden rules for planning your personal finances and using debt wisely.* Johannesburg: Creda.

MEASURING AND ASSESSING PERSONAL FINANCIAL PERFORMANCE

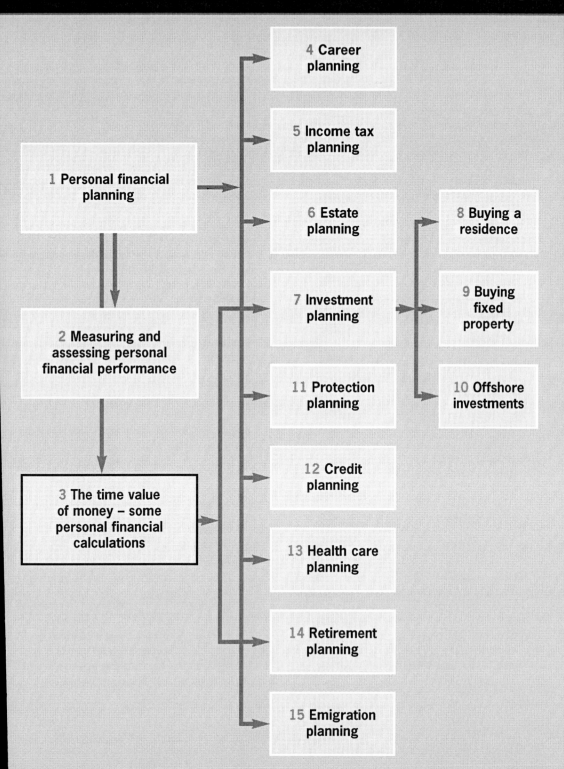

2.2 INTRODUCTION

Since we base our financial planning on our stated objectives, we also want to know whether we are in fact achieving those objectives. In other words, we would like to measure our financial performance. Annual financial statements, such as income statements and balance sheets, as well as personal budgets, are probably the most important tools we can use to measure our financial performance.

Everyone should draw up a personal budget, which should only include the income and expenditure for the household. Not everybody is capable of preparing income statements and balance sheets, however, and for that task the professional help of a chartered accountant may be enlisted.

Because income statements and personal budgets are closely related (as will be seen later), we will discuss balance sheets first.

2.3 ANNUAL FINANCIAL STATEMENTS

2.3.1 The balance sheet

A balance sheet gives an indication of your financial situation at a given time. A balance sheet primarily comprises three items:
- assets;
- liabilities; and
- net worth (owner's equity).

We will briefly discuss each of these.

2.3.1.1 Assets

Assets represent everything a person owns. Gitman (1981:26) divides the assets found in a typical household into two groups: fundamental and investment assets.

Fundamental assets can be described as those assets a family owns by reason of the function they perform in the household.

Investment assets, on the other hand, are assets acquired in order to earn a return on them. These assets do not perform a specific function in the household. Table 2.1 classifies household assets into fundamental and investment assets.

Gitman does not regard cash and deposits as investment assets. The reason for this is that these assets are employed primarily to satisfy the transaction motive, namely the conclusion of transactions with such funds. All these assets (taxed or paid off) must appear on the balance sheet, except those that are leased. Leased assets do not belong to the lessee, but to the lessor. Leased assets, therefore, only appear on the balance sheet after the last instalment (debt) has been paid off.

It should be noted, however, that cash in current accounts and deposits is in fact an investment. Once funds have been spent or invested, they are regarded as assets. Saving can be described as a restraint of spending, in other words, the money remains in your possession at your home or in your pocket. The funds in current accounts and fixed deposits are very liquid. This means the funds are readily and easily available if you wish to conclude a transaction.

Assets are further subdivided into fixed and current assets. Fixed assets comprise land and buildings, machinery, equipment, furniture, vehicles and long-term investments. Current assets comprise cash, fixed deposits, debtors (people who owe you money), marketable securities (short-term investments) and stock.

2.3.1.2 Liabilities

All debts are classified as liabilities. As with assets, some liabilities are short-term and others are long-term. Long-term liabilities may be long-term debt and mortgage bonds on fixed property, such as on a home. Short-term liabilities may be an overdrawn bank account, a loan from a private person, arrears expenditure, creditors (people to whom money is owed) and any accounts. Table 2.2 shows liabilities that may be reflected on a typical household balance sheet.

TABLE 2.1 Classification of assets
(Source: Adapted from Gitman 1981:27)

Fundamental assets	Investment assets
• Cash on hand	• Securities
• Cash in current accounts	• shares
• Deposits	• debentures
• at banks	• fixed interest-bearing securities
• at building societies	• Cash value of life and endowment insurance
• House	• Other investments
• Motor vehicles	• coins
• Equipment	
• Personal property	
• furniture	
• clothing	
• jewellery	

TABLE 2.2 Liabilities of a typical household
(Source: Adapted from Unisa 1994:6)

- Arrear accounts in respect of:
  - credit card purchases (food, clothing, holiday)
  - medical and dental services
  - repairs (motor car, refrigerator)
  - water and electricity
  - property tax (rates and taxes)
- Personal loans
- Overdrawn bank account
- Balances on hire-purchases in respect of:
  - vehicles
  - equipment
  - furniture
- Balances on mortgage bond in respect of:
  - home
  - investment in other property (holiday home, sectional title, time-share unit, business property)

The liabilities, as listed from top to bottom in the table above, have correspondingly longer repayment periods. In other words, the period of repayment for the first item is shorter than that of the last item. For example, an account for credit card purchases is normally paid within three to six months, while a home loan is normally paid off over 20 years.

A person's wealth is not measured solely by the amount of assets (in monetary value) he or she owns – the liabilities attached to such assets must also be taken into account. Of particular importance is the manner in which the assets are financed.

2.3.1.3 Net worth

A household's net worth (or owner's equity) is determined by deducting all liabilities from the total assets. Net worth is obtained by redeeming all liabilities from the available assets, even if it means that some assets have to be sold (converted into cash).

Net worth = total assets - total liabilities.

2.3.2 The income statement

A person's financial performance can be determined from an income statement. His or her income and expenditure over a certain period (financial transactions) are obtained in this case. An income statement can be divided into:
- income;
- expenditure; and
- contribution towards savings.

Each of these is briefly illustrated.

2.3.2.1 Income
All the funds a household receives, irrespective of their origin or source, are called income. Some examples of income are:
- a salary;
- a bonus (thirteenth cheque);
- commission earned;
- interest received on investments; and
- capital profit (or net profit) on the sale of assets.

The total income is obtained by adding up all income the household receives.

2.3.2.2 Expenditure
All payments for which a household is liable, whether for meeting needs or redeeming debt, are regarded as personal expenditure. This expenditure will vary from household to household. The following is a list of typical household expenditure:
- housing;
- food;
- clothing;
- short-term insurance;
- motor vehicle;
- medical;
- furniture;
- equipment;
- entertainment (television, videos, eating out);
- recreation (holiday);
- life and endowment insurance;
- rates and taxes; and
- water and electricity.

2.3.2.3 Contribution towards savings
By this is meant the difference between total expenditure and total income as is reflected in the income statement. If income for the period (usually a financial year) exceeds expenditure, the income statement reflects a net profit. This net profit constitutes a positive contribution towards savings, since it increases the person's wealth. Where expenditure exceeds income, the income reflects a net loss, which reduces the person's wealth. This constitutes a negative contribution towards savings.

2.3.3 Evaluation of financial statements

The net profit or loss is carried over to the balance sheet (from the income statement). On the balance sheet it forms part of the net worth (owner's equity), which indicates the person's wealth. By comparing two years' balance sheets, you can see whether this wealth has accumulated or diminished.

The net profit (surplus) could be used, for example, to purchase assets – see (a) – or to discharge debts – see (b). Assume that there is a net profit (surplus) of R2 000.

EXAMPLE

Balance sheet as at 28 February 2001

Assets	R100 000	Owner's equity	R40 000
		Liabilities	R60 000
	R100 000		R100 000

(a) Balance sheet as at 28 February 2002

Assets	R102 000	Owner's equity	R42 000
		Liabilities	R60 000
	R102 000		R102 000

(b) Balance sheet as at 28 February 2002

Assets	R100 000	Owner's equity	R42 000
		Liabilities	R58 000
	R100 000		R100 000

An income statement can be compared with a personal household budget. Expenditure could be reduced if the net profit is low or if a net loss is reflected. Alternatively, the household income could be supplemented by taking on additional or part-time work.

It should be noted, however, that any (possible) additional income is usually associated with additional expenditure. Care should be taken to ensure that the additional expenditure does not exceed the additional income. It is important that after-tax income should be higher than the additional expenditure. The following are possible additional costs:

- increased petrol costs;
- new clothing to wear to the office;
- full-time domestic help (or half-day help);
- care of children (pre-school);
- parking costs;
- higher income tax; and
- providing and furnishing a room for the domestic help.

As seen earlier, the income statement and the personal budget should be analysed together.

We will now look at practical examples of financial statements as adapted from Becker (1992:3, 10, 19). You will note that a statement of changes in equity has been added in this case too. The statements to be studied include the following:

- balance sheet;
- income statement;
- statement of changes in equity; and
- cash flow statement.

After studying the statements, you should note that you can use ratios to evaluate a company's financial situation. Furthermore, many individuals are involved in business themselves, and are particularly well-placed to make use of such ratios. The same goes for someone who is an employee only. Needless to say, not all ratios are relevant to an individual's financial statements. Experts agree that ratios that analyse and evaluate working capital are the most important as far as an individual's financial performance in the short- and long-term are concerned.

You will note that little is said about the accounting officer/accountant or auditor at this stage. This will be discussed in greater detail in Chapter 5 during a brief discussion of tax planning. However, I do want to mention that a qualified person will do your books (financial statements) at a relatively low cost, and according to accounting requirements. You will need to supply this person (company) with the necessary documents.

EXAMPLE

Manufacturing Company Limited
Balance sheet as at 29 February 2000

	Notes	2000 R '000	1999 R '000
ASSETS			
Non-current assets		9 220	6 413
Property, plant and equipment		6 808	4 138
At cost		9 922	7 004
Accumulated deprecation		3 114	2 866
Investments (unlisted)		2 412	2 275
Associated company		878	785
Other companies		1 534	1 490
Current assets		22 379	17 755
Inventory		12 148	9 276
Trade and other receivables		10 231	8 430
SA Revenue Services		–	17
Cash and cash equivalents		–	32
Total Assets		31 599	24 168
EQUITY AND LIABILITIES			
Capital and Reserves		18 228	16 035
Share capital		8 680	8 680
Accumulated profit		9 548	7 355
Non-current liabilities			
Interest bearing borrowing			
(long-term loans 15% p.a.)		7 000	4 000

Current liabilities	6 371	4 133
Trade and other payables	5 270	3 629
Short-term borrowing	300	-
Shareholders for dividends	588	504
Bank overdraft	118	-
SA Revenue Services	95	-
	31 599	24 168

EXAMPLE

Manufacturing Company Limited
Income statement – year ended 29 February 2000

	2000 R '000	1999 R '000
Revenue	38 945	33 024
Cost of sales	(30 959)	(26 071)
Gross profit	7 986	6 953
Other operating income		
Administration expenses	(825)	(737)
Distribution costs		
Depreciation and amortisation	(347)	(302)
Staff costs (Directors' emoluments)	(522)	(456)
Other operating expenses		
Profit/(loss) from operations	6 292	5 458
Income from investments	144	140
Dividends from unlisted investments		
Profit from ordinary activities		
before finance charges	6 436	5 598
Finance charges	(977)	(686)
Profit/(loss) before tax	5 459	4 912
Income tax expenses	(2 330)	(2 253)
Income/(loss) after tax		
from ordinary activities	3 129	2 659
Extraordinary items		
Share of after-tax income		
of associated company	93	81
Surplus on disposal of fixed assets	27	-
Net profit for the year	3 249	2 740
Earnings per ordinary share	38.1 cents	32.3 cents

EXAMPLE

Manufacturing Company Limited
Statement of changes in equity – year ended 29 February 2000

	Ordinary share capital R '000	Preference share capital R '000	Accumulated profit R '000	Total R '000
Balance at 28 February 1999	8 400	280	7 355	16 035
Net profit/(loss) for the year			3 229	3 229
Preference dividends			(28)	(28)
Ordinary dividends			(1 008)	(1 008)
Balance at 29 February 2000	8 400	280	9 548	18 228

Statement of changes in equity – year ended 28 February 1999

	Ordinary share capital R '000	Preference share capital R '000	Accumulated profit R '000	Total R '000
Balance at 28 February 1998	8 400	280	5 525	14 205
Net profit/(loss) for the year			2 740	2 740
Preference dividends			(28)	(28)
Ordinary dividends			(882)	(882)
Balance at 28 February 1999	8 400	280	7 355	16 035

Note	2000 R '000	1999 R '000
Authorised share capital		
10 000 000 Ordinary shares of R1 each	10 000	10 000
140 000 10% Cumulative preference shares of R2 each	280	280
Issued share capital		
8 400 000 Ordinary shares of R1 each	8 400	8 400
140 000 10% Cumulative preference shares of R2 each	280	280

EXAMPLE

Manufacturing Company Limited
Cash flow statement – year ended 29 February 2000

	Notes	2000 R '000	1999 R '000
Cash flows from operating activities			not available
Profit/(loss) before finance charges and tax		6 292	–
Adjustment for non-cash flow items			
Depreciation		347	
Changes in operating capital		(3 032)	–
Decrease/(increase) in inventory		(2 872)	
Decrease/(increase) in receivables		(1 801)	
Decrease/(increase) in prepayments			
Decrease/(increase) in payables		1 641	
Decrease/(increase) in provisions			
Net cash flow/(outflow) from operations		3 607	–
Cash inflow from other sources		4 172	–
Interest received			
Dividends received		144	
Rent received			
Proceeds from loans – long-term borrowings		3 000	
Proceeds from loans – short-term borrowings		418	
Proceeds from additional shares issued			
Proceeds from sale of investments			
Proceeds from sale of assets		610	
Cash flow to other sources		(7 811)	–
Interest paid		(977)	
Dividends paid		(952)	
Tax paid		(2 238)	
Purchase property, plant and equipment			
Replacement		(926)	
Additions		(2 674)	
Repayment of loans			
Addition to investments		(44)	

Repayment of hire-purchase contract		
Repayment of lease contract		
Withdrawal by directors/shareholders		
Net increase/(decrease) in cash and cash equivalents	(32)	-
Cash and cash equivalents – beginning of period	32	-
Cash and cash equivalents – end of period	-	-
Cash and cash equivalents – per balance sheet	-	

We will now briefly discuss the four statements.

The balance sheet
You probably still remember the formula:

Owner's equity = assets (fixed assets + investments + current assets) – liabilities (current liabilities + long-term debt).

Let us look at the following concepts – 'employment of capital', 'liabilities' and 'capital employed'.

Employment of capital
This aspect refers to those items on the balance sheet in which long-term funds have been invested, for example fixed assets, investments and net current assets (current assets - current liabilities). Fixed assets refer to land, buildings and machinery. Depreciation is written off over the lifetime of, for example, a machine or vehicle, and is shown on the balance sheet and the income statement. Investments in both listed and unlisted securities are also shown here. Current assets refer to, amongst others, inventory, debtors, advance expenditure (e.g. tax), accrued income (rent receivable) and cash in the bank.

Liabilities
Current liabilities refer to, amongst others, creditors, short-term loans, accrued expenses, e.g. tax payable, overdrafts and instalment sales transactions (hire-purchase). Credit cards may also be included (under 'trade and payables'), unless you have a 'budget' card. In the case of a budget card the payback period is more than a year, so it should fall under long-term loans ('non-current liabilities'). A motor-car lease, too, will not be indicated here, as it is considered to be off-balance sheet financing.

Most overspending and cash flow problems can be traced back to current assets and current liabilities. Liquidity problems refer to an inability to meet short-term obligations. Current assets are often financed with long-term funds. Solvency refers to an ability to meet long-term financial obligations.

Capital employed
The capital employed by an individual or a business could consist of, amongst others, a combination of the following, namely share capital (ordinary and preference shares), owner's equity, long-term liabilities and accumulated profit.

The income statement
The income statement shows all income and expenditure (made to earn an income), in order to calculate the net profit or income. Furthermore, this net profit for the year is used to calculate the individual's taxable income (see Chapter 5). A company will also use net profit to calculate its earnings per share.

The statement of changes in equity
The statement of changes in equity is also called the 'statement of recognised gains and losses'. Apart from its financial statements, an enterprise should present a statement of changes in equity, showing (Coetzee et al. 2000:179):
- the net profit or loss for the period;
- each income and expense item (totals);
- the correction of fundamental errors; and
- the cumulative effect of changes in accounting policy.

An enterprise should also present the following (either in the statement of changes in equity or in the notes thereto):
- capital transactions with owners;
- distributions to owners;
- the balance of accumulated profit or loss (beginning of period and at balance sheet date);
- movements for the latter period; and
- movements in the amounts of each class of equity.

The cash flow statement
Previously, the cash flow statement was called the statement of source and employment of funds. You will note the logical flow of information from the cash flow statement. Firstly, there is an indication of the cash flow that the business itself generates. Secondly, the cash flow from other sources is shown. Thirdly, the employment of cash, or the cash outflow, is indicated, for example interest, tax and dividends to shareholders. You will note that depreciation (a non-cash item) is added back or added in the cash flow statement.

Using ratios

Ratios are simply aids in order to obtain certain information regarding the financial statements, in other words the individual or business they represent. In practice, generally accepted figures for various ratios have existed within various industries and types of businesses for many years. Individuals can use ratios to interpret their own financial performance. They can also be used to evaluate a business that someone may wish to buy, or to compare businesses. Banks, creditors and other providers of funds (loans) use them to obtain more information about individuals and businesses. This is also true of the Receiver of Revenue, who analyses certain figures and situations in this way.

2.4 THE PERSONAL FINANCIAL BUDGET

A budget is a plan and a control mechanism (Weston & Brigham 1982:201). It is a plan expressed in financial terms. At the same time, it sets certain standards that have to be met in order to achieve certain objectives. In other words, it is a mechanism used in order to exercise financial control. This plan and control mechanism can benefit any household.

2.4.1 Familiarity with the preferences of the household (or knowledge of 'self')

Before the budgeting process can proceed, the compiler should be aware of the likes and dislikes of all those involved. Do the family members like the notion of investing for the future, or are they inclined to live from day to day? Some people spend all their money as it comes in, while others prefer to set aside a monthly amount for holidays twice or three times a year.

Knowledge of the personalities of all the participants in the budgeting process is consequently a prerequisite for drawing up an effective household budget. The lifestyle of the family will determine trends and tendencies (especially as regards spending) in the personal budget.

2.4.2 The purpose of a budget

A budget is a financial plan for the household over a given period. Firstly, the income and expenditure over this period must be estimated or forecast. This

> Budgeting is the most important step in the personal financial planning process – it is impossible to do personal financial planning without a personal budget (household budget).

> Budgeting is your first step towards financial success.

forecast is based on the expectations of the compiler of the budget regarding his or her future financial situation. For this reason we talk about anticipated income and anticipated expenditure.

The purpose of a budget is to enable individuals or families to achieve their objectives. A budget forces you to assess your current and future financial situation and to keep track of your income and expenditure. This results in a more careful and sensible approach to spending the funds you have in order to achieve the objectives you have set for yourself.

Before we commence with the steps involved in preparing a budget, we will discuss some principles involved in drawing up a budget. There are many more principles, but we will concentrate on those pertaining to personal financial planning.

2.4.3 Principles involved in drawing up a budget

A principle serves as a guideline for the compiler in the accomplishment of his or her task. In that way the possibility is increased that predetermined objectives will be achieved.

2.4.3.1 Involvement

All the people for whom the budget is going to serve as a plan and a control mechanism over a specified period should be involved and have a say in preparing the budget.

The household budget should have the support of all the members of the family. This will inspire confidence in the budget and everybody will have a better understanding of the nature and purpose of the planning process.

If the family serves the budget, the budget will serve the family. By this we mean that the family should realise that they have a responsibility towards keeping to the planned monthly expenditure, otherwise the budget will serve no purpose. If they do keep to the budget, it will be a means of helping them to achieve their objectives.

Involvement also implies that the budget should be used as a means of keeping track of income and expenditure to see whether there are any discrepancies between actual expenditure and anticipated expenditure. The following questions should be asked when discrepancies do occur:
- Why did they occur?
- Who or what was responsible for the discrepancy?
- What was done (what action was taken) to prevent it?

- What was done to prevent it from happening in future?
- How was it rectified?

2.4.3.2 Efficient organisation

The authority and responsibility within a family to incur certain expenses must be clearly stated. A framework should be created in which objectives can be achieved in a co-ordinated way. Each member of the family should know what is expected of him or her in the achievement of the objectives. Each (responsible) person must participate in the budgeting process, but the head of the household should be responsible for its co-ordination.

2.4.3.3 A proper administration system

An administration system is necessary, which is directly linked to specific responsibilities concerning the budgeting process and implemented for purposes of the budget. A certain person should be responsible for the administration of the budget. By administration we mean that all documents reflecting income and expenditure should be filed in an orderly manner.

If documents relating to income and expenditure are filed, the actual cost (expenditure) can be determined. Such a control system makes it easier to compare actual expenditure with planned expenditure (as well as income). Slips for all household expenditure should, therefore, be filed systematically. This will facilitate the administration process and improve control of the budget.

2.4.3.4 Good communication

Communication is a process of informing or reporting in order to achieve mutual understanding between two or more people. To achieve household objectives (for example a holiday at the end of the year), such objectives must be communicated to the whole family. Members of the family should know why their spending is restricted; for example, to save money for the planned holiday mentioned earlier. Good communication creates unity and will encourage the family to try to attain the common goal.

To a large extent, effective decision-making depends on effective communication. It should not be simply assumed that the family knows why certain discrepancies have occurred in the budget or why certain items can no longer be purchased. Such situations (in fact, all situations) should be communicated to everybody in the family in order to promote mutual understanding. Discrepancies should be accounted for fully and honestly, and corrective steps should be taken and understood by everybody. That is good communication.

Your budget would sometimes demand that you tighten your financial belt and that of the household.

2.4.3.5 A realistic budget

A prerequisite for a budget is realism. To a large extent, the care with which budget figures are calculated determines the budget's future success. For a budget to be realistic, each variable (income and cost item) that may occur should be anticipated in respect of:
- their specific time horizon; and
- an acceptable internal and external environment that will reign during that period.

For example, if for May an expenditure is anticipated, which will continue for a period of three months, the expenditure must be budgeted for May, June and July. If the expenditure will probably be higher in June (possibly because of rising interest rates), the higher amount that will apply to June and July must be budgeted for.

The family should understand that over-budgeting and under-budgeting are equally useless and negative. Realism is the solution – the figures should be as close to reality as possible.

A budget should also be flexible. Changing circumstances could result in certain expenses doubling for two or three months. For example, children may become ill in winter and the pharmacy account may be higher than usual. A motor vehicle may break down and repairs may amount to R500, which could drastically alter the budget figures for six months (or longer). In such a case, the family's objective for the year could change; for example, a cheaper holiday at another destination or even no holiday at all at the end of the year.

Budgeted figures are based on pre-estimates or forecasts. Forecasting means that certain assumptions are made about the future and certain factors, which could lead to alteration of the budget, are taken into account.

The forecasting process serves as a basis for the budget and is, therefore, a prerequisite for its preparation. No budget can be reliable if forecasts are not made.

There is an important difference between forecasting and budgeting. Forecasting indicates whether or not a future plan is feasible. Budgeting indicates how and when the stated objectives can be achieved.

Budgeting for the first time may cause the household members some 'birth-pains'.
Explain the long-term advantages to your family.

Budgeted figures too conservative	Budgeted figures too optimistic
Income: estimated too low. *Expenditure*: estimated too high.	*Income*: estimated too high. *Expenditure*: estimated to low.
Possible reasons: Where estimated income is too low, the risk of not achieving objectives will be small. Expenditures are estimated high so that expenditures are not exceeded.	*Possible reasons*: With a high estimated income, members of the family idealise what they wish to achieve and believe that this will motivate them to work harder. A low estimated expenditure is an attempt to encourage the family to save and to discourage spending. People also feel that additional expenditure should be reported immediately.
Disadvantages: Members of the family are not motivated to keep expenditure as low as possible and income as high as possible. The budgeted figures lose their value because they are not realistic.	*Disadvantages*: The family becomes demotivated because they find the budget extreme. Expenditure is so low that they will not be able to keep to it and will exceed it in any case. The result is that the budget loses its value and consequently also its purpose.

If budgeted figures exist for the previous year, it is much easier to forecast for the next year or the next planning period. For example, to accommodate the rising rate of inflation, a certain cost item, such as groceries, could be adjusted (increased) to determine the anticipated expenditure.

2.4.3.6 Planning and time

We seldom have sufficient time to do everything we wish to do. Besides, we are often restricted by our financial resources, in other words by what we can afford and when we can afford it. This is why we need to plan and budget in order to do the things we wish to do. There are two aspects of time that are important in the planning function: planning horizons and timetables. We will discuss each of these concepts briefly.

Planning horizons

Planning horizons refer to those periods in the future that must be budgeted for. For the family, this horizon is usually one year. The planning of the family's personal financial budget is done over the following 12 months. All additional expenditure the family incurs over this period will mean that the actual and the budgeted figures will differ.

Timetables

A timetable indicates the specified time within the planning horizon at which a certain decision will be implemented. For example, a planned holiday must start in March and last for two weeks, or an operation must take place after April so that the cost can be covered by an anticipated birthday bonus.

There is a planning horizon and a timetable for every household decision. Periodic planning could pertain to the day (closest to the end of the month) when the telephone account has to be paid. Firstly, a person (in the case of an employee) must have received his or her salary by that day and, secondly, he or she must have the time to go and settle the account. The timetable would also be affected by the due date for the telephone account, that is the last day on which Telkom receives monthly payments before it cuts off your telephone service.

Project planning, on the other hand, involves planning for projects undertaken from time to time, for example an overseas trip. These projects are dealt with on an *ad hoc* basis. Each project plan has its own unique timetable. The nature and scope of the project itself will determine the amount to be budgeted for.

Personal financial planning is a continuous process. Planning is done over various periods. The following periods are distinguished as far as forecasting is concerned:

- immediate (0–1 month);
- short-term (1–3 months);
- medium-term (3 months–2 years); and
- long-term (more than 2 years).

As far as the budget is concerned, the distinction looks like this:

- short-term (0–1 year);
- medium-term (1–5 years); and
- long-term (more than 5 years).

2.4.3.7 Flexible application

A budget should not be applied rigidly; in other words, it should not make rational decisions impossible. If an unforeseen expenditure occurs that was not previously identified, it must be included in the budget. A budget must be flexible so that changes (for example, an incorrect forecast) can be accommodated. Consequently, a variable budget should be drawn up reflecting the change in circumstances.

Budgeted figures must be based on certain assumptions. Once these assumptions change, the budget must also be changed. Remember that over-budgeting is as bad for the household's progress (wealth) as under-budgeting.

2.4.3.8 Human behaviour

Earlier we stated that the compiler of the household budget should know his or her own, as well as the family's, personality traits and preferences. These personality traits and preferences will to a large extent determine how a person approaches financial affairs. The family's response to too many investments and too little recreation as a result of the household budget should therefore be anticipated, otherwise problems may arise. That is why involvement and communication are so important.

A personal budget brings behaviour patterns sharply into focus. No approach can completely eliminate problems, although a partial solution is possible. The following aspects of human behaviour should be taken into account:

- Members of the same family usually differ – some may be conservative, while others may be optimistic.
- Members of the family may have different personal objectives (for example, one may want to attend a movie every week, while another may want a new dress every three months), and these must be accommodated in the budget, if funds allow.

> Budgeting will help you to apply your income, expenses and investments optimally throughout the different life cycles and to retire financially independent.

- It is essential that everybody should receive recognition for his or her contribution towards the achievement of objectives (for example, they all helped to save and to keep spending at a minimum to make the annual holiday possible).
- The family may resist change in the budget that could prevent them from achieving their personal objectives.
- The family may lose status if, for example, they have to replace their expensive car with a cheaper (ordinary) one.

2.4.3.9 Follow-up

Both good and bad performance of the household in respect of the budget must be scrutinised. This will create a framework for effective planning and control in future.

2.4.4 The appropriateness of a personal budget

The question invariably arises whether budgets are really only appropriate for business enterprises. The answer is no. The costs involved in having a budget are low, it is the best way to achieve personal objectives and it can only be to the benefit of the family. Besides, it is a simple process and can be applied without too much trouble to assist in arranging and controlling the household's finances.

> Budgeting is the best financial habit you can acquire/cultivate/possess. Incurring debt is the worst financial habit you can possess/acquire/cultivate.

EXAMPLE

Fixed budget (current budget)

	Budget	Actual figures	Discrepancy
Telephone account	R100	R120	-R20
Water and electricity	R200	R280	-R80

Variable budget (new budget)

	Budget	Actual figures	Discrepancy
Telephone account	R120	R120	R0
Water and electricity	R300	R280	+R20

2.4.5 Limitations of a personal budget

- A budget is based on assumptions. The success of a budget largely depends on the accuracy of assumptions made. These assumptions must be based on all available facts and on good judgement. Assumptions change and the budget must be adapted accordingly.
- Keeping a budget is not an automatic process. All the members of the family should contribute actively to ensure that they keep to the budgeted figures for monthly expenditure.
- A budget is not the solution to all problems. The family cannot continue overspending and then blame it on the budget. Self-discipline is essential.
- The success of the budget depends on people – all the members of the family. They must co-operate.
- A budget is based on forecasts. These forecasts may not always be accurate because it is difficult to know what is going to happen in the future.

2.4.6 Advantages of a personal budget

- A budget compels a family to do financial planning.
- It is a tool or mechanism for exercising financial control.
- Financial problems can be identified at an early stage.
- It compels a family to think about their financial future and household objectives.
- The personal objectives of each member are identified and integrated into a financial plan.
- It provides unity in objectives with the financial resources of the family.
- Thought is given specifically to unnecessary expenses incurred in the absence of a budget.
- It improves understanding between members of the family if they know why certain expenses should not be incurred.
- Priorities in the household are identified and placed in a logical sequence.
- It promotes togetherness in a family.
- It forces the family to analyse their financial situation and performance periodically.

2.4.7 Preparing the budget

A budget facilitates monthly comparison of the family's income and expenditure. Firstly, the family's anticipated income must be worked out, and then their anticipated expenditure. The next step is to compare the income and expenditure in order to determine whether there is a surplus or a shortfall in the budget.

> Budgeting is about the optimal application of your financial resources.

2.4.7.1 Estimating anticipated income

The anticipated income is estimated on a monthly basis for the next year. Income comprises the following, among others:
- joint net salary of household members;
- bonuses;
- commission earned;
- interest received on investments;
- dividends received on investments;
- annuities received; and
- capital profit (or net profit) on the sale of assets.

Amounts of money which are received but which are repayable are regarded as a liability (loan) and not as an income. The total income is calculated by adding up all the income that the household has received.

2.4.7.2 Estimating anticipated expenditure

Like income, expenditure is estimated on a monthly basis for the next year. A distinction can be made between fixed and variable expenditure. Fixed expenditure includes the following:
- housing (mortgage bond repayments);
- short- and long-term insurance (although premiums may be adjusted for inflation purposes);
- transport costs;
- regular household expenses;
- property tax;
- water and electricity; and
- regular repayments (motor vehicle, furniture – which are regarded as fixed until paid up).

Depending on certain assumptions, some fixed expenditure may also be regarded as variable and vice versa. Variable expenditure includes the following, amongst others:
- clothing;
- service or repairs (motor vehicles);
- medical costs (excluding deductions for medical scheme);
- donations;
- gifts;
- entertainment costs;
- recreation; and
- investments.

2.4.7.3 Comparing estimated income and expenditure

Here the estimated income and expenditure are compared in order to calculate the financial surplus or shortfall on a monthly basis. A surplus means that income exceeds expenditure for a specified period. A shortfall occurs where expenditure for a specified month exceeds income for that month.

Budget for the following year

	Jan.	Feb.	...	Dec.	Total
Income					
(a)					
(b)					
(1) Total income					
Expenditure					
(a)					
(b)					
(2) Total expenditure					
(3) Surplus (+) or shortfall (-)					
(1 - 2)					
(4) Cumulative surplus or shortfall					

At the end of the month, the budgeted figures must be compared with the actual figures. The totals of the actual figures for expenditure are obtained from the family's record system. Documentary proof for each item of expenditure must be kept and used to calculate the monthly total for each item.

The compiler of the budget must take rectifying steps for the months during which a shortfall has been forecast. Certain variable expenses could, for example, be carried over to months for which a surplus has been forecast. It may even be possible to avoid certain expenses completely.

It is important to note that the annual surplus or loss should be as close to nil as possible. In other words, you should not over- or under-budget. The family should also try to keep to the budgeted figures (objectives) as far as possible. Adjustments should be made on a monthly basis in order to keep the surplus or shortfall more or less at a nil.

Comparison between budgeted and actual figures

Month	Budgeted figures (R)	Actual figures (R)	Surplus or loss (R)	Cumulative surplus or loss (R)
Jan.				
Feb.				
March				
April				
May				
June				
July				
Aug.				
Sept.				
Oct.				
Nov.				
Dec.				
TOTALS				

Should a family find that they cannot balance their income and expenditure, they should seriously consider their financial affairs. Various actions or corrective steps are possible in such a case, and these are not always pleasant. The following are some alternatives:

• Repay a loan over a longer period. Such an arrangement will have to be made with the person or institution providing the loan. If permission for an extension cannot be obtained, a second loan with better terms (for example, with a longer repayment period) can be obtained to redeem the original loan.

• Where a person has a housing bond, the repayment term could be extended. The mortgagee could be approached for permission to extend the term of repayment from 20 to 30 years. The monthly bond instalments will be lower over 30 years. It must be kept in mind, however, that the total amount paid in interest will be much more over 30 years.

- Sometimes a person pays a higher bond instalment on his or her home than the mortgagee expects. The reason is usually to save interest by repaying the bond loan over a shorter period (for example, 12 years instead of 20 years). These higher monthly instalments could be reduced to the required instalment to repay the mortgage bond over the normal period of 20 years.
- A personal loan can be taken over a short period (three months). In this way a temporary financial crisis is avoided which may have arisen as a result of unforeseen events such as a motor vehicle breaking down. Usually unforeseen events are not budgeted for.
- Certain expenditures could be reduced, for example:
  - clothing (buy at sales);
  - food (never buy food when you are hungry, use discount coupons, avoid impulsive buying, avoid impulsive visits to restaurants);
  - telephone (make fewer telephone calls, use the telephone in the evening at lower rates, control calls made by children);
  - electricity (use fewer lights at night, do not have lights burning through the night, use weaker bulbs – 60 watts instead of 100 watts – run the swimming pool pump for shorter periods);
  - gifts (give less expensive gifts, limit gifts to family members);
  - donations (stop or make smaller donations);
  - recreation (relax at home, invite guests for a 'bring-and-braai' , avoid long trips with high petrol costs, and entrance fees for recreation – relax with the family at home instead); and
  - entertainment (eat out less, eat out at cheaper restaurants, watch television at home instead of going to the movies, entertain the family at home).
- Defer certain expenses for three or four months. Where a family was planning to buy a new television set on hire-purchase in May, they could defer this to August or September.
- Use an existing investment to defray expenses. However, some investments cannot be commuted to cash at short notice (a month), but an investment that could be called within one day could be used to defray unexpected costs.
- Use an existing investment as security to take out a loan. Where an investment cannot be cashed or claimed, a loan could be arranged with such investment as a contra-investment (security).
- Sell one of the family's possessions. For example, the family may have an asset they never use (a white elephant), which could be sold for cash. A

> Your personal budget should discipline you to plan your spending – before as well as after retirement.

caravan, motor vehicle or piano are examples.

- Close an account, for example a clothing account, for the next six months. This will eliminate further expenses, as well as the temptation to buy and pay later.
- A final, less pleasant alternative, is to lower the family's standard of living. Such a decision will not be readily accepted by the family. They usually worry about what other people will say. It should be kept in mind, however, that other people will find it even more strange if the family eventually goes into liquidation, simply because they were not prepared to lower their standard of living. A family's standard of living can be lowered in one or more of the following ways:
  - Sell the existing home and buy a smaller one, for example without a swimming pool. The electricity account will be smaller, and certain costs associated with, for instance, a swimming pool (equipment, chloride, acid and water for periodic replenishment) will be eliminated. A smaller garden means less water and no need for a gardener or garden service. Housework could be managed without employing a domestic worker. One lounge suite could be sold because there is only one living room. A cheaper residential area would also mean lower rates and taxes.
  - Sell the expensive motor car and buy a cheaper one. A smaller motor car usually means lower vehicle insurance, maintenance and petrol costs.

2.4.7.4 Residential area and cost of living

Block et al. (1988:36) explain how cost of living is affected by the residential area a family lives in. The residential area a person chooses to live in determines, to a great extent, what kind of salary or income he or she should be earning to cover his or her cost of living or to maintain a certain standard of living. It is important to mention here that when a person decides to change jobs, he or she should consider not only the salary package but also the cost of living involved in the area he or she intends moving to. A cheaper residential area requires a lower income than a more expensive area in order to maintain the same standard of living.

The following higher costs are associated with more expensive residential areas:
- property tax (rates and taxes);
- home insurance;

Assume that the cost of living associated with 20 residential areas in Gauteng is calculated and added up. This total cost of living is divided by 20 to determine the average cost of living for these 20 residential areas. Make these average costs of living equal to 100. The cost of living for all 20 residential areas can now be listed in terms of the average cost of living for 100. Assume that the cost of living in Standerton in relation to the average cost of living (100) is 90, while that of Sandton is 120. We wish to calculate a similar salary required in Sandton (taking into account cost of living) if a person in Standerton earns R50 000 per annum.

Calculations

(1) Calculation of index figure for Standerton (average = 100)

$$\text{Index} = \frac{\text{Cost of living in Standerton in rands}}{\text{Average cost of living in 20 residential areas}} \times \frac{100}{1}$$

$$= \frac{\text{R36 000}}{\text{R40 000}} \times \frac{100}{1}$$

$$= 90 \text{ (in example)}$$

(2) Calculation of index figure for Sandton

$$\text{Index} = \frac{\text{Cost of living in Sandton in rands}}{\text{Average cost of living in 20 residential areas}} \times \frac{100}{1}$$

$$= \frac{\text{R48 000}}{\text{R40 000}} \times \frac{100}{1}$$

$$= 120 \text{ (in example)}$$

(3) Comparable salary in Sandton

(a) Calculation of factor (comparable)

$$\text{Index} = \frac{\text{Cost of living in Sandton}}{\text{Cost of living in Standerton}}$$

$$= \frac{120}{90}$$

$$= 1.33$$

(b) Calculation of salary (comparable)

$$= \text{Annual salary in Standerton} \times \text{comparable factor}$$

$$= \text{R50 000} \times 1.33$$

$$= \text{R 66 666 (approximately)}$$

Thus, if a person in Standerton earns R50 000 per annum, he or she must earn R66 666 in Sandton to maintain the same standard of living. The above-mentioned figures are not based on research, they merely serve as an example to explain the basic method. Should a person wish to accept a job in Sandton, for example, he or she should carefully consider the cost of living before making a decision. In the example, a suburban residential area (Standerton) was compared with a metropolitan area (Sandton). The cost of living in the latter area would be higher in every respect than the first-mentioned area, although higher salaries would compensate for it.

- travel costs to workplace and schools; and
- maintenance of the home (swimming pool, larger garden, domestic helper, gardener or garden service).

2.4.8 Record system

For the purpose of a personal budget it is particularly important that documentary proof be kept of income, expenditure, accounts and financial agreements. This makes it possible to determine the actual expenditure, which must then be compared with the budgeted figures. Besides, documents are essential to prove that certain agreements have taken place, as well as to prove that debt has been paid off, should proof be necessary at some stage. If accounts are kept, it will also be possible to check the balance on accounts when necessary.

The absence of such a system may even lead to unnecessary costs. A person will have to telephone or drive to the institution or business to find out what the balance of the account is if a mistaken reminder is received. If you have proof of the payment before the due date, you know that you can safely ignore the reminder.

The importance of immediate access to financial agreements can hardly be overemphasised. If one party to an agreement is uncertain about any aspect of his or her liability, he or she can take out the relevant file and check. The same applies to a will, of which a copy should be kept in the home. The executor of a person's estate should also be in possession of the original copy.

Documentary proof is not kept solely for purposes of a personal budget but also for income tax purposes. Certain expenses incurred by the family (to earn an income) are deductible when calculating the family's income tax liability. Such deductions are only allowed if the family is able to provide documentary proof that the expenditure was in fact incurred.

Documents such as invoices for purchases are kept to protect a person's consumer rights. For example, when goods are purchased, a guarantee is sometimes supplied. If the goods turn out to be faulty, the guarantee certificate has to be produced to prove that the goods are still under guarantee. Remember always to complete the guarantee certificate accompanying a product or goods your purchase and to file it in a safe place.

If a person's will (held by the family lawyer) disappears or is destroyed, this will cause problems and great upheaval in the family. The deceased's estate will be divided according to the laws of intestate succession if the deceased dies intestate (without leaving a will), if the will is invalid or if there is no trace of the will. A copy will protect the family in the event of the death of the testator, particularly if the inheritance is in terms of the intestate hereditary right (as you will see later).

A family's records must be kept in a safe place, out of the reach of children. A will left lying around and accessible to children, especially older children, could cause considerable family problems. The fairness or unfairness of certain decisions could become an issue. Small children, on the other hand, could destroy important proof and cause financial distress to the family.

The head of the family should determine which documents are to be kept and where they are to be kept safely, depending on the family's current situation.

The following are some documents a family should keep in their record system:

- used cheque books (make sure all the counterfoils have been filled in);
- cancelled cheques (cancel the counterfoil as well to avoid uncertainty in future);
- monthly bank statements (you can compare the balance on the bank statement with the balance in your cheque book on the counterfoil);
- receipts (paid accounts);
- purchase slips with guarantees (where applicable);
- all expenditures that may be claimed from income tax at a later stage;
- proof of interest received;
- proof of dividends received;
- tax returns for previous years and possible

Help your children to cultivate this financial habit – to use a personal budget – and to take financial responsibility for their own financial future – empower your children with this wonderful life skill. lead by example.

payments or repayments;
- all proof of credit card purchases;
- credit card numbers;
- account numbers;
- assessment certificates (furniture, ring, watch – especially for short-term insurance claims);
- contracts (hire-purchase agreements, hiring agreements, purchase agreements);
- insurance policies;
- birth certificates;
- will;
- funeral booklet;
- title deed of property (home, erf);
- memorandum of association (trust);
- financial annual statements;
- marriage certificate;
- proof of investments (financial assets – shares, debentures);
- proof of personal loans taken or granted; and
- deposit slips.

It is important that both husband and wife have access to the record system, especially in the event of the death of one of them. It is recommended that the family's lawyer and/or accountant should have access as well, and that he or she should be informed of the system in the event of the simultaneous death of both parents.

Older (adult) children should be informed of the system, although they should not have access to the will before a parent's death.

The above-mentioned list is not the alpha and omega of what should be kept in a record system. Such a list will vary from one family to another and will largely depend on the financial means (wealth) and scope of the family's financial activities. A record system is nevertheless essential for any family, irrespective of their financial resources or the size of the family. Even a single person should implement and use such a system.

2.5 SUMMARY

Annual financial statements and household budgets enable people to evaluate their financial performance on an annual or a monthly basis. Even where a chartered accountant is employed to deal with the household's financial statements, individuals should draw up their own household budget. In this way they can determine, on a continuous basis, whether or not the household's stated objectives are being achieved. Knowledge of budgeting principles, as well as an efficient recording system, are prerequisites for the achievement of objectives in a household's personal finances.

2.6 SELF-ASSESSMENT

- Explain how you would measure your own personal financial performance.
- Briefly discuss the principles you would apply when compiling your household budget.
- Explain the steps you would follow to draw up a budget.
- List the advantages of having a household budget.

BIBLIOGRAPHY

Becker, H. 1992. *How to read financial statements.* Cape Town: Juta.

Block, S.B., Peavy, J.W. & Thornton, J.H. 1988. *Personal financial management.* New York: Harper & Row.

Coetzee, D., Stegman, N., Van Schalkwyk, C.J. & Wesson, N. 2000. *Corporate financial reporting.* 2nd edn. Durban: Butterworths.

Gitman, L.J. 1981. *Personal finance.* Hinsdale: Dryden.

Unisa. 1994. *Personal financial management.* (Study guide.) Pretoria: Unisa.

Weston, J.F. & Brigham, E.F. 1982. *Managerial finance.* New York: Holt, Rinehart & Winston.

CHAPTER 3

THE TIME VALUE OF MONEY – SOME PERSONAL FINANCIAL CALCULATIONS

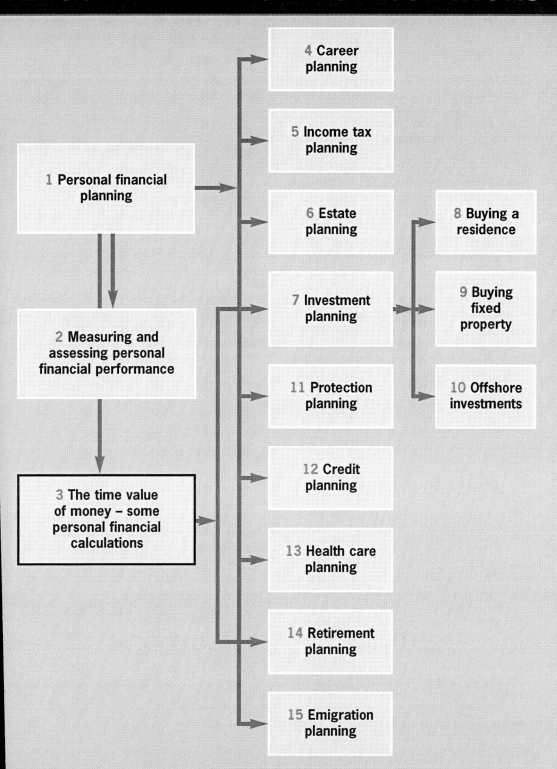

3.1 LEARNING OUTCOMES

After studying this chapter, you will be able to:

- Explain the meaning of 'the time value of money'.
- Demonstrate different calculations regarding time value of money.
- Demonstrate the influence of time value on personal finances.

3.2 INTRODUCTION

The time value of money is a concept that has major implications for personal financial planning. When time value is taken into account, it gives personal financial planning an entirely new meaning. In its simplest form, the time value of money means that R1 is worth far more today than it will be worth in a year's time. You can, therefore, buy more for R1 today than in a year's time. The longer these periods stretch into the future (for example, five or ten years) the less R1 will be able to buy, until eventually it will buy practically nothing (have almost no value).

It should be clear at this point that this concept affects all personal financial calculations, particularly the future return on investments, and it applies to everybody, wealthy or poor, employee or employer.

In the following discussion we will make use of four tables to make some elementary personal financial calculations. We will be dealing with the concepts of future and present value. We are also going to make future and present value calculations in respect of an annuity and a mixed annual cash stream (cash flow, cash income or cash expenditure). This will be followed by special applications of interest tables. (Keep in mind that the same calculations can be done with a financial pocket calculator). Examples of calculations using a pocket calculator are then presented.

3.3 SOME CALCULATIONS

3.3.1 Calculation of future value – lump sum investment

Problem

When a person invests money for a specific period (say five years) at a specific rate of return (say 15%), he or she would normally want to know what the future value of the investment will be. For example, if you were to invest R1 000, you would want to know how this amount would grow over a period of five years.

The calculation of a future value is based on the principle of compound interest. Compound interest means that the interest earned each year on an invested amount (a capital sum) becomes part of the initial investment (R1 000 in our example). In other words, we are talking about interest earned on interest.

The following formula is used to calculate future value (note that a simpler solution using interest tables follows after each formula):

Solution: formula

$FVL = C \times (1 + i)^n$

where:

FVL = future value of a lump sum

C = capital invested

i = annual interest rate

n = period in years

$(1 + i)^n = FVIF_{i,n}$

Now use the above-mentioned investment in the formula.

$FVL = R1\ 000 \times (1 + 0.15)^5$

The tables can now be used to replace the bracketed part of the formula. The capital sum invested is now multiplied by a factor in order to calculate the future value of the investment. For this we use Table 3.1. Look up the factor opposite a term of five years and an interest rate of 15%. The future value factor (FVIF) is 2.011.

Solution: interest tables

$FVL = C \times (FVIF_{i,n})$

where:

$FVIF_{i,n} = (1 + i)^n$

$FVL = R1\ 000 \times (2.011)$

$\quad\ \ = R2\ 011$

Thus, the investor will have R2 011 in his or her investment account at the end of year five. You will notice that where future value is calculated, a factor greater than 1 is always used. This is because 1 in the formula (which represents the capital sum) must be multiplied by a factor greater than itself in order to allow the capital sum (investment amount) to increase. The future value must always be greater than the initial amount invested.

TABLE 3.1 Future-value interest factors for R1,00 compounded at k % for n periods: $FVIF_{k,n} = (1 + k)^n$

Period	1%	2%	3%	4%	5%	6%	7%	8%	9%	10%	11%	12%	13%	14%	15%	16%	20%	25%	30%	35%
1	1.010	1.020	1.030	1.040	1.050	1.060	1.070	1.080	1.090	1.100	1.110	1.120	1.130	1.140	1.150	1.160	1.200	1.250	1.300	1.350
2	1.020	1.040	1.061	1.082	1.103	1.124	1.145	1.166	1.188	1.210	1.232	1.254	1.277	1.300	1.323	1.346	1.440	1.563	1.690	1.823
3	1.030	1.061	1.093	1.125	1.158	1.191	1.225	1.260	1.295	1.331	1.368	1.405	1.443	1.482	1.521	1.561	1.728	1.953	2.197	2.460
4	1.041	1.082	1.126	1.170	1.216	1.262	1.311	1.360	1.412	1.464	1.518	1.574	1.630	1.689	1.749	1.811	2.074	2.441	2.856	3.322
5	1.051	1.104	1.159	1.217	1.276	1.338	1.403	1.469	1.539	1.611	1.685	1.762	1.842	1.925	2.011	2.100	2.488	3.052	3.713	4.484
6	1.062	1.126	1.194	1.265	1.340	1.419	1.501	1.587	1.677	1.772	1.870	1.974	2.082	2.195	2.313	2.436	2.986	3.815	4.827	6.053
7	1.072	1.149	1.230	1.316	1.407	1.504	1.606	1.714	1.828	1.949	2.076	2.211	2.353	2.502	2.660	2.826	3.583	4.768	6.275	8.172
8	1.083	1.172	1.267	1.369	1.477	1.594	1.718	1.851	1.993	2.144	2.305	2.476	2.658	2.853	3.059	3.278	4.300	5.960	8.157	11.032
9	1.094	1.195	1.305	1.423	1.551	1.689	1.838	1.999	2.172	2.358	2.558	2.773	3.004	3.252	3.518	3.803	5.160	7.451	10.604	14.894
10	1.105	1.219	1.344	1.480	1.629	1.791	1.967	2.159	2.367	2.594	2.839	3.106	3.395	3.707	4.046	4.411	6.192	9.313	13.786	20.107
11	1.116	1.243	1.384	1.539	1.710	1.898	2.105	2.332	2.580	2.853	3.152	3.479	3.836	4.226	4.652	5.117	7.430	11.642	17.922	27.144
12	1.127	1.268	1.426	1.601	1.796	2.012	2.252	2.518	2.813	3.138	3.498	3.896	4.335	4.818	5.350	5.936	8.916	14.552	23.298	36.644
13	1.138	1.294	1.469	1.665	1.886	2.133	2.410	2.720	3.066	3.452	3.883	4.363	4.898	5.492	6.153	6.886	10.699	18.190	30.288	49.470
14	1.149	1.319	1.513	1.732	1.980	2.261	2.579	2.937	3.342	3.797	4.310	4.887	5.535	6.261	7.076	7.988	12.839	22.737	39.374	66.784
15	1.161	1.346	1.558	1.801	2.079	2.397	2.759	3.172	3.642	4.177	4.785	5.474	6.254	7.138	8.137	9.266	15.407	28.422	51.186	90.158
16	1.173	1.373	1.605	1.873	2.183	2.540	2.952	3.426	3.970	4.595	5.311	6.130	7.067	8.137	9.358	10.748	18.488	35.527	66.542	121.714
17	1.184	1.400	1.653	1.948	2.292	2.693	3.159	3.700	4.328	5.054	5.895	6.866	7.986	9.276	10.761	12.468	22.186	44.409	86.504	164.314
18	1.196	1.428	1.702	2.026	2.407	2.854	3.380	3.996	4.717	5.560	6.544	7.690	9.024	10.575	12.375	14.463	26.623	55.511	112.455	221.824
19	1.208	1.457	1.754	2.107	2.527	3.026	3.617	4.316	5.142	6.116	7.263	8.613	10.197	12.056	14.232	16.777	31.948	69.389	146.192	299.462
20	1.220	1.486	1.806	2.191	2.653	3.207	3.870	4.661	5.604	6.727	8.062	9.646	11.523	13.743	16.367	19.461	38.338	86.736	190.050	404.274
21	1.232	1.516	1.860	2.279	2.786	3.400	4.141	5.034	6.109	7.400	8.949	10.804	13.021	15.668	18.822	22.574	46.005	108.420	247.065	546.769
22	1.245	1.546	1.916	2.370	2.925	3.604	4.430	5.437	6.659	8.140	9.934	12.100	14.714	17.861	21.645	26.186	55.206	135.525	321.184	735.789
23	1.257	1.577	1.974	2.465	3.072	3.820	4.741	5.871	7.258	8.954	11.026	13.552	16.627	20.362	24.891	30.376	66.247	169.407	417.539	993.653
24	1.270	1.608	2.033	2.563	3.225	4.049	5.072	6.341	7.911	9.850	12.239	15.179	18.788	23.212	28.625	35.236	79.497	211.758	542.801	1342.797
25	1.282	1.641	2.094	2.666	3.386	4.292	5.427	6.848	8.623	10.835	13.585	17.000	21.231	26.462	32.919	40.874	95.396	264.698	705.641	1812.776
30	1.348	1.811	2.427	3.243	4.322	5.743	7.612	10.063	13.268	17.449	22.892	29.960	39.116	50.950	66.21	85.85	237.38	807.79	2620.00	8128.55
35	1.417	2.000	2.814	3.946	5.516	7.686	10.677	14.785	20.414	28.102	38.575	52.800	72.07	98.10	133.18	180.31	590.67	2465.19	9727.86	36448.69
40	1.489	2.208	3.262	4.801	7.040	10.286	14.974	21.725	31.409	45.259	65.001	93.051	132.78	188.88	267.86	378.72	1469.77	7523.16	36118.85	
45	1.565	2.438	3.782	5.841	8.985	13.765	21.002	31.920	48.327	72.890	109.53	163.99	244.64	363.68	538.77	795.44	3657.26	22958.87		
50	1.645	2.692	4.384	7.107	11.467	18.420	29.457	46.902	74.358	117.39	184.55	289.00	450.74	700.23	1083.66	1670.70	9100.44	70064.92		

TABLE 3.2 Future-value interest factors for R1,00 annuity compounded at k % for n periods: $FVIFA_{k,n} = \sum_{t=1}^{n} (1 + k)^{t-1}$

Period	1%	2%	3%	4%	5%	6%	7%	8%	9%	10%	11%	12%	13%	14%	15%	16%	20%	25%	30%	35%
1	1.000	1.000	1.000	1.000	1.000	1.000	1.000	1.000	1.000	1.000	1.000	1.000	1.000	1.000	1.000	1.000	1.000	1.000	1.000	1.000
2	2.010	2.020	2.030	2.040	2.050	2.060	2.070	2.080	2.090	2.100	2.110	2.120	2.130	2.140	2.150	2.160	2.200	2.250	2.300	2.350
3	3.030	3.060	3.090	3.121	3.152	3.183	3.214	3.246	3.278	3.310	3.342	3.374	3.406	3.439	3.472	3.505	3.640	3.812	3.990	4.172
4	4.060	4.121	4.184	4.246	4.310	4.374	4.439	4.506	4.573	4.641	4.709	4.779	4.849	4.921	4.993	5.066	5.368	5.765	6.187	6.632
5	5.101	5.204	5.309	5.416	5.526	5.637	5.751	5.866	5.985	6.105	6.228	6.353	6.480	6.610	6.742	6.877	7.442	8.207	9.043	9.954
6	6.152	6.308	6.468	6.633	6.802	6.975	7.153	7.336	7.523	7.716	7.913	8.115	8.323	8.536	8.754	8.977	9.930	11.259	12.756	14.438
7	7.214	7.434	7.662	7.898	8.142	8.394	8.654	8.923	9.200	9.487	9.783	10.089	10.405	10.730	11.067	11.414	12.916	15.073	17.583	20.492
8	8.286	8.583	8.892	9.214	9.549	9.897	10.260	10.637	11.028	11.436	11.859	12.300	12.757	13.233	13.727	14.240	16.499	19.842	23.858	28.664
9	9.369	9.755	10.159	10.583	11.027	11.491	11.978	12.488	13.021	13.579	14.164	14.776	15.416	16.085	16.786	17.519	20.799	25.802	32.015	39.696
10	10.462	10.950	11.464	12.006	12.578	13.181	13.816	14.487	15.193	15.937	16.722	17.549	18.420	19.337	20.304	21.321	25.959	33.253	42.619	54.590
11	11.567	12.169	12.808	13.486	14.207	14.972	15.784	16.645	17.560	18.531	19.561	20.655	21.814	23.045	24.349	25.733	32.150	42.566	56.405	74.697
12	12.683	13.412	14.192	15.026	15.917	16.870	17.888	18.977	20.141	21.384	22.713	24.133	25.650	27.271	29.002	30.850	39.581	54.208	74.327	101.841
13	13.809	14.680	15.618	16.627	17.713	18.882	20.141	21.495	22.953	24.523	26.212	28.029	29.985	32.089	34.352	36.786	48.497	68.760	97.625	138.485
14	14.947	15.974	17.086	18.292	19.599	21.015	22.550	24.215	26.019	27.975	30.095	32.393	34.883	37.581	40.505	43.672	59.196	86.949	127.913	187.954
15	16.097	17.293	18.599	20.024	21.579	23.276	25.129	27.152	29.361	31.772	34.405	37.280	40.417	43.842	47.580	51.660	72.035	109.687	167.286	254.738
16	17.258	18.639	20.157	21.825	23.657	25.673	27.888	30.324	33.003	35.950	39.190	42.753	46.672	50.980	55.717	60.925	87.442	138.109	218.472	344.897
17	18.430	20.012	21.762	23.698	25.840	28.213	30.840	33.750	36.974	40.545	44.501	48.884	53.739	59.118	65.075	71.673	105.931	173.636	285.014	466.611
18	19.615	21.412	23.414	25.645	28.132	30.906	33.999	37.450	41.301	45.599	50.396	55.750	61.725	68.394	75.836	84.141	128.117	218.045	371.518	630.925
19	20.811	22.841	25.117	27.671	30.539	33.760	37.379	41.446	46.018	51.159	56.939	63.440	70.749	78.969	88.212	98.603	154.740	273.556	483.973	852.748
20	22.019	24.297	26.870	29.778	33.066	36.786	40.995	45.762	51.160	57.275	64.203	72.052	80.947	91.025	102.444	115.380	186.688	342.945	630.165	1152.210
21	23.239	25.783	28.676	31.969	35.719	39.993	44.865	50.423	56.765	64.002	72.265	81.699	92.470	104.768	118.810	134.841	225.026	429.681	820.215	1556.484
22	24.472	27.299	30.537	34.248	38.505	43.392	49.006	55.457	62.873	71.403	81.214	92.503	105.491	120.436	137.632	157.415	271.031	538.101	1067.280	2102.253
23	25.716	28.845	32.453	36.618	41.430	46.996	53.436	60.893	69.532	79.543	91.148	104.603	120.205	138.297	159.276	183.601	326.237	673.626	1388.464	2838.042
24	26.973	30.422	34.426	39.083	44.502	50.816	58.177	66.765	76.790	88.497	102.174	118.155	136.831	158.659	184.168	213.978	392.484	843.033	1806.003	3833.706
25	28.243	32.030	36.459	41.646	47.727	54.865	63.249	73.106	84.701	98.347	114.413	133.334	155.620	181.871	212.793	249.214	471.981	1054.791	2348.803	5176.504
30	34.785	40.568	47.575	56.085	66.439	79.058	94.461	113.283	136.308	164.494	199.021	241.333	293.199	356.787	434.745	530.312	1181.882	3227.174	8729.985	23221.570
35	41.660	49.994	60.462	73.652	90.320	111.435	138.237	172.317	215.711	271.024	341.590	431.663	546.681	693.573	881.170	1120.713	2948.341	9856.761	32422.868	104136.251
40	48.886	60.402	75.401	95.026	120.800	154.762	199.635	259.057	337.882	442.593	581.826	767.091	1013.704	1342.025	1779.090	2360.757	7343.858	30088.655	120392.883	466960.385
45	56.481	71.893	92.720	121.029	159.700	212.744	285.749	386.506	525.859	718.905	986.639	1358.230	1874.165	2590.565	3585.128	4965.274	18281.310	91831.496	447019.389	2093876.590
50	64.463	84.579	112.797	152.667	209.348	290.336	406.529	573.770	815.084	1163.909	1668.771	2400.018	3459.507	4994.521	7217.716	10435.649	45497.191	280255.693	1659760.743	9389019.650

3.3.2 Calculations of future value – annuity

Problem

An annuity is an equal annual sum of money. For example, a person invests R1 000 per annum (every year) for the next five years at a rate of 7%. At the end of the five years the person will not have invested R5 000 (R1 000 × 5), but considerably more, because he or she has earned interest on interest (compound interest).

Solution: formula

$$FVA = A \times \sum_{t-1}^{n} (1 + i)^{t-1}$$

where:

FVA = future value of annuity
A = annuity (annual amount invested)
i = annual interest rate
n = period in years

$$\sum_{t-1}^{n} (1 + i)^{t-1} = FVIFA_{i,n}$$

Now use the above-mentioned annual investment in the formula.

FVA = R1 000 × (1 311 + 1 225 + 1 145 + 1 070 + 1 000 = 5751)

Solution: interest tables

$$FVA = A \times FVIFA_{i,n}$$

where:

$$FVIFA_{i,n} = \sum_{t-1}^{n} (1 + i)^{t-1}$$

You will notice that we are using FVIFA here instead of FVIF. The reason for this is that the future value factor for an annuity (A) is used in this calculation. Now use Table 3.2 to look up the correct factor at 7% for five years.

FVA = R1 000 × 5.751
   = R5 751

The invested amount at the end of the five-year period is R5 751, which is considerably more than the R5 000 originally invested.

We will now take a look at the calculation of present values instead of future values.

3.3.3 Calculation of present value – lump sum

The calculation of the present value of a lump sum is the opposite of the future value of a lump sum. The process for calculating a present value is called discounting. The formula used to calculate a present value is the opposite of the formula for calculating a future value.

Problem

A person anticipates an inheritance of R10 000 in ten years time. He or she wants to know what the R10 000 is worth today (in terms of present monetary value), if it is discounted at a rate of 15%.

Solution: formula

$$PVL = C \times \frac{1}{(1 + i)^n}$$

where:

PVL = present value of a lump sum
C = capital sum
i = annual interest rate (discounting rate)
n = period in years
Now insert the figures in the formula:

$$PVL = R10\ 000 \times \frac{1}{(1 + 0.15)^{10}}$$

Again, the tables can be used to replace the bracketed part. Table 3.3 is used now to calculate a present value at an interest rate of 15% and over a period of ten years. The present value factor is 0.247 (PVIF).

Solution: interest tables

PVL = 10 000 × (0.247)
   = 2 470

The factor is smaller than 1, because the present value of the lump sum should be lower than when it is received in ten year's time. Therefore, the R10 000 is worth only R2 470 in terms of today's money (value). This means that in ten year's time the R10 000 will only buy as much as R2 470 would buy today.

The present value of a mixed cash stream can also be calculated. A mixed cash stream is where the annual cash stream consists of several amounts, in contrast to an annuity which means equal annual amounts.

3.3.4 Calculation of present value – mixed annual cash stream

The calculation of the present value of a mixed annual cash stream is similar to the previous calculation. The difference lies in the fact that present values are calculated for different amounts, after which they are added up to obtain a single present value.

Problem

A person receives five different annual amounts over a period of five years. If the amounts are discounted at 15%, calculate the present value of his or her money.

TABLE 3.3 Present-value interest factors for R1,00 discounted at k % for n periods: PVIF$_{k,n}$ = $\dfrac{1}{(1+k)^n}$

Period	1%	2%	3%	4%	5%	6%	7%	8%	9%	10%	11%	12%	13%	14%	15%	16%	20%	25%	30%	35%
1	0.990	0.980	0.971	0.962	0.952	0.943	0.935	0.926	0.917	0.909	0.901	0.893	0.885	0.877	0.870	0.862	0.833	0.800	0.769	0.741
2	0.980	0.961	0.943	0.925	0.907	0.890	0.873	0.857	0.842	0.826	0.812	0.797	0.783	0.769	0.756	0.743	0.694	0.640	0.592	0.549
3	0.971	0.942	0.915	0.889	0.864	0.840	0.816	0.794	0.772	0.751	0.731	0.712	0.693	0.675	0.658	0.641	0.579	0.512	0.455	0.406
4	0.961	0.924	0.888	0.855	0.823	0.792	0.763	0.735	0.708	0.683	0.659	0.636	0.613	0.592	0.572	0.552	0.482	0.410	0.350	0.301
5	0.951	0.906	0.863	0.822	0.784	0.747	0.713	0.681	0.650	0.621	0.593	0.567	0.543	0.519	0.497	0.476	0.402	0.328	0.269	0.223
6	0.942	0.888	0.837	0.790	0.746	0.705	0.666	0.630	0.596	0.564	0.535	0.507	0.480	0.456	0.432	0.410	0.335	0.262	0.207	0.165
7	0.933	0.871	0.813	0.760	0.711	0.665	0.623	0.583	0.547	0.513	0.482	0.452	0.425	0.400	0.376	0.354	0.279	0.210	0.159	0.122
8	0.923	0.853	0.789	0.731	0.677	0.627	0.582	0.540	0.502	0.467	0.434	0.404	0.376	0.351	0.327	0.305	0.233	0.168	0.123	0.091
9	0.914	0.837	0.766	0.703	0.645	0.592	0.544	0.500	0.460	0.424	0.391	0.361	0.333	0.308	0.284	0.263	0.194	0.134	0.094	0.067
10	0.905	0.820	0.744	0.676	0.614	0.558	0.508	0.463	0.422	0.386	0.352	0.322	0.295	0.270	0.247	0.227	0.162	0.107	0.073	0.050
11	0.896	0.804	0.722	0.650	0.585	0.527	0.475	0.429	0.388	0.350	0.317	0.287	0.261	0.237	0.215	0.195	0.135	0.086	0.056	0.037
12	0.887	0.788	0.701	0.625	0.557	0.497	0.444	0.397	0.356	0.319	0.286	0.257	0.231	0.208	0.187	0.168	0.112	0.069	0.043	0.027
13	0.879	0.773	0.681	0.601	0.530	0.469	0.415	0.368	0.326	0.290	0.258	0.229	0.204	0.182	0.163	0.145	0.093	0.055	0.033	0.020
14	0.870	0.758	0.661	0.577	0.505	0.442	0.388	0.340	0.299	0.263	0.232	0.205	0.181	0.160	0.141	0.125	0.078	0.044	0.025	0.015
15	0.861	0.743	0.642	0.555	0.481	0.417	0.362	0.315	0.275	0.239	0.209	0.183	0.160	0.140	0.123	0.108	0.065	0.035	0.020	0.011
16	0.853	0.728	0.623	0.534	0.458	0.394	0.339	0.292	0.252	0.218	0.188	0.163	0.141	0.123	0.107	0.093	0.054	0.028	0.015	0.008
17	0.844	0.714	0.605	0.513	0.436	0.371	0.317	0.270	0.231	0.198	0.170	0.146	0.125	0.108	0.093	0.080	0.045	0.023	0.012	0.006
18	0.836	0.700	0.587	0.494	0.416	0.350	0.296	0.250	0.212	0.180	0.153	0.130	0.111	0.095	0.081	0.069	0.038	0.018	0.009	0.005
19	0.828	0.686	0.570	0.475	0.396	0.331	0.277	0.232	0.194	0.164	0.138	0.116	0.098	0.083	0.070	0.060	0.031	0.014	0.007	0.003
20	0.820	0.673	0.554	0.456	0.377	0.312	0.258	0.215	0.178	0.149	0.124	0.104	0.087	0.073	0.061	0.051	0.026	0.012	0.005	0.002
21	0.811	0.660	0.538	0.439	0.359	0.294	0.242	0.199	0.164	0.135	0.112	0.093	0.077	0.064	0.053	0.044	0.022	0.009	0.004	0.002
22	0.803	0.647	0.522	0.422	0.342	0.278	0.226	0.184	0.150	0.123	0.101	0.083	0.068	0.056	0.046	0.038	0.018	0.007	0.003	0.001
23	0.795	0.634	0.507	0.406	0.326	0.262	0.211	0.170	0.138	0.112	0.091	0.074	0.060	0.049	0.040	0.033	0.015	0.006	0.002	0.001
24	0.788	0.622	0.492	0.390	0.310	0.247	0.197	0.158	0.126	0.102	0.082	0.066	0.053	0.043	0.035	0.028	0.013	0.005	0.002	0.001
25	0.780	0.610	0.478	0.375	0.295	0.233	0.184	0.146	0.116	0.092	0.074	0.059	0.047	0.038	0.030	0.024	0.010	0.004	0.001	0.001
30	0.742	0.552	0.412	0.308	0.231	0.174	0.131	0.099	0.075	0.057	0.044	0.033	0.026	0.020	0.015	0.012	0.004	0.001		
35	0.706	0.500	0.355	0.253	0.181	0.130	0.094	0.068	0.049	0.036	0.026	0.019	0.014	0.010	0.008	0.005	0.002			
40	0.672	0.453	0.307	0.208	0.142	0.097	0.067	0.046	0.032	0.022	0.015	0.011	0.008	0.005	0.004	0.003	0.001			
45	0.639	0.410	0.264	0.171	0.111	0.073	0.048	0.031	0.021	0.014	0.009	0.006	0.004	0.003	0.002	0.001				
50	0.608	0.372	0.228	0.141	0.087	0.054	0.034	0.021	0.013	0.009	0.005	0.003	0.002	0.001	0.001	0.001				

	Cash stream (R)	PVIF (15%)	Present values (R)
1	1 000	0.870	870
2	2 000	0.756	1 512
3	3 000	0.658	1 974
4	4 000	0.572	2 288
5	5 000	0.497	2 485
Present value of mixed cash stream			9 129

Table 3.3 shows the present value factors at a discounted rate of 15% for years 1–5. The present value factors are again smaller than 1. The factor (PVIF) for year 2 must be looked up in the table opposite year 2. Like all the others, these sums of money are received (or invested) at the end of the year. An amount of R1 000 received at the end of year 1 is therefore only worth R870 today (one year earlier). The initial cash stream (before discounting) amounts to R15 000. The present value amounts to only R9 129.

3.3.5 Calculation of present value – annuity (equal annual cash stream)

In this case, the person receives equal sums of money. The present value calculation differs from the previous calculation.

Problem
A person receives five equal amounts of R1 000 each (at the end of each year) over a period of five years. Calculate the present value of the money at a discounted rate of 15%.

Solution: interest tables
In this case, we use a present value factor for an annuity (PVIFA). This factor appears in Table 3.4. We will not have a separate calculation for each year as we had previously, but only one calculation, because we are dealing with an annuity. So we only look up a single factor in Table 3.4. Once again, we take five years at a discounted rate of 15%, that is 3.352.
PVA = A × (PVIFA$_{i,n}$)
where:
PVA = present value of annuity
A = annuity (equal annual cash stream)
i = annual interest rate
n = period in years
Now insert the figures in the formula:
PVA = R1 000 × 3.352
    = R3 352

Although the person will ultimately receive R5 000 (R1 000 × 5), this amount is worth only R3 352 today.

3.3.6 Interest calculated more than once a year

So far, all calculations have been based on an annual interest rate, in other words, interest per annum. However, interest may be calculated more than once a year, for example, half-yearly, quarterly, monthly or daily. This has important implications for personal financial planning and calculations. The more often interest is calculated over one year, the higher the interest rate and the larger the amount of interest to be paid or received. If a person invests money, the interest he or she receives will be more if interest is calculated half-yearly than if it is calculated once a year. If interest is calculated quarterly, the investor will receive even more interest, and if it is calculated monthly, still more.

When money has to be invested, the investor should not merely accept that an interest rate (investment rate) of 15.5% is higher than another interest rate of 12.25%. If the interest rate is an annual amount, this would in fact be the case. However, if the interest in the case of 15.5% is calculated annually and in the case of 12.25% quarterly, a calculation should be made first.

3.3.6.1 Interest calculated annually
Assume that R10 000 is invested for five years at 16% annual compound interest. Calculate the investment amount after five years.
FVL = C × (1 + i)^n
    = R10 000 × (1 + 0.16)^5
    = R10 000 × 2.1 (FVIF – Table 3.1)
    = R21 000
where:
FVL = future value of a lump sum
C = capital amount
i = annual interest rate
n = period in years

The formula is now adapted to calculate cases where interest is calculated more than once a year. Interest can be calculated quarterly in this case.
FVL = C × (1 + i/m)$^{n \times m}$
where:
FVL = future value of a lump sum
C = capital amount
m = period of interest rate
$n \times m$ = periods (number) for which interest is calculated

TABLE 3.4 Present-value interest factors for R1,00 annuity discounted at k % for n periods: $PVIFA_{k,n} = \sum_{t=1}^{n} \frac{1}{(1+k)^t}$

Period	1%	2%	3%	4%	5%	6%	7%	8%	9%	10%	11%	12%	13%	14%	15%	16%	20%	25%	30%	35%
1	0.990	0.980	0.971	0.962	0.952	0.943	0.935	0.926	0.917	0.909	0.901	0.893	0.885	0.877	0.870	0.862	0.833	0.800	0.769	0.741
2	1.970	1.942	1.913	1.886	1.859	1.833	1.808	1.783	1.759	1.736	1.713	1.690	1.668	1.647	1.626	1.605	1.528	1.440	1.361	1.289
3	2.941	2.884	2.829	2.775	2.723	2.673	2.624	2.577	2.531	2.487	2.444	2.402	2.361	2.322	2.283	2.246	2.106	1.952	1.816	1.696
4	3.902	3.808	3.717	3.630	3.546	3.465	3.387	3.312	3.240	3.170	3.102	3.037	2.974	2.914	2.855	2.798	2.589	2.362	2.166	1.997
5	4.853	4.713	4.580	4.452	4.329	4.212	4.100	3.993	3.890	3.791	3.696	3.605	3.517	3.433	3.352	3.274	2.991	2.689	2.436	2.220
6	5.795	5.601	5.417	5.242	5.076	4.917	4.767	4.623	4.486	4.355	4.231	4.111	3.998	3.889	3.784	3.685	3.326	2.951	2.643	2.385
7	6.728	6.472	6.230	6.002	5.786	5.582	5.389	5.206	5.033	4.868	4.712	4.564	4.423	4.288	4.160	4.039	3.605	3.161	2.802	2.508
8	7.652	7.325	7.020	6.733	6.463	6.210	5.971	5.747	5.535	5.335	5.146	4.968	4.799	4.639	4.487	4.344	3.837	3.329	2.925	2.598
9	8.566	8.162	7.786	7.435	7.108	6.802	6.515	6.247	5.995	5.759	5.537	5.328	5.132	4.946	4.772	4.607	4.031	3.463	3.019	2.665
10	9.471	8.983	8.530	8.111	7.722	7.360	7.024	6.710	6.418	6.145	5.889	5.650	5.426	5.216	5.019	4.833	4.192	3.571	3.092	2.715
11	10.368	9.787	9.253	8.760	8.306	7.887	7.499	7.139	6.805	6.495	6.207	5.938	5.687	5.453	5.234	5.029	4.327	3.656	3.147	2.752
12	11.255	10.575	9.954	9.385	8.863	8.384	7.943	7.536	7.161	6.814	6.492	6.194	5.918	5.660	5.421	5.197	4.439	3.725	3.190	2.779
13	12.134	11.348	10.635	9.986	9.394	8.853	8.358	7.904	7.487	7.103	6.750	6.424	6.122	5.842	5.583	5.342	4.533	3.780	3.223	2.799
14	13.004	12.106	11.296	10.563	9.899	9.295	8.745	8.244	7.786	7.367	6.982	6.628	6.302	6.002	5.724	5.468	4.611	3.824	3.249	2.814
15	13.865	12.849	11.938	11.118	10.380	9.712	9.108	8.559	8.061	7.606	7.191	6.811	6.462	6.142	5.847	5.575	4.675	3.859	3.268	2.825
16	14.718	13.578	12.561	11.652	10.838	10.106	9.447	8.851	8.313	7.824	7.379	6.974	6.604	6.265	5.954	5.668	4.730	3.887	3.283	2.834
17	15.562	14.292	13.166	12.166	11.274	10.477	9.763	9.122	8.544	8.022	7.549	7.120	6.729	6.373	6.047	5.749	4.775	3.910	3.295	2.840
18	16.398	14.992	13.754	12.659	11.690	10.828	10.059	9.372	8.756	8.201	7.702	7.250	6.840	6.467	6.128	5.818	4.812	3.928	3.304	2.844
19	17.226	15.678	14.324	13.134	12.085	11.158	10.336	9.604	8.950	8.365	7.839	7.366	6.938	6.550	6.198	5.877	4.843	3.942	3.311	2.848
20	18.046	16.351	14.877	13.590	12.462	11.470	10.594	9.818	9.129	8.514	7.963	7.469	7.025	6.623	6.259	5.929	4.870	3.954	3.316	2.850
21	18.857	17.011	15.415	14.029	12.821	11.764	10.836	10.017	9.292	8.649	8.075	7.562	7.102	6.687	6.312	5.973	4.891	3.963	3.320	2.852
22	19.660	17.658	15.937	14.451	13.163	12.042	11.061	10.201	9.442	8.772	8.176	7.645	7.170	6.743	6.359	6.011	4.909	3.970	3.323	2.853
23	20.456	18.292	16.444	14.857	13.489	12.303	11.272	10.371	9.580	8.883	8.266	7.718	7.230	6.792	6.399	6.044	4.925	3.976	3.325	2.854
24	21.243	18.914	16.936	15.247	13.799	12.550	11.469	10.529	9.707	8.985	8.348	7.784	7.283	6.835	6.434	6.073	4.937	3.981	3.327	2.855
25	22.023	19.523	17.413	15.622	14.094	12.783	11.654	10.675	9.823	9.077	8.422	7.843	7.330	6.873	6.464	6.097	4.948	3.985	3.329	2.856
30	25.808	22.396	19.600	17.292	15.372	13.765	12.409	11.258	10.274	9.427	8.694	8.055	7.496	7.003	6.566	6.177	4.979	3.995	3.332	2.857
35	29.409	24.999	21.487	18.665	16.374	14.498	12.948	11.655	10.567	9.644	8.855	8.176	7.586	7.070	6.617	6.215	4.992	3.998	3.333	2.857
40	32.835	27.355	23.115	19.793	17.159	15.046	13.332	11.925	10.757	9.779	8.951	8.244	7.634	7.105	6.642	6.233	4.997	3.999	3.333	2.857
45	36.095	29.490	24.519	20.720	17.774	15.456	13.606	12.108	10.881	9.863	9.008	8.283	7.661	7.123	6.654	6.242	4.999	4.000	3.333	2.857
50	39.195	31.424	25.730	21.482	18.256	15.762	13.801	12.233	10.962	9.915	9.042	8.304	7.675	7.133	6.661	6.246	4.999	4.000	3.333	2.857

Where interest is calculated more than once a year, both the interest rate (i) and the number of periods (n) for which interest is calculated change. The m will be 2, for example, where interest is calculated half-yearly, and 4 where the interest is calculated quarterly. The annual interest rate, therefore, is divided by the m, while the period in years is multiplied by the m.

3.3.6.2 Interest calculated half-yearly

$FVL = R10\,000 \times (1 + 0.16/2)^{5 \times 2}$
$\quad = R10\,000 \times (1 + 0.08)^{10}$
$\quad = R10\,000 \times 2.159 \text{ (FVIF – Table 3.1)}$
$\quad = R\,21\,590$

where:
8 = interest rate; and
10 = number of periods for which interest is calculated

3.3.6.3 Interest calculated quarterly

$FVL = R10\,000 \times (1 + 0.16/4)^{5 \times 4}$
$\quad = R10\,000 \times (1 + 0.04)^{20}$
$\quad = R10\,000 \times 2.191$
$\quad = R\,21\,910$

The interest rate now is 4% and the number of periods for which interest must be calculated is 20. Table 3.1 is used for an interest rate of 4% and for 20 periods. A factor (FVIF) of 2.191 is obtained.

Capital sum: a comparison

	Capital sum
Annual interest	R21 000
Half-yearly interest	R21 590
Quarterly interest	R21 910

It should be clear now that the more often interest is calculated, the more interest is earned and the larger the ultimate capital or investment amount will be.

3.3.7 Nominal and effective interest rate

The same principles (as discussed above) apply when a person wishes to borrow money, for example to buy furniture or a motor vehicle. Usually a person is told that he or she will be charged a certain interest rate on the borrowed amount, for example 20%. This quoted interest rate is called the contract interest rate or nominal interest rate. However, it is seldom mentioned how interest will be calculated – annually, half-yearly or quarterly.

When a person borrows money, he or she should find out what the actual interest rate will be for the money being borrowed. The actual interest rate is called the effective interest rate. If a person has to choose between different interest rates calculated over different periods, he or she should first estab-

lish the actual or effective rates of the different alternatives for the loan. In this way proper comparisons can be made. The contract or nominal interest rate should, therefore, not be accepted without due consideration.

Gitman (1988:179) provides the following formula for the calculation of effective interest rate:
$k_{eff} = (1 + i/m)^m - 1$
where:
i = nominal interest rate
m = number of periods for which interest is calculated

This formula is used for the calculation of the effective interest rate if interest is calculated annually, half-yearly or quarterly. A nominal interest rate of 20% is used. Interest will be calculated 1, 2 and 4 times per annum.

3.3.7.1 Annual interest

$k_{eff} = (1 + 0.20/1)^1 - 1$
$\quad = (1 + 0.20)^1 - 1$
$\quad = 1 + 0.20 - 1$
$\quad = 0.20$
Effective interest rate = 20% = nominal interest rate

3.3.7.2 Half-yearly interest

$k_{eff} = (1 + 0.20/2)^2 - 1$
$\quad = (1 + 0.10)^2 - 1$
$\quad = 1.210 - 1 \text{ (where } 1.210 = \text{FVIF, Table 3.1)}$
$\quad = 0.210$
Effective interest rate = 21%

3.3.7.3 Quarterly interest

$k_{eff} = (1 + 0.20/4)^4 - 1$
$\quad = (1 + 0.05)^4 - 1$
$\quad = 1.216 - 1 \text{ (where } 1.216 = \text{FVIF, Table 3.1)}$
$\quad = 0.216$
Effective interest rate = 21.6%

From the calculations it can be seen that the more often interest is calculated per annum, the higher the effective interest rate (actual interest rate). When people borrow money, they should make sure that they have calculated the effective rate(s).

3.4 SOME SPECIAL APPLICATIONS OF TIME VALUE

Future and present value techniques have several applications. Some of these applications are illustrated below:
• deposits required for a future sum of money;
• repayment of a loan;
• determination of interest rates; and
• determination of growth rates.

3.4.1 Deposits required for a future sum of money

Problem

People often wish to know what amount they should invest in order to obtain a certain amount over a certain period. Assume that someone wishes to buy a house over five years and requires a deposit of R20 000. He or she would like to know the amount that would have to be invested annually in order to have an amount of R20 000 in his or her investment account in five year's time. The account in which the annual investment is made at the end of each year pays 6% interest.

Solution

$FVA = A \times FVIFA_{i,n}$

where:

FVA = future value of an annuity
A = annuity (annual investment amount)
$FVIFA$ = future value interest factor for an annuity
i = annual interest rate
n = period in years

Now insert all available numbers and figures in this formula.

$R20\ 000 = A \times (FVIFA_{6,5})$ – see Table 3.2
$R20\ 000 = A \times 5.637$
We wish to calculate A, however:
$A = R20\ 000/5.637$
   $= R3\ 547,99$

If an amount of R3 547,99 were to be invested at 6% at the end of each year for the following five years, the investment amount at the end of the five-year period would be R20 000, that is, the deposit for the purchase of a house would be available.

3.4.2 Repayment of a loan (amortisation)

In this instance, a person wishes to calculate what equal annual instalments (repayments) will have to be made in order to redeem a certain loan amount over a certain period at a certain interest rate. In the previous problem, we worked with an uncertain future amount (which still needed to be acquired). Here we have an amount that already exists (or will be borrowed), so we will use the present value interest factor (PFIVA) for an annuity in this case.

Problem

A person borrows R20 000 at 20% interest per annum. The person wants to know what equal sums he or she would have to pay in order to pay off the loan in ten years.

Solution

$PVA = A \times (PVIFA_{i,n})$
where:
PVA = present value of an annuity
A = annuity (equal annual instalment)
$PVIFA$ = present value interest factor for an annuity
i = annual interest rate
n = period in years

Now insert all available numbers and figures in this formula.
$R20\ 000 = A \times (PVIFA_{20,10})$ (see Table 3.4)
$R20\ 000 = A \times 4.192$
However, we wish to calculate A:
$A = R20\ 000/4.192$
   $= R4\ 770,99$
   $= R4\ 771$ (approximately)

The person would have to pay R4 771 at the end of each year for a period of ten years to redeem the loan of R20 000 at an interest rate of 20%.

3.4.3 Determination of interest rates

It may happen that a person would like to know what interest rate he or she would have to pay on an equal-instalment loan.

Problem

A person borrows R2 000 from a bank, and has to repay the bank for the loan in five equal instalments of R530 each. Calculate the interest rate at which he or she borrows the money.

Solution

$PVIFA_{i,n} = C/A$
where:
$PVIFA$ = present value factor for an annuity
i = annual interest rate
n = period in years
C = capital amount (loan amount)
A = annuity (equal annual instalments)
Now insert all available figures in the formula.
$PVIFA_{i,5} = R2\ 000/R530$
       $= 3.7736$

Use Table 3.4 and look up 5 years and the factor closest to 3.7736. The closest factor is 3.791. This factor appears opposite an interest rate of 10%. Thus, the interest rate on the equal-instalment loan is approximately 10%.

3.4.4 Determination of growth rates

Sometimes a person wants to know at what rate his or her money in a bank account will grow. Where the investment is already five years old, it is possible to calculate the growth rate. Gitman (1988:196) points out that future value factors as well as present value factors are used for this purpose.

Problem

A person wishes to determine the growth rate on an investment. He or she invested R1 250 in an account in 1997. Up to and including 2001, the investment grew annually as follows:

Year	Cash	Growth in years
2001	R1 520	4
2000	R1 480	3
1999	R1 420	2
1998	R1 320	1
1997	R1 250	

Calculate the growth rate of the investment.

Solution

The investment grew for 4 years. The present value interest factor (PVIF – Table 3.3) is used in this calculation. The amount in 1997 (R1 250) is divided by the amount in 2001 (R1 520) in order to determine the present value interest factor for a period of 4 years (the period over which growth occurred). R1 250 ÷ R1 520 = 0.822

The present value interest factor closest to 0.822 and a period of 4 years is 0.823. This is opposite the interest rate of 5%. Thus, the person's investment has grown at 5%.

3.5 CALCULATIONS WITH A FINANCIAL POCKET CALCULATOR

You will notice that calculations relating to the time value of money can be performed using either interest tables or a personal financial pocket calculator. However, interest tables will assist you to understand what is meant by the time value of money (the theory of compound interest). Nevertheless, it is recommended that you buy a personal financial calculator so that you will be able to perform your own personal financial calculations (when purchasing a dwelling, a motor vehicle and furniture, making investments or borrowing money). Everyday financial transactions and even retirement planning are influenced by the time value of money.

> Without a knowledge of the time value of money, it is impossible to understand personal financial planning.

Smal (1992:3) points out that until the mid-seventies all time value of money calculations were done by means of interest tables. According to him the tables were very handy because interest rates in excess of 20% were unheard of. In practice, a need occurred for more comprehensive calculations that could be used in all situations. The appearance of pocket calculators in the mid-seventies created a revolution, because calculations were not limited to fixed terms and interest rates. All financial calculations could now be done with the greatest of ease.

Many pocket calculators can be used for the purposes of these calculations. I suggest you buy the Sharp EL733, unless you already have another type – just as long as it is able to do financial calculations.

We will now do a number of calculations with the Sharp EL733 pocket calculator, and then do the calculations with other pocket calculators as well. First, note the following guidelines regarding your calculations.

How to use the Sharp EL733:

- Press 2ndF MODE to switch to the financial mode (repeat – financial mode, not STAT mode).
- Press 2ndF TAB2 (to set the number of decimal places to 2 – TAB3 for 3 decimal places).
- Press 2ndF C·CE before every calculation to clear the financial memory.
- $n(\times 12)$ is the number of periods.
- $i(\div 12)$ is the interest rate.
- PV is the present value.
- FV is the future value.
- ± PMT to key in outflowing annuities.
- PMT to key in inflowing annuities.
- COMP PV to calculate the present value.
- COMP PMT to calculate the instalment.
- COMP i to calculate the interest rate.
- COMP n to calculate the number of periods (term).
- AMRT to calculate the capital paid, the interest paid and the outstanding balance of a mortgage.
- BGN for a prepaid annuity (for example where rent is received in advance).
- APR for calculating the nominal interest rate (in the calculation).
- EFF for calculating the effective interest rate (in the calculation).

Let us consider the following example in order to calculate the difference between nominal and effective interest rates. You invest R100 and, at the end of

Remember that in the case of a prepaid annuity, you must press BGN (for the Sharp EL733) at the start of your calculations. Ensure that you know when ± must be pressed, for example for expenditure as well as when you use both present and future value in your calculation. CF*i* is used in the case of income (cash flow), '*i*' for the interest rate and '*n*' for the period. An instalment is calculated by pressing COMP and PMT at the end of your calculation. The capital that is paid off on a bond, the total interest already paid and the outstanding balance are calculated by pressing AMRT, AMRT and AMRT. If you wish to calculate the above at the end of ten years, you will have to calculate the instalment (PMT). Then enter the months (10 × 12 = 120) and, directly thereafter, press AMRT. Each AMRT will give you an answer to one of the three relevant calculations (questions). You will also be expected to calculate the net present value (NPV) and the internal rate of return (IRR).

the year, have R114,93. What nominal interest rate did you receive if interest was calculated monthly?
Calculation: 12   2ndF   APR

14.93	=	14 (13.996)
Answer	=	14%

If you receive 14% nominal interest, and the effective rate is required, the calculation is as follows:
Calculation: 12   2ndF   EFF

14	=	14.93
Answer	=	14.93%

ACTIVITY 3.1

You purchase a dwelling (house, flat, duplex) for R250 000 and finance the purchase by way of a R200 000 mortgage bond. The mortgage bond interest rate amounts to 18% per year and the period of the bond is 20 years. You wish to calculate the following:

- The monthly mortgage bond instalment.
  Calculation: (clear the financial memory of the pocket calculator (first press the yellow 2ndF button and then the orange C-CE button)
  - 200 000, ± , PV
  - 18 2ndF *ii*
  - 20 2ndF *nn*
  - COMP
  - PMT
    Answer = R3 086,62

- The new mortgage bond instalment if interest rates rise to 23% per year.

Calculation: (store your previous answer together with the relevant calculations in the memory of your pocket calculator and then press)
- 23 2ndF *ii*
- COMP
- PMT
  Answer = R3 874

- The new mortgage bond instalment should you have to extend the mortgage bond period to 30 years as a result of a cash-flow problem.
  Calculation: (store your previous answer together with the relevant calculations in the memory of your pocket calculator and then press)
  - 30 2ndF *nn*
  - COMP
  - PMT
    Answer = R3 837,46

Note that even though the mortgage bond instalment is reduced by R36,54 (R3 874 – R3 837,46), you will, however, pay considerably more in interest.

ACTIVITY 3.2

You purchase a dwelling for R300 000 at an interest rate of 18% per annum. The mortgage bond period is 20 years. After 10 years, you wish to calculate the following:
- The amount of capital amortised by the 120th instalment.
  Calculation: (clear the financial memory)
  - 300 000, ± , PV
  - 18 2ndF *ii*
  - 20 2ndF *nn*
  - COMP
  - PMT = R4 629,93
  - 120 AMRT (120 = 10 years × 12 months)
    Answer = R764,16

- The amount of interest amortised by the 120th instalment.
  Again press AMRT (you are still busy with the same calculation)
  Answer = R3 865,78

- The outstanding balance on your mortgage bond.
  Again press AMRT
  Answer = R256 954,21

ACTIVITY 3.3

You have borrowed a certain amount of money from your father in order to buy a house. Compound interest of 15% is calculated at the end of each year. The loan, together with interest, must be repaid after five years, and the amount will then be R120 682. How much did you borrow from your father?

Calculation: (clear the financial memory)

- 120 682, ±, FV
- 15 i
- 5 n
- COMP
- PV

Answer = R60 000

ACTIVITY 3.4

You borrowed R60 000 from your father to buy a house. Compound interest amounting to 15% is calculated at the end of each year. You eventually repaid your father R120 682. For how many years did you borrow the money?

Calculation: (clear the financial memory)

- 60 000, ±, PV
- 15 i
- 120 682, FV
- COMP
- n

Answer = 5 years

ACTIVITY 3.5

You borrowed R60 000 for five years from your father in order to buy a house. After five years, you had to repay your father R120 682. What amount of interest, compounded once a year, did he require you to pay?

Calculation: (clear the financial memory)

- 60 000, ±, PV
- 5 n
- 120 682, FV
- COMP
- i

Answer = 15%

ACTIVITY 3.6

Your client invested money in his/her savings account for one year. The nominal interest rate, calculated monthly at the end of each month on his/her investment, was 14%. Calculate his/her effective interest rate.

Calculation: (clear the financial memory)

- 12 2ndF EFF
- 14 =

Answer = 14.93%

ACTIVITY 3.7

You borrowed a certain sum of money from your father to buy a house. Interest was calculated at 15% at the end of each month, and the loan was repayable after two years together with interest. At such time, the amount

repayable was R80 841,06. How much did you borrow from your father?

Calculation: (clear the financial memory)

- 15 ÷ 12 = i
- 2 × 12 = n
- 80 841,06, ±, FV
- COMP
- PV

Answer = R60 000

ACTIVITY 3.8

Mr Smit has been granted a mortgage loan of R30 000. Money is worth 11% per annum, compounded monthly at the end of each month. Mr Smit's monthly instalment is R286,99. Calculate the period of the loan.

Calculation: (clear the financial memory)

- 30 000, ±, PV
- 11 ÷ 12 = i
- 286.99 PMT
- COMP
- n
- ÷ 12 (months)

Answer = 29 years

ACTIVITY 3.9

An investor analyses an industrial property and finds that it will yield a net income of R20 000, R25 000 and R30 000 over the next three years respectively. At the end of this period, the property can be sold for R300 000. If the investor requires at least 12% on his/her investment, what is the maximum amount which he/she should pay for the property?

Calculation: (clear the financial memory)

- 12 i
- 0 CFi
- 20 000 CFi
- 25 000 CFi
- 330 000 CFi (330 000 = 30 000 + 300 000)
- NPV

Answer = R272 674

3.5.1 Calculations using both the tables and a pocket calculator

1. You invest R2 000 for 3 years at 12% interest per year. What will your investment be worth after 3 years?

   Table:

   R2 000 × $FVIF_{k,n}$

   = R2 000 × $FVIF_{12,3}$

   = R2 000 × 1.405

   = R2 810

   Pocket calculator:

$2000 \pm PV$

$12\ i$

$3\ n$

COMP

FV = R2 810 (approximated)

2. You invest R1 000 per year for 5 years at an annual interest rate of 15%. What will the investment be worth in 5 years' time?

Table:

$R1\ 000 \times FVIFA_{k,n}$

$R1\ 000 \times FVIFA_{15,5}$

$R1\ 000 \times 6.742$

R6 742

Pocket calculator:

$2^{nd}F$ C.CE (to clear the financial memory)

$1000 \pm PMT$

$15\ i$

$5\ n$

COMP

FV = R6 742 (approximated)

3. Your uncle says you will inherit an amount of R100 000 from him in 10 years' time. If money is worth 10% per year, what is the present value of your future inheritance?

Table:

$R100\ 000 \times PVIF_{k,n}$

$= R100\ 000 \times PVIF_{10,10}$

$= R100\ 000 \times 0.386$

$= R38\ 600$

Pocket calculator:

$100\ 000 \pm FV$

$10\ i$

$10\ n$

COMP

PV = R38 554 (approximated)

4. You receive R1 000 per year from a trust for the next 8 years. Calculate the present value of your income if money is worth 8% per year.

Table:

$R1\ 000 \times PVIFA_{k,n}$

$= R1\ 000 \times PVIFA_{8,8}$

$= R1\ 000 \times 5.747$

$= R5\ 747$

Pocket calculator:

$1\ 000 \pm PMT$

$8\ i$

$8\ n$

COMP

PV = R5 747 (approximated)

5. Calculate the amount you have to invest at 10% compound interest to produce R20 000 after 3 years.

Table:

$R20\ 000 \times PVIF_{k,n}$

$= R20\ 000 \times PVIF_{10,3}$

$= R20\ 000 \times 0.751$

= R15 020

Pocket calculator:

$20\ 000 \pm FV$

$10\ i$

$3\ n$

COMP

PV = R15 026

6. You want to buy a house in 2 years' time. The deposit you need (in 2 years' time) is R30 000. How much should you invest per year at 12% per year to accumulate the deposit?

Table:

$R30\ 000 \times FVIFA_{k,n}$

$= R30\ 000 \times FVIFA_{12,2}$

$= R30\ 000 \times 2.120$

$= R14\ 151$

Pocket calculator:

$30\ 000$ FV

$2\ n$

$12\ i$

COMP

PMT = R14 151

7. Say you get an amount of R1 000 per year for the rest of your life. It then goes to your heirs in perpetuity (i.e. 'everlasting' income). The value of money decreases at a rate of 10% per year. Calculate the present value of your income in perpetuity.

Table: First calculate the present value.

PV = 1 000 ÷ 0.10 (10%)

= R10 000

(In this case, therefore, you need not use the Tables.)

Pocket calculator:

Assume that you will live for another 50 years.

$50\ n$

$10\ i$

$1\ 000$ PMT

COMP

PV = R10 000 (R9 915 – approximated)

8. You invest R20 000 for a period of 5 years at an interest rate of 12% per year. What will your investment be worth if interest is calculated quarterly?

Table:

$R20\ 000 \times FVIF_{k,n}$

$= R20\ 000 \times FVIF_{(12 \div 4),(5 \times 4)}$

$= R20\ 000 \times FVIF3,20$

$= R20\ 000 \times 1.806$

$= R36\ 120$

Pocket calculator:

$20\ 000 \pm PV$

$12 \div 4 = i$

$5 \times 4 = n$

COMP

FV = R36 122

9. Say someone invests R10 000 for one year and six months at an interest rate of 10% per year. Calculate the interest the person will receive after 18 months.

Table:

R10 000 × FVIF$_{k,n}$
= R10 000 × FVIF$_{10,1.5}$
= R10 000 × (1.100 + 1.210) ÷ 2
= R10 000 × 1.155
= R11 550

Interest = R11 550 (capital plus interest) – R10 000 (capital)
= R1 550

Pocket calculator:

1 000 ± PV
10 i
1.5 n
COMP
FV = R11 537 (approximated)
Interest = R11 537 (capital plus interest) – R10 000 (capital)
= R1 537

10. You invested an amount of R2 000 in unit trusts 3 years ago. It is currently worth R3 100. At what rate per year did your investment grow?

Table:

2 000 ÷ 3 100 = 0.645
look under 3 years in Table 3.4 (PVIFA) for factor closest to 0.645
this is 0.641
now look at the % interest rate above it, namely 16%
as you can see, 0.645 is a little above 0.641, but far below 0.658,
so it is closer to16% than 15%
so we will pick 15.7% or 15.8%, for example

Pocket calculator:

2 000 ± PV
3 100 FV
3 n
COMP
i = 15.7% (approximated)

11. Say an investment of R1 000 increases to R2 500 over a period of 3 years. At which *simple rate of interest* did the investment increase?

Table:

FV = PV $(1 + i \times n)$
2 500 = 1 000 $(1 + 3i)$
$(1 + 3i)$ = 2 500 ÷ 1 000
$(1 + 3i)$ = 2.5 – 1
3i = 2.5 – 1
3i = 1.5
1 = 1.5 ÷ 3
= 0.5
Simple interest rate = 50%
(Adapted from Steyn *et al.* 1998:114)

Pocket calculator:

This calculation cannot be done on a pocket calculator. Pocket calculators are programmed for *compound interest*, not simple interest (Steyn *et al.* 1998:114).

In the case of simple interest, the interest is calculated only on the capital. Therefore, interest is not added to the capital, i.e. it is not reinvested. In the case of simple interest, the interest earned is calculated by subtracting the capital initially invested from the future value.

Simple interest = Pay-out amount (end value) – Initial amount

12. Person A invests R2 000 at 10% simple interest for 3 years. Person B invests R2 000 for 3 years at 10% compound interest. Calculate the simple interest earned by person A, and the compound interest earned by person B.

Person A:
R2 000 × 10% = R200
R200 × 3 years = R600
Simple interest = R600

Person B:
Calculator:
2 000 ± PV
3 n
10 i
COMP
FV = R2 662
Compound interest = R662
(R2 662 – R2 000 = R662)

In the case of compound interest (interest and capital on interest), one receives more interest than in the case of simple interest (interest on capital only).

13. Your rich aunt will give you an annual amount of R1 000 (at the end of each year) in 3 years' time. You will, therefore, receive the R1 000 at the end of years 3, 4, 5, 6 and 7. Calculate the present value of your future receipts at a rate of 10%.

Solution:
a) First calculate the present value at the start of year 3.
b) Then calculate the present value of this amount over a period of 2 years.

Table:

a) Present value start of year 3:
   R1 000 × PVIFA$_{k,n}$
   = R1 000 × PVIFA$_{10,5}$
   = R1 000 × 3.791
   = R3 791

b) Present value of R3 791 today:
   R3 791 × PVIF$_{k,n}$
   = R3 791 × PVIF$_{10,2}$
   = R3 791 × 0.826
   = R3 131 (approximated)

Pocket calculator:

a) Present value start of year 3:

1 000 ± PMT

5 *n*

10 *i*

COMP

PV = R3 791

b) Present value of R3 791 today:

1 000 ± FV

2 *n*

10 *i*

COMP

PV = R 3 133

3.5.2 Calculations using the Sharp EL-733, the Sharp EL-735 and the Hewlett-Packard 12C (HP 12C) financial pocket calculators

Before we compare these three financial pocket calculators for various calculations, we need to explain some aspects regarding their general functioning.

Sharp EL-733 and EL-735

Although these two Sharp pocket calculators basically function in the same manner, you should particularly note the following in the case of the Sharp EL-735 (Smal 1992:111):

- In order to change the mode of the pocket calculator from financial mode to statistical mode, you do not press 2ndF MODE, but rather (EL-735) 2ndF STAT.
- Where you would press BGN where payments of receipts occur in advance, 2ndF BGN/END is pressed in the case of the EL-735.
- To convert the annual periods to monthly periods (e.g. 3 years to months), 3 2ndF × 12 is pressed in the case of the EL-735 – the answer of 36 is stored automatically.
- If we want to change an annual interest rate to a monthly interest rate (e.g. 12% per year to x% per month), press 12 2ndF ÷ 12 in the case of the EL-735 – the answer of 1% is stored automatically.
- Where the capital portion of a future instalment is calculated with the aid of AMRT, the EL-735 shows PRINCIPAL =.
- When the interest portion of a future instalment is calculated, the EL-735 shows INTEREST =.
- For the future balance following an instalment, the EL-735 shows BALANCE =.

Hewlett-Packard 12C (HP 12C)

Smal (1992:112) points out the following keys used with the HP 12C for the calculations of the time value of money:

- f (yellow): is used for the second function, which is indicated in yellow above certain keys – f is pressed first, and then the appropriate key.
- g (blue): this key is used for the third function – g is pressed first, and then the other key.
- f (FIN): these keys clear the pocket calculator's financial memory.
- g (BEG): these keys are used for calculations where payments occur at the start of a period (e.g. where rent is paid in advance).
- g12x: these keys are used to convert annual periods to monthly periods (e.g. 3 years: 3 g12×) – the answer is stored automatically.
- g12÷: these keys are used to convert the annual interest rates to monthly interest rates (e.g. 12% per year: 12g12÷) – the answer is also stored automatically.
- *n*: the number of periods.
- *i*: the interest rate per interest period.
- PV: present value.
- PMT: payments.
- FV: future value.
- CHS: this key changes the sign of a number.
- f AMORT: this is used to calculate the interest and capital portions of a future instalment, and the outstanding balance – as is the case with the Sharp EL-733 and EL-735, this key can only be used if *n*, *i*, PV and PMT have already been entered in the pocket calculator.

1. Calculate the future value of an investment of R1 000 for a period of 5 years at an interest rate of 10% per year.
   Sharp EL-733:
   2ndF C-CE
   1 000 ± PV
   5 *n*
   10 *i*
   COMP
   FV
   Sharp EL-735: As with Sharp EL-733
   HP 12C:
   f FIN
   1 000 CHS PV
   5 *n*
   10 *i*
   FV

2. Calculate the future value of R1 000 over a period of 5 years at an interest rate of 10% per year if interest is calculated semi-annually.
   Sharp EL-733:
   2ndF C-CE
   1 000 ± PV

10 n
5 i
COMP
FV
Sharp EL-735: As with Sharp EL-733
HP 12C:
f FIN
1 000 CHS PV
5 i
10 n
PV

3. Calculate the monthly effective interest rate if the nominal interest rate is 10%.
Sharp EL-733:
12 2ndF EFF
10 =
Sharp EL-735: As with Sharp EL-733
HP 12C:
f FIN
10 E
12 $n \div i$
CHS PMT FV

4. You will receive R10 000 in 10 years' time. Calculate its present value at an interest rate of 10% per year.
Sharp EL-733:
2ndF C-CE
10 n
10 i
10 000 ± FV
COMP
PV
Sharp EL-735: As with Sharp EL-733
HP 12C:
f FIN
10 i
10 n
1 000 FV
PV

5. You invest R2 000 per year for a period of 20 years at an interest rate of 10% per year. Calculate the future value of your investment.
Sharp EL-733:
2ndF C-CE
2 000 ± PMT
20 n
10 i
COMP
FV
Sharp EL-735: As with Sharp EL-733
HP 12C:
f FIN
g END (if it is to be invested at the end of the year)
10 i
20 n

2 000 CHS PMT
FV

6. Calculate the payment you need to make annually at the end of the year in order to accumulate R10 000 over a period of 5 years at an annual interest rate of 10% (a sinking fund).
Sharp EL-733:
2ndF C-CE
10 i
5 n
10 000 FV
COMP
PMT
Sharp EL-735: As with Sharp EL-733
HP 12C:
f FIN
g END
10 i
5 n
10 000 FV
PMT

7. You receive R1 000 per year for 10 years at the end of each year. Calculate the current value of your receipts at an interest rate of 10% per year.
Sharp EL-733:
2ndF C-CE
10 i
10 n
1 000 ± PMT
COMP
PV
Sharp EL-735: As with Sharp EL-733
HP 12C:
f FIN
g END
10 i
10 n
1 000 CHS PMT
PV

8. You have borrowed R1 000. Calculate the instalment to amortise the loan in 10 equal instalments. The interest rate is 10% per annum and the instalments are paid at the end of each year.
Sharp EL-733:
2ndF C-CE
1 000 PV
10 i
10 n
COMP
PMT
Sharp EL-735: As with Sharp EL-733
HP 12C:
f FIN
g END
1 000 PV
10 i

10 n
PMT

9. You have a mortgage bond of R100 000 that you have been paying off for 10 years. You want to know the balance of the mortgage. The interest rate is 15%.

Sharp EL-733:
2ndF C-CE
100 000 ± PV
15 2ndF ÷ 12 i
20 2ndF × 12 n
COMP
PMT
10 × 12 = AMRT (capital 120th instalment)
AMRT (interest 120th instalment)
AMRT (balance after 120th instalment)
Sharp EL-735: As with Sharp EL-733
HP 12C:
f FIN
g END
100 000 PV
15 g 12 ÷
20 g 12 ×
PMT
0 n
10 E 12 × f AMORT
RCL PV

10. A project shows the following expected incomes and expenditures:

	Incomes	Expenditures
End year 1:	1 000	
End year 2:		15 000
End year 3:	2 000	
End year 4:		6 000
End year 5:	1 500	

Calculate the net present value at a rate of 20% per year.

Sharp EL-733:
2ndF C-CE
20 i
0 cFi
1 000 cFi
15 000 ± cFi
2 000 cFi
6 000 ± cFi
1 500 cFi
NPV
Sharp EL-735:
RCL CF 2ndF CA ENT
20 i
0 cFi
1 000 cFi
15 000 ± cFi
2 000 cFi
6 000 ± cFi
1 500 cFi

NPV

HP 12C:
f FIN
g END
20 i
1 n
1 000 CHS FV PV STO + 1
2 n 15 000 FV PV STO + 1
3 n 2 000 CHS FV PV STO + 1
4 n 6 000 FV PV STO + 1
5 n 15 000 CHS FV PV STO + 1
RCL 1

The following two examples are adapted from Vashist (1997: 8, 9):

12. You invest R35 000 in a building you have bought. You receive a six-monthly rental payment of R6 000 per year for the next 8 years. Calculate the internal rate of return on your investment.

HP 12C:
f FIN
35 000 CHS
g cF$_0$
3 000 g cF$_j$
16 g N$_j$
f IRR
2 ×

Sharp EL-733:
35 000 ± cF$_i$
3 000 cF$_i$ (press 16 times)
IRR

13. You buy a business that requires an initial cash flow of R6 500 000. The expected cash inflow over the next 6 years looks as follows:

Year 1: R1 000 000
Year 2: R1 000 000
Year 3: R900 000
Year 4: R900 000
Year 5: R750 000
Year 6: R60 000 000

Calculate the internal rate of return on the project.

HP 12C:
f FIN
6 500 000 CHS
g cF$_0$
1 000 000 g cF$_j$
2 g N$_j$
900 000 g cF$_j$
2 g N$_j$
750 000 g cF$_j$
60 000 000 g cF$_j$
f IRR

Sharp EL-733:
6 500 000 ± cF$_i$
1 000 000 cF$_i$ (press twice)

900 000 cF$_i$ (press twice)
750 000 cF$_i$
60 000 000 cF$_i$
IRR

3.6 SUMMARY

Everybody should be able to make these personal financial calculations. It is important when you wish to borrow money and to compare different loan rates (interest rates). The more often interest is calculated per annum, the more interest is paid and the higher the loan rate. Similarly, more interest is earned on an investment when the interest is calculated (earned) more than once a year than when it is calculated only once a year. The time value of money has far-reaching implications for personal financial planning and calculations.

You can think particularly about the influence of compound interest on investments for retirement. Of course, the time value of money will be the enemy of those who have not begun investing for their retirement at an early age.

3.7 SELF-ASSESSMENT

- Discuss the influence of the time value of money on your personal financial planning.

BIBLIOGRAPHY

Gitman, L.J. 1988. *Principles of managerial finance.* 5th edn. New York: Harper & Row.

Smal, C. 1992. *The time value of money: A practical approach.* 2nd edn. Durban: Butterworths.

Steyn, B.L., Warren, B.O. & Jonker, W.D. 1998. *Fundamentele aspekte van finansiële bestuur.* Pretoria: Renall.

Swart, N.J. 1998. *Real estate: Only study guide for MNS202 -T.* Pretoria: University of South Africa.

Swart, N.J. 1999. *Personal financial management: Only study guide for MNF303-8.* Pretoria: University of South Africa.

Swart, N.J. & Coetzee, M. 2000. *My money matters: Six golden rules for planning your money matters and using debt wisely.* Johannesburg: Creda.

Vashist, M. 1997. *Using financial and business calculators.* New York: Addison-Wesley.

CHAPTER 4

CAREER PLANNING

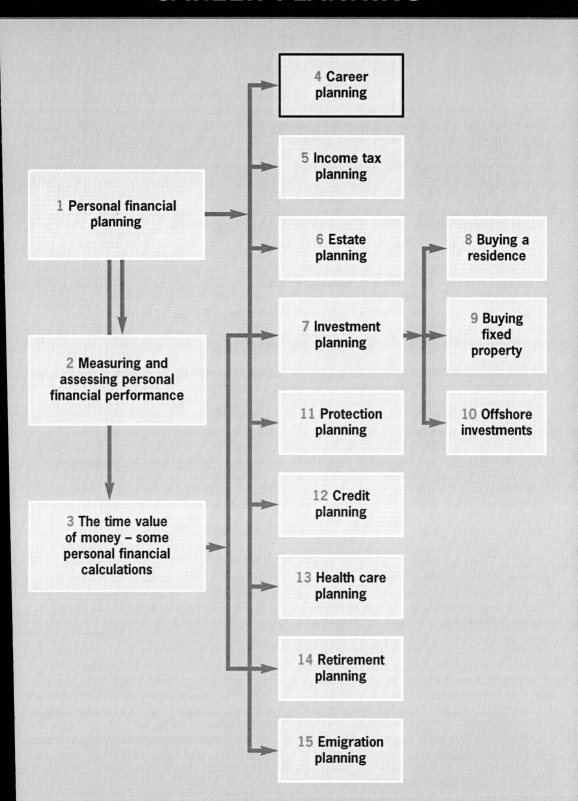

4 Career planning

5 Income tax planning

1 Personal financial planning

6 Estate planning

8 Buying a residence

7 Investment planning

9 Buying fixed property

2 Measuring and assessing personal financial performance

11 Protection planning

10 Offshore investments

12 Credit planning

3 The time value of money – some personal financial calculations

13 Health care planning

14 Retirement planning

15 Emigration planning

4.1 LEARNING OUTCOMES

After studying this chapter, you will be able to:
- Explain the importance of career planning.
- Explain what choosing a career involves.
- Explain the influence of studies and continued education on personal finances.
- Quantify the cost of studying.
- Decide whether you should start your own business rather than work for someone else.
- Find employment during times of unemployment.

4.2 INTRODUCTION

Pursuing a career is intricately linked to the significance that work or working has in people's lives. Work sustains life in the sense of biological survival, it is a source of lifetime earnings and it can sustain the quality of life of the individual, the family and the broader community. In many ways, over the years, the idea of having a job or work has become synonymous to following a career, because of the perceived stability it provides in terms of life earnings.

Various meanings are assigned to the concept *career*, namely career as *advancement*, career as *profession*, career as a *lifelong sequence of work experiences* and career as a *lifelong sequence of role-related experiences* (Hall 1976; Schreuder & Theron 1997). Bird (1994:325) defines a career as *the accumulation of information and knowledge embodied in skills, expertise and relationship networks acquired through an evolving sequence of work experiences over time.* Work experiences are not in themselves a career; they constitute the primary mechanism by which careers occur. The nature or quality of a career is defined by the information and knowledge that is accumulated.

However, for the purposes of this book, 'career' is defined as the lifelong process of accumulating knowledge through an evolving sequence of work experiences over time. The nature and quality of knowledge and skills individuals acquire over their lifetime determine their employability and thus their earning potential.

As organisations all over the world are changing in terms of structure, labour composition, reward systems, service contracts, technology and information, as a result of technological, economic and political developments, careers are to be viewed in terms of opportunities for lifelong learning and evolving the capacity to be employable, rather than in terms of having a stable job with the possibility of upward movement within an organisation.

Within this context, the concept of the 'boundaryless' or entrepreneurial career is emerging. In contrast to the traditional ideas on employment, which emphasise stability, hierarchy and clearly defined job positions for career progression, the new type of organisation will require employees to base their feelings of security on processes rather than on structures, on skills instead of job titles, and on a feeling of fulfilling a certain role rather than on advancing up the career ladder. Schreuder & Theron (1997:113) point out that the traditional view of the career path (moving upward) is being replaced by the notion of moving easily across functional boundaries and organisations, thus emphasising the importance of multiple skills. Career success is assessed by the amount of learning that has taken place, the nature and quality of knowledge that has been accumulated over a period, and thus by the marketable skills of the individual.

4.3 THE IMPORTANCE OF CAREER PLANNING

In this chapter, the emphasis falls on individual career planning as an important aspect of personal financial planning. The ultimate or primary objective of personal financial planning is to achieve financial independence before and after retirement. Despite the different individual interpretations of financial independence, the role played by career planning as a prerequisite for achieving personal financial objectives cannot be overemphasised.

Career planning can be described as the process by which individuals determine short- and long-term career goals. These goals are determined through a process of obtaining self-knowledge (which includes knowledge of values, personality type and preferences, interests and abilities) and information about the ideal career role, the work environment within which the career will be pursued and the lifetime earnings that can be achieved.

Career development is defined as 'an ongoing process by which individuals progress through a series of stages, each of which is characterised by a relatively unique set of issues, themes or tasks' (Greenhaus & Callanan 1994:7). Schreuder & Theron (1997:16) note in this regard that a career consists of different stages and the individual is confronted with different issues during each of these stages. Effective career management requires knowledge of the distinctive physical and psychological needs of the individual. The career needs of the trainee, those of the employee in mid-career and those of an employee approaching retirement are not the same.

Each of the various stages will involve decisions based on particular criteria, which may be objective (financial and other economic conditions, sociological factors such as family and education) and/or subjective (personal preferences, aspirations, orientations and interventions). These decisions will eventually affect the individual's earning power and ultimately his or her net worth or wealth. Your standard of living can only be as high as your chosen career allows, unless you also take on a part-time job.

4.4 CHOOSING A CAREER

Lindhard (1988:5) points out that a career is a way of life. In other words, a career is not merely a means of earning money in order to keep the wolf from the door. Lindhard believes that a career should be in line with the lifestyle to which you aspire.

Donald Super's theory on career choice is as follows (in Lindhard 1998:7): 'A person expresses his idea of the kind of person he is in the kind of career he chooses. Work then becomes a chosen life style which matches his abilities, interests and values.' In the process of choosing a career, people tend to project their image onto various careers in order to find the most suitable one.

The changing nature of jobs and organisations necessitates a perspective on career choice and planning that emphasises the need to experience personal meaning in work and to find a purpose in life. Schreuder & Theron (1997:121) note in this regard that success is seen as embracing not only economic gain, but also spiritual and emotional development.

It is important to choose the career with the best potential. Boone & Kurtz (1989:32) stress that growth in a specific industry is the most important indication of continuous career opportunities. It is generally accepted that the service industry is experiencing the greatest growth at present. The manufacturing industry is showing slower growth, while there are few employment opportunities in the mining and agricultural industries.

Growth and the concomitant employment opportunities also differ within the same industry (for example, the service industry). The area in which jobs are available determines the potential of such jobs. Obviously, an area with economic growth will hold better future prospects within a specific career. Similarly, growth in a specific company is associated with better career opportunities.

Some careers offer several possibilities. For example, training in financial management provides a person with a wide spectrum of career opportunities. Financial training qualifies you for a career in banking, investment, stockbroking or estate agency.

Employees or potential employees should study trends in the economy during their career planning. Gerber et al. (1988:256) point out that employers should find out which skills are required during shortages of labour, which technological changes are taking place and how government policy may influence the labour market in the future.

Information on careers in South Africa can be obtained from school and public libraries, as well as from the career guidance services of universities.

When you decide on a career, you must have a sound knowledge of self. You must know who you are, what you like and what you dislike. Block et al. (1988:13) suggest asking the following questions:

- Do I like working with people, or do I prefer working by myself?
- Do I enjoy taking risks, or do I prefer stability and predictability in my work?
- Do I prefer initiating my own work, or do I prefer well-structured work?
- Am I primarily motivated by money, or do other factors play a bigger role?
- Am I prepared to travel, or do I prefer working in one place?
- Do I prefer work which requires a university degree as a prerequisite or not?

You could do a personal stocktaking. Boone & Kurtz (1989:32) list the following questions you could ask yourself:

- What are my career objectives? What kind of work am I doing at present and where would I like to see myself in five years' time? Is any training required in order to achieve my objectives?
- What are my personal interests? What do I like most about my work or what I have been involved in until the present moment? What do I enjoy most (working with people, figures or machines)?
- What skills do I possess (verbal, numerical)? (Aptitude tests can be very useful in this respect.)
- What is my educational background? (This refers to school performance and tertiary education. You should try to relate your educational background to a specific career.)
- What positions have I held (for example, prefect at school) or what kind of work have I done up to this point? What kind of responsibility was attached to these positions? (Try to establish which aspects of these positions were pleasant and which were unpleasant.)
- What are my hobbies and personal interests?

Answers to these and similar questions should give you an indication of the kind of work you would enjoy. Personality traits, such as humour, leadership, friendliness and patience, can make a person suitable or unsuitable for a specific kind of job. For example, it is highly unlikely that an introvert would be a successful personnel manager.

Personal values also play a role in career choice. By personal values, we mean what a person expects from a career and how he or she should go about accomplishing his or her tasks. A very honest person will feel extremely frustrated (and ultimately resign) if his or her employer expects him or her to tell lies a great deal of the time.

Lindhard (1988:21) defines values as enduring personal convictions, that is believing that certain behaviour patterns and life expectations are more important to you than other behaviour patterns or expectations. He believes that people will never experience career satisfaction if their values and work activities are not in harmony.

Individual values differ considerably. For many people money is top of the list, while for others security, status or independence are the most important aspects of their jobs.

Schreuder & Theron (1997:122) note that all capabilities involved in each previous phase of an individual's life should be examined. It is also necessary to analyse the skills that would be required in your ideal career, because some of them will have to be acquired. This will determine your learning goals, for example goals concerning practical skills in personal financial planning.

The personal resources you presently possess can be identified by engaging in some form of assessment. This can range from self-assessment and gaining feedback from friends and colleagues to more formal assessment by a psychologist or counsellor for recommendations on career issues, taking into account personality traits, personal situation and the willingness to take risks.

The assessment will need to address a number of areas, including your qualities, knowledge, skills, attitudes and beliefs, and will depend on the change you are seeking. You will then need to compare your personal resources with those that will be necessary if you are to reach your goals and maintain yourself satisfactorily when you get there.

4.5 THE NEED FOR EDUCATION AND TRAINING

The need for education and training, whether in-service (on-the-job) training or further studies, cannot be overemphasised. Whether job opportunities are scarce or plentiful, candidates with the best marketable skills, knowledge and attitude will always be best equipped to achieve their career objectives. The costs involved in education and training should be regarded as an investment for a successful career leading towards the ultimate goals of achieving financial independence early in life. However, education and training do not necessarily guarantee a successful career, since other factors also play a role.

To begin with, it is important to draw a distinction between education and training. Education is a process that stretches over your entire life. Conversely, training is the learning of specific abilities in order to follow a certain career path. Today's employers are looking for more than what has been learnt at school or in formal education studies. They want people with a package of broad practical and personal skills that will be an asset to their organisation. Because the job market is so competitive, it is a case of doing proper homework on what is required by industry and equipping yourself with the knowledge and skills to ensure that you are marketable.

The transformation process in South Africa has resulted in numerous initiatives and change-drivers on a national level to redress the past unfair discrimination in education, training and employment opportunities. A central theme in all the prevalent transformation initiatives is co-operation and partnership between government, industry and formal and private educational and training institutions in enhancing the skills of the labour force to contribute to the social and economic development of the nation at large.

4.5.1 The cost of studying

The costs involved in studying at a college, technikon or university are high, so it is essential to choose the correct study plan. If you find that you want to change your career after two or three years of study or in a job, you have incurred unnecessary costs. Sometimes it takes years and even a lifetime to make up this lost ground.

It is very important that prospective students weigh the costs involved in a certain study direction against the financial dividends (salary) they will eventually receive. Someone who studies for seven years and then decides to become a teacher probably will feel frustrated at having incurred all the costs for relatively poor remuneration. On the other hand, a medical practitioner will have the opposite experience and feel that his or her investment in studying (also for seven years) was financially worthwhile.

It is generally anticipated that the costs involved in post-matriculation education (tertiary education) are going to rise dramatically. Parents should plan for possible study costs for their children if they intend studying further. We are not implying that the financial dividends attached to certain careers are of equal importance to everyone. Nevertheless, the return on any investment should always be kept in mind.

In order to avoid unnecessary or wasted study money, parents should help their children to find information on possible study directions that match their children's abilities and interests. It should be noted that a hobby does not guarantee a successful career in the same field. Often, hobbies are replaced with others within a few years.

Parents who see that their children are uncertain about possible careers could advise them to start jobs at banks or building societies. In this way they might learn more about themselves and about the careers that will best suit them. Youngsters could be advised to take any job for a while to stimulate them and possibly to lead them in specific study directions.

Besides knowledge about your field of study, you also gain from the experience and ideas of lecturers and friends during your study period. People who attend university or technikon usually have a wider frame of reference than those who do not have this opportunity.

Potential students who do not have the funds for full-time study could study part-time. They could find a job and pay for their studies over a longer period. Evening classes could be attended at under- or postgraduate levels at educational institutions.

Distance education is another possibility. The University of South Africa (Unisa) offers correspondence courses. Technikon SA in Florida also offers distance education. More self-discipline is demanded for this method of studying than is the case at residential universities and technikons.

Costs are also involved in the following aspects:
- the distance between home and the educational institution;
- the number of classes to be attended involving travelling;
- the availability of transport (a motor car) or the cost of public transport;
- the closeness to a library and/or lectures;
- the availability of a study loan from an institution or employer;
- the availability of state subsidies;
- the specific course to be followed;
- the number of subjects to be taken at a given time; and
- the number of persons in the same household intending to study.

Bursaries are sometimes granted for high scholastic performance (five As in Grade 12) or high symbols at a university. Application forms for bursaries can be obtained from educational institutions. However, not all bursaries are free. Some bursaries are granted on condition that the recipient works for the institution for the same number of years as the bursary was granted. Potential holders of bursaries should make sure that they are prepared to work for three to five years for a certain institution as part of their bursary obligations.

Vacation work is another method of covering the costs involved in studying. Afternoon or evening work could be considered, depending on the time during which classes have to be attended. Students may consider selling products for a commission over weekends.

4.5.2 A must

Many writers on career planning agree that further education and training have become 'a must'. They regard it as a prerequisite for effective career planning in South Africa. The supply of labour exceeds the demand by far, and this situation will not change overnight. On the one hand, there is a population explosion and, on the other hand, there is poor economic growth, which means that sufficient job opportunities can never be created.

There is intense competition for the jobs available. Those with the best educational qualifications are in a better position to obtain jobs, to keep their jobs or to be promoted to higher positions. Posts that were filled by matriculants in the past are now being filled by graduates. This fact reinforces the argument for higher educational qualifications after school.

4.6 FACTORS THAT INFLUENCE EARNING POWER

Boone & Kurtz (1989:26) list the following factors that may affect a person's earning power:
- educational qualifications;
- earnings in specific careers;
- specific industries (growth industries); and
- geographical considerations (workplace).

We referred to these aspects earlier.

Someone who is prepared to accept risks will normally earn more money as a result of the positive relationship (correlation) between risk and return. Those who work harder will normally earn more than their colleagues in a similar post will.

The importance of continuing education and training must be emphasised. Nobody can afford to be content because he or she studied 12 or 20 years ago. Because the work environment is so dynamic today, every worker should adapt to the demands of the workplace and increase his or her level of education and training on a continuous basis. Thus, continued education and training is also a must.

4.7 JOB-HUNTING

Looking for a job is a full-time job in itself as it takes a lot of time and effort, but it can also be exciting and challenging. Although job-hunting can be daunting and stressful, there is no way around it; you need to find out what you want and expose yourself to as many opportunities as possible. Success depends on how well you plan your strategy, determination and sheer persistence.

Nelson (1996:73–76) provides the guidelines below pertaining to job-hunting.

(a) Do research:
- Read as much as you can about each job you investigate, then eliminate those you are not so sure about.
- Make a list of all the careers that interest you.
- Reduce your list to the three careers that interest you the most.

(b) Ask questions:
- What is the financial potential in this field, both immediately and in the future?
- What employment possibilities exist?
- What is the potential for personal growth and development?
- What are the prospects for career advancement?
- Do I have the qualifications? If not, what do I need to do to qualify?
- What will training cost?
- Will I enjoy working in the type of environment offered; for example, will I be required to work indoors or outdoors?
- What is the dress code? Am I prepared to wear a suit every day?
- Will I have to commute and, if so, how far? How much will this cost?
- Will I have to move in order to get this type of job?
- Will I be able to study further while I am working?
- Do the ethics involved in this career conform to my own values?
- Will I have to work long hours or shifts?
- Is there any possibility that this job may become obsolete in future?

(c) Make lists:
- List the pros and cons for each career.
- List everything you think you will enjoy about the job.
- Now list the things you think you will dislike.
- If your likes outweigh your dislikes, you are on the right track.

(d) Know the company:
- Find out which companies would be suitable as possible employers.
- Contact your local Chamber of Commerce, look in the Yellow Pages or contact the Department of Labour.
- List names and telephone numbers, and the names of the people to contact as well as their titles and positions.
- Find out as much as possible about the company – it can be crucial when you go for an interview.
- Keep information neatly filed and easily accessible. By the time you have gone for a few interviews, you may become confused. Insufficient knowledge of the company and people you are dealing with could lose you the job.

(e) Take action:
- Approach the market-place confidently and well prepared.
- Be assertive in your search without being aggressive.
- Maintain a positive attitude. People sense when you are depressed or pessimistic and will respond in a negative way.
- Be realistic – job-hunting may take weeks, even months.
- Remain motivated, even when it seems as if you will never find the job you want.

(f) Where to look for a job:
- Read the job advertisement section in the newspapers.
- Send your CV and/or application form to your list of possible employers.
- Register with an employment agency.
- Telephone possible employers and set up interviews. This is possibly the most effective way of finding work, as many jobs are never advertised. You may telephone at just the right moment.

(g) Job-hunting tips:
- Make sure that you are in a quiet place when you telephone prospective employers.
- Before making the call, double-check who it is that you want to speak to and ask to speak to the person by name.
- Rehearse what you want to say. It is easy to become tongue-tied and flustered when you are nervous.
- Have the following items close by: a pen and paper so you can take down details such as directions if you get an interview; a diary, in case you need to make an appointment; and your CV, so that you can answer questions clearly without hesitation.

- If you are responding to an advertisement in the newspaper, have it with you so that you can describe which one you are responding to. Big companies often advertise more than one job at a time.
- Your telephone manner will be your first opportunity to impress a possible employer. Speak calmly and clearly and try to convey confidence as well as a positive attitude. Be polite and friendly, but not over-familiar. Try to sense when the person you are speaking to wants to end the conversation but do not be abrupt. Practice a few telephone calls with a friend.
- If you get an interview, offer to deliver your CV to the interviewer. This will give him or her an opportunity to study it and understand your skills and abilities. The result will be a far more positive and constructive interview.
- At the end of the conversation, thank the person politely for his or her time, even if it appears that you are unsuitable for the job or that the vacancy has already been filled. You never know when you may need to apply to the company again in future.
- A professional approach is vital. Treat your job-hunting as a job in itself. It may be tedious and take a while, but if you do it properly and in a disciplined manner, it will pay off in the end.
- 'Temping' is now seen as a respected career choice, and is great for trying a few different fields before you commit yourself. It looks better on your CV than job-hopping, and many employment agencies have an abundance of short- and long-term positions readily available.
- Key attributes sought by employers include ambition, motivation, interpersonal skills, self-confidence, direction, initiative, imagination, communication skills, maturity, enthusiasm, time management, teamwork, leadership and the ability to handle conflict.

Job-hunting is not merely sending out hundreds of CVs and waiting for a reply. Networking can be a powerful and useful strategy that you can employ. Nelson (1996:77) notes in this regard that networking is simply identifying people and organisations that could be of use to you in your job-seeking, and then approaching them.

An information interview is also an active job-hunting technique. In an information interview the job-seeker does the interviewing by discussing opportunities, the practicalities of the job and trying to expand the list of contacts with a person who is already occupied in the field he or she is trying to break into.

Information interviews can help you to increase your knowledge about a field of interest, help to clarify and redefine career goals, allow you to introduce yourself to potential employers in a pleasant, low stress atmosphere, and help you to establish a network of contacts that could lead to future employment.

4.8 YOUR OWN BUSINESS

Instead of working for someone else, you might want to start your own business and work for yourself. Someone who can organise and manage resources (human, physical/material and financial) in such a way that he or she makes a profit out of these resources is called an entrepreneur. Such a person possesses certain characteristics that people who earn a salary do not possess. Perseverance, a healthy attitude towards risk-taking and an ability to solve problems are probably the most important characteristics.

For a school-leaver or person who has recently completed his or her studies, the decision to start an own business does not hold too great a risk. It is often said that it is the best time to start a business, because the person has only an old motor car to lose if the business does not succeed. A middle-aged person, or someone about to retire, could stand to lose everything he or she has collected over many years if the enterprise fails.

A young entrepreneur usually has very little knowledge, financial means or business experience. The latter does not disqualify him or her from starting a business, however. Numerous big companies throughout the world began in this way. What is important, though, is that apart from making use of opportunities that arise, an entrepreneur should be prepared to accept many risks and take chances. People who prefer the security that a job in the public service offers fall outside this category. Usually, quality of life does not play too great a role in an entrepreneur's life. A true entrepreneur is constantly seeking challenges.

People should decide for themselves whether they prefer working very hard for themselves, are prepared to take big risks and pay for all mistakes made in the enterprise. This means that they have to pay for others' mistakes as well, whether they like it or not. Managing people will be the primary task and problem area, after the profit objective. The survival of the enterprise is just as important, because it is a continuation of the primary objective of any business enterprise, namely maximum wealth over the long term for the owners of the enterprise.

Potential entrepreneurs should also note that certain enterprises could initially be conducted from their homes. This saves costs on renting a building, office or premises, which means that more money is available for stock or other equipment.

In the case of someone who inherits a sum of money or an asset, this could be used to buy an existing business. However, for a retired person living on a pension, the risks involved in investing this money in a risky business should be weighed up against the certainty of realising sufficient profits. Besides, older (retired) people no longer have the time or physical energy to start providing for their retirement all over again. They may also be sick and unable to compete with younger people in a dynamic labour market.

4.9 BEING UNEMPLOYED

An unemployed person is someone who does not have a job. Unemployment causes frustration because of the lack of money to buy food and other necessities. An unemployed person compares him- or herself with others and feels like a failure. Self-image suffers and he or she feels inferior in the company of friends. If he or she is the breadwinner of the family, this has far-reaching consequences for the wife or husband and children.

4.9.1 Reasons for unemployment

There are numerous reasons why people are unemployed or lose their jobs. As companies close down or leave the country, thousands of workers are often dismissed. The enormous population growth makes it virtually impossible, given the country's economic growth, to create sufficient job opportunities. People are also dismissed when they are no longer capable of doing a certain job, or of doing it as well as others. Some people become too old for a job, while others become disabled at a relatively young age as a result of diseases or accidents. Others have no training or educational qualifications and, therefore, remain unable to enter the labour market.

The unemployment problem is here to stay, irrespective of how the problem is going to be addressed.

4.9.2 How to tackle unemployment

4.9.2.1 Be positive
Firstly, it is essential never to come to terms with unemployment. An unemployed person should make a conscious decision to tackle this problem or situation in a positive manner and with a positive attitude. A person who accepts his or her unemployment with resignation is a defeated person. He or she must decide to do everything in his or her power to find a job, regardless of the nature of the job. It is vitally important that an unemployed person should be prepared to do any (morally acceptable) job to maintain him- or herself and the household (if applicable).

4.9.2.2 Make plans
Secondly, plans must be made to find a job. It will certainly not help to sit at home and wait for work to arrive on the doorstep. All comes to those who wait, if they work while they are waiting. Action is required. If a person who works on a computer becomes unemployed, he or she could learn to work on other programs. In other words, he or she could improve on his or her existing skills. He or she could consult books in libraries for information about other or similar careers in which jobs may be available.

An unemployed person could also register for a course (for example, a six-month course in secretarial work) and borrow money from friends or family to pay the course fees. The course should be in a field (for example, technical) that holds reasonable promise of work, that is, where there is a shortage of trained workers. Obviously funds, whether available or borrowed, will be needed for these suggestions.

There are several alternative jobs or even odd jobs a person can do without the need for large sums of money or even any money. For example, cars can be washed around shopping centres or malls. Being ashamed of certain jobs will not bring food to the table. A hungry person cannot afford to pick and choose when it comes to work (which is scarce in any case). A person could go from door to door to wash windows or dogs for a small fee. The same applies to painting, removing garbage and carrying parcels in shopping malls.

Whatever job a person does, the important thing is that it should be done well. In this way, a person can use his or her previous job (for example, at the house next door) as a reference for a job at another house. If he or she did a good job, people will be happy to recommend him or her. People should realise that such work may be their last chance of finding any work. Similarly, they should realise that this work, if done thoroughly, dutifully and with pride, could be the beginning of a flourishing business.

4.9.2.3 Persevere in your efforts
Thirdly, an unemployed person should consult every possible source of jobs on a continuous basis. An up-to-date CV can be a great help. Several copies should be made and the CVs submitted to as many employers or personnel agencies as possible.

All unemployed people should register with the Department of Labour.

Newspapers, the radio and television should be consulted daily for available (vacant) posts. If a person cannot afford a newspaper, he or she could ask people to give him or her theirs after they have read them. A morning newspaper must be obtained and read within 24 hours, otherwise the information may be too old to use. It creates a very bad impression if a person telephones an employer about a vacant post that was filled two weeks earlier. It is a waste of time to read the previous week's newspaper.

Not all vacant posts are advertised. Unemployed people could go from company to company to enquire about vacant posts. They should take their CVs with them so that they can submit them if the opportunity arises. They should even be prepared for an unexpected interview with an employer.

Friends and family are always a source of information for an unemployed person. Hopefully, they will be concerned about him or her and try to help. Friends and family may even have their own business enterprises and be prepared to employ an unemployed family member or friend, either temporarily or permanently. Any kind of assistance, even for a month or three, should be grabbed with both hands by an unemployed person.

4.10 SUMMARY

Career planning is vitally important since it leads to the achievement of objectives. Without the necessary planning, these objectives may never be achieved. It is important, however, that as a prospective employee you know who you are and what you want to do with your life. You should try to match abilities, skills, interests and values with the nature of a planned career. This career should preferably be in a growth industry in order to ensure a successful career.

A person should constantly seek to improve his or her educational qualifications and training in order to keep up to date with the requirements of the labour market. You should know how to market yourself in the labour market by means of a neat application form, being well prepared for a personal interview and having an immediately available, updated CV. Unemployed people should remain positive, try to improve their skills (if possible) and persevere in their attempts to find any job available.

Amling & Droms (1986:36) suggest the following indicators or signposts for a successful career:

- Acquire adequate educational qualifications and training.

- Choose a career you will enjoy.
- Choose a career in a growth industry.
- Consider the salary in the chosen career over 15 and 20 years.
- Be sure to continue your training in your chosen career.
- Consider the possibility of starting your own business at any stage in your career.
- Be sufficiently flexible to change career at any stage.

4.11 SELF-ASSESSMENT

- Briefly motivate whether you would start your own business rather than work for someone else.
- Explain the importance of career planning, as well as what choosing a career involves.
- Explain the cost of studies and the influence of studies and continued education on personal finances.

BIBLIOGRAPHY

Bird, A. 1994. Careers as repositories of knowledge: A new perspective on boundaryless careers. *Journal of Organizational Behaviour.* Vol. 15, 325–344.

Block, S.B., Peavy, J.W. & Thornton, J.H. 1988. *Personal financial management.* New York: Harper & Row.

Boone, L.E. & Kurtz, D.L. 1989. *Personal financial management.* Homewood: Irwin.

Gerber, P.H., Nel, P.S. & Van Dyk, P.S. 1988. *Mannekragbestuur.* Johannesburg: Southern.

Greenhaus, J.H. & Callanan, G.A. 1994. *Career management.* New York: The Dryden Press.

Hall, D.T. 1976. *Careers in organizations.* California: Goodyear Publishing Company.

Lindhard, N. 1988. *Beroepsbeplanning.* Cape Town: College.

Nelson, D. 1996. *Planning your future: A strategy for a successful career.* Cape Town: Edson-Clyde.

Schreuder, A. & Theron, A. 1997. *Careers: An organizational perspective.* 1st edn. Cape Town: Juta & Co. Ltd.

CHAPTER 5

INCOME TAX PLANNING

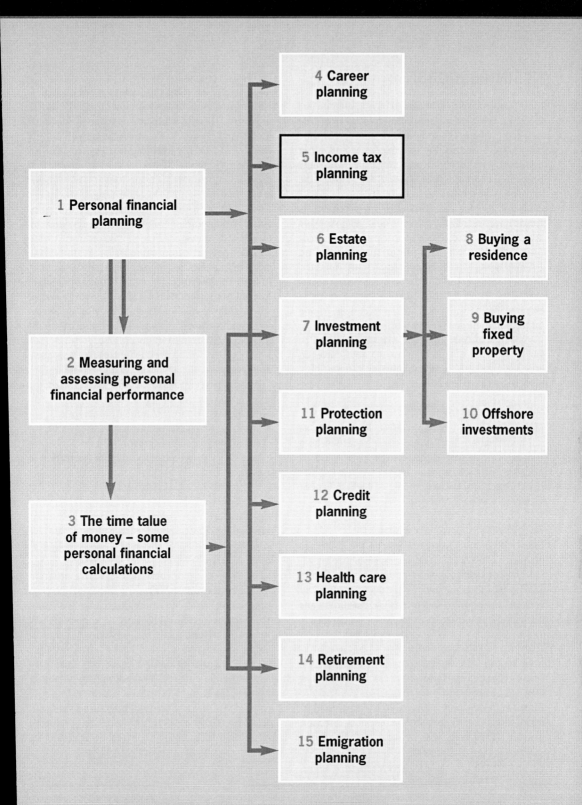

5.1 LEARNING OUTCOMES

After studying this chapter, you will be able to:
- Explain the importance of income tax planning.
- Calculate your own income tax liability with the help of an income tax guide.
- Identify some income tax pitfalls.
- Apply tax avoidance methods to avoid paying too much income tax.
- Explain the influence of tax planning on retirement packages.

5.2 INTRODUCTION

Most people have a resistance to paying income tax. However, the state supplies numerous services that have to be financed in some way or another. Income tax provides finance for these services and other essential state expenditure. Regardless of how people feel about the state 'wasting' their money, the payment of income tax is here to stay!

As far as personal financial management is concerned, we have to accept that all taxpayers should make their fair contribution towards financing the administration of the country and essential services. It is equally important, however, that taxpayers should not pay more tax than the law stipulates. To avoid this, income tax planning is essential, since it can prevent taxpayers from paying unnecessary amounts in tax to the state.

Ignorance of this important aspect could lead to wrong decisions, which in turn could have an extremely negative effect on your wealth and ultimate financial independence.

What is income tax?

Malan & Cronje (1987:7) define income tax as follows: 'Income tax should ... be regarded as a mandatory contribution which the various members of society make towards defraying the costs of certain services rendered and which benefit society as a whole.'

Tax avoidance versus tax evasion

Everybody should clearly understand the difference between tax avoidance and tax evasion. Tax avoidance means that a taxpayer reduces his or her tax liability in a legal manner, by means of methodical personal financial management. Tax evasion means that illegal methods are used to reduce tax liability.

Taxation in the 21st century

Nobody can say exactly when tax laws may be amended, and how. However, we can be certain that they will be subject to constant change. Tax laws are amended as new policy directions are instituted in regard to a country's tax system. This policy direction is made public every year by means of the annual budget. Of course the layperson cannot fathom the long-term policy simply by looking at the budget.

More and more of the loopholes used by individuals are closed, and tax avoidance becomes increasingly difficult. Eventually there will be very few ways of legally avoiding tax. Perhaps the last significant loophole left was to convert income into capital. Unfortunately this no longer always makes sense, because capital became taxable as from 1 April 2001 with the introduction of capital gains tax. It is, therefore, becoming increasingly difficult to convert rental or dividend income into non-taxable income. In the same way, it is difficult to move investments to countries with low or no taxation: in this instance, we are thinking of the South African tax system, which taxes all income earned abroad. However, should you already have paid tax on earnings abroad, this tax can be indicated on the IRP5 and deducted from tax payable.

A tax expert would need to be consulted on questions regarding the applicable exchange rate.

In the 21st century we should assume that the long-term strategy of any tax system (in First World countries) will be aimed, amongst others, at:
- stimulating job creation;
- stimulating economic growth; and
- ensuring the welfare of a country's population as a whole.

Similarly we would have to take account of policy regarding taxation, foreign investments and international business activities. In South Africa, we would have to place particular emphasis on stimulating small businesses.

The Nits (New Income Tax System) program bought by the South African Revenue Service gives us an idea of what lies in the future. Tax avoidance will become increasingly difficult and extremely limited in nature, while tax evasion will result in people landing in a great deal of trouble. One wonders whether those accountants who may have helped their clients with tax evasion would land in hot water too.

Using Nits, the Receiver will keep up to date with all business and property transactions conducted by individuals. Amongst others the following information will be immediately accessible as soon as someone completes an action (Duvenage 1999:1):

- vehicle odometer readings as soon as licences are renewed;
- odometer readings at the time of any vehicle sales;
- immediate information regarding a deceased's estate;
- information about close corporations and companies;
- provident and pension fund pay-outs;
- policy pay-outs;
- transactions on the Johannesburg Securities Exchange (thanks to tax numbers being provided when shares are bought and sold);
- a comparison between VAT payments and declared income;
- PAYE; and
- taxes paid to a regional services board.

5.3 KINDS OF TAX

A distinction is made between direct and indirect tax. We will briefly illustrate each.

Direct tax

Income tax and property tax are examples of direct tax. Direct tax is based on the principle that people should contribute to the wealth of the state to the same extent that they are able to contribute toward their own wealth. Income tax liability is calculated according to tables based on a sliding scale. All taxpayers are fully aware of the fact that they are obliged by law to pay this kind of tax. Property tax is not paid by people who do not own fixed property, such as a building or a plot. Property tax is discussed in Chapter 8, when we take a look at purchasing a home.

Indirect tax

Indirect tax is usually levied on consumer goods. Some examples are:

- value-added tax (VAT);
- excise duty (on cigarettes and alcohol); and
- import tax (on articles that are imported).

Through indirect tax, the tax base is broadened and more money flows to the state.

5.3.1 Value-added tax (VAT)

Value-added tax means that a tax is levied via registered businesses (vendors) on:

- the goods or services rendered;
- the import of goods; and
- the supply of imported services.

Only a registered vendor can charge VAT. The VAT that a person/body charges for goods and/or services is called output tax. This person/body then pays input tax to other suppliers of goods and/or services. Input tax is refunded by the Receiver, but can be claimed only for payments made during the assessment period.

Registration

Any person running a business must register for VAT (and in so doing become a 'vendor') if:

- the total turnover (the vendor's gross income) exceeds R300 000 per year (February 2001);
- it is expected that the income will exceed R300 000; or
- an average monthly income of R20 000 is expected.

Capital expenditure may be claimed from VAT, and depreciation, for example, is claimed for income-tax purposes, so VAT and income tax are two separate matters. Indeed, there are certain expenditures (inputs) on which VAT is not paid, with the result that these may be claimed as expenses for tax purposes.

Of course, a business must be run before someone can register for VAT. Small businesses that are not liable to register for VAT because of their limited turnover may, however, voluntarily apply for registration. This means that input tax can be claimed from the Receiver. Similarly, output tax will have to be levied on all goods and services.

This decision will be influenced by the following, amongst other things:

- whether those paying VAT are themselves registered for VAT (vendors) or not (private users);
- the proportion of input tax (which can be claimed) and output tax (which may be claimed only by other vendors);
- the administrative burden that VAT registration holds for a vendor; and
- the VAT costs (output tax) payable at a later stage in the case of a possible deregistration for VAT purposes by the vendor.

Tax periods

There are various VAT periods, amongst others, one month, two months and six months (e.g. a farmer). These periods are determined by the value of taxable supplies. Output tax normally exceeds input tax. The difference should be paid to the Receiver. Those expecting input tax to be less than the output tax (and who would therefore have to pay in) should try to negotiate a longer VAT period. On the other hand, those who expect input tax to exceed output tax (and will therefore receive a refund from the Receiver) should try to negotiate a shorter VAT period.

The VAT rate is currently 14% (May 2002). As with all other tax laws, VAT determinations and rates are amended from time to time, so make sure of current legislation before registering as a vendor or taking any other VAT decisions (as a vendor).

5.3.2 Capital gains tax (CGT)

Capital gains tax may have been the greatest shock to hit South Africans in the budget speech in years. The 'quiet' of the capital portion of our lives and possessions has disappeared, and even more people want to leave the country. Whereas before we were able to speculate with cars and property on a small scale and make a profit without being taxed, the situation has now changed completely. The profit on certain investments has also become taxable, whether you are a full-time speculator or not.

The Receiver of Revenue no longer distinguishes between capital and income in this regard, and tax is now payable on capital gains. According to PriceWaterhouse Coopers (2000:7), the Receiver put forward the following three reasons, amongst others, for this decision:

- to stop the transfer of taxable income to non-taxable capital as part of a tax strategy;
- capital income contributes as much to someone's ability to pay as income itself (a most uniformed view); and
- CGT is accepted internationally (it is extremely unwise to compare South Africa with First World countries; for example, Australia has CGT, but no estate duty).

Immediately prior to the introduction of CGT, arguments were advanced against CGT, which is a wealth tax and amounts to the redistribution of wealth by diminishing existing estates (see Swart 2000:3). Although the tax base is not broadened in this way, the tax burden of the same group of taxpayers is significantly increased, without a concomitant increase in income.

From April 2001 South Africans will be taxed on inflation. The same legislator who did not want to introduce capital gains tax a few years earlier, decided to go ahead and do it anyway. The prior argument went that, in the first place, you could not tax individuals on inflation, and secondly, the administrative cost of such a system would be too high for the limited financial benefit accruing from it. In the same budget in which plans were made to peg the inflation rate at between 3% and 6% for the future, it was determined that certain South Africans will be taxed for the inflation of the past.

The concept of capital gains implies that a profit has been realised on capital. For example, we speak of a 12% return on an investment. If the inflation rate is 7% and income tax amounts to more than the difference between 12% and 5%, then we have a negative return, and the value of the investment has declined in real terms. Say we bought a property ten years ago. If the value (total growth) of the investment after ten years is not higher than the inflation rate over the same period, then there has been no capital growth. Consequently, there have been no capital gains and the property in question should not be taxed on capital gains, unless tax is payable on inflation. Consider the following example:

- Suppose we built a block of flats in May 2001 at a cost of R150 000 per flat. At the average interest rate of 10% per annum, the value of the flat would be R626 587 after 15 years. If we then sell the flat for R626 587 after January 2016 we will have gained no capital on it and there can be no question of capital gains tax on the sale. Wrong – the legislator and the Receiver of Revenue maintain that we have gained capital to the tune of R466 587 (R626 587 – R150 000 – R10 000[discount]) and must be taxed on 25% of this amount (R116 647) at our marginal tax rate (e.g. 42%). This brings us to an amount of R48 992, which may not sound like much, but is it fair since it cannot be explained, except to say that it actually amounts to a wealth tax?
- If the flat were sold for R526 587, which means a capital loss of R100 000, then inflation tax still has to be paid on the R526 587 – R150 000 – R10 000 = R93 897 (R366 587 × 25%) 'profit', namely R38 492 (R91 647 × 42%) – and that after a capital loss of R100 000. This is similar to rent control, because the value of an asset can never be adjusted for inflation, which means that according to the legislator, inflation has no influence on the future value of immovable (fixed) property, movable property and certain kinds of financial investments. This makes one wonder how to explain the concepts of capital growth, inflation and profit.
- According to the Receiver, in order not to incur a capital loss, we would have to sell the flat for less than R150 000, 15 years later. In essence, we can assume that no capital loss will ever be incurred on a property that is older than five years, because historic cost prices are used for tax purposes. Even if we sold the flat for R50 we would not receive a cheque from the Receiver. At best, the loss could be written off someday in the future (in the same year or within a year) against some capital gain or other, whenever such a gain materialises according to the same definitions of profit, capital growth and capital gains, and according to the same formula.

Fortunately, the rate at which we have to pay tax on inflation is relatively low – provided it stays that way forever.

A more equitable proposition would have been to introduce the same capital gains tax on all properties bought after 1 October 2001, but to then adjust the value annually for inflation, and to tax real capital growth (growth after inflation). Furthermore, capital losses should be paid back to property owners within the same year, in order to protect and handle the cash-flow positions of those concerned in the only equitable way, failing which, the loss should be regarded as a loan to the state at market-related interest rates. The term of the loan should naturally last until the entire loss has been repaid or, in the event of the property owner's death, it should be paid back to his or her estate.

It is also important to look at the kind of property under discussion. A person who operates and owns a profitable restaurant, for example, generates so much cash that there can never be cash-flow problems with the selling and taxation of the property. Unfortunately capital gains tax will cause cash-flow problems for people who own vacant land in wrong places, however, such as farmland on which no income is earned, and old property in small towns, particularly if a bond still has to be paid off on such a property – even at the 'low' rate of capital gains tax.

With the introduction of capital gains tax, South Africans will now have a different perception of capital generated with a view to financial independence after retirement. Many initiatives of existing and prospective entrepreneurs are gone forever. People are going to wonder more than ever for whom they go to work early, stay up late and collect South African possessions. After a lifetime of paying taxes, the same people must brace themselves for estate duty.

So far we have looked at a second property, because people's dwellings, in which they reside permanently, are not subject to capital gains tax. The problem is, however, that in the process of efficient estate planning these persons often have already placed their permanent dwellings in a trust (trust *inter vivos* – during their lifetime), with the result that this private dwelling is now also subject to capital gains tax, that is to say, tax on inflation, if this dwelling were to be sold. However, the rate is 50% of the 'profit' and not 25%, as it is for private individuals.

People should, therefore, not place their homes in a trust unless they are quite sure that they are not doing it with a view to conducting business, in other words, that they are doing it purely for estate-planning purposes. By same token, people who possess dwellings in a trust should leave them there for the latter reason and not try to remove them from the trust too hastily.

However, since October 2001, a catch-22 situation has arisen. Property owners are expected to have their properties evaluated, or more precisely to have them re-evaluated in order to determine the value of the property as at 1 October 2001. The problem that now arises is that, on the one hand, owners would want to have the evaluation fixed at the lowest possible figure with a view to future estate duty. But on the other hand, the low value would mean that a higher capital gain will be realised at the future sale of the property, partly because inflation is ignored in the calculation.

Persons who are sure that they are not going to sell their property, should have it evaluated as low as possible, with a view to estate duty after their decease. Those who are reasonably certain that they will have to sell their property at some stage, for some reason, are advised to have it evaluated higher, with a view to lower capital gains tax.

Property owners will no longer be so concerned about the possibility of overcapitalising on their private dwellings, because such properties are exempt from capital gains tax. Henceforth, more money will be invested in private homes. Because capital gains tax is also applicable to other financial assets, investments in real estate should not be avoided, but should be planned with due care.

In Table 5.1, Preen (2000:4) points out the possible influence of CGT on various types of investments. Firstly, he names the type of investment, then the influence of CGT, and he makes his own comments in the third column.

A basic framework for making CGT calculations and decisions is proposed by Du Plessis (2000:102) as follows:

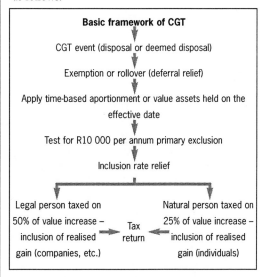

FIGURE 5.1 **Capital gains tax (CGT)**

TABLE 5.1 How capital gains tax is likely to affect your investments

Investment	How it will be taxed under CGT	Comments
Bank investments	These will not be affected by CGT, as interest is already fully taxed as income.	Relative to other investments, bank investments will now be slightly more attractive.
Shares	All capital gains realised upon shares sold will be taxed in the hands of the investor.	The payment of this tax will add to the administrative burden to the private share investor.
Unit trusts (rand-denominated)	The capital gains will be levied on the selling of shares within the unit trust portfolio and will be the responsibility of the unit trust manager. Investors selling or switching unit trusts will therefore not be taxed on the gains.	The total after–tax return of unit trusts will decrease slightly, but the individual investor will not be responsible for any CGT.
Endowments and life policies	The capital gains will be levied on the selling of shares within the underlying investment portfolio and will be the responsibility of the portfolio manager. Original policy owners will therefore not be taxed on the gains.	The total after tax return of life and endowment policies will decrease slightly, but the individual investor will not be responsible for any CGT.
Second-hand policies	The operative word for endowment and life policies is 'original' owner. Therefore, policies that have been acquired from previous owners will be subject to CGT upon disposal.	This tax will undoubtedly make the second-hand policy route less attractive, although there are many within the industry who believe that this tax will not be able to be effectively policed by the Receiver.
Retirement funds	The capital gains will be levied on the selling of shares within the underlying investment portfolio and will be the responsibility of the portfolio manager. Original policy owners will therefore not be taxed on the gains.	The total after–tax return of retirement funds will decrease slightly, but the individual investor will not be responsible for any CGT.
New generation guaranteed products	The tax on these products is still being finalised, but there will likely be a once-off tax levied on the total gain at disposal of the product.	The total after–tax return on these products will decrease slightly.
Property	Every taxpayer will be allowed one 'home' property which will be exempt from CGT. This property must be registered in the individual's name (not a CC or a trust). All other properties will be taxed on capital gains realised.	Owning your own home will become more attractive as an investment, as it is one of the few exemptions from CGT.
Business interests	CGT will be levied on the capital profit realised upon the sale of any business interests.	Business people selling business interests will have to factor this new tax into their transactions.
Offshore unit trusts	Unlike local unit trusts (were the Receiver is getting revenue from the unit trust manager), offshore unit trusts will be fully taxed on the realised appreciation in the hands of the unit holder.	The case for putting long-term offshore investments into offshore trusts will be strengthened considerably.
Offshore life policies	It appears as if offshore life policies will, at this stage, be exempt from CGT, although this seems unfair when compared to the treatment of unit trusts.	For the meantime, offshore life policies will have an advantage although this is likely to be levelled out soon.

Du Plessis then also briefly answers some questions about the unique character of CGT in South Africa:

a) Who is liable for CGT?
b) Which capital assets are affected?
c) What is included in the basic costs of affected assets?
d) What events cause CGT to arise?
e) What is excluded from CGT?
f) When does a deferral of CGT occur?
g) How are capital gains or losses determined?
h) What steps does SARS take to counter CGT avoidance?
i) What happens to capital assets acquired prior to the effective date of CGT?
j) What relief is there from CGT?
k) What records must be kept for the purposes of CGT?
l) What is the administrative procedure for the payment of CGT?
m) Who may value property for CGT purposes?

We will now briefly discuss each of these questions.

a) *Who is liable for CGT?*
- Any natural person (individual) and any juristic person (company, closed corporation or trust) that is a South African citizen (individual) or is situated and registered here (juristic persons), in regard to capital assets in South Africa or abroad.
- If a natural person or juristic person that is not resident/registered in South Africa owns property or an interest in property in South Africa, and a CGT event occurs, such person is liable for CGT.
- Such foreign persons in respect of assets utilised in a trading activity.

b) *Which capital assets are affected?*
Some assets/investments affected by CGT have already been mentioned in Table 5.1. Basically they are:
- all assets (movable and fixed, tangible and intangible);
- including all trading stock but excluding mining assets (which qualify for an income tax rebate as a capital expense).

Of course there are specific exceptions, as you will see later.

c) *What is included in the basic costs of affected assets?*
- Acquiring costs (all costs incurred – unless the cost has been claimed for income tax purposes).
- Legal fees, agent's commission, stamp duty, transfer duty, cost of conveyance, advertising costs, broker's fees and valuation costs.

- Costs of disputes regarding the above are excluded.
- Legal costs to maintain the property/interest in property.
- Improvement costs forming part of initial cost of purchase.
- VAT (paid and not claimed).
- Operating costs are excluded (interest, maintenance, insurance, rates and taxes – part of revenue account for income tax purposes).
- Record-keeping costs for the determination of base cost.

d) *What events cause CGT to arise?*
CGT arises as soon as a CGT event occurs, which may be the disposal or deemed disposal of a capital asset, namely if it is:
- sold;
- given away;
- scrapped;
- exchanged;
- lost;
- destroyed; or
- cancelled.

Disposal also occurs as soon as:
- a natural person/juristic person is no longer a South African resident;
- there is no change of ownership (for example, derivatives); or
- where a trust beneficiary changes.

e) *What is excluded from CGT?*
- A primary, own dwelling (only one).
- Private cars (not company cars) belonging to natural persons.
- Personal belongings (boats, caravans, aircraft, share certificates, gold and silver coins) of natural persons.
- Lump sum benefits (annuities, policies, but not second-hand policies).
- Compensation for injuries or illness.
- Winnings from lotteries and competitions.
- Foreign exchange gains (on converting foreign currency into rands).
- Gains or losses made by foreign agencies.
- Small business assets disposed of for retirement (persons older than 55).
- Fully exempt institutions (government local authorities and 'approved' public benefit organisations).

f) *When does a deferral of CGT occur?*
Where assets are swapped, for example, there is a deferral (rollover) of the basic costs. The latter is relevant only where assets have been transferred to South African residents. Other examples are:
- share incentive ownership;

- transfer of assets in exchange for shares in a company;
- transfer of business assets to a company;
- transfer from a deceased estate to an heir or legatee;
- donations of property;
- transfer between spouses;
- some transfers with regard to rationalisation, unbundling, restructuring, etc.; and
- business asset disposal and reinvestment in similar asset.

g) *How are capital gains or losses determined?*
According to Du Plessis (2000:112): 'A capital gain or loss is the difference between the base cost of an affected asset and the consideration realised or deemed to be realised upon the disposal, or deemed disposal, of that same asset.'
A rebate of R10 000 is granted. A capital loss may be carried forward to subsequent tax years.

h) *What steps does SARS take to counter CGT avoidance?*
Many transactions are examined and counter-steps planned.

i) *What happens to capital assets acquired prior to the effective date of CGT?*
All assets acquired before the effective date and dealt with subsequently are subject to CGT in terms of:
- the time-based apportionment basis; or
- the valuation basis.
CGT is payable on all capital gains after the effective date. Up to that date, no CGT is payable.

j) *What relief is there from CGT?*
A portion of the capital gain is taxed; for example:
- 50% in the case of companies (at company tax rate); and
- 25% in the case of individuals (at individual's tax rate).

k) *What records must be kept for CGT purposes?*
It is very important to obtain and keep all records and information regarding the acquisition of assets. If necessary, you will then be able to prove the base costs of an asset.
When purchasing an asset, Du Plessis (2000:132) suggests that the following documents/information should be kept:
- date of acquisition;
- amounts that may form part of the base costs;
- the date you dispose of the asset; and
- exchange details.
Documents may include deeds of sale, market valuations and services rendered.
If you do not have the records, you could:
- approach a lawyer or agent for help; or
- get copies of invoices.
Remember to keep business records when you inherit assets.

l) *What is the administrative procedure for the payment of CGT?*
CGT is brought into account in the tax return as part of the annual income tax. A taxpayer may also reach an agreement with the South African Revenue Services (SARS) about the payment of CGT (and interest, naturally). A

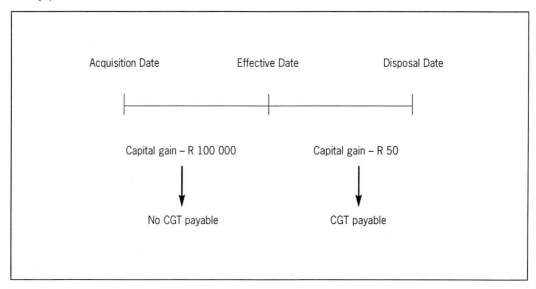

DIAGRAM 5.1 **At what date CGT becomes payable**

SITE taxpayer would need to fill in an additional form for CGT.

m) *Who may value property for CGT purposes?*
According to the SARS it is not a legal requirement to employ a registered valuer to value your fixed property, for example. However, should you wish to use someone like that, you may contact the SA Institute of Valuers at: Tel. (021) 762- 3312, Fax. (012) 762-2329, E-mail: gen@saiv.org.za.

You may ask an estate agent for a valuation, or value the asset yourself.

Of course, you must realise the long-term implications of this valuation for CGT and estate planning purposes.

- If your valuation is too low – you will pay more estate duty (if your gross estate exceeds R1.5 million) and more CGT when you sell.
- If your valuation is too high – you will pay more CGT if the SARS decides your valuation was done to evade CGT.

It is, furthermore, important to document the valuation method for the purposes of subsequent enquiries. Du Plessis refers to the time-apportionment method of valuation. This is the valuation method to determine a realistic market value on the effective date of CGT.

The market value is, therefore, determined as at that date, the basic costs are subtracted and CGT is then paid on the profit according to the rates applicable for natural persons and legal entities. Losses are dealt with as mentioned earlier.

Persons who have no records for calculating the basic costs must leave this to the SARS, according to the 20% rule. Du Plessis (2000:131) states that in such a case (and where assets were acquired prior to the effective date), 20% of the returns (e.g. selling price) will be used as the base cost for calculating CGT. This means 80% will be profit and 20% (25% of 80) will, therefore, constitute taxable capital gain in the case of individuals. Individuals will then pay tax on this 20% according to their marginal tax rate (with a rebate of R10 000).

According to Louw (2001:7), CGT means that the estate duty and donations tax rates will have to be reduced. The reason is that inheritances and gifts are now also subject to CGT. She says: 'Estate duty taxes the full value of an asset and CGT only taxes the gain. So we can't abolish estate duty completely.'

However, remember that CGT also applies to an own, private dwelling, unless the profit a person makes on it is less than R1 million.

5.3.3 Donations tax

If a person or other entity donates an amount of money or assets with a value of greater than R30 000, donations tax is payable on the amount of the value over R30 000. The donations tax rate is currently 20% (July 2002), the same as the estate duty rate. Each person (e.g. man and wife) can currently donate R30 000 per year without donations tax being payable. Both the husband and wife can therefore donate R30 000 each, if the gift does not form part of the joint estate. In such a case, the joint (once-off) donation may amount to only R30 000 – each spouse, therefore, donates R15 000. As you will notice, the Act contains many exemptions in regard to donations tax. Such annual gifts may be used quite effectively in estate planning in order to reduce the value of the net estate for the purposes of estate duty.

5.3.4 Estate duty

Estate duty is payable after someone's death. The estate duty rate in South Africa is currently 20% in the case of an estate with a net value in excess of R1.5 million. As with income tax, a formula is used to calculate the amount of estate duty payable to the state.

The formula for calculating estate duty is as follows:

Property	Rx
Plus : Property deemed to be property	Rx
Gross value of estate	Rx
Less : Allowable deductions	Rx
Net value of estate	Rx
Less : Rebate	R1 500 000
Estate duty payable	Rx

You can reduce or even eliminate estate duty through proper estate planning. Estate planning is discussed in Chapter 6. You will notice that one of the purposes of estate planning (the primary goal) is to reduce the amount payable in estate duty to nil or as close to it as possible.

5.4 THE INCOME TAX ACT

Income tax is levied in terms of the Income Tax Act 58 of 1962, as amended. Income tax scales are revised and adjusted annually. Various publications, such as Old Mutual's *Income Tax Guide*, contain legislation and summaries of the Act. By consulting such books, taxpayers can study and analyse the implications of possible amendments to the Act and base their personal financial planning on these findings. Although income tax is incorporated into every personal financial decision, everybody has to do income tax planning at least once a year.

You could discuss the amendments and their implications with your broker and accountant (or auditor) in order to clear up any uncertainties. However, remember that your broker is seldom (if ever) a tax expert. If your bookkeeper is a qualified accountant, he or she should be able to give you the necessary tax advice. However, it is important to know the basic principles and at least to read or study a tax guide every year. This will give you the required background to put questions to your accountant so that you can be properly helped.

Basic principles: Capital or income
Until 1 October 2001, it was essential to be able to distinguish between capital and income in order to calculate tax liability. Capital gains were not taxed. An example of an untaxed capital gain transaction was the sale of your second house at a profit. Since 1 October 2001, however, we have to pay tax on capital profit, namely capital gains tax (see Section 5.3.2).

5.5 THE TAX YEAR

Income tax is calculated and paid over a period of one year. This period normally stretches from 1 March until the last day of February (of the following year). An assessment period of less than a year does exist in the event of death (the period extends from 1 March until the date of death).

Taxpayers should consult a specialist if they are uncertain about any related aspects, but they must be prepared for their assessment at the end of the tax year. For this reason, documentary proof should be kept of all expenditure incurred in order to earn an income (this expenditure is tax-deductible). It is not a good idea to start wondering at the last moment which expenditures should be listed in the income tax assessment form.

If a taxpayer anticipates a much higher income than in the year to follow (for example, an endow-

> Tax planning is becoming increasingly important, and the SARS (South African Revenue Services) is closing more and more loopholes in the Act, and rooting out methods of avoiding tax.

> It no longer matters if you are only an investor. The Act regards you as a speculator for the purposes of CGT.

ment policy matures in the year of assessment), he or she can defer receipt of the money to the next year (if his or her other income is, in fact, going to be much lower in the next year). This is no longer possible in the case of someone who intends retiring at the end of February and will not receive a salary in the following tax year. More about this further on.

5.6 STANDARD INCOME TAX ON EMPLOYEES (SITE)

Metz (1998:11) regards a taxpayer as any person who:
- must pay tax; and
- must file a tax return, even if such a person does not have to pay tax.

Yes, paying tax is unpleasant. Of course, the opposite is even worse, as stated by Lord Than R Duwar: 'What is worse than paying tax, is if you do not have to pay tax.'

The Act currently distinguishes between various taxpayers as follows:
- companies (any association, corporation, company, juristic person, close corporation and trust);
- natural persons; and
- persons other than natural persons.

The tax rates for companies and natural persons differ as follows:
- It is a fixed rate in the case of companies.
- It is a sliding rate in the case of natural persons, which increases as income increases (according to particular tax scales).

Paying tax is based on the principle that someone contributes to the state's welfare in the same proportion as he or she contributes to his or her own welfare. This is why you pay more tax the more you earn.
- Paying tax is based on a minimum, below which a person does not pay tax (this amount is reviewed constantly).
- It is also based on age (in the main, there is a distinction between persons older or younger than 65 years).

Just as we need money monthly (or weekly) to exist on and to pay certain expenses, the state also needs a regular income to pay government expenses. The result is that the state tries to collect taxes on a continuous basis – i.e. throughout the year.

This is why the following systems are used:
- SITE;
- PAYE; and
- provisional tax

We will now look at each of these three methods of tax collection. As indicated by the heading to the section, SITE is dealt with first.

SITE is part of the Pay-As-You-Earn (PAYE) system. With SITE, employers pay their employees' tax liabilities. The Receiver no longer makes a separate or additional calculation that is then compared to that of the employer. Those who pay only SITE do not file a tax return at the end of the tax year.

This SITE system lays down a minimum income tax for most employees. According to the SITE system, an employer is compelled to deduct tax from employees' salaries. At the end of the tax year, a SITE calculation is made for each employee and the correct amount is paid to the Receiver of Revenue. Usually the employer does this calculation.

EXAMPLE

Say someone's net remuneration is R77 700 for the year. That person's employer would then have deducted R980,74 per month from the employee's salary for tax purposes. The table below (from SARS 2002:281) shows that an amount of R11 768,88 is deducted from the taxpayer's salary (for the year) as tax.
An amount of R7 340 is in regard to SITE and R4 428,88 for PAYE. The latter calculation is only made at the end of the tax year to determine which amounts are regarded as PAYE and which as SITE.

The annual deduction tables for persons under 65 years are shown in Table 5.2.

Metz (1998:51) further points out instances where SITE applies, namely:
- those who earn a net remuneration (net remu-

neration is determined by deducting certain legally permitted deductions from the legislative definition of remuneration);
- for the annual equivalent of the net remuneration (for example, someone who has worked only for four months); and
- when no more than R60 000 was earned during the tax period (such a person pays SITE only, and need not fill in and render a tax return – the R6 000 [for persons younger than 65; R10 000 for those who are older] interest income which could be received free of tax in 2002 may, for example, not form part of the R60 000).

SITE is, therefore, the minimum income someone has to pay in tax. Metz points out that SITE is not applicable in the following cases:
- where a person has other taxable income as well;
- where a person earns more than R60 000 (net); and
- if deductible expenses exceed 1% of your remuneration.

5.7 PAY-AS-YOU-EARN (PAYE)

Persons earning more than R60 000 (net) per year are called PAYE taxpayers. Such persons have no choice, and must (quite apart form SITE payments) complete a tax form every year and render this return.

PAYE is deducted from an employee's salary monthly, after provision has been made for particular deductions in regard to pension, medical aid and annuities. In 2001, negotiations were underway to deduct long-term policies from remuneration as well, mainly because of individuals' large debt burden, and the great number of policies. PAYE is paid to the Receiver monthly on behalf of employees.

Some people do not pay employee tax. These people pay the Receiver of Revenue estimated amounts of tax at specific intervals (provisional tax). Some employees pay employee tax as well as provisional tax.

TABLE 5.2 **Annual deduction tables for persons under 65 years**

Remuneration R	SITE R	PAYE R	TOTAL R
77 641 – 77 790	7 340,00	4 428,88	11 768,88
77 791 – 77 940	7 340,00	4 466,38	11 806,38
77 941 – 78 090	7 340,00	4 503,88	11 843,88
78 091 – 78 240	7 340,00	4 541,38	11 881,38
78 241 – 78 390	7 340,00	4 578,88	11 918,88

5.8 PROVISIONAL TAX

Provisional tax is payable on all income not regarded as remuneration. It is not paid monthly or deducted from anything. It is paid six-monthly as follows:
- the first payment is at the end of the first six months of the tax year (before or on 31 August); and
- the second payment is made at the end of the second six months (before or on the last day of February).

Someone registered as a provisional taxpayer, therefore, pays tax for the previous six months' income (twice yearly). Persons whose taxable income (note, not net income) exceeds R50 000 may make a third payment within seven months of the end of the tax year, namely before 30 September of the following year.

Should a person's tax year fall on any other date, such a person has six months after that date to make a voluntary third payment of provisional tax.

Penalties
Various penalties are payable for late tax payments. Penalties are charged at a relatively high rate (15%) for each full month in arrears, apart from a penalty of 10% on the amount owed. Additional tax may also be levied on the difference between the tax payable and the amount you have already paid (only if the tax already paid was paid in time). Otherwise the penalty applies to the total tax payable (including the amount already paid at a rate of 20%).

Registration
A person must register for provisional tax within 30 days of having become a provisional taxpayer; according to Cronje *et al.* (2000:29) that is if:
- your taxable income (apart from remuneration) exceeds R1 000;
- you have become a member of a close corporation;
- you have become a director of a private company;
- you have your own business;
- your taxable interest income exceeds R1 000;
- you are a company; or
- you are a person informed by the Commissioner that you are a provisional taxpayer.

If you have paid too much
If your taxable income is less than R50 000:
- you are not refunded the amount;
- you receive no interest on the amount; and
- you get a credit balance for the next return.

Unfortunately provisional tax is often spent on holidays, clothes, furniture and other items.

If your taxable income exceeds R50 000:
- you are refunded the amount; and
- you receive interest on the amount.

Of course, those with accountants or auditors will be reminded of the due dates for payment by such persons. If you co-operate with your bookkeeper, you should not have any penalty problems.

The advantage of provisional tax is that the tax payable (which would otherwise have to be paid monthly) can, amongst others:
- be utilised for business purposes;
- be invested, which can earn a return; and
- be used to repay debt, which could save a great deal of unnecessary interest (of course such an investment in, for example, a mortgage bond, will later have to be withdrawn and applied to paying the provisional tax on the due date).

Humans being what they are, financial discipline is a major problem.

5.9 HOW TO COMPLETE YOUR TAX RETURN

The Receiver supplies an information brochure that helps people to fill in their tax returns (those who do it themselves, and do not leave it to someone else). There are two brochures that may be of help:
- the IT12 S(B) brochure for individuals; and
- the IT14 (B) brochure for companies and close corporations.

5.10 YOUR ACCOUNTANT AND/OR AUDITOR

The word auditor is often used incorrectly to refer simply to a bookkeeper, accountant or accounting officer. However, the Auditors' Board does not permit simply anyone to be called an auditor. If a bookkeeper, accountant or accounting officer is a CA (SA) (Chartered Accountant), such a person may be referred to as an auditor. The fact that someone doing the books is registered with a particular body (e.g. a CFA (SA) registration), does not turn such a person into an auditor. There is, however, reference

---

Provisional tax is not paid in advance, but six months in arrears!

Rather use your partially paid-up mortgage bond as a tax fund.

to a company's internal auditor (not a CA (SA)) and external auditor (who is a CA (SA)).

The cost of having financial statements drawn up is relatively cheap, compared to the bother of having to do it yourself.

Next we will look at the various types of business in regard to the following:
- Who may/must draw up the financial statements?
- Who must sign the financial statements?
- Who must sign the tax form?

TABLE 5.3 **Types of business and persons responsible**

Type of business	Who can/must draw up the financial statements?	Who must sign the financial statements?	Who must sign the tax form?
1. Company	Only someone who is a practising Chartered Accountant and is registered with the CA (SA) Institute.	Directors and Auditor – CA (SA).	The company's secretary or internal accountant or the external auditor – CA (SA).
2. Close corporation	A CA (SA) or someone who is a practising accountant with one of the following Institutes: • Commercial and Financial Accountant of SA, or CFA (SA) • Associated General Accountant, or AGA (SA) with the Institute for CA (SA). There are ACCAs (Associate Certified Chartered Accountants) whose members can do CCs. The application to do companies as well has not yet been approved in South Africa.	Members of the CC and accounting officer: • CFA (SA) • CA (SA) • AGA (SA)	Members themselves or accounting officer.
3. Trust	Same as a close corporation.	Trustees and accounting officer.	Trustees or accounting officer.
4. Partnership	Partners can draw up the statements themselves, or as for close corporation and company.	Partners and accounting officer (if appointed).	Partners or accountant.
5. One-person business	Owner, or as for close corporation and company.	Owner and accounting officer (if appointed).	Owner or accountant.

5.11 HOW TO CALCULATE TAX LIABILITY

The calculation of personal tax involves a number of steps. These steps are almost identical for employer and employee, except that the employer is entitled to other exemptions. Briefly, the steps for calculation are as follows:

Gross income
Less: Exempt income
Less: Deductions allowed
Taxable income
Tax per scale
Less: Rebates
Tax liability

5.11.1 Employees

5.11.1.1 Calculating gross income

The term 'gross income' means all income before any deductions have been made, such as exempt income, allowable deductions, rebates and any expenditure. The total income for the tax year must be reflected on the tax assessment form. Income of a capital nature is reflected as part of the taxpayer's gross income, since 1 October 2001.

Consult a chartered accountant for more details. An accountant's fee is seldom high in comparison with the money you can save as result of professional advice.

Fringe benefits

A fringe benefit may be regarded as a benefit, additional to salary or remuneration, which an employee receives from an employer. Any fringe benefit an employee receives is quantified (expressed in monetary terms) by the Act in order to add it to the employee's gross income.

Any fringe benefit received must be added to income in order to prevent tax evasion (and the associated fine or imprisonment). The following are examples of fringe benefits (Deloitte, Pim & Goldby 1991:5–18):
* the use of a vehicle belonging to the employer;
* accommodation provided by the employer (a permanent home);
* holiday accommodation;
* an inexpensive or interest-free loan;
* a housing subsidy;
* assistance in the acquisition of assets;
* the use of assets (apart from vehicles and accommodation);
* meals and refreshments; and
* the acquisition of shares in terms of an employer's share scheme, or in which the employer has an interest.

Allowances

An allowance differs from a fringe benefit in that an employee receives an amount of money (an allowance) to acquire an asset or a service. Instead of receiving a company vehicle, for example, the employee receives a monthly subsidy to help him or her pay off the instalments on a motor car. Employees must reflect this allowance in the same way as fringe benefits, as part of their gross annual income. Examples of allowances are:
* vehicle and travel allowance;
* entertainment allowance;
* accommodation allowance; and
* allowance to cover any other business-related costs.

A strategy for employees

Assume that an employee uses a private telephone at home for business purposes. The average monthly telephone account amounts to R237,30. Besides the monthly rental for the telephone of R37,30, which must be paid in any case, 90% of the rest of the telephone account is for calls made in the service of the employer. These calls cost R180 (90% of R200) per month.

The employee can do one of two things. Firstly, he or she can convince the employer to pay a monthly allowance in order to recover these costs, but then there are two problems. The employee will pay tax on this allowance. He or she is also going to find it difficult to convince the Receiver of Revenue that R180 of the telephone account, which amounts to R200, was employed exclusively for business purposes.

Secondly, he or she can ask the employer to pay the R180 on his or her behalf. The employee will not have the problem of trying to convince the Receiver of Revenue of his or her honesty in the matter and neither will he or she have to pay tax on an allowance received. It would be easier to convince the employer than the Receiver of Revenue.

5.11.1.2 Exempt income

A taxpayer must determine which of his or her income is exempt from tax, and to what extent. Examples of exempt income are:
* to government and certain non-profit organisations;
* receipts and accruals to certain funds, public institutions, clubs, societies and associations;
* pensions;
* interest;
* dividends;
* copyright;
* national service salaries;
* UIF benefits;
* uniform allowances;
* bursaries and scholarships;

- to non-South African organisations;
- lump sums on retirement;
- rebates and subsidies; and
- exempt annuities.

Taxpayers must know precisely which income is exempt from income tax. All exempt income is added up and the total is deducted from gross income.

5.11.1.3 Deductions allowed

'All expenditure' incurred in order to earn a living (not applicable to those earning a salary only) can be deducted from the taxpayer's gross income. For example, employees are nowadays allowed to deduct a certain amount in the case of the use (to earn a living) of their home studies (see next discussion).

5.11.1.4 Taxable income

The taxpayer's taxable income is calculated by deducting all allowable deductions and exempt income from this gross income. Capital gains are added to this amount.

5.11.1.5 Tax per scale

Having calculated the taxable income, the tax on this income is calculated from the tax tables.

The correct tax table must be used to avoid incorrect calculation of tax liability. If a divorced person with children wishes to know which table to use, a specialist or the Act should be consulted.

5.11.1.6 Tax rebates

Various rebates are granted in the tax per scale. A taxpayer's liability is calculated by deducting these rebates (as applicable) from the tax per scale. The following are examples of rebates:
- primary rebate;
- rebates for dependants;
- rebates for certain age groups (people over 65 years); and
- rebate for an assessment period shorter than one year.

Taxpayers must check the various rebates to determine whether or not they apply to themselves.

5.11.1.7 Tax liability

After deducting the rebates, the taxpayer's total tax liability is obtained. This amount is payable to the Receiver of Revenue every year. Where a person has already made payments during the year, these payments are deducted from the tax liability. Such payments usually occur where:
- an employer makes monthly tax deductions from the employee's salary;
- a person pays provisional tax; or

- voluntary additional tax payments are made to the Receiver of Revenue throughout the year.

5.11.2 Juristic persons and tax

5.11.2.1 Partnerships

The Income Tax Act does not recognise a partnership as a separate tax entity, because it is not a separate juristic person (like a close corporation or company). The profit or loss of a partnership is divided amongst the partners according to the partnership agreement, which determines each partner's stake in the partnership.

Cronje *et al.* (2000:471) point out that Section 24H of the Act determines that:
- each partner conducts the partnership's business;
- partnership income accrues to each partner in a fixed proportion; and
- each partner receives a portion of each deduction for calculating taxable income.

The partnership has the further advantage that each partner can, for example, deal as follows with the partnership loss (in proportion to the partners' interests):
- deduct it from personal income in the year concerned; and
- carry it over to the next assessment year (in the case of a CC or company the loss stays just there).

Where partners receive a salary, the salary must:
- be shown as a deduction to determine the partnership profit; and
- be taxed together with the partnership's profit portion in the hands of the partners concerned.

5.11.2.2 Companies

'A company is also a juristic person where the liability of its shareholders (or members) is limited. This means that the company is liable for its own debts and not the shareholders personally (although there are circumstances where the shareholders and the directors can be held liable).' (Lupton 1999:5)

The following four types of company are distinguished:
- private companies (no more than 50 shareholders, shares are not offered to the public, shares are first sold to existing shareholders);
- public companies (any number of shareholders, shares are freely tradable, sometimes listed on the stock exchange, annual statements are made available to the public);
- Section 21 companies (non-profit companies, mostly for charity); and
- incorporated companies (shareholder liability is limited to guarantees, mostly legal, medical and accounting firms).

A company is governed by its Memorandum of Association (regulates its dealings with the outside world) and the Articles of Association (regulates the division of authority between shareholders and the directors).

You need the following forms for the formation of a company (Lupton 1999:31):

CM1 (2 copies)	–	Certificate of Incorporation
CM2, 2A, B, C or D (2 copies)	–	Memorandum of Association
CM44, CM44C	–	Articles of Association or D (2 copies)
CM22 (2 copies)	–	Registered Office Address
CM27	–	Consent to Act as a Director (1 copy per director)
CM29 (1 copy)	–	Register of Directors, Auditors & Officers
CM31 (2 copies)	–	Appointment of Auditor
CM46 (1 copy)	–	Certificate to Commence Business
CM47 (1 copy per director)	–	Statement as to Adequacy of Capital
Notarial certificate (2)	–	Certificate by a notary to the effect that the copy is a true copy of the original
Special Power of Attorney	–	Authorises attorneys to lodge the documents (one for each subscriber)

Conversion of a company to a close corporation

A company may be converted to a close corporation or CC (Lupton 1999:52) if:

- the company has no more than ten shareholders;
- all the company's shareholders qualify to be members of the CC (no juristic persons as shareholders);
- all the shareholders agree to convert, and show this in the minutes of a meeting;
- form CK4 (original and a copy) has been signed by all shareholders;
- a letter has been obtained from the company's auditor to indicate that there is no contravention of any regulations; and
- the Founding Statement form CK1 (in duplicate) and auditor's certificate have been completed and stamped with a R100 revenue stamp.

In this discussion we will not look at mutual conversions between private and public companies. For more information, consult Lupton (1999:53).

Tax provisions applicable to companies

SARS classifies companies in the following categories:

Type	Rate of tax
Companies:	30%
Small Business Corporations:	
R0 – R150 000	15%
R150 001 and above	30%
Employment Companies:	35%
Foreign Resident Companies:	35%

Cronje *et al.* (2000:580) point out that companies' taxable income is calculated within the same framework as for individuals, namely:

		Total income
Minus:		Capital income
		Foreign income
	=	Gross income
Minus:		Exempt income
	=	Income
Minus:		Allowable deductions
	=	Taxable income (plus CGT)

However, you must take note of the following differences between companies and individuals:
- gross income;
- exempt income;
- allowable deductions; and
- donations to educational institutions (limited to 5% of a company's taxable income).

You can, therefore, not simply calculate your own private company's tax in the same manner as your own individual tax. Consult the Companies Act together with the Income Tax Act. Note each of the aspects above to determine what you must fill in on the tax form for companies. This form also differs from those for individuals.

You must also refer to Section 1 of the Companies Act to see what is defined as a company and what is not. The association or corporation you run or are planning to run may be regarded as a company in terms of the Act.

Provisional tax

- Companies pay tax at a fixed rate. In 2002 this rate was 30%.
- Furthermore, a company is a provisional taxpayer and pays provisional tax at six-monthly intervals, just as individuals do.
- The provisional tax payable is calculated in basically the same manner as for individuals.
- Companies pay interest on an underpayment of provisional tax if the taxable income exceeds R20 000 (R50 000 for individuals).
- A third provisional tax payment is possible within six months of the year-end (seven months if the year-end falls on the last day of February).

Secondary tax on companies

Companies pay secondary tax on dividends they declare. Sections 64B and 64C of the Income Tax Act deal with secondary tax on companies. In 2002 the secondary tax rate was 12.5% of the net amount of the dividend. According to Cronje *et al.* (2000:592) secondary tax is payable on:

- the last day of the month that follows on the month in which the dividend cycle for the dividend concerned ends.

The word 'month' means a calendar month in this case. The Commissioner may issue an assessment notice if insufficient tax has been paid. Secondary tax is paid after completion of a particular return, and is done by the company, not the individual shareholders.

As in the case of individuals, companies are fined for late payment of their tax. In 2002 the interest rate was 13% on the balance owed, calculated from the end of the period concerned.

5.11.2.3 Close corporations

Lupton (1999:5) defines a close corporation (CC) as follows:

> *A Close Corporation is a juristic person, i.e. a person created by law and has the right to own property, incur debt and sue and be sued in its own right.*

You need the following forms for creating a CC:

- CK7 (Reservation of name in duplicate on yellow);
- CK1 (Founding Statement in duplicate on blue);
- CK2 (Amended Founding Statement in duplicate on yellow about name, main business and change of members); and
- CK2A (also an Amended Founding Statement in duplicate about the accounting officer and registered office address).

A close corporation is controlled and managed in terms of the Close Corporations Act 69 of 1984 and the Close Corporations Administrative Regulations.

Conversion of a close corporation to a company

According to Lupton (1999:51) a close corporation can be changed into a company by, amongst others:

- the written permission of all the members of the CC; and
- if all these members also become the founding members of the Memorandum and Articles of Association of the company.

The existing close corporation remains intact, but now functions under a new name and is regulated by the Companies Act instead of the Close Corporations Act (similar to forming a new company). Apart from the forms one normally fills in on creating a company, the following forms and letters need to be completed and attached:

- a reservation of name form (CM5) (the name will either end with '(Pty) Ltd' or 'Ltd' – the name will be the same as the CC or change);
- type the following words at the bottom of the certificate of incorporation (form CM1): 'THIS IS TO CERTIFY THAT ON .... THE ABOVE COMPANY WAS CONVERTED FROM A CLOSE CORPORATION: XyzCC CK 99/12345/23.'
- a letter (signed by each member of the close corporation) to the Registrar of Companies with
  - the name of the CC,
  - the CC's registration number, and
  - the words: 'CONVERSION FROM CLOSE CORPORATION TO COMPANY'; and
- a letter from the CC's accounting officer which declares that there is no contravention of any of the rules of the Close Corporations Act.

If an accumulated profit is involved in the conversion, secondary tax on companies is also a factor. Normally businesses first wait and 'work off' the profit before contemplating such a conversion.

Tax on close corporations

A close corporation pays tax at the same fixed rate of 30% (2002) as a company. Secondary tax on companies also applies to close corporations. Note that dividends received by a close corporation are, as for individuals, tax-exempt. SARS perceives a CC as a company for income tax purposes.

5.11.2.4 Trusts

Section 1 of the Income Tax Act defines a trust as:

> *any trust fund consisting of cash or other assets administered and controlled by a person acting in a fiduciary capacity where the person has been appointed in terms of a trust deed or agreement in terms of the will of a deceased.*

A 'special trust' is a trust created for someone who cannot generate sufficient sustenance themselves due to a mental condition or serious physical disability.

Apart from a special trust, trusts are taxed at a rate of:

- 35% for an income up to R100 000; and
- 45% for all income above R100 000.

The rates applicable to ordinary persons are used for special trusts.

We can distinguish between testamentary trusts and *inter vivos* trusts.

Testamentary trusts

A trust created in terms of someone's will is known as a testamentary trust (*mortis causa*). The income from a testamentary trust is taxable:

- in the hands of the beneficiaries; or
- in the hands of the trust.

A beneficiary with a vested interest in the trust income will be taxed on that portion of the trust income to which the beneficiary has a right. Of course a trustee's discretionary powers may determine that further income (over and above the rights of a beneficiary) may be paid over to the beneficiary. The trust will, of necessity, be taxed on the income remaining in the trust. This income is regarded as capital if, for example, it is paid to the beneficiary in ten years' time. The beneficiary will then pay no tax on it.

If a trust does not have a beneficiary with a vested interest in receiving the income (for example, if the beneficiary is too young), the trust income is paid into the trust itself (the trustee is the responsible person in this case).

Income retains its character in a trust. In terms of Section 25B of the Act, a trust's income retains its character, which implies that:

- interest income accruing to a beneficiary qualifies for the interest exemption (currently R6 000 per person, or R10 000 if older than 65 – 2002);
- income of a capital nature remains capital income; and
- foreign income remains foreign income, no matter where the trust is situated.

Inter vivos trusts

As soon as a person creates a trust in his or her lifetime, it is known as an *inter vivos* trust. In the case of an *inter vivos* trust, tax may be payable by three parties, namely:

- a donor of assets to the trust;
- the beneficiaries; or
- the trust.

Sections 7(3) to 7(7) of the Act deal with taxing the donor. Income is regarded as the income of the donor until the event that entitles the beneficiary to the income has taken place (for example, a child or beneficiary's 25th birthday), or the death of the donor.

Beneficiaries pay tax on income if the assets are donated to the trust and the beneficiaries have a vested interest in the income. A minor is not taxed, but in such a case you should look at Sections 7(3) and 7(4) of the Act. A beneficiary is taxed on income (already earned and accumulating in the trust) if:

- the donor dies; or
- the assets were sold to the trust at a lower value than the actual market value (according to the proportion of the selling price to the reasonable market value).

Income that is not taxable in the hands of the creator/donor, is taxed in the hands of the trustees. Normal expenses are deducted (Cronje *et al.* 2000:567), for example:

- administrative costs;
- trustee compensation;
- interest paid to the donor; and
- the premium on surety.

As with a testamentary trust, income in an *inter vivos* trust retains its character.

5.11.2.5 Deceased estates

For tax purposes there are two tax periods for deceased estates (Cronje *et al.* 2000:544):

- the period that ends with death; and
- the period that begins with death and ends when the estate is wound up.

If a taxpayer dies, the executor of the estate is responsible for paying tax (and must ensure that the tax form is filled in and taxes are paid). The taxpayer's (deceased's) tax period now runs from the beginning of the tax year (1 March) to the date of death. Consequently tax is payable for this period, which will usually be less than a year. The rebates such a person would have been entitled to are reduced accordingly for this period. If such a person only pays SITE, the tax period ends on the date of death. No further tax returns, therefore, need be completed or rendered.

Most estates being administered earn some income during the winding-up period, be it:

- interest income; or
- rental income from buildings/land.

The executor must render an income tax return for this period. Tax is calculated according to the normal rates applicable to living natural persons.

5.11.2.6 Insolvent estates

If a taxpayer's estate is sequestrated (voluntarily or forced), the estate's tax period ends on the date of sequestration. Taxable income is calculated for the period, and rebates are reduced accordingly. The insolvent estate is regarded as a new taxpayer for tax purposes from the date of sequestration. Furthermore, the estate (excluding businesses) before sequestration and the insolvent estate are regarded as one estate for income tax purposes.

5.11.3 Employers

Taxpayers with their own business undertakings are entitled to special deductions over and above the usual exempt income and allowable deductions. The following are examples of special deductions:
- maintenance costs (for vehicles, machinery, tools, implements and installations);
- bad debts;
- employee housing;
- doubtful debts;
- the demolition of a business building;
- depreciation of factory equipment;
- export allowances; and
- employee training costs.

Employers must determine for themselves whether they are entitled to a special deduction for purposes of income tax. Many taxpayers are unaware of the deductions they may make. All expenditure incurred for the purpose of earning an income can be deducted from gross income.

5.12 INCOME TAX PITFALLS AND HOW TO AVOID THEM

Tax liability is one of a long list of investment criteria that individuals and investors should keep in mind when they consider different investments. You should, of course, try to pay as little tax as possible. There are various ways of avoiding tax, and they are legal. Tax evasion, however, is not. We will now look at some methods of avoiding tax.
- If you have received money tax-free, avoid making it taxable again. For example, when you have already been taxed on your package when it was paid out, you should not invest in an annuity right away (you will be taxed on your income). If you need the income to live on, that is another matter. If possible, invest your money for as long as possible while enjoying capital growth and avoiding tax.
- If you have to transfer your package to your new employer's retirement fund, or if you want to leave it in a preservation fund, you should have it transferred directly from your current employer's retirement fund. If you first transfer it to your bank account you will definitely be taxed.
- Invest tax-free in your mortgage bond by paying it off.

- The tax-free allowance for interest earned is R6 000 per person (R12 000 for a husband and wife).
- At present dividends are tax-free.
- Your investment is taxable if you invest in certain capital growth investments.
- The following cost items are tax-deductible when you invest in income-producing property (property that you buy and then let to somebody else):
  - interest on your bond;
  - maintenance;
  - municipal rates, water and electricity or a levy;
  - short-term insurance premiums; and
  - administration fees.
- If you invest in an annuity, your bookkeeper should make the necessary tax-deduction.
- If you receive money in terms of a deferred compensation scheme, an amount of R30 000 will be tax-free. This has nothing to do with the one-off R120 000 that your are allowed to deduct as a lump sum.
- With a provident fund, a tax deduction of R24 000 applies if the total amount you receive is more than R24 000.
- You may donate R30 000 a year to a spouse, child, other person, institution or trust without having to pay donations tax. A married couple may, therefore, donate R60 000 per year.
- Sell fixed assets to heirs or trusts, or buy these assets in their names and lend them the purchase price. Bequeath these interest-free loans to them in your will (if you prefer). Also donate R30 000 per year to them (either from the loan or over and above the loan).
- Reduce estate duty by:
  - buying assets in the name of a child or a trust;
  - selling assets to a child or a trust;
  - making investments in the name of a trust or a child;
  - making provision in your will for establishing a testamentary trust (after your death;)
  - appointing the surviving spouse (in your will) and thereafter a child (or two) as the executor(s) of your estate after your death; and
  - bequeathing everything to your spouse.
- Make sure that you receive the maximum tax-free lump sum from your pension, provident and/or retirement annuity fund. Ask an accountant or tax specialist to help you, particularly if you belong to more than one of these funds simultaneously. The Receiver of Revenue will look at the number of years of simultaneous membership, as well as the specific fund you choose, to calculate this amount.
- You could also invest your money with the aim of trading in, say, listed shares or linked unit trusts.

You are legally entitled to deduct investment costs such as the following, for tax purposes:
- broker's fees (fees and/or commission);
- books, magazines and newspapers;
- computer;
- computer and share programs;
- Internet fees; and
- the cost of managing your business and office (even if you are working from home). Again consult a tax specialist.

- Open a bank and/or investment account for your children so that they are taxed on the income from your investments.
- If you need to borrow money, rather borrow from your spouse (or from his or her investments) so that he or she earns the interest that you have to pay as income (particularly where he or she has a much lower income). The interest is now tax-deductible.
- Invest in an educational trust for your children. They will have to pay less tax and your estate will be smaller.
- Make better use of investments from which you receive dividends instead of interest, because dividends are tax-free while interest is taxable.
- Involve your children in your business in order to share and lower the tax liability.
- Divide as much of your income as possible between yourself and your spouse.
- Make sure that you use the income from your financial investments at the latest possible stage of your life. By doing this you will postpone the payment of tax, your investments will have time to grow, and you will probably receive this income when you no longer receive income from other sources – so you will have to pay less tax.
- It is also possible to buy multiple properties and rent them in order to reduce your tax liability and increase your long-term prosperity (the instalments, maintenance, short- and long-term insurance are tax-deductible, so you are using tax money to increase your prosperity).
- Make some home study deductions for tax purposes if possible.
- Restructure your salary package.

5.12.1 Structure/restructure your salary package

Persons working for a company are in a good position to structure their salary or remuneration package in such a way that they get certain income tax benefits (after-tax benefits). If you start working for a new employer, you must therefore make sure that you know how and why, so that you can nego-

- Avoid tax (pay as little as possible).
- Make tax-free investments (for capital growth).
- Postpone the payment of tax for as long as possible.

tiate the structuring of the remuneration package with your employer.

De Villiers (1996:4) refers to the 'Taxmaster' that was developed by International Compensation. This Windows program makes possible the restructuring of remuneration packages at low cost (to employers). Employees can choose from amongst various options in regard to:
- additional salary; or
- reduced salary (sacrificing salary portions).

Companies could save a great deal in regard to employing tax consultants, and employees have a say in the structuring in order to put in place some tax avoidance.

De Villiers, furthermore, points out that it is better to pay too little tax (legally) than too much. The onus then rests on the Receiver to prove that you should pay more.

Kruger (1999:9) highlights various allowances that can help to structure a salary package with tax advantages:
- Vehicle or transport related expenses (petrol, maintenance, insurance, instalments).
- Entertainment costs (R2 500 per year in 2002).
- The lesser of: the actual expenditure, or R2 500, or R3 000 plus 5% of the taxable income (before this deduction) in excess of R6 000 derived during the year of assessment from any trade in connection with which the expenditure was incurred.
- A contributory pension fund (if you contribute the maximum amount – the greater of R1 750 or 7.5% of your retirement funding employment income; the remaining amount can be paid by your employer as part of your salary package).
- If you belong to a provident fund, it should be more advantageous to ensure that the employer makes all the contributions.

Ramantsi (2000:22) indicates that salary structuring addresses the following aspects, amongst others:
- fringe benefits (remuneration other than cash);
- allowances (when your employer pays you cash to meet business expenses); and
- basic salary (cash).

If you pay too much tax, getting the money back is your problem (the burden of proof rests on you). A structured remuneration package can help in this regard.

In order to determine whether you should receive allowances rather than a bigger salary, you need to compare the tax you would have to pay in the various cases. Ramantsi points out the tax advantage of a person receiving a travel allowance rather than a bigger salary. The portion of any allowance (for example, a travel allowance) that you do not use is taxable in your hands. In the case of some allowances you do not actually have to use them, and for some you need to keep all records as proof of tax expenses for the Receiver.

Therefore, ensure that your remuneration package is structured in such a way that your personal financial needs and goals as served optimally.

5.13 RETIREMENT/SEVERANCE PACKAGES AND TAX PLANNING

Each year thousands of South Africans receive severance packages. Thousands of people also receive their retirement packages every year. It is very important to apply these packages carefully and purposefully, after proper personal financial planning. The package must be applied after thorough consideration of all possible areas of personal financial planning, particularly tax planning.

Study Chapter 14 for more information on retirement planning and the tax decisions that go with it. You will notice that any investments you make for life after your retirement must take proper account of the tax aspects. Always consult a tax expert regarding this aspect of your personal financial planning. This expert could be your accountant or professional broker.

5.14 SUMMARY

The payment of income tax affects the financial position (wealth) of every household. Careful planning is essential in order to avoid paying unnecessary tax. Knowledge of the tax environment is a prerequisite for effective tax planning. Tax must be avoided legally and it is recommended that a tax specialist be consulted for tax planning. A tax specialist is familiar with income tax legislation, which is amended annually.

You don't simply give the state money:

- for which you have worked your entire life; and
- on which you have already paid tax for your entire life.

5.15 SELF-ASSESSMENT

- Briefly discuss the steps you should follow in order to calculate your income tax liability.
- Briefly explain the different income tax pitfalls and ways to avoid them.

BIBLIOGRAPHY

Cronje, M., Stack, E.M. & Hamel, E.H. 2000. *Die belasting van individue en maatskappye*. Durban: Butterwoths.

Deloitte, Pim & Goldby. 1991. *Pay less tax*. Cape Town: Deloitte, Pim & Goldby.

De Villiers, T.J. 1996. Gestruktureerde pakket se voordele. *Finansies & Tegniek*: 22, col. 1–3, Oct. 4.

Duvenage, H. 1999. Ontvanger weet al hoe meer van jou geldsake. *Sake-Rapport*: 1, col. 3–5, April 4.

Du Plessis, F. 2000. *Tax Update 2000*. CFA seminar. In Touch Conference Centre. Pretoria: Aug. 16.

Kruger, D. 1999. Pay less tax by structuring your salary package effectively. *Sunday Times Business Times – Money*: 12, col. 1–7, May 9.

Laurie, H. de G. 1991a. Begroting se geskenk aan getroudes. *Finansies & Tegniek*: 28, col. 2, April 5.

Laurie, H. de G. 1991b. Toevlugsoorde om belasting te vermy. *Finansies & Tegniek*: 30, col. 2, 5 Feb. 5.

Lupton, J.A. 1999. *A practical guide to company secretarial practice*. Durban: Butterworths.

Malan, E.M. & Cronje, P.M. 1987. *Income tax study guide for Tax 201-P and Itx 201-P*. Revised edn. Pretoria: Unisa.

Metz, R. 1998. *Minder vir Jan Taks*. Goodwood: Metz.

Preen, C. Here's your guide to the new capital gains tax. *Personal Finance*: 4, col. 3–6, April 22.

PriceWaterhouse Coopers. 2000. Welcome to capital gains tax! *The Accountant*: 7, col.1–3, October.

Ramantsi, T. 1999. A tax frame to work from. *Personal Finance*: 4, col. 5–7, Nov. 20.

Ramantsi, T. 2000. Tailoring a salary package to suit you. *Personal Finance*: 3, col. 1, Jan. 22.

South Africa (Republic). 1962. Acts of the Republic of South Africa – Income Tax Act 58 of 1962. Pretoria: Government Printer. (Income Tax Act, as amended).

Swart, N.J. 2000. Capital gains tax – a tax on inflation. *Property Professional*: 3–6, col. 1–2, June/July.

CHAPTER 6

ESTATE PLANNING

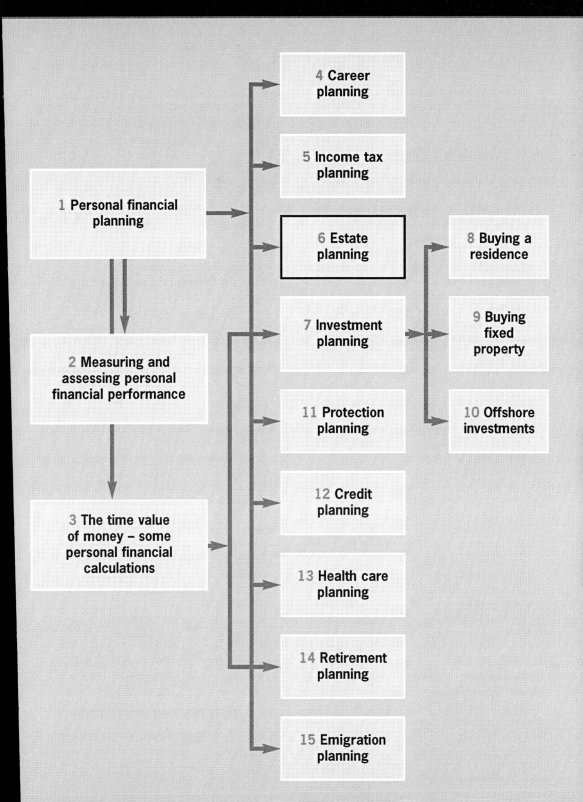

1 Personal financial planning

4 Career planning

5 Income tax planning

6 Estate planning

8 Buying a residence

2 Measuring and assessing personal financial performance

7 Investment planning

9 Buying fixed property

11 Protection planning

10 Offshore investments

3 The time value of money – some personal financial calculations

12 Credit planning

13 Health care planning

14 Retirement planning

15 Emigration planning

6.1 LEARNING OUTCOMES

After studying this chapter, you will be able to:
- Define the meaning of the concept 'estate planning'.
- Explain the importance of timely and continuous estate planning.
- Identify the different steps in the estate planning process.
- Recognise estate planning pitfalls and identify methods to avoid them.
- Recognise the influence of your lifestyle on estate planning and personal finances.
- Identify the different steps in the administration of an estate (winding up).
- Draw up a cohabitation agreement, an antenuptial contract and a will.
- Identify the uses of a trust.
- Explain the effect of a matrimonial property regime on estate planning and personal finances.
- Identify techniques to decrease the size of your estate and to avoid paying estate duty.

6.2 INTRODUCTION

The term 'estate' is the collective name for everything a person owns. Abrie & Graham (1989:2) describe estate planning as a plan that a person draws up, setting out how he or she wishes to deal with his or her possessions. According to Amling & Droms (1986:542), estate planning refers to all activities leading to the accumulation of, as well as the management of, assets or possessions. These activities take place during a person's lifetime and also apply to the transfer of possessions after death.

Amling & Droms (1986:542) refer to three phases in a person's financial life:
- building up an estate;
- preserving (protecting) the estate; and
- transferring the estate.

Planning areas in later chapters deal with the building up of an estate (investment planning), as well as the preservation of an estate (protection planning). During this discussion on estate planning, the transfer of an estate will be examined. As far as the transfer aspects of an estate are concerned, the following financial objectives are important:
- the minimisation of transfer costs (particularly estate duty, CGT, costs of administration and the cost involved in the transfer of fixed property to heirs, institutions or trusts);
- the protection (retention) of assets; and
- the provision of sufficient (liquid) funds to make transfer possible.

Estate plans are normally structured in such a way that the transfer of the estate is associated with the least difficulty and, particularly, the lowest costs. The testator/testatrix (the person whose estate has to be transferred after his/her death) or estate owner cannot take care of the transfer of his or her estate after his or her death. In other words, estate planning also refers to circumstances when the estate owner can no longer implement the estate plan him- or herself.

Many people neglect to plan their estates. Besides, estates also vary in size in financial terms. Abrie & Graham (1989:2) distinguish three approaches to estate planning:
- no estate planning;
- elementary estate planning; and
- comprehensive estate planning.

6.2.1 No estate planning

This does not imply that a person has not collected any possessions or assets during his or her lifetime. What is meant is that the person or estate owner has not made provision for the transfer of the estate to persons (dependants) or institutions after his or her death. The estate owner has also failed to draw up a will to indicate how the estate (large or small) should be transferred.

In such a case, the person's estate will be distributed in terms of the Intestate Succession Act 81 of 1987. The distribution of the estate in terms of this Act makes no provision for the transfer of the estate according to the wishes of the owner, since such wishes are not known. This could result in people who have not been acceptable to the estate owner inheriting his or her possessions. For that reason, it is advisable to draw up a will (unless the estate is very small – this will be further illustrated when we discuss the Act).

Administration of an estate refers to the process during which transfer of the estate takes place. The process is much more difficult if there is no estate plan in writing (a will). An elementary estate plan is, therefore, recommended.

6.2.2 Elementary estate planning

A relatively small estate requires only an elementary estate plan. The estate owner's wishes in respect of the transfer of the estate appear in his or her will, which will simplify matters after his or her death.

6.2.3 Comprehensive estate planning

Comprehensive estate planning refers to an estate plan that involves far more than merely drawing up a simple will. A person with a fairly large estate will use such an estate plan.

Abrie & Graham (1989:6) divide comprehensive estate planning into the following:
- timely planning (during the life of the estate owner – for example, the trust *inter vivos* technique);
- testamentary planning (in his or her will); and
- other planning (for example, insurance).

Comprehensive estate planning requires knowledge of specialised fields such as law, investment, income tax and insurance, and it is recommended that professional advice be sought from attorneys, accountants and insurance advisers.

6.3 THE ESTATE PLANNING PROCESS

Estate planning is a continuous process during which attention should be paid to changing circumstances (of the estate owner and his or her heirs). Block *et al.* (1988:539) refer to the following six steps in the estate planning process:

Step 1: Set objectives
- identify heirs;
- decide what each heir should inherit; and
- decide who should control the assets.

Step 2: Take stock
- identify estate property; and
- establish the value of the estate.

Step 3: Establish the estate's liabilities
- assess estate duty liabilities;
- assess other estate costs; and
- analyse liquidity of assets.

Step 4: Choose estate planning techniques
- identify a team of professional planners;
- establish available techniques; and
- select the most suitable techniques.

Step 5: Implement the estate plan
- draw up the necessary documents; and
- inform heirs of the plan.

Step 6: Revise the estate plan

These steps are interrelated – each contributes to the total plan. Step 1 should actually be placed after Step 3, since it is impossible to determine what heirs should inherit and who should control assets before the estate property and the associated liabilities have been identified. We will discuss each of the six steps.

6.3.1 Step 1: Set objectives

Before estate planning can take place, attention must first be given to the objectives the person wishes to achieve – exactly as for any other type of planning. Tale 6.1 was drawn up on the basis of research completed in 1985 about the most important factors in an estate plan. The factors appear in order of priority.

TABLE 6.1 **Factors affecting an estate plan**
(Source: Abrie & Graham 1989:53)

Factors that affect the form of an estate plan	Importance expressed in %
1. Care of dependants	95
2. Estate duty considerations	87
3. Retention of control over estate assets	73
4. Protection of estate assets	73
5. Income tax considerations	71
6. Avoidance of red tape	70
7. Transfer duty considerations	47
8. Stamp duty considerations	34

From the table, it can be seen that the care of dependants is the most important objective of an estate. Items 2–8 cover the protection and retention of estate assets. A larger estate (more assets) will obviously mean that dependants are better off. However, the eight factors are interrelated and are aimed at the protection objective.

These factors together form part of one of the personal planning areas – protection planning. They also form part of income tax planning, project planning, estate planning, investment planning and retirement planning. These personal planning areas are also interrelated and each one has an effect on the others.

The personal financial objectives that precede this planning area should support and supplement each other. If the objectives in one area are achieved or not achieved, this will either promote or restrict (or make impossible) the achievement of objectives in the other planning areas. For example, if a person cannot even support his or her household on a monthly basis (home, food, clothing – the protection objective), he or she will never achieve the investment objective.

Households should strive for the achievement of their objectives in order of priority. It would be unwise to concentrate on the retirement objective while the household does not have sufficient food and is living in unhygienic conditions. There should be a balance between objectives; in other words, a household should have a balanced objectives programme.

Earlier, we mentioned that the transfer costs of the estate should be kept at a minimum and that sufficient funds for such transfer should be available. Similarly, estate assets should be protected.

6.3.1.1. Identify heirs

The estate owner (the testator or the person to whom the will belongs) must decide who is going to inherit the estate; in other words, among which persons, institutions or trusts the estate is going to be distributed.

6.3.1.2 Decide what each heir should inherit

Having identified one heir or more, the will must state what each heir will inherit; in other words, the size of the respective inheritances must be determined.

6.3.1.3 Decide who should control the assets

It is important that the estate owner should be aware of the fact that only competent heirs should be entrusted with the control of the estate. For example, people such as the following should not be given control of an estate:

- an heir who does not have a sensible approach towards money and possessions (for example, someone who would be inclined to spend money recklessly or to sell off assets for cash);
- an heir who is mentally retarded;
- an heir who is severely physically handicapped and therefore not physically capable of taking control of the property;
- an heir who has relatives by marriage who are not honest with money; and
- minors.

Certain estate planning techniques can solve the above-mentioned problems. For example, a trust could be created, in which inheritances are held. Reliable trustees could then control the trust on behalf of the heirs, subject to the conditions attached to the trust as set out in the deed of trust or the will. This technique is discussed further under Step 4.

6.3.2 Step 2: Take stock

In this step, the asset side of the estate is calculated. A value is also attached to the property of the estate.

6.3.2.1 Identify estate property

All property, fixed as well as current assets, belonging to the estate owner must be identified. Fixed assets include buildings, plots and farms. Current assets include a motor car, a boat, furniture, jewellery, tools, collections, guns or rifles, cash, investments, insurance policies, annuities and pension benefits. An interest in property or a business is also regarded as an estate asset.

In terms of the Estate Duty Act 45 of 1955, right of use and enjoyment and usufruct are also regarded as property, or rather as interests in or rights to property. A right of use (fiduciary right) arises when an estate owner bequeaths possessions to an heir on condition that the possessions go to a second heir after the first heir's death, if the second heir is still living. The first heir may use the property but he or she may not sell it.

Usufruct gives a person (for example, a widow) the right to enjoy the fruits (income) of an asset. The property, however, belongs to another person or an institution. This means that the usufructuary is not given the full right of the property (it is a limited right), as another person or institution has full property rights.

The Estate Duty Act excludes certain property for estate duty purposes in view of the fact that the estate owner (deceased) did not reside inside the Republic of South Africa. Other exclusions are:

- payments to widows by the Railways and Harbours Provident Fund;

- trust money held by attorneys (Attorneys, Notaries and Conveyancers Admission Act 23 of 1934);
- benefits from a pension fund controlled by the Minister of Social Development; and
- the return on certain insurance policies.

6.3.2.2 Establish the value of the estate

Estate duty is calculated on the net value of an estate. During this step, the gross value of the estate is calculated; in other words, a value is attached to everything belonging to the estate.

The valuation of the property

A registered valuer is normally used to calculate the market value of the estate assets. In terms of the Expropriation Act 63 of 1975, market value means the amount of money that could be obtained for the property (assets of the estate in this case) if it were sold on a specific date by a willing seller to a willing buyer on the open market. Book values or replacement values of estate assets are not taken into account for the purposes of valuation for estate duty.

The valuation of an interest in a property

As in the case of property (for example, a residential home) being transferred to an heir after the death of the estate owner, an interest in property (for example, right of use, fiduciary right and usufruct) is also transferred. For example, a son inherits the use of the home to which his mother was entitled (after the death of his father). By inheriting the usufruct, the son benefits because now he has the full use of the property for the rest of his life without the encumbrance of the usufruct.

A formula is used for the calculation of the value of an interest in property (right of use, usufruct, *habitatio*). This formula capitalises the annual value of the interest or right over the following terms:
- the expectation of life of the beneficiary; or
- the term for which the interest or right applies.

The following tables by Abrie & Graham (1989:459) can be used for the calculation of the value of limited interest. Table 6.2 is used when the value of the interest or right is linked to the beneficiary's or heir's life expectancy. Table 6.3 is used if the value of an interest has to be calculated over a certain term.

TABLE 6.2 **Life expectancy and the present value of R1 p.a. for life, capitalised at 12%**
(Source: Abrie & Graham 1989:459)

Age	Life expectancy		Present value of R1 per annum for life		Age
	Man	Woman	Man	Woman	
0	64.74	72.36	8.327 91	8.331 05	0
1	65.37	72.74	8.328 28	8.331 14	1
2	64.50	71.87	8.327 76	8.330 91	2
3	63.57	70.93	8.327 14	8.330 64	3
4	62.63	69.97	8.326 44	8.330 33	4
5	61.69	69.02	8.325 67	8.329 99	5
6	60.74	68.06	8.325 80	8.329 61	6
7	59.78	67.09	8.323 81	8.329 18	7
8	58.81	66.11	8.322 71	8.328 69	8
9	57.83	65.14	8.321 46	8.326 84	9
10	56.85	64.15	8.320 07	8.327 53	10
11	55.86	63.16	8.318 49	8.326 81	11
12	54.87	62.18	8.316 73	8.326 08	12
13	53.90	61.19	8.314 80	8.325 22	13
14	52.93	30.21	8.312 65	8.324 27	14
15	51.98	59.23	8.310 29	8.323 20	15
16	51.04	58.26	8.307 70	8.322 03	16
17	50.12	57.29	8.304 89	8.320 71	17
18	49.21	56.33	8.301 80	8.319 26	18

19	48.31	55.37	8.298 41	8.317 64	19
20	47.42	54.41	8.294 71	8.315 84	20
21	46.53	53.45	8.290 61	8.313 83	21
22	45.65	52.50	8.286 13	8.311 61	22
23	44.77	51.54	8.281 17	8.309 12	23
24	43.88	50.58	8.275 64	8.306 33	24
25	43.00	49.63	8.269 59	8.303 26	25
26	42.10	48.67	8.262 74	8.299 81	26
27	41.20	47.71	8.255 16	8.295 95	27
28	40.30	46.76	8.246 77	8.291 71	28
29	39.39	45.81	8.237 37	8.286 97	29
30	38.48	44.86	8.266 94	8.281 70	30
31	37.57	43.91	8.215 38	8.275 83	31
32	36.66	42.96	8.202 57	8.269 30	32
33	35.75	42.02	8.188 36	8.262 10	33
34	34.84	41.07	8.172 62	8.245 00	34
35	33.94	40.13	8.155 36	8.245 09	35
36	33.05	39.19	8.136 47	8.235 17	36
37	32.16	38.26	8.115 58	8.224 26	37
38	31.28	37.32	8.092 74	8.211 99	38
39	30.41	36.40	8.067 81	8.198 66	39
40	29.54	35.48	8.040 30	8.183 86	40
41	28.69	34.57	8.010 67	8.167 62	41
42	27.85	33.67	7.978 44	8.149 83	42
43	27.02	32.77	7.943 44	8.130 12	43
44	26.20	31.89	7.905 47	8.108 81	44
45	25.38	31.01	7.863 80	8.085 27	45
46	24.58	30.14	7.819 24	8.059 56	46
47	23.79	29.27	7.771 09	8.031 19	47
48	23.00	28.41	7.718 43	8.000 26	48
49	22.23	27.55	7.662 36	7.966 17	49
50	21.17	26.71	7.602 01	7.929 50	50
51	20.72	25.88	7.537 13	7.889 67	51
52	19.98	25.06	7.467 48	7.846 46	52
53	19.26	24.25	7.393 87	7.799 65	53
54	18.56	23.44	7.316 31	7.748 34	54
55	17.86	22.65	7.232 34	7.693 55	55
56	17.18	21.86	7.144 14	7.633 63	56
57	16.52	21.08	7.051 78	7.568 96	57
58	15.86	20.31	6.952 25	7.499 27	58
59	15.23	19.54	6.850 04	7.423 21	59
60	14.61	18.78	6.742 06	7.341 35	60
61	14.01	18.04	6.630 10	7.254 57	61
62	13.42	17.30	6.512 32	7.160 20	62
63	12.86	16.58	6.393 01	7.060 46	63
64	12.31	15.88	6.268 22	6.955 37	64
65	11.77	15.18	6.137 89	6.811 61	65

66	11.26	14.51	6.007 26	6.723 93	66
67	10.76	13.85	5.871 65	6.598 93	67
68	10.28	13.20	5.734 03	6.466 35	68
69	9.81	12.57	5.591 82	6.328 18	69
70	9.37	11.96	5.451 65	6.184 66	70
71	8.94	11.37	5.307 75	3.036 07	71
72	8.54	10.80	5.167 44	5.882 78	72
73	8.15	10.24	5.024 37	5.772 22	73
74	7.77	9.70	4.878 76	5.557 43	74
75	7.41	9.18	4.732 90	5.388 93	75
76	7.07	8.68	4.593 54	5.217 27	76
77	6.73	8.21	4.446 63	5.016 79	77
78	6.41	7.75	4.303 09	4.870 92	78
79	6.10	7.31	4.158 98	4.693 89	79
80	5.82	6.89	4.024 40	4.516 47	80
81	5.55	6.50	3.890 51	4.343 99	81
82	5.31	6.13	3.768 02	4.173 15	82
83	5.09	5.78	3.652 76	4.004 82	83
84	4.89	5.45	3.545 46	3.839 88	84
85	4.72	5.14	3.452 32	3.679 21	85
86	4.57	4.85	3.368 64	3.523 71	86
87	4.45	4.58	3.300 66	3.374 26	87
88	4.36	4.33	3.249 07	3.231 75	88
89	4.32	4.11	3.225 97	3.102 96	89
90	4.30	3.92	3.214 38	2.989 12	90

Note: The age must be taken as on the birthday following the date on which the right was obtained.

EXAMPLE

Find the present value of an annuity or usufruct of R100 per annum for life of:
(a) a female who becomes entitled thereto at the age of 42 years 3 months; or
(b) a male who becomes entitled thereto at the age of 65 years 9 months.

	(a)	(b)
Age when acquired	42 years	65 years
	3 months	9 months
Age next birthday	43 years	66 years
Present value of R1 per annum for life	R8,130 12	R6,007 26
Present value of R100 per annum for life	R813,01	R600,73

TABLE 6.3 **Present value of R1 p.a. capitalised at 12% over fixed periods**
(Source: Abrie & Graham 1989:459)

Years	Amount	Years	Amount	Years	Amount	Years	Amount
1	0.892 9	26	7.895 7	51	8.307 6	76	8.331 8
2	1.690 0	27	7.942 6	52	8.310 4	77	8.332 0
3	2.401 8	28	7.984 4	53	8.312 8	78	8.332 1
4	3.037 4	29	8.021 8	54	8.315 0	79	8.332 3
5	3.604 8	30	8.055 2	55	8.317 0	80	8.332 4
6	4.111 4	31	8.085 0	56	8.318 7	81	8.332 5
7	4.563 8	32	8.111 6	57	8.320 3	82	8.332 6
8	4.967 6	33	8.135 4	58	8.312 7	83	8.332 6
9	5.328 2	34	8.156 6	59	8.322 9	84	8.332 7
10	5.650 2	35	8.175 5	60	8.324 0	85	8.332 8
11	5.937 7	36	8.192 4	61	8.325 0	86	8.332 8
12	6.194 4	37	8.207 5	62	8.325 9	87	8.332 9
13	6.423 6	38	8.221 0	63	8.326 7	88	8.333 0
14	6.628 2	39	8.233 0	64	8.327 4	89	8.333 0
15	6.810 9	40	8.243 8	65	8.328 1	90	8.333 0
16	6.974 0	41	8.253 4	66	8.328 6	91	8.333 1
17	7.119 6	42	8.261 9	67	8.329 1	92	8.333 1
18	7.249 7	43	8.269 6	68	8.329 6	93	8.333 1
19	7.365 8	44	8.276 4	69	8.330 0	94	8.333 1
20	7.469 4	45	8.282 5	70	8.330 3	95	8.333 2
21	7.562 0	46	8.288 0	71	8.330 7	96	8.333 2
22	7.644 6	47	8.292 8	72	8.331 0	97	8.333 2
23	7.718 4	48	8.297 2	73	8.331 2	98	8.333 2
24	7.784 3	49	8.301 0	74	8.331 4	99	8.333 2
25	7.843 1	50	8.304 5	75	8.331 6	100	8.333 2

Note: When using the table, fractions of a year should be disregarded.

The valuation of specific interests in property (limited interests or rights) will be discussed next, illustrated with examples. The following limited interests are distinguished (Abrie & Graham 1989:24):

- fiduciary right (right of use and enjoyment);
- usufruct;
- bare dominium;
- an annuity charged upon property; and
- other annuities.

A fiduciary right (the right of use)
A fiduciary right is the right to use and enjoy the fruits of a property.

EXAMPLE

Assume that a person dies and bequeaths a property of R100 000 to his son, subject to a *fideicommissum*. The son is 46 years and 7 months old. Calculate the value of the fiduciary right that has passed to the son.

Solution

Value of the property	R100 000
Annual value at 12%	R12 000
Age of son at next birthday	47 years
Factor for male person of 47 years (Table 6.2)	7.771 09
Value of son's fiduciary right = (R12 000 x 7.771 09)	R93 253,08

This calculation, as well as those for the other four interests in property, is based on Section 5(1)(b) of the Estate Duty Act 45 of 1955.

Usufruct

It is important to note that, in the case of a fiduciary right, a separate bare dominium does not exist, whereas in the case of usufruct, a separate bare dominium does exist.

EXAMPLE

Assume that a person held usufruct over a farm during his lifetime. The bare dominium belongs to his daughter, who is 30 years 11 months old. Calculate the value of the usufruct for the daughter if the market value of the farm was R100 000 at the time of her father's death.

Solution

Value of the property	R100 000
Annual value at 12%	R12 000
Age of daughter at next birthday	31 years
Factor for female person of 31 years (Table 6.2)	8.275 83
Value of daughter's fiduciary right = (R12 000 x 8.275 83)	R99 309,96

Bare dominium

Bare dominium means that a property is merely registered in a person's name. For example, he or she may not live in the property, or let it or use the income derived from it, because these interests in the property do not belong to him or her, but to someone else. Had these interests in the property belonged to him or her, it could be said that he or she has full ownership of the property.

Full ownership = bare dominium + usufruct (interest in the property).

EXAMPLE

Assume that a person dies and leaves a property valued at R100 000. The property was subject to a usufruct in favour of a daughter. If the daughter is 20 years and 2 months old, calculate the value of her bare dominium.

Solution

Value of the property	R100 000
Annual value at 12%	R12 000
Age of daughter at next birthday	21 years
Factor for female person of 21 years (Table 6.2)	8.313 83
Value of daughter's usufruct = (R12 000 x 8.313 83)	R99 765,96
Value of daughter's bare dominium = (R100 000 – R99 765,90)	R234,04

An annuity charged upon property

The calculation of the value of an annuity charged upon property is the same as for a fiduciary right and usufruct.

The following are some rules that apply to the valuation of an annuity charged upon property in terms of the Estate Duty Act 45 of 1955:

- If a person inherits an annuity, it is capitalised over the heir's life expectancy – Section 5(1)(c)(i).
- If the heir of an annuity receives it for a shorter period than his or her life expectancy, it is capitalised over the shorter period – Section 5(1)(c)(i).
- If an annuity does not accrue to someone else, it is capitalised over the life expectancy of the owner of the property – Section 5(1)(c)(ii).

If there is uncertainty about who the heir (beneficiary) is, the value of the interest is capitalised over a period of 50 years. The same applies to money where the heir is not a natural person, but a legal person (for example, a company) – Section 5(3).

An annuity charged upon a property is deducted from the return on the property or fund. The payment thus occurs from the property or fund – Section 3(2)(a). Another annuity, on the other hand, means that the person must pay the annuity him- or herself (for example, the heir of a farm). Where he or she is going to find these funds is the heir's problem – Section 3(2)(b).

Assume that a person receives an annuity of R12 000 from a business belonging to a 50-year-old woman. At the death of the person who received the annuity, the annuity goes to a 30-year-old son. Calculate the value of the annuity the son receives.

Solution

Value of annuity	R12 000
Age of son at next birthday	31 years
Factor for male person of 31 years (Table 6.2)	8.215 38
Value of annuity = (R12 000 x 8.215 38)	R98 584,56

Calculate the value of the annuity if the son receives the annuity for only 20 years. From Table 6.2 we can see that a 31-year-old male has a life expectancy of another 37.57 years. The 20-year term is shorter than the life expectancy, with the result that the shorter term is used for purposes of capitalisation. Use Table 6.3 for a specific term.

Solution

Value of annuity	R12 000
Term	20 years
Factor for a term of 20 years (Table 6.3)	7.469 4
Value of annuity = (R12 000 x 7.469 4)	R89 632,80

Assume that the annuity ceases after the death of the 50-year-old woman. Consequently, nobody inherits the annuity. The woman's (estate owner's) next birthday is used in this case to find the applicable factor.

Solution

Value of annuity	R12 000
Woman's age at next birthday	51 years
Factor for female person of 51 years (Table 6.2)	7.889 67
Value of annuity = (R12 000 x 7.889 67)	R94 676,04

It is important to remember why these values of interests in property are calculated. The main reason is for estate duty purposes, but it is also done to determine the value of the estate. The values of interests or rights in property are added to the market value of other property (property over which the owner has full property rights) in order to calculate the gross value of the total estate.

Other annuities

In contrast to an annuity charged upon property, other annuities do not form part of the deceased's estate for estate duty purposes. If an annuity ceases after a person's death, it does not form part of his or her estate. Therefore, in the case of other annuities (not charged with property), the R94 676,04 (in the example above) will not be regarded as an asset of the estate (interest in property) at the woman's death.

Other annuities refer to annuities without encumbered property. In this case, the person who has to pay an annuity to someone is not obligated to do so in terms of a will.

Assume that a person receives an annuity of R10 000 without encumbered property. Calculate the value of the annuity in the case of the person's death.

Solution

The value of the annuity is nil since it ceases at his or her death.

6.3.3 Step 3: Establish the estate's liabilities

Very few estates are completely unencumbered. Inevitably, some debts are outstanding at the time of the death of the owner. A residential home often has a mortgage bond attached to it, or hire-purchase instalments still have to be paid on a motor car. There are many more examples, such as an overdrawn bank account, which have to be taken into account before the estate's liabilities and other estate costs can be calculated.

All outstanding loans and accounts (creditors) must be listed and the amounts added up. This amount is subtracted from the gross estate value. Certain rebates are also subtracted in order to determine the net value of the estate. A person's estate duty liability is calculated on the basis of this net estate value.

It is important to note that a person's matrimonial property dispensation can greatly affect the value, and particularly the net value, of an estate. Three kinds of matrimonial property regime are distinguished in South Africa (after 1984):

- marriage in community of property;
- marriage out of community of property, with exclusion of the accrual system; and
- marriage out of community of property, with inclusion of the accrual system.

6.3.3.1 Allowable deductions

Once the estate liabilities (debts) have been deducted from the estate assets, there are certain allowable deductions in terms of Section 4 of the Estate Duty Act 45 of 1995. Miller & Irwin (1990:13) list these deductions as follows:

- funeral and deathbed expenses;
- debts owed to persons residing in South Africa;
- administration and liquidation costs;
- donations to charities, educational and religious institutions, on condition that the value of these donations has not already been deducted in terms of this section;
- donations to political parties registered in terms of the Electoral Act of 1998; and
- the amount equal to the accrual of the spouse of the deceased, where they were married with inclusion of the accrual system.

Meyerowitz (1989:28-1) supplements the list above with the following:

- all costs incurred during the administration and liquidation of the estate;
- the maintenance costs of assets (which have to be converted into cash) from the date of death to the date of liquidation;
- food and grazing costs for animals or stock that form part of the estate and must be sold;
- executor's fees (whether determined in the will or as laid down by law);
- improvements made by a next of kin in respect of property owned by the deceased (with the latter's permission), which increase the value of the interest in the property, mean that the increase in the interest can be deducted from the estate value of the deceased; and
- the value of works of art, books and pictures loaned to the state for educational purposes.

6.3.3.2 Assess estate duty liability

Estate duty is payable on the net value of the estate. The estate duty scale at present is 20% of net or taxable value of the estate. This tax scale applies to all persons who died on or after 16 March 1988. In the past, donations were added to the value of the estate from which they were made in order to levy estate duty on them. This is no longer done since the donor has to pay 20% donations tax at the time of the donation.

6.3.3.3 Assess other estate costs

The winding up of an estate costs money, since administration costs arise during the process. Administration costs may include the following items:

- *The cost of providing security.* The executor of an estate is normally exempted in the will from providing security. If this exemption has not been granted, the executor must provide the Master of the High Court with security for the proper performance of his or her duties. The costs of this security will eventually have to be recovered from the estate, and it could amount to hundreds and even thousands of rands.
- *Advertising costs.* The executor must place more than one notice in respect of the deceased's estate. Among others, creditors must be invited to submit claims against the estate of the deceased.
- *Transfer fees of immovable property.* Immovable property is often transferred to a natural person or a legal person. Transfer fees are payable and the estate must bear these costs.
- *The cost of liquidating assets.* Assets that have to be sold (usually at an auction) must be advertised. Advertising costs and auctioneer's commission arise as a result and these must be paid from the estate. Abrie & Graham (1989:224) refer to another cost item that may arise, namely the executor's account, which is calculated on the gross proceeds of assets sold (this is over and above the 3.5% on the gross value of the estate).
- *Master's fees.* Master's fees are payable in all estates with a gross value exceeding R15 000. If the deceased was married out of community of property, the master's fees are payable only on the deceased's estate. In the case of a joint estate (in community of property), master's fees are levied on the joint estate. Master's fees are levied on the gross value of the estate, but are not payable on income received after the deceased's date of death (Abrie & Graham 1989:226).
- *Executor's remuneration.* This remuneration is payable to the person or institution who administers the deceased estate. The executor is usually appointed in the will and often the remuneration is also stipulated in the will. In the absence of such a testamentary arrangement, the executor's remuneration amounts to 3.5% of the gross value of the estate. A further commission is received in terms of the gross value of all assets that had to be converted into cash.

It is recommended that a family member or relative, or even a friend, should be appointed as executor. Even if that person does not have the necessary expertise, he or she could appoint an executor (attorney or financial institution) and pay half the executor's remuneration to that executor. In other words, half the remuneration would be payable to the original executor and the other half to the 'assistant executor'.

Capital gains tax (CGT)

This new estate duty item has come to stay. All assets in a person's estate are subject to CGT. This is why the estate duty rate has been reduced from 25% to 20%. However, the difference is that whether estate duty is payable on the estate or not (estate duty is payable only if the net value of the estate exceeds R1.5 million), CGT is applicable to the estate's assets. The capital growth of 'all' estate assets (as defined by the Act) are determined, and CGT is calculated as an estate cost (payable to the Receiver of Revenue).

For more information on CGT, consult the relevant sections in Chapters 5 and 10.

6.3.3.4 Analyse liquidity of assets

An estate should have sufficient funds to cover the estate costs. In the absence of such funds, the assets would have to be converted into cash. An estate seldom has sufficient liquid assets, with the result that fixed assets (for example, a house) often have to be sold. Heirs often have the unhappy experience of seeing the family's business or farm being sold in order to redeem the costs of the estate.

Effective estate planning can prevent a shortage of funds, for example by taking out one or more life policies. Business insurance policies are another alternative. For more information, consult Chapter 11, which deals with protection planning.

6.3.4 Step 4: Choose estate planning techniques

There are various estate planning techniques. Some techniques can be used during a person's lifetime, while others have to be provided for in a will. Abrie & Graham (1989:93) describe an estate planning technique as: 'a method or technique used in an estate plan to solve an estate planning problem, in order to achieve a stated objective'.

6.3.4.1 Identify a team of professional planners

Estate planning techniques are normally used by people with fairly large estates. No single person (average person) possesses sufficient knowledge to apply all of the different estate planning techniques. For this reason, it is advisable to consult a team of professionals for each of the following areas:
- income tax (chartered accountant);
- insurance (a specialist in insurance);
- legal aspects (an attorney);
- investments (a broker or property consultant); and
- property (an estate agent).

6.3.4.2 Establish available techniques

Knowledge is required of the estate planning techniques available. We will consider the following techniques:
- the trust *inter vivos* technique;
- company-based techniques;
- testamentary techniques (testamentary trusts, usufruct, *habitatio*, *fideicommissum*, donations, annuities, massing/joint estates); and
- other techniques (investments, insurance, rental, the matrimonial property regime).

The trust inter vivos technique

If a trust is formed in a person's lifetime, it is called a trust *inter vivos*. The person establishing the trust is called the founder. In terms of this kind of trust, the founder donates certain assets to the trust, while the trustees manage the assets on behalf of one or more beneficiaries.

Conceptual framework

A trust *inter vivos* is a contractual arrangement between a testator (the founder) and trustees in favour of a third party or parties (the beneficiary or beneficiaries).

Purpose

The purpose of a trust *inter vivos* is to transfer certain assets to a trust while still retaining control over the assets. The assets are administered in favour of a third party (a natural person and/or a legal person) and are not created for the benefit of the founder.

Legal requirements

There are legal requirements for setting up a trust, of which the following are the most important:
- The donation agreement must be contained in a written deed of trust.
- The donor (founder) and the trustee(s) must have legal (or contractual) capacity.
- A copy of the deed of trust must be submitted to the Master of the High Court.
- The trust assets must be transferred legally from the founder to the trustees.
- A transfer of property rights over the assets must take place.

- An obligation must arise to administer the assets on behalf of the beneficiary/beneficiaries.
- There must be no doubt about the identity of the assets to be transferred.
- The beneficiaries or group of persons (even legal persons) from whom the beneficiaries can be selected must be clearly described.

Different uses of a trust

A trust has the following uses, among others:
- A lack of management and investment experience among beneficiaries is eliminated.
- It solves the problem of assets that are difficult to dispose of.
- Growth of the estate is frozen in this manner.
- Assets can be protected from minors until they come of age (have contractual capacity).
- Assets can be administered for mentally retarded heirs to allow them the benefit of an income (not as capital-beneficiaries) for the rest of their lives.
- It ensures the transfer of the inheritance to successive generations.
- Estate duty benefits are obtained.
- It provides for the education and maintenance of children and/or grandchildren.
- It provides funds to religious, charity and political organisations.
- Assets can be transferred at an early stage by creating a trust for each heir.

Founding a trust

A trust *inter vivos* is set up by means of a contract, called the deed of trust. It is important that the intention of the donor (founder) should be clearly apparent from the wording of the deed of trust. The powers and duties of the trustees must be indicated, as well as when and how the trust must be terminated.

Flexibility

Because a trust is flexible as an estate planning technique, it can easily be adapted to changing circumstances. The flexibility of a trust lies in the stipulations of the deed of trust. The founder has discretionary powers to:
- change the number of trustees;
- appoint or replace trustees;
- grant trustees discretionary powers;
- adjust administrative procedures;
- retain certain administrative tasks for him- or herself;
- act as trustee him- or herself;
- grant the trustees discretionary powers in respect of the benefits that the beneficiaries are to receive;

- indicate the date on which the beneficiaries are to receive benefits, or indicate that benefits be transferred to them at any future period;
- control the period for which the assets must be kept in trust; and
- transfer assets on a continuous basis in order to restrict the growth of the (founder's) estate.

How many trusts are necessary?

The estate plan can make provision for several trusts. This lends even more flexibility. More than one trust is particularly effective in a large estate that runs into several millions and where the estate owner needs to undertake comprehensive estate planning. Where a person has a large estate with several heirs, it is particularly effective if a separate trust is created for each heir. The circumstances of the heirs could differ as follows:
- their ages could differ considerably;
- their financial positions could differ considerably;
- their financial needs and obligations could differ considerably;
- one or more of them could be regarded as spend-thrifts;
- one or more of them could be severely psychologically disturbed or ill;
- their spouses could be dishonest and come from a family with a criminal record, for example where breach of contract, financial fraud and several liquidations have occurred; and
- the matrimonial property dispensations of heirs could differ considerably, which could make them vulnerable to financial ruin in the case of dishonest, avaricious in-laws.

How the donations can be made

Assume that the founder (donor) of a trust is selling R1 million worth of assets to the trust. In this way, he or she is lending the money to the trust and bequeaths the loan to the trust in his or her will. The trustees do not have to repay the loan to the founder at a later stage.

Transferring assets to a trust is expensive. Many people have come to realise, at their cost, that they cannot simply transfer their assets to another person or body willy-nilly. Large costs are involved, both in the case of movable assets (a car or caravan) or fixed assets (any fixed property such as an undeveloped plot, a flat, a dwelling or business premises).

Before transferring any assets, the cost aspect should, therefore, be examined thoroughly. Some cost aspects regarding the transfer of both movable and fixed assets are discussed below. Furthermore, a distinction is made between donations and sales transactions. The cost aspects of creating and administering a trust are also dealt with.

A donation

Every taxpayer may donate goods to the value of R30 000 annually without paying donations tax. Donations tax is levied at 20% of the amount by which the value of the gift exceeds R30 000. If a donation is made from a joint estate, each spouse is therefore actually donating R15 000.

In the case of both movable and fixed assets, the donations tax rate is 20% above R30 000. Furthermore, in the case of fixed assets, transfer duties are payable by either the receiver or the donor (as agreed).

In the case of a natural person, transfer duties are 1% up to R100 000, 5% on R100 001 to R300 000 and 8% on R300 001 and above. Juristic persons (companies and trusts) pay transfer duties of 10%. Donations tax on shares is also 20% above R30 000. Trade stock duty is 0.25% of the market value of the donation in regard to the total amount/value.

A sales transaction

When movable assets are sold, VAT at 14% is payable, over and above the selling price. When selling fixed assets, the buyer has to pay transfer duty or VAT. The rates for both are as indicated above.

In the case of shares being traded, trade stock duty is payable as well (rate as indicated above).

A trust

Assets are often donated or sold to a trust to reduce estate duty. The legal costs of establishing a trust (drawing up the trust deed) amount to between R1 500 and R4 000. The trustee must accept the capital at a cost of about 1.5% of the capital plus VAT on the cost.

Commission is payable on the income accumulated for the benefit of the trust (trust beneficiary), and this may amount to 2.5%–7.5% of the gross income. A management fee may be charged, as well as an administration fee.

The trust administrator must render two tax returns, which may cost R400–R800. Should the trust be terminated (the assets are distributed), a distribution fee is charged (which may amount to 2% of the capital value plus VAT).

For investment, income tax, estate and retirement planning purposes it is important to take account of the costs on the transfer of assets. The cost aspect is of great importance for the transferor's (donor/seller's) and transferee's (receiver/buyer's) liquidity position.

What is an offshore trust?

A trust is known as an offshore trust when it is registered in one of the world's 'tax havens'. Examples of tax havens are countries or dependencies such as Jersey, The Isle of Man, Guernsey, Luxembourg, Monaco, Lichtenstein and Nassau.

For more information on offshore trusts, consult Chapter 10, which deals with offshore investments.

Company-based techniques

A company can be utilised in several ways for purposes of estate planning:
- as a form of business enterprise; and
- to protect the growth of the estate from estate duty.

A company can be used as an estate planning technique. The estate owner establishes a company and ensures that his or her heirs retain the ordinary shares in the company. The growth in share value increases the value of the heir's estates and not that of the estate owner. When this technique is used, an estate owner should keep the following in mind:
- the costs involved in the establishment of a company (in other words, whether the benefits justify the costs involved);
- the Income Tax Act;
- the Estate Duty Act;
- the control he or she would like to retain over the assets; and
- the stipulations of the Companies Act.

Conceptual framework

A company is an association or body corporate that is established in terms of the Companies Act. The Companies Act regulates the establishment, formalities and administration in order to ensure the orderly functioning of the company as a body corporate.

The memorandum of association and the articles form the basis of a company. The memorandum of association determines the following, among others:
- the name of the company;
- the main objective and the type of business;
- the share capital;
- additional objectives; and
- the founding clause.

The articles, on the other hand, order the internal control of the company. A company with share capital is necessary for estate planning purposes. A distinction is made between a public and a private company, but a private investment company is discussed for purposes of estate planning. This kind of company is used mainly in order to prevent donations tax (where assets are donated to a trust), as well as because a trust is not regarded as a body corporate, but as a natural person. The estate owner who sells assets to a company becomes a creditor of the company.

General considerations

- *A farm.* An estate holder must remember that a farm that is not purchased in his or her name is valued at a higher rate in his or her estate. If he or she were to transfer a farm in the name of a company, the Land Bank valuations would no longer apply. Instead, an ordinary valuation would be made, which is generally 20% higher. A Land Bank valuation is based on the production value of the farm, whereas an ordinary valuation is based on supply and demand. For the purposes of estate duty, it would consequently be more profitable to retain the farm in the estate owner's name. There is a requirement, though, that a registered mortgage bond on the farm should be lodged with the Land Bank.
- *Various business enterprises.* If a different company is established for each business, the transferability is facilitated.
- *More than one fixed property.* It is recommended that a separate company should be established for each fixed property. When a property is sold, the transferability is simplified because no transfer duty or transfer costs are payable. The new purchaser does not have to register a new mortgage bond. The shares in the company are transferred to the purchaser (new owner).
- *Listed and unlisted shares.* As stated earlier, it is preferable to retain listed and unlisted shares in separate companies. A purchaser may only be interested in the unlisted shares and withdraw because he or she is not prepared to purchase a company with listed shares as well.
- *Company schemes.* Various company schemes can be used for purposes of estate planning. These schemes correspond in that the estate owner possesses the major share in all the companies and, consequently, controls the companies. He or she also has more voting power than his or her heirs as a result of the majority shares. The financing method of the various schemes may differ, however. Professionals (for example, an attorney and a chartered accountant) should be consulted if an estate owner is considering the establishment of one or more companies as part of his or her estate planning. Abrie & Graham (1989:106) distinguish between two types of company scheme: companies employed in a series, and companies combined with trusts.
  - *Companies employed in a series.* The estate owner determines the value of his or her assets and then sells them to the company. Financing of the company is in the form of a loan to the company by the estate owner. If the money is donated to the company, donations tax is payable at 20%. Share capital is issued and the estate owner establishes various companies, each with a share in the other, and controlled by him or her as a result of a majority share holding. These companies possess the company to which the estate assets are sold. The companies are linked in a series. Abrie & Graham (1989:107) point out that this technique can be improved upon by combining preference shares and a trust with companies.
  - *Companies combined with trusts.* In this case, the estate owner sells assets to a company. He or she issues more preference shares than ordinary shares. The preference shares with their voting rights are issued to him- or herself so that control over the company is retained. The ordinary shares belong to a trust established in favour of one or more beneficiaries. The increase in value, therefore, passes to a trust via the ordinary shares, where the trustees manage these shares on behalf of the beneficiaries.
- *Close corporations.* Abrie & Graham (1989:110) refer to the smaller role that close corporations play in estate planning in contrast to the role companies and trusts play. The reasons for this are:
  - Only natural persons and trustees of testamentary trusts may be members of a close corporation.
  - Companies and trustees (being trustees of trusts *inter vivos*) may not be members of close corporations.

This means that a close corporation, as a form of business, cannot serve as the basis of an estate plan.

Testamentary techniques

The will

It is possible to use a will as an effective estate planning instrument. The larger the estate, the more effective the use of a will as an estate planning technique can be. It is also possible to use a will for purposes of elementary estate planning (in the case of a small estate).

Conceptual framework

A will contains a person's wishes with regard to the disposal of that person's possessions after his or her death. These possessions can be transferred to heirs and/or other institutions (including legal persons or bodies corporate). These heirs and/or institutions are called beneficiaries in terms of the will.

A testator is an estate owner who draws up his will himself or requests an attorney or specialist to do so. A testatrix is an estate owner who draws up her will herself or requests an attorney or specialist to do so. What is applicable to a testator will also be applicable to a testatrix throughout this discussion.

A codicil can be drawn up in addition to the will. A codicil is an addition to an existing will made by the testator. This legal document, which forms part of the will, should supplement the will. A codicil usually contains amendments, additions and further details that the testator wishes to include in the will.

The executor is the person who is appointed in the will to administer the testator's estate. Administration of an estate takes place when the executor transfers the assets of the estate to the designated heirs or institutions, pays all outstanding debts, collects all outstanding moneys owned to the estate, and dispatches the final liquidation and distribution accounts to the Master of the High Court for final approval.

It is essential that a testator should possess a valid will. If the will is not valid for some reason or another at the death of the testator, the law of intestate succession (Intestate Succession Act) applies, which will be discussed at a later stage.

Legal requirements for validity. In order to be enforceable, a will must meet the following legal requirements:

- The testator must sign all the pages of the will.
- The testator must be at least 16 years old.
- Two witnesses must sign the will on the last page.
- The two witnesses must be at least 14 years old.
- The testator, as well as two witnesses, must sign every deletion, amendment, alteration, addition and interlineations.
- No person signing the will as a witness may derive any benefit from the will or act as the executor of the will.
- All requirements mentioned so far are applicable to a valid codicil as well.

The ordinary will

Abrie & Graham (1989:36) divide the ordinary will into three categories: a single will, a joint will and a mutual will. In a single will, one person makes his or her wishes known. In a joint will, more than one person make their wishes known. A mutual will is one in which testators bestow benefits upon each other.

The preamble. It is important that a will should indicate whose will it is. It must also be clear whether it is a single or a joint will. The testator's first names, surname and identity number are required here.

Revocation clause. All previous wills and codicils must be revoked when a new will is being drawn up.

This is mainly to prevent confusion about which will is valid and which is not.

Beneficiaries. Any person or institution who is to receive benefits from the testator in the future must be named in the will. In order to avoid any uncertainty, their full names and identity numbers must be supplied. Any possible relationship between the testator and the beneficiaries should also be mentioned to avoid any doubt or uncertainty.

Bequests. The will must state explicitly which beneficiary or beneficiaries should inherit which asset(s). It should also be indicated clearly whether a specific bequest is made to a specific person or institution on certain conditions (conditional or unconditional).

Appoint the executor. In the will, a testator must appoint an executor to administer the estate. A person (or persons) or institution can be appointed as executor(s). When an executor has not been appointed, the Master of the High Court will do so.

Appoint the administrator. A testator must appoint an administrator if the estate or a portion of the estate is to be transferred to a trust. If a trust is not at issue, the appointment of the administrator is not necessary.

List all assets and liabilities. It is particularly important that the executor is informed of all assets and liabilities in respect of the estate he or she is to administer. This will provide a better idea of what to do and what to expect in the absence of the testator. It will also help the testator to ensure that there are heirs for all the assets, and it will enable a consideration of the size of bequests to the heirs. Furthermore, it will enable the testator to renew attempts to provide for the repayment of liabilities (debts and mortgages).

Testamentary trusts. This aspect is illustrated in the next section. Aspects of importance here are the following: the names of trusts; income and/or capital beneficiaries; the name of the administrator; names of trustees; the contents of the deed of trust; and when and how the trust is to be terminated.

Simultaneous death. A will must make provision for several scenarios. In the case of a single will, alternative beneficiaries, executors, administrators (if applicable), trustees and institutions must be designated. If this is not done, the testator's will, on which the estate plan hinges, may ultimately be worthless. It would be fruitless, for example, if the sole heir were to die at the same time as the testator. For this reason, alternative beneficiaries should be designated. Similarly, a husband and wife could die simultaneously, leaving a mutual will that would no longer serve its purpose. If they have no children, for example, other relatives would inherit their assets in terms of the law of intestate succession.

The same would apply in the case of a couple with children (the only beneficiaries) who all die simultaneously in an aeroplane accident.

Usufruct, annuities, occupation, right of use, fideicommissum. Each of these must be set out clearly in the will. It must be clear which beneficiary is entitled to what, when a benefit commences and how and when it is terminated.

Exemption from lodging security. An executor is usually required to lodge security for the proper execution of his or her duties. It is recommended that, in the will, the testator provides exemption to the executor regarding the lodging of security.

Power of assumption. Normally, an executor is appointed in a will. This executor is not always (in fact, seldom) competent to administer an estate in the legal sense, usually because of a lack of legal knowledge. If the testator grants an executor powers of assumption in a will, an inexperienced executor may appoint a professional (attorney) or a financial institution to administer the estate on his or her behalf. The two executors would then share the executor's fee on the basis of a percentage division as mutually agreed upon (each would receive x% of the 3.5%).

Guardianship of minors. It is essential to nominate a guardian for minors, in the event of both parents dying at the same time. It is equally important that a household or person with integrity be appointed. The testator must certainly avoid appointing anyone who is known to be dishonest with money as the guardian of the beneficiaries. Such people should never be entrusted with other people's money or possessions and even less so with children. They would be inclined to enrich themselves at the expense of the children and their inheritance.

Bequests to minors. Usually, the guardian of a minor receives immovable and other property on behalf of the minor. It is recommended that a trust be established for minors. The child or children would then receive the property when they come of age. In the meantime, the administrators would have the authority to employ the income of the trust in favour of the child or children. It is even possible that capital received from buildings, a farm or investments could be employed for the child's education. In the case of a handicapped child, the same can be done.

Exclusion of community of property. The testator must exclude all inheritances from the heir's matrimonial property regimes. This is to ensure that the estate remains in the hands of future generations of the testators family. This will prevent the inheritance from passing into the hands of unscrupulous in-laws. In the case of a divorce, a child's spouse would receive half of the testator's (as well as the heir's or child's) estate.

For this reason, it is important that the testator stipulates in the will that all inheritances will be free from any matrimonial contracts whereby heirs are married or may be married in the future. All benefits in terms of the will should, therefore, be excluded from the joint estate or accrual in estates which may exist between an heir and a spouse. Benefits should also be excluded from divorce settlements between an heir and a spouse.

Avoid public auctions. It is recommended that the testator stipulates that public auctions are not to be used in the event of assets having to be sold. The reason is that assets are very seldom sold at market value in this way.

Executor's remuneration. If more than one executor is appointed, the testator should indicate how each one should be remunerated. Professionals will set their own fees (as laid down by law).

Bequests with encumbered and unencumbered property. A testator must indicate whether he wishes to bequeath encumbered or unencumbered property. For example, a house may be bequeathed with mortgage bond and all (encumbered) to an heir, or the testator could pay the mortgage bond from his estate, in which case the house will be unencumbered. The testator must indicate how debt and mortgage bonds are to be redeemed.

Maintenance of dependants during the winding up of the estate. The testator must indicate how dependants are to be provided with subsistence during the winding up of the estate. The winding up process usually takes about nine months, but it could also take years (especially with larger estates). Often, the spouse and children do not have access to accounts and, consequently, have no funds for the duration of this process to provide for their needs.

Bringing in. 'Bringing in' is an obligation on the part of an heir and/or descendant of the estate owner (testator) to return all goods ('inherited' during the testator's life) to the executor. These goods must be returned before they can be inherited from the testator. This is applicable to such goods when bringing in has been included in a will. Where bringing in has explicitly been excluded, such goods do not have to be returned.

Practical considerations. A testator must always ensure that the estate will be continued, even if this occurs in the hands of heirs or a trust. Where a business is owned, the continuity of the business is essential. Heirs should not be allowed to destroy a business within a couple of months.

Tax is an important consideration. Income tax, estate duty and donations tax must be thoroughly investigated during estate planning. It is essential that capital growth in assets will be continued. The correct estate planning technique will make provision for this aspect. The testator must also pay particular attention to the necessary liquidity in order to be able to meet estate obligations.

Letter of last requests. This is not a legally enforceable document, but serves the purpose of helping the executor to fulfil his or her duties. In the letter of last requests, the testator gives the executor more details about the structure of the will and directs a few last requests to him or her. Secret information can be conveyed in this manner; for example, where they key of a safe containing money and jewellery is hidden. This letter must be kept with the will.

The absence of a will
Some people do not have a valid will at the time of their death. An invalid will includes the following:
- a will that does not meet legal requirements;
- a will containing contradictions; and
- a will that has been torn up or destroyed.

In such cases, the deceased will have died intestate and the rules of intestate succession (Intestate Succession Act) will apply. The wishes of the testator would no longer be applicable since these wishes do not exist. Disinheritance will result in terms of certain rules of law, and undesirable people may be able to take possession of the testator's estate. A spouse may be a spendthrift and could inherit everything and the children nothing.

In the absence of a will, the estate will be distributed in the following order: spouses, children, parents, brothers and sisters, grandfathers and grandmothers. If the spouse is deceased, the estate goes to the children. If there are no children, it goes to the parents and so forth.

The guardian's fund. If a person dies without leaving a will and there are no descendants (as indicated), the Master of the High Court will place the funds of the estate into a guardian's fund. Abrie & Graham (1989:338) state that if no descendants come forward to claim the funds for the next 30 years, these funds will be declared forfeited to the state.

An offshore will
For more information about offshore wills, consult Chapter 10, which deals with offshore investments.

Testamentary trusts
As the name indicates, a testamentary trust arises from the will of a deceased. The testator, therefore, stipulates in the will that a trust must be set up in favour of one or more beneficiaries. The legal requirements for setting up this type of trust are similar to that of a trust *inter vivos*. A trust *inter vivos* is created during the lifetime of the founder.

An important difference occurs in the deed of trust. In the case of a testamentary trust, the stipulations of the deed of trust are deduced and drawn up according to the testator's will. The Master of the High Court compares the stipulations of the will that are applicable to the trust to be set up with the stipulations of the deed of trust.

With a testamentary trust, usufruct and *fideicommissum* are used. The deed of trust usually stipulates that assets are bequeathed to certain heirs (for example, children) after the death of the other spouse. During the surviving spouse's lifetime, the spouse retains usufruct of all income from the rental of buildings that are part of the estate.

The testator stipulates the duration of the trust in the will. Usually this stipulates that the trust can be terminated once the beneficiaries of capital have been paid out or have received their assets. A testamentary trust may be revoked at any time before the testator's death merely by drawing up another will. Often the will stipulates that the trust cannot be terminated before the death of the surviving spouse.

Perpetual testamentary trusts
Not all testamentary trusts are terminated. Some are perpetual, which means that they continue from generation to generation and the capital is not transferred to one or more beneficiaries. Such trusts usually have only income beneficiaries (beneficiaries entitled to the income from the estate) and not capital beneficiaries (beneficiaries entitled to capital assets).

Usually the income beneficiary (or beneficiaries) is a handicapped child, a legal person or an institution such as a church (for example, funds for evangelism and the distribution of bibles). This kind of trust can also be used for a minor, particularly where the testator knows that the other spouse is unreliable and cannot be trusted with the estate. This is particularly true of a spouse who has a separate estate and did not contribute towards the testator's estate. The possibility of the funds that have been set aside for minors eventually passing into the hands of dishonest or unscrupulous in-laws should also be avoided at all costs.

Usufruct
The testator of an estate may bequeath the usufruct of a farm or a block of flats to a natural or legal person. The person who receives the usufruct is called the usufructuary. This could include the natural proceeds (harvest) from the farm, or the income or interest derived from the farm (Delport 1987:56).

For example, in his will a man could bequeath a farm to his son while retaining the usufruct on the farm himself. The usufruct would pass to the mother/surviving spouse after the testator's death. Such a usufruct would be taxable in either the husband's or the wife's estate. The son would have bare dominium on the farm, since the testator or the mother would hold the usufruct. The bare dominium would fall away after the mother's (surviving spouse's) death (because the usufruct falls away) and the son would obtain full property rights.

Full property rights = bare dominium + usufruct.

Right of use
A person could give another person the right to use a certain property for his or her subsistence. The person who obtains the right of use can only meet the requirements of his or her family's needs and excess 'fruit' cannot be sold or rented.

Habitatio (occupation)
A husband can give his wife (and vice versa) the right to live in a house for the rest of her life. After her death, the right of occupation naturally falls away. Such a right usually means that the holder of the right may let the house. However, a specific right can be defined in the will. Where the testator (estate owner) is still alive, he can register a personal servitude in favour of a specific person or persons regarding usufruct, right of use and occupation.

Fideicommissum (a fiduciary ownership)
A *fideicommissum* is a testamentary bequest to a person on condition that the bequest goes to another person (the *fideicommissarius*) after that person's death. For example, a father may bequeath a building to his son (the *fiduciarius*) on condition that it goes to his grandson (the *fideicommissarius*) after the son's death. The fiduciarius may not sell or encumber the property with a mortgage bond. The property must be protected against the *fiduciarius's* actions in order to retain it for the *fideicommissarius*. Legally, it is possible to nominate only two *fideicommissaria*.

For example, a father may attach a great deal of value to a building and, therefore, wish to retain it for future generations. He wants to make sure that it stays in the family and that it passes from generation to generation. At the time of his estate planning, the father accepts, however, that the situation existing at the time of drawing up his will, is not going to change.

Donations
A person may make donations to natural and/or legal persons during his or her lifetime. The law allows an individual to make donations of up to R30 000 a year to another individual, without paying donations tax

on it. If the donation exceeds R30 000 in one year, tax at a rate of 20% is levied (donations tax).

For example, a father could give his daughter a house valued at R300 000 and apply this amount over a period of 10 years. In that way he will not have to pay donations tax. He could include this amount of R300 000 as a loan to his daughter in his financial statements.

For estate tax purposes, two types of donation can be distinguished:
- a donation *mortis causa*; and
- a donation *inter vivos*.

A donation *mortis causa* means that the testator makes a donation in his will in contemplation of his death. This donation may be revoked at any time before the testator's death (if his reasons for making the donation fall away). Conditions or restrictions that the donations are subject to are described in the will.

In terms of a donation *inter vivos*, a testator donates something to a beneficiary (a natural or legal person) during his lifetime. Once the beneficiary or trustee or director (in the case of a trust or company) accepts the donation, it cannot be revoked. It is always best to consult a specialist to determine whether or not a donation will be subject to tax.

Annuities
A person may donate an annuity to a person or an institution. There are two kinds of annuity:
- an annuity charged upon property; and
- other annuities.

It is possible for a person to be entitled to an annuity charged upon property (for example, a building). In this way, the beneficiary is entitled to an annuity arising from the proceeds of the building (for example, the rental derived from the building). The annuity (payable from the rental income) is, therefore, known and exists (for example, a block of flats that are leased). This kind of annuity forms part of the person's estate.

Other annuities refer to an obligation that exists to pay an annuity, irrespective of where it is derived from. This kind of annuity only forms part of a person's estate if it is transferred to another person at his or her death.

Massing
Massing takes place when two or more people (for example, a husband and wife) draw up a joint will. They dispose of their separate and/or joint estate (including all assets, liabilities, rights and obligations) in one will. Any person can draw up a joint will. They do not have to be married or related. The

joint document takes effect at the death of the first-dying as his or her will.

Such a will has two or more testators. Any of these testators may revoke or amend his or her part of the will without the knowledge of the other(s). Such amendments are only possible where there is no question of a joint estate (for example, where persons are married in community of property). One testator may not make any decisions on property that also belongs to the other testator (for example, where two friends own a beach house together).

If a married man (married in community of property) dies and he and his wife have a joint will, his wife will have the choice after his death of accepting or rejecting (adiating or repudiating) the testamentary disposal of her part of the joint estate. Acceptance or adiation means that the executor can administer the estate according to all the stipulations in the will. If the surviving spouse (wife) refuses to accept the stipulations of the will in respect of her portion of the estate, it is called repudiation.

The Master of the High Court requires a single document from the surviving spouse, indicating whether the testamentary stipulations in the case of a joint will are adiated or repudiated by the surviving spouse. The surviving spouse may repudiate the stipulations and decide for herself on the future of one half of the estate (or a portion of the estate, whatever the case may be).

Massing can, therefore, take place only if the surviving spouse accepts the stipulations of the will after the death of the other testator. Where two or more people dispose of their property in a joint will, it is subject to a limited right (a fiduciary right, a usufruct or an annuity) in favour of the surviving spouse.

In the case of massing, additional estate duty on the estate of the first-dying is not payable. When the first party dies, estate duty is paid only in respect of his or her assets in the joint estate. A consequence of the massing of estates is that less tax is paid in respect of the estate of the surviving spouse.

The reason for this is that the surviving spouse retains only a limited interest in the property of the estate, for example usufruct. The surviving spouse's estate is reduced because the value of a limited interest is always smaller than the value of the full property right. The savings in estate duty will depend on the kind of limited interest, namely a fiduciary interest, an annuity or a usufruct. It will also depend on whether the limited interest applies to a portion of or to all the estate assets.

The type of limited interest will, therefore, determine the amount of estate duty payable, as well as who is responsible for paying it. Where, for example, usufruct was not claimed as a rebate in the estate of the first-dying, it will not be taxable in the surviving spouse's estate. The property for which the interest exists must have formed part of the first-dying spouse's estate.

Other techniques

An estate owner can use various techniques to make provision for dependants. These techniques can also form part of his or her protection and retirement planning and can be supplementary to timely estate planning techniques. They are, therefore, employed particularly for the establishment and preservation of an estate and not so much for the transfer of the estate.

Investments

Investments can be made for your own use (purchasing a home), a rental income (a block of flats), capital appreciation (a second home or shares) and for speculative profit (the sale of fixed property or shares). A business can also be established or purchased in order to make provision for dependants. These investment possibilities would not solve an estate problem where, for example, an estate owner has five heirs. This problem could be solved, however, by setting up a separate trust or company for each heir.

Insurance

An estate owner can take out one or more endowment and/or life policies and nominate his or her heirs as beneficiaries of the policies. Where a new heir is born, an existing policy can be ceded to him or her, or a new policy can be taken out nominating him or her as the beneficiary. For the purposes of estate planning, it is essential that the estate owner's estate should be as small as possible at the time of his or her death. Nevertheless, the estate owner should ensure that he or she is still capable of discharging the estate duty that would arise at his or her death.

Rental (income)

In this instance, an estate owner attempts to protect an asset he or she has bequeathed (or intends bequeathing) to someone. It is almost the same as in the case of a trust inter vivos, where an asset (or assets) is bequeathed or sold, while the estate owner still retains control over the assets. A father could bequeath a block of flats to his son, for example, while he (the father) still receives the rental. In this way, the father is protecting his own estate while at the same time reducing it for purposes of estate planning.

Matrimonial property regime

In the case of a matrimonial property regime that includes the accrual system, the spouse with the larger estate can reduce his or her estate as a result of the accrual system. The same benefits can be derived as in the case of people who have joint estates (massing) or who are married in community of property.

Assume that the accrual system is applicable to a marriage and one spouse dies. The other spouse will now share in the growth of the deceased spouse's estate, if the latter's estate was the larger or has shown the most growth. People who intend making use of this system are warned that one or more of the following factors could lead to the destruction of his or her own estate:

- dishonest in-laws who are inclined to have financial problems because of their avarice (especially those who have been liquidated on more than one occasion);
- strong family ties between a future spouse and such a family;
- where the future spouse fully supports such a family, irrespective of their lies, breach of contract and fraud;
- the fact that the future spouse will support all their efforts to obtain money for their next 'scheme';
- the possibility that the future spouse and his or her family may attempt to enforce this system, even before the wedding, without obvious misrepresentation;
- the certainty that such a future spouse would not lightly go to court and testify against his or her own dishonest family's criminal deeds (even if it is for his or her own household); and
- the certainty that such a spouse may use the accrual system to blackmail the other spouse and to protect his or her own family every time family conflict arises (because of borrowed money, stolen money, breach of contract and fraud).

If any of the above factors are in evidence before the intended marriage, a marriage including the accrual system or a marriage in community of property should never be contemplated. In fact, it would be advisable, under such circumstances, not to get married at all. In-laws of this kind should be avoided at all costs. An estate owner should protect his or her estate from any of these possibilities.

The choice of matrimonial property regime is probably one of the most important decisions in personal financial planning and management a person will make in his or her life. A bad decision in this respect could have far-reaching and disastrous consequences for personal finances.

6.3.4.3 Select the most suitable techniques

Once all the different estate planning techniques have been analysed, the most suitable must be chosen. The most suitable techniques are those that will help in the achievement of estate planning objectives. Usually this will be a combination of techniques, and it is advisable to get professional advice before making a selection.

6.3.5 Step 5: Implement the estate plan

Once an estate plan has been designed with the assistance of professionals, it must be implemented. The implementation is easier and less time-consuming than the previous steps in this process. At this stage, the estate planning objectives have been established and the most suitable techniques selected.

6.3.5.1 Draw up the necessary documents

Now the estate owner must ensure that the necessary documents are drawn up in order to implement the estate plan. The team of professionals must go about drafting the will as follows:

- the attorney or specialist must draw up the new will that reflects the last wishes of the estate holder;
- the chartered accountant must work with the attorney in drawing up trust *inter vivos* documents and stipulations in the trust deed;
- the insurance broker must take out one or more policies bearing the names of the beneficiaries; and
- the share broker must put together a share portfolio that will ensure the necessary capital growth in the estate.

6.3.5.2 Inform the heirs of the plan

It is advisable to discuss the estate plan with heirs in order to inform them of prospective future inheritances. This step must be approached with the greatest circumspection in order to avoid or limit conflict between heirs. It could nevertheless remove great uncertainty, for example where there are five possible heirs to a family farm. They may feel better if they know that a trust is being created or if the farm will be sold and the proceeds divided equally among them.

6.3.6 Step 6: Revise the estate plan

An estate plan must always be modelled on the personal and financial positions of the estate owner and his or her family (and/or heirs). Any significant change in such positions should be an indication that the estate plan requires attention and amendment.

An outdated estate plan that no longer meets the requirements for achieving the estate objectives bodes ill for the dependants.

Several changes may take place, and the following are some of the most important:
- a significant change in the value of the estate or certain estate assets;
- changes in tax legislation;
- a change in marital status of a person or persons;
- the death, disability or illness of an heir, a trustee or a guardian named in the estate owner's will;
- where heirs or appointees are liquidated or declared insane;
- heirs with mercenary in-laws; and
- heirs who are of age but do not appreciate the value of money.

6.4 ESTATE PLANNING PITFALLS AND HOW TO AVOID THEM

Estate planning is involved when an individual's assets are transferred to heirs (who may be natural persons or legal entities) during his or her lifetime or after death. The following financial objectives should be kept in mind when an estate is transferred:
- transfer costs should be minimised (particularly estate duty, the cost of administering the estate and the cost of transferring fixed property to heirs, institutions or trusts);
- assets should be protected; and
- provision should be made for sufficient funds (liquid means) to transfer your possessions (assets).

It is important that the necessary estate planning is done while you are still alive. After your death you will not be able to do anything about it and the executor will have to administer your estate in terms of the relevant legislation.

Beware of the pitfalls discussed below.

6.4.1 Pitfall 1: No estate planning (your will)

Every person should have a valid will. Without a will, your goods are disposed of in terms of the Intestate Succession Act. This means family or other persons may inherit your possessions contrary to your wishes.

6.4.2 Pitfall 2: Insufficient estate planning

As soon as your assets increase in value – for example, when you receive a retrenchment package – you should consider doing comprehensive estate planning. This involves more than drawing up a simple will. Among other things, you may decide to set up a trust (before or after your death) and establish a close corporation or a company.

As comprehensive estate planning requires knowledge of a number of specialised fields, such as law, investments, tax and insurance, professional people should be consulted to assist the owner of the estate. Examples are experts in personal finance, lawyers, accountants and insurance advisers (as well as the institutions they work for). We will now briefly discuss trusts again.

When should I set up a trust?
People often wonder what a trust really is, how it functions, and what type of trust they should establish. There are two main types of trust that may be used as estate planning techniques: testamentary trusts and trusts *inter vivos*. It is important to know the objectives of each type of trust, as well as the financial implications for the person who establishes it and the beneficiaries. It is also essential to plan the trust deed very carefully, because it has legal implications when decisions have to be made about how the trust assets (capital) and income from the trust are to be utilised. People who are considering setting up a trust should first find out more about the legal requirements.

A trust is used in estate planning to reach certain objectives and to solve one or more estate planning problems, and may be employed in the following circumstances, for example:
- Suppose someone owns a large number of shares and unit trusts and he manages (invests, sells, converts) his portfolio himself. His only child and heir (besides his wife) is 30 years old and has no knowledge of investments and the stock exchange. He does not show any interest in such investments and refuses to learn.
  The father may establish a trust (preferably in his will) to take care of his investments after his death. He may also appoint a broker in his will to manage the share portfolio on behalf of his child. The benefits to which the child is entitled – income and/or capital – are stipulated in the will as part of the contents of the trust deed of the trust that is to be established. The father then includes the contents of the trust deed in his will. In his will the father stipulates that the child will be the beneficiary of the trust. In this way the

child's lack of managerial and investment experience is countered.

- A man lives in Sandton and has five young heirs. His luxury home is his only asset and he does not know how to bequeath it to his heirs, as it will not be possible to divide the house. He could now establish a testamentary trust and place his house in the trust. As his oldest child is ten years old, he could state in his will that all the children may live in the house until the age of 25. After that the house must be sold and the return divided equally among the surviving children. He could do exactly the same if he owns a farm. This is one way of solving the problem of assets that cannot be divided easily.
- A woman owns a large number of properties, including two houses, a holiday home, a block of flats and various business properties. She realises that she (not to mention her heirs) has a major estate planning problem, namely estate duty. For generations to come her heirs will lose the largest part of their assets (or a large part, if insufficient provision has been made for estate duty). A trust will offer a solution and she should transfer all her assets to a perpetual testamentary trust. This means that estate duty will have to be paid only once – by her. In the meantime, she could use various estate planning techniques to reduce the value of her estate. As far as possible, the heirs should be named as income beneficiaries in the perpetual testamentary trust. Capital growth will take place in the trust and the heirs will not have to pay estate duty again.
- A trust could be established (in a will) for a minor. The parent could stipulate that the return on his or her life policy or assets should be placed in the trust and that the child is to receive the capital and/or income on his or her 21st birthday.
- If someone has an heir who is mentally impaired (such as a child with Down's syndrome) a trust could be established for the heir, because he or she will never be able to manage the assets. The heir must be named in the will as an income beneficiary (in which case he or she will receive a monthly subsistence income) and a capital beneficiary. In the case of a testamentary trust, the wording of the will should be such that dishonest family members will be prevented from receiving and spending the income on behalf of the heir (e.g. through fraud or frequent liquidations). Nor should such people ever be allowed to act as administrators, trustees or beneficiaries of this trust (or any other trust).
- A cash amount could be placed in a trust for the education of your children or grandchildren. Use the wording 'until it is needed by the beneficiaries' to protect the income or capital.

- A childless couple could establish a testamentary 'special' trust with an organisation for mentally handicapped persons as beneficiary/beneficiaries (unless they prefer to maintain a higher standard of living and spend all their money during their lifetime). Because of the nature of the beneficiary/beneficiaries, no estate duty will be payable.
- Suppose a man and his wife own five properties and have five heirs. They could set up a separate trust for each heir, with the properties as trust assets.

Which type of trust?

It is too expensive to transfer an individual's fixed assets to a trust *inter vivos*, because of the exorbitant amount that has to be paid in the form of transfer duty. The law has created liquidity problems for individuals, and a testamentary trust is the only way to solve the problem. If you want to establish such a trust, however, you must have sufficient life cover (one or more life policies) to pay estate duty. Group insurance or annuities that do not form part of your estate are not sufficient.

If you already own a lot of assets, you should buy any additional fixed assets in the name of a trust *inter vivos* (or in the name of a company or close corporation). This will allow you to avoid the double payment of transfer duty and to save on estate duty and capital gains tax.

Plan carefully with the help of an attorney and/or chartered accountant before you set up any kind of trust.

If you are thinking about emigrating at some stage you should consider setting up an offshore trust. This is particularly important if your children or grandchildren might later emigrate, or study or work abroad.

Since 1 July 1997 offshore trusts have held certain benefits for South Africans. An offshore trust counters the devastating effect of tax legislation on an individual's hard-earned assets.

6.4.3 Pitfall 3: Insufficient liquid assets (funds) for transferring the estate

Make sure that there are sufficient funds in your estate to wind up the administration process. Here financial investments such as life policies could be particularly useful.

6.4.4 Pitfall 4: Building your estate without doing continuous estate planning

You should make deliberate efforts and follow specific strategies to reduce the value of your estate (after your death), particularly if you have to invest or reinvest a package. These should be determined by your personal financial situation. Here are a few strategies:

- Sell property to your heirs but lend them the money to make the purchase. Bequeath this loan to the heirs in your will.
- Donate an amount or R30 000 to each child every year. Then deduct an amount of R30 000 every year from the loan that is bequeathed to each (in case the legislation is amended).
- Never include the accrual system in your antenuptial contract.
- People with large estates who expect to pay a lot of estate duty should not bequeath their life policies to other people (heirs). The yield of these policies should form part of the estate.
- Use a trust to buy fixed assets with an expected high capital growth.
- Take out a life policy as soon as you buy a fixed asset and adjust the premiums annually to keep up with inflation.
- Buy further fixed assets in the names of the heirs or trusts.
- Do not allow your retired father or mother to take out a policy in his or her name (except to make provision for estate costs). Rather take out a policy in the name of the child as applicant, but on the life of the parent.
- Remember that a large number of policies may lower your standard of living (because you have too many fixed assets). Rather establish a trust, a company or a close corporation and save money.
- If you cannot make provision for estate costs (e.g. because of medical disability) you should convert some of your fixed assets into cash while you can still make decisions and are still in control of your affairs.
  - You and your spouse may donate R30 000 every year to a child, a spouse or a trust.
  - A man and his wife may jointly donate R60 000 per year to a trust. The next year they may borrow R60 000 from the trust and then donate it to the trust again within the same year. After five years their financial position will be as follows:
  - Their estate has been reduced by R300 000.
  - They have borrowed R240 000 (R60 000 x 4) from the trust in the four years and they, therefore, owe the trust R240 000. In terms of

estate duty, their estate is now R540 000 smaller (the donation of R300 000 plus the loan of R240 000). There is also a rebate of R1.5 million, which means that no estate duty will be payable if the estate is worth less then R1.5 million. In addition, the surviving spouse may have a 50% joint share in the joint estate. If the complete estate is bequeathed to the surviving spouse no estate duty will be payable.

- The value of the assets in the trust (initially R300 000) has already grown to, say, R400 000. The growth of the estate, therefore, took place in the trust and not in their estate.

6.5 YOUR LIFESTYLE AND ESTATE PLANNING

Your lifestyle will have an influence on your money matters and influence them positively or negatively throughout your life. It will determine how much money you have for investment/spending, your retirement (financially independent or not), your career advancement as employee/employer and the extent to which estate planning is necessary. It also determines the type and size of the financial claims you could expect on your estate in the case of death or divorce.

We will now look at some aspects that will determine your type of financial planning in the following instances:

- if you are cohabiting with someone;
- if you are engaged;
- if you are married; and
- if you are in the process of a divorce.

6.5.1 Living together: Your cohabitation agreement

What does cohabiting mean?
You are cohabiting if you live with someone in the same home without being legally married. Two people who live together can be of the same or the opposite gender.

No protection from the law
The law offers little if any protection to people who live together, unless children are born of such a relationship. The law regards marriage as the institution that forms the basis of family life. This is why so many legal requirements have been created to prevent confusion when a marriage is dissolved.

Watch out for financial pitfalls

Many hidden financial problems arise when people who have lived together decide to separate. Here are a few examples:

- The wealthy partner gives the other party a car but keeps it registered in his or her own name. The other party is so impressed by this that he or she hands over all his or her income to the first partner for investment in a bright future together. The wealthy partner again makes all the investments in his or her own name. When the relationship ends, one party has all the assets.
- A male couple decide to share a flat. One pays the rent, water and electricity and buys the food. The other buys furniture and a car in his own name. Were this relationship to end, the party who has virtually been supported by the other would, in addition, be entitled to the furniture and the car.
- A man and a woman who live together buy furniture using the man's cheque account, but the woman contributes her share. The man incurs too much debt and is declared insolvent. The furniture that was actually bought jointly is not attached. The woman would be able to retain her share of the furniture only if she could prove that she paid for it, which could be difficult in circumstances like these.
- After Dave and Linda have lived together for 40 years, Dave dies of cancer. Over the years he and Linda have bought a lot of expensive furniture and have paid for it together, but everything was bought in Dave's name. Unfortunately, he dies intestate. Linda gets none of their furniture. His estranged brother (the only living relative) inherits all Dave's possessions. However unfair it may seem, the law does not protect Linda at all.
- Danie and Marinda live together and buy a flat registered in both their names. They are granted a bond to finance their purchase. (Building societies and banks do grant loans to people who live together. However, both must have an income and the instalment that is paid monthly must not exceed 30% of their joint income.) They later decide to end the relationship. Danie suggests they sell the flat but Marinda does not want to. Danie tries to sell his share in the flat to Marinda, but she refuses to buy. Danie offers to buy Marinda's share, but again she refuses. Without a cohabitation agreement Danie cannot force Marinda to accept any of his proposals. Both are entitled to live in the flat and the situation becomes unbearable. If Danie had bought the flat in his own name, in the absence of a written agreement between the two, Marinda would have had to leave the property. She would not have been entitled to even a single month's accommodation.

- Jack and Jenny live together. He works and she does not. He dies in an accident at work and Jenny applies for unemployment insurance benefits (benefits to which certain unemployed persons are entitled). However, Jack is still married to another woman. This woman, therefore, receives these benefits and not Jenny.
- A serious problem arises when a child is born of a relationship such as this and the relationship is terminated. Roman-Dutch law held that a father who did not legitimise his child by marrying the mother should be punished – the man was, therefore, obliged to pay maintenance but he was not entitled to see his own child. This was his lot, regardless of whether or not it was the woman who did not want to get married. Recent legislation has changed this. Children have greater rights, and so do fathers. Consult an attorney for further information.

Draw up a cohabitation agreement

The only practical way of preventing most of the above problems is a cohabitation agreement. This must be a purely financial agreement between two parties. It is particularly important to include the following matters in the agreement:

- which expenses will be shared and in what proportion;
- how these will be paid (from a joint account or separate accounts);
- the keeping of separate savings accounts;
- how investments will be made and in whose name (separate accounts in own names are recommended);
- how the assets will be divided if the relationship is terminated;
- how an interest in a joint business (if applicable) will be dealt with (also in the event of the relationship ending);
- whether maintenance will be paid after separation;
- what rights and obligations will issue from ownership of a home during and after the relationship;
- how a lease contract will be managed during the relationship (for example, will it be done in both names), in the event of death (would one party be able to take over the lease) and after separation;
- how property will be bought (jointly, separately); and
- how joint assets will be divided if the relationship is terminated.

Common law marriage

As at September 2002, there was no legislation governing common law marriage. For more information consult an attorney, as this field is quite complicated.

Customary marriage

Traditional marriages used to be characterised by legal imbalances between a man and his wife or wives. When new legislation came into force on 15 November 2000, it liberated millions of South African women from second-class citizenship (McCracken 2002:24).

According to traditional marriages, women became minors after getting married in the traditional way. This implies that these women could no longer have a bank account or enter into a contract of purchase or sale. In the case of the death of the husband, the oldest son would inherit everything and the wife was left with nothing.

According to the new law, a man may have more than one wife (polygamous). Every time the husband considers marrying an additional wife, a meeting must be held to determine the 'future' of all the assets. They will determine how the assets will be divided in the case of the death of the husband as well as in the case of divorce. Problems regarding property settlements, guardianship of children, child support and division of the estate are thus 'solved'.

Customary marriages could be changed, by registration of the marriage, until 14 November 2002 to obtain these new legal benefits for married women.

> Breaking off an engagement may have negative financial implications for one or both parties.

McCracken (2002:25) explains the differences between unregistered and registered customary marriages in Table 6.4.

6.5.2 Your engagement: Financial implications

Most people planning to marry become engaged at some stage. Just as 75% of marriages end in divorce, many people break off their engagement. Let us take it further. Just as divorce has definite financial implications, breaking off an engagement may also have negative financial implications. We could say that there are certain requirements for an engagement, just as there are for a marriage. If these requirements are not met, the engagement or marriage would be invalid.

As soon as an engagement or marriage exists legally, it has certain implications for the parties. The legal standing of the relationship between spouses is informed by Matrimonial Law as part of Family Law, which also regulates the termination of both an engagement and marriage.

Table 6.5 shows some requirements and characteristics of the engagement contract as opposed to other contracts; and Table 6.6 shows requirements regarding the validity of an engagement.

TABLE 6.4 **Customary marriages: Then and now**
(Source: McCracken 2002:25)

Unregistered (Then)	Registered (Now)
• Children could get married (or be betrothed)	• Parties must be older than 18 years
• Families could enforce marriages	• There must be a meeting of the minds (consent from parents/guardian is necessary if one party is younger than 21 years)
• The marriage was not recorded on paper (except under the Zulu code)	• The marriage must be registered
• The wife had minor status	• The wife (wives) has (have) adult status
• Man needed no agreement with wife for further marriages regarding assets division	• Man must agree with wife or wives regarding division of assets
• No agreement had to be registered	• Agreements must be registered
• Marriage was not recognised by employer or state	• Marriage recognised by employers and state
• Difficult to get a divorce	• Easier to get a divorce
• Wife could not own property	• Wife can own property
• Only the oldest son of the first marriage could inherit from his father	• Estate is divided in accordance with customary marriage contract
• No marriage contract	• Registered marriage contract

TABLE 6.5 Comparison between an engagement contract and other contracts
(Source: Unisa 1997:30)

	Engagement contract	Other contracts
Postal contract	An engagement contract concluded by post comes into effect at the place where and at the time when the offeror is informed of the acceptance of the offer by the addressee.	A commercial contract concluded by post comes into effect at the place where and at the time when the letter of acceptance is posted.
Legal capacity	Only persons legally capable of being married to one another may become engaged to one another. For example, a girl younger than 15 years and a boy younger than 18 years need permission from their parents and the Presidency to get married.	In the case of a commercial contract concluded by a minor, only the parent/guardian of the minor need give permission.
Withdrawal	In certain circumstances an engagement may be broken off unilaterally on good grounds.	A party may withdraw (unilaterally) from a contract only if the other party to the contract is guilty of breach of contract.
Specific performance	To claim specific performance would mean that the one party would force the other party to marry him or her. In South Africa no one may be forced to marry. Specific performance can, therefore, not be claimed.	A party is entitled to claim specific performance from the other party.
Damages	Calculating damages is *sui generis* in the sense that the damages awarded are calculated according to positive and negative interest.	The rule for damages is that damages awarded are calculated only according to positive interest.

TABLE 6.6 Validity of an engagement
(Source: Unisa 1997:34)

Types of cases	Person(s) whose permission is (are) required
When both parents of a minor are still living	Both parents
When only one parent of the minor is still living	The surviving parent
When only one parent has custody of a minor	Only the parent who has exclusive custody
When both parents of the minor are deceased	The legal guardian
When the minor is emancipated	Both parents
When the minor was married, but is divorced	No permission required
When the minor was married, but his/her spouse is deceased	No permission required
When the minor has been declared emancipated in terms of the Emancipation Age Act 57 of 1972	No permission required
When the minor is a boy under 18 years or a girl under 15 years	The Presidency and parents
When the parents of the minor conclude an engagement on behalf of the latter	The minor

It is particularly important to know that an engagement cannot simply be broken off with no liability for paying damages or satisfaction to the other party. There may be claims and court cases, with serious financial consequences for the party breaking off the engagement.

Table 6.7 points out that both a claim for damages and a claim for satisfaction may be instituted if an engaged party commits a breach of contract. Apart from damages and satisfaction, an innocent party may also claim/reclaim that which was given to the other party, and keep what was received from the other party. The latter will be subtracted from the amount of damages.

TABLE 6.7 **Claim for damages and satisfaction**
(Source: Unisa 1997:30)

Action for damages	Action for satisfaction
This is the action instituted by the 'innocent' party for compensation for the patrimonial loss he or she suffered. Patrimonial loss constitutes damages that reduce your estate.	This is the action instituted by the 'innocent' party for compensation for the non-patrimonial loss he or she suffered. Non-patrimonial loss constitutes damages that do not reduce your estate, but do affect your person or personality.

As with any contract, the following requirements must be met in the case of an engagement: the parties must have legal capacity, there must be consensus, it must be permissible and juristically and factually possible.

An engagement may be terminated as follows: matrimony, death of a fiancé/fiancée, mutual agreement, withdrawal of parental permission in the case of a minor, unilateral withdrawal on suitable grounds and breach of contract (Unisa 1997:36).

6.5.3 Getting married

'A marriage is defined as the legally acknowledged life-long voluntary association between one man and one woman to the exclusion of all other persons.' (Unisa 1997:45)

To be valid, a marriage must satisfy, amongst others, the following: legal capacity, consensus, proper sanction and satisfaction of the prescribed formalities.

The persons indicated in Table 6.8 enjoy no legal capacity to marry.

TABLE 6.8 **Persons with no legal capacity to marry**
(Source: Unisa 1997:47)

Concept	Meaning
Infans	A child younger than 7 years.
Minor	A child between the ages of 7 and 21 years.
Wastrel	A person with normal mental abilities but who is incapable of managing his or her own affairs due to an incapacity regarding his or her powers of discretion or character which causes him or her to waste his or her assets in an irresponsible and reckless manner.
Mentally incapacitated person	A person with a mental incapacity who can, as a result, not understand the nature and consequences of his or her actions.

Persons between the ages of 7 and 21 years, i.e. minors, may marry with the required permission.

Where minors were married before or have been declared emancipated, they need nobody's permission to conclude a marriage.

Table 6.9 shows the requirements for a valid marriage between minors, or one that involves a minor.

TABLE 6.9 **Validity of the marriage of a minor**
(Source: Unisa 1997:62)

Types of cases	Person(s) whose permission is (are) required
If both parents of the minor are still living	Both parents, even if they are divorced
If one parent of the minor is deceased	The surviving parent
If both parents of the minor are deceased	The legal guardian
If one or both parent(s) of the minor are absent, insane or otherwise has/have no legal capacity, or if the minor has no legal guardian	The Commissioner of Child Welfare
If one or both parent(s) of the minor, the guardian of the minor or the Commissioner of Child Welfare refuse permission	The High Court
If the minor is a boy younger than 18 years or a girl younger than 15 years	Apart from one of the above-mentioned parties, the Presidency as well

Furthermore, in the case of an invalid marriage, the status of the 'spouses' is that of unmarried persons, and any children conceived will be regarded as illegitimate.

Where minors have married without permission, the marriage may be dissolved by the court or not. If it is not dissolved, the following pertains in regard to the matrimonial property regime:

- if there is no antenuptial contract (ANC), community of property pertains; and
- the ANC will be valid if accrual is included, i.e. a marriage out of community of property with inclusion of the accrual system.

Handling money, and matters pertaining thereto, is the main reason why people experience so much marital conflict, and eventually divorce. It is, therefore, essential for both spouses to have certain financial knowledge, in order to realise the role money will play in the marriage. This will form the basis on which each household should determine particular guidelines for spending money according to the household and individual budget.

With a view to the long-term prosperity of both parties, two completely separate estates with the accrual system excluded, and personal financial planning, is suggested.

This is why it is so important for those intending to marry to think carefully about the following two vital matters beforehand:

- the specific matrimonial property regime they will use when drawing up their ANC; and
- the specific manner in which household income, joint and/or several, is to be invested and spent.

The choice of a matrimonial property regime is particularly important, taking into account current legislation, financial principles, self-protection, protection of the family assets and, especially, personal financial planning. The particular assets the two parties bring to the proposed marriage, as well as those of their parents, will also play a major role.

You must decide for yourself how you are going to manage the household's money matters to the satisfaction of all parties.

6.5.4 Your matrimonial property regime – your antenuptial contract (ANC)

'We're getting married. Where do we sign?' People, especially young people, are so in love when they get married that they want to sign and get it over with as quickly as possible. Young people (who are often naïve) regard an antenuptial contract as an emotional document – something like a declaration of their love, because they 'will never get divorced'. Their marriage 'is going to be unique'. However, the fact is that one in every two people (50%) will be divorced and that this percentage becomes 75% if second, third and fourth marriages are included. An antenuptial contract should, therefore, be regarded as a purely financial agreement and should be drawn up with the possibility of divorce in mind, because of the high risk, particularly when the accrual system is included.

Because of the rate at which marriages break down these days, it seems almost incredible that the possibility of a divorce and the financial consequences thereof are not dealt with in the antenuptial contract. Should the couple later decide to divorce, it will be very difficult to reach a settlement about the division of assets without going to court. At this stage it is usually too late for reason.

How important is an antenuptial contract?

The antenuptial contract is the most important document a person entering a marriage will sign in his or her life. It will affect and even determine all your financial decisions for the rest of your life. It may also determine what you do with the possessions you accumulate in your lifetime. In particular, the matrimonial property regime you choose will have an influence on your financial future – especially if you should divorce.

Personal financial matters are based on three aspects: the accumulation, protection and transfer of assets. Your antenuptial contract will have a direct effect on all of these.

People are worried about the risk involved in investments. They will carefully choose a less risky unit trust or a share with a higher yield. It is shocking, then, that most people sign an antenuptial contract blindly, when statistically there is a 50% chance that they could lose a part of their possessions within the next seven years as a result of divorce. Investment risks seem negligible compared with the risks involved in an antenuptial contract.

Your antenuptial contract will even have a direct influence on your career. Say you want to mortgage your house to buy a business or exploit a business opportunity. If your spouse jointly owns the house in terms of your antenuptial contract you need his or her signature to get the loan. Your spouse may refuse to sign (may have other plans) and you will be left high and dry.

The antenuptial contract will also affect your estate planning.

Where does the problem arise?

Drawing up a suitable antenuptial contract should be taught as part of personal financial skills. After all, knowledge of personal finances is the most important life skill young people could have.

What is the problem?

Young people (or other people who are getting married) usually are not aware of the importance of the antenuptial contract or its financial implications. People who want to get married also usually neglect to find out more about the various types of matrimonial property dispensation and their financial consequences.

Your attorney should explain the various matrimonial property regimes to you long before you sign the contract, but usually you quickly sign your contract, pay your fee and leave. You are often under the impression that you have no option but to include the accrual system.

Many married people still do not know that the accrual system is included if you marry out of community of property unless you explicitly exclude it. Nobody bothers to tell them, as is evident from the numerous court applications by couples who want to change their antenuptial contracts because they did not know that the accrual system could be excluded. The dangers of the accrual system in case of divorce are not explained to parties either, presumably because it could be construed as cheap or free financial advice.

The assets and investments of naïve and well-meaning parents may also unwittingly and innocently become part of the accrual and they may incur immense financial losses when their child divorces.

But the biggest danger is the inflexibility of divorce legislation, because your antenuptial contract has a direct bearing on your divorce (something that few people realise).

The purpose of an antenuptial contract

Some of the purposes of an antenuptial contract are: to determine what the two parties possess at the time, how assets will be accumulated for the rest of their lives, and to help the executor with the administration of the estate of a deceased spouse. In case of divorce, the antenuptial contract should help the attorney or advocate to establish what each spouse is entitled to. Unless specific arrangements are made and specified in the antenuptial contract, the law will determine what is going to happen to the possessions of the parties in a divorce – often with disastrous consequences.

Who should draw up the antenuptial contract?

An antenuptial contract must be drawn up by an attorney. When two people want to get married they usually go to the nearest attorney, who is supposed to explain to them the financial implications of the various matrimonial property regimes. Unfortunately, this seldom happens and the couple often have to go to court to change their antenuptial contracts at a later stage.

Types of matrimonial property regime

The law stipulates that when two people marry they have to choose a specific matrimonial regime, which is then registered in their antenuptial contract.

People may choose to marry in community of property. This means that their assets and liabilities will be divided equally (50/50) and they will jointly own all their assets for the rest of their married lives.

The matrimonial property regime that you choose will also determine whether you need the approval of your spouse to perform certain actions. If you are married in community of property you will not need approval for actions such as selling listed shares to buy others, making a deposit in your own name, or mortgaging, selling or ceding building society shares in your own name. For others you will need informal (oral) approval (e.g. for selling or pawning loose assets of the joint estate, or disposing of money that belongs to the other spouse or the joint estate). In some cases, written approval will be required, for example when disposing of fixed assets in the joint estate, entering into agreements about fixed assets, standing surety, making a purchase in terms of the Alienation of Land Act and entering into a credit agreement.

Table 6.10 points out the debt position of parties married in community of property.

Another option is to marry out of community of property with exclusion of the accrual system. Each spouse will then possess his or her own assets and will have his or her own liabilities. This system is strongly recommended, because many hidden problems in the accrual system can be avoided.

A third possibility is to marry out of community of property with inclusion of the accrual system.

The accrual system applies to all marriages concluded after 1 November 1984. People who want to get married now have a choice: to marry out of community of property with inclusion of the accrual system (which happens automatically), or to marry out of community of property with exclusion of the accrual system (this should be stipulated in their antenuptial contract). Each spouse must make a list of his or her own assets and liabilities that should be excluded from the accrual. This list should form part of the antenuptial contract.

Here are some examples of the pitfalls you may encounter:

- Mr A (who has a large estate) and Mrs B (who owns only a car) get married with inclusion of the accrual system. A month later, Mrs B's lover comes to fetch her and three months later the marriage ends in divorce. Mr A has acquired a property worth R1 million on their honeymoon. Mrs B is now entitled to half of the accrual of their estate, namely R500 000, and Mr A is obliged to pay it to her.
- Mr C (who has many assets) and Mrs D (who has no assets) marry with inclusion of the accrual system. He lists his assets in the antenuptial contract and puts their value at R500 000 but does not use a sworn valuator. The actual value of his assets is R1 million. Mrs D is a fortune seeker and six months later they are divorced. The law says that Mrs D is now entitled to the R500 000 by which Mr C undervalued his assets, irrespective of whether or not he was able to assess their value and where he is to get the money. Remember that in terms of the law, ignorance of the law is no excuse.
- Mr E (who has few assets) and Mrs F (who has three farms worth about R200 000) marry with inclusion of the accrual system. Mrs F dies, and by then the farms are worth R500 000. The law says that there has been a R300 000 (R500 000 less R200 000) growth in Mrs F's estate and that half of that (R150 000) must be paid to Mr E. Unfortunately the estate is not liquid enough (there are insufficient funds or cash) and all three farms have to be sold in uncertain times for only R150 000. Her bequests are now worthless and her two children do not inherit anything.

TABLE 6.10 **Marriage in community of property – liability for debt**
(Source: Unisa 1997:118)

Debt	Liable party (parties)
Debt regarding household necessities	• Both spouses jointly • Either spouse severally
Other debts binding the joint estate	• Both spouses jointly • Spouse who created the debt
Debts regarding a spouse's separate goods	• Spouse whose separate goods are involved

Because of the many practical problems, you will be well advised to consider your options very carefully before marrying with inclusion of the accrual system.

Calculation of accrual:
  Net final value of estate
  Minus net initial value of estate
  Minus assets excluded (according to ANC)
  = accrual

Calculation of accrual charge:
  Accrual charge = 1/2 (greatest accrual – smallest accrual)

Parents do not always realise that their assets could be at stake when their children get divorced. For example, a father donates a building complex to his son and daughter-in-law. The complex consists of a residential unit (for the parents) and an adjoining shop. They agree (verbally) that the father and mother should have the residential unit (they may live there until they die) and usufruct on the shop that is being leased (they may live off the rental). This is the only pension the parents have.

The son marries out of community of property with inclusion of the accrual system and gets divorced five years later. The former daughter-in-law decides to claim her share – which includes half the building complex. The father and mother are forced to move out, and lose their pension because the complex has to be sold to give the daughter-in-law half of the proceeds.

The antenuptial contract: Important aspects
Here are some of the most important aspects that should be addressed in an antenuptial contract.

- A list should be made of each party's possessions (mainly fixed assets, vehicles and furniture) with their market values as determined by a sworn valuator. This is very important in a marriage out of community of property.
- When a couple gets married in community of property, it should be stipulated beforehand who is to retain what in the event of a divorce, what is to be sold and how the proceeds are to be divided. In marriages in community of property it should be stipulated who is going to keep what, what should be sold, and whether the proceeds should be divided between the spouses. The same should happen if the accrual system is included (not excluded) and future property may be involved.
- Stipulate whether future inheritances will form part of the settlement agreement. All future inheritances (assets, or income earned on assets or investments) should be carefully excluded when assets are divided. Also stipulate that no income that is inherited in one way or another may be taken into account when maintenance is determined in the case of divorce. Parents should make similar stipulations in their wills about inheritances that may come to their children.
- Decide who is going to be the legal guardian of one or more of the children. This may prevent future legal costs.
- Possible future claims for maintenance should be dealt with at this early stage. Beware of 'the R1 clause'. This can be increased after a divorce to hundreds and even thousands of rands.
- You must also stipulate whether one spouse will be responsible for the medical expenses of the other and for what period. After divorce, an ex-spouse is no longer a dependant as far as medical aid funds are concerned and does not have to remain on the other's medical aid fund, unless he or she is medically disabled. Many people destroy their former spouses if their medical expenses are allowed to remain the responsibility of the ex-spouse, because they have the entire pharmacopoeia and all doctors and operations at their disposal.
- Determine how custody of the children will be arranged. Choose unrestricted access during the week (with the necessary arrangements), access every second weekend and alternate short and long holidays. This prevents a situation in which the children are used as emotional footballs after a divorce.
- Stipulate that no party will be entitled to any policy of the other party in case of divorce (unless he or she has contributed to it) and that no policies need to be maintained or ceded to children (for their education). This will ensure that the affected ex-spouse will be able to lead a more 'normal' life, because he or she will not be forced to meet greater financial demands with less money.
- Stipulate that neither party will be entitled to any investment of the other party, even if it is ostensibly to be used for the children's education. The children should also not be entitled to any investment.
- Stipulate that a reasonable amount will be paid for the maintenance of the children. This maintenance should be indicated as a percentage of net income. Indicate how this net income will be calculated and stipulate further that the two parties will share equally the reasonable costs for the maintenance of the children. Also stipulate that proof must be given of how the maintenance is spent.
- Children will automatically remain dependants on the existing medical aid fund. It may create a major

problem if the children are listed as dependants on the medical aid scheme of a parent who does not have custody – particularly if the parent does not meet his or her financial obligations. Medical aid benefits can be abused and could eventually include all medicine, therapists (whether therapy is necessary or not) and other costs not covered by the fund. An unscrupulous parent could simply give the name and medical aid number of the other parent and then abuse medical aid services while the other has to pay the bill.

- Stipulate who is going to be the legal guardian of the children (later this could become a very emotional affair). This will protect the children from being used for financial gain – something that happens very often and is allowed by a loophole in the legislation.
- Stipulate who is to be held responsible for legal costs (of the divorce). It is advisable to stipulate that the legal costs will be shared equally if a settlement is reached out of court within 30 days, otherwise one party may refuse to pay any legal costs or push up the costs in an unreasonable manner. A settlement out of court should not cost more than R3 000. If attorneys are consulted over months, this amount could grow to tens of thousands of rands – even if the parties settle out of court. It may also be stipulated that the party who institutes divorce proceedings will have to pay all the legal costs.
- Stipulate that furniture that was borrowed from parents will not form part of the settlement agreement. This will prevent a spouse from selling furniture that belongs to his or her in-laws or from storing it elsewhere. Enter into a joint loan agreement with your spouse.
- Children often borrow money from their parents for a specific project. It is important to stipulate that if both spouses sign for such a loan (e.g. to partially pay off a mortgage bond) both will be held responsible for repaying the loan if they are divorced. Determine this beforehand, because if one party flatly refuses to pay his or her share after the divorce, it can leave the other party with a substantial financial burden.
- Stipulate that where fixed property is owned jointly and the parties are divorced, the party who did not contribute to the mortgage payments will be responsible for repaying half of what has been paid at that stage. This would be when the property is owned on a 50/50 basis, unless the other party has made similar financial contributions.

Probably the biggest question is whether an antenuptial contract should be short or detailed. Attorneys rightly suggest that the shorter and simpler an antenuptial agreement the 'easier' things will be in the case of death or divorce. But there are two problems in drawing up an antenuptial contract:

- the accrual system; and
- divorce laws.

The accrual system was introduced to end past discrimination against women. Unfortunately it is often problematic when applied in practice. Avoid it, and warn your children against it, mainly because it is very difficult to divide assets and call up investments if you divorce, and even more difficult to determine which assets and investments belong to whom.

An antenuptial contract should not only be drawn up to facilitate financial arrangements after the death of a spouse. It is also essential when a marriage that began in good faith ends up in the divorce court. Plan your antenuptial contract in advance and become involved in the planning of your children's contracts when they get married.

Protect yourself against:

- yourself;
- your spouse;
- your family;
- your in-laws;
- third parties;
- the laws of the country;
- your spouse's insolvency;
- poor estate planning, investment planning, retirement planning as well as poor income tax and career planning; and
- no possibilities for personal financial planning.

6.5.5 Managing your joint finances

If your spouse has little knowledge of money matters, you must help him or her to attain that knowledge. While you were dating, you must have had an inkling whether your future spouse has such knowledge or not, just as you would have gained some insight into your spouse's values – whether he or she just takes, or is also willing to make a financial contribution. In other words, you must already know whether you will need to create a culture that would force both parties to make a contribution, in order to keep the debt collectors from your door. Any debt demands should be watched carefully, and followed up.

Emotions and love-sickness on the part of spouses, or one of them, often mean that they go through the following phases without ever knowing

Life does not revolve around money – money is a means to an end and has a place in our lives. Unfortunately money is often the reason why some people marry, but also the reason for divorce.

who the other spouse really is, or how the other person feels about money or spends it, or will be spending it. These phases are:
- the dating phase;
- the cohabiting phase;
- the engagement phase;
- the marriage phase; and eventually
- the divorce phase.

Keep an eye on your friend throughout all these phases to see how money is handled: that is, to influence you, to disadvantage others, for personal enrichment or to deceive someone. The same strategy may later be used against you. Forget all about emotions and love-sickness and make sure that rational thinking (also that of your parents/best friends) helps you to examine and analyse matters thoroughly.

However, let us stick to money management in order to:
- manage the household's money matters efficiently; and
- avoid conflict (which can result in divorce).

Some guidelines
- Each spouse's income should go into a separate bank account.
- Spread the payment of household expenses fairly (this does not necessarily mean equally, because one spouse often earns more than the other).
- Make notes of your distributions/payments and keep this on record. The party contributing less (and who can still remember this) must not claim the greater part of the estate during the divorce proceedings, but only what he or she is, in all fairness, entitled to.
- Make sure that you know which assets are owned and bought jointly.
- Each spouse should use his or her own chequebooks, accounts and credit cards.
- It is important that each party should build up a good credit record (paying clothing accounts promptly, for example) for future reference.
- It is only logical that the spouse owning property in his or her own right should singly be responsible for expenses associated with it (the other spouse should then help to pay for things like the telephone, food and suchlike, and also save something towards his or her own property or retirement, to ensure that he or she does not one day walk away with only a full belly – not that it always works out that way, particularly because children are usually involved, and quite possibly a lover with a place of his or her own).
- Invest together to reach joint goals that will help to strengthen the foundations of the marriage.

- Each spouse should be able to spend a certain amount at his or her own discretion, so as to promote independent growth and reach personal goals – without it, the spouse with the greater income may be able to dictate everything, financially speaking.
- Both spouses must at all times be aware of the state of the household finances, in order to promote peace and security (from matters such as investments, to the joint will or individual wills).
- Make a positive contribution to the joint management of the household's funds, and do not simply voice criticism.
- Of course, one spouse may have so much knowledge that management of the money matters may safely be left solely in his or her hands (as the other party, you should still remain informed of that party's decisions, spending and state of your own money matters).
- Both spouses should ensure that they will be able to retire with financial independence, and adjust their investments, annuities, wills and trusts accordingly.
- Do not simply sign as surety for the other spouse's debts – you could lose everything you own (a spouse should not put the other in such a financial position).
- Through conversations and communication, involve the housekeeping as part of your budget and planning at all times.
- If a spouse works for the other spouse, the full 'business relationship' should be put on paper to prevent someone having to walk out without a bean after many years' hard work.
- If spouses are involved in a joint business, it is even more important to keep written records of all business activities.
- Make very sure that a deed of sale is drawn up and linked to a life policy (business assurance policy) – in this way one party can buy the other's share in case of a divorce, or they can continue with the business relationship after the divorce, or the one spouse could buy the other's share after his or her death, using the proceeds of the policy.
- If one spouse earns much more than the other, or if the other does not work, the spouse with the smaller or no income could work for the other as part of an own business, in order to spread the income and to reduce and spread the load of income tax.
- However, keep in mind that household tensions could increase if spouses work together and bring home business problems involving transactions (income and expenditure).
- The value of the parties' share in the specific type

of business must be determined, because it could become an issue if the business is dissolved (or after a divorce).

- When drawing up the business agreement for that type of business, and the deed of sale, it is very important to determine the basis for valuing the business interest.

Sometimes, persons in the process of a divorce receive a package. The other partner then (rightly or wrongly) often claims half of the package as part of the settlement agreement. The matrimonial property regime under which the parties were married will no longer solely determine whether the package must be divided between them in this way. Let us look at examples where a package (i.e. pension benefits) is regarded as part of a person's assets in a divorce.

Pension benefits have been regarded as part of a person's estate since 1989 and are, therefore, also considered to be part of that person's estate in case of divorce. Nowadays, one spouse is entitled to a part of the other spouse's pension (calculated on the date of the divorce) payable at retirement. Consult Chapter 14 for more information on divorce and retirement benefits.

These rules apply to pension funds, provident funds, preservation funds and retirement annuities.

6.5.6 Divorce: Your divorce settlement

Protect yourself
During the divorce process, make sure of the following:

- that your spouse will not be allowed to buy on your account(s);
- that your spouse will not be allowed to liquidate your joint investments and use the money elsewhere (e.g. for buying shares);
- arrange for the continued payment of policies;
- arrange for the payment of debts that you were also involved in (make sure that creditors do not come looking for you);
- arrange that business and financial transactions may occur only under the signature of both spouses – particularly where you are in business together;
- keep records of all income and expenditure until the divorce is finalised;
- arrange with your bank (or other institution) that only you may use your credit card; and
- draw up a new will for yourself.

> Divorce is really the disentanglement of two people's personal financial lives. These financial lives can often not be separated to the satisfaction of both spouses or even one of them.

An attorney
Get the help of an attorney to handle a divorce. The attorney should simply direct the legal process and not represent one party or the other. This is practical where both parties have some financial knowledge and know exactly what they are letting themselves in for (not that there are many people with this kind of knowledge).

In other cases, you should consult an attorney, without letting yourself become involved in a process that will disadvantage the other spouse unfairly.

Handling your own divorce
An attorney's help is usually sought in most divorce cases, to represent one or both parties. Of course an attorney saves a great deal of time, especially if the parties have already agreed on a settlement and regard the division of assets and possessions as fair.

Lombard (1994) points out, however, that it is legally permissible to handle the divorce yourselves, as long as you work very accurately and both spouses agree to it (i.e. an uncontested divorce). This can save much money for one or both of the parties. The actual legal aspects of the divorce will cost only a few hundred rand. Of course, you would need to put forward good reasons why the marriage should be dissolved.

Perhaps the most difficult aspect of a divorce is the distribution of assets and possessions. After many years of married life and accumulation it is not always easy to say exactly who is entitled to what. An attorney specialising in family law is the best person to consult at this very late stage, to advise on the distribution of assets in the light of your particular matrimonial property regime as reflected in the antenuptial contract (ANC).

6.6 THE ADMINISTRATION OF AN ESTATE (WINDING UP)

The administration of an estate (winding up) involves many steps that may differ from case to case. The steps are not determined only by the size of the estate, but also its solvency/insolvency.

Abrie *et al.* (2000:8) point out the use of computer programs that can ease the task of the administrator. The programs not only provide for drawing up the liquidation and distribution accounts, but also for calculating all manner of estate costs. The administration process is completed step by step.

It is only logical that a program cannot replace a person or the user thereof, especially not one with the required knowledge of the administration process and the applicable legislation, amongst others the:

- Wills Act 7 of 1953;
- Intestate Succession Act 81 of 1987;
- Control over Trust Property Act 57 of 1988;
- Estate Duty Act 45 of 1955;
- Matrimonial Goods Act 88 of 1984;
- Surviving Spouses Support Act 27 of 1990;
- Abolition or Amendment of Restrictions on Fixed Property Act 94 of 1965;
- Subdivision of Agricultural Land Act 70 of 1970; and
- Deeds Registration Act 47 of 1937.

An estate must be administered as soon and as accurately as possible. The administrator must put the needs of the beneficiaries first and always take account of their wishes.

In the discussion below, we will briefly look at the executor's tasks during the administration of solvent and insolvent estates.

6.6.1 Solvent deceased estates

A deceased's estate is administered by an executor, who may be the surviving spouse and/or child(ren) of the deceased, a lawyer, an accountant, a financial institution or an agent of the executor. The executor is responsible for executing all tasks during the process of administering the estate, and this takes place under the watchful eye of the Master of the High Court. Surviving spouses and/or child(ren) appointed as executors in a will often prefer to take on this task themselves, in other words not to approach an agent (for example, a lawyer, accountant or financial institution) to help carry out the task.

You need to distinguish between estates with an estate value of smaller or larger than R50 000, and also between solvent and insolvent estates.

Appointing an executor
An executor is appointed by the Master, in the form of a letter of executorship, when the following have been forwarded to the Master: a death notice, the original will, an inventory of the assets of the estate, an acceptance of executorship in duplicate and proof of surety (where applicable).

If the executor wishes to appoint a co-executor, the following need to be forwarded to the Master: an acceptance of co-executorship in duplicate, the

deed of assumption signed by the executor and the co-executor, as well as the original letter of executorship (which the executor originally received from the Master). The Master issues a certificate that must be attached to the letter of executorship.

In the case of a Section 18(3) appointment, the following is handed to the Master: a death notice, an inventory of assets, a will (if any), a list and description of estate debts, acceptance of the Master's instruction (appointment), signed by the applicant or the surviving spouse, if these are two persons (Form J155 at the office of the Master) and a declaration by the next of kin (Form J192) for an intestate estate (no will, or an invalid will). All documents should preferably be handed in at the same time (together with a covering letter), and copies of all documents should be retained.

Executor's remuneration
The minimum executor's fee is R350. The fee may be determined in the will, or according to a prescribed tariff, namely 3.5% of the gross value of the estate and 6% of the gross accumulated and collected income following the date of death. An executor appointed in terms of Section 18(3) must arrange contractual remuneration with the beneficiaries.

Solvent estate to the value of R50 000 or less
The Master may make a Section 18(3) appointment (an instruction to one or more persons to administer the estate) even if an executor has been appointed in terms of a will. In such a case, no notices to creditors need be published, and no estate account need be drawn up. A small estate can, therefore, be administered quickly and cheaply.

Solvent estate to the value of more than R50 000
Tasks prior to an appointment as executor
1. Interview with next of kin. There must be a rapport with the next of kin. The surviving spouse and/or next of kin must sign the death notice, inventory and acceptance of executorship. Documents such as the original will, identity document, title deeds, death certificate, policies and other proof of investments must be obtained.
2. A death notice must be issued within 14 days of the date of death.
3. An inventory of estate assets must be drawn up (with estimated values) for the deceased only, for the joint estate (married in community of property) and for the consolidated estate (Form J243).

4. The original or duplicate of the original will must be obtained. In the case of a hand-written will, the writer's name and relationship to the testator and beneficiaries must be obtained.

5. For acceptance of the executorship, Form J190 must be completed in duplicate and signed by the executor and two witnesses (one copy to the Master and one to the Receiver of Revenue).

6. Forward the documents to the Master.

7. Open files for documents, assets, liabilities, cheque account, correspondence and liquidation and distribution account.

8. Value the estate's assets (fixed, movable, balances, investment amounts) and determine the amounts of the liabilities.

9. Get the forms for the income tax return from the tax office.

Tasks after appointment as executor (on receiving the letter of executorship)

1. When a co-executor (or agent) is appointed, the initial executor must give written power of attorney to the agent.

2. Ensure that firearms are kept safely until the beneficiaries have obtained licences. Protect estate assets.

3. The estate notice is published in the Government Gazette (Form J193) as well as in a newspaper circulating in the deceased's district. Creditors are requested to claim against the estate within 30 days. Forward a copy of the notice in the local newspaper to the Master.

4. A cheque account must be opened in the name of the estate as soon as more than R100 in estate money is available. All estate money must first be paid into the estate cheque account before it can be applied or invested.

5. If an executor needs to provide security, a Section 27 inventory (additional) must be drawn up and submitted.

6. Income tax is payable from 1 March to the date of death (in the same tax year).

7. Ensure that there is a valid valuation of all assets.

8. At this stage, the executor will be able to determine whether the estate is solvent, i.e. whether the value of the assets exceeds the value of the liabilities. Report an insolvent estate to the Master immediately.

9. Liquidate the estate, taking into account the following: the estate debts and how they are to be paid, the assets and how to dispose of them, the beneficiaries, the testamentary prescrip-tions, the interests and wishes of the beneficiaries, the practicability of a particular plan. Liquidation methods include the following: allocating assets to beneficiaries, partial sale of assets, a general sale of assets, redistribution of assets amongst the beneficiaries, and a Section 38 acquisition of assets by the surviving spouse.

10. The executor must ensure that the surviving spouse and/or dependant children entitled to maintenance do, in fact, receive the maintenance. The executor could also apply to the Master for maintenance for the deceased's family.

11. Advances to beneficiaries and legatees may be made at own risk if the executor finds that the estate is solvent and liquid enough. A nominated executor need, therefore, not freeze an estate.

12. Although not legally required, estate debts should be paid as soon as possible in order to reduce interest payments.

13. If it is not possible to submit the liquidation and distribution accounts to the Master within the required six months, an application for an extension must be submitted within six months (with full reasons).

14. The liquidation and distribution account may be submitted without proof of assets and liabilities, unless the Master requests these, or estate duty is payable, or beneficiaries are minors or a Section 38 acquisition occurs.

15. An estate duty form (Income Form 267(a)) is required together with the letter of executorship. On completion, the form must be signed in the presence of a Commissioner of Oaths.

16. As soon as the Master has approved the liquidation and distribution account, it must be made available for inspection at the Master's office and in the deceased's district for 21 days. Notice of this must appear in the Government Gazette and a local newspaper.

17. If no objections are received after the account has been available for inspection, the outstanding debts must be paid and the estate's assets distributed amongst the beneficiaries in accordance with the account. Lastly, the Master's memorandum of requirements must show proof that the Master's fees have been paid, fixed assets have been transferred and the estate cheque account has been properly dealt with.

You must decide for yourself whether you are prepared to act as executor in the case of a relatively small estate; it is often not really worth it.

6.6.2 Insolvent estates

The purpose here is not to repeat parts of Chapter 12 on Credit Planning. However, it is important to know that someone's estate may be administered under the following circumstances, namely where:
- a deceased person's estate is solvent (see Section 6.6.1);
- a surviving person's estate is insolvent (see Section 6.6.2); and
- a deceased person's estate is insolvent (see Section 6.6.3).

The brief discussion below links directly to the chapter on credit planning. We will briefly look at the administration process that occurs when:
- the court has made a sequestration order;
- the insolvent person's estate has passed on to the Master of the High Court;
- the curator has been appointed; and
- the insolvent person's estate has been passed on from the Master to the curator.

Let us briefly look at the steps in the administration process (Abrie *et al.* 2000:53).

Creditors' meeting and proof of claims
The Insolvency Act provides for various meetings during which creditors may prove their claims against the insolvent estate, amongst others: a first meeting, a second meeting, a general meeting, a special meeting and a meeting to consider an offer of accommodation. At this meeting, claims are proven, others are withdrawn and a curator is appointed.

Examinations
Assets are traced by means of an examination of the insolvent and other persons. The creditors and the curator are also examined by the Master.

Assets are liquidated
Creditors instruct the curator to sell certain assets before and after the second meeting. The purpose is to get hold of cash that may be distributed amongst themselves.

Returns
The returns from sold assets and assets that could not be sold (insured assets serving as security for certain creditors) are now allocated to the various types of creditor in order of priority, namely insured preference creditors, uninsured preference creditors and uninsured creditors.

Curator's account
The curator must draw up an account that includes the following:
- the liquidation account (how assets may be converted into cash);
- the distribution account (how the returns/assets are to be divided amongst the creditors);
- the contribution account (how creditors helped to cover the costs);
- a trading account (if the curator also had to trade on behalf of the estate);
- the final accounts of the above-mentioned accounts; and
- and a pro rata costs schedule (reflecting all the administration costs).

6.6.3 Insolvent deceased estates

During the administration process, creditors are given an opportunity to submit and prove claims. The executor must at this stage determine whether the estate is solvent or insolvent. If the estate is insolvent, all creditors must be informed of this in writing.

Abrie *et al.* (2000:146) point out that an insolvent deceased estate may be administered in terms of the Estates Act or the Insolvency Act. The latter may occur if the executor asks the creditors which they would prefer. The wish of the majority, in number and in value, is accepted and applied as the given administration process. Let us now look at the terms of each.

6.6.4 Insolvent partnerships

A partnership is not an independent juristic person that exists apart from the partners. It comes into being when the partners start a joint business and run it with a profit motive in terms of a partnership agreement.

Abrie *et al.* (2000:159) point out the following regarding the sequestration of partnership estates in terms of Section 13(1) of the Insolvency Act: 'If the court sequestrates the estate of a partnership (either provisionally or finally on acceptance of surrender of the estate), it also sequestrates the estate of each member of that partnership.' As soon as a partnership estate is sequestrated, the estate of each partner in the partnership is sequestrated as well. Sequestration may occur by means of surrender of the estate (all the partners must apply jointly and also for their own estates) or by means of forced sequestration.

The curator draws up a separate account for each estate. Otherwise, the administration process is the same as for the estates of normal individuals, except for the following:

TABLE 6.11 Administration of an insolvent deceased estate

Administration in terms of the	
Estates Act	Insolvency Act
Executor does the administration	Curator does the administration
Executor has fewer powers	Curator has more powers and may cancel deleterious transactions made by the deceased, and trace assets by means of an examination process
Creditors need not contribute to the outstanding sequestration costs	Creditors may be requested to contribute to outstanding sequestration costs
Estate cannot be rehabilitated, because the estate has not been declared insolvent	Estate may be rehabilitated because it has been declared insolvent
Payment of creditors occurs in terms of the Estates Act	Creditors are paid in sequence in terms of the Insolvency Act

- Estate costs are divided amongst all the estates.
- If a partner's estate shows a surplus after sequestration, the curator applies it to pay creditors.
- If the partnership estate shows a surplus after sequestration, this is paid to the personal estates of the partners (in accordance with the partnership proportion).

6.6.5 The liquidation of close corporations

A close corporation (CC) is liquidated in terms of the Close Corporations Act 69 of 1984. The liquidation is much the same as for companies. Abrie *et al.* (2000:192) point out that liquidation may be initiated as follows:
- Voluntary liquidation by members or creditors:
  - all members must agree to this in writing during a meeting and submit such resolution to the Registrar of Close Corporations with the required payment;
  - the Registrar registers the resolution; and
  - voluntary liquidation is possible only if the CC has no debt, or where the previous 12 months' debt can be paid.
- Forced liquidation by the court:
  - a CC is usually provisionally liquidated first; and
  - there are many reasons for forced liquidation by the court.

The Master appoints the liquidator after granting a provisional liquidation order. A meeting of creditors is held, and another meeting to inform members of the CC about the state of affairs. On completion of the liquidation/administration process, the CC is dissolved in terms of Section 419 of the Companies Act.

6.6.6 The liquidation of companies

A company is also a juristic person that exists independently of its members, as is a close corporation. A company is liquidated in terms of the Companies Act, and not the Insolvency Act. However, Section 339 of the Companies Act provides that it is possible to use the Insolvency Act for liquidation purposes, namely where:
- the company cannot pay creditors; and
- there are aspects for which the Companies Act makes no provision.

Abrie *et al.* (2000:165) point out the major differences between liquidation and deregistration:
- liquidation results in dissolution; and
- deregistration does not result in dissolution, but permits the company to continue trading as an association without juristic personality.

As for a CC, the company may be voluntarily liquidated by members or creditors, or by the court. After a liquidation order has been issued, a provisional liquidator is appointed until a liquidator is appointed during a meeting of creditors. With a few exceptions, the liquidator performs basically the same functions as a curator.

Abrie *et al.* (2000:189) emphasise the possibility of placing a company under judicial management rather than liquidating it. With judicial management (which cannot apply to close corporations), a company experiencing temporary financial problems due to poor management or mismanagement is given new management (a judicial manager). This management is appointed by the court and has certain rights and powers in terms of a final judicial management order.

6.6.7 The sequestration of a trust *inter vivos*

A trust is sequestrated in accordance with the Insolvency Act. For more information consult the Act.

6.7 SUMMARY

It is very important to do the necessary estate planning at an early stage in your life. A person's unique, individual situation will determine whether elementary or comprehensive estate planning is required. People who are not familiar with financial matters should employ the services of professionals to help them with their estate planning.

The estate owner should be acquainted with the estate planning process in order to draw up an estate plan that will help him or her achieve the objectives he or she has set. He or she should progress through each step of the process systematically and with the help of professionals. In this way, dependants will be taken care of after his or her death and the estate will be reduced in order to save on estate duty.

The estate owner and planner must employ timely (where applicable) testamentary estate planning techniques in order to keep the estate small, while at the same time protecting the estate in favour of eventual heirs. A prerequisite for effective estate planning is knowledge of the matrimonial property regimes and their implications for an estate.

In this chapter, we concentrated on the transfer of the estate. Investment and protection planning as mechanisms for creating and protecting an estate are discussed in later chapters.

6.8 SELF–ASSESSMENT

- Explain the importance of timely estate planning.
- Briefly discuss the different steps in the estate planning process.
- Briefly discuss estate planning pitfalls.
- Briefly discuss the influence of your lifestyle on your estate.
- Explain the different uses of a trust.
- Explain the influence of your matrimonial property regime on your personal financial planning.

BIBLIOGRAPHY

Abrie, W. & Graham, C.R. 1989. *Estates: Planning and administration.* Pretoria: Proplus.

Abrie, W., Graham, C.R. & Evans, R.G. 2000. *Boedels: Beplanning en bereddering.* Volume 2. Bereddering van insolvente boedels. Pretoria: ProPlus.

Abrie, W., Graham. C.R., Schoeman-Malan, M.C.R. & Van der Spuy, P. de W. 2000. *Boedels: Beplanning en bereddering.* Vol. 1. Bereddering van bestorwe boedels. Pretoria: ProPlus.

Armling, F. & Droms, W.G. 1986. *Personal financial management.* 2nd edn. Homewood: Irwin.

Block, S.B., Peavy, J.W. & Thornton, J.H. 1988. *Personal financial management.* New York: Harper & Row.

Delport, H.J. 1987. *South African property practice and the law.* Cape Town: Juta.

Lombard, H. 1994. *Hanteer jou eie egskeiding.* Pretoria: Kagiso.

McCracken, P. 2002. Marrying past and present. *Bona*: 24–25, col.1–3, April.

Meyerowitz, D. 1989. *The law and practice of administration of estates and estate duty.* 6th edn. Cape Town: Pioneer.

Miller, J.J. & Irwin, W. 1990. *Tax advantages of life assurance.* 15th edn. Cape Town: MDR.

South Africa (Republic). 1934. Acts of the Republic of South Africa – (Act 23 of 1934). Pretoria: Government Printer. (Attorneys, Notaries and Conveyancers Admission Act).

South Africa (Republic). 1955. Acts of the Republic of South Africa – Income (Act 45 of 1955). Pretoria: Government Printer. (Estate Duty Act).

South Africa (Republic). 1975. Acts of the Republic of South Africa – Land (Act 63 of 1975). Pretoria: Government Printer. (Expropriation Act).

South Africa (Republic). 1984. Acts of the Republic of South Africa – Husband and wife (Act 88 of 1984). Pretoria: Government Printer. (Matrimonial Property Act).

Unisa. 1997. *Familiereg studiehandleiding (PRL102-4).* Pretoria: University of South Africa.

CHAPTER 7

INVESTMENT PLANNING

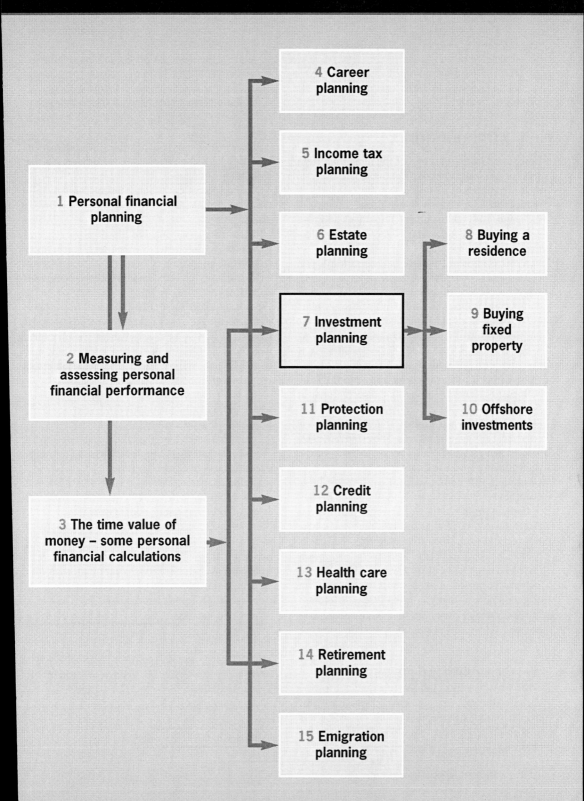

7.1 LEARNING OUTCOMES

After studying this chapter, you will be able to:

- Evaluate investments by means of general investment principles.
- Evaluate investments based on the different investment criteria.
- Explain how to avoid investment pitfalls.
- Choose a broker.
- Explain the functioning of the different types of investment in both the money and the capital markets.
- Apply different investment approaches.
- Evaluate ordinary shares, preference shares and fixed-interest-bearing securities.
- Interpret share prices and other information in the newspapers.
- Analyse the meaning of the various economic indicators on television.
- Explain the functioning of retirement packages.
- Evaluate personal financial planning models.

7.2 INTRODUCTION

Investment planning is one of the most important areas of personal financial planning. It is an integral part of retirement planning and a direct induce-ment to protection planning. Financial independence after and during retirement, and with a view to your estate, is largely determined by effec-tive investment planning.

In this discussion, we will be concentrating on private individuals investing in financial assets. Many people tend to regard financial assets such as endowment policies as a burden insurance agents are determined to place on them. However, this is far from the truth, since financial assets can be worth as much as fixed assets. The only difference is that, in the case of a policy, it is an 'invisible' asset.

The same applies to stocks and shares. Many people are afraid of investing in such financial assets. They feel that it is too risky and that they could easily lose their capital. There are numerous fallacies and generalisations about investment, usually as a result of ignorance on the part of the general public or the small investor.

Although this book may confirm some of these fears, an attempt will nevertheless be made to shed more light on the subject of investing in financial assets. People, in general, are ignorant about how transactions on the Johannesburg Securities Exchange take place. There is a general perception that investing on the stock exchange is similar to 'playing the horses', in other words, that it is a form of gambling and that you often lose your money. The fact remains, however, that some people have become very wealthy as a result of such investments.

7.3 CONCEPTUAL FRAMEWORK

Various concepts are explained throughout this chapter, but for the purposes of this discussion it is important that you should understand the following concepts:

Investment management involves the employment of funds with the purpose of earning an income from them.

Assets consist of everything a person can purchase, whether capital (productive), financial or current assets.

Productive assets include fixed property and machinery (equipment) that are purchased in order to generate an income.

Current assets include, amongst others, stock, cash and debtors.

Financial assets refer to investments in ordinary shares, preference shares and debentures on the capital market, as well as bank acceptances, treasury bills, negotiable certificates of deposit, project bills and trade bills in the money market. The discussion in this chapter centres on investment in financial assets.

The money market refers to an abstract market, where supply and demand for funds over the short term come together.

The capital market, on the other hand, refers to an abstract market where supply and demand for funds over the long term come together.

All financial assets are negotiable. *Negotiable* is a concept that indicates whether a certain financial asset (in this case) can be bought or sold.

Not all financial assets are listed. The concept *listed* means that a company's shares have been granted a listing on the Johannesburg Securities Exchange, which means that the shares appear on the securities exchange's official list and can be traded on the secu-rities exchange. Some financial assets, such as shares

Read this chapter, particularly Section 7.6, together with Section 14.5 dealing with methods of providing for retirement in Chapter 14. This will help you to realise how many alternatives there are for investment purposes, be it for short- or medium-term goals, or retirement. See also Chapter 10 dealing with offshore investments.

in an unlisted company, bank acceptances, negotiable certificates of deposit, treasury bills, trade bills and project bills are unlisted financial assets.

The Johannesburg Securities Exchange (JSE) is a licensed and organised market where listed financial assets are traded.

The *official list* refers to the complete list of all the companies whose stocks and shares are traded on the Johannesburg Securities Exchange.

Institutional investors are bodies such as insurance companies, banks, building societies, pension funds and other companies.

An *offer* refers to an offer to purchase a given listed share or security (debenture) at a specific price. An offer usually takes place through a stockbroker.

A *stockbroker* is a member of the Johannesburg Securities Exchange, who acts as a trader in stocks or shares.

Brokerage refers to the commission a stockbroker receives for buying and selling stocks and shares or for buying (not selling) unit trusts.

A *stockbroker's note* is the contract letter a stockbroker sends to his or her client after a transaction has taken place. This note contains full details about the transaction, the brokerage, the basic charge, the tax payable, the settlement period, the purchase or sale and the amount owing or due to the client.

Portfolio (in this discussion) refers to all the financial assets an individual owns, whether listed or unlisted, and marketable or unmarketable.

Financial assets are issued in the primary market and traded in the secondary market. The *primary market* is that market in which financial assets are created and issued for the first time. The *secondary market* arises after financial assets have been issued for the first time; in other words, once these assets are sold again.

From Diagram 7.1, it is clear that savings are a prerequisite for investments; in other words, money must be available first (savings) before an investment can take place. The investment can then be used to make a capital investment, for example money is drawn from an investment account (savings account) to be used as a deposit for buying a house. Savings (the amount available) are usually insufficient for making a capital investment (for example, buying a farm).

Savings refer to money a person has at his or her disposal that he or she does not spend, and that may be kept at home, for example. Such money will be readily accessible, and increases the owner's liquidity. The moment the person uses these savings or transfers the money to a savings account or fixed deposit account, it becomes a financial investment (a financial asset). When savings are employed to buy a capital asset (e.g. a building), the savings become a capital investment. In other words, savings imply that the money is not spent.

Investment is the transfer of purchasing or buying power (funds) to third parties for the purchase of assets (for example, krugerrands, diamonds, coins, stamps, antiques and securities) aimed at earning an income or a return (for example, interest or dividends), taking into account the risk involved (Brümmer & Rademeyer 1982:5). The risk arises because there is no certainty about the future interest, dividends or profit (for example, from the sale of diamonds). An attempt is, therefore, also made to obtain capital profit from an investment. An individual investor will attempt to maximise the return or rate of return for a given risk, or to minimise the risk involved in a specific investment for a given return. If it is impossible to increase the return on an investment, an effort will be made to lower the risk attached to the investment or that of the portfolio of investments. Portfolios in this instance refer to the total amount of investments a person owns.

Investment trusts are companies that specialise in investing in stocks and shares (Brümmer & Rademeyer 1982:5). Unit and property trusts are examples of investment trusts, and refer to trusts in which individuals can buy units (subunits) and sell them back at a later stage.

Capital investment refers to the employment of funds to buy land, buildings, machinery and equipment in order to earn a return or an income. For the purposes of our discussion, this definition is sufficient.

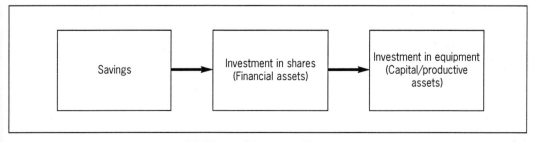

DIAGRAM 7.1 **Savings and investments**

7.4 INVESTMENT PRINCIPLES

In practice, there are various investment principles a person should know about when considering personal financial management and planning. Although the same investment principles apply to both individuals and institutions, we will limit our discussion to the application of these principles for personal purposes.

It is generally accepted that investors are risk avoiders. This assumption is not always true, particularly when you consider entrepreneurs and those who always prefer risky investments. An illustration of risk, return, time, value and risk preferences follows. The relationship between these concepts should be noted.

Gitman (1988:211) describes risk as the possibility of suffering a loss. He refers to the possibility that the actual return on an investment may be lower than the anticipated return (in other words, the variability of the anticipated return). We can talk about the risk attached to a single asset or investment or to a portfolio of assets or investments.

'Return' refers to the income or profit on an asset, or the possible loss involved in owning such an asset or investment. In general, an investor would anticipate a higher return on an investment with a high risk and a lower return on an investment with a low risk. Risk and return are, therefore, positively correlated; in other words, the higher the risk, the higher the anticipated return, while the lower the risk, the lower the anticipated return.

Time plays a major role in risk and return. Risk is an increasing function of time; in other words, the longer the time period (or investment period), the greater the anticipated risk and the greater the anticipated return on an investment or asset. The longer the time period, the greater the variability of the anticipated return.

A potential investor can determine the value of an investment by establishing the risk and anticipated return involved, as well as the time period of the investment. The price of a share (therefore its value) is determined by evaluating the risk-return characteristics. A person's attitude towards risk or risk preference will, consequently, influence his or her decision to undertake a certain investment. Different attitudes towards risk are discussed next.

7.4.1 Risk preferences

Risk decisions, as with any other personal decisions, are subjective by nature. Such decisions are taken on the basis of a person's likes and dislikes. Risk preference refers to a specific person's attitude towards risk; in other words, to what extent a person will be prepared to accept risk or not be prepared to accept risk, and particularly what compensation is required for certain levels of risk. Gitman (1988:212) distinguishes between three different risk preferences: risk indifferent people, risk acceptors and risk avoiders.

7.4.1.1 Risk indifferent people

Here the person's attitude towards risk is such that no change (increase) in return (compensation) is required for an increase in risk.

7.4.1.2 Risk acceptors

This attitude towards risk is one where even a reduction in return is accepted for an increase in risk.

7.4.1.3 Risk avoiders

Risk avoiders want a higher return for a higher risk.

Investors always compare the anticipated rate of return of a particular investment with the anticipated risk of the investment. Of equal importance is an evaluation of the effect a particular investment will have on the risk and return of your portfolio (total investments). For example, an investor may make an investment with a very low return and add it to his or her portfolio, thereby lowering the total (joint) risk of the portfolio, if the risk of the portfolio was higher than that of the new investment.

This process of lowering the risk of a portfolio by the addition of investments with a lower risk, is called diversification. Investors usually try to increase their wealth by increasing the rate of return on an investment and lowering the risk.

A person may decide to invest in stocks and shares only if he or she has saved enough for this purpose. People in the middle income group do not normally invest in shares. Brümmer & Rademeyer (1982:28) point out that a large group of people in the higher income group also do not invest in shares, chiefly as a result of financial conservatism and a strong risk avoiding attitude, in general. They also refer to the following financial requirements that investors should meet before investing in shares: sufficient life insurance, housing, instalment sales and consumer credit and sufficient savings. Each of these aspects is discussed below.

7.4.2 Financial prerequisites

7.4.2.1 Sufficient life insurance

The scope of life insurance depends on the scope of a person's asset structure, income, health, age, life expectancy, financial obligations (debt) and number of next-of-kin (inheritances). Life insurance is discussed in greater detail in Chapter 11 on protection planning.

7.4.2.2 Housing

Most people buy their homes by means of bond loans. The monthly bond instalment lowers the homeowner's disposable income to such an extent that there are hardly sufficient funds left for investments in shares. Once the home has been paid off (the bond loan has been redeemed), investments become possible.

7.4.2.3 Instalment sales and consumer credit

Instalment sales (hire-purchase) should be small in relation to the household's income, particularly because interest rates on instalment sales are so high. Brümmer & Rademeyer (1982:29) recommend that instalments should not exceed one-fifth of the household's net annual income. Instalments should also not be higher than 20% of the net monthly income. The practice of someone with large instalment sale commitments borrowing money to invest in shares is not recommended.

7.4.2.4 Sufficient savings

A household must possess sufficient funds to meet the demands of the transaction motive and the precaution or provident motive. An investor should have sufficient money to afford normal domestic transactions. Funds should be retained to provide for unforeseen events; for example, a washing machine or motor car breaking down or the costs involved in hospitalisation. Before these two motives have been addressed, investment in shares is not an option. Money must be saved in order to ensure the necessary liquidity.

7.5 INVESTMENT PITFALLS AND HOW TO AVOID THEM

There are many investment pitfalls that most of us will fall into at some stage. Some pitfalls are obvious, but to avoid others you will need to know a lot about investments and investment planning.

7.5.1 Pitfall 1: Comparing the return of the investment with the purpose

Comparing the return of a specific investment with the purpose of that investment is definitely the primary pitfall these days. For example, you should never compare the return of an investment in your own home with the return on a risky share. Never evaluate the investment in a home only in terms of money.

When it comes to money matters, surely the most basic right is the right to do what you like with your money – this is what personal finance is all about. We have already learned that we should try to be financially independent after retirement, but very few people attain this objective. Each individual is and remains entitled to deal with his or her hard-earned money during his or her lifetime as he or she thinks fit.

In this discussion, we look at the financial reasons for buying or renting a home, as well as the non-financial ones. The aim of investing in your own home will hopefully be placed in perspective. Remember that we are not talking about an investment in a second house, but in a home to live in.

What is the argument all about?

Suddenly the media paint a scenario that makes many of us wonder whether we have wasted our lives! We often read (and are told by many brokers) that it is more profitable to rent a house and invest our money in unit trusts or shares. So, sell your house and immediately rent a cheaper house. Invest your 'profits' lucratively. People who are thinking about buying their first house are also advised to rent forever and never buy a house. Invest the difference between the rent and the higher amount that you would have spent on your own home in unit trusts or shares, it is said.

But do we all feel like this about money and the return we will earn from it? Are all of us motivated by money to the same extent? The answer is a definite 'no'. If this was the case, most of us would complete the same studies, do the same work, rent single rooms and measure all our daily activities and our lives against the return on our investments. People are motivated by different things, as has been proven time and again in literally thousands of educational and management books.

What about your other possessions?

If we argue in favour of renting a house we should also weigh up the value of our furniture, jewellery, expensive holidays, social activities and private schools, for example, against the possible return on our money (our investment). This would mean that you should not own anything on which you could have earned a return somewhere else. This is the argument in favour of renting a house.

If this argument is true, you should also sell your car and invest the money. People who want to buy cars should rather invest the instalments. Everybody will then have to use 'cheap' public transport. However, the market mechanism (the way in which the market is operating, i.e. supply and demand) will lead to an increase in the demand for bus transport and this demand will push up the monthly bus fares. At the new rates, it would be better to buy your own car and invest the 'bus fare instalments' somewhere else.

Financial considerations when you are renting a home

The same argument holds when you are renting a house instead of buying one. If you rent a house, you are using your own money and you do not take out a bond. This means that your money is particularly expensive, because you do not make use of 'leverage financing'. The less money of your own that you put into a house or business, the higher the return on your money (usually). If you use only your own money, you will also not be able to rent such a big, expensive house as you would be able to buy.

Nor will you always know when the rent will be increased and by how much. You can never be certain that the house you are renting will not be sold, and if it is sold, you may have to move because you cannot enter into a new contract with the new owner (who wants to move into the house).

In the past 15 years the return on houses has outperformed the return on shares. When you buy a house, you may use the house as security, but financial institutions will not easily lend you money to invest in shares if you do not have security.

Retirees and people who are old or sick and who are no longer physically or financially able to look after their own homes may rent or buy property (in a full title/sectional title/group-housing/retirement scheme) that will be maintained on their behalf.

Neither technology nor the 21st century will change the fact that we all want to own our own homes. We want to have control over this aspect of our lives at least. Even the high interest rates that were experienced in South Africa in the second half of 1998 did not affect the arguments against renting and in favour of buying, particularly over the long term and over a lifetime.

When you rent a home you run the risk of losing your accommodation at any time, but you do not need to pay maintenance, insurance or property tax, and there are no implications for your estate. If the rent becomes too high, you simply move again. There are also myriad households risks attached to owning an own home. These possible expenses are absent or minimal when you rent a home.

Many people rent for years. When you get along with the owner, you may even benefit financially (e.g. you look after the garden and pay less rent, or you may have a first option to buy).

Financial considerations when you buy a home

People usually buy houses when they are about 25 years old, and most people own houses by the time they are 45. Because you can buy a house with borrowed money, you can buy a bigger house while you are using very little of your own money (usually only the deposit). You, thus, receive a higher return on your money. Even though your house gets older, it increases in value because of inflation. The value of the stand usually increases continuously because less land and fewer stands are available.

When we consider that nowadays children live with their parents for quite a few years after they leave school (without paying rent elsewhere or even to their parents) homeownership holds a lot of financial and other benefits, particularly if the children are unemployed and their parents would have had to pay rent on their behalf.

Buying a house in Clifton, for example, made some people so rich that others can hardly understand how anyone could have bought a house in such an expensive neighbourhood. A housing subsidy from your employer makes it even more beneficial to own a house. It is an immense financial benefit to receive this amount every month for about 20 years.

A house may be used as security for further loans and a paid-up (or partly paid) mortgage bond may serve as a lifelong emergency fund.

The positive aspect is that the house becomes your property at the end of the repayment period. However, you pay a lot more for the house because of increases in the interest rate, maintenance, property tax, extensions, upgrading and repairs, for example. Increases in interest rates or sudden unemployment, for example, could mean that you can no longer afford your monthly instalments and that you may lose your house (it may then be sold at auction) as well as all the money you have spent on your house. The result of this, compared with renting, will also be that you will 'have nothing', and you may be in a worse situation than if you had rented a house. If your employer transfers you and you are forced to sell your house, you may also lose a large percentage of your money, particularly if you have to sell the house for less than it is worth. Also, the area in which your house is situated may no longer be regarded as an 'elite' area, which will affect its value. The market may also have a negative effect on your investment. A paid-up house, however, has many benefits for heirs – it gives them security and creditworthiness.

7.5.2 Pitfall 2: Misconceptions about investing in a life policy

Nowadays, another common pitfall and investment mistake is the misconception that shares will give you a higher return than a life policy. Your investment aims (reasons for investing) and financial needs should never be confused with the return on your investment on, say, a life policy, or on another investment such as shares.

A life policy is an asset, like a house or a block of flats. It is a non-tangible investment that enables you to transfer your largest financial risks to an insurance company. In return for the monthly premiums, the policyholder receives an acceptable yield on an investment with very low risk, not to mention peace of mind.

A life policy may be used in various fields of personal financial planning. As an investment alternative it is surely the most flexible investment instrument, because it can be used in so many different ways. A policyholder may use a life policy to cover 90% of his or her risks, irrespective of whether he or she is poor, rich, earning a salary or has an own business.

Refer to Chapter 11 on protection planning for more detail about the advantages of a life policy.

7.5.3 Pitfall 3: Underestimating the negative effect of inflation

The third major investment pitfall for investors is underestimating the negative effect of inflation on provision for retirement.

Inflation is the best friend of those who have sufficient fixed property (particularly in the right place) but is a monster for those:

- who have not made sufficient provision for retirement;
- who have to rely on income producing investments (and are dependent on them);
- who do not have any investments that produce capital growth;
- who, after retirement, have to rent a place to stay at a market-related fee (i.e. who do not own property and do not have sufficient investments with the necessary capital growth); and
- whose policies have not been adjusted for inflation each year, particularly if they have to rely on these policies for retirement.

Many South Africans will find themselves in a difficult financial situation after retirement, particularly if they live for many years and/or are in bad health and do not have a medical aid scheme.

The inflation rate

The effect of inflation is calculated by using the factor 72 formula. Suppose the rate of inflation is 12%. The value of an investment will then be halved every six years (72 ÷ 12 = 6). This means that in six years' time, an investment of R50 000 (if it does not provide capital growth against inflation) will be worth only R25 000 in today's money.

The effect of inflation can be countered if an investment produces an after-tax return (where the investment produces taxable income) that is higher than the rate of inflation.

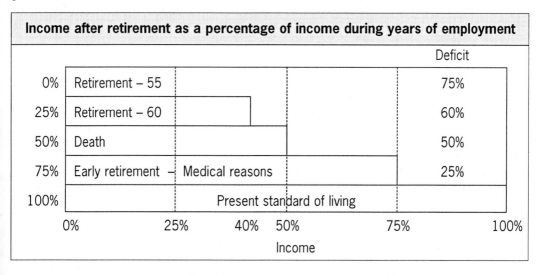

FIGURE 7.1 **Shortfall in income after retirement**

Future inflation rate

From 1960 onwards there has been a drastic rise in the rate of inflation. The histogram in Figure 7.1 emphasises this deficit in the event of death, early retirement for medical reasons and retirement at the age 55 and 60. The current standard of living of each individual is set at 100% (of the standard after retirement). The histogram and the far-reaching financial implications of inflation after retirement will be different for each individual.

For those who do not have sufficient investments for retirement, inflation will increase the income shortfall in each of the four instances. If a person lives for a very long time, inflation will eventually reduce the buying power of his or her money to below the breadline. Retirement then becomes a race between inflation and death.

The only answer is to make investments that will offer capital growth over the longest possible period. Retired people, or those who invest packages when they are near retirement age, must allow their investments with capital growth to grow, and postpone using the income from these investments for as long as possible. By doing this they let compound interest (i.e. interest on interest) work for them.

7.5.4 Pitfall 4: Having insufficient knowledge of investment principles

Usually, investors have little or no knowledge of investment principles. A basic investment principle is that investments with a higher return are more risky than investments with a lower return. Good fund managers have an immense influence on this principle. As a result, we find that in the case of unit trusts:

- A higher return could accompany a lower risk.
- A lower return could accompany a higher risk.

7.5.5 Pitfall 5: Being uninformed about the investment criteria

Another pitfall is that investors are not informed about the various investment criteria. Compare these criteria with your financial objectives and resources before you choose an investment. Choosing a specific investment will be determined by a combination of some of the following investment criteria:

- income (do you need it?);
- capital growth (do you need it?);
- whether the investment is safe (do you want a guarantee that your investment amount will be paid out, or do you want to speculate with it and risk losing it or receiving only part of it back?);
- flexibility (are you looking for the possibility of switching to another investment because of certain other needs you may have in the future?);
- liquidity (do you perhaps need the investment within a week or a day?);
- taxability of the investment (do you already pay the maximum tax and do you want to make a tax-free investment?);
- ease of management (do you want to manage your investment, or do you want to leave it in the hands of a fund manager?);
- risk (do you like taking risks?);
- amount (do you have a lump sum to invest, and what amount do you need for the investment you have in mind?);
- the term of the investment (for what period do you want to invest your money, and when will you need it?);
- your marginal tax rate (have you already reached the maximum tax rate?);
- transaction costs (what will it cost you to invest your money, do you have the necessary funds, or would you rather invest somewhere else because of the high costs?);
- timing (remember the economic cycle and its effect on specific industries);
- diversification (spread your investments to lower your risk);
- control (how much control do you want to have over your investment or its utilisation?);
- knowledge/management requirements (an investment in shares or a holiday resort will require knowledge as well as certain managerial skills);
- inflation (protect yourself against inflation when choosing an investment – invest for capital growth); and
- your investment objectives (the most important criterion of all).

7.5.6 More pitfalls

- Many people do not know the difference between investing and gambling. If you invest money for a very short period and there is a possibility that you may lose it, you are actually gambling. You have definitely not invested the money, neither have you speculated with it. The investment term also determines whether you are saving, gambling, speculating or investing. When you gamble with your investment, the term is usually very short. When you speculate (if you invest with a view to making money from fluctuations in the market, e.g. with shares) the term is longer. When you invest, the term will be longer still.

This does not mean that you are gambling if you sell your unit trusts a month after investing in them. The most important factor is your objective when you make an investment.

- It is dangerous to make an investment before you have determined the following:
  - your personal financial situation;
  - your household risks, and whether you have already made provision for them;
  - your risk profile; and
  - your short-, medium- and long-term financial objectives.
- People often do not know how to choose a broker.
- Often, income tax planning, estate planning and retirement planning are not kept in mind when the investment decision is made.
- The investment decision is made without taking the stage of your life cycle into account, in other words your present standard of living as well as your age and marital status (i.e. your lifestyle). A younger person (single, with no children) should choose an aggressive investment portfolio; a young family, a growth portfolio; a financially established person, a balanced portfolio; and a retiree a conservative portfolio (i.e. a less aggressive investment strategy).
- Often, people do not have proper investment strategies. You should use specific strategies to increase the return on your investment (to maximise the return in relation to your risk or to minimise your risk in relation to your return).
- People often go through life without empowering themselves in the field of personal finance.
- People often invest their money without consulting a financial specialist.
- People often decide about investments without being aware of the role of these investments in their personal financial planning. You should know why you are making the investment and where it is going to fit into the scheme of your personal financial planning.
- Many people want to make a specific investment because their rich friends or acquaintances have done so. You should never compare yourself with others. Your investment has nothing to do with them. Invest with your own objectives, limitations and financial situation in mind.
- Never allow buzzwords such as 'shares' to confuse you and force you into making a hurried investment. There are lots of investment opportunities that will make you financially independent after retirement, and there are many ways of making provision for retirement.
- Remember, you must protect your income, fight inflation, protect your capital and weigh up the risk and returns against your personal risk profile.
- Many people make investments without any long-term objective in mind. Do strategic planning before you invest your funds.
- Never allow fear to determine the type of investment you make. For instance, do not blindly invest in shares with a high yield, if you are afraid that you have not made sufficient provision for retirement. And do not allow fear of losing your money on the securities exchange prevent you from ever investing in shares.
- Do not allow greed to influence your investment strategy. Rather plan purposefully and base your planning on professional advice.
- Do not call up your investments because of mass hysteria in the market (caused by high interest rates, low share prices, etc.). An example is when you feel you should sell your shares when the market is weak (share prices are low). Rather keep your shares until the market recovers, or else you will convert your paper loss into a real financial loss.

7.6 CHOOSING A BROKER

'Media brokers' confuse me, what should I do? Some people in the media, and some brokers who have personal interests in publications on personal finance, are confusing the South African public. They are creating an erroneous impression about matters pertinent to the personal finances of investors. Some who earn a living by writing articles, and some who want to market their private businesses often quote a few particular investments and investment yields (of 1% or less) out of context to prove their point. Self-interest has become so common, to some, that the interests of the public are no longer part of the agenda.

7.6.1 Beware of glossy brochures and buzzwords

Buzzwords, catch-phrases, 'golden rules', 'last warnings', 'ultimate wealth', 'golden opportunities' and 'golden schemes' are all aimed at catching public attention. Some brokers use the media to tell the public that they need only make one more ultimate investment; as soon as they have invested money in this particular scheme, they will have 'arrived'. The 'media broker' who catches enough people with this strategy is actually the only person who 'arrives', with the millions he or she earns as commission.

7.6.2 Investors need more information

The time has come for people to be more assertive and to demand objective personal financial information, so that they can make informed decisions and assume responsibility for their own personal finances.

For example, certain advisers compare owning a house with the yield of unit trusts over a period of twenty years. You may wonder where these people are going to stay during this period (in unit trusts?). And then second properties. Here they concentrate on the selling price of the second property after a certain period. What about all the tax deductions, the fact that it is a business opportunity and the financial discipline it has established? Your return is increased, because much more is tax-deductible.

People certainly do not need to make a new investment every week to replace their existing investments (Swart 1999:11).

7.6.3 Solid financial principles are the keywords

The driving forces behind your personal finances are the economic and social realities of your country, as well as financial principles.

You should not be guided by what the richest people in the world have done (these are only pretty stories and pipe dreams). Use your own personal financial situation, based on your own financial resources, as the starting point, and keep your household budget constantly in mind. Then you should start investing for prosperity before and after retirement.

Purposeful personal financial planning is the answer, not mass planning for own profit, based on buzzwords and fear.

7.6.4 How do you choose a broker?

Of course, you expect that:
- You will realise your investment objectives.
- You will have peace of mind.
- The broker will have the necessary knowledge, qualifications and resources (computer system, research team).
- You will receive transparent advice.
- The fees will be reasonable.
- You will be part of the eventual investment decision.
- Investment planning will be proactive.
- Investment strategies will be based on your risk profile as well as your expected return.
- The broker will look after your interests.
- You will continue to receive dedicated advice and after-sales service for the duration (life) of the investment.

7.6.5 What do you expect of your broker?

If you take up a broker's time and pay for it (which is the right thing to do) you are entitled to expect a lot from him or her. If you only want advice, you should expect less than when you want to make an investment, in which case you would expect a proper after-sales service. If you expect a quarterly summary or report from your broker, you should ask for it and make sure that you receive it. Make sure that you get service for the fee (for advice only) or the fee and commission (if you invest money) that you pay your broker.

If you do not pay anything, you should not expect too much, as you will not be entitled to much. Nor can you expect much time or advice for R20 or R50. People often expect to pay a small one-off fee and then make use of the broker's time and knowledge repeatedly. Remember, the broker's time and money are just as valuable as your own.

7.6.6 What does your broker expect of you?

Brokers naturally expect to get money from you. This is what the occupation is all about. There is nothing wrong with this principle, as long as they earn the money. Do not allow a broker simply to take your money – he or she must earn it.

A broker will expect the investor to be serious and not to shop around for ten or 15 quotations (investment options) from different brokers in a short period.

Show that you are serious as soon as you have decided on a course of action, particularly if you have decided to use the services of a specific broker. This broker also expects you, the client, to enter into a long-term relationship based on honesty, openness and good communication.

Inform your broker of any changes in your financial situation, so that you can discuss the effects on your financial plans. These include changes in your income, expenses, assets, liabilities, the composition of your family and the standard of living you intend to maintain after retirement. Allow your broker to become an integral part of your life.

7.6.7 Wrong perceptions

Before we have a closer look at a few types of financial adviser, we should discuss some misconceptions that are prevalent among the investment public. Some people think all financial advisers are 'policy hawkers'; others think all financial advisers are brokers or stockbrokers. The person in the street often feels that all 'policy hawkers' want to make money quickly and easily, without fully informing the policy owner or providing proper after-sales service. Another misconception is that legal advice should be obtained only when people are getting married, divorced or want to draw up contracts of purchase and sale. Some people think that tax matters only crop up when drawing up financial statements (income statements and balance sheets), while others let people in the industry work hard (provide a lot of advice and waste a lot of time) and then buy a policy from or invest money with someone else.

Other obstacles to choosing a financial adviser are conflicting financial advice, advertisements in the media, people's attitudes to risk, their financial position and the political and economic situation in the country.

Potential investors should know that an investment portfolio should include various types of investment, and that these make provision for different needs over differing periods of time. For instance, people's needs may increase (cost of living), decrease (debts that are paid off), remain constant, or be permanent, temporary or unpredictable. It is, therefore, only logical that an individual should make different types of investment. (Note at this stage that most needs and risks are covered by insurance products.)

So if we do not like 'policy hawkers', we should find a way of distinguishing between the good and the 'others' (we should establish criteria). Our discussion is aimed specifically at helping the investment public to choose a financial adviser.

It is certainly not our intention to offend any type of broker or group of people. We also accept that any group or type of broker will have its specialists in the field of personal financial management.

7.6.8 Types of broker

Traditionally, brokers have been divided into four main categories: insurance agents, bank brokers, independent brokers and stockbrokers.

We can differentiate between financial advisers in insurance companies (employees of insurance companies) and those outside insurance companies (individuals who work for themselves or a financial institution).

The following people market insurance products for insurance companies:

- representatives;
- insurance advisers;
- senior insurance advisers;
- financial advisers; and
- senior financial advisers.

The new trend in the market is to have advisers licensed to sell specific products and to service specific markets. The onus is on the consumer to find out which products an adviser is entitled to sell. You, therefore, need to find out whether the adviser is licensed and what his or her qualifications are.

Independent brokers and bank brokers operate outside insurance companies. Their experience, knowledge, level of education and training, and, therefore, ability to provide effective personal financial advice, will place them on the equivalent of any one of the five levels indicated above.

By now it should be clear that 'broker' is a very wide concept.

The best advice will be provided by a fellow of the FPI (The Financial Planning Institute). This is a marketer who has obtained the professional qualification of the Financial Planning Institute.

Only about 1 500 of the approximately 60 000 marketers in South Africa have this qualification, which is endorsed by the Luyt Centre for Insurance Law at the University of the Free State. Only a few candidates are successful in the two examinations that have to be passed. About 17% to 30% pass the entrance examination and only 19% the final examination. In order to act in the best interests of their clients, FPI fellows subscribe to a very strict ethical code when they conduct their business. Fellows are entitled to levy a professional fee for services or advice and can, therefore, be held accountable by law for their advice. They provide advice over the broad spectrum of personal financial planning and are by far the best to consult when you want to buy an insurance product. In particular, fellows will be able to explain the long-term implications of investments to investors and, therefore, they should provide better advice than bank brokers or independent brokers who do not have these qualifications.

FPI has three levels of membership:
- associate;
- ordinary member; and
- fellow.

Bank brokers
Bank brokers may act on behalf of all insurance companies, but they are often encouraged by the banking group that employs them to promote its products (e.g. Standard Bank and Liberty, Nedbank and Old Mutual, and Absa and Sanlam).

They have more knowledge of the products offered by different companies than, say, insurance representatives. (Obviously it is difficult to have an in-depth knowledge of all available products.)

Bank brokers usually earn commission only and have to pay part of their commission to the bank. They are often transferred, which means that they cannot provide a long-term after-sales service. The newly appointed bank broker will be expected to render an after-sales service for policies that were sold by somebody else and on which he or she did not receive commission (which may happen with other brokers as well.)

Bank brokers often have only a basic knowledge, and work for a specific bank because the bank gives them business (they do not have to generate business themselves). They get their business from the bank manager, who gets a percentage of the commission. As a result, the product on which the highest commission is earned is often marketed (something which may also happen with other brokers).

Usually these brokers will also draw up a will 'free of charge'. Later, however, the broker will be the executor of the estate and will earn thousands of rands. The same can be said about insurance brokers.

Independent brokers

Independent brokers have access to the entire financial market. Independent brokers are not pressured by a particular institution to sell only its products. However, they also sometimes recommend products on which they earn a higher commission.

Independent brokers offer advice on estate and tax matters, and can assist in drawing up a comprehensive financial plan. They earn commission on the products they sell, or levy consultation fees when they only give advice.

Independent brokers should have proven experience or knowledge, or an FPI qualification. However, it is questionable whether a single individual can have knowledge of the entire spectrum of products, particularly when he or she is doing business on his or her own. To be able to give comprehensive financial advice, any broker will need a research team; this is what is meant by the term 'full-service broker'.

Stockbrokers

The following steps are useful when you choose a stockbroker:

Remember: All brokers are human beings. A single broker is not representative of the entire industry or a specific type of broker. Exceptions exist all over the field of personal finance.

- Arrange a personal meeting with members of the broker's firm.
- Try to get to know a few brokers.
- Listen to what other investors have to say about specific brokers.
- Ask your bank manager to recommend a competent broker.
- Find out how long the firm you are considering has been doing business on the stock exchange. A good record and many years of experience will be a positive sign.
- Find out whether the research team includes an expert on the economy, tax matters, computers, statistical analysis and psychological aspects (how people react – the role of fear and greed).
- Find out whether the broker maintains a good relationship with his or her clients.
- Find out whether the broker is also interested in the small investor, not only in institutional investors such as pension funds and insurance companies.
- Make sure that the broker can or will offer the investment services you require.
- Find out whether the broker will require a cash deposit. The broker will keep this for a few years until he or she knows you, particularly your creditworthiness, better.
- Consult a number of friends, investors and brokers before you decide on a specific broker.
- The broker must have access to large international institutions and markets.
- The business must have an effective administration section.
- Consult advertisements placed by brokers to find out what services they offer and in what markets they specialise.

Also decide what type of account you want to have with a stockbroker. You can manage your own share portfolio or authorise a broker to manage it on your behalf. When you manage your own portfolio, you instruct the broker to buy or sell shares on your behalf in terms of a direct agreement. When you have an indirect agreement, a broker acts as your intermediary.

Under a non-discretionary agreement, the broker will manage and administer your portfolio, but you reserve the right to decide which shares should be bought and/or sold. Under a discretionary agreement, the broker will manage your shares and make all the decisions about buying and selling.

Attorneys

You should consult an attorney about all legal matters, such as your will and establishing a trust (or trusts). An attorney with whom you have done business in the past and with whom you have a reasonably good relationship should be able to give you sound advice. Do not confuse an attorney with a financial adviser, even though they may be the same person.

Accountants

The same argument holds. Because of their qualifications, accountants should be able to give you excellent advice on tax matters and the different business forms (sole proprietorships, partnerships, close corporations, companies, etc.). However, remember that accountants usually work with accounting principles: your entrepreneurship, financial goals and challenges are not so important to them. Nevertheless, you may use the services of an attorney or accountant who meets the criteria for choosing a broker (we will discuss these later).

Pension fund, provident fund and personnel officers

One of the most unethical practices of our time is that such officials sometimes abuse their positions and earn commission by acting as intermediaries between brokers and investors. Of course, the innocent investor will know nothing about this. The following scenarios are possible when people (potential investors) are given details about their retirement benefits:

- The potential investor is handed a business card from the official's own broker (the commission is later shared).
- The official praises that specific broker.
- All other brokers and their products are criticised.
- Practical examples with fictitious figures are quoted to discourage the potential investor from using other brokers.
- The official makes it sound as if his or her broker will put an end to all the potential investor's financial concerns.

Imagine what this official could earn in commission. Of course, only a few officials are guilty. However, beware of those who hand out business cards. If you do use the card, be sure to follow the guidelines (discussed later) before you make your final decision.

'Share-lecturers' (also stockbrokers)

If we were to divide the subject of Personal Financial Management into its constituent parts, shares would only be one of 30 subjects. Imagine what effect an adviser whose knowledge is limited to shares could have on your other financial needs. Naturally, there are people who are knowledgeable about shares and other subjects in the field of personal finance. Shares play an important role when investing financial assets as part of investment planning. Investment planning, in turn, forms part of one of the various planning areas in the wide field of personal financial management.

At the moment, 'shares' is a buzzword in South Africa. You do not have to invest in shares, but if all your other financial needs have been provided for, you should invest directly in shares in order to obtain capital growth (given your age).

Journalists

Very few journalists have been trained in the occupation about which they air their views every day or every week. Journalists report mainly on something that has already happened and do not always place it in a context you can understand or which suits your needs. However, they do provide a valuable service in supplying information about the industry.

Trust companies

A visit to a trust company may be the answer for people with larger estates, who have to invest their funds when they are already involved in comprehensive estate planning. A trust company may be consulted when trusts or companies, for example, have to be established and need to be included in a will.

Remember, the above remarks are intended only as guidelines; they are not generalisations.

You will decide for yourself what type of adviser's or broker's services you should use for your particular financial needs. The Financial Services Board has instituted comprehensive initiatives to protect the investing public in their dealings with advisers and brokers. Presently, these guidelines are being revised and improved.

You should pay particular attention to the protection the investing public is currently afforded by law in their dealings with and investments through brokers and advisers. Take careful note of the part in Section 7.16 dealing with investor protection. Take note, amongst others, of the provisions of the Long-Term Insurance Act No 52 of 1998 as regards:

- Policyholder Protection Rules (PPR)
- The Statutory Notice for Policyholders
- The Financial Advisers and Intermediaries Act

7.6.9 Your relationship with your broker

Eventually, you will have a certain relationship with your broker and this relationship should last for many years. As this is no simple matter, you should choose your broker with a long-term financial relationship in mind.

Will the broker manage your relationship properly?

In other words, can you trust the broker with your financial needs, objectives, time and money over a long period of time? You should not only make good investments but also appropriate investments continuously. Managing this process involves, amongst others, the following:

- understanding and respecting your financial situation;
- providing continuous financial advice in line with your financial objectives;
- following up and controlling your investment portfolio continuously;
- communicating regularly (over the telephone and in writing);
- reporting opportunities and dangers regarding your investment(s) immediately;
- managing aspects other than your account; and
- understanding your risk profile, the time horizon of investments and expected returns (investment performance).

Guidelines for evaluating brokers

The criteria for choosing a broker may be divided into three main categories:

- Academic qualifications, professional qualifications and training.
- The specific firm the broker is working for.
- The person (broker) who is sitting in front of you.

Academic qualifications, professional qualifications and training

In theory, you should consult publications (positive and negative) about the broker and by the broker. Are there indications of media involvement, and does he or she for some reason enjoy high esteem? Ask for a CV (curriculum vitae) based on the broker's achievements in the field of personal finance. Follow up personal references supplied by the broker and contact existing and potential clients for references as well. Consider the reasons given by satisfied, as well as dissatisfied, clients. Does the broker have adequate knowledge and/or the applicable professional qualifications? Does he or she perform well and can this performance be substantiated (e.g. by awards)?

The specific firm

Make enquiries about the broker's business (either as employer or employee). What is the history of the business (positive or negative)? Does the business enjoy positive media coverage? Remember, however, that some 'media brokers' will invariably put other businesses in a bad light because of the financial benefits this will hold for them. Does the firm employ other brokers as well? Does it have a competent research team?

The person (broker) sitting in front of you

- Note how your negotiations with the broker are going. Do you like what he or she is saying?
- Is the broker interested in a long-term relationship, or do you get the idea that he or she is only interested in a quick commission?
- Try to determine the extent of the broker's integrity. Beware of an attitude of 'give me all your money'.
- Does the broker have empathy with your financial situation and/or needs? Get away as soon as possible from a broker who immediate starts criticising other brokers and their investment proposals. Remember that there are various ways of attaining your investment objectives.
- Be wary of a broker (any broker) who immediately wants to call up all your policies and invest this money as well.
- The same is true of a broker whose investment proposals are limited to offshore investments or shares. Is he or she really a good broker?
- What type of client does the broker usually have?
- Are the broker's financial or investment proposals clear enough for you to understand?
- Be wary of a broker who puts return first, without making sure that the financial product will satisfy your investment needs and objectives.
- What after-sales service can you expect?
- Does the broker have someone who can take over if necessary, or could your long-term relationship come to a sudden end?

7.6.10 Can I be my own broker?

Many people would like to make their own decisions about their personal finances and would prefer to invest their own packages, for example. Can you do it on our own? Evaluate yourself and circle the mark for each criterion on the left in Table 7.1.

A transaction has remuneration as its objective and nothing more; a relationship has a longer-term aim.

TABLE 7.1 **Can I be my own broker?**

Criterion	Mark				
	Low		Medium		High
Knowledge (investments)	1	2	3	4	5
Training	1	2	3	4	5
Experience	1	2	3	4	5
Time (information, research)	1	2	3	4	5
Managerial abilities	1	2	3	4	5

Now add up your marks:
- 20–25: You will definitely be able to handle your own financial matters.
- 15–19: You will be able to make most decisions on your own, but you need the assistance of a financial adviser/broker.
- 1–14: You will not be able to make any decisions about your financial matters on your own; you will need a financial adviser/broker.

This is only a rough indication to help you determine how much financial advice you might need.

Whether you decide to be your own broker or not, it is important to consult as many sources of financial information as possible, such as:
- scientific books on personal finances;
- academic books on personal financial management (These books cover the total area of personal financial planning. These are the only books that explain the structure underlying personal financial planning. They do not need to be updated every year because they contain pure financial principles that have been tested through the years. The authors are not trying to sell certain products to the readers.);
- financial articles in magazines and newspapers (make sure that you place the contents in perspective – do not be prompted into changing your investments every week);
- brokers;
- banks;
- insurance companies;
- the Internet;
- suppliers of electronic financial information (e.g. Reuters, Intelligent Network, Dow Jones Telerate Southern Africa, McGregor Information Services);
- the South African Reserve Bank;
- Statistics South Africa;
- the International Monetary Fund;
- the Bureau for Economic Research at the University of Stellenbosch;
- the Bureau for Financial Analysis at the University of Pretoria; and
- the Bureau for Market Research at the University of South Africa.

7.6.11 What are the costs of investing?

Traditionally, brokers earn commission, a fee or both. Because the investment has to be managed over a long term, a management fee is levied as well.

When you are investing in a single financial product (e.g. an endowment policy, a lump sum endowment policy or a voluntary annuity) the cost of the investment usually amounts to 1.75% of the total amount of the investment.

If an investment is made with a stockbroker, the broker's fees may vary depending on the services that will be rendered in future. However, the following cost items will be involved in buying and selling shares:
- Buying: x number of shares at × cents each
  Plus: broker's fees at x% of the amount invested
  Plus: marketable securities tax (MST) at x%
- Selling: only broker's fees (no MST)

With unit trusts, the following costs will be involved (an example):
- *Initial fee*. The unit trust management company will charge initial fees of up to 0.25% on funds. Compulsory fees for MST at 0.25%, broker's fees and VAT at 14% will also be levied.
- *Annual management fees*. An annual management fee, as determined by the trust deed, will be levied. These costs are negotiable. The management fee will be deducted from the income before it is declared and paid out.
- *Be careful*. It could be expensive to transfer a certain unit trust investment to another fund. Timing is very important here, because you may incur a loss. The conversion entails selling units in the old fund and then buying units in the new fund. The new costs will amount to under 1% if the same broker handles the conversion. The actual costs will be determined by the difference in the market value of the initial investment (buying) and the market value at the time of sale.

The cost of an investment in a product that is linked to unit trusts are made up of the following cost elements:

- *Initial costs* (administration fees of 5%–7%). These include annual management fees (1% for the unit trust company plus 0.5–1% as a management fee for companies with linked products, plus VAT).
- *Total costs.* These will depend on the amount that is invested, the product to which the unit trust is linked and the broker's commission.
- *Broker's fees.* Besides the initial fees already included in the costs, brokers receive a further 0.5% per year.
- *Statutory or compulsory costs.* 0.75–0.25% marketable securities tax plus a broker's fee of 0.5%.

When money is invested in fixed property, the initial costs comprise transfer duty, conveyancing fees, interim interest, occupational rent, the costs involved when the property is unoccupied and the agent's commission.

When investing a lump sum in a 'package product' (an investment product in which all types of financial product are found and in which you may constantly switch between products at virtually no cost), the costs will be 5% of the amount invested (consisting of 2.5% commission and 2.5% administration fees). Remember that this commission is negotiable. The 5% does not include the management fee. Suppose you invest R500 000 in such a product. The costs may be as follows:

EXAMPLE

Initial fees
Single investment (R500 000)

	Amount (%) VAT excl.	Amount (%) VAT incl.
Financial advisor	R12 500 (2.50%)	R14 250 (2.85%)
Administration	R5 500 (1.10%)	R6 270 (1.25%)
TOTAL	R18 000 (3.60%)	R20 520 (4.10%)

Recurring investment (e.g. monthly)

			% (VAT excl.)	% (VAT incl.)
Financial adviser			0.00%	0.00%
	From	To	% (VAT excl.)	% (VAT incl.)
Administration	R0,00	R2 500	2.50%	2.85%
	R2 500	Plus	1.50%	1.71%

Annual fees

			% pa payable monthly (VAT excl.)	% pa payable monthly (VAT incl.)
Financial adviser: service fee			0.50%	0.57%

			% pa payable monthly (VAT excl.)	% pa payable monthly (VAT incl.)
Administration: service fee	R0,00	R2 500 000	0.50%	0.57%
	R2 500 000	R5 000 000	0.40%	0.46%
	R5 000 000	Plus	0.30%	0.34%

Note: Annual fees will be recovered as a percentage of the investment fund.
The tables below indicate that the costs of your investment will decrease as the investment amount increases.

Initial fee on single investment	Rate (VAT excl.)
On the first R100 000	1.75%
On the next R100 000	1.25%
On the next R100 000	1.00%
On the next R200 000	0.75%
On the next R500 000	0.50%
On the next R4 000 000	0.25%
R5 000 000 and more	0.00%

Initial fee on recurring investments	Rate (VAT excl.)
R0 – R2 500	2.50%
R2 500 and more	1.50%

Administration service fee (yearly)	Rate (VAT excl.)
R0 – R2 500 000	0.50%
R2 500 000 – R5 000 000	0.40%
R5 000 000 and more	0.30%

- *Financial adviser's initial fee*. Can be negotiated – between 0% and 5%.
- *Financial adviser's annual administration service fee*. Can be negotiated – between 0% and 1%.
- *Annual administration fee*. Will be recovered monthly from the investor's plan according to a sliding scale.

Conversion fees
- *Within the same management company*. No fees except compulsory costs are levied on conversions between investment funds that are managed by the same management company.
- *Between different management companies*. Compulsory costs and a levy of 0.25% on conversions between funds that are managed by different management companies.

7.7 INVESTMENT STRATEGIES FOR DIFFERENT AGES

People often find it difficult to start investing early in their working lives and to continue with different investments throughout life. Unfortunately, investment strategies are a prerequisite for financial independence and even survival after retirement. Retirement can last 20 to 30 years, during which time inflation will decrease the purchasing power of your investments, and the different kinds of taxes will eat away at the remainder of your hard-earned assets.

Every person needs an investment strategy for his or her goals in life, for the many needs that demand particular provision and for protection against possible and certain financial risks. Your unique situation, and especially your age and place in the life cycle, will determine the particular investment strategy. The key term for financial independence is financial discipline. If possible, you should invest as long as you live. Then, too, the correct investments should be made at the right time. You do not want to start in life (at the age of 30) buying a car for R180 000, while renting a flat and not contributing to any other investments.

Investment strategies over a period of sixty years, starting in the working years, are recommended. For the purposes of this section, we assume that education will continue to the age of 20, although it could be closer to 30. Investment strategies are required for the following life stages: the young years, the family years, the career years, the pre-retirement years and the retirement years. It is important to know that throughout the five life stages, continuous and diverse investments should be made.

7.7.1. The young years (20–30)

Financial discipline ought to be formed during this period. An investment with capital growth over the long term, such as an endowment policy, is a necessity. It is important to accumulate a deposit for a dwelling (flat, townhouse or house) or to finance the purchase with a 100% bond.

Use your employer's 100% housing scheme, if possible, and do not forget the housing subsidy (or allowance) in your calculations, if applicable. Take out a life policy to cover your bond (an access-type bond), from the same financial institution, with the option to use the lump sum after 20 years.

Make use of the tax benefits of a retirement annuity by investing in one. If possible, invest monthly in a specialist unit trust fund. Cover your household risks by means of short-term insurance and take out disability and dread disease cover. If you change jobs, transfer the money from the pension fund or provident fund to that of the new employer. Start making investments to cover the needs of young children. You could also start a family business.

7.7.2 The family years (30–40)

Although the needs of children will be a priority for households in this group, parents should maintain current investments. Try to increase your life coverage and make sure that you and your spouse make use of the maximum tax advantages when it comes to contributions to retirement annuities. Take out endowment policies for the children and invest all additional funds in your mortgage bond. This will ensure a high tax-free return on your money and, at the same time, create an emergency fund through your access bond. Investing in shares though a professional broker is also recommended.

7.7.3 The career years (40–50)

At this stage, the children will start moving out of the house and, as a result (hopefully), more funds will be available for investment. More attention should be given to investments with capital growth, with a view to retirement. You can move to a smaller dwelling, if necessary. Your bond should be paid during this period and a second property can be bought in the name of a child or trust. Children can stay in the dwelling or it can be let.

7.7.4 The pre-retirement years (50–60)

Serious attention should be given to retirement and all possible funds ought to be put into investments with capital growth, like property or endowment policies. Contributions to pension or provident funds, retirement annuities or deferred compensation schemes should be increased. It is important to diversify your investments in order to spread your risk.

7.7.5 The retirement years (60 and over)

Avoid risky investments and concentrate on capital growth. Concentrate on the protection of your hard-earned investments (for your retirement and for your children's inheritances). Put some of your money into fixed deposits to earn interest. Guaranteed income and capital plans (obtainable from insurers) are recommended investments. An investment in a second-hand endowment policy is also possible. Remember that all existing investments should be maintained. Get rid of all debt.

7.8 INVESTMENT CRITERIA

Before a person invests money (buys financial assets) he or she must be aware of the various criteria for evaluating investments. Various aspects affect the choice of investment options, of which the following are the most important.

7.8.1 Income

Not all investors are interested in capital growth. Some prefer a regular, fixed income, even though the value of the investment decreases as a result of inflation. For a 20-year-old person, such a decision could be disastrous over the long term, but for a 70-year-old person, it could be a good decision.

People who are not interested in capital growth will, therefore, make use of some savings plan or another. They will invest money saved in a savings plan in order to earn a monthly income from it.

Potential investors who want a fixed income can also invest in participation bonds. The capital is still safe (repayment of funds is guaranteed), but the money must be invested on a fixed basis for five years.

If a potential investor who wants a regular income is prepared to accept a greater risk, a much higher return can be obtained. Capital growth may also occur to a certain extent, which means that inflation will not absorb the investor's money.

Fixed-interest-bearing securities or trusts offer a fixed income while repayment of the principal sum is guaranteed. This type of investment is not ideal for the 'small' investor.

Unit trusts, however, do offer the small investor an investment opportunity aimed at income. Income trusts are a good example. Unit trusts are a long-term investment, however, and people who want their money within three years are advised to invest in the right unit trusts. The same applies to property trusts and money market funds.

7.8.2 Growth

By growth we mean capital growth; in other words, a rise in the value of the investment, for example a home. It is important that an investment should show capital growth in order to improve the investor's cash position after the sale of the investment. Investments in shares or long-term unit trust investments are further examples. With capital growth, we mean that the value of the investment should increase annually by at least as much as inflation. If the annual increase in value is less than the inflation rate, we call it a negative growth or negative real growth.

7.8.3 Safety of capital

The safety of an investment means that the investment must survive for as long as it pleases the investor. If an amount of R100 000 is invested, the investor must be sure that the money is safe and that he or she will receive not less than R100 000 (apart from the fact that the investor will receive less in real terms, as a result of inflation and tax on interest income, for example).

Where a young person loses his or her investment, he or she may be able to recoup the loss over the years from other income sources. Older people, particularly retired investors, will not be able to regain a lost investment over the years. The result is that older people usually prefer less risky investments, where the safety of the capital amount (invested amount) is guaranteed.

7.8.4 Flexibility

A potential investor must find out whether it will be possible to make adjustments to his or her investment at a later stage. An example is where the contents of a policy can be adjusted to provide for changing circumstances. Note should also be taken, for example, of the possibility of converting one kind of share to another kind.

7.8.5 Liquidity

It is particularly important to certain investors that their investment can be converted to cash fairly easily and at short notice. Even with short-term securities, the more liquid securities will be chosen. If the investor urgently needs his or her cash (investment), it must be available.

7.8.6 Taxability

Certain types of investment are preferred above others, as a result of the taxability of the return on investments. People with a high taxable income will prefer investments that are partially taxable or that yield tax-free returns. High returns are, therefore, played down against tax-free income.

7.8.7 Ease of management

Potential investors have to decide themselves whether they have sufficient expertise to manage an investment or investments. Where a shares portfolio requires specialised knowledge, for example, the management should preferably be left to an expert (a stockbroker). From a management point of view, it is advisable to evaluate investments continuously and to decide whether they should be replaced with other or similar investments. The obligatory investment term will determine when an investment can be altered.

The average investor does not possess the necessary expertise to manage investments him- or herself. It is recommended that investments are discussed with an expert (according to the kind of investment) at least once a year. Older people (especially after retirement) sometimes have enough time to spare, but do not always have the energy to undertake their own share transactions.

7.8.8 Risk

Risk refers to the possibility of suffering a loss. A person's attitude towards risk determines which investments he or she will prefer. The risk involved in investment in shares, for example, is higher than for unit trusts. In turn, unit trusts are more risky than property trusts.

7.8.9 Return

Earlier, we referred to the fact that risk and return are positively correlated; in other words, when risk rises the anticipated return will also rise and vice versa. A lower risk is associated with a lower anticipated return.

7.8.10 Amount

The amount of money a potential investor has at his or her disposal will determine which investments are possible and which are not. Small amounts of money can be deposited in a savings account. Fairly small amounts can also be invested monthly in unit trusts. An investment in listed shares, however, requires a larger investment amount, which is generally out of the reach of the average investor.

7.8.11 Term of investment

The specific term of an investment is very important to a potential investor. If the investor may need his or her money in a year's time, he or she should not consider an investment with a longer term. An investment in shares requires that funds are invested over a longer term, unless the shares are sold. Listed shares are fairly easily negotiable.

The term, therefore, is particularly important where money is invested for a fixed term (for example five years) and where negotiability is not an issue. Where a decline in interest rates is anticipated, it is better to make a fixed investment over a longer period. Where interest rates are about to rise, the investor loses by making a fixed investment over a long term at a specific interest rate. The need for money and the anticipated interest rates, therefore, play an important role in the desirability of a specific investment term for the potential investor.

Further, it is important to realise over what term a specific investment will benefit the investor. Unit trusts, for example, are a long-term investment. For terms that are shorter than three to five years, the investor may suffer a loss, particularly if he or she wishes to sell within that period. Over the long term, the possibility of a loss is smaller if the investor's motive was capital growth.

7.8.12 Investor's tax rate

An investor's marginal tax rate will largely determine the kind of investment he or she chooses. If an investor falls into a relatively high income category, with the associated high tax liabilities, a tax-free investment or an investment with capital growth rather than a regular income is preferable. Certain institutions still offer tax-free and partially tax-free investments.

7.8.13 Transaction costs

The purchase and sale of assets is usually accompanied by some form of transaction costs. Financial assets (the area of investment during this discussion) have to do with stockbrokerage. In certain cases (certain kinds of investments), transaction costs are paid for both the purchase and the sale of financial assets.

For example, transaction costs can be lower where shares or unit trusts are bought regularly (for example monthly). The reason for this is that the average price per share or unit trust is lower.

7.8.14 Timing

Earlier, we explained how an anticipated rise or fall in interest rates affects the fixed investment of money. A fixed investment at the right time (when interest rates are going to rise) can generate considerably more income in the form of higher interest for the investor.

In the case of shares, timing is almost as important as the choice of the right shares in the right industry. For those who want to speculate with shares, the timing of buying and selling is crucial. Shares should, therefore, be bought at the time the investor (or stockbroker) regards them as undervalued and sold at a time when they are regarded as overvalued.

To avoid buying shares at the wrong time, a method can be followed that is called 'rand cost averaging'. This means that an amount is invested on a regular basis (for example monthly). Even if prices vary, the average costs paid over time (for example a year) are lower than they would have been in the case of once-only purchases (investments).

7.8.15 Diversification

It is important that a potential investor is aware of this aspect, particularly during the evaluation of potential investments. Diversification means the spreading of risk over a number of investments with the purpose of lowering the total level of risk. If the risk of an investor's portfolio is already very high, he or she should rather choose an investment with a lower risk in order to lower the total risk of his or her portfolio. Again, the investor's attitude towards risk plays an important role during investment and, consequently, during diversification.

7.8.16 Control

The potential investor must decide whether he or she wants to exercise control over the investments, and how much control he or she desires. This will depend on his or her personality type. In the case of financial assets, the investor can manage the shares portfolio him- or herself, and undertake the buying and selling of shares without the assistance of a stockbroker.

Savings accounts or fixed deposits do not require any control on the part of the investor. An investor may, however, require a stockbroker to manage a shares portfolio. A stockbroker may be asked to take complete control over the portfolio and make all the decisions for buying and selling, or the investor may retain a measure of control. In the latter case, the stockbroker will ask the investor's permission to buy and/or sell, in which case transactions will take place only with the permission of the investor.

7.8.17 Knowledge/management requirements

Certain financial assets (investments) require a large amount of knowledge and expertise. Very few people possess the necessary knowledge, time or skill to manage their own shares portfolio. A stockbroker may, therefore, be appointed to manage the portfolio. Saving money in a savings account or fixed deposit, however, does not require much knowledge or expertise. Even an illiterate person can make such investments.

7.8.18 Protection against inflation

The pre-tax return on an investment should be higher than the inflation rate (the South African inflation rate was about 9% in 2002). An investment may also have a higher capital growth than the inflation rate. Protection against inflation means the retention of the buying power of the investor's money. Investments seldom offer a positive (real) after-tax rate of return, in other words, higher than the inflation rate.

The current inflation rate makes investment on the share market essential. Earlier, when the inflation rate was 3 to 4% and the return on a fixed deposit was about 8%, an investor (with a marginal tax rate of 25%) could expect an after-tax return of 6%. Today, an after-tax return that is higher than the inflation rate is unthinkable. Potential investors are therefore referred to the importance of the before-tax investment rate, the inflation rate and particularly the investor's marginal tax rate.

Posel (1990:15) points out that individual households have their own inflation rate, depending on their bond loans and/or number of children. The investment plan for each household is therefore based on this unique inflation rate. The investment techniques they adopt will also be determined by this factor. The purpose of an investment or investment plan is, after all, to obtain a positive (in real terms) after-tax return. Real in this context means after-tax return minus the inflation rate.

Posel (1990:29) comes to the conclusion that the consumer expenditure index and not the consumer price index should be used to calculate the actual inflation rate. Individual households should therefore take note of this real fact during their personal financial planning.

7.8.19 The investor's objectives

The investor's investment objectives will largely determine which investment criteria are the most important personally. These investment objectives will determine which investments (in financial assets) he or she will consider and which he or she will avoid. A potential investor's investment objectives will be determined by the following personal factors:

- current financial situation (wealth or financial independence);
- age;
- physical abilities;
- educational level;
- present career;
- single or married with a family;
- attitude towards risks;
- management ability;
- nature of income (regular or on a commission basis); and
- source of funds and purpose of investment.

Existing investments will, therefore, be assessed differently by different people, based on their own personal situations. However, both existing and potential investors should be aware of the different investment criteria. This will equip them with the necessary knowledge to make sensible investments that will meet their investment objectives.

7.9 TYPES OF FINANCIAL INVESTMENT

Potential investors have several financial investments to choose from. They will accept or reject investments on the basis of their investment objectives by using certain investment criteria. These types of financial investment form part of the investor's portfolio and may include:

- money market investments; and
- capital market investments.

Now we will discuss some investment options in the money and capital markets.

7.9.1 The money market

In the money market, the potential investor may invest in the following financial assets:

- bank acceptances;
- treasury bills;
- negotiable certificates of deposit;
- participation bonds;
- deposits;
- project bills;
- trade bills; and
- money market funds.

7.9.1.1 Bank acceptances

Bank acceptances are the oldest form of credit in the world, and can be traced back to the 4th century BC (Falkena *et al.* 1989:209). At present, bank acceptances are the most traded securities in the money market. A bank acceptance is a bill of exchange issued by a business enterprise (after borrowing money) in which it undertakes to pay a stated sum of money after a stated period. This period is usually three months (90 days). The bill of exchange is usually accepted by the bank, which means that the bank guarantees the payment of the sum of the bill of exchange on maturity.

Bank acceptances are usually issued in the following amounts: R5 000 000, R1 000 000, R500 000, R200 000, R150 000, R100 000, R50 000, R20 000, R10 000 and R5 000.

The primary market
Bank acceptances are issued by banks.

The holders of bank acceptances
The holder of a bank acceptance is that institution or individual who is entitled to a certain sum of money on a certain date. Holders may be individual people, state institutions, pension funds and insurance companies.

The secondary market
An active secondary market exists for bank acceptances. Investors may sell bank acceptances of high quality in the market at any time. Bank acceptances are bought for terms of three years, but they may be sold within this period, although the holder will usually lose out, because the return over the short term is lower than over the long term, or because the rate of return has fallen.

7.9.1.2 Treasury bills
A treasury bill is issued by the bank and is proof that the estate has borrowed money from a person or institution. The loan term is three months. The bill itself does not provide much information, but the following does appear on it: date of issue, date of maturity (on which the debt must be paid) and the sight value (nominal value) that must be paid to the holder of the treasury bill on the date of maturity.

Treasury bills are issued in the following amounts: R5 000 000, R2 000 000, R1 000 000, R500 000, R200 000, R100 000, R50 000 and R10 000. The minimum amount borrowed, however, is R100 000. Individuals or institutions may issue (request) tenders for treasury bills on Fridays.

The primary market
The South African Reserve Bank issues treasury bills on behalf of the state. Loan amounts are incurred in descending order until all loan amounts (according to the state's need of funds) are exhausted. Two types of treasury bill are distinguished: those issued weekly with a tenure of 91 days, and special issues with a tenure of 92 to 365 days. On the maturity dates, the treasury bills are offered at the Reserve Bank, which redeems the outstanding debt.

Holders of treasury bills
Banks, building societies, insurance companies, pension funds, mining houses, discount houses and individuals may be holders of treasury bills.

The secondary market
A treasury bill is transferred merely by tendering it (handing it over), unless the name of the original supplier of funds appears on it. In that case, the investor must endorse (sign) the treasury bill at the back on tendering it.

7.9.1.3 Negotiable certificates of deposit
These certificates are issued (by banks, for example) as an indication that funds (capital plus interest) will be paid on a stated date to the holder of the certificates. A negotiable certificate of deposit contains the following information: name of issuer (bank or building society), date of issue, date of maturity, amount of deposit, value on date of maturity and interest rate per year.

Negotiable certificates of deposit are issued for periods of up to five years. If issued for a period shorter than a year, interest is paid at the end of the period. For periods of one to five years, interest is paid at the end of the period or every six months. These certificates are usually issued for large amounts: R1 000 000, R500 000 and, in exceptional cases, in multiples of R100 000.

The primary market
Banks and building societies issue such certificates.

Holders of certificates
Building societies, discount houses, mining houses, pension funds, companies, government institutions, municipalities, and individual people may be holders of certificates.

The secondary market
Certificates are transferable merely by tendering, unless the depositor's name appears on them. In that case, the depositor must endorse the certificate on the back. The certificate is offered for payment on the date of maturity at the bank or building society. The issuer will then pay the sight value (deposit) plus interest to the holder of the certificate. The interest rate applies up to the date of maturity.

Assume that a certificate is issued on 31 June and matures on 31 December of the same year. At an interest rate of 12% per year, the buyer pays 100% for the certificate and six months later receives 106% ($12/100 \times 6/12$). If the certificate is traded after three months, the price is the discounted value of 106%, that is 103.085% of the original purchase price (Laurie 1990:15).

7.9.1.4 Participation bonds
Individuals can invest in participation bonds. The minimum investment amount is R1 000 and the term is five years. During this period, the funds may not be withdrawn, except in the case of the death or liquidation of the investor. After five years, the money may be withdrawn or reinvested. However, three months' notice must be given.

The interest rate varies and is not fixed over the five-year period. Even though inflation may lower the value of the investment, the risk is low and this type of investment is particularly suitable for retired people. Interest is paid out in one of four ways: quarterly in advance, monthly in advance, quarterly in arrears and monthly in arrears. Some calculations are, therefore, necessary in order to determine which financial institution pays the highest interest on the basis of the method of interest payments used.

7.9.1.5 Deposits

Deposits may be made at a bank or building society (deposit receiving intermediaries). Smaller deposits are placed in savings deposits. Deposits for fairly large amounts (for example, R50 000) are called deposits on demand. The 'small investor' will, therefore, make use of a savings account (savings deposit).

A minimum amount usually has to be left in a savings account, in order to ensure a higher rate of return for the investor. The number of withdrawals per month is also limited. Fixed-term and notice deposits have a higher interest rate than a pure savings account (for example, accounts used to deposit monthly income).

However, inflation is the enemy of savings account investors, because the purchasing power of money decreases over time. Nevertheless, such funds are necessary for unforeseen events. Each household and individual should have some money in a savings account (in spite of the decline in value) as a safety measure.

Trade bills, project bills, promissory notes, government stock, municipal stock and Land Bank bills are all part of the money market. Investments in these instruments require very large sums of money and are not suitable for small investors. We will not discuss money market instruments any further.

It is not always easy to distinguish between the money market and the capital market. Normally, investments for terms of up to three years are regarded as part of the money market, while longer-term investments are regarded as part of the capital market. When a capital market instrument, with a normal tenure or term of five years, is sold after two years, it becomes part of the money market.

7.9.2 The capital market

The capital market offers individuals the opportunity of investing their savings over the long term. The various investment options in the capital market are called capital market instruments. Opportunities are created in the capital market for investing as well as trading in such investments (long-term investments). The capital market consists of a large number of financial institutions or intermediaries who offer a large variety of financial instruments (capital market instruments), each with different risk/return features.

Financial instruments in which potential investors can invest in the capital market are:
- ordinary shares;
- preference shares;
- fixed-interest-bearing securities;
- unit trusts;
- property trusts;
- listed property companies; and
- derivatives.

Although there are similar instruments, they are not relevant to our discussion, since we are primarily interested in the small, individual investor. We will now discuss each of the above instruments.

7.9.2.1 Ordinary shares

Companies with a limited liability usually issue ordinary shares. Individuals and institutions may invest in these shares. An investor would have limited liability if the company was liquidated, which means that he or she cannot lose more than 100% of his or her investment. The names of people who buy shares appear in the company's member register and they receive share certificates as proof of their investment. This is the case of an investment in a public company.

An investment in ordinary shares implies that the investor puts his or her money at the disposal of the company for an unlimited period. Should the investor need this money (for whatever reason), he or she may not withdraw it from the company. Shares are transferable, however, and can be traded.

Ordinary shareholders may receive dividends after all fixed interest obligations and preference dividends (payable to preference shareholders) have been paid. Dividends are not always paid out to shareholders; sometimes, they are retained to finance further projects. Depending on the needs (preferences) of ordinary shareholders, they would choose companies for investment, which either pay regular dividends or which reinvest dividends. Consequently, there is a choice between income (distribution of dividends) and capital growth (reinvestment of dividends).

The risk is great for ordinary shareholders for the following reasons, amongst others:
- There is no certainty that an ordinary shareholder will, in fact, receive dividends.
- There is no judicial (legal) obligation on the company to pay back the borrowed money (the capital invested in ordinary shares by the shareholders).
- The legal obligation is to first pay interest and preference dividends from the profits.
- Industrial results and company policy determine the payment of dividends and the repayment of capital.
- During liquidation of the company, ordinary shareholders will be compensated last if sufficient funds remain after the payment of creditors and preference shareholders.

Ordinary shareholders have a say, since they have voting rights in accordance with their share holding on important matters at annual general meetings.

They decide on the following, among others: who should serve on the board of directors, the approval of the financial annual statements, the dividend policy and the investment policy of the company.

The high risk associated with ordinary shares implies that a high return on such investments may be expected. The return is received in the form of dividends, capital growth and a rise in share prices. The return should also be higher than an investor would receive for an investment with a similar risk elsewhere.

Ordinary shareholders are regarded as owners of the company, because they carry most of the risk of all the suppliers of capital.

7.9.2.2 Preference shares

Preference shares have features of both ordinary shares and debentures. They are also called mixed forms. Normally, preference shares are created for special circumstances.

The risk of preference shares is lower than for ordinary shares, for the following reasons, amongst others:
- Preference dividends are paid before dividends are paid on ordinary shares.
- Preference shares enjoy preference above ordinary shares, in the case of the company being liquidated.

Preference shareholders do not possess voting rights. Preference dividends are paid out after interest on capital, because preference dividends are paid out of net profit after tax, whereas interest is paid from before-tax income. The following income statement illustrates the position of holders of debentures, preference shares and ordinary shares in terms of their income demands and profit-sharing in the event of liquidation:

Profit before interest and tax	Rx
Minus: Interest obligations	—
Profit after interest before tax	Rx
Minus: Tax	—
Profit after interest and tax	Rx
Minus: Preference dividends	—
Profit available for distribution among ordinary shareholders (or reinvestment in the company)	Rx

We see that interest must be paid first (to creditors), secondly, preference dividends (to preference shareholders) and, thirdly, dividends on ordinary shares (to ordinary shareholders). The same sequence is retained if funds or assets remain after a company's liquidation. Preference shareholders receive a lower return then ordinary shareholders, with a lower risk attached to their investment because of the fixed

obligation to pay out dividends (except for cumulative preference shares).

Preference shareholders do not have voting rights and are not regarded as owners of the company. In cases where dividend payments are in arrears (have accumulated), preference shareholders may have voting rights.

The following types of preference shares are distinguished:
- *Fixed-interest shares*: a fixed rate of return is paid on the coupon rate of the preference share.
- *Variable interest preference shares*: rates of return are linked either to money market or to capital market rates.
- *Cumulative preference shares*: there are not always sufficient funds (profits) in a specific year to pay out dividends. The dividends are, therefore, accumulated for a year when there are sufficient profits for the payment of dividends.
- *Participation preference shares*: here, preference shareholders receive dividends and share in the surplus profit (after dividend payments).
- *Redeemable preference shares*: in this case, the company may buy back preference shares at a fixed date or over a fixed period. Investors are usually wary of the latter.
- *Convertible preference shares*: preference shares may be converted (changed) to ordinary shares with a higher return but also with a higher risk. Convertible preference shares are more expensive than other types of preference shares.

7.9.2.3 Fixed-interest-bearing securities

The concept 'fixed-interest-bearing securities' includes a wide variety of investment alternatives:
- gilt-edged stock – IOUs issued by the government;
- semi-gilt-edged stock – IOUs issued by government subsidised institutions (for example Eskom), as well as the larger municipalities; and
- debentures – IOUs issued by companies.

Each of these will now be briefly discussed.

Gilt-edged stock

The government offers a 100% guarantee that all capital plus interest will be paid to the investor in gilt-edged stocks. Investors know beforehand how much interest they are going to receive. Interest payments are usually made every six months. Gilt-edged stocks are not without any risk, though, as will be seen in the discussion on debentures.

Semi-gilt-edged stock

These stocks are similar to gild-edged stocks but the risk is slightly higher.

Because of the higher risk, a higher interest rate is paid to investors. The risk and return can be directly linked to the financial situation of the institution (e.g. Eskom, the South African Transport Services) or municipality concerned.

Debentures

A debenture is a written IOU that a person or an institution receives as proof of money lent to the person or institution. A debenture-holder is actually a creditor who is entitled to his or her borrowed capital plus interest. The exact manner and period of payment is set out in the IOU. Normally, interest is paid annually, while the borrowed amount is paid at the end of the borrowing period.

Gilt-edged and semi-gilt-edged stocks are issued by the government, government institutions and municipalities in order to obtain funds. Companies, on the other hand, issue IOUs to obtain funds, over and above issuing shares. Fixed-interest-bearing stocks represent long-term loans to (or long-term investments in) these institutions.

There is always a possibility that a company may be liquidated (for whatever reason). Consequently, the risk of IOUs is higher than in the case of gilt-edged or semi-gilt-edged stocks. A higher interest rate is, therefore, paid to holders of debentures. As mentioned earlier, holders of debentures have a preference demand above ordinary preference shareholders in the event of the liquidation of the company. Holders of debentures have no voting rights, except where interest payments are in arrears. The following types of debentures are distinguished:

- *Secured debentures*: these debentures are issued with assets (moving or non-moving) as security (in the event of the liquidation of the company).
- *Unsecured debentures*: here, no security is offered and no preference above other creditors in the event of liquidation is obtained.
- *Guaranteed debentures*: a holding company guarantees the debentures of a subsidiary company.
- *Participating debentures*: holders of debentures receive annual interest payments and also participate in surplus profits.
- *Convertible debentures*: holders of debentures may convert their debentures to ordinary shares. It is agreed beforehand on the number of shares as well as the stated date of conversion.
- *Redeemable debentures*: the company may redeem the loan before the maturity date agreed upon. The investor may be stuck with a large amount of cash while interest rates are low and there are no similar investments (with the same returns as the redeemable debentures) in the market.

7.9.2.4 Unit trusts

An investment in unit trusts is a method whereby the fairly small investor can form part of the share market without being directly involved. Professionals are responsible for the management of such investments and they have the necessary time and expertise. People who buy unit trusts generally do not want to be responsible for analysing the market.

Unit trusts are large investment portfolios that may include a wide variety of shares and fixed-interest-bearing trusts. These portfolios are diversified, with the result that the risk for the investor or potential buyer is lower, since the law requires that each unit trust keep at least 20 different investments. The return consists of interest and dividends. Capital profit earned when the unit trusts are sold is taxable (capital gains tax is payable).

The investor can claim repayment on his or her units at any stage. The price received for the units will be determined by their price at the time of repayment and not when they were bought. Investors also have the right to request that dividends be reinstated. Various kinds of unit trust exist, which gives investors the opportunity to choose their own investment area. Laurie (1990:12) points out that this conflicts with the idea that investment decisions are left to the managing company.

Specialists regard regular investments over fairly long periods as the only way of investing in unit trusts. Unit trusts are an ideal investment for the person in the street who uses a monthly income to invest. Investors who possess large amounts of capital would most probably invest in shares.

The functioning of a unit trust is illustrated in Diagram 7.2.

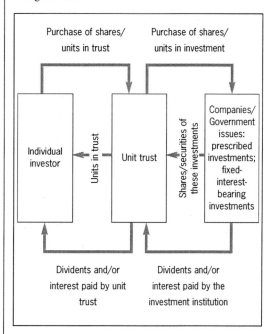

DIAGRAM 7.2 **The functioning of a unit trust**

Advantages of unit trusts

- *Liquidity.* Unit trusts are 100% liquid and may be called up at any time, because legislation compels the fund to buy back units.
- *Well-diversified.* Risk is spread over a large number of different investments.
- *Flexibility.* Contributions to unit trusts may be altered or even stopped.
- *Hedge against inflation.* Like investments in fixed property and shares, an investment in unit trusts offers a hedge against inflation. The return is, therefore, higher than the inflation rate. An average rate of return of +20% is generally obtained in the five best unit trusts over a term of five to 20 years.
- *Purchase unit.* Units may even be divided into fractions. Laurie (1990:117) points out that unit trusts may be bought in smaller units than shares. For example, shares may be bought like milk in litres. Unit trusts, on the other hand, may be bought like petrol, even in cents.
- *Rate of return against insurance.* An investment in unit trusts will beat the return on an endowment policy and even a retirement annuity over the long term.
- *Lower costs.* The costs involved in an investment in a unit trust are lower than for insurance.

Disadvantages of unit trusts

- *No guarantees.* Unit trusts offer no guarantees for the safety of the investments. Over the short term they are risky investments.
- Rates of return, or growth rates, of the various unit trusts vary from year to year. If a specific unit trust provides the highest return in 2002, it may provide the fifth or sixth highest rate of return the following year.

Types of unit trust

There are three main groups of unit trusts in which the individual investor may choose to invest: general, specialised and income trusts. Each of these will now be discussed briefly.

General unit trusts

These unit trusts invest in shares over a wide spectrum of sectors on the Johannesburg Securities Exchange. This ensures diversification; in other words, the risk is spread over a large number of investments. Potential investors who prefer spreading their risk will usually invest in general unit trusts. Stable medium- and long-term growth is obtained, even though the dividend income is fairly low.

Specialised unit trusts

These trusts invest in specific sectors, such as gold mines, because of their faith in the sector or sectors. The risk and return of these trusts are higher than for general trusts. Individuals who have confidence in a specific sector should choose a trust that invests in that sector.

Income unit trusts

Income unit trusts only invest in fixed-interest-bearing assets such as gilt-edged securities (issued by the government), semi-gilt-edged securities (stocks issued by government institutions and municipalities) and debentures. The safety of the investment amount plus interest is ensured. Individual investors who will invest in these unit trusts are usually those who want a high income (rather than capital growth). These unit trusts are particularly suitable for retired people, as well as for people who want a short-term investment. It is not an investment that beats inflation or that provides capital growth over the long term.

The choice of unit trusts

Just as you would face certain choices when buying a home, you also have certain choices when buying unit trusts. The following steps may be taken:
- choose an industry or business sector;
- decide on the type of trust;
- determine the investment term;
- decide whether to reinvest dividends or not; and
- choose a broker.

Potential investors should be aware of the fact that an investment in a certain type of unit trust does not mean that funds need to be kept in that trust indefinitely. The investment may be switched to another kind of trust at a minimum cost. If financial risks increase, funds may be transferred from a general trust to an income trust. In this way, the investor guarantees that his or her capital investment amount plus interest will be paid back to him or her.

Unit trusts may be bought from a broker as well as an insurance broker or agent. Because of the low commission they receive, insurance agents do not try to sell unit trusts to the public. They prefer marketing insurance, for which they receive sufficient commission. People who already have insurance are advised to buy their unit trusts through their insurance agent. These agents do this as an additional service to their clients. However, unit trusts may be bought from a bank.

A broker has more knowledge than an insurance agent about investments in unit trusts. It can, therefore, be left to the discretion of the stockbroker to buy unit trusts in line with the investor's investment purposes and needs. An insurance agent will certainly not be able to render this service, mainly because his or her attention is focused on insurance products.

Charges involved in purchasing unit trusts
Even an investment in unit trusts involves costs for the investor. There are no charges involved in the selling of the trusts. The following cost-items are distinguished:

- *An initial charge.* When unit trusts are bought, an initial charge of 5% of the purchase amount (investment amount) is levied.
- *A service charge.* Service charges are calculated at 1/16 of 1% of the market value of the investor's portfolio at the end of each month.

7.9.2.5 Property unit trusts (PUTs)
Property unit trusts were originally created to offer investors the opportunity of investing in fixed property.

The following are some of the advantages of an investment in property trusts:

- a small amount of money may be invested (unlike an investment in shares);
- units are bought back relatively quickly if potential investors exist;
- the investment is liquid;
- the investor's risk is spread;
- investment expertise and management are obtained at relatively low charges; and
- the 'handing over' of management and administration problems to the company's management.

Disadvantages of property trusts are the following:
- the income from dividends is fully taxable in the hands of the investor (the holder of units);
- the normal dividend release is not applicable; and
- it is not an attractive investment for individual investors with a high marginal tax rate.

It is recommended that units in property trusts be bought through a stockbroker. Even though the prices of property trusts (units) are published daily, an investment requires knowledge of the market and requires a lot of time. Stockbrokers have a research team at their disposal who supply them with information, which enables them to make professional investment decisions.

For more detail, refer to Section 9 in Chapter 9 on buying fixed property.

7.9.2.6 Property loan stock
For more information, consult Section 9 in Chapter 9.

7.9.2.7 Derivatives: Options
Bernstein (1995:7) defines a derivative as follows: 'A derivative is simply a financial instrument derived from an underlying asset or stock.'

Du Plessis (1997) defines a derivative as 'a contract designed to provide for the future delivery of assets'. He points out that derivatives are used to manage risk, so the risk/return calculation must be done extremely accurately for every financial transaction.

Morris & Siegel (1993:124) point out that derivatives are used mainly for one of two reasons, namely:
- to reduce risk (hedging by hedgers); and
- to trade them (speculating by speculators).

Derivatives have become increasingly important in the financial world, and are actively traded on many exchanges. They are also regularly traded outside exchanges by financial institutions, fund managers and corporations in the 'over-the-counter' market. The prices of derivatives can depend on almost any underlying variable, for example, stock, cattle, shares, rainfall and the movement in oil prices (Hull 2000:1). The ownership of oil stocks is not the issue, but rather a bet on the upward or downward movement in oil prices (or the price of oil stocks).

Diagram 7.3 illustrates the nature of derivatives. You will note that the main group of derivatives, the manner of trading and the underlying assets are indicated.

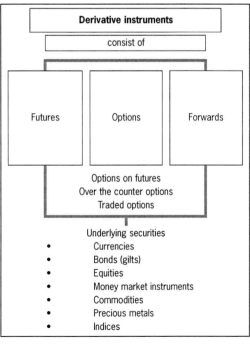

DIAGRAM 7.3 **The nature of derivatives**
(*Source: Du Plessis et al. 1997:313*)

Furthermore Du Plessis *et al.* (1997:328) distinguish between an option, a future and a forward as follows:

- An option is the right to buy or sell a standard amount of a specified asset on a future date at a price agreed to by the parties on drawing up the contract.
- A future is an obligation to buy or sell a standard amount of a specified asset on a future date at a price agreed to by the parties on drawing up the contract.
- A forward is an obligation to buy or sell a specified amount of a specified asset on a future date at a price agreed to by the parties on drawing up the contract.

Note the main difference between a right and an obligation.

In the following discussion on derivatives, we will briefly look at options, futures and some other types of derivatives. Because of the vast scope of this subject, we will only be able to touch on it superficially. Not a great deal is said about forwards in this brief discussion, apart from the following:

- Forward contracts have been known as future contracts for some time.
- According to Alexander (1996:16) a futures contract is: 'merely a standardised, exchange-traded forward contract. The major difference between the two instruments is that a future is a "standardised package" and is traded through an exchange, whereas a forward contract may apply to any quantity of an asset, and with any delivery date.'

Types of option

There are mainly two types of option, namely a call option and a put option. Alexander (1996:52) defines them as follows:

- 'A call option gives the holder (purchaser) the right to buy the underlying asset from the writer at the exercise price.'
- 'A put option gives the holder (purchaser) the right to sell the underlying asset to the writer at the exercise price.'

As you can deduce, there are two parties to the options contract, namely the purchaser and the writer. Options, therefore, give persons (hedgers and speculators) the opportunity to make buy-and-sell decisions on the basis of the state of the market and market trends. The market price of an option will rise or fall according to the performance of the underlying investment on which the option is based.

Call option

Those buying a call option believe that the value of the underlying asset will rise. Let us explain this by using an example. Assume someone believes the value of a building will rise in the next three months. However, the owner of the building believes the exact opposite, namely that the value of the building will decline or remain the same. The potential buyer of the building is prepared to buy a call option at a premium. This gives him or her the right to buy the building within the three-month period at the strike or exercise price.

The owner is prepared to sell such an option at a premium. Example: Increase in value to R550 000:

Profit	= R550 000	Market value	= strike plus premium
	− R520 000	Break even	= R500 000 + R20 000
	= R30 000		= R520 000

By exercising the call option and buying the property, the holder will, therefore, make a profit of R30 000. The purchaser profile can also be called a *long call*, and the writer profile a *short call*. Example: Decrease in value to R480 000:

Loss	= R520 000	Break even	
	− R480 000	Market value	(R500 000 + R20 000)
	= R40 000		

If the building were bought while its value was declining (i.e. the call option is exercised), it would result in a loss of R40 000. By exercising the option and not buying the building at R520 000 (while its market value is only R480 000), only the premium of R20 000 will be lost.

Put option

Assume the owner of a building expects the value of his or her property to decrease within the next three months. He or she may now buy a sell or put option at a premium, which gives him or her the choice of exercising the option (or not) and selling the building at a particular price. However, someone else believes that the price of the building will rise or stay the same in the three-month period. Furthermore, he or she is prepared to write a sell or put option at a premium.

EXAMPLE

Market value declines to R350 000

Strike price	=	R400 000
Minus: premium	=	R20 000
		R380 000
Minus: market value	=	R350 000
Profit	=	R30 000

Profit if the option is exercised (the building is sold at R400 000).

Market value increases to R420 000

The option will not be exercised, and the option holder's loss is equal to the amount of the premium, namely R20 000. Remember that an option is a right owned by the option holder, and not an obligation. The owner of the building will not sell it, because it has not increased in value. The rise in value (R20 000) equals the premium of R20 000.

Option trading occurs on the Securities Exchange, in the over-the-counter (OTC) market as well as the South African Futures Exchange (SAFEX).

Table 7.9 provides a comparison between call options and put options from the viewpoint of both the owner of the options (or owners-in-waiting – 'naked callers') and the writers (sellers) of the options. We may also call them hedgers and speculators.

Morris & Siegel (1993:142) also provide the following proven guidelines in regard to options:

- The greater the difference between the exercise price and the actual price, the cheaper the premium, because there is less chance of the option being exercised.
- The closer the expiration date of an 'out-of-money option' (actual price below strike price for a call and above for a put), the cheaper the price.
- The more time there is until expiration, the larger the premiums, because the chance of reaching the strike price is greater.
- Call and put options move in position. Call options rise in value as the underlying market prices go up. Put options rise in value as market prices go down.

Other types of option

Morris & Siegel (1993:146) distinguish between the following further types of option, which are used as protection for investments or for the purposes of speculation:

- options on stock indexes;
- options on currency;
- options on interest rates;
- trading options; and
- options on future contracts.

Call and put options can be bought and sold on all of these.

7.9.2.8 Derivatives: Futures

As indicated earlier, futures are obligations to buy or sell a specific commodity, share or even a stock index. Alexander (1996:15) defines a futures contract as: 'An agreement to buy or sell a standard quantity and type of commodity/financial asset/national asset on a specified future date at a price predetermined at the time of entering into the contract.'

Futures contracts are available through SAFEX (South African Futures Exchange) and consist mainly of commodity futures or financial futures.

Risk

In the case of futures, you can lose much more than your initial investment. Comparing futures, shares and options, the risk position is as follows:

- *futures*: more than investment;
- *shares*: total investment; and
- *options*: premium.

Underlying assets

Futures contracts are based on underlying assets, such as commodities, equities, gilts and money market instruments. The value of these underlying assets determines the value of the futures contact. Futures contracts include the following: All Share Index, Gold Index, Financial and Industrial Index, Krugerrand, Long Bond (1) and (2) as well as Short-term Interest Rate (Du Plessis *et al.* 1997:345).

Unlike the case with options, futures are obligations to buy or sell at a specified date, no matter the extent of the loss.

In the case of a futures contract, the buyer takes a long position and the seller a short position. The buyer profits if the market moves up and loses if the

TABLE 7.9 **A comparison between call and put options**
(Source: Adapted from Morris & Siegel 1993:141)

	Call	Put
Buy (hedger)	The right to buy the underlying item at the strike price until the expiration date.	The right to sell the underlying item at the strike price until the expiration date.
Sell (speculator)	Selling the right to buy the underlying item from you at the strike price until the expiration date. Known as writing a call.	Selling the right to sell the underlying item to you until the expiration date. Known as writing a put.

market moves down. The seller's position is the exact opposite (Jordan 2000:239).

Bernstein (1995:23) explains the functioning of a futures contract as follows. Assume a farmer produces 10 000 tons of wheat. The production costs are R10 per ton and the end sale price is R12 per ton – a profit of R2 per ton. Harvesting will only occur in two months' time, and there could be any number of disasters that could push the price down to R7 per ton, which would mean a loss of R3 per ton. The answer is to buy a futures contract.

You would buy a futures contract that will guarantee the future delivery of the wheat at a price of R12 per ton. The price of the futures contract will reduce your profit (R2 per ton), but will protect you against a possible loss.

7.10 INVESTMENT APPROACHES

Individual investors who wish to handle their own transactions on the Securities Exchange should be aware of the various investment approaches. Stockbrokers use these approaches through their professional research teams. As will be seen in a later discussion, shares are bought when they are undervalued and sold when they are overvalued.

An undervalued share has a higher value than perceived in the market. An investor will buy this share because he or she believes that it is worth more than the value the owner of the share (shareholder) attaches to it. In turn, the owner believes that the share is worth less than the value the buyer attaches to it and, consequently, wishes to sell.

Buyers, whether private investors or institutions, have their own personal approaches to the buying and selling of listed shares. Numerous factors influence the decisions buyers and sellers make in respect of the share market. There are three principal approaches towards stock exchange analysis and investment decisions: the fundamental, the technical and the modern portfolio theory. Each of these will now be briefly discussed.

7.10.1 The fundamental approach

This approach consists of three main steps:
- a macro-economic analysis, which attempts to determine and explain the state of the economy in general;
- a business sector analysis; and
- an analysis of the individual company.

7.10.1.1 Macro-economic analysis

This approach requires knowledge about numerous economic variables, such as the money supply, interest rates, consumer spending and production. The purpose is to determine turning points in trends, in other words, when trends swing downwards and when upwards. Because of the huge amount of information required, and which has to be collected and processed, this analysis is out of the reach of individual investors (the person in the street). Stockbrokers are in a position to undertake such analysis on an ongoing basis.

7.10.1.2 Business sector analysis

Business sector analysis is largely aimed at determining growth potential within a business sector. This growth potential determines the investment potential of a certain business sector, for example electronics. The analyst, therefore, attempts to identify a business sector that offers profitable investment opportunities. The following factors must be considered during the analysis of a certain business sector:
- historical trends for sale and profits;
- the permanent nature of the business sector;
- the type of product within the business sector;
- competition and competitors;
- labour activities; and
- extent of government interference.

Business sector analysis must be undertaken in conjunction with the current status of the economy as well as future economic trends. On the basis of the investment principles and the preferences of the investor, industrial sectors must be chosen that exhibit rapid growth. These business sectors should perform better than the general economy, especially in times of economic growth.

7.10.1.3 Analysis of the individual company

Just as the business sector with the best growth prospects must be chosen, so individual business enterprises within the sector with the best growth prospects, and thus investment potential, must be sought. A business enterprise's future dividend and capital return must be determined and weighed against the risk involved in the investment in a specific enterprise.

Financial analyses, in particular, are used in this case. A financial analysis establishes a business enterprise's present and future position by analysing its annual financial statements. Possible present and future problems, and the causes thereof, are identified. Various ratios are used for further analysis.

The business enterprise's shares are valued by means of various valuation models, in order to determine the value of the business enterprise from the viewpoint of the individual investor.

7.10.2 The technical approach

With this approach, the historical movements of share prices are analysed. Trends and patterns are investigated, in order to find guidelines on possible trends in share prices in the future. Technical analysts work from the viewpoint that patterns in share prices are recurrent by nature, because they reflect recurrent changes in investment sentiment (emotional actions by buyers and sellers on the market).

Actions by buyers and sellers repeat themselves as soon as similar market conditions prevail. It is merely logical, therefore, according to this approach, that trends in share prices will repeat themselves. These trends repeat themselves not only in terms of the share market as a whole but also as far as individual shares are concerned.

The Dow theory is aimed exclusively at forecasting trends in the share market as a whole. This theory compares the share market with an ocean in which tides (larger trends) cause waves (average trends) and ripples (smaller trends). It is very difficult, and even impossible, to forecast the direction, size and frequency of waves and ripples. A graphic representation of the above-mentioned trends enables you to determine the tide (larger trends) in the share market as a whole.

Analysts who use the technical approach attempt to understand the 'psychology of the market'. They try to determine the emotional trends of thinking (investment sentiment) on the share market. In this way, opportunities and threats can be identified with a view to the selling and/or buying of shares.

This approach can never be used in isolation for investments in the share market. It is not a proven method that provides reliable results. Further, the ability to make forecasts has never been properly proved. However, it is a useful tool.

Examples of technical analysis
There is a wide variety of graphs that may be used for technical analysis, most of which may be generated by computer programs. The following are a few examples of charts used for technical analysis: Moving average; on balance volume (OBV); overbought/oversold (OBI/OS); relative strength index (RSI); Momentum; and relative strength.

Comparison: the fundamental versus the technical approach
The technical approach is more of a guideline for short-term investment. Here we have to do with speculation, where the investor utilises a surplus of supply and demand to his or her own advantage.

The fundamental approach is more suitable for long-term investment. This is the reason why the future growth potential (earning ability) of certain industries and individual business enterprises must be determined.

Individual (small) investors do not have the ability to use the technical approach towards investment in shares. It is possible for individual investors to analyse certain business sectors and business enterprises on a small scale.

The technical approach gives an indication of a possible swing or revolution in share prices. The fundamental approach cannot identify turning points but it can identify under- and/or overvalued shares.

7.10.3 The modern portfolio approach

The previous approaches to investment analysis are also called traditional approaches. The emphasis is mainly on the price of shares and earnings per share. Return on investment is the most important factor. However, it is an error to focus only on return when investing in shares.

The modern approach does not look at return only, but at the combination of risk and return. Risk is the chance of suffering a loss or a variation in anticipated return (for whatever reason). Investors should consider both the risk and the return involved in shares before deciding on investing in a certain business sector, business enterprise or share.

Furthermore, investors should keep the risk of their total portfolio of investment in mind. They should attempt to put together an effective portfolio. An effective portfolio can be described as a selection of a variety of investments that:
- maximise the return for a certain risk level; or
- minimise the risk involved for a specific return.

7.11 COMPUTER PROGRAMS AVAILABLE

Some people do prefer managing their own share portfolios. They prefer not to make use of a broker. Several computer programs are available to such investors to facilitate their task. Although they do not have a research team with expertise at their disposal, they do have motivation (interest in the success of their own portfolio) with which a broker cannot compete.

Computer programs are generally based on the technical approach towards share market analysis. The motive is usually to speculate and not to invest over the long term. Trends have to be assessed on a daily basis in order to judge whether shares should be bought or sold. Although numerous techniques exist that supporters of the technical approach can use, computer programs are generally based on only five or six techniques.

Basic techniques are also included in these programs, which enable investors to keep an eye on their long-term investments as well.

Individual investors who wish to handle their own share investments are advised to complete one of the several courses offered to prepare speculators for share transactions and to equip them with knowledge of the share market as a whole. Courses are offered by several institutions.

7.11.1 Software

Several software programs are available. People who are relatively unfamiliar with the share market could buy a fairly simple package.

Before buying a program, find out whether the supplier also provides historical data. Suppliers of programs provide updated information on a daily basis to buyers. Beginners should also complete a short computer course to make themselves more familiar with the program they choose. There are also advanced courses in computer training for investors.

7.11.2 Hardware

A simple and fairly inexpensive computer can be used for the purposes of share investment. All software can be used on a basic personal computer. As with buying a computer for general use, it is often necessary to progress to a computer with a bigger memory, because of the large amount of information to be stored.

7.12 THE JOHANNESBURG SECURITIES EXCHANGE

The Johannesburg Securities Exchange (formerly the Johannesburg Stock Exchange) is the place where shareholders gather to buy and sell securities (financial assets). The Exchange is regarded as a perfect market because:

- There are many buyers and sellers.
- It has an effective communications system, which enables buyers and sellers to remain in close contact with one another.
- Each individual investor can act at his or her own discretion (there is no collusion between buyers and sellers).

The Exchange itself does not buy and sell securities; that is done by members of the Exchange. The main functions of the Exchange are as follows:

- It provides a place where securities can be marketed.
- It decides who may become members and who may make use of its facilities.
- It establishes rules to be adhered to during transactions.
- It assists with the settlement of disputes about transactions.
- It distributes information on prices and transactions of securities.

The Johannesburg Securities Exchange is a national exchange. A national exchange is one where transactions are restricted to the securities of the country in which the exchange is situated. Fewer securities are traded than on an international market. An international market is one where securities are not restricted to those of a specific country. Securities also include those issued by other countries. The stock exchanges in London and New York are examples of international markets.

A great variety of transactions take place on the Exchange. Two main groups may be distinguished: investment transactions and speculative transactions. The main purpose of investment transactions is not to make speculative profit, but to invest money in securities in order to earn income in the form of dividends or interest on capital.

Speculative transactions are aimed at making capital profit. These transactions have given rise to two types of speculator: the rising price speculator (bull) and the falling price speculator (bear).

The rising price speculator buys shares with a view to selling them at a profit. For example, he or she will buy shares at a price of R1 each in the hope of selling them at a higher price, say R1,25 each.

The falling price speculator sells shares he or she does not own at the time of the sale. For example, he or she will sell shares at R1 each, hoping to buy them at 75 cents before the time of delivery.

Various other markets have established themselves on the Exchange, such as the development capital market, the options market and the futures markets. However, we will not discuss these here.

7.13 VALUATION METHODS

7.13.1 The valuation of ordinary shares

Valuation is the process whereby risk and reward factors are attributed to a share in order to determine its value.

Gitman (1988:266) mentions four methods of determining the value of shares:

- the basic valuation model;

- the book value method;
- the liquidation value method; and
- the price-earnings multiplier.

7.13.1.1 The basic valuation model
The basic valuation model may be used to determine the value of an investment, such as ordinary shares. This model calculates the present value of the sum of all net cash inflow (dividends) anticipated over the investment term. The basic valuation model is as follows:

$$\text{Value (V)} = \frac{\text{Income (I)}}{\text{Cost (C)}}$$

where:

Income = anticipated future dividends
Cost = the discounted rate of return to the investor

The anticipated future dividends of a share are discounted by the investor at a certain rate in order to determine its present value. In this way, the value of an ordinary share is determined. It is not easy to determine anticipated dividends in the case of ordinary shares, mainly for the following reasons:
- There is no certainty that a dividend will be received in a certain year.
- The size (amount) of the anticipated dividend is difficult to determine.
- Circumstances could compel the company to reinvest all retained profit (undistributed dividends).

Since the company is not obligated to repay the capital invested to an ordinary shareholder on a declared future date, only the anticipated future dividends are relevant during valuation. In fact, investors who sell shares relinquish their right to receive future dividends. Conversely, investors in ordinary shares buy in anticipation of future dividends. So it is only right that the present value of these anticipated dividends should determine the value of an ordinary share.

The intrinsic value of ordinary shares may be calculated by means of three models:
- the zero growth model (when no growth is forecast for anticipated dividends);
- the constant growth model (e.g. that dividends will grow annually at a constant rate of 5%); and
- the variable growth model (where the dividend growth rate changes annually).

For the purpose of calculation, it is recommended that you accept that the anticipated future dividends will grow at a constant rate. This makes the calculation easier, and a more realistic present value is

achieved. The basic valuation model is recommended for the valuation of ordinary shares.

7.13.1.2 The book value method
With this method, the value of a share is the value indicated in the financial statements. Because of its historical nature, this value can never be regarded as the actual market value of a share. This method is not recommended for the purposes of valuation.

7.13.1.3 The liquidation value method
The liquidation value of a share is the actual amount each ordinary shareholder will receive:
- if the assets of the company are sold;
- after creditors and preference shareholders have been paid; and
- the remaining money is distributed among the ordinary shareholders.

This method is more realistic for determining market value, but does not take the earning capacity of the company's assets into consideration.

7.13.1.4 The price-earnings multiplier
This method is used to value a share by multiplying the anticipated earnings per share by the average price-earnings ratio of the relevant business sector. Assume that a share has an earning of R2,60 and the price-earnings ratio for the business sector is 7. The value of the share will be 7 times its current earning of R2,60, namely R18,20. This method is preferred above the book value and the liquidation method, because it is based on future earnings. Like the basic valuation model, it is commonly used in practice by investors and brokers.

There are various valuation methods that all aim at identifying under- and overvalued shares. The investor's funds, objectives, knowledge, time and attitude towards risk will largely determine whether he or she wishes to buy shares for the purpose of speculation or as a long-term investment.

7.13.2 The valuation of preference shares

The same calculation (the basic valuation model) is used to determine the present value of a preference share. The calculation is simplified by the following:
- a preference dividend is paid annually, except in the case of cumulative preference shares; and
- this dividend is paid even if ordinary shareholders do not receive any dividends.

The zero growth model is recommended for the valuation of preference shares. The time value of money principle applies here as well, since future income (anticipated dividends) is discounted to a present value.

7.13.3 The valuation of debentures

The value of a debenture is the present value of all annual income (interest) that the investor is entitled to receive from the borrower in terms of the contract. An investor receives a debenture from a company as proof that the company has borrowed funds from him or her. It is indicated on the debenture when (that is, over how many years) the borrowed amount will be repaid to the investor. This borrowed amount is called the face value or issue value of the debenture.

The company pays annual interest to the holders of debentures according to a declared rate, the coupon rate. The investor receives an annual interest income on his or her investment, and at the end of the investment term (the date of maturity of the debenture) he or she receives the original investment amount (face value or issue value).

Debentures, like shares, are negotiable. A buyer will want to buy a debenture in order to obtain the interest income for a number of years (the tenure of the debenture). Before buying, however, the investor will first want to value the debenture, in order to determine what price he or she is prepared to pay. Since both repayment of the loan amount and the interest are guaranteed, both must be discounted over the tenure, in order to determine the present value of the debenture.

The basic valuation model for debentures is as follows:

$$Bo = I(PVIFA_{k,n}) + M(PVIF_{k,n})$$

where Bo = the value of the debenture (market value)

I = the annual interest payment (coupon rate)

PVIFA = the present value interest factor for an annuity

M = the face or issue value of the debenture

PVIF = the present value interest factor for a lump sum

k = the discount rate

Some aspects of the above-mentioned concepts will now be explained.

7.13.3.1 The face value or issue value (par value)

The face value is the value that the borrower promises to pay on the redemption date, and is independent of market value. Market value here refers to the price at which the debenture will be traded. The market value fluctuates constantly because of market factors, whereas the face value remains constant.

7.13.3.2 The coupon rate

The interest amount is expressed as a percentage of the face value (par value). This percentage is called the coupon rate.

7.13.3.3 The rate of return

The rate of return and the coupon rate are often confused. The rate of return is the rate earned on the current market price, and varies as the market fluctuates. If the market price or market value is lower than the face value (par value), the debenture trades at a discount and the rate of return is higher than the coupon rate. If the market value is higher than the face value, the debenture trades at a premium and the rate of return is lower than the coupon rate.

A change in the market price may result in capital profits or capital losses, as well as fluctuations in the interest income and rates of return. If an investor buys a debenture at a low market price, he or she can expect an interest income that is considerably higher than the coupon rate.

A change in market interest rates may lead to considerable capital profits or losses, and may affect the market price of debentures. The influence that market interest rates exercise varies according to the following:

- the redemption term (period to maturity date);
- rates of return; and
- coupon rates.

Investors are advised to pay attention to the following guidelines and the associated strategies in respect of debentures.

Guideline 1
For a given change in interest rate, the price of a debenture with a longer period before maturity date (redemption period) varies more than that of a debenture with a shorter redemption period (Makiel 1962:197–218).

Investment strategy
Mittra & Goosen (1981:191) recommend that a debenture with a long redemption period should be bought when a decline in interest rates is anticipated. If a rise in interest rates is anticipated, a debenture with a short redemption time should be bought.

Guideline 2

As the redemption date becomes longer, the decline in the market price of a debenture becomes progressively less as a result of an increase in interest rates.

Investment strategy

When market interest rates decline, a debenture should be sold as quickly as possible, because the largest price increases occur within a short period. When interest rates rise, debentures should be retained in order to minimise losses.

Guideline 3

The market prices of debentures with lower coupon rates vary to a greater extent when changes take place in market interest rates than do those of debentures with high coupon rates.

Investment strategy

When a rise in market interest rates is anticipated, debentures with a high coupon rate should be bought. When a decline in market interest rates is anticipated, debentures with a low coupon rate should be bought. The important factor is the market price and not the interest that will be received.

Guideline 4

The higher the market interest rates, the greater the change in the market prices of debentures for a specific change in market interest rates.

Investment strategy

Buy debentures when a decline from a high level in market interest rates is anticipated, since this will result in a large increase in the market price.

7.13.4 Risk

Earlier, we said that the valuation process involves the consideration of both risk and return. Until now we have been discussing the anticipated return and the methods used to calculate this return. Our discussion will now focus on determining the risk when evaluating ordinary shares, preference shares and debentures. To begin with, some concepts must be defined.

7.13.4.1 Probability (P) and anticipated return (R)

Probabilities may be used to determine the risk attached to a share. The probability of a particular return is the percentage probability the return has of being realised. For example, if the probability of a return is 80%, it means that return will occur 8 out of 10 times. The weighted average return is the sum of the probabilities that can be allocated to the various anticipated returns.

The anticipated returns of a share may be calculated as follows, by means of probabilities:

TABLE 7.9 **A probability distribution**
(Source: Krüger 1990:52)

P × R	=	P.R
(a) x (b)	=	(c)
0.10 × 76%	=	7.6
0.15 × 63%	=	9.5
0.30 × 46%	=	13.8
0.25 × 32%	=	8.0
0.20 × 16%	=	3.2
0.10 × 3.6%	=	0.3
Anticipated value (R)	=	42.4%

where:
P   =   probability that a certain return will be realised
R   =   the rate of return
P.R =   P × R = (R) = anticipated rate of return

From the probability distribution, it appears that the anticipated return (R) for the share is 42.4%. Returns consist of the dividends anticipated (DIV) and the selling price of the share at the end of the term (PI), expressed as a percentage of the original investment (PO). The anticipated return (R) may be represented as follows:

$$R = PI + DIV \div PO \times 100$$

The anticipated value (R) is calculated by adding together the various possible rates of return.

7.13.4.2 Standard deviation (σ)

The most common criterion for risk is the standard deviation. The larger the share's standard deviation, the greater the risk. The standard deviation measures the average deviation (of all returns – R) of the anticipated return (R). The equation for the calculation of the standard deviation is as follows:

$$\sigma = \sqrt{\sum_{i=1}^{n} [R - (R)]^2 \times P \atop i = t}$$

where:
σ   =   standard deviation
R   =   rate of return
(R) =   anticipated rate of return
P   =   probability linked to a certain return

From the probability distribution the standard deviation may be calculated as follows:

$$\sigma = \sqrt{\sum_{i=1}^{n} [R - (R)]^2 \times P}$$

$$
\begin{aligned}
(76 - 42.4)^2 \times 0.10 &= 112.9 \\
(63 - 42.4)^2 \times 1.15 &= 63.7 \\
(46 - 42.4)^2 \times 0.30 &= 3.88 \\
(32 - 42.4)^2 \times 0.25 &= 27.04 \\
(16 - 42.4)^2 \times 0.20 &= 139.40 \\
(3 - 42.4)^2 \times 0.10 &= 155.24
\end{aligned}
$$

$$
\begin{aligned}
\Sigma &= 502.16 \\
\sigma &= \sqrt{502.16} \\
&= 22.4
\end{aligned}
$$

7.13.4.3 Coefficient of variation (CV)

This criterion of risk is calculated by dividing the standard deviation of the share by the anticipated return. The following formula may be used:

$$CV = \frac{\sigma}{(R)}$$

where:

CV = coefficient of variation
σ = standard deviation
(R) = anticipated return

The larger the coefficient of variation of a share, the greater the risk involved. The coefficient of variation is calculated below:

$$CV = \frac{22.4}{42.4}$$

$$= 0.53$$

7.13.4.4 σ versus CV

The standard deviation is an absolute criterion of risk. Hence, it is used only to calculate the risk involved in a share without taking the anticipated return into account. Conversely, the coefficient of variation is a relative criterion of risk; in other words, it is used to calculate risk relative to the anticipated return. The following illustration serves as an example:

	Share A (our example)	Share B (another example)
(1) Anticipated return	42.4	30
(2) Standard deviation	22.4	20
(3) Coefficient of variation [(2) ÷(1)]	0.53	0.67

Where an investor has to choose the share with the lowest risk, based only on the standard deviation of two shares, he or she will choose Share B (the smaller the standard deviation, the smaller the risk). Where the coefficient of variation is calculated (which takes anticipated return into account), however, the investor will find that Share A holds a smaller risk (smaller coefficient of variation). Share A will now be chosen instead of Share B.

Several shares may be evaluated in this manner, based on their risk-return characteristics. Brokers make use of such calculations, but individual investors do not. It is essential, however, because a share cannot be valued in any other way. The investor should standardise the risk and return of shares he or she values, in order to make meaningful investment decisions.

During a valuation process, the investor should determine the following:

- the anticipated return (dividends or interest);
- the risk attached to the investment; and
- whether the return is sufficient to compensate for the risk.

7.14 BUYING SHARES

Just as it is said, 'marry in haste, repent at leisure', it is necessary to proceed with caution before buying shares. Firstly, you need a large amount of money; secondly, you need a lot of time; thirdly, you need sufficient knowledge of and experience in the global share market. Several factors should be considered before deciding to buy:

- your investment objective;
- the type of business sector;
- the type of business enterprise;
- the type of share;
- the right time to buy;
- the costs involved;
- the composition of your shares portfolio;
- an annual revision of your portfolio; and
- your choice of broker.

7.14.1 The motive for an investment in shares

Individual investors have different motives for buying property, of whatever nature. The following are some of the most important motives for buying shares:

- An investor can sell his or her shares in a fairly short period and convert such investments into cash.
- The value of shares rises at a faster rate than the inflation rate, because the value of the property in which a company invests rises rapidly.
- A regular income may be received in the form of dividends.
- Dividends in the hands of the investor are tax-free at present.
- Investors interested in capital growth can reinvest their dividends, in other words, request that the company retain them to invest in further projects.

7.14.2 The method of investment in shares

Firstly, a potential investor in shares may invest directly or indirectly. A direct investment means buying shares that are traded on the Johannesburg Securities Exchange. An indirect investment implies that unit trusts or property trusts are bought; in other words, the investor invests in the shares of other companies.

Secondly, the individual investor may make this direct or indirect investment in shares him- or herself or may do so through a broker (stockbroker or insurance broker/insurance agent).

We discussed unit trusts earlier in this chapter and will, therefore, concentrate on buying shares (a direct investment in shares) in this discussion. First, we give potential investors who wish to do the buying themselves some pointers, after which we will discuss the broker's role.

7.14.2.1 The investor who handles his or her own buying

Before making a decision to buy, an investor should first consider his or her investment objective. In terms of buying shares, this objective has a dual nature:

- to buy with the objective of investing; or
- to buy with the objective of speculating.

An investment

Where shares are bought in order to keep them, the investment will be a long-term one. The investor buys shares and holds them for a relatively long period, for example ten to 50 years. Capital growth over the long term is the objective.

Speculation

In the case of speculation, shares are bought with the objective of making a profit from them. A speculator invests over the short term and is not interested in capital growth. For example, a share may be bought today and sold in two weeks' time. This period may be shorter or longer. The investor will buy a share if he or she believes it is under-valued and will sell it as soon as he or she believes it is overvalued.

7.14.2.2 Buying and selling through a broker

A broker is a person who possesses specialist knowledge of and experience in certain products or services. He or she usually has a research team, consisting of experts in specific areas, at his or her disposal.

Broker services

Brokers offer a variety of services. Van Rensburg (1989:117) distinguishes the following types of service that brokers offer their clients.

A direct agreement

With a direct agreement, the broker buys or sells shares on the instruction of the client (the investor or potential investor). The agreement between the investor and the broker is verbal; that is, in person or over the telephone. The client informs the broker of the maximum price he or she is prepared to pay, as well as the minimum price at which he or she is prepared to sell the shares concerned.

Once shares have been bought, the purchase sum must be paid within seven days of the purchase date. If such payment is not made within 14 days, the broker will sell these shares within 60 days. If the return on such shares does not cover the original purchase sum, the broker will sell some of the investor's shares to cover the shortfall.

Where shares are bought, the client must deliver the transfer deed to the broker within seven days. The share certificate must also be included in the transfer deed.

Advantages:
- This method is fairly inexpensive in terms of brokerage and tax on marketable securities.

Disadvantages:
- Very little advice is given to the client on buying and selling opportunities.
- Danger signs in the market are not always pointed out to the client.
- All administration (buying, selling, dividends) is left to the client.

- A lot of time is wasted trying to keep up with market activities.
- The broker's research team is not used to the advantage of the client.
- Investors seldom have sufficient expertise (particularly small investors) to make their own buying and selling decisions or to manage their own shares portfolio.

Agreement with broker and bank

The broker acts as an agent between the investor and his or her bank. The bank safeguards all share certificates, as well as transfer deeds. When shares are bought, the bank takes possession of the new share certificates and transfer deeds, and pays the purchase sum to the broker within seven days. When shares are sold, the opposite occurs. Banks also receive the dividends.

Advantages:
- All problems associated with administration are carried over to the bank.

Disadvantages:
- Administration costs charged by the bank increase the total cost (administration costs and brokerage plus tax) borne by the investor.

Managed client agreement

Here, the investor has two choices. Firstly, he or she may give the broker limited discretionary powers. The broker is given possession of the shares portfolio, but cannot make decisions by him- or herself. The expertise of the broker and the broker's research team is not utilised, and the investor makes decisions based on his or her own expertise. In this case, investors should have sufficient time at their disposal.

Secondly, the investor may give the broker full discretionary powers. The broker manages the shares portfolio and makes all the investment decisions in respect of buying and selling shares. The broker employs the investor's money at his or her own discretion. Investors who do not have sufficient expertise and time to manage their own portfolios are advised to choose this option.

Non-discretionary client agreement

In this case, the broker is in possession of the client's money, transfer deeds and share certificates. When shares are bought, they are registered in the name of the broker's nominated company.

Discretionary agreement

The client hands over his or her total portfolio to the broker to manage it. The broker is in full control of the shares portfolio and makes all the buying and selling decisions. The broker regularly sends the client statements and dividends received.

The charge for such a service varies between 1/8 of 1% to 1% of the market value of the portfolio. Further costs include brokerage, tax for trading and a fee for safeguarding the client's documents.

A potential investor must decide what kind of agreement he or she wishes to conclude with a broker. This decision will be based on the client's own expertise, time at his or her disposal for research and transactions, the costs he or she is prepared to incur, as well as his or her willingness to handle the administration.

Choice of broker

Not everybody can be a broker. A broker must be a member of the Johannesburg Securities Exchange. The Exchange requires a broker to have at least three rights to the exchange. Furthermore, a broker must provide the Exchange with certain guarantees, and he or she must have a certain net value (asset value). Brokers are also required to pass an entry examination.

The general investor public is protected against fraudulent and dishonest brokers. The Exchange has established a Guarantee Fund for this purpose, and strict action is taken against those who do not keep to the Exchange's motto 'Bound by my word'.

It is particularly important that client and broker should have the same approach towards risks. Some brokers like buying risky shares and this may not be what the client has in mind. The choice of a broker is no easy task. However, it is a very important decision, since clients place a large amount of money in the hands of their brokers. The decision should, therefore, be made with care.

7.14.3 Costs involved in buying and selling

There are costs involved in buying and selling most investments, and shares are no exception. Both buying and selling shares are associated with certain costs.

7.14.3.1 Costs involved in buying shares
- A basic charge of Rx per transaction is levied.
- Brokerage is based on the purchase sum.
- Marketable securities tax (MST) is payable immediately when shares are sold. This tax is levied at a rate of x% of the purchase sum.

7.14.3.2 Costs involved in selling shares

As with buying shares, there are also basic charges and brokerage when selling shares. However, no tax is payable on marketable securities when shares are sold.

7.14.4 Which shares to buy

Probably the most difficult decision investors are faced with is what kind of shares to buy. Often the investor public is inspired by the growth performance of certain shares offered by some company or another. These shares are bought because investor sentiment perceives them as being the 'right' shares.

De Lange (1991:14) gives the following tips on what to do to determine which shares are the best to buy:

- Examine the company's growth performance over the past five years (the growth rate, particularly the dividend growth rate, must exceed the inflation rate).
- The company management must be leaders in the market who set the pace for new developments (innovations).
- Those who seek winning shares (for example, the 100 top shares) must accept that this process requires hard work and is very time-consuming.
- Investors should attempt to buy shares that will limit possible losses by means of effective portfolio management.

7.14.5 The right time

Once an investor has decided which shares to buy, he or she must choose the right time to buy them. Those who are interested in investing over the long term should buy as quickly as possible. Even if they have to pay a higher price initially, the average price will fall if they buy on a regular basis (the average costs are lower).

Speculators, on the other hand, should buy shares on which they can make a profit when they sell them. The secret of successful speculation is to buy shares at the right time and to sell them at the right time. Timing is of much greater importance when investing in the short term.

7.14.6 Setting up a shares portfolio

When setting up a shares portfolio, the same investment criteria apply as discussed earlier. A shares portfolio refers to all the shares an investor owns. Probably the most difficult decision is the balance between a growing return, on the one hand, and an acceptable risk level, on the other hand.

Laurie (1989:40) mentions the success achieved by an investment portfolio that is published annually in the British newspaper, *The Investor's Chronicle*. He suggests the following type of investment portfolio, based on their rules:

- Choose shares on the basis of dividend growth rather than short-term capital appreciation.
- Choose a minimum of ten shares, in order to spread the risk.
- The amount invested in each of the ten shares should be more or less equal.
- The portfolio should remain unchanged for at least one year.
- From the second year, the portfolio should be revised annually.
- A minimum of transactions should take place.
- Profit should only be taken if the market value of a share is at least 50% higher than the average market value of the portfolio.
- Shares should only be sold in emergencies.
- Dividends and interest should be reinvested, preferably in shares already included in the portfolio.
- The primary purpose of the portfolio should be never to sell a share if at all possible.
- During reinvestment, the share in the portfolio with the best prospects for long-term dividend growth should be chosen.

De Lange (1991:38) lists two additional factors that should be kept in mind when composing a portfolio:

- Access all investments and anticipated results over the long term.
- Build up your own expertise in order to manage your shares portfolio.

7.14.7 Do's and don'ts

There is no blueprint on buying and selling shares. Nevertheless, certain guidelines, based on years of experience, can be valuable when investing in shares, whether over the long or the short term. The share market offers investment opportunities for all. There are also many pitfalls, especially for potential or inexperienced investors.

The following is a list of do's and don'ts in respect of investment in shares:

- Do not expect to become wealthy overnight.
- Do not try to manage your own shares portfolio if you are a novice.
- Do not attempt to manage your own shares portfolio if you do not have sufficient time.
- Do not try to speculate if you do not have a computer (with a suitable program).
- Do not try to speculate if you do not receive up-to-date, daily information about the closing prices of shares.
- Do not buy shares blindly (without the necessary research).

- Do not borrow money to buy shares.
- Do not buy shares just because everybody (the investment public) is doing it.
- Do not sell shares because others are selling.
- Do not participate in panic selling – this is usually what inexperienced investors do.
- Do not become attached to a certain share.
- Do not try to 'play' broker.
- Do not overreact on the basis of so-called hot tips.
- Do analyse a company's financial status before buying its shares.
- Do study your shares carefully.
- Do evaluate shares on the basis of their current performance, as well as their future potential.
- Do invest in the 'stronger' companies in growth sectors.
- Do try to buy only quality shares.
- Do keep abreast of economic and political events.
- Do obtain your information from several sources (not only newspapers).
- Do remain on a good footing with other brokers.
- Do work hard and spend enough time on research.
- Do obtain information and knowledge from professional investors.
- Do revise your portfolio and be meticulous with your administrative tasks.

7.15 SHARE PRICES IN NEWSPAPERS

Newspapers are a source of a great deal of information on share prices. Because abbreviations are used, which uninformed readers may not understand, they are briefly discussed below.

High	1.30
Low	1.20
Share	De Beers
Last sale	1.25
Buy	1.22
Sell	1.28
Div %	20%
Dividend return	15.3
Price/Dist Incr	6.3
Rise/Fall	+3
Vol	300

- *High*: The highest share price for the year. This price can be compared with other prices (the same share) in order to determine abnormal rising and falling.
- *Low*: The lowest share price for the year.
- *Last sale*: The last sale price paid for a share the previous day (R1,25).

- *Buy*: The last offer made the previous day by buyers for a De Beers share, namely R1,22.
- *Sell*: The last price charged by a seller the previous day, namely R1,28.
- *Div%*: The dividend which shareholders were paid as a percentage of the nominal share value. For example, a company has 10 000 000 shares at a nominal value of R1 each. The dividend per share is 20c and the dividend percentage is 20% (20/100 × 100). High dividends are usually preferred.
- *Dividend return*: The dividend return on the actual price the investor pays (not the nominal value). Assume that the purchase price is R2 per share, and the dividend remains 20c per share. The dividend return will be 10% (20/200 × 100).
- *Price-earning ratio*: If the dividend return amounts to 20c and the share price is R1,20, it means that the share is sold at 6 times its earnings. The ratio is 6.
- *Rise/Fall*: Here, it is shown whether the last selling price is higher or lower than the last selling price of the previous day.
- *Vol*: This shows the number of shares sold weekly or monthly.

The abbreviations in the *Business Report* will differ slightly from the above. However, investors get a good idea of what is happening with certain shares and transactions. Where a novice has difficulty understanding the tables in newspapers, professional investors and brokers have no problems.

7.16 THE ECONOMIC INDICATORS ON TELEVISION

Economic indicators that appear on television every day have certain implications for investors in financial assets. The most important indicators are briefly discussed below.

7.16.1 The gold price

The gold price is indicated in American dollars and reflects the price of gold as at the afternoon fix in London. A rise in the gold price results in a rise in government revenue as well as that of the gold mines. More money is consequently available for the economy. A fall in the gold price has the opposite result. The gold price affects the economic trend of a country.

7.16.2 The rand/dollar exchange rate (R/$ exchange rate)

This exchange rate indicates how many rands are needed to buy one dollar. Trade with foreign countries occurs in dollars and this rate is extremely important to businesspeople.

7.16.3 The dollar/euro exchange rate ($/´ exchange rate)

This exchange rate is of great importance to those who trade with Western Europe. Some prices are indicated in euros, so they must first be converted to dollars.

7.16.4 The bank acceptance rate (BA rate)

Earlier, we referred to bank acceptances as money market instruments and discussed them briefly. The bank acceptance rate is a good indicator (forecaster) of short-term interest rates. When this rate drops and the trend continues, a drop in short-term rates can be expected. The opposite is also true.

7.16.5 Capital market rates

This concept was explained earlier. A rise in capital market rates is an indicator (forecaster) of a rise in interest rates over the long term. A drop in these rates forecasts a drop in long-term interest rates.

7.16.6 The gold index

The gold index is calculated by adding the market price (value) of a number of selected gold shares together and determining the average value/price of the shares. This average value is called the gold index. If the gold index rises continually, it means that the value of gold shares rises in general. It may well happen that the prices of individual gold shares may drop. When the gold index drops, the opposite is true.

7.16.7 The industrial index

The industrial index is calculated in the same way as the gold index. Instead of gold shares, specific industrial shares are selected. The industrial sector is relevant here.

7.16.8 The consumer price index

We have already discussed this concept. The consumer price index is called the inflation rate and gives an indication of the annual rise in consumer prices.

7.17 SEVERANCE OR RETIREMENT PACKAGES: HOW TO INVEST?

The decision to invest the proceeds of a package involves a great many decisions and much homework regarding all aspects of personal finance. Experts need to be consulted about the investment of you package.

This section should be studied together with Chapter 14 on retirement planning.

7.17.1 What is the meaning of the word 'package'?

The concept of a 'package' is not new in the new South Africa. In fact, the only question is when we will be offered a package and how it will compensate us for the loss of years of service and retirement benefits. Nowadays South Africans who decide to take packages (and there are many) are confronted with a large number of difficult decisions. Unfortunately they get very little assistance, if any, in the form of timely financial advice (Swart 1999:5).

People may be offered packages because of:
- the dissolution of the employer's pension or provident fund;
- voluntary breach of service (resignation) by an employee;
- compulsory breach of service (dismissal);
- staff retrenchments by an employer; or
- retirement.

A package may be in the form of a severance package or a retirement package. Remember that any large lump sum should be invested in the same way as a package. The same investment principles, investment criteria and investment alternatives will be valid and should be applied when investing lump sums such as:
- policies that are sold;
- a policy that matures;
- the one-third lump sum of an annuity;
- inheritances;

Your possessions are the sum total of your life and energy.

- group benefits received on the death of a spouse;
- money received when a couple divorce;
- any investment that has to be reinvested; and
- when fixed or moveable property is converted into cash.

How important is your package?

The capital amount of your package may be the sum total of your life at that moment – good or bad; in other words, a small or a large amount (Swart 1999:6). This is what you own and you have to make decisions that will affect the rest of your life.

Your investment decision (the utilisation of your package) is of vital importance because it will largely determine:

- what the next few years of your life will be like; and
- what the rest of your life will be like.

This decision is much more important than you could ever have imagined, in particular when you are an older person. A wrong decision or investment could mean that you will outlive your financial resources in your retirement years. Your retirement should not become a race between inflation and death (a race that is won by inflation in the lives of 94% of retired people). Inflation can devour your investments long before you die. You have to make a decision about your life; rather give back the application form unsigned than sign it while you are uncertain about the action you should take.

When a relatively young person receives a package, the investment decision means more than a decision about a career or an own business. Those who are 55 years and older will decide how to invest their packages with a view to retirement. Therefore, retirement planning is more important for older people than for those who still have to build a career. During their career years people are also planning for retirement, even when they have established or bought their own businesses. Also keep in mind that your package represents your existing provision for retirement.

This does not mean that you should not use money from your package to pay for that long-awaited overseas trip or new car; it depends on whether you can afford it at this stage. Remember, however, that the package is intended to make provision for your retirement and that this long-term objective must be pursued at all times. Unless you have sufficient money for retirement, your package should not be used in any other way. Someone who is still relatively young can begin to make provision for retirement from scratch, but the closer you are to retirement, the less your chances of doing this. You may not even have the chance. Be

extra careful with your package in this situation; preserve its capital value for as long as possible.

Should I take my retirement package?

People often have a choice of whether to take their packages or not. It is difficult to provide simple guidelines for everybody, but a few facts will enable you to make a better-informed decision.

Should everybody take the package immediately?

The answer is an emphatic 'no!'. The financial situations of individuals differ to a large extent, so almost all of their personal financial decisions will differ too, even when it is the same type of decision. Do not allow people to confuse you. Those who do not see a future in the country will want to take the package and utilise it as they think best. Their decisions are usually politically or emotionally motivated, and have nothing to do with those who are not considering leaving the country. Many South Africans will have much less of a future in a foreign country, and have no choice but to make the best possible use of their possessions in South Africa.

Should I take my package five years before retirement?

If you want to establish your own business and intend to use a large part of the package for this purpose, you may feel that the business will generate more retirement benefits than the fund (if everything goes well). You may then leave the money in the fund or appoint a broker to manage the package on your behalf. Is it wise, however, to withdraw money from the fund in the last five years before retirement? Remember that the amount in the fund will more than double over the final five years, mainly because of the effect of compound interest.

Let us look at the example of two employees who invest R100 per month from the age of 40 until retirement. The annual growth rate is 15%. One of the employees retires at 60 while the other retires at 65.

The term, amount, interest rate and end value are:

A: 20 years R100 per month 15% R149 723,95
B: 25 years R100 per month 15% R324 563,96

B will, therefore, mainly because of compound interest, receive more than twice the amount that A does, because B is prepared to work five years longer.

As a further example, a person who takes a package three years before retirement will lose, amongst others, the following benefits:

- three years' salary;
- three years' growth in his or her present fund;
- three years' contributions by the employer;
- possible promotion over three years;
- salary adjustments; and
- accumulated leave pay-outs.

How will the new legislation affect me?

The amended legislation will affect whether you take a package or not. It is expected that the amount of R120 000 in the tax-free lump sum calculation will be lowered to R50 000. It is also expected that higher tax will be levied on the lump sum, and this makes estimates and calculations even more difficult. These aspects should be weighed against what you may lose in the years until retirement (as mentioned above) as well as the capital growth of your investments if you do not take the package.

And the return in the fund?

In South Africa, investment funds are usually placed with pension and provident funds, insurance companies and deposit-taking financial institutions (banks and building societies). There will be more and more pressure on these institutions to provide for the never-ending needs of the new South Africa and its reconstruction programmes. It is only logical to assume that when the funds are utilised elsewhere, their eventual yield will be considerably lower. Only time will tell precisely when this is going to happen. The illustrative yields of earlier policies were 12% and 15% – at the moment, they are only 6% and 12%. In future they will drop even further. The same will happen to the yields of other funds. Therefore risky investments with a high capital growth (30% to 60%) have to be seriously considered (depending on your age).

What about future packages?

Funds will probably not be able to offer packages much longer, mainly because the level of funding will eventually become too low. This is one of the main reasons that fund members wish to lay their hands on their money while the money is still available and there is still money in the funds. To decide whether to take a package is, therefore, no easy task, and there are no answers that are absolutely correct or completely wrong.

Where should I invest my package?

It is just as important to know what to do with a package as it is to decide whether to take a package. The personal situation or objectives of the individual or fund member will be crucial in both cases. Different investment instruments will have different tax implications. The Receiver of Revenue expects people to use their packages to make provision for retirement. The package should be deposited in the retirement fund or your new employer or in an annuity or preservation fund, otherwise you will be penalised by having to pay tax. Whether you start working for a new employer, or want to start your own business or choose to retire, will determine, to a large extent, how the package should be utilised.

7.17.2 Personal financial planning models in South Africa: Research recommendations

Most people who have a lump sum or a package to invest or apply have no idea of what to do with it. They are under the misapprehension that an investment in a particular product will provide the solution for their financial future. They consult a broker or brokers, who are expected to sell them a product, or a package product, of some sort. Unfortunately, this investment has to be integrated with a personal financial plan that is uniquely adapted for the individual concerned. The problem is made worse by the fact that brokers do not always know what personal financial planning is and how it should be done. Moreover, there are hardly any proposals and programmes on offer from brokers that are designed to take care of the personal financial planning of individuals and potential investors. Brokers confuse personal financial planning with making an investment.

What happens when packages are offered?

Confusion and uncertainty are rife among individuals about their financial future when they receive an offer of a package. At this stage, the employer is blamed for a lifetime's lack of personal financial planning. What choice do people have by then? After all, they left school so long ago that they can hardly blame the principal, the teachers and the minister of education for the fact that the most important life skill of all (handling your own money – personal financial management) was not taught at school. They also do not blame tertiary institutions for the fact that personal financial management is not made compulsory for all studies undertaken after completing school. Of course, employers should be blamed for not helping their employees to acquire this indispensable life skill.

What happens when packages have to be invested?

There is even greater confusion and uncertainty than before. As many brokers as possible have to be consulted as quickly as possible to obtain as many investment proposals as possible; but then, the investors have no idea as to which proposal they should accept, because they cannot evaluate the proposals they have solicited. In addition, of course, they still do not know what is actually meant by financial planning. Some investors remain unwilling to put any real effort into deciding how to use or invest their package. Many investors like to invest with a group of investors, because it makes them feel safer. They do not want to be the only one to lose a part of their package or 'everything'. Brokers' knowledge, proposals and past investment records are bandied about and criticised by investors, and even by some brokers. Among those who bay most loudly for the blood of an innocent broker, and are the keenest to tarnish his or her reputation, are those who have suffered losses by their own doing (e.g. by selling off shares when the market was low, thus turning a loss on paper into a real financial loss).

Another mistake made by investors is to compare the long-term record for service of one broker with that of an independent group of brokers, even if the single broker represents a financial institution that is a thousand times larger than the independent group. What bothers investors who have thrown in their lot with such a single broker is that this individual could die, and the reason for this concern is that they fail to realise the strength of the large institution. Moreover, these prospective investors like to keep an expert on hand who can serve as a rubber stamp of approval when they have received a few investment proposals.

Very few investors (if any at all) decide to include the finances and financial situation of their spouses in their package investment proposals. Consequently, the package is invested without taking account of the financial needs and future of the spouse, or of how the finances of the couple will react individually, or will interact, under the influence of the financial strategy adopted. This is not personal financial planning.

Many people who receive packages are already 55 years of age and older, and have to take vital decisions about their financial future (i.e. invest their life savings, which account for their total financial accomplishment over their entire lifetime) at this 'late' stage of their lives, without the knowledge required to do so. Information received in good time about personal financial planning and the investment of a package could make a big difference in these cases. This lack of information received at the right time is the reason why a package investment is merely seen as an investment, and not as part of the whole personal financial planning process.

People who receive a relatively small package still have to deal with the realities of income, capital and a particular lifestyle after retirement. Some people whose packages amount to as little as R200 000 still want to travel overseas, although they do not have a spouse who can help them cope with the costs of subsistence later.

Many package recipients can only say that they started with nothing 15 or 30 years ago and that, regardless of the fact that they were employed over that entire period, they still have most of it left. This is a rather paltry achievement, compared to what it should be in order to offer the individual the financial security he or she needs.

Then there are those who are disinclined to take much trouble over the investment of their packages. They have been indolent all their lives and intend to go on like that regardless of their abysmal ignorance about money matters. They are reluctant to disclose additional personal information to brokers and obstinately refuse to fill in forms that provide such information, with the result that brokers cannot factor the required information into their usually limited models (you will see below why these models are regarded as limited or deficient).

Potential investors are always ready to give credence to a 'story', for example a rumour that someone has lost money placed with financial institution X, insurance company Y or broker Z. Of course, money has been lost in every conceivable place with every broker, but that is not necessarily the fault of the place or the broker. Often, it is a matter of the economic cycle, interest rates, the stock exchange and especially the investor's own fault. Uninformed investors are easily panicked into calling up their investments when rates of return decline. This is usually a mistake, but investors are reluctant to accept responsibility for their own actions. Instead, they look for someone or something else to blame.

Many investors are stubborn and it is only too clear why their financial situation is so unfortunate – they have stubbornly resisted expert advice throughout their lives.

Package investors are apparently irresistibly attracted to brokers whose business cards have been given to them by someone in the organisation they work for who:

- slanders other brokers;
- cites fictitious examples of invested amounts that have been lost; and
- reserves praise exclusively for the broker whose business card he or she gives out (naturally at a shared

commission), citing exorbitant rates of return without pointing out the higher attendant risk.

Investors are also inclined to allow themselves to be led by what their colleagues do with their money. If you can learn from what your colleagues do, certainly, but other people's actions have no intrinsic bearing on what you do with your own individual or household planning. Colleagues are accompanied to as many presentations as possible, because the refreshments served after the presentation are attractive and we all feel so rich and important together.

An investment proposal that lacks substance is often compared to a thick, glossy brochure, and inferences are drawn from it concerning:
- the quality of service that will be received;
- the rates of return that will be realised;
- the size of the organisation concerned; and
- the organisation's affectionate concern for the potential investor.

Remember, brokers do not want their proposals or detailed planning to become known to other brokers. Every broker believes that secrets will be given away if this is done. Consequently, some brokers first make an insubstantial proposal that is followed at a later stage, when they believe that the investment will actually materialise, by voluminous glamorously detailed planning documentation. Do not be seduced into blind acceptance of an extensively detailed proposal that often merely provides additional information about different types of investment.

In some instances a particular investment proposal is accepted immediately, 'because, you see, we are leaving for the seaside at four this afternoon on our annual vacation'. There we will sit and have 'investor's blues' about what we should have done with our package. We do not have the time to sit and agonise over the issue here and now.

A negative factor that stands in the way of sound planning is the fact that brokers are played off against each other in a sort of bidding war to save on commission. Well and good, but do not take it so far that after the broker has wasted three weeks on you, he or she effectively has to pay you to invest your package. Similarly, commission is paid to any other broker in preference to a colleague's husband or wife, regardless of the relevant spouse's professional expertise and qualifications. Yes, brokers who are the spouses of colleagues are summarily slandered and brought into ill repute, in order to prevent the colleague's household from being enriched. Of course, it stands to reason that disclosure of confidential information may play a small role here.

The benighted notion still exists that an insurance broker is a hack, compared to other independent brokers. Remember, insurance brokers can also be independent and can market any product. A lack of information is always dangerous, regardless of whether personal financial planning, investments, off-shore investments or package investments are at issue.

Mistakes in investment proposals

Investment proposals are exactly what the name indicates, namely a proposal to invest your package in one or several products. Some proposals 'touch' on financial planning by referring to it somewhere along the line, while others indicate the cash flow of the individual (package recipient) over a period of, say, ten to 20 years. Proposals are still aimed at the sale of products and do not take account of the following aspects of the individual's financial position:
- the influence of the package on the spouse's financial situation as regards income, taxation, standard of living, early retirement, deferred retirement and estate planning;
- interaction between the above factors;
- cash flow projections for the financial future of both spouses;
- linking the investment to trusts; and
- the introduction of annuities that may fall away in the future, and the resultant influence on the individual's tax position.

In other words, most models are not concerned with the investor's personal financial planning, but are merely aimed at marketing products for commission. This is why it should be stressed that personal financial planning must be separated from the exclusive marketing of products (up to a point); thereafter, products can be marketed with a view to the individual investor's personal needs and aims, risks and risk profile.

What is personal financial planning?

Investment planning is an aspect of, and not synonymous with, personal financial planning.

After studying several hundred investment proposals, the conclusion is that there is one model that can accommodate total personal financial planning for the individual (Swart 1999). The most important considerations about the model are that it:
- follows all the steps in the personal financial planning process (as defined in the theory and in academic books);
- is budget driven;
- recognises the importance of cash flow as a prerequisite for a financial future and financial independence after retirement;

- integrates investment, estate, tax and retirement planning in the process of personal financial planning;
- indicates exactly how future cash flow shortages will be financed, and also how future surpluses will be invested or applied;
- furnishes the client with an event or activity report, and thereby assists the client with his or her personal financial planning at every step;
- does what many other 'models' (i.e. investment proposals) aimed at the sale of specific financial products, fail to do;
- indicates exactly when retirement should be brought forward, take place or be deferred;
- integrates the personal financial planning of spouses and indicates how the finances of spouses interact with each other;
- gives the good as well as the bad news concerning future cash flow patterns and needs;
- informs clients of possible courses of action in the case of inadequate, adequate or more than adequate provision for retirement;
- is not product driven, but is planning driven and based on the client's needs and objectives;
- deals with total/comprehensive personal financial planning;
- does not take it as given that a further investment is the solution to the client's needs;
- actively involves the client in the provision of personal information by asking him or her for an average of ten to 13 pages of information;
- requires repeated interaction with the client;
- makes personal financial planning understandable to the client;
- will prove very useful to financial institutions and the insurance industry;
- will help individuals to develop a realistic vision of the future and to take appropriate financial precautions in an early state;
- can help prevent retirement blues;
- points out possible compromises that individuals/clients may have to make, in order to maintain a particular standard of living after retirement;
- gives the client a realistic projection of how short-, medium- and long-term goals can be achieved;
- combines the personal financial planning of two spouses with up to three trusts; and
- provides objective advice, before selling any financial products.

Without the necessary cash flow projections, personal financial planning remains a pipe-dream. A budget is, in fact, the individual's plan expressed in financial terms. (For more information, see Swart 1999.)

7.18 THE ECONOMIC CYCLE – YOUR INVESTMENT CYCLE

7.18.1 Industries and the economic cycle

The state of the South African economy has a direct influence on the return you get on your investment. We are thinking in particular of the specific investment instrument in which you invest your money (e.g. property, shares or government stocks). Your investment decision may vary considerably depending on the specific phase (upswing, downswing or recession) of the economic cycle (business cycle). A professional broker should be able to advise you when you have to decide how to invest your funds. Selecting the right time to invest is of paramount importance.

For example, if you know that the price of unit trusts has just begun to decline and that this decline is expected to continue for a few years, it would be foolish to invest all your money in unit trusts at that stage. The right time is even more important if you want to speculate with your money, in other words when you want to buy shares and sell them at a profit. For people who are investing in shares over the long term, the state of the economy is also important. Certain shares are very sensitive to the state of the economy while others are scarcely influenced at all.

You should know how a specific industry is related to the state of the economy (the economic cycle). Certain industries move with the economy while others move in the opposite direction.

Let us look at a few industries, namely growth industries, defensive industries, cyclical industries, interest-rate-sensitive industries and rand-hedging industries (Swart 1999:136,137).

Growth industries
An investment in a growth industry, such as computers, the financial sector and electronics will usually perform well, irrespective of the state of the economy. It is important to determine which industries will grow in future.

Defensive industries
The economic cycle has very little effect (almost none) on defensive industries. People eat, drink and use financial services even in a recession. An investment in the food, beverage and financial services industries will, therefore, always offer a relatively good return, irrespective of the economic cycle.

Cyclical industries
The economic cycle has the biggest influence on cyclical industries, which include durable goods

such as cars and furniture. For example, in a recession, people will be satisfied with their old cars and old furniture and will not attempt to replace them. You would be well advised to find out more about the state of the economy before you invest in a cyclical industry.

Interest-rate-sensitive industries

These industries are largely affected by expectations of rising or declining interest rates. Examples are the building industry, the property industry and the financial sector (banks).

Rand-hedging industries

You may also invest in an industry to protect your investment against the depreciation in the value of the rand (rand hedging). Income is usually received in a foreign currency such as dollars or pounds. The costs, however, are paid in rands. Shares such as Richemont and Minorco are good examples.

7.18.2 What does the economic cycle look like?

In simple terms, the cycle consists of an economic recovery phase, an upswing, a downswing and then a recession.

7.18.3 How do I invest during the economic cycle?

The returns you are going to earn on your investment will be determined mainly by the decision, during a specific cycle, to buy (to invest) or sell (to withdraw and reinvest money).

- *Economic recovery*. In a phase of economic recovery, short-term interest rates are at a low. You should now invest particularly in commodities (metals and minerals), because of increased demand during the next economic phase, the upswing.
- *Economic upswing*. In this phase, investors usually sell government securities, shares and property. Short-term interest rates rise, the inflation rate begins to rise too and company profits decrease. During an economic upswing, new businesses are established and more people are employed.
- *Economic downswing*. In this phase, commodities are sold because of an expected drop in demand. Short-term interest rates are very high and government securities are bought, because a drop in short-term interest rates and a recession are expected.
- *Recession*. A recession causes negative economic growth. Short-term interest rates drop and investors mostly buy shares and property.

The primary problems

First, you should know the state of the economy; in other words, the current state and which stage in the economic cycle is expected to follow. Then, you should know the different types of industry (remember, there are five) and how they react to a specific stage in the economic cycle.

If you invest in fixed property as a speculator, the cycle will be of the utmost importance, even more important than the location of the property. The timing of your investment is, therefore, more important than where you invest. Make sure that you invest in the right place at the right time, especially if you want to speculate. It takes the property cycle about 17 years to move from a low to a high. The return on your investment will be best if you can buy when the cycle is at a low and sell when it is at a high (after about 17 years). The term of a bond is usually 20 years. This is particularly relevant if you have to borrow money (take out a bond) and rent out the property. If you buy when the property cycle is at a low, you will have the best protection against rising interest rates.

Of course, you should know your individual risk profile and the stage you have reached in your life cycle, in other words your investment profile. Let us look briefly again at investment decisions in the various life stages (see Section 7.7): youth, family years, career years, years before retirement and years after retirement.

- *Youth (20–30)*. At this stage, you have to learn financial discipline. Any funds you receive in these years should be invested for capital growth. Risky investments are recommended because of your age and the number of years before retirement. Invest in property (your own home), unit trusts and shares.
- *The family years (30–40)*. You should still invest for capital growth with a view to your children's future financial needs (as well as your own).
- *The career years (40–50)*. The children leave home and you will probably have more money of your own to invest for retirement. Investments for capital growth are still recommended. If you are temporarily or permanently unemployed, you should also invest for a monthly income.
- *The years before retirement (50–55)*. Investments for capital growth should now be less risky. Increase your annuities and diversify your investment (spread your investment risk – never put all your eggs in one basket).
- *The years of retirement and afterwards (55 and older)*. Avoid risky investments but concentrate

on capital growth if your income needs permit it. Pay off your debts and manage your credit. Protect your investments (your provision for retirement) against inflation.

It is, therefore, very important to be well informed about:
- the economic cycle;
- investments in various products in various industries;
- how different industries react in different economic cycles;
- the stage of your life cycle; and
- timing when you are making an investment decision.

If you think that the rand will continue to drop for many years to come, you should invest in products and industries that will protect the value of_your rand. To repeat – first think of your needs, risks and objectives.

7.19 INVESTOR PROTECTION

For many years, investors have deserved some form of protection when it comes to financial matters, especially when they have large funds and investments that were made years ago (usually with a view to retirement). Many people and institutions have campaigned for this protection, and the first positive signs are now visible on the investment horizon.

A new insurance industry
The days when the insurance industry was characterised by policy hawkers are over. A new industry has developed that may be forced by law to offer not only information but also protection to the public. After all, you as a consumer (investor) deserve to be protected against making uninformed decisions.

Let us look at some positive aspects of the industry.

Consumer information
Since 1 April 1997, insurers have been providing the estimated value of the policy at the end of each period of five years. This enables the consumer to see that the initial return is low but that it increases during the term of the policy. The status of the broker is also made known to the consumer by the LOA (Life Offices Association).

The insurance company also supplies the name of the representative of the company, with whom complaints may be lodged, and the address of the ombudsman (protector) of the industry. In this way,

the company takes responsibility for brokers' actions (advice).

Consumer protection
Since 1 June 1997 consumers have a cooling-off period of 21 days after taking out a policy. In this period, the new policyholder may cancel the policy if it seems to be the wrong product, or if the broker pressurised him or her to take out the policy.

If a policy is cancelled, all the premiums that have been paid will be paid back to the policyholder, who will not lose anything.

The industry is trying to be more transparent.

New philosophy
When selling insurance, the industry's objective is to offer value-adding solutions to consumers. Full financial planning, services and particularly products are now aimed at establishing a positive long-term relationship with consumers.

New protection
Comprehensive protection measures has been introduced whereby investment services will be improved and regulated to protect investors. The 'Masterbond' and 'Supreme' scandals should never be allowed to happen again. The new legislation puts special emphasis on making public all the relevant facts concerning the investment as well as the investor. For example:
- Investors should be able to make an informed decision about the nature of the product, the contract, the expected returns and risks, and the investment criteria.
- They should receive all the information they require.
- The legislation should apply to the whole industry and should be enforced by legal sanctions.

The Financial Planning Institute
In 1996 ILPA (The Institute For Life and Pension Advisers), currently the Financial Planning Institute (FPI), compiled a code of conduct for its members in its Generally Accepted Planning Practice (GAPP). The code has practical guidelines to help intermediaries (brokers or marketers) perform their tasks. GAPP stipulates that members must always act professionally and maintain a relationship of trust with their clients (investors), avoid conflict of interests and make the relevant facts known. Nothing should be kept secret. All investors enjoy this protection when they do business (place investments) with brokers who have an ILPA (FPI) qualification.

Brokers and protection

To protect clients (the investing public), the Financial Services Board has laid down guidelines to which brokers must adhere. You must know what they are, so that you will know which brokers may market which products to you, and what information you must be given.

These guidelines are constantly being adapted and improved to provide better protection for clients in their dealings with brokers.

One can but hope that the investing public will not only have rights, but will show certain responsibilities towards brokers. This will create a sounder investment environment for the adviser/broker and the client, based not only on the rights of the parties, but also on certain responsibilities. Furthermore, the public needs to be educated in regard to financial life skills, and be prepared to take responsibility for their personal finances and financial future themselves.

Sections 44 to 65 of the Long-term Insurance Act 52 of 1998 stipulate many guidelines that protect policyholders. The guidelines urge advisors and brokers very strongly to offer clients a professional service.

The Policyholder Protection Rules (PPR), issued under the Long-term Insurance Act became effective on 1 July 2001. These Rules apply to all intermediaries (advisors and brokers) as well as to insurers, and only apply to the insurance business. The Rules demand transparency, which, in turn, promotes understanding and trust. This is an ideal foundation to build long-term and profitable relationships with your clients.

The Rules place certain obligations on intermediaries during the sales process, and prescribe the following:

The contact stage – before business is discussed with the client

1. The Statutory Notice for Policyholders, without changes, must be handed to the client. This is a bill of clients' rights, in terms whereof a client has the right to the following information:
   - the right to know who the intermediary is;
   - the right to be informed of the impact the decision to take out life assurance will have on him or her;
   - the right to be informed of the implications (e.g. costs) if a policy is replaced;
   - the right to know who the insurer is;
   - the right to cancel a transaction; and
   - detail regarding the complaints handling process, if a client is dissatisfied.

2. A personal information document, known as a permit, must be handed to the client. It contains the following:
   - your full names, title, address, and telephone number(s) and legal status;
   - details of your relevant experience;
   - details of the insurers who have mandated you to sell their products;
   - details of product accreditation confirming that you have the necessary competency, knowledge and proficiency to sell specific insurers' policies;
   - detail of any professional indemnity cover you may or may not have;
   - whether you hold more than 10% of shares directly or indirectly in any insurer whose products you are authorised to sell, or whether you have received more than 30% of total commission and remuneration from a particular insurer over the previous calendar year; and
   - any service fees (separately negotiated fees for services rendered) that you will be charging, if you are allowed to.

3. Keep records of all disclosures until at least three years after the termination of a policy (the burden of proof lies with you to prove that these disclosures were made, should a complaint or dispute arise).

The quotation stage

1. Do not allow a client to sign blank or incomplete forms. It is illegal to do so.

2. If a replacement policy is involved, you must advise the client as to any costs and the implications of the replacement policy. A specific form (Advice Record for Policy Replacement) must be completed. It explains the financial implications of a policy replacement.

3. Within six months from the effective date of the Rules, monitoring systems must be in place to measure compliance, e.g. keeping a register of client complaints.

4. There should be a thorough analysis of each client's financial situation.

5. The client should be given a choice of three different products.

6. The broker should take out liability insurance.

Investors are expected to fill in a declaration that indicates the following, amongst others: that the correct information was received, analysed and presented, and that it was understood. Spouses sign the declaration as well if married in community of property. The intermediary also signs the declaration.

You are also referred to the Financial Advisors and Intermediaries Act. This Act regulates entry into the broking industry, the requirements that advisors and brokers must meet, and the rights and duties of brokers (and the investing public).

Money kept by attorneys

If, for some reason, you invest a lump sum via an attorney, you must make sure that your money will enjoy the same protection as trust money. If this is not the case, you should rather invest via another type of broker where your money will be protected. Find out whether the investment is protected by the Guarantee Fund of the Attorneys Act (Swart 1999:132).

A cooling-off period for home buyers

Home buyers are now given five days to 'cool off' by the Estate Agents Act 112 of 1976, as amended. In this period they may decide whether they want to go through with the purchase. This period excludes the day on which the contract was signed, as well as Saturdays, Sundays and public holidays. The cooling-off period applies only to residences with a value of less than R250 000 and will, therefore, not apply in the following cases (Swart 1999:133,134):

- When a property is valued at more than R250 000.
- When the buyer had an option to buy the property.
- When a property is sold at a public auction that has been advertised.
- When a transaction is concluded where the buyer and the seller have previously been involved with the same property.
- Where the buyer is a legal entity.
- If the buyer reserves the right to appoint another person to act as buyer.
- If the buyer makes an offer on a second property before exercising his or her rights regarding the first property (in this case the cooling-off period for the first property will lapse).

This means that if you invest in a house, you will have five working days to reconsider your decision to purchase as well as the terms of the deed of purchase (with the above provisos). If you are not satisfied with your purchase, you may cancel the contract and make an offer on another property (or invest or use your money elsewhere).

If you are selling your house, the buyer has this cooling-off period, so you should not take on any long-term obligations before you are sure that the transaction will go through. If not, you may have to pay the instalments on two houses or use all your funds to buy a new house (when you wanted to use the money from the sale of your old house but now have to rent it out because you were not able to sell it).

Through its code of conduct for agents, the Estate Agents Act offers further protection for buyers during negotiations with agents. In terms of a new amendment, a fine can be imposed if an agent's conduct is not in line with the code. The buyer will be entitled to receive up to 80% of this amount.

The cooling-off period also applies to a private sale, when buying from a plan, and when you are buying a house through an estate agent.

If you sell your own house the cooling-off period holds no advantages.

Because the buyer may still cancel the contract there will be a period of uncertainty, because you will not know whether your house has actually been sold. An unscrupulous buyer could waste the seller's time and money because the seller may lose other opportunities to sell the house during the five-day period.

The period may also be used (misused) to negotiate a lower price. If a buyer has reserved the right to nominate a third party in the contract, he or she could also use your house to speculate. Sellers are defenceless against this sort of protection. So remember that you as a buyer will sometimes also be the seller.

Have you invested in sloppy work?

You can also invest in building a new house. Often, no written agreement is concluded with the building contractor and all the money is paid before the building work has been completed. You can imagine how many things could go wrong.

At present all home builders are forced by law to register with the National Home Builders Registration Council (NHBRC). The council has every house inspected before it issues a guarantee of approval, which stipulates that:

- Sloppy work must be rectified within three months of occupation.
- Leaking roofs must be repaired within 12 months.
- Major structural faults should be repaired within five years.
- The building material must comply with the minimum quality requirements.
- The foundations must be suitable for the type of soil.

Complaints about sloppy work should be directed to the National Home Builders Registration Council at: (011) 886 3636. Assistance is free of charge. If your complaints are valid, the board will approach the builder and act as an intermediary until repairs have been completed, even if another builder has to be paid from the Guarantee Fund to do the repairs. The following information is also available from the council:

- the names of all registered builders;
- registrations that have been cancelled;
- the number of houses built; and
- previous complaints about a builder.

You are strongly advised to find out more about a builder's work, before you invest your money in a new building project.

7.19.1 Sources of information and protection

Financial Services Board (FSB)
P O Box 35655
Menlo Park 0102
Pretoria

Chief Executive Officer of FSB & Registrar of Pensions
Mr Rick Cottrell
P O Box 35655
Menlo Park
Tel: (012) 428 8000
Fax: (012) 347 0221

Deputy Executive Officer of FSB & Deputy Registrar of Pensions
Mr André Swanepoel
P O Box 35655
Menlo Park
Tel: (012) 428 8000
Fax: (012) 347 0221

Ombudsman for Short-term Insurance
Mr Michael Bennett
P O Box 30619
Braamfontein 2017
Tel: (011) 339 6525
Fax: (011) 339 7063

Ombudsman for Life Assurance
Judge Jan Steyn
P O Box 4967
Cape Town 8000
Tel: (021) 674 0330
Fax: (021) 674 0902

Ombudsman for Banking
Mr Charl Cilliers
P O Box 5728
Johannesburg 2000
Tel: (011) 838 0035
Fax: (011) 838 0043

Pension Fund Adjudicator
Professor John Murphy
P O Box 23005
Claremont 7735
Cape Town 8000
Tel: (021) 674 0209
Fax: (021) 674 0185

Life Offices Association of SA
Executive Director:
Mr Gerhard Joubert
P O Box 5023
Cape Town 8000
Tel: (021) 423 2233
Fax: (021) 423 0222

The ombudsmen do not act as financial advisers. They deal only with specific disputes.

Pension funds
There are various important aspects regarding complaints that may arise about pension funds. We will discuss some of them.

Everyone who is a member of a pension fund that falls under the Pension Funds Amendment Act 22 of 1996 has three years to submit complaints to the Ombudsman for Pension Funds. Complaints may be submitted by any person and any institution that has an interest in a pension fund, including present and former members of the fund, beneficiaries, employers, the Financial Services Board, The Registrar of Pensions and insurance companies. Complaints may deal with issues such as the administration of the fund, the investment of funds and the incorrect interpretation of the rules of the fund.

Certain steps must be followed when you submit a complaint:

- Submit a written complaint to your employer or pension fund.
- The employer or fund must react to this complaint within 30 days.
- Submit a written complaint to the Ombudsman for Pension Funds (include personal particulars as well as information about your work and pension fund, proof that the complaint has been submitted to your employer/pension fund, as well as the response you received from them, information about where your employer/pension fund can be contacted, and your solution to the problem).
- After this, a meeting may be arranged with you and a representative of your pension fund.
- The Ombudsman makes a decision about the case and both parties have the right to appeal against this decision in the High Court.
- If no appeal is lodged the decision is accepted as binding.

If marketers (brokers) are found guilty, various sanctions may be implemented against them. Such sanctions may be:

- administrative (marketers are no longer allowed to sell certain products);
- civil (the courts become involved); and
- criminal law cases (offences are made known to the public and the marketer will lose his or her good reputation).

7.20 SUMMARY

An investment in financial assets offers the investor numerous benefits. Probably the most important benefits are the fact that long-term investments exceed the inflation rate in terms of capital growth. The growth rate of some investments is as much as twice the inflation rate. In this way, an investment is obtained with a positive real return.

Individual investors should decide on the kind of investment they want to make on the basis of their own investment objectives.

Further, they should decide whether they are going to manage their own investment portfolio or whether they are going to employ a broker to do it for them. The compensation the broker receives must be weighed up against the investor's time and knowledge of the specific market.

Investment planning and participation in financial investments, however, is essential. A potential investor can begin by buying unit trusts on a monthly basis. The risk is relatively low in comparison with the long-term (five to 50 years) rate of return. The benefits involved in such an investment exceed the disadvantages by far.

It is important that an investor should be aware of his or her current financial situation and attitude toward risk. Once he or she has compared and reconciled these aspects with his or her financial needs, the investor can proceed with his or her chosen financial investments.

7.21 SELF-ASSESSMENT

- Explain the functioning of the different types of investment in both the money and the capital markets.
- Explain how you would go about choosing a broker.
- Identify the different investment approaches.

BIBLIOGRAPHY

Alexander, R. 1996. *Futures and options: A South African guide to derivatives.* Wynberg: Zebra.

Bernstein, S. 1995. *Understand derivatives in a day.* Harrogate: Take That.

Brümmer, L.M. & Rademeyer, W.F. 1982. *Beleggingsbestuur:* 1st edn. Pretoria: Van Schaik.

De Lange, L. 1991. Eienskappe van die beurs se 100 wenners. *Finansies & Tegniek:* 12–14, col. 2–3, Sept. 20.

De Lange, L. 1991. Hoe om 'n wen-portefeulje saam te stel. *Finansies & Tegniek:* 38, col. 1–3, Nov. 15.

Du Plessis, P G. et al. 1997. *The investment decision.* Pretoria: Van Schaik.

Falkena, H.B., Fourie, L.J.& Kok, W.J. 1989. *The mechanics of the South African financial system.* 3rd edn. London: Macmillan.

Finansies & Tegniek. 1995:74, col. 1, May 26.

Gitman L.J. 1988. *Principles of managerial finance.* 5th edn. New York: Harper Collins.

Hull, J.C. 2000. *Options, futures & other derivatives.* 4th edn. London: Prentice-Hall.

Jordan, L. 2000. *Options plain and simple: Successful strategies without rocket science.* New York: Prentice Hall.

Krüger, A. 1990. Bereken risiko vir 'n beter opbrengs. *Finansies & Tegniek:* 52, col. 1–3, Feb. 23.

Laurie, H de G. 1989. Jaarlikse portefeulje-hersiening. *Finansies & Tegniek:* 40, col. 1–3, June 29.

Laurie, H de G. 1989. Só vaar ons portefeulje. *Finansies & Tegniek:* 38, col. 1–3, Oct. 6.

Laurie, H de G. 1990. *Sukses met beleggings.* 1st edn. Pretoria: Van Schaik.

Malkiel, B.G. 1962. Expectations, bond prices and the term structure of interest rates. *Quarterly Journal of Economics.* May.

McGowan, D.A. 1981. *Contemporary personal finance.* Boston: Houghton Mifflin.

Mittra, S. & Goosen, C. 1981. *Investment analysis and portfolio selection.* New York: Harcourt Brace Jovanovich.

Morris, K.M. & Siegel, A.M. 1993. *The Wall Street Journal guide to understanding money and investing.* New York: Lightbulb.

Posel, K. 1990. *Enjoy investing on the stock exchange.* Durban: Butterworths.

Schwichtenberg, D. 1991. How to set up your own trading system. *Personal Wealth – A Financial Mail Publication:* 24, col. 2–3, Nov. 30.

Swart, N.J. 1999. *Investing your package: All you need to know.* Pretoria: University of South Africa.

Van Rensburg, J.C. 1989. *Everyone's guide to investment.* Cape Town: Don Nelson.

CHAPTER 8

BUYING A RESIDENCE

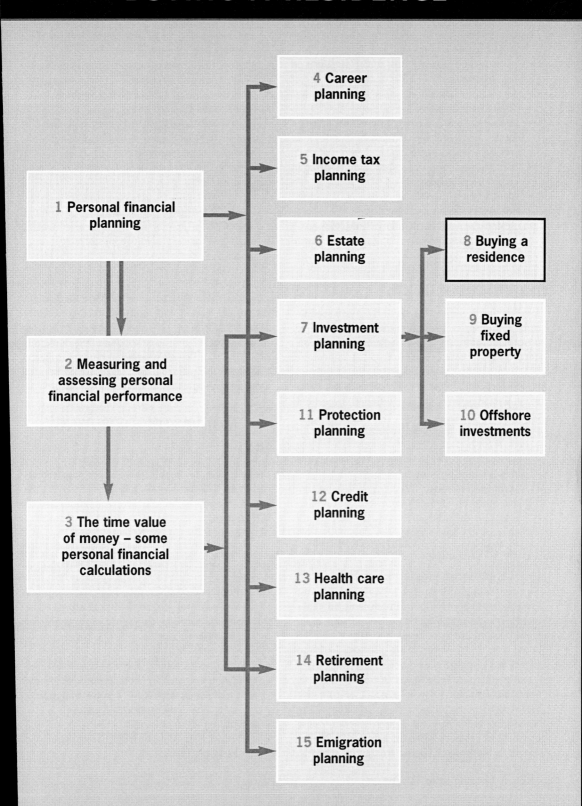

4 Career planning

5 Income tax planning

1 Personal financial planning

6 Estate planning

8 Buying a residence

7 Investment planning

9 Buying fixed property

2 Measuring and assessing personal financial performance

11 Protection planning

10 Offshore investments

12 Credit planning

3 The time value of money – some personal financial calculations

13 Health care planning

14 Retirement planning

15 Emigration planning

8.1 LEARNING OUTCOMES

After studying this chapter, you will be able to:

- Explain the financial implications of buying a home.
- Realise the importance of the decision to buy.
- Demonstrate some aspects regarding the value and valuation of a house.
- Identify and quantify the costs involved in buying a house.
- Be aware of the Board and the Institute that regulate the conduct of estate agents.
- Explain the position of trust that exists between estate agents and their principals (the buyer or seller).
- Identify what services estate agents offer in return for a commission.
- Identify the situations when estate agents are entitled to receive a commission.
- Define the various mandates that may arise between the seller of a house and an estate agent.
- Explain under which circumstances you should make use of a particular type of mandate.
- Explain which parties (natural persons and legal persons) may or may not be involved in the purchase and sale of a house.
- Identify the financial implications that the Rent Control Act may have for buyers and sellers.
- Identify some of the financing methods that may be used to buy a house.
- Explain the various types of mortgage bond.
- Explain the functioning of mortgage bonds and mortgage bond payments.
- Identify the most important sources of long-term financing.
- Identify possible sources of finance when financing is difficult to obtain.
- Demonstrate the practical steps involved when buying or selling a house or when moving house.

8.2 INTRODUCTION

Investment in immovable property, more specifically a house, is generally the greatest single investment most people ever make. Before a potential investor or buyer decides to invest in a house, he or she should first compare the specific features of the property with his or her requirements or investment objectives. Investors have different investment objectives, such as:

- investment for own use (the investor wishes to occupy the house);
- investment in order to obtain a regular income (intends letting the house);
- investment for capital growth (intends selling the house at a profit in the future); and
- investment to build an estate (the house will form part of his or her estate as a bequest to his or her heirs).

First, we will discuss investing in a house for your own use. Immovable property is, almost without exception, not a very liquid investment; in other words, it cannot readily be converted into cash. However, a house owner does not have to sell the house if he or she requires cash, as it is possible to negotiate a loan with the house as security.

Two main risks are involved in buying a house: operating risk and financial risk. Operating risk means that the factors affecting the value of the house are of such a nature that the value of the house may be lower than the investor paid for it. Factors that affect the value of a house are the site, the loca-

tion, institutional factors, the property market and economic, social and political factors (Maritz 1983:295). Financial risk refers to the need to borrow money (obtain a mortgage bond) and the numerous obligations and costs involved in buying property. The bigger the loan in relation to the market value of a property, the greater the financial risk.

8.3 MOTIVATION FOR BUYING A HOUSE

Before we discuss the valuation and cost implications of buying a home, we will take a brief look at the reasons for taking this step. People are motivated by various needs to buy a house or other type of dwelling, of which the following are the most important.

8.3.1 Self- and family-orientated needs

Underlying self- and family-orientated needs are psychological and economic motivations. The following are some psychological motivations for buying a house:

- a dwelling place (a place to live);
- the safety of the family (a safe place to live);
- independence and freedom (your own home with a garden and space for a growing family);
- creativity (the design and use of a house);
- adventure (finding the right house);
- the expansion of knowledge (learning about contracts and financing);

- peace of mind (no rent increase); and
- emotional factors (love in a home and living in a particular residential area).
  (Seldin 1980:912)

8.3.2 Economic motivations

- Buyer's credit position improves (better loan terms, improved credit terms);
- amortisation (repayment of loan);
- appreciation (value of property increases); and
- peace of mind (financial security).
  (Seldin 1980:912)

8.3.3 Group-orientated needs

Group-orientated needs associated with buying a house usually revolve around a person's position in the community and his or her participation in politics. Having a 'position in the community' implies that a person:

- is a respectable resident (an element of stability in the residential area);
- shares in the interests of the community (the upholding of the community); and
- has a positive attitude about the area (an interest in the improvement of the residential area).
  (Seldin 1980:913)

Political participation by a homeowner may lead to:

- participation in the interests of the country (interested in a stable government); and
- public support (contributes to national prosperity by investing in a house).
  (Seldin 1980:913)

Seldin (1980:913) states that most first-home buyers are families consisting of a husband, a wife and pre-school children. Home ownership usually begins at the age of 25 and increases after the age of 45. Under normal circumstances, a family's assets or net value never reach a maximum before the age of 35.

Thousands of houses are bought and sold every month. Estate agents, therefore, have an important role to play in providing home buyers with financial advice.

Estate agents should structure their financial advice around their client's motivation for buying or selling. Seldin (1980:481) points out that the seller should be motivated to sell a specific property, and that he or she should be able to define this motivation. The estate agent, on the other hand, should be able to identify this motivation. If a seller is unable to define the motivation, he or she would most likely be wasting his or her own time, as well as that of the estate agent, the potential buyer and

the person or organisation providing the finance (bondholder).

Examples of motivations are illustrated below.

8.3.4 Other motivations

People are motivated to sell their house and purchase another house for various reasons, such as:

- they are transferred to another town;
- they need a larger house;
- they have bought a new house before the old one has been sold;
- divorce;
- the prospects of a more profitable investment;
- the death of a spouse; and
- insolvency.
  (Seldin 1980:481)

8.3.4.1 Transfer to another town

Many large companies give their employees financial aid when they are transferred. An estate agent will want to establish whether this is the case, whether the company will pay the commission, transfer costs and valuation costs, whether the company intends buying the existing house and, if so, at what price. Furthermore, if the seller is forced to sell during an economic slump, the estate agent will want to know whether the company will compensate him or her for this.

The most important financial advice centres on the timing of the buying of the new house and the selling of the existing house. This time difference could result in financial loss, since the person may have to pay two mortgage bonds until the existing house has been sold and registered.

A person may also be obliged to rent a house in the new city or town and repay the bond on the existing house until it is sold. Other scenarios are that occupational interest may have to be paid, or the person may have to secure a bridging loan at a time when his or her creditworthiness is exhausted. A levy or commission is payable on a bridging loan.

Further costs may arise from the need to move from a rented house to a new house; in other words, the person would have to pay removal costs twice. If a telephone is required, it would mean paying double installation fees. Estate agents should point out all these cost implications to buyers and sellers, who should take them into account before they move.

8.3.4.2 A larger house

The need for a larger house has several financial implications. It may lead to a larger or smaller mortgage instalment, payment of rates and taxes, maintenance costs and particularly transfer fees.

Assume that a natural person buys a larger house for R480 000. The purchase price of the previous house was R300 000. In both cases, the buyer makes use of a 90% mortgage loan. The following costs will ensue:

	Old house (R300 000)	New house (R480 000)
Transfer duties & Conveyancing costs	16 211,00	32 515,00
Mortgage registration costs and stamp charges (VAT inclusive)	4 109,00	6 031,00
	R20 320,00	R38 546,00

These figures show that a buyer of a larger house needs an additional R18 226 (R38 546,00 – R20 320,00) in cash before the higher mortgage payments come into effect. However, the sale of the previous house may contribute towards the payment of these additional costs, depending on the capital redeemed.

8.3.4.3 Buying before selling

If a person has already bought another house, but still has to sell the previous house, he or she may have to secure another loan in order to meet the second (or new) obligation. He or she will have to pay interest on this second bridging loan until the previous house has been sold and one obligation has been met. The longer it takes to sell the house, the more his or her financial liability will increase. This often results in the person reducing the price of the first house and consequently suffering a considerable financial loss.

Estate agents should (if possible) advise their clients about buying a second house before the first one is sold, and they should ensure that the selling price of the previous house remains realistic and in keeping with current market trends. Other estate agents may spread the word that the seller is in financial trouble and buyers may consequently make lower offers for the house, hoping that the seller will be forced eventually to agree to a lower price.

8.3.4.4 Divorce

A divorce may adversely affect a couple's financial position, unless they agree to a period within which their house should be sold, as well as the price. An estate agent's advice could be valuable in such a case. The husband may wish to sell the house as quickly as possible and may be willing to drop the price. The wife, on the other hand, may need some time to acquire a new house and be willing to wait for a better offer, or the wife may wish to live with her parents and be prepared to sell the house for less

than her husband is asking. The estate agent should try to ensure that the husband and wife come to a reasonable agreement before a potential buyer makes an offer, thereby preventing a financial loss for one or both of them.

The estate agent must point out to them that they will invariably suffer a financial loss, as one or both will have to purchase or rent a new house. To minimise this loss, they should agree on a realistic price for the house, as well as the period within which they want to sell. This will enable them to improve their financial planning, since neither of them will have to rent a house temporarily while the house is on the market. A sole mandate may be effective in this case in order to ensure that the house is sold at a market-related price within the proposed time.

If the house is in need of repairs, the estate agent should advise them to sell at a lower price rather than incur additional expenses.

8.3.4.5 Investment purposes

People often decide to buy a house in another residential area as a result of their personal evaluation of current and future developments in that area. They believe that buying a house there would be a good investment. Estate agents should be up to date with developments in residential areas that may reduce or increase the value of houses. Property values may drop as a result of the erection of factories, industries, mines, freeways, prisons, a school for problem children or business concerns in the vicinity or close to the residential area. A newspaper report on development in a particular area could, for example, result in property prices rising or falling.

Estate agents should be able to advise clients who wish to move to another residential area for investment purposes. If they are unable to do so, a property consultant may be approached. A hasty decision without proper advice could well lead to a lower selling price and a higher buying price than necessary and unnecessary expenses may be incurred, thereby cancelling any investment benefits.

Estate agents should point out to clients that it is not advisable to buy a fairly inexpensive house in a particular area unless it can be resold at a relatively good price. If the demand for houses in a particular residential area is low, buyers should be cautioned against buying there for investment purposes. In such residential areas, the market value of houses increases at a slower rate than in areas with a greater demand for houses. Even in a fairly poor residential area, the general costs involved in buying a house are still payable, and the buyer will find it more difficult to recover these expenses from the sale of the house in the long term.

Falkena (1988:22) believes that the leverage effect of mortgage financing is the most important reason for investing in a house. Assume that you buy a house for R100 000 with a deposit of R10 000 and a 90% mortgage loan. You could recover this deposit within a year if property prices increase by 15% during that period.

8.3.4.6 Death of a spouse

Seldin (1980:14) discusses the case of someone of mature age acquiring a house after the death of his or her spouse. Usually, such a person would find a smaller place to live, leaving the original house to fall into disrepair. Under these circumstances, an estate agent should advise his or her client to improve the house in order to sell it at a market related price. Improvements to a house that has been on the market for some time may stimulate estate agents to renew their efforts to sell the house.

8.3.4.7 Insolvency

Insolvency may motivate a person to buy or sell a house. The meaning of the word 'insolvent' in terms of the law is:

- someone whose estate is under sequestration in terms of the Insolvency Act 24 of 1936;
- any insolvent deceased estate which is dealt with in terms of Section 34(5) of the Administration of Estates Act 66 of 1995;
- a legal person under liquidation who cannot pay his or her debts; or
- a person whose estate is dealt with in terms of Section 28(5) of the Agricultural Credit Act 28 of 1966 or Section 28(5) of the Alienation of Land Act 68 of 1981.

Once a person has been declared insolvent, he or she may not enter into property transactions involving the insolvent estate. An unrehabilitated insolvent may purchase movable (as well as immovable) property with income earned in the form of a salary or through providing professional or other services (Delport 1982:6). Any newly acquired property will be placed in his or her second estate. An attorney should be consulted before entering into any business with an insolvent. Normally, a certificate is obtained from the trustee of an insolvent estate, stating that the purchase price of any new property is to be financed by funds to which the trustee and/or the insolvent estate has no claim and that the trustee, therefore, has no objection to the new acquisition.

It is particularly important that young buyers should buy a house they can afford. It is better to buy a smaller house and make additions at a later stage when your financial position improves. Look

for a smaller site, better utilisation of space and cheaper construction methods.

Botha (1987:4) stresses the importance of advising potential young buyers, particularly as the future depends on them. They need to be advised to match their housing needs with their income. It was for exactly this reason that projects for basic or first homes were initiated at Albertville and Elandspoort. Estate agents should encourage young buyers to investigate similar projects before they take the plunge.

It is essential that potential home buyers should be fully aware of the factors that determine the value of a house. These factors are discussed below.

8.4 VALUATION OF A HOUSE

8.4.1 Factors that determine the value of a house

The most important factors that determine the value of a house, apart from the property market and general economic conditions, are:

- physical features (site and improvements);
- location; and
- institutional factors.
  (Maritz 1983:301)

8.4.1.1 Physical features

When a potential buyer views a house, he or she is given information on the site or plot and the house itself. The size and slope of the site should be viewed, and the potential buyer should find out about the municipal services available (water, electricity, garbage removal). Note should be taken of important features of the house, such as size (square metres), finish, quality of construction and age.

8.4.1.2 Location

As far as the location of the house is concerned, particular attention should be paid to the convenience and exposure network. The convenience network is related to aspects such as the proximity of shopping centres, schools, churches, freeways and recreation grounds. The exposure network refers to sensory factors that affect living in a house, such as a noisy factory across the road (sound), a chemical manufacturing concern close to the house (smell) or a refuse dump visible from the house (sight).

8.4.1.3 Institutional factors

Institutional factors refer to private and public legal circumscriptions; in other words, what rights you have as the owner of the property or house.

Information on private legal circumscriptions may be obtained from the Deeds Office, and include factors such as: in whose name(s) the property has been registered, neighbour law (lateral support, infringement on the natural flow of water), rules of law apart from neighbour law, and limited real rights (real servitude, private servitude, public servitude, mineral rights, quitrent-tenure, tenancy, leasehold, real security rights) (Maritz 1983:41).

Public legal circumscription refers to the control exercised by government in the interests of the public. Such information may be obtained from the local municipality and includes taxes, control measures and expropriation. Rates and taxes, as well as control factors, such as zoning and building by-laws (usage, density, floor area ratio, height, coverage and the regulation of space around buildings) are of particular importance to a potential buyer (Maritz 1983:83).

Swart (1988:52, 53) mentions the following additional factors that increase the value of a house. Most buyers are more interested in the number rather than the size of the rooms. In order of preference this includes a family room, kitchen, main bedroom, bathroom and finally a study. Something as simple as a veranda may be important to a buyer. The size of a covered veranda is regarded as part of the house, even if it is not enclosed at the sides.

Home improvements in a more expensive neighbourhood produce a better return than in a cheaper neighbourhood. For this reason, it is better to buy a small house in a better suburb than to undertake extensive repairs to a house in a poorer suburb. Moving to a better suburb holds distinct advantages.

Employees who receive a good housing package can improve their financial position by moving regularly, although not so frequently that the Receiver of Revenue regards the profits made as a source of income. Banks and building society staff usually move to a better house on average every four years because of subsidised interest rates of four or five percent. As a result, the fourth house may even be paid for in cash after 16 years.

Overcapitalisation usually occurs when homeowners like their residential area and decide to build onto the house in view of retiring there. However, if they happen to be transferred shortly afterwards, they may find that the profit they made on selling the house does not cover the cost of the extensions.

The owner of a house in a poorer residential area who has already repaid R30 000, for example, could increase his or her personal wealth by selling the house and buying one in a better residential area, provided that he or she can afford the additional instalment (on R30 000). The value of the house would rise and he or she would be less likely to overcapitalise.

A homeowner may live in a good residential area but spend about R500 per month on petrol to get to work. In such a case, it may be better to look for a house in a similar area but closer to work. The R500 could then be used to pay off a higher mortgage loan. However, if he or she receives a petrol allowance, another set of rules would apply.

Many people currently prefer brick walls to plastered walls. The marketability (and therefore the investment value) of a house could be increased by building a small bar, hanging mirrors at strategic places, building a braai or laying out a tropical garden. Potential buyers or investors should consider all these factors to improve the value of their house.

8.4.2 Assessing the price of a house

There are three main methods of assessing the value (price) of a property:
- the method of comparable selling prices;
- the income method; and
- the cost method.

As most people are primarily interested in the value or price of a house (as far as immovable property is concerned), only the first method will be dealt with. It is assumed that the buyer or investor would occupy the property him- or herself.

8.4.2.1 The method of comparable selling prices

This method determines the value or price of a house according to the house or property market (consisting of buyers, sellers and estate agents). This market value reflects the price which buyers and sellers would be prepared to pay for a house at any given time. The method of comparable selling prices is also referred to as the market approach.

The principle of substitution is applicable here. This means that a buyer or an investor would not be prepared to pay more for a property than the amount/price for which he or she could buy a similar property. For this reason, it is essential to compare various properties (houses). In comparing the selling prices of two houses, particular attention should be paid to the following:
- the factors determining the value (as explained before);
- the *bona fide* status of the sales transaction (for example, a transaction between family members, a liquidation sale, a sale from an estate – in other words, whether an equal bargaining position existed between buyer and seller);
- the date of the sale (the market conditions should have been more or less similar before a comparison would be significant);
- the nature of the sales transaction (a cash sale or a bond being taken); and

- what was purchased (what other items besides the house were included in the sales transaction).

Once the potential buyer has identified two houses of which the selling prices (on the basis of the above-mentioned criteria) can be compared with the house in which he or she is interested, he or she will see what its market value is. Next, the market value (according to the method of comparable selling prices) is compared with the investment value of the house.

Market value represents the maximum price that should be paid. If the market value is higher than the investment value (the specific value for the investor), the house must be bought at investment value or not at all. If the market value is considerably lower than the investment value, a buyer should not pay more than the market value.

The method of comparable selling prices is based on real sales and prices paid under comparable conditions. However, it is not that simple to compare houses. Maritz (1983:261) points out that recent sales can only give an indication of historic market value and not of current market value.

8.4.2.2 The income method
Consult Chapter 9 for more information.

8.4.2.3 The cost method
Consult Chapter 9 for more information.

To understand the origin of certain costs, it is necessary to take a brief look at the registration procedure of deeds of transfer and mortgage bonds. Estate agents should inform the parties concerned about the period of time involved in this process and the costs that may arise during this period (for example occupational interest until the house has been sold).

8.5 COST IMPLICATIONS OF THE REGISTRATION PROCEDURE OF DEEDS OF TRANSFER AND MORTGAGE BONDS

The registration of deeds is the legal process that puts into effect the objectives of preceding legal actions regarding registrable immovable property (mainly the disposal of property) (Laurens 1984:1). The South African system of registration of deeds is concerned only with the registration of real rights regarding immovable property (Laurens 1984:231). Section 16 of the Deeds Registries Act 47 of 1937 provides that ownership of property may be transferred from one

person to another only by means of a deed of transfer signed and attested by the Registrar.

Some concepts are explained below.

8.5.1 Conceptual framework

A deed of transfer is a document that states the facts of a transaction in which property is sold and that the transferee is entitled to the property (Technikon RSA 1985:6). The person who transfers the property (the seller) is called the transferor, while the transferee is the person to whom the property is transferred (the buyer). The transfer of other real rights in property may take place only by means of a deed of transfer attested by a notary and registered by the Registrar. The basis of the registration of deeds in the Republic of South Africa is the Republic's survey system. The primary aim of the registration system is to inform the public on property rights as well as limited real rights over property (Laurens 1984:24,25).

The role of the conveyancer during the registration process of deeds of transfer will be explained next.

8.5.2 The role of the conveyancer

Once a contract for the sale of property (agreement of sale) has been concluded, the conveyancer is instructed to put the agreement into effect in terms of Section 16 of the Deeds Registries Act 47 of 1937. Such instruction is normally given to the conveyancer nominated by the parties to the agreement. If no nomination has been made, the seller nominates a conveyancer. In KwaZulu-Natal, the buyer nominates a conveyancer. The cancellation of an existing mortgage bond on a house and the registration of a new mortgage bond by a buyer are handled by a conveyancer of the financial institution(s) concerned. If the old and new mortgage bonds have been granted by two financial institutions, the conveyancer will take the following steps after receipt of the instruction:
- request the financial institution to provide the title deed and details of guarantees that are required in order to cancel the seller's mortgage bond;
- make an enquiry at the Deeds Office to ensure that no interdict has been registered against the property;
- check the names and dates of birth of the parties to the contract as well as the description of the property;
- apply to the local authority for a tax assessment and, if applicable, a water clearance certificate; and

- inform the financial institution granting the mortgage bond to the buyer that he or she will handle the transfer.
(Delport 1982:9)

Delport (1982:100) explains that the financial institution's conveyancer will respond to the inquiries after completion of the tasks mentioned above. The requested information will then either be provided or certain information requested (for example, regarding the new mortgage bond).

The estate agent must advise the parties during the registration of mortgage bonds. The role of the estate agent as honest broker will be explained next.

8.5.3 The role of the estate agent

Estate agents must inform both the buyer and the seller of the financial implications of guarantees by the other party (buyer or seller), parties with whom these parties have already concluded contracts or are about to conclude contracts, and financial institutions that have granted or are about to grant mortgage bonds. All those involved in the transaction will want to be assured of their rights and obligations after the conclusion of the transaction. The assurance is provided by obtaining and/or providing certain guarantees. In other words, a guarantee that the money and/or property will be available on the registration date of the transaction. Usually, the guarantees which the various parties must produce appear in the agreement sale.

Among others, a financial institution will guarantee that, in the case of a cash sale, the purchase sum will be available in cash on the registration date. Otherwise, the institution will guarantee that either the cash deposit or mortgage bond amount (for example, 90% of the value of the property) or both (in the case of a covering bond from a bank) will be available on the registration date. Estate agents must ensure that their principals receive such guarantees by means of the inclusion of suspensive conditions in the agreement of sale in order to indemnify them against financial loss.

A seller should be advised not to purchase a second house before he or she has received a guarantee from a financial institution regarding the sale of the first house, to avoid finding him- or herself financially liable for two houses. The buyer should also obtain a guarantee from the financial institution regarding the sale of the house he or she intends buying, before selling his or her own house. Otherwise, a buyer may end up either with a second house (if he or she cannot sell the first house) or without a house (if he or she actually sells the first house and cannot purchase the other house, as the seller has not

obtained guarantees to finalise the transaction). Clearly, financial advice regarding similar transactions can be of great value to both parties.

Delport (1982:90) points out the importance of the time these guarantees are issued. Guarantees are not issued when a financial institution grants a mortgage loan or when the financial institution's conveyancer is instructed to undertake the registration of the mortgage bond. The guarantee is issued after the conveyancer has sent a copy of the new deed of transfer in the name of the buyer (draft deed) to the financial institution's conveyancer and provided him or her with certain information.

A guarantee is also issued after the conveyancer has provided the financial institution with an authorisation (signed at the mortgage bond attorney's office) for the issuing of the guarantee, and after signing the power of attorney to pass the mortgage bond.

One or more conveyancers may be involved in a sales transaction:
- the transfer attorney (conveyancer appointed by the seller or buyer); and
- the mortgage bond attorney(s) of one or more financial institutions (where the parties register or cancel mortgage bonds at different financial institutions).

Once all the transfer documents have been signed, the guarantees issued, the tax and water clearance certificates obtained, and the transfer duty indemnity certificate or transfer duty receipt obtained, these documents can be lodged at the Deeds Office for registration. Estate agents must point out to buyers and sellers that it may take two or three months before these documents are finalised, and that they should take this into account when planning their own transactions.

Occupational interest is an important factor to take into account as well, since the longer the registration process takes, the longer occupational rent will have to be paid. The registration of transfer is very important, as property rights to immovable property are transferred to the buyer on the date of registration in the Deeds Office.

An estate agent can assist in preventing delays in the registration of property (which will be to the advantage of both the mortgagor and the conveyancer) by providing clear and well-prepared documents with regard to the sales transaction. This will also eliminate unnecessary telephone calls and correspondence. Estate agents should provide the conveyancer with the following:
- a signed copy of the sales transaction;
- information on where the deed of transfer for the property is kept;

- the name of the mortgagee;
- the telephone numbers of the parties and where they can be contacted;
- confirmation of compliance with all suspensive and resolutive conditions in the agreement of sale; and
- any other information relevant to the agreement of sale.
(Reid 1987:216)

We will now look at the identification and quantification of the various costs related to buying a house. We will not discuss buying a house from an estate (deceased or insolvent), at an auction, for investment purposes, for tax purposes or with the view to improvements. We are concerned only with buying a house to live in and the role it plays in personal financial management.

8.6 COST-ITEMS RELATED TO BUYING A HOUSE

Swart (1988:160) points out how important it is that buyers should know exactly what they are letting themselves in for. In the discussion that follows, the cost factors related to buying a house are explained. Potential buyers should be aware of the role that estate agents play in such a transaction and of the importance in the long-term of a decision to buy a house.

A great many houses are bought and sold in South Africa every day. The majority of these houses are bought and sold through estate agents.

As a result of an upswing in the property market, many ambitious individuals, untrained salespersons and opportunistic entrepreneurs entered the market as estate agents. Unfortunately, many of these people were unable to give sound professional financial advice to buyers and sellers. Buyers and sellers conclude transactions involving several hundreds of thousands of rands, and untrained estate agents form part of the negotiating team in these deals. Estate agents simply leave the industry if they do not earn sufficient commission, but the new homeowners are contractually bound to the financial contract for 20 to 30 years, and therefore have much more to lose.

Buyers and sellers of houses need sound financial information before they can proceed to purchase and/or sell property. It is an open question whether parties to transactions always have adequate and relevant information at their disposal before entering into agreements. Prospective buyers often respond to misleading advertisements by developers and agents, who tend to emphasise the low monthly instalments as a prerequisite for home ownership. They neglect to mention the numerous hidden costs involved.

Estate agents are not always prepared to reveal these hidden costs to their clients as such advice could cost them their commission. Furthermore, not all agents know how to quantify the capital needs of buyers, so that only a few cost factors are mentioned.

The purpose of this discussion is to identify and quantify the various costs relating to buying a house in order to design a form which potential buyers (and estate agents) can use. This form indicates the most important costs, and the information applicable to the buyer in question is filled in on the form. In this way, the buyer can be fully informed about the total package of costs involved. However, this form will only be useful if used correctly.

8.6.1 General costs relating to buying a house

The way in which a house is acquired determines the costs involved. However, certain costs are standard whatever the method of purchase. An estate agent should point out to buyers how these costs will affect their capital needs at the time of purchase. The calculations in this section are based on a three-bedroom house at a purchase price of R450 000. A mortgage bond rate of 18% is assumed.

8.6.1.1 Transfer duty
Central government levies a tax, called a transfer duty, on the sale of immovable property. When the buyer is a natural person, transfer duty amounts to 0% of the first R100 000 of the purchase price, 5% (R100 000 – R300 000) and 8% on the balance (R300 001 and more). A legal person pays 10% of the purchase price. Transfer duty on R450 000 for a natural person and a legal person amounts to R22 000 and R45 000 respectively. A vacant plot is exempt from transfer duty up to an amount of R70 000.

8.6.1.2 Conveyancing costs
Conveyancing costs are levied for the transfer of immovable property from one natural or legal person or persons to another. The amounts payable are prescribed by legislation and levied by the transfer attorney of the property. Conveyancing costs are calculated according to a table that is revised from time to time, and published in the *Government Gazette*. On an amount of R450 000, conveyancing costs will amount to R7 545.

8.6.1.3 Occupational interest

The buyer pays occupational interest if he or she occupies the house before the transfer has been registered in his or her name. Similarly, a seller pays occupational interest if the seller remains in the house for a period after the transfer of the house. Occupational interest is normally calculated at the current bond interest rate on the full purchase price of the house and is payable monthly in advance. The owner (seller) has to pay all municipal rates on the date of transfer, irrespective of who is occupying the property at that stage.

8.6.1.4 Loss of interest on capital

Estate agents should notify buyers of a possible loss of interest on capital. A cash buyer's money is usually invested with a financial institution where it earns interest. If he or she wishes to pay the full purchase price to the seller, it is suggested that the buyer does not supply the cash before the date of registration, so that he or she earns interest on capital up to that date.

8.6.1.5 Estate agent's commission

The seller is normally responsible for paying the estate agent's commission, unless the buyer acts as principal for the estate agent. The relevant estate agency determines the percentage of commission. At the rate of 6%, the agent's commission on R450 000 will amount to R27 000. The estate agency receives the commission due after the seller has received the purchase price.

8.6.1.6 Deeds Office registration

You will pay an amount to the Deeds Office, based on the purchase price.

8.6.1.7 Rates and taxes

A registered homeowner is responsible for paying rates and taxes (municipal rates). Municipalities differ in this regard, as a person who has sold his or her house and given transfer on the 15th of the month is often responsible for the payment of rates up to and including the 1st of the next month. The buyer will subsequently be liable for such payment from the 1st of the month, even if the buyer had already taken transfer on the 15th of the previous month.

8.6.1.8 Rates clearance certificate

An amount is payable to get a certificate indicating that the rates and taxes have been paid to the local municipality. No transfer is possible until this has been paid by the buyer, the seller or both proportionally.

8.6.1.9 Valuation costs

A potential buyer may voluntarily have a house valued in order to determine its market price. These costs are compulsory, however, if a person makes use of bond financing (inspection fee). In terms of the recommended tariffs of the South African Property Valuators Board, in 2002, valuation costs on R250 000 amount to R650 (plus R3,20 per thousand). A motivated valuation report costs approximately an extra R485 per hour. If a valuator is requested to perform valuations in another town, he or she receives a further R3,50 per kilometre for travelling expenses. As travelling expenses rise from time to time as a result of increases in vehicle and petrol prices, the valuation costs will rise accordingly.

8.6.1.10 Moving expenses

Moving expenses normally arise when a house is purchased. A well-known South African transport company's tariffs for moving the contents of a three-bedroom house are discussed below.

Tariffs differ on the basis of distance as well as the time of month. Transport costs of goods to be moved within a distance of a 100km between the 7th and 21st of the month will amount to R2 700. For the rest of the month, costs over the same distance will amount to R4 500 (figures from 2002).

Packaging costs are R35 per carton and R45 for a medium carton. These costs usually include the unpacking of cartons as well (2002 tariffs).

Insurance costs will amount to approximately 1.75% (all risks; transit, 1%) of the replacement value of the goods for distances up to 150km. For distances of more than 150km costs are 2.85% (all risks) and 1% (transit) of the replacement value of the goods.

8.6.1.11 Telephone installation costs

Telephone installation costs currently (2002) amount to R239 with a further rental of about R67,72 (depending on the type of telephone). An additional telephone extension will cost extra per extension if only one telephone is used for all lines. If a second telephone is required for an extension, an additional rental is charged. When a second telephone has a different number, each connection will cost extra.

8.6.1.12 Water and electricity

Most city councils require a deposit of about twice the buyer's previous (if applicable) electricity account. Usually, no deposit is necessary for a water account.

8.6.1.13 Miscellaneous expenses

Buyers often have numerous expenses such as the replacement costs of curtains that do not fit, carpets that do not match their furniture, or they need more furniture than they had anticipated. An estate agent can point out possible miscellaneous expenses to buyers, but will not be able to determine the specific expenses.

8.6.1.14 Additional improvements (optional)

The buyer should know whether or not the house is purchased with or without immediate improvements, for example the replacement of carpets, locks/keys and painting. If immediate improvements or repairs are necessary, the buyer must take the costs of these into account when quantifying his or her capital requirements.

8.6.2 Costs relating to a bond

Those who are in the financial position to pay cash for a house only need to pay the general costs in addition to the purchase price. When the house is financed by a mortgage bond, there will be costs which are not applicable during a cash transaction. It should be borne in mind, however, that several costs are involved in both methods of purchase. The costs associated with a mortgage bond method of purchase will be dealt with briefly.

8.6.2.1 Deposit

Once an offer to purchase has been accepted and signed by both parties, it becomes an agreement of sale. Usually, the deposit is 10% of the purchase price, but it may be less, depending on the agreement with the seller. The estate agency usually keeps the deposit in a trust account. The deposit is released from the trust or savings account once all suspensive conditions have been met. At this stage, the agent's commission is deducted from the deposit and the balance is held in trust by the seller's conveyancer until the transfer has been finalised. Only then does the seller receive the purchase sum.

8.6.2.2 Bank initiation fee

The bank charges this fee for setting up the loan.

8.6.2.3 Bank administration fee

The bank charges you a monthly loan administration fee.

8.6.2.4 Bond instalments

A potential buyer who wishes to apply for a bond requires information on the monthly instalments. The monthly instalment on R150 000 (deposit deducted) at an interest rate of 18% in the case of a decreasing loan over 20 years, amounts to R2 315. If a person receives a housing subsidy (for example, a 100% housing loan by the government), the subsidy amount will be R770 and the member's contribution will be about R1 545.

8.6.2.5 Bond registration costs

Bond registration costs consist mainly of the amount paid to the attorney (bond attorney) of the financial institution (the mortgagee) plus stamp duty. Stamp duty on R150 000 amounts to R300, and bond registration costs to R2 651 – a total of R2 951. The cost of a collateral bond amounts to R100. A notarial bond may also be registered over immovable property. Stamp duty is not applicable to the following:

- covering bonds for other bonds or notarial bonds; and
- a collateral bond.

8.6.2.6 Inspection fee

Inspection fees are payable to a financial institution that endeavours to determine whether the property provides sufficient security to grant a 100% mortgage bond, for example. The inspection fees (if the mortgage bond is approved after inspection) are normally debited against the mortgage bond. If a person applies for a bond of R400 000 over a house valued at R450 000, an inspection fee is payable on the latter amount. This cost item differs considerably among financial institutions and varies between R800 and R1 000 for a house of R450 000.

8.6.2.7 Interim interest

Once a house has been registered in a buyer's name, the financial institution from which the bond has been raised pays the bond amount to the seller. The buyer's first instalment is often only payable in the following month. Consequently, the financial institution (mortgagee) charges interest on the money for the period between the date of registration and the date of payment of the first instalment. Thereafter, the normal monthly instalments are payable.

8.6.2.8 Levy commission with regard to mortgage bonds and collateral security

In the 1970s, commission was levied on loans in order to be able to obtain mortgage bonds from building societies. Commission on a loan is a negotiated percentage of the loan amount charged by financial institutions when funds are in short supply. House buyers often approach family members and acquaintances for collateral investments in order to obtain financing.

8.6.2.9 Homeowner's insurance policy

A homeowner's insurance policy provides protection to the security of the mortgagor. If a house burns down, for example, the mortgagor will lose the security on the mortgaged house. Consequently, mortgagees require that mortgagors take out a homeowner's policy according to the replacement value of the house. Insurance premiums on houses with thatched roofs are higher than for other houses due to the greater risk. Estate agents should warn those who purchase a house without bond financing about the principle of averages. Assume that the replacement value of a house is R450 000 and the homeowner insures it for R300 000. If the house is completely destroyed by fire, the insured person will receive the amount of R300 000 from the insurer(s).

If the damage amounts to R300 000, the insured person will not receive the total amount of R300 000. The payment will be proportional, according to the ratio of under-insurance (the principle of averages). As this ratio is 2:3, the insured person will receive an amount of R200 000 (two thirds of R300 000). The principle of averages is usually included in the insurance contract as a condition of the policy.

8.6.2.10 Decreasing term life insurance policy

A decreasing term life insurance policy is also called a mortgage protection policy. This policy ensures that, in the case of death or permanent disability, the amount owing on a mortgage loan is paid and that the next of kin of the deceased will own a house without a mortgage over it. The insurance premiums are paid together with the bond instalments.

An endowment policy may also be taken out instead of a term policy. Although the premium of an endowment policy is considerably higher, it has the following advantages:
- it provides capital at retirement;
- it supplies pension at retirement;
- it provides cover for dependants during the policy term;
- it has surrender value;
- it may be used as security for a loan;

- payments may be stopped with the necessary approval and cover will continue at a lower premium; and
- if payments are stopped without notice, the surrender value of the policy is used to continue the payments of the premiums.

8.6.2.11 Cancellation costs for an existing mortgage bond

The costs involved in the cancellation of a mortgage bond vary considerably among financial institutions – between R880 and R1 000 irrespective of the amount of the bond. Some institutions impose a further penalty if the mortgage bond (or bonds) is repaid within the first year. The penalty often depends on whether the buyer of a secured house has raised the mortgage bond from the same financial institution. The cancellation of every additional mortgage bond amounts to R60 per bond.

8.6.3 Summary

Estate agents should have a standard document containing all the probable costs in buying a house. When a buyer approaches an estate agent (as principal or otherwise) for an agreement of sale contract, the estate agent should analyse the buyer's situation so that all the costs applicable to that buyer appear in the document. This will provide the buyer with an overall view of the financial implications of the agreement of sale.

It is suggested that estate agents inform their clients of the existence of this, or a similar form, and fill it in for them. Buyers are advised to insist that estate agents complete such a form for their specific situation. Buyers will be more satisfied and less likely to offer resistance to the payment of commission.

An estate agent's financial advice should lead to a happy and satisfied buyer and seller. This will be achieved if he or she:
- analyses the client's financial position; and
- uses the form on p.193 (or similar form) to quantify the costs involved in order to provide the client with a package.
(Swart 1988:203)

TABLE 8.1: Checklist of costs involved in buying a house
(Source: Swart 1988:178)

GENERAL COSTS
Transfer duty   _____
Conveyancing costs   _____
Occupational interest   _____
Loss of interest on capital   _____
Agent's commission   _____
Deeds Office   _____
Rates and taxes   _____
Rates clearance certificates   _____
Valuation costs   _____
      Valuation   _____
      Travelling costs   _____
Moving expenses   _____
      Distance 0–100km (7th–21st of month) _____
      Distance 0–100km (21st–7th of following month) _____
      Distance further than 100km (7th–21st of month) _____
      Distance further than 100km (21st–7th of following month) _____
      Packing costs   _____
      Insurance costs   _____
      Storage costs   _____
Telephone installation costs   _____
      Installation of one line   _____
      Rental for one line   _____
        Type A   _____
        Type B   _____
        Type C   _____
      Installation of an extension   _____
        The same telephone number   _____
        Another telephone number   _____
      Additional rental for an extension   _____
Water and electricity   _____
Miscellaneous expenses   _____
      Carpets   _____
      Curtains   _____
      Furniture   _____
      Appliances   _____
      Garden services   _____
Additional improvements   _____
SUBTOTAL   R_____
ADDITIONAL COSTS INVOLVED WHEN THERE IS A BOND   _____
Deposit   _____
Cash (balance of purchase price not covered by mortgage bond)   _____
Bank initiation fee   _____
Bank administration fee   _____
Bond repayment   _____
      Subsidy   _____
      Member's contribution   _____
Mortgage bond registration costs   _____
Stamp duty   _____
      Collateral bond   _____
      Additional property   _____
      Notarial bond   _____
Inspection fees (financial institution)   _____
Interim interest   _____

Commission tariff for first bond, second bond, collateral security (if applicable)	_____
Homeowner's insurance policy	_____
Decreasing term life insurance policy	_____
Endowment policy	_____
Cancellation costs for existing bond	_____
Cancellation costs	_____
Penalty (if applicable)	_____
Additional bonds	_____
TOTAL	R_____

8.7 THE ESTATE AGENT: A PROFILE

8.7.1 Introduction

Until the 20th century most buying and selling transactions took place directly between buyers and sellers. Once two parties reached an agreement, an attorney was requested to draw up the agreement of sale contract and to finalise the transaction.

In the early 1890s the property business was highly disorganised and the general attitude was one of 'let the buyer beware'. In the course of time, the property business became more organised and statutory boards took control over the conclusion of property transactions through estate agencies. In the United States of America, NAREB (National Association of Real Estate Boards) was established in 1908. Legislation was passed in 1917 in California and Oregon, making it compulsory for property brokers and agents to obtain a licence before they were allowed to conclude property transactions (Ring & Dasso 1985:36).

An estate agent is someone who represents buyers and sellers in order to serve their interests during the conclusion of buying and selling transactions. This service is not free of charge, as the estate agent receives a commission for the successful completion of a transaction. To become an estate agent, you have to meet the requirements set by the Estate Agency Affairs Board (EAAB).

The EAAB is a body corporate established and controlled in terms of the Estate Agents Act 112 of 1976. This body has a code of conduct to which all estate agents must conform. The Institute of Realtors is incorporated as a non-profit making company and strives to improve the standing and knowledge of its members as a professional body.

8.7.2 Conceptual framework

The Estate Agents Act 112 of 1976 defines an estate agent as any person who, for the acquisition of gain, on his or her own account or in partnership, in any manner holds him- or herself out as a person (including a legal person such as a company or a close corporation) who, directly or indirectly advertises that he or she, on the instruction or on behalf of any other person, performs the following acts in respect of immovable property, an interest in immovable property or business undertaking:

- sells or purchases;
- negotiates to sell or purchase;
- canvasses sellers or purchasers;
- undertakes or offers to canvass sellers or purchasers;
- lets or hires;
- negotiates to let or hire;
- canvasses lessees or lessors;
- undertakes or offers to canvass lessees or lessors;
- collects or receives any moneys payable on account of a lease; or
- renders any such other service specified by the Minister, on the recommendation of the EAAB, from time to time by notice in the Government Gazette (Delport 1987:298; Maritz 1983:25; Section 1(iii) of the Estate Agents Act, 1976).

In *Rogut v Rogut* 1982 (3) SA 928 (A) an estate agent was considered to be a person holding him- or herself out as an estate agent or advertising that he or she operates as an estate agent. A distinction must always be made between estate agents who act lawfully and who are in possession of a fidelity fund certificate, and those who operate without such a certificate. The public is often unaware that a valid fidelity fund certificate is a prerequisite for an estate agent to earn a commission.

8.7.3 Estate Agency Affairs Board (EAAB)

In the following discussion emphasis is placed on the objectives of the Board, the estate agents fidelity fund, fidelity insurance, as well as the several requirements estate agents and agents are obliged to meet.

8.7.3.1 The Board's objectives

The aim of the Board is to promote and maintain the professional integrity of estate agents (Section 7 of the Estate Agents Act, 1976). Delport (1987:293) and Maritz (1983:29) mention two aspects connected with this aim:

- to protect the public in their dealings with estate agents by ensuring that persons subject to certain disqualifications do not practice as estate agents and to safeguard the money entrusted to estate agents by the public; and
- to regulate the affairs and activities of estate agents by defining their rights and responsibilities clearly by means of a code of conduct.

8.7.3.2 Estate agents fidelity fund

An estate agents fidelity fund was established by the Estate Agents Act 112 of 1976 to reimburse persons who suffer pecuniary loss as a result of theft by an estate agent of certain money or property entrusted to him or her, or failure by an estate agent to open and keep a trust account (for example, when an estate agent keeps money in his or her car and this is later stolen by a thief).

All the annual contributions of estate agents, as well as income accrued to the fund from other sources, are paid into the estate agents fidelity fund. Claims by buyers and sellers against estate agents who fall under this law, not common law, are paid from this fund. The fund is controlled and managed by the EAAB, which keeps an account of the financial position of the fund in one of the official languages. A person wishing to claim against the fund must prove that the estate agent who was responsible for the financial loss in fact complies with the definition of an estate agent (Section 1(iii) of the Estate Agents Act, 1976).

Full-time estate agents are committed to building good references and are aware of the long-term implications of the kind of service they render. Part-time estate agents sometimes do not have enough time to concentrate on good service, perhaps because they have other responsibilities and they do not intend operating as estate agents over the long-term. Unfortunately, there are many 'fly-by-night' estate agents.

Efficient estate agents normally have comparative market analyses at their disposal and are able to handle negotiations in a professional manner. An estate agent who has a proven record of successful sales in the past can be strongly recommended. The mere fact that an estate agent mentions previous achievements is not always sufficient, unless he or she can provide statistics. It was pointed out above that an estate agent must have a fidelity fund certificate.

8.7.3.3 Estate agents fidelity fund certificate

Over and above contributions to the fidelity fund, an estate agency must take out fidelity insurance in respect of every person employed by the agency, irrespective of his or her capacity. By taking out fidelity insurance, an estate agency protects itself in its capacity as an employer against theft by its employees.

An estate agent has a special relationship with the persons who instruct him or her to buy or sell on their behalf. This relationship is based on trust between the estate agent and his or her principal(s).

The position of trust between an estate agent and his or her principal resulting from the relationship between them is dealt with below.

8.7.4 Position of trust: Relationship between estate agent and principal

In this discussion, we will examine the relationship that develops when an estate agent receives an instruction from a principal (person giving the instruction) to perform a specific task for remuneration. Maritz (1983:209) points out that the estate agent is not employed by the principal when entering into an agreement with him or her, the reason being that the estate agent in fact has no obligation to render any service to or perform any task for the principal. Furthermore, the estate agent may, with the full powers of his or her principal, enter into an agreement of sale or even appoint a subagent to act as the principal's representative.

An estate agent may act as a principal's representative even though the principal does not exist at the time of the conclusion of the contract, for example when a company is about to be established. Once the company has been established, the contract is effective retrospectively. It is possible for an estate agent to enter into an agreement with a buyer or seller without revealing the principal (undisclosed principal). If a third party (buyer or seller) finds out about this undisclosed principal, he or she may choose whether to enter into the agreement with the estate agent or the principal. The undisclosed principal may also reveal him- or herself and act as if the estate agent has operated on his or her behalf from the beginning.

When a representative (the estate agent) claims that he or she has the necessary power of attorney (authority to do or act on behalf of another and to perform certain legal functions), or when a third party (buyer or seller) claims that the representative (estate agent) with whom he or she has negotiated has the necessary power of attorney, or when a principal claims that his or her representative (the estate agent) has the necessary power of attorney, the person who claims the power of attorney must prove it.

The power of attorney that an estate agent receives from his or her principal is circumscribed by express or tacit agreement between both parties. Van Jaarsveld (1983:195) points out that the principal is permitted to enter into an agreement with a third party even if the representative has not acted within the confines of his or her power of attorney.

Once an estate agent has carried out his or her instructions, this power of attorney is terminated. Similarly, the power of attorney may lapse after a specific period of time or if it is no longer possible for the estate agent to carry out the power of attorney. The latter applies when the status of either the estate agent or the principal changes, as in the following cases:
- in the event of the principal or representative becoming insane during their relationship;
- in the event of the principal being declared insolvent; and
- in the event of the principal or representative dying (Van Jaarsveld 1983:200).

An estate agent may, nevertheless, in the absence of a power of attorney, carry out certain instructions as representative of his or her principal; these include the following:
- making suggestions;
- obtaining options; and
- providing insurance (Maritz 1983:209).

An estate agent is permitted to make suggestions to potential buyers and sellers with regard to numerous matters, such as the value of the property, methods of buying or selling a house and alternative methods of raising finance. Neither the estate agent nor the principal can be held liable for suggestions made by an estate agent. Delport (1987:318) points out, however, that both the estate agent and principal could be held liable for damages in the case of misrepresentation.

An estate agent may obtain an option on behalf of his or her principal at any time, as the principal is not under an obligation to enter into the agreement. Similarly, an estate agent is not obliged to enter into the agreement in his or her own name. The relationship between an estate agent and his or her principal is primarily determined by the agreement (contract) between them. A written agreement is recommended as it excludes misunderstandings. This agreement must indicate the respective duties of the parties, the remuneration payable, as well as when it is payable. Seldin (1980:127) suggests that an attempt should be made to provide solutions in the contract in the event of problems arising if certain things occur.

With regard to the agreement between the estate agent and his or her principal, Maritz (1983:209) points out that, in terms of the Act, unless otherwise agreed, an estate agent is under no obligation to:
- conduct negotiations for the purchase;
- ensure that the agreement of sale is finalised and executed;
- establish a valid agreement of sale;
- canvass buyers; or
- introduce a buyer when the opportunity presents itself.

After appointing an estate agent to render a service, the principal may render this service or appoint another estate agent or more estate agents so sell his or her house. Such action by a principal is only possible in the absence of a sole mandate. Unless agreed otherwise, the principal may enter into agreements with as many estate agents as he or she pleases. The principal does not have to enter into a contract with a third party (buyer or seller) introduced by an estate agent.

The obligation of good faith is based on the position of trust existing between the estate agent and his or her principal. This obligation places the responsibility on the estate agent:
- to serve the interest of his or her principal;
- to ensure that his or her own interests are not in conflict with his or her obligations;
- not to make any secret profit;
- not to use secret or confidential information in an improper way;
- not to be negligent;
- to carry out the power of attorney personally; and
- to maintain professional and ethical standards (Delport 1987:318).

These points are discussed below.

8.7.4.1 The obligation to act in the interest of the principal

This obligation arises immediately. An estate agent has to make a choice between possible actions or has to refrain from doing something. If an estate agent discovers facts that may be damaging to the principal if the instruction is carried out, he or she must reveal these facts to the principal. Any action in the interest of the principal must always be to the principal's advantage, or the estate agent must refrain from taking any action if it will not be to the principal's advantage.

8.7.4.2 The obligation to ensure that there is no conflict of interest

Maritz (1983:213) points out that, during the performance of an estate agent's tasks, there may be conflicting interests between him or her and the principal. This conflict may not have a negative influence on the actions of the estate agent with regard to advising his or her principal. No estate agent should be in a position where there is conflict between his or her interests and obligations.

Joubert (1967:649) poses two questions on conflicting interests. Firstly, the question arises as to whether an estate agent (as a representative) may buy what he or she has been asked to sell and, secondly, whether the agent may sell what he or she has been asked to buy for the principal.

Both may be done, provided that it is done in good faith and transparently.

The following two cases will be dealt with briefly:

- entering into an agreement with the principal; and
- entering into an agreement in which the representative has an interest.

Upon entering into an agreement with the principal, an estate agent must bring all the relevant facts to his or her principal's attention. Facts are relevant when they affect the principal's decision to enter into an agreement with the representative (or the conditions under which he or she would do so). The acceptability of the price at which the principal should sell, is also applicable here (Joubert 1967:651).

The agreement may be declared null and void if an estate agent does not disclose all the relevant facts. Consequently, an estate agent must obtain and use all the relevant facts to the benefit of the principal. No commission may be received while entering into an agreement with the principal, unless the latter gives his or her consent (Delport 1987:319).

An estate agent's spouse may not be a party to the purchase transaction when the estate agent is acting as a representative, unless this fact has been disclosed to the third party. Seldin (1980:131) maintains that, in the absence of such consent, the estate agent might not attempt to obtain the highest price for the seller's property, because of the personal interest of the agent in the transaction.

Should the estate agent enter into an agreement on the principal's behalf, with him- or herself as the other party, without the necessary consent of the principal, the latter may uphold or reject the contract. Should the principal reject the contract, he or she may (where the representative buys what he or she has been asked to sell) reclaim the property from the estate agent at repayment of the purchase price.

8.7.4.3 The obligation not to make a secret profit

While carrying out his or her task, an estate agent may not make any secret profit without the consent of the principal. Maritz (1983:213) states that when secret profit has actually been made, it must be repaid to the principal. Making a secret profit is wrong because it is done without the consent of the principal. A bribe, for example, could be mentioned here; bribery refers to the reason for a gift.

According to Van Jaarsveld (1983:230), a bribery takes place where a representative has been promised a gift, with the view to encourage the agent to act in favour of the donor. Such a gift is a secret when it is presented without the knowledge or consent of the principal. Should the principal suffer pecuniary loss as a result of the donor's action, he or she may, among other things, claim the profit made or the loss suffered from the estate agent.

To determine what profits are secret profits, Joubert (1967:685) points out the causal relation that should exist between the profit and the representative. Additional factors that determine whether the profit is unlawful are found in the fact that the profit is contrary to the instructions of the representative. An estate agent must give to the principal what is due to the principal and may not claim more than he or she is entitled to.

8.7.4.4 The obligation to keep certain information secret

An estate agent obtains certain confidential information about the principal whilst carrying out his or her instructions. This information is entrusted to the estate agent and may be used only to promote the interests of the principal. Such an obligation exists for the duration of the contractual relationship and also thereafter. Joubert (1967:690) points out that, should the information be in writing, the representative must return it to the principal once the instructions have been carried out. Estate agents may also not use this confidential information for personal gain or to the detriment of their principal.

An estate agent must disclose all relevant information to the principal, use his or her information and discretion to benefit the principal, apply all confidential information in good faith and supply correct information to the principal with regard to the state of affairs when requested by the latter. Similarly, estate agents must disclose to the principal all information regarding the principal's business that could be used to promote the business.

8.7.4.5 The obligation not to be negligent

Where an estate agent neglects to make an offer to the owner (principal) on behalf of the principal before the expiry date, the estate agent will be liable for damages to the principal. An estate agent will also be held liable if he or she fails to obtain the signature of a co-owner for an agreement to sell a property and the buyer loses the transaction as a result. The same principle applies when an estate agent supplies incorrect information regarding the selling price of a property, current market trends or any other matter that may have a negative effect on the selling price of the property for the owner. An estate agent will not, however, be held liable for giving an honest opinion on values or other matters (Delport 1986:27; Seldin 1980:130).

An estate agent cannot base his or her financial advice to the client on random assumptions – he or she must make sure that the facts are correct. An estate agent who makes false or careless statements to buyers and sellers, or who fails to disclose certain information, could cause considerable problems for him- or herself, the principal and the agency.

Assume that a buyer purchases a house for the purpose of letting it through an estate agent who is acting on behalf of a seller. The buyer finds out (after the purchase) that the house cannot be let because it is subject to the Rent Control Act, which means that the rental income will not be a profitable investment.

In such a case, the estate agent will be held liable for non-disclosure of important information, that is, the effects of rent control. Delport (1986:27) points out the following questions that may arise from such a case:
- Could the buyer sue the seller because the agent caused this problem?
- Could the seller, if he or she is responsible for the agent's conduct, sue the agent for his or her actions?
- Could the buyer sue the agent for the false statements and the non-disclosure of essential information?
- Could the buyer sue the agency for its agent's conduct?
- What action, if any, could be taken by the EAAB in this regard?

Estate agents should pay special attention to the following questions regarding whether or not to disclose financial information to buyers and sellers:
- Should the agent inspect the property first in order to identify any defects (patent and latent defects)?
- Would it make any difference if the agent were not aware of a particular defect?
- Is an agent under an obligation to find out, for example, whether the property is rent controlled, even if he or she does not state that the property is not rent controlled?

- Would it make a difference if, for example, the buyer were not a specialist but a professional businessperson? (Delport 1986:27)

Delport (1986:27) poses these questions in another way:
- When is it better for an estate agent to disclose absolutely nothing about a specific matter?
- When is an estate agent obliged to disclose information and convey this information correctly?

An estate agent's liability for false statements is considered by answering the following question: Could the buyer sue the seller and, if so, could the seller in turn sue the estate agent to recover any resulting expenses? In *Davidson v Bonafede* 1981 (2) SA 501 (C) the court declared that the estate agent had acted in a reckless manner by not ascertaining the state of the house. The seller was liable for all expenses incurred by the buyer, since the agent had acted on his behalf (irrespective of whether or not the seller had been aware of the false statements made by the agent).

The courts view reckless conduct in the same light as fraud, even if the estate agent did not know whether his or her statement was true or false. Sellers can include a clause in the agreement of sale that indemnifies them as well as the agent with regard to false statements. Estate agents must advise sellers in this respect. However, liability for fraud cannot be excluded. A *voetstoots* clause does not exclude liability for false statements.

Consequently, the question is not whether the seller has made true statements to the estate agent, but whether the estate agent has made true statements to the buyer. As far as could be ascertained, no seller has yet been found liable for negligent or false statements made by an estate agent. Negligent statements are statements that no reasonable estate agent would make under similar circumstances (Delport 1986:28). A seller could certainly recover any expenses from the estate agent, because of the good faith that should exist between them.

A buyer cannot hold an estate agent liable for contractual damages, as no contract or mandate exists between them (unless the estate agent acts on behalf of the buyer). Delport (1986:29) indicates that he could not trace any court case in this regard. Nevertheless, the courts would hold a person liable for false or negligent statements and the particular liability would depend on the relevant facts and circumstances of each individual case.

In *Soobramoney and Another v R. Acutt & Sons (Pty) Ltd* 1965 (2) SA 899 (D) the court found an estate agent not guilty after he had indicated the incorrect boundaries for a property that was for sale. A clause in the agreement of sale relieved him of all liability, stating that the buyer had inspected the property. Estate agents must make buyers and sellers aware of the inclusion of clauses in agreements of sale. The parties must not only sign the agreement but they must also make sure that they understand the implications of all the clauses.

To be found guilty, the estate agent must not only have made negligent or false statements but such actions must have led to the buyer contracting with the seller. In order to determine when an estate agent is duty-bound not to make a negligent statement, the following factors are considered:

- the relationship between the estate agent and the buyer;
- special skills possessed by the estate agent;
- the extent to which a party may avoid a loss;
- knowledge of the extent to which an uninformed party trusts the estate agent; and
- the nature of the statement (Delport 1986:30).

Buyers often rely heavily on the estate agent because they lack knowledge of the ins and outs of buying a house. Consequently, a special relationship develops between the estate agent and the buyer. Because of the EAAB's code of conduct, as well as the Institute of Realtors' ethical code, estate agents do have special skills and are not merely salespersons.

It is a fairly simple matter for an estate agent to prevent a client from finding him- or herself in an awkward financial position by providing him or her with the necessary information. Estate agents should be able to recognise clients who are uninformed about certain aspects. In such cases, they have a particular obligation to avoid negligent statements.

This does not mean that an estate agent can always be sued for any statement after the conclusion of the contract, since the courts regard some statements as being mere exaggeration. For example, an estate agent's statement that a particular house is the most beautiful house in South Africa cannot really be regarded as a negligent or false statement.

Estate agents are advised not to make statements that do not reflect the truth. If they do not know whether information is true or false, they should indicate that they do not know, and undertake to find out.

Another question that may arise is whether an aggrieved buyer can sue an estate agency on the basis of a statement made by its employee (an estate agent) that led to the conclusion of a transaction. In this case, we are dealing with the relationship between an estate agent and his or her agency, and in particular how the parties see this relationship. If a party is under the impression that an agent is acting on behalf of an agency, this party can sue the agency for statements made by the agent. In turn, the agency can recover this expense from the agent, because the agent must act in good faith towards the agency.

Delport (1986:28) points out that, in order to avoid financial losses, an estate agent must either contract free of liability with his or her agency, or take out insurance against such liability. It is recommended that taking out insurance against professional liability be made compulsory for estate agents.

An agent's failure to make certain information known is merely another form of making a false statement. The courts, however, hold estate agents less liable for not disclosing information than for false or negligent statements.

Delport (1986:30) states that, insofar as can be established, no case exists in South Africa where an estate agent has been held liable for non-disclosure of information. On the other hand, there are numerous cases where a buyer/seller has been held liable for non-disclosure of certain information. The following cases may be consulted in this regard:

- *Glaston House (Pty) Ltd v Inag (Pty) Ltd* 1977 (2) SA 846 (A); and
- *Trotman and Another v Edwick* 1951 (1) SA 443 (A).

A positive reply to the following questions will determine whether an estate agent would be liable for damages as a result of not disclosing certain information:

- Was the agent under an obligation to disclose certain information?
- Did the estate agent fail to take reasonable steps in order to determine the true state of affairs?

The EAAB cannot be held liable by a buyer who suffered losses as a result of an estate agent's statement or the non-disclosure of certain information. The estate agent's fidelity fund does not make provision for such losses. An estate agent can only be held liable for violating the code of conduct for estate agents. If an estate agent is found guilty, he or she could be fined, or his or her fidelity fund certificate could be revoked and he or she would no longer be allowed to practise as an estate agent.

Delport (1986:31) summarises this discussion as follows: 'Sticks and stones might break your bones, but words, expressed or not, can put you out of business.'

8.7.4.6 The obligation to exercise power of attorney personally

Normally, an estate agent is expected to exercise his or her power of attorney personally when carrying out an instruction, as power of attorney is often granted to an estate agent on the basis of his or her reputation. It is permissible, however, for an estate agent to appoint a subagent to act on his or her behalf. Kerr (1972:164) defines a subagent as someone who is bound by contract to the agent and not to the principal. Such subagent must be responsible to the agent for carrying out the agent's task (instruction from principal) in its entirety or in part.

Van Jaarsveld (1983:227) and Kerr (1972:163) state that a representative (an estate agent) may in fact transfer his or her power of attorney to a subagent, with the express or tacit permission of the principal, provided that he or she ensures that the second estate agent carries out the instruction properly, as the estate agent who appointed the subagent could be held liable for damages to the principal, unless a contract has been drawn up between the principal and the subagent.

Seldin (1980:135) points out that no subagent acting without power of attorney may bind a principal to a transaction. In such a case, the subagent will be bound to the contract. To determine whether a subagent may indeed bind the principal contractually, the following questions should be asked:

- Were the subagent's actions part of the estate agent's (representative's) task? If not, the former is not defined as a subagent.
- Did the subagent possess power of attorney to perform the task of an estate agent? The principal will subsequently be bound to the contract (provided that power of attorney has been granted to the appointment of the subagent) according to the limitations of the initial power of attorney granted to the estate agent (Kerr 1972:164).

It is possible for estate agents, particularly as a result of their position of trust, to carry out their obligations towards their principals in an unethical and dishonest manner in many different ways. For that reason the express or tacit agreement with the principal must be honoured.

Estate agents' ethical obligations are discussed below.

8.7.4.7 The obligation to maintain professional and ethical standards

The IEASA (1985:7) defines professional and ethical behaviour as maintaining a standard that distinguishes between right and wrong, good or bad in practising a profession. Although estate agents do not receive payment if a service they have rendered is unsuccessful, they are by no means relieved of their responsibility towards the public. Estate agents must render service of a high quality, even though they do not receive remuneration for unsuccessful transactions.

Godi & Reyhons (1980:239) point out certain traits that professional persons have in common:

- They have a good self-image.
- They have the ability to solve problems.
- They set definite quantitative and qualitative objectives.
- They have a well-developed ability to listen, because they know that people do not always mean what they say.
- They enjoy communicating in spite of the many obstacles that occur during communication, such as buyer's and seller's preconceived ideas about the service rendered by estate agents (some people are concerned about protecting their own egos when communicating with estate agents).
- They are enthusiastic about and interested in their work (buyers and sellers sense this interest and respond to an estate agent's confidence during a presentation).
- They understand people – for example, a seller would choose an estate agent to market his or her house because the estate agent understands him or her, rather than because the seller understands the agent.
- They perform when it is expected of them (estate agents should not only have knowledge and skills but must also apply them when required by the situation).
- They are prepared to work hard.

In order to understand the difference between a property broker and an estate agent, it is necessary to define the terms intermediary, broker and commercial agent.

Intermediaries are go-betweens who do not buy and sell goods for their own account – their sole aim is to bring manufacturers and retailers together. Commercial agents and brokers are the two most important types of intermediary (Lucas 1983:391).

Brokers are not sales orientated to the same extent as commercial agents. Their service is more limited and they are normally used on account of their specialist knowledge and experience. The many variations in practice make it difficult to distinguish between brokers and commercial agents. Marx & Dekker (1982:14) point out that a broker only brings the buyer and marketer of goods and services together.

According to the Central Statistical Services, *commercial agents* are persons, such as estate agents, who receive commission as a primary source of income (Lucas 1983:332).

Apart from the requirements of the Estate Agents Act, a code of professional ethics, as compiled by the Institute of Realtors, indicates that estate agents accept an obligation to practise self-discipline. The

practical aim of such a code is to inform the public of the following:
- that the profession aims at performing its tasks effectively and in the interest of the public; and
- in exchange for the public's trust, estate agents act in the public interest.

Estate agents experience ethical problems on a daily basis in their dealings with buyers, sellers, other estate agents, as well as their employers. Conflict arises when an estate agent makes decisions based on his or her own values, especially when these values are unethical according to legislation, the property business, employers, buyers and sellers. The estate agent's ethical obligations may be divided into the following categories:
- an ethical obligation towards him- or herself;
- an ethical obligation towards other estate agents, employers and the property business; and
- an ethical obligation towards members of the public (buyers and sellers) (IEASA 1985:8).

Each of these obligations is briefly discussed below.

Every estate agent enters the business world with certain perceptions of right and wrong and often faces the temptation to act against his or her own personal standards and behaviour. Gorman (1979:408) states that ethical responsibility towards yourself begins with the choice of a business (estate agency) to work for. By avoiding any estate agency that expects its estate agents to act unethically, an estate agent can prevent many problems. Buyers and sellers should immediately report possible unethical behaviour by estate agents to the EAAB.

Estate agents are placed in a position of trust, firstly by the estate agency that employs them and secondly by the principal. Gorman (1979:408) distinguishes, among others, between the following problem areas regarding ethical conduct.

There is fierce competition among estate agents as a result of the commission involved in concluding transactions. This competition often leads to the 'wrong' property (that is, a house for our purposes) being sold to the buyer, with far-reaching consequences for the buyer and/or seller, as well as for the image of the property business. Estate agents should be prepared to share commission with another agent by allowing the other agent to sell the 'right' house to a buyer, even if the first agent introduced the buyer to the second agent. With the approval of their respective agencies, estate agents may conclude a mutual agreement to share commission. Most agencies have arrangements in this respect.

Members of the public have the right to expect ethical behaviour from estate agents, and normally do not get involved in arguments about commission between estate agents. An estate agent should not advise a party who has already been informed by another estate agent, only to persuade that party to purchase his or her own principal's house. An estate agent should not give any financial advice against his or her own convictions in order to earn a commission. Such advice is not in the interest of the country, the relevant parties or the property business.

Contradictory advice is not always unethical – an estate agent may feel duty-bound to give contradictory advice if he or she knows that a client is not receiving sound financial advice from another agent. It may be to the client's advantage to be told that the other agent's advice is not sound. However, an estate agent who makes a habit of questioning other agents' abilities to provide financial advice and is constantly warning clients about this will be guilty of unethical behaviour.

Estate agents should give advice in such a way as not to be seen as wanting only to conclude a transaction at all costs. Earning commission should not be the sole aim, as this could easily lead to unethical behaviour. The primary goal should be to make a profit for the client on a deal by rendering good service.

Examples of unethical behaviour by agents that have been identified in the past may be found in Gibson (1983:259–282), Huse (1982:508), IEASA (1985:9) and Ring & Dasso (1985:35).

Ethical behaviour is essential for the protection of the entire community, as well as the mutual protection of its members. The institutions principally involved in controlling the ethical conduct of estate agents are the EAAB (a statutory body) and the Institute of Realtors (an incorporated non-profit making association).

The services rendered by estate agents are briefly discussed below.

8.7.5 Services rendered by estate agents

8.7.5.1 Primary services
The many services rendered by estate agents may be divided into two main groups, namely primary and secondary services. Maritz (1983:3) distinguishes between the following primary services:
- finding a buyer for, or seller of, immovable property or an interest in immovable property;
- finding a lessee for, or lessor of, immovable property or an interest in immovable property; and
- finding a buyer for, or seller of, or lessee for, or lessor of, a business concern.

Among other things, an estate agent's function is to canvass a potential buyer, introduce the buyer to the canvassed property, supply information on the property in order that he or she may decide whether to purchase or not, assist the potential buyer in drawing up the offer to a seller should he or she decide to purchase, arrange financing, present the offer to the seller and advise the potential buyer about the acceptance or non-acceptance thereof.

8.7.5.2 Secondary services

Secondary services support primary services, although they may be rendered separately. As secondary services mainly comprise advice on specific aspects of property, some consultants concentrate only on these services. It should by no means be accepted that an estate agent distinguishes between primary and secondary services in the course of his or her work, since the one is usually accompanied by the other. This will be apparent throughout our discussion.

Maritz (1983:5) distinguishes between the following secondary services:

- determining the market value of a property;
- advising on property investment;
- advising on raising finance; and
- advising on property development.

Sellers often either undervalue their property (to attract buyers) or overvalue their property (which discourages potential buyers). After the finalisation of an agreement, the seller often feels that the price was too low. On the other hand, a buyer may wonder whether he or she paid too much. This is referred to as 'buyers blues'. Experience of the property market, which most estate agents have (unless they are new to the business), can greatly reduce or even eliminate these problems.

8.7.5.3 Roles estate agents play

The IEASA (1985:58) mentions the following roles that estate agents play:

- rendering a service to meet the requirements of buyers and sellers, following up these services and keeping both parties informed;
- encouraging both parties to accept current market trends (market prices) in a positive way, by informing them on a factual basis;
- convincing both parties that their actions are in the interest of both parties;
- leading the buyer and the seller to an agreement on the strength of their advice; and
- building a good reputation by means of references and testimonials from satisfied buyers, sellers and previous employers.

All properties for sale or to let must be listed and the list must be shown to other agents. Once a buyer has been found for a specific property, negotiations on the price and terms follow. An estate agent's most important role is that of negotiator. The seller should be informed of the price that the buyer can and is prepared to pay. The seller should also be advised on how to prepare the property to make it attractive to other buyers, and how to arrange visits by potential buyers.

The owner (seller) may be informed of matters regarding his or her house by mail, by telephone or in person. It is recommended that an estate agent inform his or her client in person and with enthusiasm.

An estate agent should also explain to the seller what further action he or she intends taking, as this will hopefully give the seller peace of mind about the efforts being made to market the house. If a buyer indicates that he or she will only be interested in a house if certain repairs are undertaken, the seller should be informed.

Seldin (1980:437) points out that estate agents should obtain further information in anticipation of questions potential buyers may ask when viewing the house, such as concerning the availability and accessibility of schools, transport facilities, churches, recreation facilities and proximity of freeways. If a buyer needs 30 days to obtain a mortgage bond for the purchase of the house, the estate agent must ensure that the buyer applies for a mortgage bond and then must follow up the transaction until all the formalities have been finalised.

Estate agents are also required to carry out the following ten-point plan, compiled by IEASA (1985:60), in order to perform their tasks more efficiently:

- Develop thorough knowledge of all activities related to their area of work.
- Keep records of all purchase transactions irrespective of who was responsible for the transactions.
- Always provide potential buyers and sellers with a reliable market analysis.
- Ensure that properties are listed at market-related prices.
- Have knowledge of codes of conduct (EAAB) and the code of ethics .
- Provide effective guidance when entering into the agreement of sale by informing the parties on the meaning of various clauses.
- Learn how to relate the requirements of sellers and buyers to their financial position.
- Develop the ability to determine the real buying and selling motives.
- Make both parties feel that their interests are being served on an equal basis.
- Obtain the maximum information regarding properties from, among others, books, magazines, seminars and courses.

Property in South Africa is usually bought and sold through registered estate agents. Estate agents earn their income by offering primary services, among other things, and consequently they will do everything in their power to see that transactions take place. Before a buyer or seller decides to enter into a transaction, careful consideration should be given to the role estate agents play.

An estate agent represents the property business and his or her behaviour affects and reflects the image of the business. His or her actions are based on the fact that buyers and sellers of property are brought together. Seldin (1980:435) explains that a purchasing process in fact constitutes rejection, contrary to the general idea that it constitutes making a choice. The rejection process involves reducing the number of properties for sale to a few with viewing potential. This rejection process could be difficult without the assistance of an estate agent, since professional guidelines are necessary regarding the property a buyer can afford according to his or her income and personal circumstances. In addition, an estate agent has to qualify buyers and sellers (that is, thoroughly analyse their financial situations).

Estate agents enter houses up for sale on the estate agency's books. There are other occasions for providing financial advice to buyers and sellers. Estate agents often list a house without pointing out to the seller that certain factors in the market are not conducive to the sale of the house. Godi & Reyhons (1980:113) mention five factors that determine the marketability of a house:
- area (residential area);
- condition;
- price;
- terms; and
- the seller's motive.

Estate agents should inform sellers of the demand for houses in the *area* in which the house is situated. There may be several similar houses for sale in this area and the climate (warm or cold) may either promote or adversely affect the demand. Houses may sell very slowly because of the distance to business and shopping centres. Although the house may be situated in an attractive area, the plot may be unattractive for various reasons: the slope, rockiness, a large number of stairs leading to the front door, or its size. On the other hand, the plot may be attractive, but situated in an unattractive area.

A house in a physically good condition will sell more readily and at a better price than a house in bad repair. Estate agents must point out to buyers that a house in a good *condition* is a better marketing proposition. They could make suggestions such as having the house, roof or fence painted, or improving the state of the garden. They should also find out whether the seller would be prepared to spend a certain amount of money if such improvements were necessary.

When a seller's *price* is too high, it could exclude the house from the market in that price class. Estate agents are not normally prepared to make any great effort to show a house to buyers when the price is obviously too high.

Estate agents explain to sellers that the *terms* of sale affect the marketability of a house, as well as the eventual price. If a seller demands a relatively high price for cash, he or she is unlikely to get this price. In the case of a seller wishing to sell a house on an instalment basis, a higher price could be anticipated than in the case of a cash purchase.

The seller's *motive* for selling is another factor that determines the marketability of a house. An urgent need for cash could, for example, lead to a quick sale if the price is low. The same applies when a seller has to move unexpectedly. In order to provide the most efficient service, an agent should find out about the seller's motive.

Estate agents should point out to sellers that, even though the house is in a less attractive area, it could still be sold, providing that it is in good condition, the terms are reasonable, the price is equal to or less than the market price and the seller has a strong motivation to sell.

Even though the disadvantages of an unattractive area and the condition of the house are reduced by an attractive price and terms, the seller's motive is the most important of the five factors regarding the marketability of a house. The reason for this is that it is the seller who must decide on the selling price. Having assessed these five factors affecting the marketability of a house, an estate agent will be in a position to advise the seller on the marketing plan. At this stage the agent should be ready for an interview with the seller in order to list the house (canvass for marketing purposes).

During this interview it is important that the estate agent creates a rapport with the seller in order to gain his or her trust and thus obtain more information about his or her situation. When all is said and done, financial advice can only be really effective if the agent has all the necessary facts and information about the seller. An agent should realise that a seller would place (list) a house on the agency's books only if he or she was convinced that his or her personal goals would be reached by doing so. When several estate agencies attempt to list a house on their books, the estate agent who best understands the requirements of the seller will ultimately succeed.

All sellers who sell their houses through an estate agent would normally require assistance with their decisions. Such assistance is required because sellers feel that estate agents have the necessary knowledge, and therefore agents should not disappoint them in their expectations. Estate agents should assist their clients in considering alternatives by making suggestions to solve any problems that may arise. Untrained estate agents are generally not in a position to advise sellers and will find it difficult to convince them to accept their advice. Because of the inefficient service provided by inexperienced estate agents, sellers often come to believe that no special skills or expertise are required and that they are quite capable of selling their houses themselves (Godi & Reyhons 1980:121).

Godi & Reyhons (1980:122) suggest the following four steps to help sellers reach their goals:
- identify the seller's problem;
- understand the seller's problem;
- identify with the problem; and
- solve the problem.

Estate agents should advise clients on their options for solving any problems. It is up to the estate agent to decide how to go about solving a client's problem, and the agent could make various suggestions in this regard.

An estate agent's ability to qualify buyers saves both parties time and particularly money. The buyer's financial position must be assessed in order to determine what he or she wants, can afford and should buy, depending on his or her circumstances and requirements (Seldin 1980:436). Such information helps an estate agent to come up with a better presentation in a shorter time. An estate agent qualifies the buyer by asking the 'right questions', and by establishing who will make or influence the decision to buy. The 'right questions' may comprise the following (Hopkins 1980:234; IEASA 1985:56):
- the composition of the family;
- the age of the children;
- the buyer's likes and dislikes regarding his or her existing property;
- the buyer's preference in architectural style;
- any specific preferences (for example, three garages);
- the amount of time the buyer has at his or her disposal to find a property;
- the buyer's willingness to make an immediate decision to purchase;
- when the buyer has to move; and
- whether the purchase of the property depends on the sale of another property or the raising of a bond (these aspects are called suspensive conditions).

Hopkins (1980:233) points out that many estate agents enter into agreements before they have qualified buyers. Frequently, they neglect to establish their client's needs for financial advice before concluding the contract. It is more often a case of failing to qualify buyers than of failing to finalise a transaction.

Many sellers attempt to play the role of estate agent themselves and to sell their property without the help of an estate agent. From the following discussion it may be seen that certain aspects do require the assistance of an estate agent.

8.7.6 Aspects that require the services of an estate agent

An estate agent's services are valuable for the following aspects to be effective:
- connected purchase; and
- showing a house.

Estate agents often attempt selling a house to a buyer and selling the buyer's previous house at the same time. In such a case, the estate agent will do everything in his or her power to sell the person's existing house in order to have a second house available and earn the commission.

An estate agent is in an ideal position to attract as many buyers as possible to view a show-house. Because estate agents often arrange show-houses, they are familiar with the most effective methods. A show-house gives the seller a reasonable idea of the price to expect and ensures that he or she makes the most of this opportunity; a show-house is usually only held once (Kling 1983:59).

People involved in property transactions frequently argue that they can save on the commission payable to the estate agent by selling the property themselves. This is in fact the case if everything goes according to plan. The savings can be calculated according to the estate agent's commission structure (Kling 1983:57).

However, it is not always easy to find a suitable buyer for your property without the assistance of an estate agent and transactions are seldom concluded without a hitch. Competition arises between the seller (who normally has only one property to sell) and estate agents (who have several properties on their list). A problem which may arise is that the seller has a limited number of potential buyers.

A second problem arises from the fact that buyers want to pay the lowest possible price for the property, while the seller wants the highest price possible – sufficient grounds for tempers flaring during the negotiating process! The result is that potential buyers are lost. In this case, an estate agent's primary role, namely that of negotiator, is invaluable, since he or she mediates between the parties. Particularly when a high purchase price (and consequently a large commission) is involved, the negotiating process often requires skills that may only be provided by a well-trained, professional estate agent.

Most purchase and sales transactions of immovable property take place through an estate agent; therefore, it is essential that potential buyers and sellers have the necessary information about the payment of commission. This matter is discussed below.

8.7.7 Commission

Estate agents receive commission from the principal (buyer, seller, lessee or lessor) for services rendered. The commission is arranged between the estate agent and his or her principal either tacitly or explicitly, but the amount is determined by the agency for whom the agent works.

Estate agents are entitled to remuneration for rendering a service that realises an income for the agency that employs them. The same applies to self-employed estate agents. Estate agents receive commission for the following activities:
- the selling of immovable property;
- the selling of immovable property at public auctions;
- the selling of commercial enterprises, partnerships and shares in a company;
- the attraction of capital (after services for which payment is received) in a concern;
- the collection of rental and the administration of property;
- the finding of a lessee and/or negotiations leading to a lease contract;
- the administration of sectional title buildings and company buildings occupied by owners;
- the administration of miscellaneous moneys and commissions;
- the selling of holiday accommodation; and
- rendering a service where the estate agent acts on behalf of some party or another (Espag 1984:82).

Espag (1984:19) explains how commission is distributed among agents, co-agents and the agency:
- Where the agent involved has canvassed, listed and sold a property without assistance. In this case, the estate agent is entitled to commission determined by the agency that employs him or her.
- Where the agent involved has canvassed and listed a property, and it has been sold by another estate agent in the agency. In this case, he or she will receive a percentage of the commission earned by the other agent who sold the property.
- The canvassing of an available property sold by a competitor agency on the basis of co-operation. Agencies often share commission according to an agreed ratio, and the agent who canvassed the property receives an agreed percentage of the shared commission.
- The sale of a property canvassed and listed by someone else in the agency he or she works for. Again, the policy of the relevant agency determines the distribution of commission among the agency and agents who were responsible for the listing and selling of the property respectively.
- The conclusion of management contracts (managing property portfolios) and leasing contracts. The estate agent is paid for rendering the service according to a predetermined agreement with his or her employer.

Co-operation between estate agents should be encouraged with regard to the conclusion of purchase and sales transactions. Without such co-operation, there will be unnecessary competition among estate agents for commission, and they will not be able to give effective advice. For this reason, estate agencies have a specific policy regarding the role of concluding transactions and earning commission. A particular agreement, known as a multi-mandate, exists between some estate agencies.

If an estate agent concludes a transaction on behalf of the principal, he or she is entitled to commission even if the principal does not benefit from it (*Levy v Phillips* AD 139), in other words, even if the principal's house is sold at a loss. Before this rule can be applied, the estate agent must have complied with all the provisions of the contract. This rule does not apply if the agreement states explicitly that the commission depends on whether the principal receives a special benefit in terms of the contract (Espag 1984:57).

When a contract is subject to a suspensive condition, which is not fulfilled, the estate agent will not be entitled to a commission (*Lasky v Steadmet (Edms) Bpk h/a Wessels de Villiers Agentskappe* 1976 (3) SA 696 (T); *Naidu v Naidoo* 1967 (2) SA 233 (N)). If a resolutive condition has not been fulfilled, the estate agent is entitled to commission.

8.7.7.1 Liability for the payment of commission
The party (buyer or seller) on whose behalf the estate agent acts is liable for the payment of the commission (Delport 1987:238, 335). It may also be agreed by the estate agent and the buyer that the

seller is to pay the commission. The payment of commission is determined contractually by the parties and payment may even be made jointly. Normally the seller pays the commission to the estate agent.

8.7.7.2 The amount of the commission

Parties usually agree either tacitly or explicitly to the amount of remuneration. In the absence of an express agreement, the customary remuneration (*Van Jaarsveld v Ackerman* 1975 (2) SA 753 (A)) or amount payable according to trade practice will be payable. Van Jaarsveld (1983:207) points out that, in the case of a lawsuit regarding the amount of commission, where the latter cases are not applicable, the court will determine a reasonable remuneration (*Chamotte (Pty) Ltd v Carl Coetzee (Pty) Ltd* 1973 (1) SA 644 (A)), taking into account the following factors:

- the nature of the work done or service rendered;
- the time and effort devoted to it;
- the value of the service to the principal;
- the proficiency required for the rendering of the service – *Kark v Proctor* 1961 (1) SA 752 (W);
- the responsibility for rendering the service – *Lubke v Kegel* 1913 WLD 91;
- the professional status of the representative;
- the customary remuneration paid by others for such a service – *Steer & Co v Rowland* (1897) 14 SC 358 (7CTR 400); and
- the intentions of the parties – *Totoyi v Ncuka* (1909) EDC 115.

The seller may further determine that the estate agent receives as remuneration everything the buyer pays above the minimum amount required by the seller (Joubert 1979:250). This seldom happens, however.

Once an estate agent undertakes to sell a house at a lower commission, the seller should ensure that the house is advertised as well as it would have been done at a higher commission. Better market analysis and good follow-ups are frequently the hallmark of the 'more expensive' agencies.

8.7.7.3 The point at which commission is earned

An estate agent is entitled to commission when the services rendered to a buyer or seller actually lead to the conclusion of an agreement of sale between the parties. The parties may tacitly or explicitly agree upon the event (the conclusion of, among other things, the agreement of sale), as well as upon the service to be rendered.

If no tacit or explicit agreement exists, the event, the service and the payment of commission are prescribed by law. A distinction is made between the principal as seller and the principal as buyer.

When the seller acts as principal, the service the estate agent must render is the presentation of a buyer who is ready, willing and able to buy. The buyer must be contractually capable and financially capable (capable of meeting the financial obligations of the contract) before he or she can qualify as a buyer. The event is the conclusion of a binding agreement between the buyer and seller. Commission is payable from the proceeds of the purchase price.

This also applies when the buyer acts as principal, with one exception. Unlike the seller, the buyer need not be financially capable of buying after the estate agent has found a property that meets the buyer's requirements. The buyer is liable for the payment of the estate agent's commission irrespective of whether he or she is financially capable of buying. (Maritz 1983:215, 217).

A buyer's financial position at the time of the conclusion of a contract is clearly dealt with in *Press v Jofwall Investments (Pty) Ltd* 1981 (1) SA 261 (W). Furthermore, a buyer is capable of buying even if he or she is insolvent, if he or she has sufficient assets to sell or use as collateral to borrow money (Joubert 1979:258). An estate agent should, therefore, find out as much as possible about the financial position of the buyer.

Before an estate agent is entitled to remuneration, some kind of transaction must have taken place, and the estate agent must have contributed to the conclusion of the transaction. An estate agent will be entitled to remuneration even if he or she did not introduce the ultimate buyer to the seller, provided that the agent actually caused the final agreement of sale to take place. In other words, there has to be an adequate casual relationship between the actions of the estate agent and the eventual purchase. Joubert (1979:254) poses the following questions to determine the actual cause of the conclusion of a contract. At issue is who introduced the buyer to the seller, who was responsible for negotiations running smoothly and who made it financially possible for the buyer to purchase.

The following court cases may be consulted in this regard. In *Lombard v Reed* 1948 (1) SA 30 (T) it was found that the initial estate agent was the cause of conclusion of the contract, even though a second estate agent handled the negotiations. Even when a buyer is unable to continue paying the seller, the seller has no right to claim the commission back from the estate agent, as was evident in *Beckwith v Foundation Investment Co* 1961 (4) SA 510 (A). In *Joubert and Others v Coster* 1982 (4) SA 540 (C) it was found that the estate agent was entitled to the commission, even though the potential buyer's father eventually purchased the property.

It frequently happens that an estate agent is unable to carry out the principal's instruction within a given period of time, and the seller takes over the negotiations him- or herself in order to finalise the purchasing transaction. Where an estate agent actually introduces a potential buyer to the seller within the given period and an agreement of sale is concluded, the estate agent may still claim remuneration, provided that the agent can prove that his or her introduction to the buyer was the cause of the agreement of sale. At issue in this instance is whether the estate agent performed the action on the grounds on which he or she based this claim while his or her instructions were still valid. The fact that buyers and sellers cease negotiating directly through an estate agent, therefore, does not necessarily guarantee that commission is not payable (Joubert 1979:256).

Estate agents should always inform buyers and sellers that they have an obligation to pay commission on the basis of their tacit or explicit agreement with the estate agent, since this increases their financial burden when buying a house. In order to determine which estate agent should receive remuneration, it must again be determined who was the real cause of concluding the contract. The onus of proving who should receive the remuneration is on the estate agent.

In the next section an analysis is made of the various mandates and contracts that may exist between estate agents and sellers, as well as between buyers and sellers.

8.8 THE CONTRACT

Negotiations and discussions always take place before a contract is concluded, for example when a house is sold or bought. The ultimate objective of these negotiations or discussions is to conclude a contract. Once a contract has been concluded, a set of rights and obligations in terms of both parties' promises takes effect. Legally enforceable promises are called contracts (Meyer 1979:41).

There are various kinds of contract, but for our purposes we will confine ourselves to a sole mandate, an open mandate, a multi-mandate and a purchase contract as applicable to the buying and selling of a house. Even if the parties to a purchase contract are capable of contracting, several requirements have to be met before a legal contract can be drawn up. The IEASA has provided a pro forma contract for its members' use. In order to understand how a contract affects the financial position of a buyer or seller, an

illustration is given below of the contract and the provisions applicable to buying and selling a house.

8.8.1 Conceptual framework

Gibson (1983:9) defines a *contract* as a legal agreement entered into by two or more persons within the limits of their contractual capacity, with the serious intention of establishing a legal obligation, the intention of making known without vagueness, each one to the other and in accordance with the subject, to perform positive or negative actions that may be carried out.

A contract is an agreement that indicates that the persons concluding it intend binding themselves to certain obligations (De Wet & Van Wyk 1978:7). An *obligation* is a legal relationship between two or more persons, according to which the one is entitled to a performance, while the other is bound to a performance.

For our purposes, a *purchase contract*, which De Wet & Van Wyk (1978:278) describe as a mutual agreement between two parties, is dealt with specifically with regard to immovable property. The seller undertakes to supply property (a house), and, in exchange, the buyer undertakes to pay the seller a certain amount for it.

A *mandate* is established between an estate agent and a principal (mandator) immediately the estate agent accepts a mandate (instruction) from the principal to render a specified service to the principal (Delport 1987:309). An estate agent cannot claim commission from a person unless he or she is able to prove that the person concerned has given a mandate to act on his or her behalf.

Various mandates exist, of which only the following have to be in writing:
- sole mandate; and
- a mandate containing a power of attorney to enter into a contract on behalf of the principal (Delport 1987:310; Section 2(1) of the Alienation of Land Act, 1981).

The various mandates which may exist between estate agents and sellers are explained below.

8.8.1.1 A sole mandate

In this discussion, we take note of the following points connected with a sole mandate: the period of the mandate, the reasons why sellers are unwilling to enter into such a mandate and the advantages it holds for the seller in particular. The difference between a sole mandate, an open mandate and a multi-mandate is also explained. A sole mandate is discussed in greater detail, because an estate agent's advice depends on a thorough knowledge of the concept. We will briefly refer to a multi-mandate. An open mandate does not involve agreement between an estate agent and a principal; it merely refers to the fact that any agent may sell a seller's house.

A sole mandate is concluded between an estate agent and a seller whereby the seller appoints one estate agent exclusively for a limited period agreed upon to sell a property, thereby excluding other estate agents and him- or herself from the act of selling (IEASA 1985:25). From this definition it appears that the seller's actions are restricted as a result of granting such a mandate. The mandate must be in writing to prevent:

- the seller from refusing to accept an offer corresponding with the mandate;
- the property from being sold by another estate agent;
- the seller from selling the property him- or herself;
- the seller from withdrawing the property from the market; and
- the seller from performing an act that results in the estate agent being unable to sell the property (IEASA 1985:25).

It is, therefore, important that estate agents properly inform their clients of the rights and obligations that arise from a sole mandate. The seller must know how long the period of the mandate should be and for what reason this period is decided upon; in other words, the seller must understand why a specific period would be advantageous as a result of his or her situation in the property market.

Period of a sole mandate

Experience has shown that it is not worthwhile entering into a sole mandate for too short a period under the following conditions:

- where there is no urgency to sell;
- where the selling price is unrealistically high under the current market conditions;
- where the house is new on the market; and
- where there is an over-supply of houses (IEASA 1985:29).

If such a mandate is in fact entered into under the latter conditions, it may have the following implications:

- it merely proves to the seller that his or her house is not worth selling;
- the seller may reject sole offers that are lower than the anticipated selling price; or
- another estate agent may sell the house at a later stage at a lower price than the first offer received during the period of the sole mandate (IEASA 1985:29).

A sole mandate over a relatively long period will not be worthwhile from the seller's point of view in the following circumstances:

- where the sale of the house is urgent;
- where the seller drops an initially high selling price and decides to accept the market price; and
- where other estate agents have already exposed the house to the market over a fairly long period (IEASA 1985:29).

In contrast, Jawitz (IEASA 1985:29) states that a relatively long period may be desirable for the seller in the following circumstances:

- where the seller is in no hurry to sell the house;
- where the supply of houses exceeds the demand; and
- where the selling price is much higher than the market price.

Reasons why sellers are unwilling to grant a sole mandate

Sellers are not always willing to enter into a sole mandate with an estate agent. Consequently, estate agents should inform sellers about situations in which such a mandate may be advantageous, because lack of information is usually precisely the reason for their unwillingness. Jawitz (IEASA 1985:30) lists the arguments usually raised by sellers:

- Sellers may be under the impression that if more estate agents are involved in marketing the house, there will be more opportunities to sell the house, since they represent more potential buyers and will make a greater effort in the presence of such competition, with the result that the house will sell at a higher price.
- Perhaps the seller or a friend has had an unpleasant experience with such an agreement, possibly because the estate agent, in their view, did not do his or her best to sell the house.
- The estate agent may not have allowed the introduction of other buyers through other estate agents, because he or she would have had to share the commission, resulting in the seller losing the transaction of sale.
- Or the opposite applies – the seller may not care how many estate agents market the house because he or she is waiting for a predetermined offer.
- The seller will be obliged to pay commission if he or she withdraws the property from the market and sells it through another estate agent at a later stage.
- The seller will be obliged to pay commission if he or she sells the house him- or herself.
- Other estate agents are prepared to market the house without such a mandate.

- The seller already has a friend in the property business and prefers using this friend's services.
- The specific estate agency does not appear to be active in the seller's area.
- If the seller enters into such an agreement, other estate agents may be loath to attempt selling the house.

Sellers should be made aware that estate agents are not happy with the absence of such a mandate, since there are always many other sellers who are prepared to grant them a sole mandate. Estate agents explain the following to their clients:
- An estate agent will take any low offer to the seller in order to 'earn' the commission under the noses of other estate agents who have the right to do the same.
- Potential buyers may come to the conclusion that the house's selling price is too high, because so many estate agents are involved.
- No estate agent will spend the maximum time, effort or money to advertise a house which may be sold by someone else.
- Problems regarding the commission may arise especially when two or more estate agents were involved in the transaction.
- Other estate agents may not necessarily keep the principal informed of how matters are proceeding (IEASA 1985:31).

Advantages of a sole mandate
A sole mandate offers numerous advantages, but the following are considered the most important:
- An estate agent will make a more concerted effort to convince potential buyers of the value of the seller's house, compared with other houses.
- Because of the single communication channel, the seller will know which estate agent is arriving to show his or her house.
- Disputes with other estate agents about commission will be eliminated.
- If all efforts to sell the house are unsuccessful, an estate agent will approach another agent to assist him or her and come to an agreement to share the commission.
- An estate agent will not spread rumours about reasons why buyers cannot be found for the property (IEASA 1985:32).

In practice, sellers frequently refuse to sell their houses for less than a specified amount, even if the price is unrealistic under current market conditions. If the estate agent (subject to a sole mandate) fails to sell a house at the desired price, because all the offers are too low, the frustrated seller may ask to sell the house him- or herself.

Estate agents could add a clause to the sole mandate, which permits a seller a short period in which to attempt selling the house him- or herself at a specified minimum amount. This amount is fixed at the maximum offer already made by buyers, which means that the seller may only sell the house at a higher price within the fixed period (otherwise it would be unfair towards the agency). The clause may also provide that a potential buyer who has already made an offer will be afforded an opportunity to make a similar offer or to better the offer received by the seller, before such an offer is accepted.

A seller may also decide that he or she no longer wishes to sell the house. In that case, the estate agent may end the sole mandate by asking the seller to sign a document cancelling the mandate. However, should the seller wish to sell the house in the near future, he or she will be bound (in this example) to sell it through the same estate agency. This prevents sellers from terminating their sole mandate without sound reasons.

Furthermore, should the value of the property increase in the meantime (as a result of an upswing in the property market, for example) and the seller receives a higher offer from another agent, the seller may not accept this offer. Consequently, the seller would suffer a financial loss as a result of granting a sole mandate. In spite of these factors, it still appears that a sole mandate offers a seller sufficient advantages, depending on the seller's situation.

8.8.1.2 An open mandate
In the case of an open mandate, the owner and estate agents market the house. This kind of mandate is not, in fact, a binding agreement with a chosen estate agent. A principal may appoint as many estate agents as he or she wishes to sell or let a property. With an open mandate, a seller will, for example, provide one or more agencies with information about the house for sale. Any estate agent or agency may subsequently sell the property and the seller is liable for paying the agent who sells the house commission.

In the case of an open mandate, estate agents are less inclined to advertise a seller's house as intensively as in the case of a sole mandate. Because more estate agents are involved, more potential buyers will view the house than in the case of a sole mandate. An open mandate represents a greater probability that the seller will receive his or her desired price.

An open mandate is recommended if a seller is not in a hurry to sell the property, wants a specific price for the property and wishes to retain the right to sell the property him- or herself. If a property has been on the market for a long time without being sold, a sole mandate is recommended.

8.8.1.3 A multi-mandate

Swanepoel (1987:5) defines a multi-mandate as the listing of a property made available in terms of an agreement with more than one estate agent or various estate agencies. The joint efforts of many agents improve the service to buyers and sellers. As in the case of an open mandate, there are more agents involved in the sale of the house than in the case of a sole mandate and a higher price may be negotiated.

A seller who has entered into a sole mandate with an estate agent may enter into a multi-mandate at a later stage; in other words, a sole mandate may be converted into a multi-mandate, particularly if the agency whose agent received the sole mandate is a member of MLS (Multi-Listing Services). An estate agent who receives a multi-mandate will feed information regarding the property into a computer, thereby providing all the participating agents (to the multi-mandate system) in the area with the relevant information.

Next, we discuss the legal requirements for establishing a contract between buyers and sellers.

8.8.2 Requirements for a legally binding contract

Because the basis of a contract is its validity, we will begin our discussion with the requirements for a legally binding contract, namely:

- the parties must have contractual capacity;
- there must be a meeting of minds (consensus) between the parties;
- there must be a state of juridical and physical feasibility; and
- the contract must comply with all formalities.

8.8.2.1 Parties with contractual capacity

A contractually capable party is defined by Ring & Dasso (1985:137) as a person who is legally qualified to enter into a binding contract. The parties to a transaction may be natural persons and/or legal persons (bodies corporate).

Natural persons
Husband and wife
Here, we will focus on the effects of the Matrimonial Property Act 88 of 1984 on the capability of married couples to enter into a contract with another party.

The Matrimonial Property Act 88 of 1984. It is essential that estate agents advise their clients on the effect of the Matrimonial Property Act. This Act radically changed the marital regime between husband and wife. Clients should be informed of how a husband, wife or both are affected or bound by a purchase contract as a result of the nature of their matrimonial regime.

The purpose of the Act was to create legal equality between spouses and to provide financial protection to both spouses entering into marriage after the commencement of the Act, whether married in community of property or out of community of property. The accrual system was also introduced; but, in order to offer couples the widest possible choice, they were given the opportunity of marrying with or without the application of the accrual system. Although community of property was retained, marital powers were abolished in all marriages entered into after 1 November 1984, and equal rights to administer joint possessions were included (Sections 21(1) and 4(a) of the Matrimonial Property Act). The accrual system was introduced to avoid the previous financial disadvantages associated with marriages out of community of property (Van der Spuy 1984:15).

In the section below we will first discuss the position of a husband and wife in the conclusion of contracts before the commencement of this Act, and then we will discuss the implications of the Act on buyers and sellers.

Concerning the contractual capacity of men and women, we have to distinguish between married and unmarried persons. Concerning a married man and woman, a distinction must be made between marriages before and after the Matrimonial Property Act. This Act made provision for persons married before its introduction to change their matrimonial regime. Since the Act does not affect legal persons (bodies corporate), we will confine our discussion to natural persons.

Enforcement before the commencement of the Matrimonial Property Act 88 of 1984. When reference is made to marriages concluded before the commencement of the accrual system, it means before 1 November 1984. The accrual system is applicable to marriages out of community of property entered into on or after this date (Section 4(a) of the Matrimonial Property Act).

- *Position of a husband.* A man who has never been married may, in his personal capacity, enter into a contract for purchasing, selling or letting immovable property provided he is of age, is not insane, is not an unrehabilitated insolvent, has never been declared a prodigal by a court order and is not completely under the influence of alcohol or drugs. The contractual capacity of an unmarried woman is the same as that of a man (Delport 1982:12).

A man married out of community of property before 1 November 1984 is fully contractually capable and may buy and sell immovable property without the consent or knowledge of his wife, provided that he is not insane or an unrehabilitated insolvent. Therefore, a married man may conclude transactions to buy and sell immovable property that forms part of the communal estate.

- *Position of a wife.* A woman married in community of property before 1 November 1984 falls under the marital power of her husband and may not enter into certain contracts without his consent. Therefore, she may not alienate (dispose of) or mortgage any immovable property forming part of the joint estate or her own private property without the consent of her husband. The right to share in a spouse's estate cannot be ceded or be subject to attachments during the existence of the marriage and does not form part of a spouse's insolvent estate.

If a wife buys or sells property as her husband's representative, the wife must obtain permission in writing from the husband at the stage at which she signs the contract. When a woman is married in community of property and conducts business as an estate agent, however, she does not need her husband's consent to buy and sell immovable property (Delport 1982:12; Delport 1987:185). Furthermore, being an estate agent, she should be able to provide her husband with financial advice on purchase transactions.

However, since the commencement of the Matrimonial Property Act, the contractual capacity of a wife married in community of property has undergone considerable change. A woman has full contractual capacity with regard to her own estate if she is married out of community of property with exclusion of her husband's marital power.

The following discussion deals with marriages subject to the accrual system.

Enforcement after commencement of the accrual system. Every marriage out of community of property in terms of an antenuptial contract by which community of property and community of profit and loss are excluded, which is entered into after the commencement of the Matrimonial Property Act, is subject to the accrual system, except in so far as that system is expressly excluded by the antenuptial

contract. At the dissolution of a marriage subject to the accrual system, by divorce or by death of one or both of the spouses, the spouse whose estate shows no accrual or a smaller accrual than the estate of the other spouse will derive a profit (Delport 1982:488).

- *Position of a husband.* The marital power that a husband had under the common law over the person and property of his wife was abolished in respect of marriages entered into after the commencement of the Matrimonial Property Act. The effect of the abolition of the marital power was to do away with the restrictions that the marital power placed on the capacity of a wife to contract and to litigate (Sections 11 and 12 of the Matrimonial Property Act). In the case of a marriage out of community of property, the husband has full contractual capacity regarding his own estate, but has no contractual capacity to do business with property that forms part of his wife's estate.

If the marriage is in community of property, a system of co-management is applied, according to which neither party to the marriage may perform any juristic act with regard to the joint estate without the consent of the other spouse. Consequently, one party may not do any of the following without the written consent of the other party:

- alienate, mortgage, burden with a servitude or confer any real rights in any immovable property forming part of the joint estate;
- enter into any contract in respect of the above;
- alienate, cede or pledge any shares, stock, debenture bonds, insurance policies, mortgage bonds, fixed deposits or any similar assets, or any investment by or on behalf of the other spouse in a financial institution, forming part of the joint estate;
- as a purchaser enter into a contract as defined in the Alienation of Land Act 68 of 1981 (that is, an instalment agreement); or
- allow the transfer of immovable property or the registration of real rights with regard to immovable property (Delport 1982:492; Section 15(2) of the Matrimonial Property Act).

Should a spouse wish to sell a house together with the furniture, separate consent (which may be given verbally) must be obtained from the other spouse with regard to the movable property (furniture).

- *Position of a wife.* A wife has full contractual capacity and the same powers as her husband regarding the management of the joint estate (assets and debts excluded), if she is married in community of property. The position of the wife is the same as that of a husband if she is married in community of property.

A wife married before 1 November 1984 could, in terms of the Matrimonial Property Act, change her matrimonial property regime from the old to the new property dispensation. This means that the marital power could be abolished in order that both spouses could have full contractual capacity (Sections 21(1) and 4(a) of the Matrimonial Property Act). This concession expired in November 1986.

- *Implications of the Act for buyers and sellers.* The marriage regime under which buyers and sellers are married has specific implications for themselves and other buyers and sellers with regard to immovable property (houses) and the associated purchase contracts. Such parties must know that they may not sell a house if it belongs to their husband/wife according to their marital regime, or if they do not have the written consent of their marriage partner. Similarly, a house cannot be bought using funds obtained from the other spouse's estate or from the joint estate (if married after 1 November 1984) without the written consent of the spouse. No consent is necessary, however, (despite the marital dispensation) for taking or granting an option on a house on behalf of a spouse.

Section 15(9) of the Act makes provision for the protection of a buyer in the case where a transaction is handled as though a spouse has given permission, while he or she in fact has not, if such wronged buyer did not know or could not reasonably have known about the requirements for such permission (Van der Spuy 1984:26).

Van der Spuy (1984:26) further suggests a business practice with which third parties should comply when contracts of purchase or sale are entered into. Asking the following questions may eliminate or greatly reduce this problem:

- Are you married and, if so, when were you married?
- If before 1 November 1984, were you married in or out of community of property? (Please furnish copy of marriage certificate.)
- If after 1 November 1984, were you married in or out of community of property? (Please furnish copy of marriage certificate.)
- If in community of property, do you have the consent of your spouse? (Please furnish written consent).
- Has your matrimonial property dispensation been changed in terms of Act 88 of 1984? (If so, please furnish a copy.)

Similarly, it is suggested that questions be posed to unmarried persons with regard to their age and guardianship, even though this Act is not applicable to unmarried persons.

- *Foreign law marriages.* The parties to a purchase contract regarding immovable property in the Republic of South Africa may not always be married in terms of the South African legal system (Delport 1982:12–14). This fact, if applicable, must be mentioned in the purchase contract. For example, a wife whose marriage is controlled by the law of another country may have property registered in her name if she is not subject to the marital power of her husband in terms of the law of that country.

- *The role of the estate agent.* Although an estate agent cannot play the role of an attorney (among other things because of a difference in training), he or she should be well-acquainted with the implications of this Act for buyers and sellers. A considerable amount of time and money can be saved if the marriage property dispensation of couples is determined early in the negotiation process. A spouse may, for example, negotiate to sell a house that belongs to the other spouse and, meanwhile, procure another house on the basis of this first potential transaction. If the other spouse (who is the lawful owner of the house) does not consent to the selling of the house at a later stage, both spouses may face a financial dilemma as a result of the new purchase transaction.

Buyers and sellers should be informed before they proceed to conclude a contract, otherwise the purchase may eventually be declared null and void and the parties may have rejected other attractive deals in the interim. Or a spouse may have entered into another contract, which could mean double financial responsibilities if the first contract expired. Once a potential buyer or seller has been canvassed, the estate agent should determine the effects of the Matrimonial Property Act and point out its implications to the parties throughout the negotiation process. Spouses in the process of a divorce could both suffer a financial loss if they do not make a decision about the price of their house in good time (before concluding the contract with the buyer).

A minor

A minor may act as a buyer, lessor or lessee of immovable property with the assistance of his or her father/mother and/or natural/legal guardian, but is prohibited from acting as the seller of immovable property (Section 80, Estate Duty Act, 1965) unless permission has been obtained from the High Court or the Master of the High Court (Delport 1982:12). In terms of South African law, an unmarried person under the age of 21 is considered a minor. If he or she marries, a person under the age of 21 obtains the status of an adult. A court of law may declare a minor an adult with contractual capacity. A divorced person under the age of 21 is also considered to have contractual capacity.

A legal or juridical person

Van Jaarsveld (1978:62) defines a legal or juridical person as an entity that may be the bearer of rights and obligations, in other words, a legal person may act as a debtor and/or creditor in a contract. A legal person usually has the capacity to do business with immovable property and is represented as follows: a private or public company registered in terms of the provisions of the Companies Act 61 of 1973, or a close corporation established in terms of the Close Corporations Act 69 of 1981.

Ring & Dasso (1985:138) state that contractual capacity in respect of a legal person is also important where executors, administrators, trustees, persons acting with power of attorney, agents and legal persons conduct property business. Any person conducting business with a legal person is, therefore, strongly advised to insist on proof of legal capacity.

Maritz (1983:99) points out that most contracts contain a resolution by the executive body of a legal person, in which the nature of the transaction is explained, among other things, and in which the authorised agent's nomination to act is confirmed.

An unincorporated body

A contract may be concluded on behalf of a company or close corporation that still has to be formed or incorporated (an unincorporated association or body). Authorisation to enter into a contract on behalf of an unincorporated association does not have to be in writing and the contract is known as an alienation deed. An unincorporated association has no rights or obligations in terms of a contract concluded on its behalf before the association (or enterprise) has been incorporated. The contract entered into normally stipulates whether the representative will be held liable in his or her personal capacity if the legal person does not confirm (ratify) the contract after its incorporation.

Buyers and sellers wishing to conclude a contract with a representative of an unincorporated association should obtain advice regarding liability in the event of the legal person not confirming the contract after its incorporation. Estate agents should advise buyers and sellers, if possible, or an attorney should be consulted.

8.8.2.2 Consensus between buyer and seller

The law of contract requires that the parties to a contract must declare their respective wishes in the contract. Van Jaarsveld (1983:27) states that a meeting of minds (agreement or consensus) must be apparent from the actions of the parties, although this is not sufficient for the formation of a contract. Parties who anticipate legal effects or consequences must act in such a way that the other party is involved. Agreement or consensus is established by means of an offer and acceptance. These concepts are explained below.

An offer

An offer is made by a prospective contractor as a declaration of intent, and it contains suggestions regarding the conclusion of a contract with a specific content. It is of such a nature that a contract is formed immediately the person to whom it is directed agrees to it (Christie 1981:20; Van Jaarsveld 1983:27). The function of an offer is to express the offeror's wishes and to elicit a response from the offeree(s). This means that a buyer makes an offer to the seller (the opposite is also possible) which invites the seller to respond to a particular suggestion concerning the conclusion of a contract between them.

Acceptance

Thereafter, the seller (the offeree) states his or her corresponding wish, called an acceptance, to accept the offer. Instead of accepting an offer, a seller may make a counteroffer and wait for the buyer's acceptance. If this offer is accepted, a legal contract may be formed between the parties, provided that the further requirements for the conclusion of a contract have been met.

A buyer or seller may withdraw an offer regarding the purchase or sale of a house before acceptance, even if an estate agent is handling the offer. Once the third party has accepted the offer, an agreement has been formed and the offer can no longer be withdrawn. An offer may lapse after a certain period of time (previously agreed upon, or after a reasonable period), after rejection or when a counteroffer has been accepted. For more information on offers and counteroffers, consult Coaker & Schultz (1980:2–14).

Christie (1981:46–48) points out that an offer may only be accepted by the person to whom it is addressed. An acceptance means that the person who received the offer has expressed his or her intention and declared his or her absolute consent to the proposals (Van Jaarsveld 1983:32).

8.8.2.3 Legal and physical feasibility

Legal feasibility means that the contract must not conflict with the provisions of legislation or the common law, while physical feasibility means that the subject of the contract must be practicable (Van Jaarsveld 1983:82).

Legal feasibility

Legal feasibility implies, for example, that a seller may not sell his or her house to a minor (without the assistance of a guardian). Similarly, a buyer may not purchase a house from a minor. A person may not purchase a house on behalf of a company that does not exist and may never be established.

Physical feasibility

Physical feasibility implies, for example, that a person may not sell a house that is non-existent or that does not belong to him- or herself. The reason for this is that fulfilment or performance (providing the house) is impossible at the time the contract is concluded.

Objective impossibility

As far as physical feasibility of a contract is concerned, a distinction must be made between objective and subjective impossibility to perform. Objective (absolute) impossibility occurs, for example, where, due to a natural disaster, a house is destroyed after it has been sold and, therefore, cannot be delivered to the buyer. Even if the buyer were able to offer a counter-performance, no agreement would arise and no claim could be instituted for the fulfilment of the contract.

If the buyer has already incurred expenses in view of the fulfilment of the contract (for example, bought curtains for the new house) he or she would not be able to claim damages from the seller unless he or she could prove negligence on the part of the seller. Van Jaarsveld (1983:97) points out that in the absence of any blame, the damages should rest 'where they have fallen'. This means that the buyer cannot recover expenses from a seller for purchasing curtains, for example, if the seller has not acted in a negligent manner.

Subjective impossibility

Subjective (relative) impossibility of performance exists where it is not impossible for both parties to perform, for example, where a buyer cannot pay for a house or where a seller sells a house included in his or her insolvent estate. In such cases a contract does exist between the parties.

A fourth requirement for the legality of a contract is formality or formal requirements. This is explained below.

8.8.2.4 A contract must comply with all formalities

Formal requirements are the statutory instructions that determine the appearance of a contract before it is legally enforceable (Mosterd 1972:42). The law requires that the purchase contract for immovable property must be in writing, in such a way that it contains the rights and obligations of both parties. The reason given for this is that fraud can more easily take place when a contract is not in writing; therefore, formal requirements help to prevent fraud. Coaker & Schultz (1980:202) state that the courts will not enforce a purchase contract unless it is in writing and signed by the parties or their agents, who also have authority in writing to act on their behalf.

Any amendment of a purchase contract by a buyer or seller must be in writing, but the law does not require that the termination of a contract must be in writing. A question that may be raised here is whether an offer to an option of a buyer or seller must be in writing. According to Mosterd (1972:54), it must be in writing, since the acceptance of the option in writing would establish a valid purchase contract.

Section 3 of the Alienation of Land Act, 1981 stipulates that the requirements of recording and signing and alienation deed in writing do not apply to the sale of land by public auction, unless the purchase price or any other money is payable in more than two instalments over a period of more than one year. In such a case, the provisions of this Act (applicable to most agreements in respect of immovable property) are applicable and the conditions of sale must be drawn up in terms of Section 16 of the Act and immediately read out in public before the auction. The buyer must also be provided with a copy immediately after the auction.

Although the requirements of a written contract apply, estate agents should be able to inform buyers and sellers that a purchase agreement may consist of more than one document. Mosterd (1972:55) mentions that a purchase contract often consists of an offer in writing sighed by the seller, which the buyer accepts by signing, or the buyer may accept the offer by signing a separate document. The communication of acceptance need not be in writing.

Maritz (1983:103) states that a telegraphic acceptance of an offer to purchase is legal, provided that the telegram is signed by the person accepting the offer when handed in at the post office. The conclusion of a sole mandate may occur by means of a telegraphic offer and acceptance. On the other hand, a phonogram is not considered valid. In cases where time is a critical factor for making or accepting an offer, estate agents must inform buyers and sellers that they may use a telegram. Although estate agents do not perform the duties of an attorney, they should nevertheless be capable of advising clients on the correct procedure for offers and acceptance in the property market. However, an attorney should be consulted for advice on the technical aspects.

An offer and an acceptance may also be faxed. In reality, the offer is relayed within seconds, even though the receiver may be thousands of kilometres away. Similarly, an offer may be accepted and a counteroffer made within seconds. Estate agents must be acquainted with the use of a fax machine where time is a critical factor.

Like any other contract, a purchase contract has specific features. These are dealt with below.

8.8.3 Three requirements of a purchase contract

Normally, three matters are dealt with in purchase contracts in respect of residential property:
- the nature of the contract to purchase and sell;
- the specific property involved; and
- the price at which the property will be sold (Kerr 1984:3).

The buyer and seller must reach consensus on each of these points before a purchase contact becomes legally binding. Firstly, both parties must have the intention to purchase and sell, and the buyer must receive the use and enjoyment of and powers of disposal over the subject of purchase; in other words, he or she must become the owner of the subject. Secondly, the property (house) to be sold must be described in the purchase contract in such a manner that the buyer knows which house he or she will be purchasing from the seller. Thirdly, the parties must agree on the purchase price. Kerr (1984:23) states that there must be certainty about the price, which must be indicated in monetary terms. Where a purchase contract is silent about one of these three items, it will be null and void, since it must contain exactly what has been agreed upon.

8.8.4 Standard contractual clauses

Section 83 of the Attorneys Act 53 of 1979 is applicable to the drafting of contracts. This section stipulates that no person other than an attorney may draft any contract in respect of immovable property for remuneration, or have a share in it, except for a lease with a term not exceeding five years (Delport 1982:38; Section 83 of the Attorneys Act, 1979).

A distinction is made between the following:
- cash deed of purchase;
- offer to purchase; and
- alienation deed.

Estate agents have an important role to play with regard to these, since many of the clauses require that clients be given financial advice, such as the following:

Buyers must be informed that the risk is transferred from the seller to the buyer on the date on which the contract is concluded. Consequently, the buyer must either obtain information from the seller's insurer that the property remains insured until registration or transfer, or the buyer must arrange insurance from the date on which he or she receives the property rights (the registration date). Estate agents must point out to buyers and sellers that they must come to a mutual agreement on the date on which the risk is transferred to the buyer.

The parties must also be told that they must come to an agreement on the payment of commission. Both parties must bear in mind the payment or receipt of occupational interest if the date of occupation does not coincide with the date of registration of the deed of transfer.

Buyers must know that movable property (furniture) that appears in the same agreement as immovable property, must be described separately because of the higher transfer and other costs. Sellers must also be informed that they have to pay VAT on movable property that is sold separately from immovable property.

The seller is indemnified against *latent* (invisible) defects in the property of which the seller was unaware. If the seller was aware of such defects, he or she will not be protected against the buyer's claims. On the other hand, *patent* (visible) defects are defects that would be noticed by the normal actions of a person. Kerr (1984:77) indicates that a defect is latent when it is equally possible to discover as not to discover and where in half the cases it will not be discovered.

Schaller (1984:47) explains the *voetstoots* (as it is) clause as one in which a seller gives the buyer an implied guarantee that the property does not have latent defects, in other words, defects which cannot be detected by reasonable inspection. This clause must be explained to the parties concerned, as well as the rule '*huur gaat voor koop*' (lease goes before sale) and what the implications of existing tenants are for the buyer.

The *alienation deed* is a contract which stipulates that a residential plot is being sold and that repayment will take place in more than two instalments over a period exceeding a year (Delport 1982:88–2). Estate agents should advise clients on the effects a possible rise in interest rates may have on the number of instalments to be paid.

Important aspects that form part of contracts are *suspensive* and *resolutive conditions*. Frequently, property transactions are not concluded as a result of compliance or non-compliance with these conditions, and it is important that estate agents advise potential buyers and sellers on the meaning of these conditions in a contract. The difference between a suspensive and a resolutive condition is explained below.

Van Jaarsveld (1983:279) states that a condition is *suspensive* when the commencement of the intended operation of a contract depends on something that must happen in the future, or that must not happen. Once these conditions have been fulfilled, the purchase contract takes effect, or else the contract falls away.

The following are suspensive conditions:

- where a buyer wants to sell his or her own house first;
- where a buyer who wants to sell his or her house first has to wait for a bond to be granted to the buyer of his or her house; and
- where a buyer is waiting to be granted a bond.

The position when the conclusion of a contract depends on a *resolutive* condition is the opposite of the position in the case of a suspensive condition (Van Jaarsveld 1983:280). In other words, once the condition has been fulfilled, the existing right or obligation will terminate. A buyer may include a resolutive condition in a purchase agreement, which may be the occurrence of one or more of the following events, for example:

- the erection of a prison in the vicinity of the house the buyer wishes to purchase; or
- the development of a freeway, nudist camp, defence force unit or an industrial area.

Estate agents should inform clients of these and the many other aspects relating to the contracts, or they should advise clients to consult an attorney. However, the aspects mentioned above are considered the most important.

Our next discussion involves options and the right of first refusal as agreements that may arise between two parties.

8.8.5 An option

Earlier in this chapter, we referred to making an offer in writing in order to obtain an option. Delport (1982:14) defines an option as an offer to purchase or sell property (or to lease or let property), coupled to an agreement not to revoke this offer for a certain period. An option consists of two parts:

- a general offer to purchase or sell property, which has to comply with the usual requirements for an offer in general; and
- an agreement to reserve the offer for a specific period of time.

In practice, the period for reserving the offer is usually stipulated. A seller (giver of option) may make the buyer an offer regarding the exercising of the option before the period expires to enable the buyer (option holder) to exercise this option. Consequently, the buyer may exercise the option before the expiry date by accepting the seller's offer.

8.8.5.1 Setting out an option

As in the case of a purchase agreement for immovable property, an option must clearly stipulate the specific property, the price and information regarding the relevant parties. The estate agent must ensure that an option specifies the following:

- the material terms of the agreement;
- the legal position of the parties after conclusion of the agreement;
- the date on which the payment of interest must commence;
- the dates on which the term commences and ends; and
- whether the capital sum is to be paid in instalments or not (Delport 1985:15).

Buyers and sellers could suffer financial loss in the absence of advice regarding the explanation of an option, should a court order that:

- the buyer (who was under the impression that the purchase price would be paid in instalments) has to pay the capital sum in full;
- the seller (who expected the buyer to pay the capital sum in full) has to be paid in instalments over a relatively long period, while the seller has already taken on other financial obligations and is, therefore, depending on the full payment of the purchase price;
- the buyer has an obligation to pay interest to the seller which is back-dated over a period of three years, for example;
- the seller cannot recover any interest from the buyer; or
- either the buyer or seller owes the agent a commission, while this had not been anticipated by the parties concerned.

Numerous other examples may be added. The advice of an estate agent or attorney can be of great value to make clients aware of the operation of an option.

8.8.5.2 Exercising an option

An option is exercised by the unconditional acceptance of the offer to purchase or to sell (whichever may be the case). The acceptance must be in writing and signed by both parties concerned, or by the agent who signs with the written permission of one or the other on their behalf. An option may be exercised in the same document or in another document (Delport 1985:16).

From this discussion it is clear that giving someone an option 'until Saturday' is not a valid option. To be valid, an option must be set out as follows (Delport 1985:18): 'I ... (seller) hereby grant ... (buyer) an option to purchase my house ... (address) at R ... (price) which will be payable in full at registration. The option expires ... (date and time). Signed: ... (seller).'

If a tenant, who signed a lease with the option to purchase, eventually purchases the property, the lessor is responsible for paying the agent's commission. Where the same estate agent handled both the lease and the purchase contract, the commission paid beforehand must be deducted from the commission for the purchase contract.

There is often confusion about the difference between an option and a right of first refusal. The difference can be explained as follows.

8.8.6 Right of first refusal

A person obtains the right from the owner of the property, should the owner wish to sell, to be granted the first opportunity to purchase the property. The price and terms will be the same for the holder of the right as for a bona fide third party (Maritz 1983:109).

The holder of a right of first refusal is not obliged to purchase if the opportunity should arise. Similarly, the owner is not obliged to sell the property to the holder, but is merely obliged to give the holder the first opportunity to purchase, should the seller come to such a decision. The owner may not sell the property at a better price or on better terms (of which the holder is unaware) to a person other than the holder.

Estate agents should advise buyers and sellers regarding the rights and obligations that stem from a right of first refusal and recommend this or conclude it on behalf of a principal, if it is in the interest of the principal.

The implications of the Rent Control Act for buyers and sellers of houses are discussed next.

8.8.7 The Rent Control Act 80 of 1976

Rent control was initially established in 1920 to prevent lessors from exploiting the weaker negotiation position of lessees, which arose as a result of the housing shortage at the time. At present, rent control is only applicable to older residential premises occupied by low income groups. Van Jaarsveld (1978:465) points out two objectives of this Act:
- to protect lessees against unreasonably high rentals by controlling the amount that may be charged for premises; and
- to exercise control over the impermanence of occupation, by limiting the eviction of lessees of premises.

In the following discussion, attention is given to the enforcement of the provisions of the Act, as well as to the role of estate agents as a result of the implications that the Act holds for buyers and sellers.

8.8.7.1 Enforcement and provisions
The Rent Control Act is applicable to:
- Lease contracts in respect of houses, garages and car parks that fall within the area of a rent board, and which were occupied for the first time on or before 20 October 1949.
- Lease contracts in respect of houses, garages and car parks which fall within the area of a rent board, and which were occupied after 20 October 1949 and before 1 June 1966.
- Lessees who have been living on the premises under rent control since 23 May 1980 and whose income does not exceed the limits contained in the Housing Act 4 of 1966. Should a lessee at any stage vacate the premises, or not comply with the income requirements contained in this Act, the premises no longer fall under rent control. Since 1 October 1980, the income category has been R450 per month for an unmarried person and R850 per month for a family. Only the income of the breadwinner, excluding the income of other dependants, is taken into account (Section 51(f) of the Rent Control Act, 1976).

The Rent Control Act stipulates that a lessee of premises under rent control may continue to occupy the premises for an unlimited period of time after expiry of the term contained in the contract, provided that he or she pays the rent regularly and complies with the conditions of the lease, unless:
- The lease expires as a result of being lawfully terminated by the lessor.
- The lessee causes material damage or is guilty of behaviour that offends the occupants of adjoining or neighbouring properties.
- A local authority requires the premises within reason for a city improvement scheme and the lessee is given six month's notice in writing and the relevant period expires.
- The lessor requires the premises as a whole and within reason for occupation by him- or herself, his or her parent(s) or child and the lessee is given three month's notice in writing to vacate the premises and the relevant period expires.
- The lessee was previously employed by the lessor, but is no longer in his or her employ and the

lessor requires the premises for occupation or use by someone employed by him or her.

- The premises had previously been occupied or used by the lessee and the lessee had consented in writing to vacate before or on a specific date, where this date has arrived.
- The premises are required within reason for the purposes of any reconstruction or renovation scheme, repairs, restoration or transformation which necessitates the vacation of the premises and the lessee has been given six month's notice in writing to vacate the premises and the relevant period has expired.
- Another reason exists, which a court regards as sufficient reason, taking into account all the circumstances (Section 28(d) and (e) of the Rent Control Act, 1976).

The Act further provides that a lessee becomes a statutory lessee after expiry of the lease, as a result of the passage of time or termination by the lessor. Although the common law lease is terminated, the mutual rights and responsibilities of the statutory lessee and lessor are evaluated as though the lease still exists. Apart from a few exceptions, a statutory lessee loses his or her rights if, for example, he or she sublets the premises or assigns or transfers the use of the premises to someone else. A court cannot issue an ejection order to a statutory lessee if the lessee pays the relevant rent within seven days after the agreed day of payment and complies with the other provisions of the lease (Section 34(2)(a) of the Rent Control Act, 1976).

The provisions of the Rent Control Act hold the following implications for potential buyers and sellers.

8.8.7.2 Implications of the Act for buyers and sellers

Buyers and sellers of houses subject to rent control could find themselves in a situation with negative consequences. Assume that person A buys a house from person C and sells his or her own house to person B on the agreement that person B may occupy the house at the beginning of the following month. The house originally bought is subject to rent control and the lessee is going to terminate the contract in three month's time. Person A may still occupy his or her own house for one month, but may only occupy the new house in three month's time. This means that person A has to find accommodation elsewhere for two months and pay occupational interest.

Furthermore, it may happen that person A is not allowed to occupy the house owned by person C, because of the inability of person C to evict the lessee legally. Person A may be forced to rent a house for months because he or she is unable to find the 'right' house.

If person A is buying person C's house for investment purposes only, person A may not increase the rent in future to earn more money on his or her investment. In addition, the rental for such premises is fairly low and not a good investment opportunity, unless the property is acquired at a very low price. Research has shown that uninformed buyers frequently make poor investments.

Assume also that a person owns a house that is leased subject to rent control. If he or she decides to sell the house, he or she would have to find a buyer actually wanting to occupy the house. A buyer who wants to lease the house will not necessarily be satisfied with the low rental income. The rate of return on the buyer's investment will, consequently, be very low. Existing lessees may not be given notice, unless there are legal grounds for doing so. Thus, this house must compete with other investment opportunities that are more profitable for buyers.

Research has shown that buyers and sellers cannot afford to ignore the effects of the Rent Control Act during purchase and sale transactions. We will now briefly look at the estate agent's role during such transactions.

8.8.7.3 The estate agent's role

As in the case of the Matrimonial Property Act, estate agents must obtain and provide information on the implications of the Rent Control Act from the first meeting with their clients and throughout the negotiation process. They should obtain information on, among other things, the applicability of the Act to a particular property, the possibilities of a lessee vacating the premises voluntarily, the possibilities of lessees being given notice lawfully and the willingness of a buyer to continue with the lease contract.

Buyers and sellers must be alerted to the possibility of having to pay interest on two mortgage bonds for a period of time, as well as the possibility of having to continue with such payments over a fairly long period. Potential buyers must also be advised on the desirability of such property for investment purposes.

8.9 RAISING FINANCE FOR THE PURCHASE OF A HOUSE

8.9.1 Introduction

In this section, we will discuss the methods and sources of financing available to buyers and sellers in the housing market. Finance is not only required over the long-term – people often need money to meet financial requirements for a year or two. Various institutional sources of financing exist, of which banking institutions and building societies are the most important. These institutions represent primary sources of financing for buyers and sellers of houses, who may also make use of secondary sources, for example friends and investors.

Estate agents must ensure that buyers and sellers are advised on bond repayments, since lack of information may hold considerable implications for the parties. The parties should not only be informed about obtaining a bond or loan but also about the benefits regarding the way in which they may be utilised.

Many organisations provide their employees with housing subsidies, and estate agents should explain the effects of a subsidy (if applicable) on the instalments. Subsidies are taxable and the parties should realise that the use of such fringe benefit is not for free. Estate agents should keep abreast of the various subsidy schemes that exist in order to point out the benefits to buyers and sellers.

Buying a house is a commitment with considerable financial obligations. The average buyer is seldom able to finance the purchase with his or her own cash, and usually has to borrow the difference between the purchase price and his or her own cash reserves.

The following are some methods of raising finance to buy a house.

8.9.2 Methods of raising finance to buy a house

Miller (IEASA 1985:122) distinguishes the following methods of financing a house:
- cash;
- partly cash, balance by means of a mortgage bond;
- jointly cash, balance in instalments;
- joint property rights; and
- 100% mortgage bonds.

Financing methods used at present consist of combinations of one or more of the methods mentioned above. Each of the five methods is discussed below.

8.9.2.1 Cash

In order to give their clients good advice, estate agents must establish whether a client's cash is in his or her possession or invested, and how or when the money will be available to the attorney effecting the transfer. Replies could be any of the following:

- on request;
- fixed deposit;
- shares;
- held by an attorney;
- employer will make cash available; or
- a pension scheme (IEASA 1985:122).

Cash deposited at a financial institution may be drawn *on request*, except in the case of a fixed deposit. The conditions on a savings account, for example, determine the right of the depositor to withdraw funds.

Cash is often invested with a bank or building society for a *fixed period* of, for example, 12, 24 or 36 months, during which time it may not be withdrawn. In terms of Section 21 of the Banks Act 23 of 1965, a bank must repay a fixed deposit at the expiry date and not earlier. However, if the depositor instructs the bank to reinvest this amount, the bank is not obliged to repay the money on the expiry date (Section 21 of the Financial Institutions Amendment Act 106 of 1985; Unisa 1985:93).

In exceptional cases, a bank may pay a fixed deposit before the expiry date:
- where the deposit forms part of the assets of a deceased estate;
- where the depositor is placed under judicial management or under liquidation;
- where the deposit is required by a pension fund to make deferred pension payments; or
- where the Registrar of Banks approves the early repayment (Unisa 1985:94).

Bannock *et al.* (1977:372) describe a *share* as one of a number of equal parts in the nominal capital of a company, which gives the owner of the share the right to part of the split profit and to the residual value of the company if it is liquidated. A *shareholder* is a person who owns a share in a company. A *share certificate* is issued to shareholders and is proof of ownership of shares in a company.

A *listed share* is a share which appears on an official list at the Johannesburg Securities Exchange (after approval of a listing of a company's shares on the securities exchange) and which may be sold on the securities exchange (Brümmer & Rademeyer 1982:4). Listed shares may be converted to cash almost immediately.

Unlisted shares cannot always be converted to cash immediately because there may not necessarily be an immediate buyer. Furthermore, shareholders are not always prepared to sell their shares at current share prices.

A person often sells his or her house and waits for an *attorney* to finalise the transfer. Estate agents must confirm the facts of the case with the attorney in order to determine when the money from the sale will be available for the seller's use.

In the case where an *employer provides the money*, housing schemes must be investigated. The estate agent must ascertain whether his or her client does, in fact, qualify for a certain housing scheme, how this scheme functions and, if necessary, he or she must explain it to the client.

Funds obtainable from a *pension scheme* are usually applicable to retired persons. Estate agents must make sure of the facts regarding the payment of such an amount in cash, before an agreement of purchase can be concluded.

8.9.2.2 Partly cash, balance by means of a mortgage bond

This method of purchase is the most common form of financing, and many variations are available. Assume that a person purchases a house for R100 000. He or she may have R20 000 in cash and obtain a bond for R80 000 from some institution for the balance. If he or she has only R10 000 in cash, and needs a further R10 000 (in addition to the R80 000 bond), this may be financed from the following sources, according to Miller (IEASA 1985:124):
- from the seller or another natural or legal person as a second mortgage on the house;
- from the seller by providing a promissory note;
- from the seller or another natural or legal person who invests an equal collateral amount; or
- the registration of a notarial bond, in favour of the seller, over movable property such as vehicles, furniture and equipment.

8.9.2.3 Partly cash, balance in instalments

Miller (1987:144) states that new houses are normally advertised as a total package. The seller (usually a developer) subsidies the payment of interest by the buyer for a certain period (for example one, two or three years). From the advertisement, it may appear as though the payment of interest is in fact subsidised, but this is not necessarily true. This method is known as hire-purchase (instalment sale) and is covered by the provisions of the Alienation of Land Act 68 of 1981. A seller may, for example, offer a house at a selling price of R85 000 as follows:
- a deposit of R8 500; and
- 12 or 24 monthly instalments of R850 each (at 12% per annum).

After this period of time the buyer must register a bond over the house in order to pay the seller. If the buyer is unable to raise finance, he or she must sell the house. The buyer will suffer a loss if he or she cannot sell the house at a price that could redeem the outstanding debt, although it should normally be possible because of the continuous increase in the market value of property. If the market value of the house rises, a buyer should be able to obtain a bond to settle the outstanding debt.

Estate agents must inform their clients of the benefits both parties (buyers and sellers) may derive from this type of financing. The benefits for the buyer are:
- The buyer enters the property market with little initial cash.
- The buyer becomes an owner instead of a lessee.
- The contract may be adapted with the aid of the seller to suit the financial ability and requirements of the buyer (Miller 1987:144).

The benefits for the seller are:
- The responsibility for the maintenance of the house rests with the buyer.
- If the buyer cannot continue payment at a later stage, the house will still be registered in the name of the seller.
- The seller receives a cash deposit when the agreement is concluded – a faster process than in the case of a normal transfer.
- This sales method lends itself to tax benefits (Miller 1987:145).

This contract document contains the following requirements:
- A minimum of two instalments are required.
- A cash deposit has to be paid.
- An interest rate must be indicated (even if it is nil).
- The date of conclusion (date at which the buyer must take transfer) must be indicated (Miller 1987:146).

8.9.2.4 Joint property rights

Joint property rights exist when two or more persons are joint owners of the same property, that is they share the same property in undivided shares, or they are joint owners of the property in its entirety (Delport 1987:28). The extent of each joint owner's undivided share does not have to be the same – one may own 70% of the undivided share and the other 30%. The extent of each joint owner's undivided share determines:
- his or her share in the profit and general expenses; and
- his or her rights and obligations in the event of the termination of joint property rights (Delport 1987:29).

Joint owners may arrange their rights and obligations by means of an agreement. In the absence of such an agreement, the following common-law principles apply:

- Each joint owner is entitled to use the property for the purpose for which it was bought.
- Joint owners cannot prevent one another from using the property jointly, for example by locking a door to prevent a joint owner from using a common room in a house.
- The profits must be split between joint owners according to each one's share.
- Joint owners must share any maintenance costs on a *pro rata* basis.
- All the joint owners must agree to the selling or mortgaging of the property. A majority decision is not sufficient. In the case of a lease or sale, the estate agent must make sure that all the parties sign the relevant contract. If a joint owner acts on behalf of another joint owner, he or she must have the other party's power of attorney.
- A joint owner may (depending on the mutual agreement) lease or sell his or her own undivided share without the permission of the other joint owners. If an estate agent receives an instruction to lease or sell an undivided share on behalf of a joint owner, he or she must ascertain whether this joint owner is prohibited from doing so by a mutual agreement (Delport 1978:29–30).

A person may sell a specified percentage (undivided share) of his or her house (for example, 40% or 60%) to a buyer. The seller subsequently retains part of the sold house. If the buyer sells the house at a later stage, the amount exceeding the initial purchase price (first purchase transaction) is divided among the parties according to the ratio of joint ownership.

8.9.2.5 100% mortgage bonds

This method of financing normally occurs through a company's housing scheme or through schemes that government departments offer to their employees (Miller 1987:147).

Long-term financing is financing for a period of five years and longer. The requirements for financing a house are long-term because very few people are in a position to repay the bond amount for a house over a short period; therefore, the sources and instruments of long-term financing are important for buyers and sellers. This is the main reason why deeds of mortgage are offered for the financing of housing, since bond financing is granted from funds over which long-term powers of disposal have been obtained.

The following deals with providing information on the instruments and sources available to buyers and sellers for raising finance for a house.

8.9.3 Long-term financing instruments

The money provided to finance a house is transferred by means of certain instruments. The conditions for the functioning of these instruments vary considerably and estate agents must explain them to the parties concerned. In other words, an estate agent's financial advice must include the functioning of these instruments.

Falkena *et al.* (1984:259) define a financial instrument as a written contract which states the relationship between a provider of funds (investor) and a borrower of funds. Maritz (1983:325) considers the following financial instruments as the most well-known for financing immovable property:

- a mortgage bond; and
- a contract for the alienation of land in instalments.

A mortgage bond is the most common financing instrument used by buyers and sellers of houses.

8.9.3.1 A mortgage bond

Conceptual framework
A mortgage bond is a legal action through which property is pledged in order to obtain a loan. Once a financial institution obtains the right to a buyer or seller's house, a bond is raised as security for the money lent to such parties by the institution. This document is called a mortgage bond.

The following terms related to the use of mortgage bonds are particularly important:

- conveyancer;
- deeds office;
- deed of transfer;
- mortgage deed (or hypothecation deed);
- mortgagee or bondholder;
- mortgagor;
- reducible loan; and
- fixed-term loan.

A *conveyancer* is someone who is authorised in terms of the Deeds Registries Act to draw up deeds of transfer and mortgage bonds in the province in which the Deeds Office is situated (Section 15 of the Deeds Registries Act 47 of 1937).

A *deeds office* is the government office where mortgage deeds and deeds of transfer are registered. This office is the registration office for deeds in respect of immovable property for the area in which that property is situated (Section 102 of the Deeds Registries Act, 1937).

A *mortgage deed* is a document stating the legal act between a mortgagor and the mortgagee (Technikon RSA 1986:18). A mortgage deed is a bank or building society bond, for example, where a mortgagor registers a bond over his or her property as security for the mortgagee. Immovable property is pledged against a mortgage deed. This document is attested by the registrar (Section 50 of the Deeds Registries Act, 1937).

The *mortgagee* is the financial institution (a bank or building society) that grants the funds (bond) to a buyer or seller (the *mortgagor*) against the security of immovable property. Both a natural and a legal person may act as a mortgagor or mortgagee.

Anyone with *contractual capacity* may apply for a bond at a financial institution or from another person, and may grant a bond to someone (a natural or legal person). A married woman's matrimonial regime determines her capacity to act as a mortgagor. When a husband and wife own property jointly, both are involved as mortgagors and mortgagees according to the transaction. Such persons may mortgage their separate parts of the property (where applicable), with our without permission in writing from the other party (on the basis of the relevant matrimonial regime) (Van Jaarsveld 1983:188, 189).

A *minor* must obtain permission from the Master of the High Court or the court to act as a mortgagor. Neither the guardian nor the minor may alienate immovable property without such permission.

Legal persons may act as mortgagors and mortgagees. *Insolvent persons* may not act as mortgagors or mortgagees, and certain persons, such as the executors of deceased estates, have only limited rights to mortgaged property (Van Jaarsveld 1983:189). The capacity of *churches* and *societies* to mortgage property is explained in their constitutions. If a person considered to be a farmer by definition wishes to act as mortgagor, he or she must explicitly relinquish all protection and benefits granted in terms of the Agricultural Credit Act 28 of 1966.

It is always the duty of the financial institution's conveyancer to determine whether an applicant (for a bond) has contractual capacity. An estate agent may grant a bond on behalf of the owner of a mortgaged property. Wille (1961:10) points out that a contract concluded by an agent binds the principal and not the agent.

Bonds are subdivided into reducible loans and fixed-term loans. A *reducable loan* is one where the loan is paid off in equal instalments over a period, consisting of interest and capital redemption. Such a loan must contain an agreement to indicate that the capital sum will be repaid within a certain period of time. If part of the loan (advance) is repaid or a re-advance is granted, the period for payment of the outstanding capital sum is calculated from the date on which the re-advance was granted. A reducible loan may be converted to a fixed-term loan (IEASA 1985:143).

The nature of a mortgage

A mortgage is the right (by virtue of a legal act) which one person has in and over another person's (the mortgagor's) property and which serves as security for the mortgagor's obligation towards the mortgagee. The right is secured by a mortgage deed on the debtor's immovable property by the mortgagor (Meyer 1979:76).

A real right in a mortgage is constituted on registration in the Deeds Office in the district in which the mortgaged property is situated. The registration serves as a general notice to the public in order to prevent transactions involving encumbered (mortgaged) property (Meyer 1979:76). The effects of a real right in mortgaged property are the isolation of the property as the subject of attachment in the event of default of payment, as well as the granting of a preferential right in the event of the buyer or seller becoming insolvent.

The most effective way to ensure an obligation with immovable property as security is the registration of a mortgage deed on that immovable property (Meyer 1979:77). If a person stands surety for a buyer or provides collateral security, the safest security will be the registration of a mortgage bond on immovable property (if possible).

The parties to a mortgage bond are the mortgagee and the mortgagor. The rights and obligations arising from the mortgage bond are legally enforceable. A mortgagee holds the property of the mortgagor as security until the debt has been paid. The mortgagee obtains a real right over the mortgaged property; in other words, the right is secured under all circumstances and in respect of all people. All improvements to the property, such as additional buildings, are subject to the mortgage bond.

A mortgagee can prevent a drop in the value of the mortgaged property by ensuring that no servitude may be registered over the property without his or her consent, unless the servitude is expropriated. In the case of expropriation, provision is made for notice and compensation to the mortgagee. No property on which a mortgage deed has been registered may be transferred until the mortgage bond has been cancelled or the mortgagee has consented to the sale of the property (Section 32 of the Registration of Deeds in Rehoboth Act, 1976).

In the absence of an agreement to the contrary, a mortgagor may lease the property and the lessee may enjoy all the rights of a lessee, provided that the mortgagee's interests are not prejudiced. The mortgagor never loses the right of possession (occupation) of the property through the registration of a mortgage bond. The mortgagor may sell the property, but before the property is transferred, he or she must pay everything that is owing to the mortgagee.

If payment does not occur, the new buyer and the mortgagee must agree that the buyer will take over all the mortgagor's obligations in terms of the mortgage bond. If a testator leaves a mortgaged property and the opposite intention is not evident in the will, it is the duty of the testator's executors to release the mortgage deed on the property of the effects of the mortgage deed and to transfer it to the heirs unburdened (if the estate is strong enough).

A mortgagor's indebtedness can be deduced from the bond amount, as well as the interest payable. The terms and conditions of repayment, as well as the property encumbered with a mortgage bond are described in the mortgage deed. The law does not prescribe a standard form for a mortgage deed (apart from a collateral and surety bond). Maritz (1983:327) points out that the content of a mortgage deed is determined, among other things, by the bond agreement between the parties concerned, current practice, common law and, to a certain extent, by statutory prescriptions. Registration offices normally require that a mortgage deed contains the following:
- a heading identifying it as such;
- a preamble clearly describing the mortgagor and mortgagee;
- an explanation of how the indebtedness arose;
- an acknowledgement by the mortgagor or his or her authorised agent (for example, an estate agent) in respect of such indebtedness; and
- an insurance clause in which the property for which a mortgage bond was provided is insured as prescribed by the Deeds Registries Act 47 of 1937 (Maritz 1983:329).

A mortgage bond that includes both existing and future debt may be registered on immovable property. In other words, a second bond may be registered on a house in favour of an unincorporated company or a close corporation (Meyer 1979:77). The same property may be mortgaged in favour of more than one mortgagee. In this case, a first and second bond may be registered on the same property.

Maritz (1983:329) discusses the most important clauses appearing in mortgage bonds provided by building societies, as well as the purpose of each clause. A *continuous coverage clause* makes provision for the fluctuation of the obligation (instalment) in the future without the mortgage bond becoming invalid.

Interest is payable on the sum due and normally begins to accrue once a mortgage bond has been registered. The parties may agree at a later stage to reduce or alter the interest rate and even, at the discretion of the mortgagee, to a fluctuation in the interest rate between certain limits. The mortgage deed usually stipulates that the mortgagee will give the mortgagor notice at a specified period of such changes in the interest rate.

All banks and building societies make provision for a fluctuation in interest rates (Caney 1975:333, 334). Buyers should, therefore, take into account in their financial planning that their bond instalments may fluctuate. Estate agents should inform buyers that their monthly instalments could increase at a later stage as a result of interest rates rising. This may prevent buyers from buying a house that they eventually cannot afford.

Financial institutions normally grant a reducible loan, in other words, a loan that may be redeemed over a certain period. The mortgagor pays fixed monthly instalments consisting of interest due and capital redemption. Estate agents should warn buyers that the bond amount decreases very slowly at first, because of the interest on the total amount. As the bond amount decreases, the interest also decreases, and capital redemption speeds up.

If the place of payment has not been indicated, but the date has, the onus is on the mortgagor to pay the mortgagee at a place convenient to the mortgagee. If neither the place nor the date has been indicated, the onus is on the mortgagee to call on the mortgagor and request payment. Estate agents must point out to mortgagors that they must honour their obligations according to the agreed manner and place, in order to maintain a good relationship with the mortgagee. A good relationship is essential, particularly in view of a future re-advance or a second bond.

There is always a danger that the property serving as security for the mortgagee may be destroyed partly or completely by a fire or other disaster (Caney 1975:337). Such events reduce the security of the mortgagee and consequently increase the risk. In order to indemnify the mortgagee against the risk, it is customary for a mortgage deed to stipulate carefully the following insurance details:
- how the property must be insured;
- which insurance company must be used;
- the amount of insurance; and
- that, if necessary, the mortgagee is entitled to pay insurance premiums on behalf of the mortgagor and recover this amount from the mortgagor or capitalise it on his or her bond loan (Maritz 1983:331).

The mortgagor must pay the insurance premiums under all circumstances. Estate agents must point out to mortgagors that they should not pay insurance premiums separately – the premiums must be included in the monthly instalments.

A local authority has a limited claim to a property with regard to rates and taxes (of the relevant property). The claim has preferences above any other registered bond and is limited to the outstanding amount for rates and taxes. Thus, a local authority may have the property sold, irrespective of whether there is a mortgage on the property, in order to recover any outstanding taxes. The mortgagee may only lay claim to the proceeds after the sale and deduction (payment) of these taxes.

Maritz (1983:331) points out that a mortgage deed specifies the following, precisely because of the reasons mentioned above:

- that the mortgagor must pay the local authority's taxes;
- that the mortgage bond will be breached if the mortgagor neglects to pay the taxes; and
- that the mortgagee has the right to pay municipal taxes on behalf of the mortgagor and to recover these amounts from the mortgagor. Caney (1975:337) agrees with this explanation.

It is expected of the mortgagor to maintain the property, or make the necessary improvements, in order to ensure that its market value is not reduced. In other words, the property must offer the mortgagee the same security, taking into account the property market as a whole (Caney 1975:343). A mortgagor cannot demolish a certain room in the house because he or she disapproves of it for some reason. Estate agents should point out to mortgagors that they may in no way reduce the value of the property while it is mortgaged.

Estate agents must explain the effects of rent control to mortgagors, particularly when it may be contrary to the interests of mortgagees.

In order to protect themselves against possible income and administrative losses, certain institutions have a penalty clause in the event of accelerated repayment.

A mortgagee always demands the submission of the title deed of the property in order to ensure that no transaction takes place in the Deeds Office (regarding this specific property) of which the mortgagee has no knowledge. This prevents a mortgagor from attempting to sell the mortgaged property in times of financial hardship. Estate agents must explain to mortgagors that no sales transaction in respect of a mortgaged property is possible without the mortgagee's permission.

In order to facilitate correspondence with the mortgagor, his or her postal address must appear in the mortgage deed. A mortgagor may agree to the jurisdiction of a magistrate's court to reduce the costs involved in lawsuits. Estate agents should refer mortgagors to an attorney for information in the event of potential lawsuits.

The Expropriation Act 63 of 1975 is aimed at protecting the interests of mortgagees during expro-priation, but mortgagees usually demand the inclusion of a clause granting them the right to handle all documentation, as well as receipt of compensation, on behalf of mortgagors.

Most mortgage bonds contain a foreclosure clause. A foreclosure clause stipulates that, in the event of the mortgagor neglecting to fulfil his or her obligations in terms of the mortgage bond, the mortgagee may immediately call up the capital and interest due in terms of the mortgage bond. A foreclosure clause grants the mortgagee the right to demand the capital amount due from the mortgagor by means of notice (usually six months).

If the mortgagor fails to pay the outstanding bond instalments, or neglects to comply with the conditions of the foreclosure notice, a court may declare the mortgaged property executable (in other words, the mortgagor will lose his or her right to retain possession of the property and the mortgagee has permission to sell the property). The property will consequently be sold in execution and the mortgagee may claim that a reserve price be fixed. The proceeds of the sale will go to the mortgagee and the remaining balance, after deduction of all costs, will go to the mortgagor as the former owner of the property. If the sale of the property cannot generate sufficient funds to cover the mortgagor's debt, he or she will remain liable for paying the remaining debt.

Various special clauses are included in mortgage deeds and these are dealt with below. Estate agents should refer buyers to a reliable attorney for more information regarding these clauses.

An agreement that the mortgagor will forfeit his or her right of ownership to the mortgagee, or that the mortgagee may retain possession of the mortgaged property in lieu of payment owing to default in payment, is invalid in the South African legal system. Such a clause is called a 'pactum commissorium' (Van Jaarsveld 1983:196).

On the other hand, an agreement that the mortgagee has the use of the property instead of interest is valid and is called a 'pactum antichresis' (Van Jaarsveld 1983:197). An agreement that a mortgagee may sell the mortgaged property on his or her own authority without a court order in the case of the mortgagor's default of payment ('paratge executie') is invalid if it relates to immovable property.

Certain technical arguments may be raised to nullify the purpose of a bond loan and, therefore, these arguments should be excluded in order to lend the mortgagee maximum security. Where there is an intention of lending or advancing money, the following arguments, among others, should be ruled out:

- Non causa debiti, namely that the principal debt is not legal and binding because it is not based on reasonable cause.

- If the *non numerantae pecuniae* argument is not ruled out, the mortgagee must prove (in the event of a dispute) that the money has actually been paid to the mortgagor. If the mortgagor forgoes this argument, the onus of proof that the money was not paid will rest with the mortgagor.
- The *error calculi* clause rules out errors made in the calculations, as well as the revision of accounts (Caney 1975:335).

Estate agents must inform applicants for bond loans of the importance of completing application forms as comprehensively as possible (Myburg 1987:135). Institutions require the following information (in application forms), for example:
- information about the property;
- information about the applicant; and
- general information applicable to both the property and the applicant, in order to determine the institution's risk as well as the applicant's ability to pay the bond instalments (Myburg 1987:136).

Since commission and errors on application forms unnecessarily delay the registration process, complete and accurate information will prevent such delays. Estate agents must warn applicants that they could suffer financial losses if the purchase of a house is delayed and they are obliged to pay occupational interest over a longer period than anticipated.

The following are the different types of mortgage bond estate agents should be familiar with in order to be able to advise buyers and sellers.

Types of mortgage bond

Estate agents should be familiar with the different types of mortgage bond in order to be able to:
- explain to the parties concerned when a particular kind of bond should be used;
- suggest the best type of mortgage bond under different circumstances;
- explain to the party that, for example, a covering bond can only be obtained from a banking institution; and
- explain to the parties how the different types of mortgage bond function.

A first bond

A first bond contains all the features of a mortgage bond, as well as those of a special bond, since a specified immovable property is mortgaged (Technikon RSA 1986:130). First and second bonds are the most important bonds for the purpose of our discussion. Ring & Dasso (1985:315) describe second and further bonds as 'junior bonds' because they hold greater risk for the mortgagee.

A covering bond

A covering bond secures a debt to be incurred at a future date, contrary to the normal bonds which serve as security for funds borrowed before or after registration of the mortgage deed (Section 50(2) of the Deeds Registries Act, 1937). The mortgage deed must expressly state that the bond is designed to secure a future debt, to be incurred after registration of the mortgage deed. A further requirement is that the maximum amount must be stipulated in the mortgage deed (Van Jaarsveld 1983:215). The mortgagor is free to allow fluctuation of the amount he or she borrowed within the determined maximum amount, and this will not affect the validity of the mortgage deed (Jones 1985:457).

A covering bond may be registered over immovable property to serve as security for a bank overdraft. Maritz (1983:327) states that a covering bond may be a first, second, third, fourth, etc. bond. Estate agents must warn their clients that it is not at all easy to obtain a covering bond from another financial institution once they have registered a first bond over a property. The reason for this is that the first financial institution will have first claim to the property in the event of liquidation.

New bond packages

Apart from the conventional bonds normally used to purchase a house (in more than 80% of cases), there are several new bond options for prospective buyers. Prospective buyers now have the opportunity to convert their property investment into an investment portfolio with high growth. Home bond schemes are linked to an endowment policy or a unit trust.

These new bond packages differ from a conventional bond in the sense that only interest is redeemed. The capital redemption portion is used to pay for an endowment policy or a unit trust. Although these two schemes are more expensive, a larger capital sum can be anticipated at the end of the bond term. Higher income earners prefer to use these schemes rather than conventional bonds.

The following is a brief discussion of some of the new housing financing methods.

Endowment policy option

With this option, a bond is linked to an endowment policy. The monthly instalment redeems only the interest, while the capital sum is used to take out an endowment policy in the name of the insured. Financial institutions guarantee that the bond debt will be redeemed at the end of the bond term. A further amount will be paid to the insured as a bonus. It is expected that an average home bond will be paid off approximately five to seven years earlier.

The endowment policy does not lapse automatically when the mortgagor sells his or her house, as it has been ceded to the mortgagee, who can transfer it to another house. Once the bond has been redeemed (paid off), the mortgagee will return the policy to the mortgagor. The mortgagor, in turn, may decide whether to continue or terminate the policy. If the policy is terminated within the first five years, however, the mortgagor must pay income tax on his or her returns.

Unit trust linked bond
In this case the capital expenditure portion of the premium is linked to a unit trust. Unit trusts offer a high return. Tax is payable on the dividends received. The disadvantage (or risk) attached is that there is no guarantee that a return will eventually be paid to the mortgagor.

If you compare a conventional bond, an endowment policy option and a unit trust linked bond, it can be seen that the anticipated growth rate, the investment value at the end of the term and the net return of unit trusts are considerably higher.

The access choice
The access choice has more advantages than conventional bonds. With this bond, a mortgagor has the opportunity to use the paid-off amounts at any stage and without prior permission from the mortgagee. The mortgagor will pay interest on the R50 000 and may use the additional R30 000 at any stage.

This kind of bond is convenient if a person needs money at a later stage for improvements. Repayments on the bond may be used to purchase other necessities (even short-term). The mortgagor has access to the repaid bond and may even use it to buy a lounge suite, for example. It is poor financial management, however, to use long-term funds to acquire short-term assets. The problem is that a lot more is paid for such assets.

Bond payments
A person wishing to apply for a bond of R50 000 needs information on the monthly instalment. Assume that the interest rate is 16%. The normal period of repayment for a house, in the case of a reducible loan, is 20 years, and the monthly instalment is R696. As financial institutions demand that the monthly instalment does not exceed 30% of a person's income, the gross income of the person must be at least R2 320 per month.

Interest rates will affect the monthly instalment and the term as follows:
- If the interest rate rises to 16.5%, the new monthly instalment will be R714. The mortgagor will, therefore, require an additional R18 (R714-R696) per month.
- If the interest rate drops to 15.5%, the new

monthly instalment will be R667. The mortgagor will be faced with a choice that could eventually save or cost a lot of money. If the mortgagor pays R677 per month, thereby saving R19 per month, he or she would nevertheless have to continue paying this instalment for 20 years. If the mortgagor continues paying R696 per month, however, the repayment term will be reduced to between 17 and 17.5 years (between R697 and R693).

A rise in interest rates caused by an upswing in the economy is usually accompanied by higher salaries. High income groups in particular benefit from this. Similarly, a rise in the market value of properties will compensate for the higher instalment that has to be paid. Financial institutions consequently receive greater security for bond loans already granted.

On the other hand, if there is a slump in the economy, a rise in interest rates would not be coupled with economic growth or higher salaries. Mortgagors would consequently find it much more difficult to pay their monthly instalments.

A monthly subsidy lowers the monthly instalment considerably. Therefore, a rise in interest rates would be unlikely to prevent the mortgagor from continuing payment of his or her monthly instalment. Where a monthly interest rate subsidy is received, mortgagors must take note of the following.

A person paying a subsidised interest rate of 8% will have a monthly instalment of R418. The difference between 16% (R696) and 8% (R418), namely R278, is paid by his or her employer.

If a person decides to increase the monthly instalment of R696 (16%) by R100 to R796, the period of repayment is reduced to between 11 and 11.5 years. Thousands of rands could be saved on interest payments depending on the rate of inflation, general interest rates, and the interest-to-capital ratio in an instalment.

Where a house is purchased by means of a bond of R100 000 at 14% per annum over a 20-year period, the monthly instalment is R1 243,52 and the interest-to-capital ratio will be as follows:

TABLE 8.2 **Interest-to-capital ratio during bond payments**

Month	Interest	Capital
1 – 60	R67 986,80	R6 624,45
61 – 120	R61 325,18	R13 286,07
121 – 180	R47 964,58	R26 646,67
181 – 240	R21 168,43	R53 442,81

In month 190, the interest-to-capital ratio is R688:R555. The interest-to-capital ratio fluctuates over the term of the debt. Initially, a lot of interest is paid and little capital redeemed, while the capital and interest redemption is almost the same in month 185. After this period, more capital than interest is paid off. Although it is initially better to pay more than the normal instalment, this benefit decreases as the capital redemption increases per instalment in relation to the interest redemption.

If a home loan amounts to R30 000 (over a period of 20 years and at an average interest rate of 19%) and a person increases his or her instalment (R486,21) by one tenth (R486,21 + R48 = R534,21), he or she would pay off the house more than eight years sooner and at the same time save (interest) of almost R41 884,97 (R116 690 - R74 805,43 [R534,21 x R140,03]). Such savings are possible because in this case R116 690,40 must be repaid by the mortgagor.

Table 8.3 (Trace 1985:62) gives an indication of how an amount of R50 000 at various interest rates is reduced over a period of 20 years. If we look at the 16% column, we see that R48 673 (97.35%) is still outstanding on the bond loan after three years. Initially the capital sum drops very slowly and eventually much faster.

'Saving' on interest has the same net result as 'earning' interest. Furthermore, this 'saving' is not taxable. By paying more than the required monthly instalment, the mortgagor makes a tax-free investment with the mortgagee at the bond lending rate.

Buyers could also save approximately R7 200 (interest) if they negotiate a loan of R60 000 for a period of 25 years at an interest rate of 18% instead of 18.5%. A half per cent difference in the interest rate could bring about great savings and estate agents should ensure that buyers use their money in the best way. This saving is as follows:

Interest rate	Bond instalment
18.5	R934,49
18.0	R910,46
	R24,03 x 300 months (25 years)
	= R7 209,00

The possible advantages of an increased bond payment are:
- most significant when the bond term has just begun; and
- smallest when only five years of the bond term are left.

Estate agents should know that psychological factors, such as peace of mind after retirement because a bond has been paid off, have an effect on a mortgagor's

TABLE 8.3 **Outstanding balance on a bond of R50 000**
(Source: Trace 1985:62)

Years left to pay	Annual interest rate											
	12%	13%	14%	15%	16%	17%	18%	19%	20%	21%	22%	23%
20	50 000	50 000	50 000	50 000	50 000	50 000	50 000	50 000	50 000	50 000	50 000	50 000
19	49 359	49 348	49 508	49 571	49 626	49 675	49 718	49 755	49 788	49 817	49 812	49 864
18	48 637	48 798	48 943	49 072	49 187	49 289	49 380	49 460	49 530	49 592	49 646	49 649
17	47 823	48 070	48 293	48 493	48 673	48 833	48 976	49 103	49 215	49 315	49 403	49 480
16	46 906	47 241	47 546	47 822	48 070	48 293	48 493	48 672	48 832	48 974	49 099	49 211
15	45 872	46 298	46 688	47 042	47 363	47 654	47 910	48 152	48 364	48 553	48 722	48 873
14	44 708	45 225	45 01	46 137	46 535	46 897	47 226	47 524	47 93	48 036	48 254	48 449
13	43 395	44 004	44 567	45 087	45 564	46 001	46 401	46 766	47 097	47 398	47 671	47 917
12	41 917	42 614	43 264	43 867	44 425	44 940	45 415	45 850	46 249	46 613	46 945	47 248
11	40 251	41 032	41 776	42 452	43 090	43 684	44 235	44 744	45 214	45 647	46 044	46 408
10	38 373	39 233	40 045	40 809	41 526	42 198	42 825	43 409	43 952	44 456	44 922	45 353
9	36 258	37 184	38 066	38 902	39 692	40 437	41 139	41 797	42 414	42 990	43 528	44 028
8	33 874	34 853	35 792	36 689	37 542	38 354	39 123	39 851	40 538	41 185	41 794	42 364
7	31 187	32 200	33 178	34 119	35 021	35 886	36 713	37 501	38 250	38 963	39 637	40 275
6	28 160	29 181	30 174	31 137	32 067	32 966	33 831	34 663	35 460	36 225	36 955	37 651
5	24 750	25 745	26 721	27 675	28 603	29 508	30 386	31 236	32 059	32 854	33 619	34 358
4	20 906	21 835	22 753	23 657	24 543	25 414	26 267	27 099	27 911	28 703	29 471	30 217
3	16 575	17 386	18 192	18 993	19 783	20 568	21 342	22 101	22 853	23 592	24 313	25 020
2	11 695	12 322	12 950	13 579	14 203	14 830	15 453	16 072	16 686	17 297	17 898	18 492
1	6 196	6 559	6 925	7 295	7 662	8 037	8 412	8 789	9 165	9 546	9 921	10 295

decision to increase his or her bond payments. A large existing bond could be an advantage for homeowners, particularly in times when funds are scarce. Estate agents must always be intent on keeping their clients informed of the full financial implications of alternative decisions they could make.

A seller of a house with a relatively high bond will be able to sell the house more easily, because the buyer has the opportunity to take over the existing bond. The mortgagee will receive his or her money before the seller receives the surplus (if any). A high existing bond, therefore, facilitates financing for the buyer, especially in times of a lack of funds.

Kling (1983:40) defines a re-advance as making another loan from the amount already repaid on the capital amount of a bond. Re-advances are more desirable than a second bond because of the savings on registration costs for a further bond. The monthly instalment is paid on the full bond amount from the time the re-advance is granted. The bond term (for example 20 years) is also calculated from this time. A person who negotiated an initial bond of R50 000 and has already repaid R20 000, may apply to the financial institution for a re-advance of R20 000. If the mortgagor wishes to borrow more than R20 000, a further bond will have to be registered.

Termination of bonds

Van Jaarsveld (1983:218, 219) lists the following methods of terminating bonds:
- by paying the debt;
- by renewing the debt;
- the destruction of the property;
- by a court order;
- by the mortgagee surrendering the bond;
- by judicial sale of the mortgaged property; and
- by prescription.

Mortgagors should take note, however, of the cancellation costs involved in terminating a bond within the first year of the bond term. If a person sells his or her house and the new buyer negotiates a bond at the same financial institution, a specified amount is often paid to the seller. Consequently, the seller need not pay cancellation costs.

A bond may also be terminated if the full outstanding balance on the bond loan has been paid. Kling (1983:38) writes that some financial institutions impose a penalty of 1% of the bond amount if the total bond is redeemed within the first year of the bond term. In such a case, estate agents must advise clients against repayment of the bond within the first year. Similarly, clients must be warned of the bond registration costs and cancella-

tion costs if they wish to renew a bond that has been redeemed altogether.

Renewal of debt takes place once a new security has replaced an existing security. Estate agents should point out the benefits of a re-advance above a second bond, that is, there are no registration costs. A property destroyed by fire can no longer serve as security for a mortgagee. Consequently the bond is terminated.

Although this is seldom the case, a court may declare the bond null and void. A mortgagee may tacitly or explicitly waive his or her bond rights over a particular property. A court will require a clear explanation by the mortgagee of his or her intention to waive a bond, before deciding whether the mortgagee has in fact tacitly waived the bond. Once the mortgaged property is sold after an insolvency, the bond will lapse (the bond lapses after any sales transaction).

If a mortgagor has not made any repayments on the bond loan over a period of 30 years or longer and has not acknowledged any responsibility to such an obligation, the mortagee's rights become prescribed (with regard to debt collection). Consequently, the mortgagee may no longer enforce any rights.

8.9.3.2 A contract for the alienation of land in instalments

A contract for the sale of land in instalments is another instrument of finance and not merely an alienation deed (Maritz 1985:57). Agreements for the alienation of land are regulated by the Alienation of Land Act 68 of 1981. This Act stipulates certain requirements that all agreements in respect of immovable property (with certain exceptions) must meet.

Maritz describes the following more important concepts:
- Alienate means sell, exchange or donate.
- An alienation deed (i.e. a sales contract, exchange contract or donation contact) is the written agreement embodying the alienation contract.
- Land, for the purposes of contracts for the sale of land in instalments, involves land used or intended to be used for dwelling purposes only, and does not include agricultural land or land kept in trust by the Minister for the state for any person (Section 1 of the Alienation of Land Act, 1981).

An estate agent may sign an alienation deed on behalf of a person with his or her written permission. Financing according to this method takes place under the following circumstances:
- when a buyer cannot provide a cash amount or supplementary security to obtain a bond loan; or

when, for some reason, the land cannot be registered in the name of the buyer, for example when the land has not been proclaimed yet (Maritz 1985:59).

The sale of land in instalments has the following benefits for the seller:
• The land can be repossessed fairly easy and quickly if the buyer defaults.
• Transactions can be finalised relatively quickly, because delays in financing (a bond loan, for example) for the buyers are to great extent eliminated.
• Un-proclaimed erven (which cannot be registered) can be sold.

A buyer gains the following benefits from this financing instrument:
• Occupation of and control over the property may be obtained in the absence of an initial cash repayment of the purchase sum.
• The buyer can build up (save) sufficient capital to enable him or her to redeem 20% of the purchase sum in cash, in order to obtain a bond loan. Subsequently, the outstanding portion of the purchase sum is paid off (note, to the seller, and the debt is now owed to the mortgagee) and transfer is taken of the property.

It often happens in practice that the owner of land sells the land on an instalment basis before he or she has paid for it and before it has been registered in his or her name. A new buyer may also sell the land to a third person and in this way there could be a whole series of buyers. As the initial owner (seller) has not yet given transfer of the land, the end buyer can only take transfer once all the intermediate buyers have taken transfer. Estate agents must point out to persons that one or more of these buyers (or sellers) may become insolvent or commit a breach of contract.

A person who buys land from a seller who is also a buyer and not the registered owner of the land is called a remote purchaser (Section 1 of the Alienation of Land Act, 1981).

A person who purchases land from a seller in order to sell it again, as well as a person who sells land to remote buyers, is called an intermediary (Section 1 of the Alienation of Land Act, 1981).

Any buyer or remote buyer can fulfil the obligations of an intermediary by paying a seller a sum of money (on behalf of the intermediary). The purpose of this is to make it possible for a buyer or remote buyer to help prevent the cancellation of contracts by intermediaries. Otherwise, the buyer or remote buyer him- or herself will not receive transfer of the land.

The following discussion deals with the various sources of long-term financing in order to determine the sources that provide funds on the best possible terms. The requirements set by these sources for the provision of funds are also discussed.

8.9.4 Sources of long-term financing

Sources of long-term financing are those financial institutions that provide funds over a longer period (ten years and longer). The main providers of long-term funds in South Africa are: deposit-taking institutions (banking institutions and building societies), mutual building societies, insurance companies, pension and provident funds and participation bond schemes.

The role of each of these institutions in financing houses is briefly explained.

8.9.4.1 Deposit-taking institutions

The main providers of home loan finance (long-term finance) are deposit-taking institutions. Deposit-taking institutions were created in terms of the Deposit-taking Institutions Act 94 of 1990. This Act repealed the Building Societies Act 82 of 1986 and the Banks Act 23 of 1965. We no longer make a distinction between commercial banks and building societies.

Deposit-taking institutions have no statutory prohibitions and prescriptions regarding the:
• kind of advances that may be made;
• minimum extent of transactions in housing advances;
• maximum extent of transactions in business and general advances;
• maximum amount of housing or business advances;
• registration of first and subsequent mortgages;
• collateral security to be furnished; and
• valuation of properties (Unisa 1993:183).

Financial institutions are financial intermediaries between businesses or persons with a surplus of funds, and businesses or persons with a shortage of funds. Funds are attracted by these institutions from economic units with a surplus of funds to make such funds available to economic units with a shortage of funds (Brümmer & Rademeyer 1982:561).

These institutions undertake the following:
• home loans against security of a first bond; and
• overdraft facilities against security of a covering bond.

These two methods are briefly illustrated below:

Home loans against the security of a first bond

Institutions accept a first bond as security for providing buyers with a home loan. Such a loan works as follows.

The joint income of a husband and wife (in the case of married persons) is calculated to obtain the maximum loan amount. The matrimonial regime of the applicants will determine whether they will be liable for the debt separately or jointly.

According to the IEASA (1985:136), the instalment amount of the loan may not exceed 30% of the joint gross income of the borrower(s).

The definition of a borrower's monthly income varies among different deposit-taking institutions but the following are usually taken into account:

- the borrower's gross monthly salary (no deductions are made for the payment of income tax, medical or pension fund contributions, and where the borrower is on a commission income, an average is usually taken over a specified period of time, e.g. two years);
- the gross salary of a spouse or of a joint owner if the partners are not married;
- subsidies from an employer;
- one-twelfth of an annual bonus, travel allowance, business allowance, donation or bequest, or other fringe benefits, provided that these are received on a regular basis; and
- one-twelfth of the annual interest on savings and dividends on investments, provided that such savings and investments are not being used to finance the subject property.

The inclusion of other items in the borrower's defined monthly income is at the discretion of the institution. For example:

- Overtime pay is often not taken into consideration.
- Maintenance payments to divorced persons are considered on merit.
- Some fringe benefits, such as a car allowance, may only be allowed at a fixed amount set by the institution.
- Rental received is usually included on a net basis after provision for mortgage payments and operating expenses.

In assessing affordability, institutions also look at the borrower's obligations in respect of hire-purchase agreements, unsecured credit loans and his or her assets and liabilities structure. This may result in a decision by the institution to reduce the 30% ratio to perhaps 20% of the borrower's monthly income (Unisa 1993:184).

Home loans are at present granted for an amount equal to 90% or even 100% of the value of the house, as determined by the institution. However, banks require additional security for financing above 90%.

There is large-scale competition among financial institutions for granting bond loans at the lowest possible rate. Funds are fairly easy obtainable for housing purposes, and consequently deposit-taking institutions are waging a battle to draw and/or retain clients because of the similarity of their offers in the capital market. The capital market is the physical and abstract market where supply and demand of long-term funds meet or are brought into contact with one another (Brümmer & Rademeyer 1982:35; Falkena et al. 1984:259).

A small test sample by *Finansies & Tegniek* has shown that status clients in particular obtain lower interest rates than other clients. Status clients even borrow money on overdrafts at a lower interest rate than the current prime rate (only the best clients benefit in this way). These institutions, however, deny that they are primarily concerned with attracting status clients. These clients are subsidised by less creditworthy clients, who have to pay higher interest rates (Volschenk 1987c:10).

Deposit-taking institutions avoid interest rate wars in their advertising and prefer placing the emphasis on service and reliability. Buyers should not assume that the advertising campaigns of the various institutions will ensure the best interest rates in the long term. Negotiations are a further requirement for the 'best' interest rates (Kemney 1988:701; Volschenk 1987b:14).

Institutions usually require that applicants for bond loans open a current account with them. Even if the applicant does not write out a single cheque, the administration of the current account entails costs for the holder. Estate agents should advise buyers to consult various financial institutions in order to obtain the best bond loan. Potential buyers should rather consult a financial institution that has been handling their business for a long time, if they cannot obtain a loan at the lowest interest rate.

A good bond loan is a combination of the following: the lowest available interest rate, the highest percentage of bond to purchase price of the house (lowest collateral investment), no anticipated rise in interest rates in the near future and a future interest rate rise not higher than the average bond rate required by most financial institutions.

It is suggested that the bond term should not exceed 20 years because of the large amount of interest payable. Even if an initial lower instalment looks good, this benefit is counteracted by the payment of interest in the long term. Estate agents should inform potential buyers of this aspect after analysing their financial position.

In theory, there is a connection between the risk a client holds for a financial institution and the interest rate he or she pays on a bond loan. There is a more direct connection between the negotiation ability of a client at a financial institution and the interest rate he or she will be paying. A client may, therefore, pay a higher interest rate than someone else who is less creditworthy. The reason for this is that one client may have enquired about the interest rate while the other did not.

Buyers who have to sell their house for financial reasons frequently suffer a loss if they have a 100% bond loan. Agents should, therefore, warn buyers to purchase property that matches their financial position and to include rising interest rates in their financial planning.

Home loan terms vary as follows according to the amount (in the case of reducible loans):

- less then R100 000 (30 years);
- R100 000 – R150 000 (25 years); and
- more than R150 000 (20 years).

Institutions prefer that the term of a loan does not extend beyond an applicant's 70th birthday. The age limit is meaningless, since most people of that age would prefer having paid off their house by that time. It is suggested that this age should not be more than 65, because the requirements for a relatively large house are the greatest at age 45. A 20-year bond term makes 65 a more acceptable age.

If instalments are paid over a period of 30 years, it may happen that the monthly payment on a particular amount will be lower, but the total interest payable will be considerably higher. Buyers of first houses, as well as those who wish to purchase a more expensive house, will benefit from the initial relatively low bond instalment (Volschenk 1987a:16).

A second method of financing is by means of overdraft facilities against the security of a covering bond.

Overdraft facilities against the security of a covering bond

Institutions provide overdraft facilities for the purchase of immovable property against the security of a covering bond on a particular property. Normally, overdraft facilities are provided for not more than 50% or 60% of the value of the property. Such overdraft facilities are reviewed annually (Maritz 1983:353).

Estate agents must inform potential buyers of the lower loan amount (50% or 60%) obtained according to this method of financing. Overdraft facilities should not be used to finance a house, because long-term debt should not be covered by short-term financing. The reason is that institutions may call up this debt after one or five years, which could compel the mortgagor to find a large amount of money in a relatively short period.

8.9.4.2 Mutual building societies

A mutual building society is a permanent association of persons, the principal object of which is the making, out of funds derived from the issue of shares to and the acceptance of deposits from the public or from subscriptions by members, of advances for any purpose upon the security of the mortgage of urban immovable property. (Unisa 1993:182)

Three mutual building societies decided not to be converted into public companies, namely: Eastern Province; Provincial; and Grahamstown. The Mutual Building Societies Act 24 of 1965 regulates the activities of these mutual building societies. Procedures for obtaining housing loans are similar to those of deposit-taking institutions. Mutual building societies are subject to the following principal statutory regulations:

- Kind of advances. Mutual building societies may grant:
  - a housing advance;
  - a business advance; and
  - a general advance.
- Advances and consents that are prohibited. A mutual society shall not advance money by way of a housing or business advance to any person against security of:
  - A mortgage on immovable property or on any right to immovable property that is not urban immovable property or a right to urban immovable property.
  - A second or subsequent mortgage on urban immovable property or on a right to urban immovable property, unless the first mortgage or all mortgages, as the case may be, on such property or right ranking prior to that mortgage, is or are in favour of the society.
  - A mortgage on urban immovable property or on any right to urban immovable property ranking pari passu with mortgage in favour of another person on the same property or right.
  - A mortgage on a right to urban immovable property if that right is a lease, or other right to occupy, or use the property:
    - having a remaining term of less than 20 years; or
    - which is not at the discretion of the lessee, occupier or user renewable for a period, or for continuous periods totalling, at least 20 years.

- A society shall not advance money to any person against security of a fixed deposit which the person has invested with it or a share issued by it to that person, unless the rate of interest payable on the advance is at least 1% higher than the rate of interest payable on the fixed deposit or the rate of dividend payable on the share, as the case may be.
- A society, also, shall not consent to the registration in favour of any other person or a mortgage on any property or a right to property which will rank pari passu with a mortgage held by it on the property or right (urban property is defined in the Act).
- Minimum extent of transactions in housing advances. The minimum extent of transactions in housing is prescribed.
- Maximum extent of business and general advances. The maximum extent of business and general advances is prescribed.
- Maximum amount of housing advances. Unless collateral security is furnished in favour of society, it shall not grant:
  - a housing advance in excess of 90%, in the case of a reducing mortgage, and 80% in the case of any other mortgage; or
  - a business advance in excess of 80% of the market value of the property or a right in property, provided that it may also provide the full cost of registration of the property or right in the name of the borrower.
- Collateral security. If collateral is furnished, a society shall not grant a housing or business advance which is greater than the lesser of:
  - the market value of the property or right in question; or
  - the sum of the advance which may be granted on the property or right without collateral security and the value without collateral security furnished.
- Type of collateral security to be accepted. The type of collateral acceptable is defined in the Act and the percentage of its value to be taken into account, is prescribed.
- Valuation of urban immovable property. The society is obliged by law to make a valuation of the subject property or to have such a valuation done. (Unisa 1993:202)

8.9.4.3 Insurance companies

Insurance companies are particularly interested in investments in offices, warehouses, industrial buildings, shopping centres and large shops. As a source of financing in the property market, insurance companies play a less important role than deposit-taking institutions. Insurance companies are less, or not at all interested in town development, housing, sectional title schemes, time-share schemes, share-block schemes and leasing of flats (Technikon RSA 1986:99).

Maritz (1983:359) writes that insurance companies grant few, if any, bond loans. When they do grant bond loans it involves large amounts (a million rand or more) and at high interest rates. He states that insurance companies do play an important role in lease-backs as a form of financing.

Schaller (1984:38) indicates that insurance companies, unlike building societies, are not limited to an 80% or 90% ceiling on the amount they may grant on a bond. However, few South African insurance companies grant private housing bonds and, if they do, these are usually confined to policyholders. For all these reasons, it is not necessary to discuss insurance companies as a source of finance for housing at any great length.

8.9.4.4 Pension and provident funds

Pension and provident fund organisations are organisations not for gain. A pension fund organisation is a society aimed at providing members or ex-members of that society with annuities or lump sum payments. The funds are reserved for the day members or ex-members reach retirement age, as well as for their dependants at their death (Section 1 of the Pension Fund Act, 1956a). A pension fund organisation also does business concerned with any of the objectives for establishing a mutual benefit society (Section 2 of the Friendly Societies Act, 1956b).

Because pension funds handle trust money, they are governed by specific legislation, namely the Insurance Act 27 of 1943 and the Pension Fund Act 24 of 1956. Pension and provident funds prefer investing in income-bearing commercial property and do not provide funds for housing (Maritz 1983:359).

8.9.4.5 Participation bond schemes

These schemes do not provide funds for housing and, therefore, will not be discussed further.

Although financing for housing is of a long-term nature, buyers and sellers often find themselves in a position where they need short-term financing. Many people have to approach family or friends, or deposit-taking institutions in order to obtain funds, particularly for the hidden costs involved in buying a house.

Schaller (1984:39) maintains that buyers, having paid all the costs involved (including the hidden costs) are often unable to buy extras such as carpets, curtains and furniture. One solution could be to apply for a further loan, using existing insurance policies as security, if a person has paid sufficient premiums on the policies.

8.9.4.6 Sources of financing when funds are scarce

When funds are scarce, estate agents have to be more creative. The following are some suggestions for solving the problem of a scarcity of funds.

Buyers and sellers should be encouraged to arrange financing around an existing bond (if applicable). Here an estate agent should play a prominent role in the negotiation process by informing the seller of the shortage of funds from other sources and by convincing him or her of the necessity of financing the transaction from the existing bond. The mortgagee should be asked whether the buyer may make use of the bond, and the buyer must be asked whether he or she is able (if necessary) to pay the difference between the bond and the purchase price, or whether he or she is able to make up the difference in some other way.

An estate agent could advise the buyer (applicant) to approach the institution holding the bond (the mortgagee). Assume that the selling price of a house is R350 000 with an existing bond of R180 000 at a 14% bond rate. The buyer has R70 000 in cash and therefore needs a bond loan of R280 000. The estate agent could approach the institution with an application for a R280 000 bond loan (which redeems the R180 000 bond loan) at 15% interest. The institution would be aware of the property concerned and of its value.

The seller may be approached to act as a mortgagee. This type of financing is called secondary financing. Assume that the institution provides a first bond, but the buyer does not have sufficient cash to pay the difference in the purchase price. An estate agent could attempt to obtain a second bond from the seller. The buyer will undertake to pay the seller monthly instalments over a specified period.

An estate agent could approach private persons for financing (also known as secondary financing). There are many people, such as retired persons, widows and widowers who have cash that is not being property utilised. Estate agents could approach them to obtain finance for housing. In this way, estate agents could assist in finding the necessary funds.

Buyers should be encouraged to purchase a house, in spite of initial high interest rates, particularly if a drop in interest rates is anticipated in the near future. Estate agents should inform buyers that, in time, their bond instalments would be lower, which would lighten their financial burden.

Estate agents may request a seller to let the house to a potential buyer until he or she obtains a bond. The buyer may have a certain amount available (say R1 000) which he or she could use to pay the rent. If the buyer (who should have good creditworthiness) is able to keep up this monthly rental, the seller could move in the knowledge that the buyer would pay the desired purchase price as soon as his or her application for a bond comes through.

A buyer should preferably apply for a bond loan from the financial institution where he or she has an account. The estate agent could approach the institution where the buyer has a savings account or an investment. In this way, the buyer would obtain financing much more quickly.

Another solution could be for the estate agent to approach the buyer's employee to finance the purchase (this is particularly applicable to employees who hold high positions in large companies). The treasurer of a large company would usually know the treasurer of the financial institution concerned, which may contribute to the buyer obtaining a bond loan (financing).

Estate agents have to depend on financing by financial institutions or natural persons in order to conclude agreements of sale between buyers and sellers. For that reason, and to obtain their commission, it is their task to assist in obtaining scarce financial means for potential buyers. Financial advice should, therefore, be provided regarding the possibility of obtaining financing.

Estate agents should maintain contact with various financial institutions, which will be more likely to remember the estate agent in times when funds are hard to come by. If the estate agent limits his or her negotiations to a single institution, it may be disadvantageous if he or she, as a stranger, has to apply to another institution for financing at a later stage. By negotiating with various institutions, the necessary funds may often be obtained. However, when funds are really scarce, financial institutions are inclined to limit their business, regardless of any relationship an estate agent may have built up with them. It appears then that there is not much difference between concentrating on one or more institutions.

An estate agent's task can be greatly facilitated if the management of the estate agency appoints a person who is responsible for processing completed application forms. This person would constantly liaise with various financial institutions and would be in a position to report to estate agents regarding the approval of applications. A lot of time could be saved, because estate agents would not have to consult eight or perhaps ten institutions on their own in search of financing for potential buyers. Nothing prevents an estate agent from taking loan applications personally to the institution.

Estate agents should also advise their clients on potential problems arising after they have moved into a new house or left an old house. Their service should continue after the conclusion of a contract.

The next section is about housing subsidy schemes that the state offers in order to enable buyers to obtain a house of their own.

8.9.4.7 State housing subsidy schemes and the implications of such schemes

The state is currently offering various housing subsidy schemes to alleviate the housing crisis.

Prospective buyers of new or existing houses can apply to the state for financial assistance. However, this assistance is subject to certain qualifications.

Estate agents should be acquainted with all the schemes available to state employees in order to provide them with financial advice. They should also be able to advise first-time buyers on how to go about obtaining state assistance. Buyers and sellers need to know how these schemes function.

The following properties are subsidised:
- properties classified for dwelling purposes; and
- properties within a reasonable distance of the buyer's place of work.

Estate agents must advise state employees, statutory bodies and state supported institutions on how state housing subsidies work.

100% housing loans

The state guarantees an amount equal to and not exceeding 20% of the total purchase price of the house to a building society or a bank. The building society or bank then grants a loan equal to 100% of either the purchase price or the value of the property, whichever is the lowest (IEASA 1985:129).

If the buyer is unable, for whatever reason, to keep up his or her instalments, the building society or bank will sell the property. If there is a difference between the outstanding balance (owing to the institution) and 80% of the original purchase price, it must be guaranteed by the relevant state department.

After receiving the application form from the state department (stating the maximum amount for which the property may be purchased), the employee (applicant) may conclude the purchase contract and must ensure that the granting of the 100% housing loan is included as a suspensive condition. If the employee fails to do this, and the loan is not granted, he or she will have to pay the 20% of the purchase price him- or herself, since he or she will not be allowed to withdraw the loan application.

After conclusion of the purchase contract, the buyer must complete the usual application form for a bond loan from a financial institution and submit it to the relevant financial institution either him- or herself or by means of an estate agent. Once a financial institution has valued the property, a 100% loan will be granted. The relevant state department will then guarantee the 20% portion of the loan in favour of the financial institution.

The buyer is expected to cede his or her total contribution to the pension fund (over a period of ten years), as well as one month's salary, to the relevant department. If the employee is discharged or leaves the service, he or she must repay the 20% guarantee to the financial institution within 60 days. If he or she is unable to do this, the total accrued contribution to the pension fund, as well as his or her last salary, will be paid to the financial institution.

The financial institution will usually inspect the property after a mortgagor's resignation. If the outstanding bond amount is less than or equal to 80% of the market value of the property, the mortgagor does not have to repay the mortgagee, in which case the mortgagor will be entitled to receive his or her contributions to the pension fund as well as his or her last salary.

A state employee also receives a subsidy on his or her monthly bond payment in the case of a 100% housing loan. This subsidy is only granted to a maximum bond amount of R75 000.

Assume a person has been in the employ of the state for nine months and he or she decides to purchase a house. The estate agent should inform him or her that he or she would qualify for a 100% state housing loan if he or she were to wait another three months. This would mean that it would not be necessary to find the deposit (or if there is sufficient money to pay the deposit, he or she would not have to wait for it), since the state would guarantee the deposit (usually 20%).

Selling a subsidised property

Goosen (IEASA 1985:132) points out that when an employee sells a subsidised property, the total profit made must be invested in the new property to be purchased, or he or she forfeits the right to a further subsidy or loses the 20% guarantee. Although a state employee may sell his or her first property, he or she must apply in writing to the department in order to sell a second property and purchase a third.

When first-time home buyers purchase a house through an estate agent, it is the estate agent's task to inform such buyers of the existence and functioning of subsidy schemes. In order to render an efficient service to clients, and in the best interest of the country, estate agents must be well informed on all existing subsidy schemes and how they function, as well about changes that take place.

Employees must be encouraged to obtain all possible information on their employer's company housing scheme (where applicable) before applying for financing.

8.10 PRACTICAL STEPS: HOME BUYING

8.10.1 How much can I afford?

- You can only buy the house you can afford.
- Do not commit financial suicide.
- Ask your parents/spouse/an estate agent/attorney to help you to determine what you can afford (draw up a new household budget).
- What you can afford when interest rates are low is not your most important criterion.
- Determine what you can afford if interest rates rise by 10% (think about the future as well).
- Deposit-taking financial institutions (banks) will further determine the amount you can buy for by looking at the amount you qualify for according to banking regulations.

8.10.2 How much do I qualify for?

- Banks allow you to borrow an amount with a monthly premium of 30% of your joint monthly incomes (including your spouse or partner).
- First calculate your joint annual income from all sources.
- Multiply this amount by 30% to get your maximum allowable annual bond payment.
- Divide this amount by 12 (months) to get your maximum allowable monthly bond payment.
- Once you have this amount you can ask the bank/estate agent/attorney to determine the maximum bond amount you may qualify for at the current interest rate.
- You must find out if you will qualify for a home loan equal to this amount.
- You will have to supply a deposit or give some collateral (an investment/amount in a savings account/a policy) if you would like to buy a home for a larger amount – bear this in mind once you start house-hunting or when you apply for a bond.

8.10.3 Your household budget

- Once you know the monthly bond payment, you should draw up a new household budget in order to determine if you can afford this premium (or the higher premium for your new and more expensive house).
- Remember to add all the other cost-items once you find your new home and know more about the rest of the applicable costs.
- Only if you can accommodate the total additional financial burden can you think about making an offer to the home owner or agent selling the house.
- Make sure that you will be able to make plans to afford the higher monthly premium when interest rates rise.
- If you cannot accommodate this purchase in your budget, you will have to settle for a cheaper house and repeat the personal financial planning process.
- Repeat these steps until you have your affordable home.
- Most people are very emotional about the buying of a house and often have a lot of buyer's blues to deal with eventually.
- Make sure it will be possible for you to keep your house – just think about what family, friends and neighbours will say should you have to sell the house at a lower price to get rid of some of your debt at a later stage.

8.10.4 House-hunting

- Consult advertising, magazines and newspapers.
- Use estate agents and visit estate agencies.
- Use the Internet.
- Shop around and compare costs and houses/listings.
- Obtain as much information on the following as possible:
  - The residential area in which you intend purchasing a home:
    - its convenience network (distances to schools, shopping centres, hospitals, medical services, churches);
    - its exposure network (pollution, noise, traffic, flight paths, water courses, prevailing winds, humidity, landscape);
    - its general condition (clean, old or new, streets in good condition);
    - its reputation (criminal activities);
    - its recreational facilities (parks, tennis courts, golf courses); and
    - its future potential development (schools, shopping centres, etc.).

Obtain this information by personally visiting the area, talking to residents or reading the local newspaper.

- The stand or erf itself (area and shape):
  - its zoning – business, residential, etc.); and
  - limited real rights (servitude, water and mineral rights, restrictive conditions to development).

You can obtain this information from local authorities and the title deed.

- The dwelling:
  - type and age of building;
  - floor area;
  - garden layout;
  - paint;
  - roof;
  - walls;
  - electricity;
  - plumbing;
  - windows and doors;
  - leaking swimming pool;
  - blocked drains;
  - rising damp;
  - layout;
  - security aspects;
  - possible further improvements;
  - leaks;
  - ceiling;
  - floors;
  - foundation;
  - worn carpets;
  - paving;
  - rotting wood; and
  - moisture.

Get a professional architect or engineer to help with the physical inspection.

- The financial aspects:
  - purchase price;
  - municipal value;
  - last selling price;
  - rates and taxes;
  - market value;
  - replacement value; and
  - outstanding mortgage amount.

You can also obtain this information from the local authorities, the title deed and the current bondholder.

- The following web pages will be of assistance to you:
  Aida – www.aida.co.za – company information and contact details.
  De Huizemark – www.dehuizemark.co.za – company information and contact details.

Devmark – www.devmark.co.za – Cape Town based property services company offering a property portfolio, information on home loans, auctions, FAQ and international investments.
Era – www.eraproperties.co.za – buying and selling information, as well as a national and international property search.
Homenet – www.homenet.co.za/bond.html – a property search, company information and contact details.
Lew Geffen Properties – www.lewgeffen.co.za – a property search, as well as information on finances and legislation.
Pam Golding Properties – www.pamgolding.co.za – a property search and company information.
Remax – www.remax.co.za – a property search hosted by 'homefinder', as well as contact details.
Seeff – www.seeff.com – a property search, auction properties and contact details.
Vered – www.vered.co.za – advice for first time home owners, a bond calculator, information on rentals, auctions and a property search.

8.10.5 Calculating all the cost-items

- Complete the cost-item checklist or ask an estate agent/attorney to help you.
- It may also be possible to defer certain costs, for example home improvements, to a later date.
- These 'unnecessary' costs will increase your bond and monthly instalments.
- Include this amount in your budget to see if you can proceed with the purchase.

8.10.6 The offer to purchase

After submitting your signed offer to purchase, it is the seller's prerogative to either accept or reject the offer, within the specified time period. On acceptance, your offer to purchase becomes a legally binding contract.

The offer to purchase is defined as a legally binding written contract that includes the following:

- The full name of both the seller and the purchaser.
- A full description of the property (as described in the title deed).
- The purchase price and deposit (and how this will be paid).
- The actual date of occupation (and the occupational rent, if applicable).
- The conditions of the sale (e.g. whether it is subject to the sale of the buyer's property and/or bond finance being obtained).
- All fixtures and fittings to be included in the purchase should be specified to avoid future disputes.

8.10.7 Choosing a home loan

By now you should know your income (single or joint), the maximum home loan amount you can get and afford, as well as the security/collateral you may have to supply in order to buy a more expensive house.

Decide on the interest rate
- Make sure you understand the different home loan interest rate options:
  - variable interest rate (applicable to most home loans – interest rate varies up or down according to the prime lending rate);
  - fixed interest rate (the interest rate is fixed for a period of about two years and you can budget accordingly);
  - capped interest rate (the rate will not increase above a specified rate for a specific period – you normally pay a higher premium for this privilege);
  - reducing interest rate (you will receive a monthly decrease in interest rate of 1% per year for the next three years or 0.5% every six months for the next three years); and
  - combination of fixed and variable (where part of the loan's interest rate is fixed and part is variable).
  - Negotiate on the basis of your good history with the bank for the lowest possible rate.

Decide on a bank
- Compare the different banks to decide on your mortgagee.
- Commercial banks offer home loans against the security of your house – this goes hand in hand with a life policy to redeem the bond amount in case of your death or disability, ceded to the bank of course.
- You may either cede an existing life policy (with large enough coverage to cover the bond amount) or take out a new policy at any financial/insurance institution.
- Merchant banks offer high net worth individual home loans.

Method of payment
- You can sign a debit order at your bank to deduct your monthly instalment and to transfer it to your home loan.
- Your employer may require that you sign a stop order whereby your monthly instalment will be deducted directly from your salary – mostly applicable to government departments (and companies).

8.10.8 Applying for a home loan

You can apply for a loan in one of the following ways:
- Via an estate agent or attorney.
- At a financial institution.
- On the internet:
  ABSA – www.absa.co.za – a personal banking section, an online home loan application and a homeowner's portfolio calculator.
  FNB – www.fnb.co.za – information on the FNB Lifeline Facility and the 'peace of mind option', an overview of features and benefits and a cost calculator.
  Mercantile Bank – www.mercantile.co.za – electronic banking and product information.
  NBS (BOE) (now part of Nedcor) – www.nbs.co.za/wizard – a 'financial wizard' link, including a bond calculator for various home loan options.
  Nedbank – www.nedbank.co.za – online banking, questions and answers, an overview of home loan options and checklists.
  Origin – www.origin.co.za – information regarding merchant banking for individuals with assets of R400 000 or more.
  SA Homeloans – www.sahl.co.za – information about switching costs and benefits, insurance options and a mortgage rate comparison table.
  Standard Bank – www.standardbank.co.za – an online property search, a buyer's and seller's guide, a cost calculator and an online home loan application.

8.10.9 The processing of the application

Stage 1 (day 1): With a home loan sales consultant or at your bank
- Complete an application form.
- Attach the supporting documents.
- Indicate your insurance preference.

Stage 2 (days 1–4): At the bank
- A property assessment is completed by a bank official.
- Credit department verifies documentation and prepares credit and affordability checks.
- Credit department gives final credit decision (grants or declines application).
- Credit department informs branch or consultant.
- Bank appoints registering attorney on successful application.
- Loan agreement prepared and forwarded to attorney.

Stage 3 (days 4–60): At the attorney

- Mortgage bond documents prepared.
- Advised to contract attorney and arrange to sign documentation.
- Required to pay transfer duty and other costs.
- Attorney lodges transaction with Deeds Office.

Stage 4 (day 60): At the bank

- Bank receives advice from attorney of the registration of the loan.
- The transaction is recorded.
- Funds are disbursed.

8.10.10 The legal work

Once the bank has approved your home loan, the following legal work can begin:

- A transferring attorney (normally appointed by the seller) will attend to the transfer of ownership of the property into your (the buyer's) name.
- The bank will appoint a registering attorney on your behalf to prepare the mortgage bond contract, and have it registered in the Deeds Office.
- At this stage, you may be required to pay a deposit to the transferring attorney.
- The attorneys will call on you to sign various documents necessary for the registration of the property transfer and mortgage bond.

8.10.11 Payment of deposit and other legal costs

You will now have to pay the following legal costs:

- The deposit – to either the seller's estate agent or the transferring attorney (into an interest-bearing account with you as the beneficiary).
- Assessment fee.
- Initiation fee – paid to the bank for processing the loan.
- Bond registration costs – payable to the registering attorney.
- Transfer costs (transfer duty, conveyancing fees and stamp duty) to the transferring attorney for transferring the property into your name.

8.10.12 The Deeds Office

- The attorney will apply to cancel the existing bond.
- The attorney will apply to register the new bond.
- The attorney will apply to transfer the property.
- All these applications will be made to the Deeds Office.

8.10.13 Attorney advises bank

A few weeks after the former applications, all these activities will take place:

- The attorney will advise the bank.
- The bank will disburse the money.
- The transferring attorney will advise you that the property has been registered in your name.
- You will now own the home.
- The bank will advise you when your first payment is due.

8.10.14 You, the new home owner

- If you moved into the house prior to registration, you would have to pay occupational rent.
- You can now arrange with the seller to finalise your account.

8.10.15 Build or buy?

- Depending on the current interest rates, building or buying can be more advantageous.
- Building may provide more for your needs if you build exactly what you want.
- On the other hand, an older house may be much more spacious and cost effective and provide more for your needs, not desires.
- Some areas may supply larger houses at a lower cost and better value for your money.
- To build means you pay the current building costs at inflated rates.
- If you are able to do most of the work yourself and use subcontractors, you will save up to 40% of your total building cost.
- The latter requires some knowledge and technical expertise.
- It is also wise to hire a project manager if you do not have the required knowledge.

8.10.16 Protection against defects in a new house

- The National Home Builders Registration Council (NHBRC) protects the owners of newly built houses against malpractices and bad workmanship.
- Since 1 December 1999 all builders should enrol all new houses.
- All lenders providing loans on new houses must ensure that the builder is registered with the NHBRC.
- Phone the NHBRC at 011-348 5700 for all relevant building complaints.

8.10.17 Renovating

- If you are relatively happy in your home and 'sure' that you want to stay there for the rest of your life, you can do expensive improvements.
- If not, you should not spend too much, because you may overcapitalise.
- Renovate to protect your house against deterioration.
- Overcapitalisation means you are spending so much on your house that you will never be able to recoup your investment in case you want to sell.
- Look at the rest of the neighbourhood and determine whether your house is already the most expensive one.
- If this is the case, you should not spend more on major improvements.
- It is also unwise to spend too much on an old house or a house with an old building style (except for national monuments), unless you can sell it at a profit.
- You can thus renovate if it will increase the property's value.
- Of course, you must make some renovations if you want to sell the property.
- Renovations are like personal financial management, they are personal in nature.
- Nobody can tell you not to spend money on your house if it will improve your quality of life.
- Ask professional advisers/agents/valuers to assist you in making renovation decisions.
- Together you should determine the attributes that will increase the value and suit your pocket.
- Remember, there are scores of white elephants that will certainly not increase the value of your home, unless you want to do it for yourself.
- It can be assumed that all security aspects will increase the value.
- If the value of your house is less than the average value in your neighbourhood, then you will benefit from a lot of renovations in terms of increased value.
- Get quotes for your improvements.
- Financing your renovations can be done in many ways, amongst others, by using:
  - your own resources;
  - a re-advance on your home loan – where you borrow up to the initial registered loan/bond amount;
  - a further advance – where you register an additional amount on your home loan; and
  - an access bond – using the difference between your initial loan amount and your current balance (the amount by which you have already reduced the loan amount).

8.10.18 Security

- Security is very important, not only for your personal safety, but also in terms of resale value.
- You should protect your house, as well as the contents, for your family.
- The bondholder also requires some bond protection against your death or in case the house burns down.
- Insure against any possible occurrence.

8.10.19 Squatting

- Squatting has become a major legal problem since the introduction of the Prevention of Illegal Eviction from and Unlawful Occupation of Land Act 19 of 1998.
- The High Court is fortunately siding with home owners.
- Make sure you do not fall prey to squatters in your empty house.
- It may take months to remove/evict them at a very high cost.

8.10.20 Different ways to home ownership

- The house can be purchased in your name only, especially if you are not married.
- It can also be purchased in the name of a trust (get the best possible advice with regard to the contents of the trust deed to protect your house for future use, against taxes and divorce).
- If you are married in community of property and you purchase a house, it will be registered in both your names.
- If you are married out of community of property with inclusion of the accrual system, the new house will 'belong' to both spouses (depending on its contribution to the accrual estate) irrespective of whose name it has been registered in.
- If you are married in community of property with exclusion of the accrual system, the purchaser can register the property in his or her name and the property will belong to the purchaser exclusively (the other spouse will always be entitled to the repayment of contributions to the other spouse's house).
- If you want to protect yourself and your assets against taxes, current and future legislation, divorce laws, spouses and in-laws, marry out of community of property with exclusion of the accrual system.
- Your house will be protected in a trust against your debtors (unless you have used it as security), estate

duty and your spouse, if you plan accordingly.

- When you transfer your house during your lifetime to a beneficiary, you do not have to pay any transfer costs.
- If you buy a house in the name of a trust, you will have to pay donations tax should you transfer the house to beneficiaries.
- You will have to sell your share to the beneficiaries to prevent the latter.
- Do not transfer your house to a trust while you are still alive, because you will have to pay the transfer costs all over again.
- Do not donate it during your lifetime, because you will have to pay donations tax.
- Rather buy your next/a new house in the name of a trust.
- You will have to take out the home loan in the name of the trust.
- All trustees will have to sign suretyship for the loan at the bank.
- Beware of buying a house from a trust (especially if it is the only asset in the trust) – you may be liable for the debts of the trust.
- The same applies for a close corporation.

8.10.21 Property cycles

- Just like economic cycles, we have to deal with property cycles.
- Rising and declining interest rates are responsible for our property cycles.
- These cycles may differ in various neighbourhoods based on expected property prices (property demand).
- Interest rates may determine property demand and thus property prices.
- The ideal would be to buy a house when prices are low and to sell when prices are high.
- Prices are low when interest rates are high (low demand).
- Prices are high when interest rates are low (high demand).

8.10.22 Paying off your bond

- You should try to pay off your bond as quickly as possible in order to save on interest.
- The paid-off amount will also serve as an emergency fund in the case of an access bond.
- Should you need money (for whatever purpose) you have pre-approved financing in your bond.
- Always try to make additional payments to lower your bond amount.
- Increase your monthly payments if possible.
- Stay with your increased or high payments, even if interest rates decrease.

- It will allow you to pay for your house over a shorter period, depending on your monthly payments.

8.10.23 Living together

- Draw up a cohabitation agreement indicating the rights and responsibilities of all occupants.
- Make sure you know the legal aspects if you separate from the other party to this arrangement.
- It is important to know in whose name the property is legally registered and who is paying the bond.
- Do not simply assume that because you are contributing (or paying) towards the bond instalments, you are also a co-owner – you may end up losing a lot of money, as well as the dream of owning your own home.
- Co-owners should both sign the purchasing documents.
- Ensure that you can recoup your contribution from the bond in case of a separation, unless you have received other benefits according to your cohabitation agreement.

8.10.24 Divorce

- In most cases, a divorcing couple will sell 'their' house.
- Make sure that you indicate in your signed settlement agreement the minimum price you will accept.
- Otherwise, the other spouse may refuse to accept a certain price or to sell at all (as part of the attorney's strategy).
- Make sure you indicate in your signed agreement who will be responsible for the loan payments in the meantime and how this will affect other obligations.
- You can also buy the spouse's 50% share in the house.
- If you are married in community of property, you will have to register your spouse's share in your name and pay 50% of the normal transfer fees.
- If you are married in community of property (house in your name), no transfer costs will be payable.
- With an in community of property marriage regime, you will have to ask the bank's permission to take over your spouse's share of the loan.
- Should the bank refuse, you will have to ask your spouse to continue with half of the payments or another alternative (all specified in your divorce settlement).
- If the communal house forms part of a trust or close corporation, new suretyships will have to be

obtained, the necessary documents will have to be signed and one spouse will have to purchase the other spouse's half.
- No transfer fees will be payable to obtain the other spouse's share in a trust or close corporation.

8.10.25 Sources of information

- Books, newspapers and magazines.
- Estate agents and attorneys.
- Websites.
- Useful contact numbers:
  IEASA Central Region: (011) 482 2017
  IEASA Northern Region: (012) 362 4725
  IEASA Eastern Region: (013) 667 9307
  IEASA Pietermaritzburg & Natal Interior:
  (031) 394 2205
  IEASA KwaZulu Natal Coastal Region:
  (031) 309 8831
  IEASA Border Region; (043) 722 3929
  IEASA South Eastern Cape Region:
  (041) 364 2805
  IEASA Western Cape Region (National):
  (021) 531 3180
  PA Group: (011) 476 9002
  The Estate Agency Affairs Board: (011) 883 7700
  SA Property Owners Association (SAPOA):
  (011) 883 0679
  SA Institute of Valuers: (031) 309 7431
  The College of Property Management and
  Development (CPMD): (011) 482 6378
  (IEASA is now the Institute of Realtors)

8.11 PRACTICAL STEPS: SELLING YOUR HOUSE

8.11.1 Your costs

- You will have to pay estate agent's commission.
- Other costs will include the cost of preparing your house for all the prospective buyers.
- You will also have to spend some time elsewhere at a cost on show days.

8.11.2 The estate agent(s)

- Choose reputable estate agents and agencies.
- You will have to give an estate agent a mandate to sell your house.
- Open mandate – you and several agents market the house.
- Multi-mandate – you and only one agent may sell your house.
- Sole and exclusive mandate – only one agent may sell your house.

- Give one estate agent an exclusive mandate to sell your house after a month.
- Determine what the estate agent's marketing plan for your house will be.
- Determine what the estate agent's after sales service will be.

8.11.3 The Internet

- Shop around to determine if you will be liable for a listing fee only or for commission as well.
- Commission will be payable where the estate agency uses the Internet as a marketing tool.

8.11.4 The selling price

The following factors will determine the marketability of your house and the selling price:
- Area (demand for houses).
- Condition (a higher price for a house in good physical condition).
- Price (a too high price will chase potential buyers away).
- Terms of sale (a cash transaction may yield a lower price).
- Motivation for selling (you have an urgent need for money or have already purchased another house, for example).

8.11.5 Preparing your house

Indoors
- Give the house a spring-clean. If you can, have a company clean the carpets and lounge furniture.
- Pack all the cupboards in your house neatly. If necessary, store linen and clothing that is out of season at a friend's home, this will give the impression that there is plenty of storage space.
- Create space by storing extra furniture, and position furniture so that potential viewers can move from room to room with ease.
- Fix all dripping taps. Dripping water may suggest that the plumbing is not sound and it also stains enamel surfaces.
- Keep the shades and the drapes open to let in more light, but screen unappealing views where possible.
- To make your kitchen look warm and welcoming, completely degrease the oven, wash all the work surfaces and keep the sink free of dishes. Clean the refrigerator and give the kitchen a wonderful aroma by percolating coffee or roasting cinnamon in the oven.
- Use your pot plants to their best effect by placing them in strategic spots throughout the house.

- To make your home look larger, light up the whole house and use mirrors to reflect outside light.

Outdoors
- Give the front door a wash or a fresh coat of paint. First impressions last.
- If you have a garden, mow the lawn, trim the edges and weed the flowerbeds.
- Wash any outdoor furniture you have, and if it is rusted, either paint it, store it or get rid of it.
- Make sure the doorbell works, straighten the gutters and TV aerial, and repair any broken windows. If you have a fence, give it a coat of paint and make repairs if necessary.

8.11.6 Show days

- Do not be in the estate agent's way.
- Do not be in the way of prospective buyers.
- Leave the agent with a well-prepared house.

8.11.7 Receiving an offer to purchase

- The agent will hopefully supply you with an offer to purchase.
- If you are not satisfied with the price or the conditions, make a counteroffer, if you are interested.
- Use your agent for the latter to negotiate on your behalf.

8.11.8 Appointing a transferring attorney

You will need to do this once a prospective buyer gives you a written offer to purchase, which you accept, in order to:
- transfer ownership of the property into the buyer's name; and
- receive the deposit paid by the buyer.

8.11.9 The cancelling attorney

A cancelling attorney, who is appointed by your bank if you have an existing bond on the property you are selling, will cancel your existing bond so that transfer of ownership can take place.

8.11.10 Final costs

Once you have sold your house, the following costs will need to be paid:
- commission, which you will need to pay to your estate agent for selling your property; and

- a cancellation fee, which needs to be paid to the cancelling attorney for cancelling your existing bond.

8.12 PRACTICAL STEPS: MOVING HOUSE

8.12.1 Your preparations and checklist
- Supply the purchaser of your house with your new home address (and work address, if applicable), telephone numbers, security codes in case your old alarm goes off (also inform the security company or response unit).
- Inform all your creditors (accounts payable) of your new address and telephone numbers.
- Inform all people making deliveries (newspaper, milk, bread, magazines).
- Remember to disconnect your old telephone with the help of the telephone company and to arrange for the correct accounts.
- Negotiate your water and electricity bill with the purchaser.
- Inform your garden service and arrange for different payments for you and your buyer.
- Inform the post office of your new address.
- Arrange with your short-term insurer to cover your transport risk for the day you move your furniture – it is much cheaper than insurance provided for by the removal company.
- Inform your friends and relatives about your move.
- Give your new information to:
  - the municipality;
  - bank;
  - insurance companies;
  - the SABC (TV licence);
  - accountant;
  - doctor;
  - Receiver of Revenue;
  - investment companies;
  - employer;
  - attorney;
  - dentist; and
  - psychologist.

8.12.2 Transportation costs

- These may include transport cost, packaging costs, insurance costs and storage costs.
- It is cheaper to travel in the middle of the month than at the month end.

8.12.3 The day you move and arrive

- Make a checklist for that day as well.
- Advise the movers about the placement of boxes or furniture.
- Arrange food for your family.

8.13 SUMMARY

Buying a house is arguably the biggest single investment most people make during their lifetime. The decision to buy a house holds long-term implications, and potential buyers should be informed of the numerous factors that affect this decision. The importance of purchasing the right house in the right place at the right price with the right kind of financing cannot be overemphasised.

Most sales transactions take place through an estate agent. Potential buyers should know what kind of services they can expect from estate agents, as well as the following: when commission must be paid; which kind of mandate is best; which sources and instruments of long-term financing are available; what kinds of mortgage bond are available; and what the hidden costs involved in buying a house are.

8.14 SELF-ASSESSMENT

- Briefly discuss the cost-items involved in purchasing a dwelling.
- Explain the importance of the decision to buy a residence.
- Explain how you would go about valuing a residence.
- Explain situations when an estate agent is entitled to receive a commission.
- Explain the different types of mandate.
- Briefly explain financing methods that may be used to buy a residence.
- Explain the different types of mortgage bonds
- List the practical steps involved when:
  - buying a residence;
  - selling a residence; and
  - moving house.

BIBLIOGRAPHY

Alienation of Land Act: see South Africa (Republic), 1984.

Association of Building Societies of South Africa. 1987. *The Building Societies Act.* Johannesburg.

Attorneys Act: see South Africa (Republic), 1979.

Bannock, G., Baxter, R.G. & Rees, R. 1972. *The Penguin dictionary of economics.* 1st edn. Harmondsworth: Penguin.

Belcher, C.I. 1972. *Norman's purchase and sale in South Africa.* 4th edn. Durban: Butterworths.

Botha, R.E. 1987. Jong kopers se probleme wek kommer. *Huisgids, Bylae tot Beeld*: 4, col. 1, Sep. 5.

Brümmer, L.M. & Rademeyer, W.F. eds. 1982. *Beleggingsbestuur.* Pretoria: Van Schaik.

Caney, L.R. 1975. Mortgage and pledge. In Freemantle, M.P. (ed.) *The South African encyclopaedia of forms and precedents.* Vol. 12. Durban: Butterworths. p. 273–471.

Building Societies Act: see South Africa (Republic). 1986.

Celliers, H.S. & Benadé, M.L. 1982. *Maatskappyreg.* 4th edn. Durban: Butterworths.

Christie, R.H. 1981. *The law of contract in South Africa.* Durban: Butterworths.

Coaker, J.F. & Schultz, W.P. 1980. *Wille and Millin's mercantile law of South Africa.* 17th edn. Johannesburg: Hortors.

Coetzee, J. 1991. Nuwe verbandopsies het voor- en nadele. *Finansies & Tegniek*: 36, col. 1–3. March 22.

Deeds Registries Act: see South Africa (Republic) 1937.

Delport, H.J. 1982. *Handleiding vir die eiendomsagent.* Revised edn. Cape Town: Juta.

Delport, H.J. 1985. A look at options. *Juta's South African Journal of Property*, 2(3):14–18, May 3.

Delport, H.J. 1986. An estate agent's liability for misrepresentations and non-disclosures. *Juta's South African Journal of Property*, 3(4):27–31. Sept. 10.

Delport, H.J. 1987. *Die Suid-Afrikaanse eiendomspraktyk en die reg.* Cape Town: Juta.

De Wet, J.C. & Van Wyk, A.H. 1987. *Kontraktereg en handelsreg.* 4th edn. Durban: Butterworths.

Espag, A. 1984. *'n Ondersoek na die kommissiestelsel vir eiendomsagente.* Potchefstroom. (145 pp.) M Com script, Potchefstroom University for CHE.

Estate Agents Act: see South Africa (Republic), 1976a.

Expropriation Act: see South Africa (Republic), 1975.

Falkena, H.B., Fourie, J.J. & Kok, W.J. (eds). 1984. *The mechanics of the South African financial system.* 2nd edn. Johannesburg: Macmillan.

Falkena, H.B. 1988. Skuldmaak vir tweede huis nou onwys ... maar huispryse is in 'n stygende fase. *Finansies & Tegniek* 40(1):22, Jan. 8.

Financial Institutions Amendment Act: see South Africa (Republic), 1985.

Gibson, J.T.R. 1983. *South African mercantile and company law.* 5th edn. Cape Town: Juta.

Godi, A. & Reyhons, K. 1980. *Creative listing handbook*. Chicago: RNMI.

Goosen, W. 1985. Government subsidised and guaranteed mortgage bonds. In Institute of Estate Agents of South Africa. *Real estate sales guide*. Cape Town: Juta. p. 129–133.

Gorman, W. 1979. *Selling: Personality, persuasion, strategy*. 2nd edn. Toronto: Random House.

Hopkins, T. 1980. *How to master the art of selling*. Schotsdale: Champion.

Huse, E.E. 1982. *Management*. 2nd edn. New York: West.

Institute of Estate Agents of South Africa. 1985. *Real estate sales guide*. Cape Town: Juta.

Jawitz, E. 1985. Sole selling mandate. In Institute of Estate Agents of South Africa. *Real estate sales guide*. Cape Town: Juta. p. 25–34.

Jones, R.J.M. 1985. *Conveyancing in South Africa*. 3rd edn. Cape Town: Juta.

Jordaan, J. 1987. Inflasie se verwoestende rooftog. *Finansies & Tegniek* 39(29):5 col. 1, Jul. 24.

Joubert, D.J. 1967. *Die verpligting van die verteenwoordiger in die Suid-Afrikaanse reg*. (LLD thesis). University of Pretoria.

Joubert, D.J. 1979. *Die Suid-Afrikaanse verteenwoordigingsreg*. Cape Town: Juta.

Kemney, B. 1988. Bond war: societies look to counter-strategies. *Finance Week*. 35(12):701, col.1, Jan. 6.

Kerr, A.J. 1972. *The law of agency*. Durban: Butterworths.

Kerr, A.J. 1984. *The law of sale and lease*. Durban: Butterworths.

Kling, G. 1983. *Buying, building and altering a home in South Africa*. Cape Town: Struik.

Kroncke, C.O. 1978. *Managerial finance: Essentials*. 2nd edn. New York: West.

Laurens, R.C. 1984. *Inleiding tot die studie van aktebesorging*. Pretoria: Butterworths.

Lucas, G.H. (ed.) 1983. *Die taak van die bemarkingsbestuur*. Pretoria: Van Schaik.

Maritz, N.G. 1983. *Die studiegids vir eiendomsagente: Grondbeginsels van eiendomswese*. Cape Town: Juta.

Maritz, N.G. 1985. *Byvoegsel tot die studiegids vir eiendomsagente: Grondbeginsels van eiendomswese*. Cape Town: Juta.

Marx, S. & Dekker, H. 1982. *Bemarkingsbestuur: Beginsels en besluite*. Pretoria. Gutenberg.

Meyer, M. 1979. *Eiendomsbestuur: Regsomgewing – vaste eiendom*. Study guide 1: MBL semester 5. Pretoria: Unisa.

Miller, D.M. 1985. Financing residential property. In Institute of Estate Agents of South Africa. *Real estate sales guide*. Cape Town: Juta. p. 122–128.

Miller, D.M. 1987. In Instituut van Eiendomsagente van Suid-Afrika. *Verkoopshandleiding vir vaste eiendom*. Johannesburg. p. 144.

Mosterd, D.E. 1972. *Die koopkontrak*. Durban: Butterworths.

Mutual Building Societies Act: see South Africa (Republic), 1965.

Myburg, L.J.E. 1987. Bouverenigingsaansoekvorms: die belangrike rol van die eiendomsagent. In Instituut van Eiendomsagente van Suid Afrika. *Verkoopshandleiding vir vaste eiendom*. Johannesburg. p. 135–139.

Odendal, E.E. 1985. *Verklarende handwoordeboek van die Afrikaanse taal*. 2nd edn. Johannesburg: Perskor.

Participation Bond Act: see South Africa (Republic), 1981b.

Pension Funds Act: see South Africa (Republic), 1956a.

Permanent Bank. 2000. *Home values: Turn your house into a home*. Permanent Bank.

Registration of Deeds in Rehoboth Act: see South Africa (Republic), 1976c.

Reid, B. 1987. Die rol van die aktevervaardiger. In *Verhoopshandleiding vir vaste eiendom*. Johannesburg: Instituut van Eiendomsagente van Suid-Afrika.

Rent Control Act: see South Africa (Republic), 1976b.

Ring, A.A. & Dasso, J. 1985. *Real estate: Principles and practice*. 10th edn. Englewood Cliffs: Prentice-Hall.

Schaller, R.E. 1984. *Your complete guide to buying a home in South Africa*. 6th edn. Durban: Butterworths.

Seldin, A. 1980. *The real estate handbook*. Homewood: Irwin.

South Africa (Republic). 1937. Acts of the Republic of South Africa – Deeds Office (Act 47 of 1937). Pretoria: Government Printer. (Deeds Registries Act).

South Africa (Republic). 1956a. Acts of the Republic of South Africa – Salaries and Pensions (Act 24 of 1956). Pretoria: Government Printer. (Pension Funds Act).

South Africa (Republic). 1956b. Acts of the Republic of South Africa – Building Societies (Act 25 of 1956). Pretoria: Government Printer. (Friendly Society Act).

South Africa (Republic). 1956b. Acts of the Republic of South Africa – Building Societies (Act 24 of 1956). Pretoria: Government Printer. (Mutual Building Society Act).

South Africa (Republic). 1975. Acts of the Republic of South Africa – Land (Act 63 of 1975). Pretoria: Government Printer. (Expropriation Act).

South Africa (Republic). 1976a. Acts of the Republic of South Africa – Land (Act 112 of 1976). Pretoria: Government Printer. (Estate Agents Act).

South Africa (Republic). 1976b. Acts of the Republic of South Africa – Lessee and Lessor (Act 80 of 1976). Pretoria: Government Printer. (Rent Control Act).

South Africa (Republic). 1976c. Acts of the Republic of South Africa – Deeds Office (Act 93 of 1976). Pretoria: Government Printer. (Registration of Deeds in Rehoboth Act).

South Africa (Republic). 1979. Acts of the Republic of South Africa – Legal Practitioners (Act 53 of 1979). Pretoria: Government Printer. (Attorneys Act).

South Africa (Republic). 1981a. Acts of the Republic of South Africa – Buying and Selling (Act 68 of 1981). Pretoria: Government Printer. (Alienation of Land Act).

South Africa (Republic). 1981b. Ācts of the Republic of South Africa – Companies (Act 55 of 1981). Pretoria: Government Printer. (Participation Bonds Act).

South Africa (Republic). 1984. Acts of the Republic of South Africa – Husband and Wife (Act 88 of 1984). Pretoria: Government Printer. (Matrimonial Property Act).

South Africa (Republic). 1985. Acts of the Republic of South Africa – Banking and Means of Payment (Act 106 of 1985). Pretoria: Government Printer. (Financial Institutions Amendment Act).

South Africa (Republic). 1986. Acts of the Republic of South Africa – Building Societies (Act 82 of 1986). Pretoria: Government Printer. (Building Society Act).

South Africa (Republic). 1990. Acts of the Republic of South Africa – Banks and Building Societies (Act 94 of 1990). Pretoria: Government Printer. (Deposit-taking Institutions Act).

Swanepoel, S.J.M. 1987. To multi list or not to multi list. *Real Estate Forum*, 14(1):5, Feb.

Swart, N.J. 1988. *Finansiële adviesdienste deur die eiendomsagent in die woonhuismark: 'n Bedryfsekonomiese ondersoek.* (330pp.) M Com thesis, Rand Afrikaans University.

Swart, N.J. 1996. Hoe om die waarde van jou huis te verhoog. *Finansies & Tegniek*: 52, col. 3–8, Jun. 16.

Swart, N.J. 2000. *Home values: Turn your house into a home*. Permanent Bank.

Technikon RSA. 1985. *Behuisingsbestuur 1*. (Study guide no. 5). Johannesburg.

Technikon RSA. 1986. *Eiendomsfinansies*. (Study guide no. 3). Johannesburg.

Trace, A.P. 1985. *The bond book*. Honeydew: Layman's Guide.

Unisa. 1985. *Bankbestuur*. Revised edn. (Study guide 1 for BKM201-8). Pretoria: University of South Africa.

Unisa. 1993. *Real estate*. (Study guide for BEC 206-W). Pretoria: University of South Africa.

Van der Spuy, A.S. 1984. *New Marriage Property Act 88 of 84*. Marshalltown: Cosmos.

Van Jaarsveld, S.R. 1978. *Suid-Afrikaanse handelsreg*. Cape Town: Lex Patria.

Van Jaarsveld, S.R. 1983. *Suid-Afrikaanse handelsreg*. 2nd edn. Cape Town: Lex Patria.

Volschenk, C. 1987a. Huislenings met langer looptye ... Standard wik en week nog. *Finansies & Tegniek* 39(16):16, Apr. 24.

Volschenk, C. 1987b. Banke klim met mening in. *Finansies & Tegniek* 39(37):14, Sep. 18.

Volschenk, C. 1987c. Finansiële instellings veg dat stof staan ... maar verloor hulle bloed as 'pryse' se min in die gedrang is? *Finansies & Tegniek* 39(46):10, col.1, Nov. 20.

Wille, G. 1961. *The law of mortgage and pledge in South Africa*. Cape Town: Juta.

Table of Cases

Rogut v Rogut 1982 (3) SA 928 (A)

Davidson v Bonafede 1981 (2) SA 501 (C)

Soobramoney and Another v R Acutt & Sons (Pty) Ltd 1965 (2) SA 899 (D)

Glaston House (Pty) Ltd v Inag (Pty) Ltd 1977 (2) SA 846 (A)

Trotman and Another v Edwick 1951 (1) SA 443 (A)

Levy v Phillips 1915 AD 139

Laskey and Steadmet (Edms) Bpk h/a Wessel de Villiers Agentskappe 1976 (3) SA 696 (T)

Naidu v Naidoo 1967 (2) SA 223 (N)

Van Jaarsveld v Ackerman 1975 (2) SA 753 (A)

Chamotte (Pty) Ltd v Carl Coetzee (Pty) Ltd 1973 (1) SA 644 (A)

Kark v Proctor 1961 (1) SA 752 (W)

Lubke v Kegel 1913 WLD 91

Steer & Co v Rowland (1897) 14 SC 358 (7 CTR 400)

Totoyi v Ncuka (1909) EDC 115

Pross v Jofwall Investments (Pty) Ltd 1981 (7) SA 261 (W)

Lombard v Reed 1948 (1) SA 30 (T)

Beckwith v Foundation Investment Co 1961 (4) SA 510 (A)

Joubert and Others v Coster 1982 (4) SA 540 (C)

BUYING FIXED PROPERTY

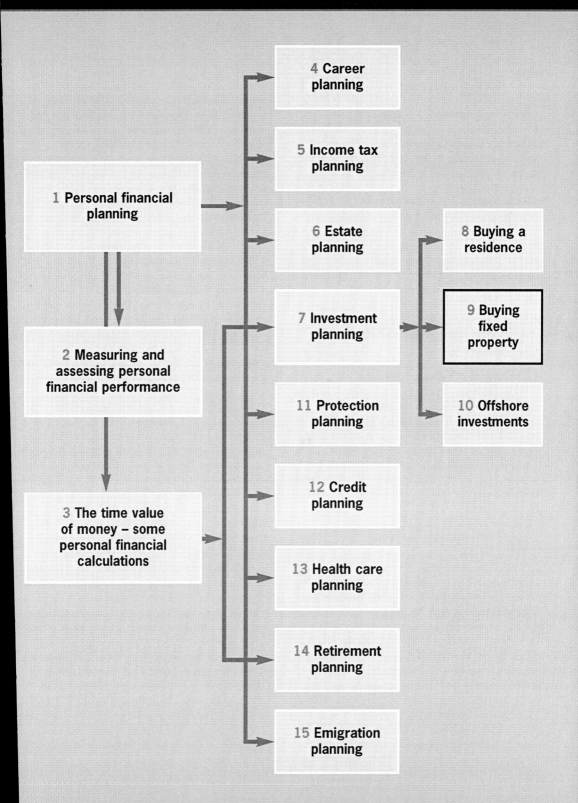

9.1 LEARNING OUTCOMES

After studying this chapter, you will be able to:

- Identify the steps involved in the process of investing in fixed property.
- Explain the functioning of the different types of fixed property.
- Explain the financing of property.
- Explain different ways to own property.
- Explain property contracts.
- Illustrate the importance of the administration of fixed property.

9.2 INTRODUCTION

Apart from purchasing a house, an investment in fixed property is not something everybody would consider. Property investment is usually out of the reach of the person in the street, at least for as long as he or she still has a housing bond to repay. However, a person may inherit or receive money from one source or another (such as a gift or a lump sum from an endowment policy), which he or she may then consider investing in fixed property. Many people with capital resources purchase fixed property in order to increase their wealth. An investment in fixed property, therefore, is one way of ensuring financial independence after retirement.

9.2.1 Why keep on investing in residential property?

An answer to the eternal question
Property as an investment instrument has sustained considerable damage from the debate on whether to rent or buy a dwelling. High interest rates do not really help the property market to get off the ground either. The misconceptions about property as an investment is currently reaching fever pitch, firstly as a result of the increase in municipal rates (land tax), and secondly owing to the introduction of capital gains tax.

The question why people should still invest in property is briefly considered below.

It is important to note at the outset that we are talking about immovable (fixed) property because, after all, the concept of property includes everything that can be owned, for example unit trusts or a car. Furthermore, we have to mention the familiar distinction between speculation and investment; that is to say, do not compare an investment in fixed property with the speculative buying of shares on the stock exchange. Compare returns on investment on the one hand, and returns on speculation on the other, after the same period. So much for returns, but what about the purpose of the investment? Only when we have to select an investment that has to serve the same short-, medium- and long-term

needs can we compare returns. So, let us choose the foremost long-term need, namely financial independence after retirement – the pre-eminent objective of personal financial management.

Surely the most important aspect or personal financial management is the human element involved. If that were not the case, we could plan like robots that achieve all objectives without fail. Unfortunately, that is not how things work, and the human element differs from person to person. We take particular investments made over a lifetime with a view to retirement as the basic premise and benchmark of comparison for the purpose of this discussion. Consequently, we look at the investments that are actually made by a person, and that are still there at retirement and afterwards. Naturally, the many investments we make during our lifetime and call up or sell do help us towards achieving the aim for retirement. Capital gains and the reinvestment of capital are prominent examples in this regard.

So what is the point, the substance, of our argument in favour of property? Financial discipline is the first and foremost answer. It is also the most important aspect of achieving personal financial goals over any term. More than any other kind of investment, fixed property requires this kind of discipline over a lifetime.

As people's needs, but especially desires, arise one financial investment after another (e.g. unit trusts) is called up and applied towards satisfying the needs and desires. People are particularly inclined to use financial investments to pay for holidays, overseas visits, study costs, weddings, deposits on a car, furniture, unnecessary purchases or for just any old debt crisis. It is easy to get rid of these investments at opportune and inopportune times. People do not readily use their property to meet expenses such as those just mentioned, however; besides, it takes a lot of time to sell property, and market conditions (interest rates and prices) are taken into account.

One of the main reasons why financially independent retirement is possible today is precisely the fact that people mistakenly believed that endowment policies should be left untouched for 30 or 40 years. As with property, it was in fact the financial discipline of maintaining such policies (regardless of the return compared to certain shares) that made this possible. Nowadays, we do not like discipline much, because we like to use our money to indulge our whims as and when we like. Financial investments are used throughout, and few, if any of them, will remain for retirement. Retirement annuities stand the best chance.

Furthermore, fixed property offers security for the present as well as the future, because it can be encumbered with a bond (a first mortgage) if you need money. You can also offer it as security to a bank for your overdrawn account by offering a covering bond on your property. You can use the paid-off part of your bond on your property as an emergency fund. For example, where a person owns three paid-off properties, the income from two can be used to purchase and pay off a fourth property. Thus, the income from the two helps to meet the monthly repayments on the new property, with the result that the new property is paid off quickly. By this means, quite a few properties are purchased and paid off over a lifetime. The income derived by renting out a portfolio of properties serves as income before and after retirement. Moreover, any of the properties can be sold at a later stage (regardless of capital gains tax) and the after-tax return can be used towards filling the income gap after retirement. If you get to the stage where you own 30 or 50 properties, you should make a sustained effort to sell poorer investments and replace them with better properties. Just remember the 'location, location, location rule'.

People talk like experts over cups of tea and around braai fires, maintaining that they would never rent out a property because other people would damage it. Decent lessees have never broken down another person's property overnight. Spend the R3 000 or R4 000 and fix the flat when your good tenant leaves after five or ten years, particularly in a city where good rentals are realised for even tiny flatlets. The problem is that many potential investors see only the possible maintenance costs, rates and short-term insurance premiums and are unwilling to assume any risk. Unfortunately, this cannot be avoided, and an investment in fixed property has to be managed as well. You must become and remain involved from the day you choose a particular property, select a tenant, finalise the lease, watch the market and do the maintenance as durably as possible within your budget. Fortunately, these expenses are tax-deductible because they are incurred to earn an income. The other taxpayers, therefore, help to pay for your investment.

You do not just squander a fixed property before your retirement for the sake of satisfying some desire or to meet a short-term need. An investment in fixed property with a view to retirement, therefore, has considerable merit as a result of the financial discipline associated with such investments. Naturally, you also have to make investments in other kinds of financial assets with a view to retirement and to meet other needs and objectives.

9.2.2 Advantages and disadvantages of property investment

Pyhrr *et al.* (in Cloete 1994:65) point out the following advantages and disadvantages.

Advantages
- Pride of ownership (the investment can be seen and 'shared' with others).
- Personal control (the owner is in control).
- Estate building (by applying financial leverage over time, property investment is an estate building process).
- Security of capital (property is perceived to be a safe investment).
- Leverage (you do not have to use your own money to invest in property).
- Tax advantages (all expenses are tax-deductible if they have been incurred to earn an income).
- Capital appreciation (especially with a good, secure location).
- Protection against inflation (the investment beats inflation over time).

Disadvantages
- Illiquidity (cannot be converted to cash in a short time).
- Management burden (property has to be managed by someone).
- Depreciation (physical, function and location depreciation decrease the value of property).
- Government control (zoning restrictions).
- Real estate cycles (property values are sensitive to business and economic influences).
- Legal complexity (knowledge of property laws is a prerequisite for property investment).
- Lack of information (not everybody has property knowledge and primary property information is scarce).

9.3 THE INVESTMENT PROCESS

A potential investor should compare the features of the property he or she intends purchasing with his or her personal investment objectives and needs before coming to a decision about the purchase. He or she should also compare the proposed investment with other similar investments. Investments in property are usually made in order to receive a rental income and/or to achieve capital growth. Fixed property offers a hedge against inflation; in other words, the value of property normally increases annually at more or less the same rate as the current rate of inflation.

The type of fixed property a potential investor would consider usually depends on one or more of the following factors:

- the amount of capital available;
- creditworthiness (i.e. his or her borrowing capacity);
- attitude towards risk;
- knowledge of the type of property;
- income tax position; and
- the management requirements of the property (in the case of a hotel or a holiday resort).

In the first place, a prospective investor looks for a suitable property, or one could say a suitable investment opportunity. The aim is to match his or her needs and requirements with a suitable property. Diagram 9.1 is a representation of the investment process.

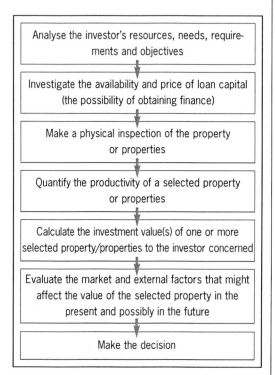

DIAGRAM 9.1 **The investment process**
(Source: Maritz 1983:291)

In the following sections, we will briefly discuss the investment process on the basis of Maritz's diagram.

9.3.1 The investor's resources

An investor who wishes to purchase fixed property requires a large amount of capital. Several additional cost items are involved, such as transfer duty, transfer costs and bond registration costs. An investor may be obliged to use other financial assets or to find co-investors in order to make the purchase physically possible. The entire investment process will have to be an attractive proposition to these co-investors before they would be interested in investing (purchasing). The special features of the property will have to suit their investment needs.

9.3.2 The investor's needs, requirements and objectives

Before investments can take place, prospective investors should ask themselves why they choose to invest in fixed property, as well as why they wish to invest in a specific property. The property or properties will have to meet certain investment criteria. Although several less important criteria could be added, the following five listed by Maritz (1983:291) should suffice:

- anticipated return on capital;
- liquidity of the investment;
- risk involved in the investment;
- income tax implications; and
- management requirements of the investment.

9.3.2.1 Return on capital

The return on investment capital is probably the principal reason for making an investment. When someone makes an investment for his or her own use (such as a home), the convenience and utility value of the home will be more important than the return on the investment. An investment with a view to receiving a regular income will ensure a cash inflow for the investor. A property investment with a view to capital growth is made because the investor hopes to make a profit when he or she sells the property at a later stage. Some people invest in property to increase the wealth of their estate.

An investor will want a certain return on the total amount of capital (own and borrowed) invested (for example 18%). He or she will also want a certain return on his or her own capital (the capital he or she provides without having to borrow it) invested (for example 21%). An investor who already owns other income-producing property would want the rate of return on the new property to exceed the rate of return on the existing property (for example 16%). The 16% is called the internal rate of return and the new investment will consequently have to provide a rate of return of 16% or more.

The use of loan capital increases the return on one's own capital. Assume that a person purchases a fixed property for R100 000 with his or her own money. He or she leases the property and receives an annual return of R20 000. The return on his or her own capital, therefore, is 20% (R20 000 ÷ R100 000 × 100%). If he or she uses only R80 000 of his or her own money, however, and borrows the other R20 000, the return on his or her own capital will be 25% (R20 000 ÷ R80 000 × 100%). As you can see, the use of loan capital increases the return on the investor's own capital. This situation is called gearing or leverage.

9.3.2.2 Liquidity

Liquidity refers to the speed and convenience with which an investment or asset can be converted into cash. Fixed property cannot be sold overnight and converted into cash, mainly because it may be difficult to find a buyer, or a potential buyer may not have sufficient funds, or the market may be unfavourable and potential buyers may find the asking price too high. In other words, fixed property is not a liquid asset. Maritz (1983:293) points out, however, that it may not always be necessary to convert fixed property into cash, since such an investment could serve as surety for a loan.

9.3.2.3 Risk

Risk may be described as the chance that a loss may be suffered, or that the actual results of an investment (for example income) may differ from the anticipated results (or income). In the case of fixed property, a distinction is made between operating risk and financial risk.

Operating risk

Operating risk refers to the risk that a fixed property (in this example) may not be capable of realising its fixed operating costs. This means that the income is too low to cover the operating costs. Maritz (1983:295) refers to the following aspects that may affect the income of fixed property:

- the physical nature of the property (an old building may require extensive maintenance costs);
- the location of the property (if a growth area is being developed, existing lessees may move to the area);
- institutional characteristics (rent control may restrict the income derived from a block of flats);
- the property market (if the market is in recession,

the demand for leasehold property may be minimal); and
- political conditions (a new political order may influence the demand for certain property in certain areas).

Financial risk

Financial risk refers to the risk that an investor may not be capable of honouring his or her financial obligations (arising from an investment). If he or she has borrowed money, making use of gearing or leverage, he or she will have certain financial obligations. For example, he or she will have to pay monthly instalments on a mortgage bond over 20 or 25 years. This means that a risk exists that he or she may not receive sufficient income to pay off the mortgage bond instalments (over and above the operating costs). The higher the mortgage bond sum in relation to the market value of the property, the higher the financial risk.

9.3.2.4 Income tax

The Income Tax Act is amended every year and prospective investors should, therefore, establish to what extent such amendments (if applicable) may affect their investment or proposed investment. For example, if an investor previously received a tax rebate on the construction of a building, he or she should not automatically assume that this rebate would be applicable to his or her next building as well.

The interest payable on a mortgage bond is tax-deductible. However, this concession is only applicable to a mortgage loan that was taken out in order to derive an income from the investment.

9.3.2.5 Management requirements

An investment in fixed property demands management. For example, a hotel, a holiday resort, a block of flats, an office block and a shopping centre would all have to be managed. A prospective investor should, therefore, decide whether he or she has the necessary expertise to manage an investment, or whether he or she would need to find someone with the necessary expertise to manage it for him or her. A skilled and trained person or persons could be found to manage a block of holiday flats by the sea, for example. However, the anticipated return on the investment would have to be sufficient to cover this kind of expense, otherwise it should not be contemplated.

9.3.3 Investigate all financing possibilities

Once an investor has identified his or her resources, objectives and needs, he or she must investigate ways of obtaining additional funds if he or she cannot provide the purchase price. Financial institutions, friends, family and even other investors could be approached for a loan. Others could also be involved as partners, directors or shareholders in order to help fund the investment.

9.3.4 Inspect the property

According to Maritz (1983:301), the following are utility or value-producing features of a property:
- its physical nature (land and renovations);
- its location; and
- its institutional characteristics.

9.3.4.1 The physical nature of the property
Physical nature refers to the following:

Land
- the size and shape of the plot;
- the slope (a very steep slope would lower the value of a block of flats);
- kind of soil (arable agricultural soil would increase the value of a farm for investment purposes); and
- services (a road, a storm-water system, electricity, water and sewerage services).

Renovations (to a building)
- size of the building;
- durability of the structure (quality of construction);
- functional effectiveness of the building (whether it suits the intended purpose or whether alterations or additions would be necessary);
- the relationship of the plot to the building (is there sufficient parking at a shopping centre or bock of flats);
- appearance of the building (whether it requires renovation or is in good condition); and
- sufficient miscellaneous facilities (whether storerooms will have to be built).

9.3.4.2 Location
The location of an investment property refers to its convenience network and exposure network.

Convenience network
An investor who is considering investing in a block of flats should investigate the convenience it offers lessees in respect of the following:
- proximity to office or place of work;
- availability of bus service;
- proximity to places of worship;
- proximity to schools; and
- proximity to shopping centres.

Exposure network
In this regard, the investor should investigate all factors to which the property is exposed. If a block of flats is situated opposite a factory that emits an unpleasant smell, it would be a poor investment in terms of its resale value. The same applies to noise, a garbage dump, a scrap-yard or a high measure of air pollution. These aspects are all important as far as the location of the investment is concerned.

9.3.4.3 Institutional characteristics of the property
These characteristics refer to any regulations pertaining to private and public circumscription of property rights. These pertain to the right of use of the property, or the maximum lawful and economic use that may be made of a property. For example, an investor may purchase a plot with the intention of constructing a block of flats on it, and then find that it has been zoned as industrial land. Or a servitude may be registered on a property, in which case the investor (purchaser) would not be allowed to build on that part of the plot.

Losses could, therefore, be avoided if an investor consults the Deeds Office and the local municipality on regulations pertaining to civil and public law property rights, such as:
- rates and taxes;
- expropriation;
- control (building regulations, storm-water drainage, retaining walls);
- real servitudes (subdivision of land, zoning, more than one house);
- personal (civil) servitudes (usufruct, occupation); and
- public servitudes (thoroughfare, the construction of a national roadway).

The aspects listed above will determine the lawful use(s) an investor may make of the property. Prospective investors should check these aspects thoroughly, or have them checked, before investing in fixed property.

9.3.5 Quantification of the productivity of the property

To quantify means to attach a value or amount to something. Productivity refers to the income derived from the investment property. A prospective investor should, therefore, determine the income he or she expects from an investment. Maritz (1983:303) points out that the income a prospective investor expects consists of one or both of the following components:

- the income stream (for example, monthly rental); and
- the terminal or residual value (for example, the amount of money received if an office block is sold after 12 years).

Maritz (1983:303) also discusses two methods for calculating income stream:
- the calculation of normalised income for the first years; and
- the calculation of the actual income stream over a certain period (say ten years), as well as the calculation of the terminal or residual value at the end of this period.

Normalised income is calculated for the property only. In this brief discussion, we will not go into the income position that includes income tax implications (benefits). Income is also calculated without taking into account the use of loan capital (borrowed money). Maritz (1983:305) states that the reason for this is that, at this stage, the prospective investor is interested in the productivity of the investment property, and not how that productivity can be increased by the use of loan capital or income tax benefits.

9.3.5.1 Calculation of normalised income for the first year

Income may be calculated in several ways. Maritz (1983:265) explains that the following incomes must be calculated in order to determine normalised annual net income:
- gross income;
- effective gross income; and
- net income (normalised annual).

Gross income refers to the income received before any deductions have been made for expenses (of whatever nature). Effective gross income is calculated by deducting losses (for example, if a building is not occupied or if debt is not collected) from gross income. Normalised annual net income is calculated by deducting operating costs from effective gross income. For the purposes of our calculation (as mentioned earlier), tax and instalments on loans are not deducted in order to provide an after-tax return on your own capital. In the following example, we calculate only up to Point 5. Net operating income actually refers to normalised annual net income (cash inflow), or NNI.

EXAMPLE

Calculation of net operating income

	R
1. Gross anticipated rental income	144 000
2. Minus: unoccupied factor and collections	7 000
3. Equal to: effective gross income	137 000
4. Minus: operating expenses	35 000
5. Net operating income	102 000

9.3.5.2 Method of comparable rates of return (capitalisation)

All investors expect a certain rate of return on their investments. This anticipated rate of return is also called the overall capitalisation rate. Once an investor has calculated the above-mentioned normalised annual net income (NNI) and the overall capitalisation rate (OCR), he or she will be able to determine the market value of the investment property.

Assume that a person expects an 8.1% rate of return on his or her capital and the property's NNI amounts to R30 000. The market value is calculated as follows:

$$\text{Market value} = \frac{\text{NNI}}{\text{OCR}}$$

$$= \frac{\text{R30 000}}{8.1\%}$$

$$= \text{R370 000}$$

The ratio between MV, NNI and OCR can be represented in a triangle as follows:

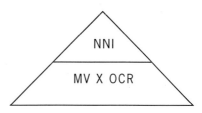

Thus NNI is equal to MV multiplied by OCR. The amount of R30 000 is equal to R370 000 × 8.1%, or OCR is equal to NNI divided by market value. In this way, rates of return, market values and incomes of various investment proposals (for example buildings) may be compared with and weighed up against one another.

This method of comparing investments is called the method of comparable rates of return (capitalisation). Our next point of discussion is the method of discounted cash flow analysis (discounting).

9.3.5.3 Method of discounted cash flow analysis (discounting)

We referred to discounting in Chapter 3. In the case of capitalisation, income for one year only is used. In the case of discounting, we use the income over several years to determine the market value of a property.

With discounted cash flow analysis (discounting), the market value of a property, or the price that may be paid for a property, is equal to the present (current) value of all net financial benefits (net income) that will be obtained from the property in future.

The following is needed for a discounted cash flow analysis:

- future income (A);
- terminal or residual value (B); and
- discount rate (C).

Calculate NNI for, say, 4 years

	1st year	2nd year	3rd year	4th year
Gross income	128 011	135 692	143 833	152 463
Estimated expenditure	30 161	32 950	43 150	45 739
	97 850	102 742	100 683	106 724

Terminal or residual value

This is calculated by the capitalisation method:

$$MV = \frac{NNI}{OCR}$$
$$= \frac{R106\ 724}{8.5\%}$$
$$= R1\ 255\ 576$$

Discounting of cash flow and terminal or residual value

If details A, B and C are available, two methods may be used to calculate the discount value: a long and short method. Assume that the discount rate is 10%.

First method (long method)

Use FV and PV on a financial pocket calculator.

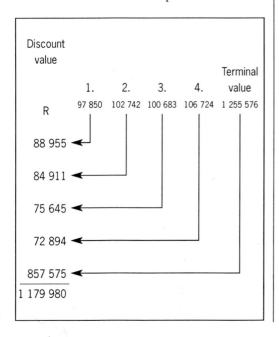

Second method (short method)

Use the CFi key on an EL 533 and EL 733 financial pocket calculator.

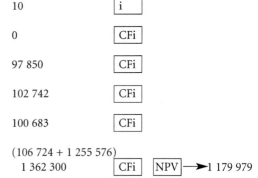

9.3.5.4 The cost method

According to the cost method, the value of a property is determined by calculating the costs incurred in substituting or reproducing the property (in the case of unique buildings) after these costs have been adjusted for depreciation. The following formula is used:

$$MV = CC - D + MVL$$

where:

MV	=	market value
CC	=	construction costs based on current costs
D	=	depreciation
MVL	=	market value of land

The income method (comparable rates of return) cannot always be used in the valuation of investment property. In such a case, the cost method (comparable costs) is used, which is based on the principle of substitution or replacement. When the replica of a building has to be valued, reproduction costs are used (churches, monuments and the Union Buildings are examples). Where similar or comparable renovations are made and have to be valued, they are referred to as replacement costs.

Construction costs

When calculating costs in practice, the cost per square metre is generally used. Expensive finishing, for example, would increase these costs. Maritz (1983:279) refers to the following factors that may increase the value of a certain fixed property in comparison with another similar property:

- extent of plan;
- height from floor to ceiling;
- height of the building;
- differences in construction methods and materials;
- differences in finishes and architectural detail;
- sanitary and other high-cost equipment;
- plot (stand);
- date of construction;
- geographical area in which constructed;
- tender condition; and
- contract period.

All costs that normally fall to the owner (builder or constructor) must be included. Maritz lists the following cost items:

- registration costs and attorney's fees;
- consultation costs, surveys and demolition permits before construction work begins;
- professional services of architects, quantity surveyors and building planners;
- property tax during the construction period;
- insurance during the construction period;
- administrative expenses; and
- the building contractor's profit, if this is not included in the building costs (direct costs).

Depreciation

According to Maritz (1983:281), depreciation (D) should be calculated and deducted from construction costs (CC) in order to determine the market value of the renovations (MR) to the building.

$$CC - D = MR$$

There are three main reasons for depreciation:

- physical or structural ageing (cracked walls, rusting roof, overdue maintenance);
- functional ageing (out-of-date design and layout, toilets outside the building); and
- economic ageing (rezoning of a residential area to an industrial area).

In practice, it is no simple matter to calculate depreciation on fixed property such as a building. Maritz mentions the following methods that may be used in practice, apart from a subjective calculation or assessment of depreciation.

The capitalisation of income method

Depreciation equals construction costs minus value as calculated according to the comparable rate of return (income method).

EXAMPLE

	R
Construction costs	120 000
Less: Value according to income method	90 000
Depreciation	30 000

The market method

The situation could be that old buildings can be sold on the market for 30% less than the current construction costs. In that case, depreciation would be 30%.

Mathematical models: the sum of the years method

Assume that a building has an economic life of five years and the construction costs amount to R5 000. Annual depreciation is calculated as follows:

EXAMPLE

$1 + 2 + 3 + 4 + 5 = 15$

Year	Calculation	R
1	5/15 x R5 000	1 667
2	4/15 x R5 000	1 333
3	3/15 x R5 000	1 000
4	2/15 x R5 000	667
5	1/15 x R5 000	333
		5 000

Market value of land

The method of comparable purchase prices is used to determine the market value of land. The calculation is similar to that for house prices. The value of a plot or land is, therefore, determined by comparing it with similar plots or land that have been sold under similar market and economic conditions. The comparable selling transactions should preferably not have taken place more than three months previously. The transactions should also contain more or less the same conditions and the site should be in more or less the same area.

9.3.6 Calculation of investment value of a property

Maritz (1983:311) emphasises the important distinction between the utility or utilitarian value of a property and its market value. Earlier we referred to market value as the price a willing buyer would pay to a willing seller at a given period in the market.

The utility or utilitarian value of a property is the value it has for a specific investor at a given stage. This value (the investment value), therefore, only has a bearing on the prospective investor, given the following:

- his or her attitude towards the risks involved in the investment;
- the funds available to him or her;
- the cost of financing the investment;
- his or her attitude in general towards any risk;
- his or her age;
- the return on his or her current investment portfolio;
- his or her liquidity and solvency; and
- his or her creditworthiness.

The utility or investment value a property holds for a specific investor can influence his or her willingness to pay more or less for the property than the market value. Maritz (1983:311) points out that if the investment value were higher than the market value, an investor would willingly buy the property at market value, believing that it was a bargain; but if the market value were higher than the investment value, the investor would not want to buy the property.

EXAMPLE

Assume that a person's attitude towards risk is to avoid it at all costs. He or she is less willing to take risks than the average investor. This investor is considering purchasing a block of flats with the following anticipated annual net cash inflows:

Year	Cash inflow	Present value factor (6.0%)	Present value
1	14 000	0.943	13 202
2	14 000	0.890	14 460
3	14 000	0.840	11 760
4	14 000	0.792	11 088
5	14 000	0.747	10 458
Total present value			58 968
Less: Initial amount invested			42 000
Net present value			16 968

The net present value (the value that a building would add to an investor's estate, for example) of a specific building is calculated for the average investor (an investor who accepts risks to a certain extent).

Should the prospective investor wish to leave more room for risk in his or her calculations, he or she could use one or both of the following methods:

- the certainty equivalent method; and
- the risk-adjusted discount rate method.

9.3.6.1 The certainty equivalent method

According to this method, the prospective investor requires greater certainty in forecasting the anticipated income of, for example, the block of flats referred to above. Because he or she wants to be sure of the income for the five years, each year's income is estimated at a reduced amount. In other words, he or she deliberately reduces the income for each year to ensure that he or she will in fact receive the income.

EXAMPLE

Year	Cash inflow	Certainty equivalent	Certain cash inflow	Factor (6%)	Present value R
1	14 000	0.90	12 600	0.943	11 882
2	14 000	0.90	12 600	0.890	11 214
3	14 000	0.80	11 200	0.840	9 408
4	14 000	0.70	9 800	0.792	7 762
5	14 000	0.60	8 400	0.747	6 275
Total present value					46 541
Minus: Initial amount invested					42 000
Net present value					4 541

From the example it can be seen how the investor reduced each year's cash inflow in order to eliminate further risk. The result is that the net present value of the block of flats is reduced. The investor does this to obtain greater certainty, hence the name 'certainty equivalent method'.

9.3.6.2 The risk-adjusted discount rate method

This is the second method that may be used to reduce the investor's risk. The investor expects a certain return on his or her investment, which is called the discount rate (see Chapter 3). With this method, the investor increases the rate of return he or she desires. An increased discount rate means that the total present value and the net present value of the block of flats, for example, are reduced. The new (higher) rate is 8%.

EXAMPLE

Year	Cash inflow	Present value factor (8%)	Present value
1	14 000	0.926	12 964
2	14 000	0.857	11 998
3	14 000	0.794	11 116
4	14 000	0.735	10 290
5	14 000	0.681	9 534
Total present value			55 902
Less: Initial amount invested			42 000
Net present value			13 902

or (14 900 X 3.993) - 42 000 = R13 902

For more information about these two methods of reducing risk, consult Brigham & Gapenski (1990:395) and Gitman (1991:346). Another method of determining the risk involved in a specific investment is discussed next.

9.3.6.3 The sensitivity analysis method

Assume that an investor wants to compare the risk involved in two projects (A and B). The investor is not only interested in the return, but wants to determine the risk as well. Table 9.1 compares the annual net cash inflow as well as the net present value of projects A and B.

The method consists of calculating an optimistic, most probable and a pessimistic value (of cash inflow, for example) for both projects. By deducting the pessimistic value (cash inflow or net present value) from the optimistic value, a zone is calculated. This zone represents the risk involved in a specific project. The larger the zone, the greater the risk.

Regarding the cash inflow, the zone for project B is four times greater than for project A. Project B is, therefore, four times as risky as project A. Similarly, project B is almost four times as risky as far as its net present value is concerned.

TABLE 9.1 **Sensitivity analysis**
(Source: Adapted from Gitman 1988:344)

	Project A	Project B
Initial amount invested	10 000	10 000
Annual net cash inflow		
Outcome		
Optimistic	2 500	4 000
Most probable	2 000	2 000
Pessimistic	1 500	0
Zone	1 000	4 000
Net present values		
Outcome		
Optimistic	9 015	20 424
Most probable	5 212	5 212
Pessimistic	1 409	– 10 000
Zone	7 606	30 424

9.3.7 Evaluation of the market and external factors that may affect the value of an investment

It is very important that a prospective investor should analyse the market for the proposed type of fixed property before he or she purchases. To buy a block of flats while half the flats are standing empty would be a poor investment decision in ordinary market conditions. Equally, purchasing a block of flats in an industrial area would be a poor investment. The resale value of such a property would be very low.

Clearly, there should be a demand for the services the property is able to offer. The best investment would be one where the demand increases as a result of growth in the area in which the property is situated. Future demand is as important as current demand. A market analysis will demonstrate the supply of and demand for services similar to those the investment property has to offer. It is, therefore, necessary to forecast changes in the demand for a certain kind of fixed property among the community (Maritz 1983:319).

Economic factors also play a role. The demand for a certain service in a certain area is determined by factors such as the resident population, as well as their incomes. Obviously, people in a higher income bracket will be in a position to pay more. Temporary workers, even if there are thousands, are not the basis for an investment in fixed property. Once their work has been completed, the workers will move away and the building will remain unoccupied.

The availability of credit is another factor to be considered. Low interest rates would increase the demand for sectional title flats and town houses. The investment value of such properties would also rise. Monetary and fiscal policies of the authorities play a definitive role in investment in fixed property.

The political situation in a country is a factor that may increase or decrease investment values. A new political order or times of political uncertainty could undermine the general confidence in the economy. Foreign investors would be scarce and property prices would fall temporarily because the demand for property would be less. Prospective investors would adopt a 'wait and see' attitude.

9.3.8 Making the decision

According to Maritz (1983:319), a decision to invest is made when buyer and seller reach agreement on the price of the property, as well as on the conditions of sale. The price will be significantly influenced by the parties' knowledge of the property market (recent transactions, similar properties, the demand for certain services, the area, the population and their income).

A prospective investor should make sure that his or her financing arrangements correspond with the price and conditions of sale. For example, it would make no sense to agree to hand over money at a date prior to receiving a loan, or to pay interest on a loan at a high rate before any money has changed hands.

9.4 TYPES OF INVESTMENT IN FIXED PROPERTY

9.4.1 Investing in your own home

This aspect is discussed in Chapter 8.

Building or buying (own home)
Probably the most frequent question prospective home buyers ask themselves is whether to build or buy a house. The cost aspects of buying a house are discussed in Chapter 8. Further cost aspects were dealt with during the discussion on the costing method (as a method of valuation).

There are several advantages and disadvantages to building a house, which prospective builders and buyers should consider. Some of the advantages are:
- The owner/builder can build a house to suit his or her taste and style.
- The owner/builder can choose the building material he or she prefers.
- The owner/builder can build a house to his or her own requirements (for example, four bedrooms and three garages).
- The maintenance costs of a new house are generally lower than those of an older one.

Some of the disadvantages are:
- Building a house is more expensive than buying an existing house (building costs tend to increase considerably every year).
- The country's economy generally determines house prices.
- The supervision of the building project can be time-consuming and even a burden to the owner/builder.
- The services of an architect increase building costs considerably.
- Because a home is most people's first experience of building, it may not turn out quite as practical as it was intended to be.
- Building costs are usually higher than budgeted for because of rising building costs and/or lack of knowledge of building costs.
- The building project usually takes longer than planned because of unforeseen events.

- There is a risk of workers on the building site calling a strike, which would contribute towards higher costs.

Renting or buying

The motivation for buying a home is discussed in Chapter 8. In this chapter, we refer to only a few aspects. Unless a person knows that he or she is not going to live in a certain place for any length of time (for example, if he or she is only working there for a few months), there is no merit in renting a house rather than buying one.

Apart from the security a home offers, it also offers a hedge against inflation. The value of a house rises annually more or less at a rate equal to the current inflation rate. There is also considerable capital appreciation in the value of a house (or any fixed property) over the long term.

Where people rent a house, they are actually paying off the property for someone else. The house will never belong to them, even if they remain in the house for the rest of their lives. In contrast to the aforementioned, they could have:
- possessed a home of their own after 20 years (the normal mortgage bond term);
- built up an estate with the house as an asset;
- built up creditworthiness, since after repayment of the home bond they could use the house as security for securing a loan; and
- purchased further assets (even fixed property, for example a second house) with the house as security.

9.4.2 Holiday homes

A holiday home is a luxury and not normally an investment option for less wealthy people. A holiday home brings about the same costs as a residential home and, like any other house, becomes progressively more expensive to maintain.

Unless the holiday home is let to tenants, the fact that it is unoccupied most of the time must be taken into account. A holiday home that can be let for R2 500 per month has an unoccupied factor (or cost) equal to R7 500. This money could have been employed to pay off the bond that was taken out to buy the house.

The distance that has to be travelled to the house is another cost factor the owner has to consider. The cost of fuel is an important consideration these days.

The unoccupied home holds great risk, particularly as far as theft is concerned. An unoccupied house today will almost certainly be burgled, irrespective of the security measures taken. If someone is appointed to look after the house, it will constitute another cost item in the form of a salary or other benefit. An alarm system will not work over a long distance and will not solve the problem. The best alternative would be to have someone living in the house.

It is important to invest in a growth area, just as for any other fixed property. A popular area (by the sea or in nature) is the best investment. An area with a poor reputation should be avoided, since the resale value in such an area would be low. It would also take longer to find a suitable buyer for such a holiday home. An area such as Plettenberg Bay would have high prices and high capital growth in the long term. Beautiful natural surroundings and/or a sea view are important considerations when buying a holiday home.

9.4.3 Sectional title schemes

In terms of the Sectional Title Act 66 of 1971, it is possible to buy a part or section of a building. This part or section may consist of a flat, an office or a shop in a shopping centre. Assume that a person buys a flat under a sectional title scheme. He or she (the owner) would then have sole proprietorship of the purchased part (the flat), together with joint ownership of the common property (for example the grounds, staircase, swimming pool, verandas and lift). A lock-up garage may be included as part of the deal.

From the date of the first sale of a sectional title unit, a body corporate is instituted for the building (sectional title scheme). The developer (until all units have been sold) and the other owners of units in a building all become members of the body corporate, which is responsible for the control, administration and management of the common building. The activities of the body corporate must always be in the interests of the owners of units. The body corporate also stipulates the monthly levy to be paid by the owners for maintaining the building.

9.4.3.1 Buying a unit

It is possible to mortgage sectional title property. It is not possible, however, to sell or to buy a unit separately from the joint property. The property rights to a sectional title unit are conferred in a sectional title certificate and are transferred by means of an endorsement on the sectional title certificate. According to Delport (1987:113), the conveyancer provides the Registrar of Deeds with a certificate during a transfer of property rights, on which the following information appears:
- the names and marital status of the parties;
- proof that all moneys have been paid to the body corporate;
- proof that the transferor is not insolvent;
- proof that the transfer has not been prohibited by an interdict; and

- proof that a person acting on behalf of a church, an association or another body corporate has been authorised to do so.

9.4.3.2 Rights and obligations of the owner(s) of a unit

An owner may either occupy the property (for example, a flat) him- or herself or may let it. He or she may not use it for any purpose (for example, as an office) other than the registered purpose. He or she must keep to the rules of the body corporate. Keeping pets (dogs and/or cats) or having a braai under the carports may be prohibited in terms of these rules.

An owner is expected to maintain his or her section and to report any need for repairs (for example, a leaking roof) to the body corporate without delay. The body corporate is entitled to inspect any unit within reasonable hours of the day. Delport (1987:122) points out that an owner (with the written consent of the trustees of the body corporate) may subdivide his or her section, consolidate two sections and even extend his or her boundaries.

When an owner insures his or her section, this insurance also applies to his or her share of the common property. No owner may close off any section of the common property (for example, a passage) for his or her own exclusive use. Furthermore, an owner may take action against the body corporate if it does not ensure that the management rules are enforced and adhered to.

Owners pay a monthly levy to the body corporate. This levy is revised and adjusted on an annual basis to help cover the costs of the body corporate.

The sectional title described here means that the owner obtains title over the unit which he or she buys. A type of scheme where title is not obtained, namely a share-block scheme, is discussed next.

9.4.4 Share-block schemes

In a share-block scheme, a person obtains a share in a company that manages a certain scheme. This scheme may consist of an office block or a block of flats. The company managing this scheme is called a share-block company. A shareholder does not take ownership of a flat, for example, which he or she intends occupying or letting, but merely obtains the right to use the flat.

A shareholder's rights and obligations are contained in the memorandum of association and articles of the share-block company. His or her rights and obligations are also determined by the use and occupation agreement concluded between the shareholder and the company. Delport (1987:124) mentions that a potential buyer may

become a shareholder of a company in one of the following ways:
- by buying shares from the developer; or
- by taking over the shares of an existing shareholder.

The Share Blocks Control Act 59 of 1980 and the Companies Act 61 of 1973 regulate the management of share-block schemes. These Acts protect the investment made by shareholders in the company. The directors are, therefore, obliged to act in the interests of the shareholders.

Delport (1987:130) describes a use and occupation agreement as 'an agreement concluded between a member (shareholder) of the share-block company and the company itself, which contains the negotiations and conditions according to which a person may occupy a specified part of a building.'

This agreement usually covers the following:
- the maintenance of the building;
- the payment of electricity accounts;
- subletting of rooms;
- loan obligations of shareholders;
- the rights and obligations of shareholders; and
- the rights and obligations of the share-block company.

The use and occupation agreement must be in writing. Initially, the parties to the agreement, according to Delport (1987:130), are the share-block developer and the share-block company. As soon as a share in a unit is sold, the rights and obligations in terms of the use and occupation agreement are ceded to the buyer (shareholder).

Potential buyers should carefully study this agreement in order to make an informed decision. Various aspects of the sale of shares are also contained in the agreement. This information is of great importance to a potential investor (shareholder), particularly in view of the resale of the shares at a later stage.

As in the case of a sectional title scheme, a share-block scheme also has a levy fund to which shareholders contribute on a monthly basis. The amount of the contribution is determined by the number of shares the shareholder holds. Furthermore, certain management rules have to be adhered to. Delport (1987:142) also points out that a share-block scheme may eventually be converted into a sectional title scheme.

9.4.5 Time-share schemes

'Time-sharing is a method in which a number of people each obtain the exclusive right of use and occupation of the accommodation during a specified period each year' (Delport 1987:144). He mentions that the period (called a time module or time unit) usually consists of one or more weeks. It may even be one day (for example, in the case of a hotel room).

A time unit usually consists of a fixed period; for example, the second week in December. The time unit may also be arranged or managed according to an exchange programme. This means that it is possible to move a time unit from December to March, for example.

In South Africa, time-share units are normally bought for holiday purposes. Several advantages arise from ownership:
- guaranteed holiday periods;
- holiday costs are protected against inflation;
- the bother of making holiday arrangements is reduced;
- holiday accommodation in a sought-after resort is assured;
- time-share interests may be exchanged; and
- the scheme management often undertake to let time-share units.

Some disadvantages are also attached to a time-share scheme (Laurie 1990:127):
- the owner is bound to one resort;
- service fees may be raised without justification;
- the resale profit is often low;
- the market for time-share units is fairly small;
- letting the unit is not very profitable; and
- it is not really an investment, except in the case of very expensive resorts.

Delport (1987:144) mentions several factors that may affect the purchase price or the resale value of a time-share interest:
- the legal basis of the scheme;
- the relevant time of the year;
- location of the project;
- recreational facilities available;
- quality of finishes;
- size of the unit;
- layout of the unit;
- furnishing and accessories of the dwelling unit;
- availability of exchange facilities; and
- the annual levy fees.

Potential investors are advised to investigate several schemes and to obtain advice before buying a time-share unit.

9.4.6 Rented houses

People sometimes consider buying a second house and letting it to tenants. The rental is used to pay off the bond instalments (or to contribute towards the repayment). The interest on the mortgage loan is tax-deductible since the loan was taken in order to earn an income from it. The house is a better hedge against inflation than, for example, a cash investment of R30 000.

Where capital growth is the main consideration, an investment in a second house would be a good idea. Return on the investment (rental income), however, is poor.

A specific, unique investment opportunity would afford an investor greater benefits than an ordinary investment situation. For example, a house for sale from an estate or at an auction at a low price would present a good investment opportunity (depending on the utility features and the property market), in view of capital growth and as a hedge against inflation.

It is difficult to say at this stage whether the Rent Control Act will still be applicable to the letting of residential property in the future (over the longterm). This Act controls the maximum rental that may be charged for residential property. An investor may purchase a second residential home with the intention of letting it and then find that the rental he or she may charge is ridiculously low. He or she may end up being unable to pay off the mortgage loan and could even have a financial crisis on his or her hands. Potential and intending investors should first determine whether the Rent Control Act is applicable to a certain property before investing in it.

9.4.7 Syndicates

It frequently occurs that a person wishes to make an investment, but does not have sufficient funds or creditworthiness. One option would be to approach other investors and convince them to join in the investment. Their joint endeavour would then be called a syndicate. In this way, it becomes possible for an individual investor to make a larger investment than would otherwise have been possible.

Several types of enterprise can be formed, such as a company or a close corporation. Laurie (1990:135) states that a syndicate investment is seldom intended as a long-term investment. The purpose is usually to make a capital profit when the property is sold at a later stage.

Four people decide to form a syndicate. Their plan is to build a shopping centre on an empty site, and then to let each of the five shops or to sell them to another investor. One of the four people owns the site, the second has an investment of R250 000, the third is a building contractor and will construct the building, while the fourth investor is an attorney who will handle all the legal aspects involved in the marketing and administration of the shops. They also agree to take out a building loan amounting to R1 000 000.

It may appear as if the construction and marketing of the building could proceed without problems, but this is not necessarily the case. There are several risks attached, namely:

- rising building costs;
- liquidation of one of the four members;
- a shortage of lessees (or tenants);
- too low initial rentals, placing financial pressure on the syndicate and compelling them to sell the shops at lower than market value; and
- a shortage of buyers for the shops.

9.4.8 The development of property (construction)

An investor may contemplate constructing a building with the purpose of letting it. If there is an existing building which has to be demolished first, the law of 'lease before sale' should always be kept in mind. This means that lessees cannot be evicted from a building while they still have a lease to live there. Prospective developers or investors should remember this.

It is not easy to distinguish between an investment analysis and a feasibility study. A feasibility study is usually undertaken when a building is to be erected. Maritz (1983:365) distinguishes the following four phases in the property development process:

- the feasibility study phase;
- the design phase;
- the construction phase; and
- the property administration phase.

The feasibility phase is undertaken by an architect (where applicable). The building contractor normally handles the design and construction phase, while the letting agent is involved in the property administration phase. Some aspects of the feasibility phase will be discussed now.

Throughout the process, the prospective 'investor/developer' must reconcile his or her own objectives with the feasibility of the property development. If he or she has decided that a return of at least 16% is required, he or she should not begin a project than can deliver only a 5% return. In other words, the project should not only be feasible but it should also fit the investor's objectives.

When an investor intends undertaking a development project, he or she should pay particular attention to the applicable market. An investor should determine, for example, whether there is a demand for a shopping centre in a particular residential area. He or she should investigate factors such as the features of the plot, where it is located and what kind of convenience and exposure networks are offered.

It must be possible to offer a service from the plot. The investor should examine the most economic and legal use of the plot. The residual land value of a plot is calculated in Table 9.2. For example, the investor should consider whether a building should be erected for leasing as a bottle store or as an office building.

TABLE 9.2 Calculation of residual land values
(Source: Adapted from Maritz 1983:371)

Item	Bottle store	Office building
1. Lettable areas	800m^2	800m^2 + 800m^2
2. Rent per m^2	R40	R20 + R40
3. Rental income per annum	R384 000	R576 000
4. Capitalisation rate	16%	16%
5. Value of project for developer requiring 6% return on capital	R2 400 000	R3 600 000
6. Construction costs of improvements	-R1 600 000	-R3 000 000
7. Residual land value	R800 000	R 600 000

The residual land value of the bottle store appears to be more than that of an office building. The investor would, therefore, decide to construct the building and let it as a bottle store.

Assume that another plot has to be purchased at a price or market value of R700 000. It is clear that the land value of R600 000 of the office building would not be considered at all, since it is lower than the market value of R700 000. The bottle store, on the other hand, has a land value of R800 000, which is higher than the market value of R700 000. The latter development would, therefore, be considered.

The prospective developer would consequently have to obtain financing in order to purchase the plot and erect the building.

A syndicate could be considered. If the decision is to build a bottle store, the costs would amount to:

market value of plot	R700 000
construction costs of building	R1 600 000
	R2 300 000

The developer would have to consider several financing options if he or she decides to proceed with the development. The residual land value of R800 000 means that the developer could pay R800 000 more for the project than the anticipated R2 300 000 and still earn 16% on his or her capital.

9.4.9 Retail shops/shopping centres

An investor could buy a share in a shopping centre, buy a few shops or decide to build a shopping centre and lease the shops. The third requires very thorough planning by the investor/developer (who has to act as entrepreneur as well), particularly in regard to financing the project and marketing the shops. Developing and marketing a shopping centre is expensive and requires careful planning.

This type of investment is usually financed by the developer him- or herself, or by the developer with the help of retail groups or an insurance company. Before deciding to act as developer/investor yourself, you should make use of the services and knowledge of professional developers. Rather pay 'cheaply' now for all the very expensive mistakes you would otherwise make later. Your research and planning must include, amongst others, location, building regulations, the building site itself, the market, competitors, tenants and accessibility.

The basic budget should already give you some idea of the scope of such a development, and of the rental income you should be generating to ensure the success of the project. The lease contract is of cardinal importance to generate rental income, but also to find and keep tenants. You should, furthermore, think about replacements and subleases in order to ensure continuity in the centre. Picking the right tenants is of critical importance in the case of a shopping centre, especially as regards the value of the centre as a whole. A few 'bad' tenants could derail the entire project for yourself and other investors.

Of course, a shopping centre also has a life cycle, just like a product. Effective management of a shopping centre can increase its economic life, because you may well find yourself in with new shopping centres. You may have noticed, in your neighbourhood, that shopping centres become obsolete in 10 to 20 years, and must then be regenerated through further investment by the owners/investors. The public does not like shopping in a run-down centre. They also find it unacceptable if the toilets or elevators do not work properly, particularly if this is the case for an unacceptably long period. Such aspects may attract customers or drive them away for ever (Cloete 1993:93).

9.4.10 Office space

An office development embraces all aspects in and outside an office itself, amongst others, parking, the work environment, the site, office lay-out, elevators and stairs. The management of an office building is, therefore, of particular importance to investors, especially as regards the type of tenants the building attracts. The latter will determine the return on your investment.

As with shopping centres, offices must meet the needs of the tenants. Tenants must always feel good about the level of their business, without sacrificing their corporate image and losing clients. Their physical needs must be met, and the rental must be acceptable. As a prospective investor, it is vital that you should do research and consult experts on tenants' needs. This should give you a better idea of the ins and outs of an office block as a rental and investment medium.

It is also important to distinguish between the risks attached to a new office development and those attached to an established office block. You must decide for yourself which type of risk-return relationship you want, and can live with. A property expert could point out certain market factors to you, which could largely determine the short-, medium- and long-term sustainability of a particular office block (or proposed development) – over and above the management and marketing aspects involved. Therefore, compare various similar office blocks with the help of an expert before investing in one.

In the case of a new development, you must be sure that the rental income will cover the costs, and that the projected rental income will by far exceed the required rental payment. Of course, a cost calculation and knowledge of the tenants in the market are prerequisites for these comparisons and calculations (Cloete 1993:5,165).

9.4.11 Industrial property

Industrial property includes factories and warehouses, as well as undeveloped industrial land on which a factory is still to be built. As in the case of all other types of fixed property, the zoning will determine what such property can be used for. The demand for products manufactured in a factory, for example, will largely determine the demand for industrial property as an investment medium. The same goes for the demand for warehouses. Large-scale technological change (or obsolescence) could negatively affect the value of industrial property, for example because existing technology can no longer be used for manufacturing certain products. This is particularly the case where specialised equipment is used.

Other factors that directly influence the investment value include changes in the industry, the proximity of clients, the source of raw materials or semi-finished products and distance from export ports. It is only logical that tenants of industrial property will have more technical requirements than would be the case with other types of property. Therefore, make sure that such tenants remain happy that their demands are being met, and will wish to renew their leases.

In general, the return on an investment is higher for shopping centres (retail property) and office blocks than for industrial property. Someone marketing this type of property will also have to display greater technical expertise than with other types of property. Therefore, make sure that such a person indeed has the necessary knowledge, and also consult other experts about this specific type of investment. You can be sure that this type of property will also have to satisfy many legal requirements before it can be leased to a tenant (Cloete 1993:187).

9.4.12 Undeveloped residential property (stands)

Undeveloped residential property may be one of the best investments of our time. Of course, this refers to locations ranging from acceptable to very good. Obviously, the more expensive residential areas will imply more expensive plots, but also far greater profits when these stands are sold after two to five years. The main reason, of course, is that land becomes scarcer and the demand for it higher. Plots in security areas, in particular, can currently be sold

at a considerable profit after two to three years (often even within the first year). You must be able to obtain the required financing, and be able to pay the rates and taxes until you are able to sell the plot again. Stands in security precincts that include golf course developments may offer the highest returns of all types of property investment (and even some other types of investment). However, they do cost a great deal more.

9.4.13 Undeveloped business property (stands)

Do not simply accept that whatever pertains to undeveloped residential property also goes for undeveloped business property. Of course, the location of an undeveloped business property is the prime determinant of its value. However, the most economic (the highest residual land value for the property) and legal (in terms of its zoning) use thereof will determine its investment value now and in the future. An estate agent can help you to determine the most economic and legal use for a property. Investments are usually made in such properties with a view to development, either for own use or for lease or sale.

Developing a business property should be accompanied by a feasibility study. In this way, it can be ascertained at the right time whether the utility and productivity of the property (proposed development) match the needs (objectives and goals) of the developer. Any such investment must, therefore, be undertaken with the expertise of a developer and a business consultant who would possibly be able to market the property. Someone with such a property would, therefore, seek a developer who is able to act as co-investor and co-owner. Of course, the property must be managed after the construction phase to ensure that it becomes and remains profitable.

Potential investors will invest in an undeveloped business property if the projected return on the total investment and development is lower than the internal rate of return of the developed property (Cloete 1993:147).

9.4.14 Retirement villages

People buying into a retirement village usually regard it as the last investment of their lives. At this stage of their lives, they simply do not want to take the chance that something could go wrong with their investment and (often last) funds. Those contemplating such an investment must, therefore, make quite sure that they know what they are letting themselves in for. The help of their children could be very useful in this case with, amongst others:

- tracing a few similar schemes;
- research regarding the advantages and disadvantages of every type of scheme, and comparable schemes;
- financing a scheme;
- linking the investment to a valid and updated will;
- moving to their new home; and
- overcoming any orientation or adaptation problems subsequent to the move.

If there are no children, a broker can be employed to help. It is also a good idea to speak to current residents about the advantages and disadvantages of a scheme. This may help in avoiding many financial and other pitfalls. Of course, children could invest in a scheme of this nature on behalf of their parents, for example by buying a life interest. The scheme will buy back such an interest after the death of the owner, and the scheme will pay the proceeds into the deceased's estate. After the death of the occupant(s) the unit is then sold to someone else.

Retirement villages are particularly suited to persons who believe in communal living. The health facilities are most attractive to infirm persons. Investors will, if possible, choose schemes with facilities that suit their pockets and medical conditions. Make sure that you know exactly what facilities (including meals and recreational facilities) the scheme offers before investing in it. Also be certain that the scheme you are contemplating will ensure your independence. Remember that you will be required to pay a levy, so you must be able to afford any increases in this levy (Cloete 1994:86–88).

9.4.15 Hotels

You can invest in a hotel on a time-share or sectional title basis. Because of the nature of the constant use, the investment amount needed for a time-share unit is much lower than for the ownership that results from a sectional title investment. In the latter case, you may use the hotel room or unit registered in your name personally for 30 days of the year. When used by the owner, the room is withdrawn from the rental pool, and during this time the owner does not share in the returns rendered by the room.

The hotel is managed by a hotel group, which rents the room or unit to guests or holidaymakers for the rest of the year. During occupation by the owner, only a cleaning fee is charged. The owner receives a monthly statement indicating the owner's income from the rental pool into which all rental income is placed. Running costs, a levy fee and days of usage by the owner are subtracted from the owner's quota, and then his or her income is paid.

If the hotel is situated inland, it will be marketed to businesspeople and tourists. It is easier to use tourism to market a hotel at the coast (or in the Kruger National Park), especially if there are facilities for business seminars, and business accommodation as well. You should not rely on the hotel to help pay your mortgage bond, but should rather regard this as a lifestyle investment. Make such an investment in order to realise capital growth in the long term (if you are investing in an upmarket area), and because you feel you owe it to yourself (for many years of hard work).

Investors are usually expected to buy their rooms or units in the name of a close corporation or company. Investors are under the impression that they can write off the mortgage bond interest against their own income. Unfortunately, this is not the case if the property is not registered in the investor's own name. As a result, the hotel will usually not provide enough income to write off any interest against the corporation's or company's tax. Even worse, the property may become so expensive that it cannot really be called an investment – after all, an investment must at some stage render a positive after-tax return.

9.4.16 Group housing schemes

A group housing scheme is not, as with a sectional title or time-share scheme, regulated by specific legislation. Consequently, we can define it as a housing development that is not a sectional title or share-block development. It is of the greatest importance that the deed of sale for a unit in such a scheme be drawn up very carefully, in order to ensure that the buyer keeps to the scheme's rules and that the requirements of the home-owners' association are met.

If the land on which a group housing scheme is developed can be subdivided, each house will be on its own stand. The owner of the house is also the owner of the stand, and is responsible for paying rates and taxes, water, electricity and insurance. If subdivision is possible, all the normal rules for home ownership apply.

If the land on which the group housing scheme is to be developed cannot be subdivided, the following pertains: the owners become co-owners of the land and all improvements, and are jointly responsible for paying rates and taxes, water, electricity and insurance.

The owner (or co-owner) of each house in a scheme belongs to a home-owners' association.

Furthermore, all owners and co-owners sign an agreement on the usage of open areas and communal facilities. A levy is paid to the association if the scheme includes communal or open areas.

9.4.17 Student flats

It is possible to invest in student flats, which differ from ordinary flats. The first examples of this type of investment were erected near the University of Pretoria and the University of Stellenbosch. The student flats are rented out to students during the semester, and to holiday-makers during university holidays. They should prove very popular amongst students who prefer to share these three- and four-bedroom flats with other students rather than living in a residence. The income is placed in a rental pool, which is used to pay all running costs. The owners must pay the mortgage, but the rental income can be used to help pay the bond instalments (Van Tonder 2000:1).

9.4.18 Golf estates

Why have golf estates become so popular and expensive? The answer is quite simple. People are seeking protection from the high levels of crime in South Africa. Currently, the most profitable investment in the country is in the more expensive golf estates, especially if you have a package you can invest. You may also buy in one of the cheaper estates, either to live there yourself (and sell later), to sell the plot later or to develop the plot and then sell it. Do the necessary homework before making the investment. You will notice that where owners live on the estate themselves, the prices will be higher.

9.4.19 Property unit trusts (PUTS)

Just as you can invest in unit trusts, you can also invest in property unit trusts (PUTS). As the name indicates, the underlying assets in this type of investment are fixed property. PUTS give investors the opportunity of investing in property without managing it themselves. PUTS are closed unit trusts, which means that units are issued immediately when the trust is established. The controlling company decides when to issue new units. The number of units issued usually remains the same over a long period.

In this regard, they differ from unit trusts, which are open trusts. Units are issued as the demand for them arises on the market. New units are issued continuously, and issued units are bought back according to demand. In the case of PUTS, units have to be bought back from existing investors, if they wish to sell. You should buy PUTS through a stockbroker with knowledge of the market.

PUTS invest in gilt-edged commercial, industrial, retail and residential property. An investment in PUTS ensures capital growth over the long term, which beats the inflation rate. Rental income rises annually, as well as the value of the property invested in.

Advantages of an investment in PUTS are the following:
- a small amount of money may be invested;
- the investor's risk is spread;
- investment management and expertise are obtained at relatively low charges; and
- there is no property administration to worry about.

9.4.20 Property loan stock (PLS)

Property loan stock (PLS) is quoted on the Johannesburg Securities Exchange (JSE). It is controlled by a trust deed, and trustees are appointed to handle claims by shareholders. PLS companies obtain financing by issuing shares and debentures. A property management company manages the property in which PLS companies invest. Diagram 9.2 illustrates the functioning of a PLS company.

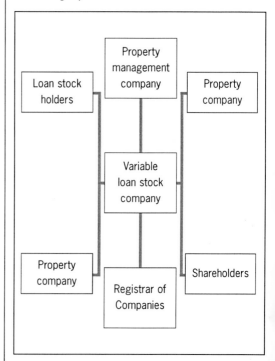

DIAGRAM 9.2 **The functioning of a PLS company**

PLS companies are flexible because they can invest in new properties quite rapidly by issuing shares and debentures. The value of a particular PLS company is shown in the newspapers. Units (shares in the PLS company) can be bought and sold on the JSE.

You should not overestimate the growth in the value of either PUTS or PLS companies. Property income grows slowly, and the value of PUTS and PLS companies will mainly be determined by rental income. As with other types of fixed property, future earnings determine the value of these investments. In the case of PLS companies, it is not just the location of particular property (office, retail, industrial), but also a matter of reliable tenants who will renew their leases. Furthermore, investors have a real choice between high- and low-risk PLS companies (Fife 2001:21).

9.4.21 Flats

Apart from living in a flat yourself, you can invest in a flat with the intention of renting it. In general, a flat is cheaper than a townhouse, especially if it is located close to the city centre. Mainly low-income groups will invest in a single flat in the city centre, in order to earn an income that will help to pay the mortgage bond, levy and short-term insurance premium.

An investor with good tenants (who pay regularly) will be able to build up an estate in this way. Still, you must remember that although the flat may be sold at a later stage:
- there is unlikely to be much capital growth in a flat;
- the Rent Control Act may apply in certain cases, or be made applicable later; and
- the value and future selling potential will largely be determined by neighbours and inner-city decay.

Flats are a better investment in rural areas, mainly because:
- Rural towns are generally retirement towns with thousands of retirees who no longer want to maintain a farm or town plot.
- Retired persons do have a culture of paying and looking after someone else's flat as if it were their own.
- There is peace and quiet at a distance from city life.
- Retirement packages that may not be worth much in city terms may be worth much more in rural areas with a cheaper lifestyle, compared with urban areas (especially, low rentals – a two-bedroom flat in a rural area will cost between R400 and R800 per month, while it will cost between R1 500 and R3 000 per month in the city).

- City rentals are constantly rising, while it is merely adjusted for inflation in rural areas; this is bad for investors, but it is easier to get and keep tenants.

A flat in an upmarket area is always a better investment. Not only will it attract better tenants, but it will also ensure long term capital growth. Flats interspersed with houses are also a better investment than those massed together in a city centre. However, rather try a town house as an investment, for the same reason.

9.4.22 Town houses

The same arguments used in the case of flats relate to town houses. Town houses in cities or near the sea may offer wonderful capital growth (and income), particularly if they are situated in a security area or golf development, with or without a view of the sea. At this stage, you are already aware of the cost aspects, valuation, financing and investments that pertain to a flat as much as to a town house. It is important to buy a town house at a price that will be in line with future rent; that is, the mortgage bond instalments must be in line with the rental income obtained. If town houses are not situated in a security area, golf estate or near the sea, they should be situated amidst as many residences as possible. The marketability and capital growth is always higher in such a case than where town houses are grouped together in their thousands.

9.4.23 Offshore property

See Chapter 10 on offshore investments.

9.5 PROPERTY FINANCING

You cannot invest in property without the necessary financing. This financing may consist of your own or borrowed funds. Never use only your own money to invest in rental property, because that means losing all the tax benefits of rental deductions from bond instalments or on a loan. If you make use of borrowed money for the investment, it is called leverage. Leverage means that you use borrowed money to increase the after-tax return on your own money.

9.5.1 Sources and forms of financing

Depending on the specific fixed property being discussed for investment purposes, you may use various sources and forms of financing. Sources include banks, insurance companies, pension funds, other investors (natural persons) and developers and retailers.

Financing involves, amongst others, some form of collateral (loan security) for the supplier of the funds, bridging finance or long-term financing, which could take various forms. We will discuss each of these briefly.

Collateral (security for the loan)

As when buying a dwelling (house, town house, flat), the supplier of funds will expect security in the form of collateral if 100% financing (with the aid of bonds and loans) cannot be obtained. Also, the value of the property will have to exceed the purchase price (or financing amount). The supplier of funds will also judge the creditworthiness of the leverage buyer and decide on further collateral, especially if there seems to be doubt about repayment of the entire financing. A collateral bond may also be used (see the discussion below on long-term financing).

Bridging finance

If somebody invests in a property development, for example, bridging finance is often required until the long-term loan or bond has been registered and starts to deliver funds. Bridging finance may take the form of an overdraft or term loan, and these are also available at banks.

Long-term finance

Long-term finance may be in the form of one of the following.

A term loan

This is money borrowed for a fixed term, for example ten years.

A bank overdraft

Although this type of debt is repayable annually, it can be used for long-term financing.

A mortgage

You are already familiar with the concept of a mortgage and its functioning. This may be a first or second bond.

A collateral bond

A collateral bond is an auxiliary bond to the primary bond, which is registered by a mortgagor in favour of the same mortgagee as security for debt already paid. The following is an illustration of a collateral bond: assume that a person wishes to purchase a house for R80 000. He or she may register a first bond of R60 000 over the house at a bank. He or she has R10 000 in cash and, therefore, needs a further R10 000, which can be obtained by registering a collateral bond over an erf he or she owns, for example (Delport 1987:73; Jones 1985:473; Kling 1983:41).

A debenture bond

Listed public companies use debentures as a form of long-term financing. A natural person may also issue a debenture. Celliers & Benadé (1982:143) describe a debenture as a certificate issued by a natural or legal person as an acknowledgement of indebtedness of a specified amount. The certificate also indicates the interest rate, date on which payment (capital plus interest) must commence and the instalment conditions. A debenture may be single, in other words, it may be issued to a single person, but it may also be a portion of a series of debentures issued to several holders.

Celliers & Benadé (1982:144) indicate that a bond over immovable property as security for a debenture or several debentures occurs by registering a debenture bond. A house may serve as security for a debenture or several debentures through the registration of a debenture bond. Kroncke (1978:298) points out that all debentures have equal preference in respect of a natural or a legal person's assets in the event of liquidation.

A debenture bond is registered in favour of a trustee for all the debenture holders. Such mortgage deeds are registered in cases where a specific security (immovable property) is presented for the debt. If the enterprise (company) or person fails to comply with the conditions of the mortgage deed, the trustee may act on behalf of the debenture holders (mortgagees) and sell the insured assets, after which the proceeds may be used to pay the debenture holders. Van Jaarsveld (1983:609) mentions that if the proceeds are less than the outstanding loan amount, the debenture holders become general creditors of the enterprise (company).

A participation bond

Such bonds are a source of finance for office blocks, shopping centres, blocks of flats and industrial properties. Maritz (1983:327) defines a participation bond as a first bond registered over immovable property in favour of a designated natural or legal person.

In a participation bond scheme, several participating lenders invest cash amounts in an investment company, which in turn lends the collective amount against the security of a mortgage bond, in favour of the investment company. Although the bond is registered in the name of the nominated company, the participants to the bond have the same rights as though they are the registered mortgagees (Falkena et al. 1984:151).

The nominated company's sole aim is the keeping of participation bonds in trust as the nominee for, or the representative of, the participants to each specific bond registered in its name. In the event of insolvency of the nominated company, the participation bond will not form part of the insolvent estate. This means that participants cannot suffer any losses.

Investors in participation bonds are usually pension funds, charity organisations and persons whose after-tax incomes from participation bonds are higher than could be realised elsewhere. The attractive feature of participation bonds is the fact that the scheme manager (of the nominated company) makes a conservative estimate of the value of the immovable property and then lends only two thirds of the value of the bond (Falkena *et al.* 1984:152).

According to the Participation Bonds Act 55 of 1981, participants must invest their funds for a minimum period of five years. At the end of this period, the capital remains invested, but may be withdrawn at three months' notice, provided that the scheme manager can transfer the investment to another investor or take up the investment personally. Estate agents must inform buyers and sellers who wish to enter into such a transaction about the possible withdrawal of funds and the period for which funds must remain invested, if a party is relying on the use of such funds.

After the expiry of the five-year period, capital is normally redeemed over a 20-year period in annual or half-yearly instalments. Redemption requirements vary among participation schemes.

A covering bond

Covering bonds are dealt with in Chapter 8, but they may be used to finance properties other than houses.

A special mortgage bond

An immovable, incorporeal object, such as a registered long-term lease, may be mortgaged by a special bond (Van Jaarsveld 1983:216). Consequently, potential buyers may, with a special bond, mortgage a lease attached to a property that they are leasing in order to purchase a property.

A building loan

A building loan entails the granting and registration of a mortgage bond, where debts are incurred over the period that it takes to erect the building. A bank undertakes to pay as the work progresses. Interest is collected on a daily basis on the mortgage amount and capitalised monthly. The mortgagor (or buyer) of the plot (on which the building is to be erected) must make provision for this interest plus inspection fees against the total amount of the loan, or else

he or she must pay in cash. This interest is called interim interest (Maritz 1983:333–349; Technikon RSA 1986:132).

A building contractor has the right (at common law) to retain the keys of a building until he or she has been paid the full contract price. This right is called the right of retention or builder's lien. Banks require that the builder waives his or her right of retention in writing, since it takes priority over the bond registered by the bank (Caney 1975:383; Delport 1987:78).

9.5.2 Purchase and leaseback of property

People who are considering an investment can buy an existing property from its owner and then let it to the owner (seller) to run his or her business from. The previous owner becomes the lessee of the building. He or she receives a capital amount for the sale and, in turn, pays rent to the new owner (the lessor). The sale of the building enables the previous owner to obtain operating capital, for example.

The agreement concluded between the buyer (investor) and the seller (lessee), is called a leaseback agreement. Maritz (1983:341) describes a leaseback agreement as 'the transfer of property rights to a buyer-investor with simultaneous leaseback of the property to the seller-leaseholder for a specified time at an agreed rental'. He states that the rental is usually known as net receipts for the investor (buyer-investor). The reason for this is that the leaseholder (seller-leaseholder) is responsible for the payment of all expenses such as property tax, insurance, operating costs and maintenance.

Advantages for the seller-leaseholder
- Operating capital is increased, because the purchase sum (net) can be employed to purchase stock, for example.
- The rental may be indicated as an expenditure for tax purposes.
- The problems of ownership are carried over to the buyer-investor.
- The purchase sum may be employed in such a manner that a maximum return is obtained.

Advantages for the buyer-investor
- A building is acquired, allowing him or her to achieve capital growth over the long term.
- At the end of the lease period, the property remains in the hands of the buyer-investor.
- The investment does not require as many management requirements as the purchase of an existing business, for example.

- The risk is particularly low in comparison with, for example, the share market.

A prospective investor should, therefore, consider a purchase and leaseback agreement as an investment option. The building may not always be exactly what the investor is looking for, but he or she invests for the sake of the rental income. Laurie (1990:134) emphasises that it is important that the buyer-investor should check the creditworthiness of the leaseholder (seller-leaseholder). He or she must also look into the possibility of letting the building to someone else in the event of the seller-leaseholder becoming insolvent.

9.6 DIFFERENT WAYS TO OWN PROPERTY

You may own property in various ways, amongst others as sole owner (in full), as sole owner (partly) or with other people or co-owners (who have invested in it jointly). From the discussion so far you have become familiar with the concepts of sectional title, share block, syndications, companies and trusts. These are ways of owning property on your own or together with others.

Ownership is the greatest right that a person can have over a property. An interest in immovable property is a lesser right than ownership. An interest in immovable property limits the ownership of such property and has certain implications as far as the value and utilisation of the property are concerned. Consequently, before purchasing or selling an immovable property, it is essential that you ascertain whether someone has a specific interest in such property.

Normally, you can determine who the registered owner of immovable property is by inspecting the title deeds of the property in the Deeds Office. In the following cases, someone other than the registered owner (according to the title deeds) may be the owner or co-owner of the property: as a result of prescription (note the 30-year requirement), expropriation, statutory vesting (the state acquires ownership without registration), a marriage in community of property or where the system of accrual has been included, the insolvency of the registered owner, the death of the owner or the deregistration of a company and abandonment (e.g. the owner dies without leaving an heir or disappears).

Joint ownership comes into being once an immovable property is registered in the names of two or more persons. Each joint owner has a specific share (percentage interest) in the property. Specific rights and obligations exist among joint owners (as well as regards their negotiations with third parties). Like ownership, joint ownership can be terminated. In addition to common law provisions governing the rights and obligations of joint owners, joint owners can contractually agree on actions concerning their property. Joint ownership does, however, have specific implications for the future sale or marketing of the undivided shares, that is, for the joint owner (seller) or buyer. Ensure that you have a thorough understanding of both the advantages and disadvantages of joint ownership for joint owners.

Remember that total or full ownership consists of the following:
bare dominium + usufruct = total/full ownership (dominium)

You must decide for yourself what type of ownership you require, just as you need to decide about buying property in your own name, or in the name of a close corporation or a trust. In order to make these decisions, you need to evaluate the property you have decided on in terms of your:
- specific matrimonial property regime;
- various investment criteria;
- investment goals;
- income tax goals;
- estate planning goals; and
- retirement planning goals.

9.7 PROPERTY CONTRACTS

When immovable property is disposed of, use is made of property contracts. The same applies in the case of the leasing of immovable property. Such contracts must be valid and must be concluded by parties (themselves or on behalf of an institution) who have contractual capacity. Depending on the type of contract and the situation concerned, different conditions will be included in such property contracts. The matter or property contracts will now be discussed on the basis of the following questions.
- What general principles apply to property contracts?
- What is meant by 'the purchase and sale of immovable property'?
- What is meant by 'the sale of land in instalments'?
- What aspects should be dealt with in a contract of lease?

9.7.1 General principles

A contract comes into being as soon as two or more parties conclude an agreement. In the case of alienation of immovable property, the contract must be in writing. In order to be valid, a contract must comply with certain general requirements:

- The parties must have contractual capacity.
- There must be a meeting of the minds, or consensus, between the parties.
- The contract must be lawful.
- Performance in terms of the contract must be possible at the time of conclusion of the contract.
- The prescribed formalities must be complied with.

Make sure that you understand what is meant by each of the above five requirements. Refer to Chapter 8 in this regard.

Both natural and legal persons can be parties to a contract. In addition, there is no limit to the number of persons who may be parties to a contract of purchase and sale or to a contract of lease. Make sure that you understand how a partnership (the partners), a close corporation or company (that is currently in existence or that must still be established) and a trust (the trustees, on behalf of a trust that already exists) can be a party to a contract of purchase and sale or to a contract of lease. Property can, however, be purchased on behalf of a trust that still has to be established if the agreement is drawn up to the benefit of a third party (*stipulatio alteri*) or as an ordinary nominate transaction ('x or his/her nominee').

In many cases, suspensive and resolutive conditions are prerequisites for the coming into being of a contract. An example of a suspensive condition is where a buyer states that his or her offer is subject to the grant to him or her of a mortgage loan by a bank within a period of, say, six weeks. In terms of a resolutive condition, an offer to purchase would lapse if, for example, a road were to be built through a residential area within three months. Should the mortgage loan be granted a contract comes into being, but if the road is built, the offer to purchase lapses and consequently so does the contract.

An option may be described as an offer to purchase (or to sell or lease) property that includes an undertaking not to withdraw the offer within a specific period (i.e. from the point of view of the person granting the option). As soon as the person to whom the option has been granted (the addressee) accepts the option, a contract is concluded. Both the option and the acceptance thereof must be in writing. You must know when it is advisable to obtain an option in respect of immovable property.

A right of first refusal, or a pre-emptive right, gives the holder the right to purchase a specific property in the future should the owner thereof wish to sell the property. In contrast to an option, the owner thereof does not have to sell the property. However, the owner must give the holder of the right preference should he or she (the owner) wish to sell the property concerned. In the case of an option, the person granting the option (the owner) is obliged to sell the property should the holder of the option exercise (accept) the option.

Standard-form contracts relating to immovable property can be obtained from the Estate Agency Affairs Board as well as the Institute of Realtors.

9.7.2 The purchase and sale of immovable property

You must note that the general principles of the law of contract are also applicable to a contract for the purchase and sale of immovable property. Just as ownership does not necessarily always vest in the registered owner, so the seller does not have to be the owner of the thing being bought or sold.

If you are wondering what is and is not included in the purchase of immovable property, refresh your memory by reconsidering the definition of immovable property. In particular, note permanent improvements, permanent fixtures, and all movable assets that permanently serve the immovable property.

Frequently, a contract of purchase and sale is concluded between family members for the purpose of estate planning. In many cases of this nature, the purchase price is set unreasonably low in order to save on transfer duty and conveyancing fees. However, the law regards such a transaction as one that is not concluded in good faith, and will ensure that the necessary costs are paid.

A seller can be held liable for defects in the property that is sold if:

- A written guarantee has been given to the effect that no defects exist.
- A misrepresentation has been made regarding the condition of the property.
- There are hidden (latent or dormant) defects in the property of which the seller is aware.

The seller is, however, not liable for patent (visible) defects in the property. It is also important that you know when the risk attaching to the object being sold passes from the seller to the buyer. Especially note the influence of suspensive and resolutive conditions on the passing of risk.

A *voetstoots* clause in a contract of purchase and sale excludes a seller's liability for hidden (latent or dormant) defects, but not his or her liability for misrepresentation (concerning, for instance, defects of which he or she was aware).

Remember that estate agent's commission is payable where the actions of the agent (on the basis of a mandate) result in the conclusion of a contract of purchase and sale (or a contract of lease or the sale of land in instalments). Normally, the seller pays the commission (unless the agent has a mandate from the buyer), but the parties can agree otherwise.

Immovable property can also be sold by auction (voluntary or in execution in terms of a court order). If the auction is subject to a reserve, the auctioneer is not obliged to accept any offer that is lower than the reserve or minimum price. In the case of an auction without reserve, the property is sold to the highest bidder. With an auction subject to confirmation, the seller can accept a higher bid during the period of confirmation. In such a case, the person making the previous highest offer is afforded the opportunity of buying the property at this new bid price.

A company can purchase property through a person who has the necessary written mandate to contract on behalf of the company. Company property may only be sold after the necessary approval has been obtained for such sale at the annual general meeting. The sale of shares in a private company is governed by the company's articles of association.

Written permission representing 75% of the members' interests in a close corporation is required for the purchase or sale of immovable property. A person who has a written mandate from a close corporation can purchase land, a share block or a time-share interest. Members' interests may be sold only to a member, to the close corporation itself or to another person who qualifies to become a member. Only natural persons and testamentary trusts may be members of a close corporation.

9.7.3 The sale of land in instalments

The sale of land on instalments is governed by the Alienation of Land Act 65 of 1981. In terms of a transaction for the sale of land in instalments, the purchase price of the land is payable in more than two instalments over a period longer than a year. Land that is destined to be used mainly for residential purposes may be sold by way of an instalment transaction.

It is especially important that you know that the parties to a sale of land in instalments may also be known as a remote party and an intermediary. Always make sure if this is in fact the case.

9.7.4 The leasing of immovable property

A contract of lease is a contract for the letting and hiring of immovable property. A lessor and lessee may conclude a contract of lease by agreeing only on the thing to be leased and on the payment of rental. It is, however, advisable to refer in a contract of lease to the date of occupation, the duration of the contract and the place of payment of rental. In this way, misunderstandings can be avoided.

A contract of lease for longer than ten years should be registered against the title deed of the property concerned. The advantage of registration is that it ensures that the contract of lease will be binding on the lessor's successor in title. Successors in title are not always aware of long leases. A lessor and a lessee have numerous rights and obligations that, if not included in the contract, will be regulated by the common law.

Certain immovable property that is leased is subject to rent control. The primary purpose of rent control is to provide the poor with accommodation by ensuring that the rental in respect of a property is fixed by a rent board. In addition, lessees are protected in large measure against eviction from their dwelling places. Where immovable property is sold, the rights of all lessees (not only those in rent controlled premises) enjoy preference over the rights of the new owner; hence the expression, *huur gaat voor koop*.

The importance of contracts of lease for the property market can never be overemphasised. Both lessees and lessors must ensure that their rights (over and above those provided under the common law) are protected in contracts of lease. Likewise, they must familiarise themselves with their obligations.

9.8 GOVERNMENT CONTROL OVER PROPERTY

The government exercises control over immovable property. When a specific property is analysed for the purpose of purchasing, leasing or valuing it, such government control can have either a positive or a negative influence on the value of the property. Consequently, it is extremely important to note both the nature and degree of government control over immovable property. Such control will be discussed on the basis of the following question: In what ways does the government exercise control over the real estate industry?

Government control over immovable property is exercised mainly in the following three ways:
- government control measures;
- taxation; and
- expropriation.

Consult a legal expert well versed in leases to help you with drawing up and/or interpreting leases.

For the purpose of our discussion on government control measures, it is especially important that you have some knowledge of town planning schemes. The object of these schemes is to bring about co-ordinated and harmonious development in order to promote the general welfare (health, safety, order and convenience) of the community. In addition, the aim is to promote the attractiveness of the environment in the most effective and economic way.

A town planning scheme is a legal document which comprises the following:
• provisions in the clauses of the scheme;
• the identification of the land to which the scheme applies; and
• scheme maps, appendices or schedules in respect of the latter.

The clauses of a scheme deal with, among other things, the following: the use of the land, drainage, the dumping of waste products and refuse, streets, zoning, erf sizes, regulation of the construction of buildings, control over advertisements, the planning of developed or undeveloped areas and control over the development of land containing dolomite, clay or subsiding soil.

The identification of land and buildings refers to the following:
• the purposes for which land may be used or buildings may be constructed (e.g. a dwelling unit);
• where construction of a building may be undertaken only with the permission of the local authority concerned (e.g. the building of a church or school); and
• the purposes for which land may not be used or for which buildings may not be constructed (e.g. any use other than for residential purposes).

Among other things, the maps, appendices or schedules for a scheme comprise:
• a map indicating all matters to which a scheme applies (e.g. the scale, the boundaries and name of township areas, farms, smallholdings and erven, the position and names of streets, roads, squares and open areas, every railway siding, cadastral information, and permissible land uses); and
• appendices or schedules indicating special rights as well as special conditions in respect of specific properties.
(Ghyoot 1996:106)

Information concerning a scheme can be obtained from the relevant local authority. You must know what information is included in such a scheme, as well as what the information means. Also ensure that you have a knowledge of, among other things,

building regulations and the control over township establishment and agricultural and industrial land.

You must make certain that you know how property taxes are calculated on the basis of property value in the various provinces. Property taxes have a considerable influence on the productivity and value of a property. Make sure that you understand this.

Immovable property is often required by the state for use in the public interest. The process by which such property is acquired by the state is termed 'expropriation'. Make sure that you know how the compensation paid by the state is calculated. It is very important to know what influence possible future expropriation may have on the value of a property for potential buyers or lessees.

Consequently, as far as land is concerned, the state determines, among other things, what products may be sold in the industry, what rights may be acquired over such products, how these rights may be transferred, restrictions with regard to certain rights (zoning, subdivision, building within two-year standards, health and safety) and administrative control (inspections, acceptance or rejection of applications, permits, licences, fines and registrations) (Ghyoot 1997).

According to Ghyoot (1997), the influence of the state is far greater than is actually indicated in the preceding discussion and includes the following strategies adopted by the government:
• indirect intervention by way of monetary and fiscal policy;
• intervention via the market mechanism; and
• direct participation for own advantage.

Indirect intervention by way of monetary and fiscal policy encompasses the exertion of a financial influence by the state. In the monetary sphere, the supply and cost of credit (e.g. mortgage interest rates) are controlled, which, among other things, influences the demand for houses, the prices of houses and sales in the residential property market. As far as fiscal policy is concerned, high property taxes may be levied in order to discourage development. The converse is also possible. In addition, subsidies or low-cost loans may be permitted with a view to achieving specific government objectives.

Intervention via the market mechanism may occur in the following ways: by manipulating demand and supply (e.g. by making state land available or by facilitating subdivision), zoning (e.g. for public use), rent control, by freezing development (until such time as the state decides to purchase or use the property concerned), by confiscating property (e.g. where it is used illegally, say, to manufacture drugs) and by means of land restitution (e.g. where it is returned to the original inhabitants).

The state also participates directly in the activities of the real estate industry for its own benefit. In order to do this, the state's involvement includes all those activities normally performed by estate agents, property valuers, property investors and property developers in the private sector.

9.9 THE ADMINISTRATION OF PROPERTY

Almost any fixed property, even a home, requires a measure of administration. There are aspects such as rates and taxes, water and electricity, telephone accounts, insurance of the building against fire damage, as well as insurance of the contents of the house against possible loss. In the case of rented property, the administrative aspect involves a great deal more.

Owners may let rented property themselves or employ an attorney, an estate agent or a business specialising in letting fixed property. Where the owner has the necessary knowledge and time, he or she would do the letting, which would be much cheaper than using the services of others or another business.

Administrative expenses and aspects involved in the letting of fixed property involve the following:
- collection costs;
- the payment of rates and taxes;
- repairs and maintenance costs;
- finding lessees (tenants);
- drawing up rental contracts;
- the insurance of buildings against fire and storm damage, as well as political unrest;
- insurance against possible interruptions in the running of the business (if a building burns down, it may take six months to repair the damage, during which time there would be no rental income); and
- the risk of not being able to find occupants or tenants.

9.10 SOURCES OF INFORMATION IN THE REAL ESTATE INDUSTRY

Participants in the real estate industry require information concerning immovable property and the property market. Such information can be obtained from specific sources and it is, therefore, important to know what sources exist.

In terms of the code of conduct for estate agents, an agent should convey all relevant information about a property to a prospective buyer or lessee. An estate agent is not expected to climb onto the roof or to make specific excavations, but he or she is expected to acquaint him- or herself with those facts that can be ascertained fairly easily and to convey these facts to prospective buyers or lessees.

This topic will, therefore, be discussed on the basis of the following question: What information does a market participant require, and where does he or she obtain such information?

Prospective buyers and lessees require information concerning the following (Estate Agents Board 1993:70):
- the residential area;
- the erf (without improvements);
- improvements to the erf (dwelling, duplex); and
- financial aspects concerning the property.

Important information concerning a specific area includes:
- the convenience network of the residential area (distance to schools, shopping centres, hospitals, medical services, churches and the midpoint of a town or city);
- exposure network (pollution, noise, flooding);
- the general condition of the residential area (clean, old or new, streets in good condition);
- reputation of the residential area (type of people, criminal activities);
- recreational facilities (parks, tennis courts, golf courses); and
- zoning and future developments (shopping centres, schools).

An agent can obtain information regarding a residential area in the following ways: by personally inspecting the area, by interviewing residents, through local newspapers and from the local authority.

An undeveloped erf considerably limits the potential uses to which it can be put by a buyer who wishes to develop such an erf. Limited real rights (e.g. a servitude), specific building regulations, the type of land, and the shape, slope and size of the erf are examples of the type of information that an agent must gather concerning a property. Such information may be acquired by visiting the erf, by consulting local authorities and by obtaining a copy of the title deed in respect of the property.

The following information should be gathered concerning improvements: type of building material, slope of the roof, age of the improvements, the layout of the improvements, floor area of all improvements, apartments attached to, for example, a dwelling, the kitchen area of a dwelling, security aspects, movable property that is not included in the improvements, garden layout, appearance, general condition of improvements and possibilities for further improvement. The property may be inspected physically in order to obtain the aforementioned information.

Information concerning financial aspects includes information on the selling price, the market value of the property, the municipal value, the possible replacement value (insurance value), the last selling price, the mortgage amount involved and the name of the mortgagee, and the rates and taxes (or levy) payable.

Note, however, that information sources embrace far more than merely the data that can be gathered by means of a physical inspection of the residential area, and of the land and improvements. A lack of local, available information on property is one of the biggest problems faced by the South African real estate industry. It is, therefore, important that you know about the numerous sources of secondary data that are at your disposal. By 'secondary data' we mean data that has already been gathered by some person or organisation and which is hopefully available somewhere for your use. Also note that the accuracy of secondary data must be determined, and that such data has a limited useful lifespan owning to the dynamic nature of the property market.

We shall now consider briefly the following secondary sources of data encountered in the South African real estate industry:

- internal and informal sources;
- statutory and professional bodies;
- collective sales networks;
- syndicated property research services;
- state sources;
- private surveying and mapping companies;
- research and tertiary institutions;
- commercial marketing research firms; and
- other sources.

Internal and informal sources of data include the following: internal records concerning clients, their preferences, type of property, market areas and income levels, sales figures, budgets, correspondence, reports and service records pertaining to a property.

Statutory and professional bodies in the real estate industry have already been discussed in the overview of the real estate industry.

Collective sales networks provide secondary data concerning property sales and the leasing of property in particular. Examples of such networks are Multi Listing Services (MLS) and Comprehensive Property Services (CPS).

Syndicated property research services are provided by firms that conduct surveys on the various sectors in the property market. In South Africa, Rode & Associates provides such a service by way of, among other things, the *Rode's Report*. In addition, the BMI Building Research Strategy Consulting Group conducts research for the construction industry.

State data sources, such as central, regional and local authorities as well as semi-state data sources, contain valuable records pertaining to the real estate industry. In most cases, the public may inspect these records, often for a small fee. The Offices of the Surveyor-General provide cadastral records for the purposes of land surveying and registration.

Maps and aerial photographs are available to the public from the Offices of the Director: Mapping, and from the Government Printer in Pretoria. Cadastral maps indicate, among other things, the following aspects concerning a property: beacons, boundaries, servitudes, co-ordinates and physical and institutional particulars. Particulars on properties, and of the persons or institutions having acquired real rights in immovable property, may be obtained from the various Deeds Offices. However, a person wishing to obtain such particulars must know the full name of the owner, his or her identity number or date of birth, or the description of the property (name of farm, or number of smallholding or erf).

The Central Statistical Service (CSS) provides official statistics for the Republic of South Africa. In addition to conducting a population census every five years, the CSS also provides statistics covering a wide field. Data on rental properties, property development and property developers are provided either in printed form or on magnetic tape.

Local and regional authorities provide, for example, guide and structure plans, town planning schemes (maps and clauses), general town plans, individual building plans and valuation rolls.

Private firms and mapping companies have offices in most of the large cities and provide numerous types of aerial photographs and maps. Examples of such firms or companies are AOC Holdings and Map Studios.

The Human Sciences Research Council (HSRC) and the Council for Scientific and Industrial Research (CSIR) also possess data on aspects of the real estate industry.

The following institutions at universities also provide relevant data: The Bureau for Economic Research at the University of Stellenbosch, The Institute for Planning Research (IPR) at the University of Port Elizabeth, The Bureau for Financial Analysis at the University of Pretoria and The Bureau of Market Research at the University of South Africa.

Commercial research firms possess data that can be of use to the real estate industry.

Other sources of secondary data include large real estate agencies, developers and investors. These sources often have specific and relevant publications at their disposal.

9.11 SUMMARY

Investment in fixed property constitutes a process called the investment process. During this process, the potential investor must be aware of aspects such as: his or her needs, objectives and resources, the availability of his or her own and borrowed funds, the physical nature of the property, the utility value or productivity of the property, the investment value of the property and the market, economic and other factors that may affect the value of the property. Once all these factors have been investigated, the investment decision can be made.

Several kinds of investment (investment options) are open to an investor: building, buying or renting a home, holiday homes, sectional title schemes, share-block schemes, time-share schemes, rented houses, purchase and leaseback of property, syndicates and the development of property. Further, the investor should be aware of the management and administrative aspects involved in an investment in fixed property.

9.12 SELF-ASSESSMENT

- Briefly discuss the steps you would follow regarding an investment in fixed property.
- Briefly discuss the functioning of 20 different types of fixed property.
- Explain ways to finance fixed property.
- Briefly explain different ways to own property.
- Explain the functioning and key aspects of property contracts.
- Motivate the importance of a well-organised property administration system.

BIBLIOGRAPHY

Brigham, E.F. & Gapenski, L.C. 1990. *Intermediate financial management.* 3rd edn. London: Dryden.

Caney, L.R. 1975. Mortgage and pledge. In Freemantle, M.P. (ed.) *The South African encyclopaedia of forms and precedents.* Vol. 12. Durban: Butterworths. pp. 273–471.

Celliers, H.S. & Benadé, M.L. 1982. *Maatskappyreg.* 4th edn. Durban: Butterworths.

Cloete, C.E. 1993. *Eiendomsbemarking 11: Nasionale Eiendomsopleidingskommittee, studiegids 3.* 1st edn. Florida: Technikon SA.

Cloete, C.E. 1994. *Eiendomsbemarking 11: Nasionale Eiendomsopleidingskommittee, studiegids 2.* 1st edn. Florida: Technikon SA.

Cloete, C.E. 1994. *Property education series: Property finance,* Vol. 1. 1st edn. Florida: Technikon SA.

Cloete, C.E. 1994. *Property education series: Property Finance,* Vol. 2. 1st edn. Florida: Technikon SA.

Delport, H.J. 1987. *Die Suid-Afrikaanse eiendomspraktyk en die reg.* Cape Town: Juta.

Estate Agents Board. 1993. *An introduction to the fundamental principles of estate agency.* Johannesburg: Estate Agents Board.

Falkena, H.B., Fourie, L.J. & Kok, W.J. (eds). 1984. *The mechanics of the South African financial system.* 2nd edn. Johannesburg: Macmillan.

Fife, I. 2001. Listed property: Real choice. *Financial Mail:* 88, col. 1–3, Sept. 21.

Ghyoot, V.G. 1996. *Property education series: Property marketing research.* Revised edition. Florida: Technikon SA.

Ghyoot, V.G. 1997. *Public sector policy in the property industry.* Unpublished manuscript.

Gitman, L.J. 1988. *Principles of managerial finance.* 5th edn. New York: Harper Collins.

Gitman, L.J. 1991. *Principles of managerial finance.* 6th edn. New York: Harper Collins.

Jones, R.J.M. 1985. *Conveyancing in South Africa.* 3rd edn. Cape Town: Juta.

Kling, G. 1983. *Buying, building and altering a home in South Africa.* Cape Town: Struik.

Kroncke, C.O. 1978. *Managerial finance: Essentials.* 2nd edn. New York: West.

Laurie, H. de G. 1990. *Sukses met beleggings.* 1st edn. Pretoria: Van Schaik.

Maritz, N.G. 1983. *Die studiegids vir eiendomsagente: Grondbeginsels van eiendomswese.* 3rd edn. Cape Town: Juta.

South Africa (Republic). 1971. Acts of the Republic of South Africa – Land (Act 66 of 1971). Pretoria: Government Printer. (Sectional Titles Act).

South Africa (Republic). 1973. Acts of the Republic of South Africa – Comapnies (Act 61 of 1973). Pretoria: Government Printer. (Companies Act).

South Africa (Republic). 1980. Acts of the Republic of South Africa – Land (Act 59 of 1980). Pretoria: Government Printer. (Share Blocks Control Act).

Swart, N.J. 1998. *Real estate.* Only study guide for MNS202-T. Pretoria: University of South Africa.

Swart, N.J. 1999. *Personal financial management.* Only study guide for MNF303-8. Pretoria: University of South Africa.

Van Jaarsveld, S.R. 1983. *Suid-Afrikaanse handelsreg.* 2nd edn. Cape Town: Lex Patria.

Van Tonder, J. 2000. Studentewoonstelle kan belegging vir ouers wees. *Geld – Rapport:* col. 1–4, April 16.

OFFSHORE INVESTMENTS

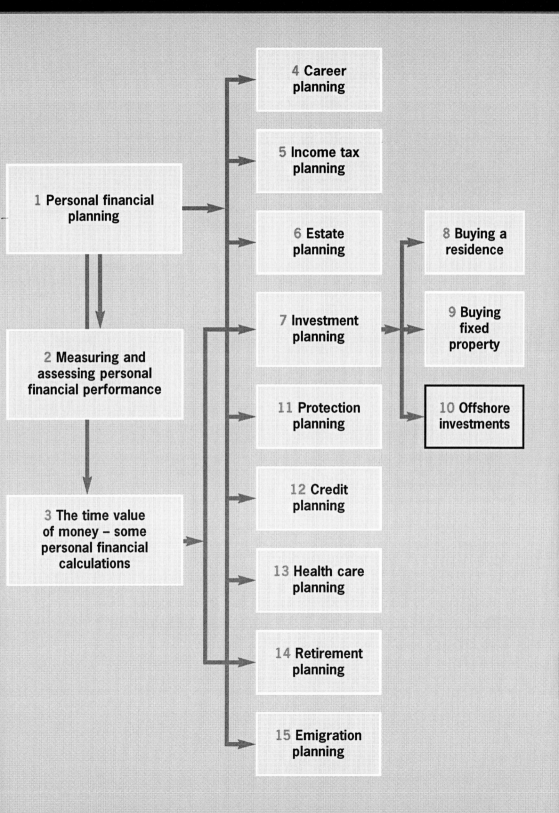

10.1 LEARNING OUTCOMES

After studying this chapter, you will be able to:

- Explain the motivation for offshore investments.
- Identify the research required before investing in foreign countries.
- Explain the different types of offshore investment.
- Illustrate the relationship between offshore investments and your estate.

10.2 INTRODUCTION

'Offshore investments' are currently buzzwords in the South African financial world, particularly in the media. Whether you are young, old, poor, rich, have your own business, are a farmer or are unemployed, you want to know more about offshore investments. If you have a retirement package to invest, you will obviously consider this type of investment. However, if your package is just big enough (or not even big enough) to survive on, you should rather not make any risky investments (locally or internationally). Offshore investments are not necessarily risky, but they are clouded in a lot of uncertainty and confusion that will remain with us for many years.

There is not a great deal of transparency about offshore investments and sometimes we even have difficulty locating the country where we want to invest on a world map. Brokers find it just as difficult. When making offshore investments, your peace of mind will depend on whether you have acquired the necessary information and knowledge.

South Africans have been torn from their relaxed public service background with its prospects of a peaceful retirement. Suddenly, we are living in an information environment. We are informed about offshore investments, wills, trusts, tax havens, income tax systems, donations tax and estate duty. To add to our confusion, all these differ in one way or another (or even totally) in various countries.

Suddenly, the whole world's investment products are being sold on our doorsteps or inside our homes via the Internet. South Africans can invest and reinvest on other continents within seconds. South African investors are therefore ripped from their comfort zones by the realisation that most of us have all our financial eggs (assets) in one basket (in South Africa). In addition, the value of our currency is constantly dropping against those of developed countries.

We are waking up to the fact that our investment portfolios by no means meet international standards. What about South African investors whose

> Do not rush in where angels fear to tread.

investment portfolios do not even meet South African standards, or who do not even have local portfolios? We have to restructure our investment portfolios to prevent ourselves becoming poorer all the time.

10.2.1 Why do we have exchange control?

The South African government applies exchange control to prevent large amounts of capital from flowing out of the country as a result of factors such as:

- local political shocks;
- a poor economy (markets); and
- changes in legislation (particularly regarding income tax and estate duty).

Exchange control amounts to government control over the buying and selling of foreign currencies. This restricts the free market system. Of course, South African investors also want to be free to invest where they wish to. This would help them to cope with the increasing financial demands the government is making on their assets.

10.2.2 The abolition of exchange control

South Africans may, among others:

- invest R750 000 (2002) per person above the age of 18 years in overseas countries;
- open a South African foreign bank account and use a foreign currency of their choice (e.g. invest in overseas countries);
- open a foreign exchange bank account;
- buy property overseas (including fixed property); and
- invest in various overseas financial assets (e.g. unit trusts and shares).

> Most South Africans do not even know how to invest in South Africa, where they have been living all their lives, let alone overseas.

> We do not have a choice – we must find out more about offshore investments and apply this knowledge.

The Reserve Bank, however, has set a prerequisite, namely that South Africans must pay their taxes before they can invest in foreign countries. (These investments will be discussed later.)

We expect exchange control to be relaxed gradually and ultimately abolished. Only then will foreign countries and foreign investors see that the government has faith in investment opportunities in its own country, and the average South African investor will be able to escape from the 'investment jail'.

Advantages of the abolition of exchange control

If exchange control is abolished, investors will be able to invest in various overseas products, each with its own unique advantages. The risk of limiting our investments to South Africa will increase. By investing in foreign countries we will be able to increase our returns and lower our risks. We will be able to reduce our risks in international terms and apply international diversification.

10.2.3 Why invest offshore?

There are numerous reasons why you should invest offshore. Investors are motivated by a number of factors, but the main reasons are:

- protection against fluctuations of a single currency and market;
- thousands of new investment opportunities;
- the expertise of offshore fund managers who know the foreign markets;
- a balanced portfolio; and
- the possibility of increasing the return of your portfolio on an after-tax basis.

The following groups of investors should invest in the international market:

- all investors – about 10% to 20% of their investments (total belongings) depending on the composition of their asset portfolio;
- wealthier people – up to 50% of their assets;
- those who are considering emigration – as much as possible (set up an offshore trust, make assets liquid, buy an expensive timeshare that may be exchanged later for an overseas timeshare);
- people with children who may later want to emigrate or work in overseas countries and/or who want to send their children (or grandchildren) overseas;
- people whose income is sufficient to live on after they have invested part of their retirement packages offshore; and
- if you think you may live for another 10, 20 or 30 years – your international investment will later be worth a lot in rand terms if you bring it back to South Africa, because the value of the rand will

Remember, the value of the rand is falling but the value of First World currencies is rising – a double blow for South Africans.

continue to drop, compared with the currencies of the strong economies of developed First World countries.

What should we do? Firstly, we should make provision for rand hedging (to protect ourselves against a falling rand) and, secondly, we should diversify our investments internationally. We will now look at these two actions.

Protect yourself against the falling rand

The value of the South African rand is falling and will keep on falling for many years to come. Low productivity and high real wages are placing more and more pressure on our inflation rate. If we add the overseas influences and perceptions about Africa and South Africa to these factors, it is only logical that we should keep a falling rand in mind when we do our financial planning.

Overseas investors find out more about what is happening here every day. The most important realities include increasing violence, lack of law enforcement, corruption, mismanagement, the tax burden on investors, and the influence of the trade unions on the government, not to mention the unrealistic socio-economic expectations of millions of South Africans.

Let us look at a few methods that can be used to protect your money against a falling rand. You will see that one (or more) of these options is within your reach (after your needs and objectives have been taken into account). Your broker or advisor can help you. Note that the risks and terms of an exchange account (that invests in a call account and fixed deposits) are lower than those of an offshore investment in shares. The various rand protectors/offshore investments fall in the Figure 10.1 spectrum as far as risk is concerned.

Other than the two extremes, each investor will have a different perception of the risks of the various types of offshore investment. Unfortunately, you will have to take these risks if you want to protect your rands, whether you like it or not.

The long-term tendency of the value of the rand is downwards, because of negative perceptions of our country and economy internationally (as well as locally).

*Low risk
and return*

	Local/international exchange account (call money, fixed deposits)
	Policies
	Linked unit trust products
	Local unit trusts
	Structured funds
	Guaranteed share schemes
	Offshore property trusts
	Fixed property
	Containers
	Offshore unit trusts
	Offshore share portfolios

*High risk
and return*

FIGURE 10.1 **The spectrum of risks and returns**

International Diversification

International diversification means the following, among others:

- You invest in different countries.
- You invest in different offshore investment products in different industries or sectors.
- Your investments are internationalised.
- Your total investment risk is lowered and the returns on your investments are higher over the long term.
- You protect yourself against a decrease in your real wealth.
- Your international risk is smaller and your international wealth increases.

At this stage, informed South Africans have accepted the fact that offshore investments should form part of their investment portfolios. The collapse of emerging markets in 1998, in particular, contributed towards this realisation. The investment world regards South Africa as an emerging market (and more particularly as part of Africa), and nothing will change this fact and perception. As a result, foreign investors will be prepared to place only a small part of their investments in South Africa.

Do not place more than 1% of your investment portfolio in emerging countries – there is simply too much risk that you may lose it all. Everything you own is already tied up in an emerging country, namely South Africa. Totally avoid further investments in emerging countries.

It is never easy for the government of an emerging country to attract foreign investment, particularly if funds are withdrawn because of some economic or political situation or event in that country. Often, the only method is to raise interest rates, and this has the following far-reaching financial implications, amongst others, for the local population and country:

- higher mortgage bond interest rates;
- higher rates for overdraft facilities;
- higher credit card rates;
- a great deal of money is spent on interest payments;
- there is less money for saving and investing;
- household budgets no longer balance;
- no or little money is available for sustenance and household necessities;

- lower profits for businesses;
- lower share prices;
- lower unit trust values;
- people sell investments at a loss;
- people try to obtain money to avoid going bankrupt;
- thousands of people do go bankrupt;
- more unemployment;
- less money/income tax for the requirements of the state and country;
- more political unrest and socio-economic problems;
- still less foreign investment; and
- yet more withdrawals of foreign investment.

This vicious circle is endless in the case of emerging countries, markets and their people.

The question that arises is whether something similar does not also happen in developed countries. Of course, unpleasant events occur there as well, but the financial influence thereof on investors, the people of the country and the country itself is very small. The situation also returns to 'normal' much more quickly than in emerging countries.

The fact is that the wealthy sector of the South African population has spirited away millions of rands abroad that they cannot bring back easily because it was taken out of the country illegally before the easing of exchange controls. On the other hand, the average South African investor should start an offshore investment portfolio when he or she can afford it. The millions of poor people will probably never own foreign assets.

An advantage of offshore investments is the greater choice of investment products this offers investors, for example, hedge funds and shares in the largest and most profitable companies in the world.

Stick to well-known companies and products. Do not allow greed, on the one hand, or the cunning of a dishonest salesperson/broker, on the other, to cause you simply to throw away money. Rather deal with a well-known and reputable South African investment firm. In this way, you reduce your risk and also enjoy peace of mind. Consult the Financial

Services Board if you have any doubts about an investment scheme.

However, much research must be done before and after an investment, because it must be monitored continually in order to guard against changes.

10.2.4 Types of offshore investor

It is only logical that various types of investor will invest offshore. Their financial situations differ widely, and so, too, the reasons why they want to and must invest abroad. Some may never emigrate, while others who do emigrate may wish to return to the country at a later stage. It may be fashionable for some, but for those living in emerging countries, who have both a job and the financial means, it is an essential requirement. Others spot investment opportunities and realise there is no international co-operation regarding the tax liability of individuals/juristic persons. As an individual's wealth increases, offshore investments become essential. According to Gough (1998:16), the primary reason is mostly protection of current assets, rather than making money. 'Whatever their reasons for investing offshore, all these groups are taking advantage of the anomalies that exist between the financial and tax regimes of the different nations of the world.' (Gough, 1998:2)

10.3 RESEARCH BEFORE INVESTING IN FOREIGN COUNTRIES

Before you decide to make any offshore investment you have to do a lot of research. Never make an offshore investment impulsively. After you have talked to a few people and brokers, you should realise that one uninformed decision could have a snowball effect. As you go through the learning curve and learning process, you will soon find out that an uninformed person is on a dangerous route.

Let us look at the research you should do before you invest overseas:

- Remember that you want to invest your money in such a way that you will be financially inde-

pendent after your retirement.
- Consult various sources of information about offshore investments (we discuss this later).
- Consult various brokers and experts.
- Make sure that you know why you want to invest in a foreign country.
- Determine your risk profile.
- Find out whether your investment objectives fit in with your retirement objectives.

Decide which product, countries and currencies you want to invest in, and then:
- Avoid swindlers and never be too optimistic or too pessimistic – always be realistic.
- Find out whether you have to obtain the approval of the Reserve Bank for your investment.
- Make sure that you know which forms to complete for the Reserve Bank and your own bank, and what additional proof they may require.
- Find out whether the company's way of doing business will be acceptable to you (how they operate overseas – their services, confidentiality and the products they offer).
- What is the situation in the countries where you want to invest? Find out more about political stability, language, religion, acceptance, the strength of their currencies, tax legislation (income tax, donations tax and estate duty) and legislation affecting trusts and companies.
- Let a broker or institution help you to determine the exact time when your investment should be converted into the other currency.
- Identify the economic cycles of overseas countries and invest in countries in which the cycle is favourable for the growth of your investment (e.g. during a phase of economic restructuring).
- Evaluate the investment risks of specific overseas countries.
- Ascertain the management style, reputation, infrastructure and performance record of the offshore fund manager (particularly when markets are weak).
- Find out about the inflation rates and interest rates of the various countries.
- Analyse these countries' investment histories for investors.

10.3.1 Offshore investment pitfalls

If an investor has no knowledge of the investment traps in South Africa (based on financial principles, personal needs and goals), the broader picture and other pitfalls will be missed as well. A knowledge of local investment pitfalls must, therefore, be regarded as a prerequisite for offshore investments.

In discussions of offshore investments there may have been warnings against a particular person, event or legislation (local and abroad). It bears repeating that research must be done before contemplating any offshore investment. Only proper research, knowledge of personal planning and the help of experts in foreign legislation can result in purposeful offshore investments.

10.3.2 Money laundering

The process whereby illicit money becomes part of the system and is invested in legal products with financial institutions, is known as 'money laundering'. Brokers found guilty of such investments in South Africa can land in a great deal of trouble.

10.3.3 Where can I get information about foreign investments?

Consult the following sources:
- information pamphlets issued by brokers;
- newsletters of financial institutions, insurance companies and brokers;
- the Internet (www.businessweek.com, www.yahoo.com, www.micropal.com, etc.);
- local newspapers;
- overseas newspapers (*Financial Times, Asia Money, Money Observer, International Money Marketing*, etc.);
- local information business (International Information Business and Stock Press);
- computerised investment analysis (Micropal, Money Mate); and
- the University of Pretoria's quarterly survey of unit trusts.

10.3.4 How much am I allowed to invest offshore?

At the moment, R750 000 per person may permanently be invested offshore. The usual requirements of the Reserve Bank will apply because the money does not have to be returned to South Africa.

If you want to invest overseas in the form of an offshore investment, you may invest any amount (there is no maximum) because the investment will have to come back to South Africa and may not be used in a foreign country.

It is, of course, possible to invest more than R750 000 overseas, through a donation to a spouse (who does not have R750 000) and interest-free loans to family members (and/or your parents).

10.3.5 How much should I invest offshore?

The average investor should not invest more than 20% of a portfolio offshore. A wealthy investor, who has sufficient assets and is in a position to invest offshore without incurring any debts, may invest up to 50% of a portfolio. It is impossible to determine a fixed percentage. Decide where you fit in, after you have obtained the necessary information.

10.3.6 In which currency should I invest?

The American dollar and the British pound are still the most popular currencies. Another possibility is Europe's new currency, the euro. The dollar remains the number one choice.

10.3.7 In which country (or countries) should I invest?

Emerging markets usually offer good investment opportunities (so international investors tell us). Even South Africa appears on the list of countries that are regarded as emerging markets.

The USA, the United Kingdom and Western Europe offer long-term benefits.

Find out whether it would be better to invest in tax-friendly countries and use a trust (or trusts) for your investment or business. South African investors usually prefer the Isle of Man and the English-speaking (British) Channel Islands of Guernsey and Jersey as tax havens. The British government gave them total financial independence to protect their investors in an acceptable manner and at an acceptable level. The legal system and tax systems are also acceptable to South Africans.

10.3.8 Investment guidelines – your international investment strategy

- Decide how much money you have to invest.
- Are you going to invest a lump sum, or are you going to invest on a monthly basis from another source/investment?
- Decide whether you want to invest money locally or internationally.
- Choose one or more investment products; for example, a container, unit trusts and shares.
- Choose, for example, a certain type of unit trust in a specific industry.
- Diversify further by not investing only in a single unit trust but in, say, five different unit trusts.

- Your investment choices must meet your needs for income or capital growth.
- Choose safe countries, particularly tax-friendly countries, for your investment.
- Establish a trust if it can help you to avoid paying income tax in a tax-friendly country.
- Use the Internet and personal references by brokers (but do your homework first) and choose a management company for your investment.
- Make sure that you understand the investment risk.
- Use the Internet to monitor your investment performance.
- Never make impulsive, emotional decisions about your long-term investment.
- Always keep your investment objectives in mind.
- Compare your international investment strategy with your retirement planning process and make sure that you will achieve your retirement goals.
- Beware of investing only in emerging countries (markets). They are all influenced by more or less the same factors, and you are already exposed to an emerging market in South Africa (with all the risks).
- Regard your investment in an emerging market as a medium- to long-term investment.

These are only a few general guidelines that should be evaluated together with a lot of other information. Use them to make more informed and sensible investment decisions on your offshore investments.

10.3.9 How do South African companies handle offshore investments?

Local companies that market unit trusts have added an overseas component to their companies. They have used various methods for this:
- Some companies opened offices in overseas countries.
- Others formed partnerships with overseas institutions.
- Alliances were formed between local and overseas institutions with the local institutions acting as agents for their counterparts overseas.
- Various offshore fund managers were appointed at different institutions. They handle offshore investments in a specific product as the need arises.

Overseas institutions are already doing business in South Africa to attract offshore investments.

Banks and insurance companies have also appointed offshore fund managers in various countries where South Africans can invest their R750 000. Brokers, financial institutions and insurance companies all over South Africa use one or more of these methods (and combinations of these) in their offshore investment sections.

These institutions also offer the following types of offshore fund: global or international funds, sector funds, share funds, government securities, money market funds and currency funds.

10.3.10 What are the costs of investing in a foreign country?

It would be impossible to specify the costs of offshore investments. You have to establish the initial costs and the annual fees (or management charges). It is safe to assume that the costs of an offshore investment will always be higher than the costs of South African investments. As a result, you will receive a lower return on your offshore investment, particularly in the beginning.

For example, if we invest the R750 000 in an offshore fund, the costs will be as follows:

Initial cost	5%
Service charge	1.15%
Compulsory charge	0.6%
Initial cost of reinvesting the income	5%

To put things in perspective, the benefits of such an investment should be compared with the costs.

10.3.11 Which factors determine the return on offshore investments?

Firstly, the type of investment will determine the return on your investment. Over the long term, shares seem to beat cash, government securities and fixed property. Secondly, the weight (percentage of the total portfolio) of the type of investment should be determined, for example:

Shares: 60%
Government securities: 20%
Property: 10%
Cash: 10%

Then you have to decide on the type of economy where you want to invest, namely a developed country or an emerging country, for example:

Developed countries (e.g. USA): 60%

Emerging markets (Brazil, Singapore, Malaysia, etc.): 40%

Always compare the costs with the benefits (income/capital growth).

As a last step, decide on the specific currency in a specific country, for example:

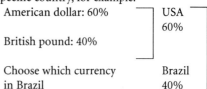

American dollar: 60%   USA 60%

British pound: 40%

Choose which currency in Brazil   Brazil 40%

All these decisions (and many others, such as the decisions of the fund manager) will affect the returns on your offshore investment.

10.3.12 An international currency exchange guide

If you want to find out how much a specific currency (e.g. the rand) is worth in another currency (e.g. the French franc) you may consult an international exchange guide, which can be obtained from the Reserve Bank and other banks. The guide will enable you to calculate how much your offshore investment is worth in the currency of a specific country. The exchange rate between the rand and the American dollar or the British pound is also quoted on radio and TV.

According to Gough (1998:150): 'An exchange rate is simply the ratio at which one currency can be exchanged for another at a given time.' Furthermore, you can distinguish between the nominal and the effective/real exchange rate, where the latter also takes into account the price levels of the two countries that are compared. It is never easy to predict the specific exchange rate, because a great many factors determine and influence it, amongst others:

- inflation;
- trade figures;
- flows of capital;
- interest rates;
- investment abroad;
- money flowing to a country's stock market;
- productivity;
- savings;
- bank intervention;
- confidence in a country;
- bull and bear markets; and
- events like war and crime.

10.3.13 Tax on offshore investments

For various reasons it is not possible to discuss the tax position regarding offshore investment here. Some of these reasons are:

- Tax systems and the basis of income tax calculation differ from country to country.
- Not all countries have entered into tax agreements that eliminate double taxation of investors.
- Different countries attach different meanings to the term 'offshore investment'.

You will, therefore, have to consult an international tax expert in order to evaluate and accept or reject the tax implications regarding your offshore investment.

If you invest in an overseas country that has not entered into an agreement with South Africa to avoid the payment of double tax, you will have to pay tax in both countries. Let us look briefly at the tax position of a few offshore investments:

- Interest earned overseas – interest will be taxable unless it is received by an offshore trust in a tax haven.
- Interest on a local foreign exchange account – interest will be taxable.
- The exchange rate profit that results when the offshore interest income is converted into rands – taxable.
- Income from the leasing of buildings – rent is taxable unless received by an offshore trust in a tax haven.
- Income from the leasing of a container – rent is taxable unless received by a trust in a tax haven.
- Dividends from unit trusts and shares are taxable (not all countries distinguish between the interest part and the dividends of unit trusts, however).
- Capital growth – taxable.
- Capital profit – taxable unless received by a trust in a tax haven (study residence based taxation).

It is important to realise, firstly, that the tax base differs in different countries, so offshore investments will be treated differently by various tax authorities. It is not the purpose of this book to point out the myriad differences, because that would require a book all of its own, which would, furthermore, have to be revised every year. However, the main tax categories comprise the following: income tax, capital gains tax, estate duty and withholding tax (tax on income from an investment by a non-resident). Do consult an international tax expert for information regarding your particular case. In particular, find out more about tax havens and their various positions regarding tax. Always remember that, as is the case with other investment criteria, you should also give attention to tax matters. After all, you do expect a positive after-tax return on your investments.

Especially remember the following in regard to the taxability of a South African's offshore investments:

- Capital gains tax is applicable to local as well as foreign assets (not in a trust, unless controlled from South Africa or permanently in an offshore financial centre as part of an offshore investment).
- Because of residence-based tax, all income derived from a foreign source is taxable.
- Although dividends earned in South Africa remain tax free, dividends from a foreign source are taxable (certain exemptions exist).
- Withholding tax paid abroad is tax deductible in South Africa.

Any capital gain or taxable income will be payable in South Africa and should be declared in your tax return form.

10.3.14 Capital gains tax (CGT)

Capital gains tax (CGT) was discussed in Chapter 5, dealing with income tax planning. The fact that CGT applies to all assets/investments owned by South Africans, wherever they may be in the world, is of great importance. That is why another discussion of CGT is warranted in this book. If you want to reach specific estate goals, it is also of great importance to understand the influence of CGT on estate planning. Kruger *et al.* (2001:44) provide a practical illustration of this relationship in Table 10.1.

The introduction of CGT resulted in a reduction in the estate duty rate and the donations tax rate from 25% to 20%. Where CGT is paid on the disposal of assets in a foreign country, a credit is granted by the South African tax authorities so as to prevent duplicating CGT payments. All South African citizens must pay CGT if assets are disposed of, or a deemed disposal takes place. In some cases, non-residents may also be liable for paying CGT. The concept of 'assets' means all assets anywhere in the world, and any interest in such assets. It is also important to know that the concept of disposal or deemed disposal includes basically any action or event that affects your assets. Some actions that are excluded are, amongst others, where assets serve as security for debt, obtaining debt financing, obtaining shares in a company, a change in trustees and the distribution of trust assets to a beneficiary already entitled to them. The latter implies that trust assets may not be distributed willy-nilly without certain CGT implications, depending on the type of trust, the rights of the trustees and the rights of beneficiaries.

TABLE 10.1 Income tax and CGT
(Source: Kruger et al. 2001:44)

Income tax liability	Capital gains tax liability

Gross Income
    Minus Exemptions
= Income
    minus Deductions
= Taxable Income
    Apply rates of tax
       to Taxable Income
    Deduct rebates
= Normal SA tax payable
	Disposal or deemed disposal of an asset
	⇩
	Proceeds or deemed proceeds
	⇩
	Deduct base cost of the asset
	⇩
	Capital gain or Capital loss
	⇩
	Exclusions?
	⇩
	Sum of all capital gains and losses reduced by the annual exclusion of R10 000—
	
	   > R0 or < R0
	   ⇩ ⇩
	Aggregate capital gain Aggregate capital loss
	⇩
	Deduct previous assessed capital loss
	⇩ (if applicable) ⇩
	Net capital gain x inclusion rate Assessed capital loss carried forward
	⇩ ⇩
	
	Taxable capital gain included in taxable income (follow steps in left-hand column)

Amounts excluded from CGT are, amongst others:
- R1 000 000 of your primary dwelling (occupied by a person for certain times, temporarily employed elsewhere, parts not used for business purposes or in which a special trust has an interest); and
- R10 000 per year for a natural person and a special trust.

Personal assets that are excluded are, amongst others: car, furniture, household appliances, a boat (less than 10 metres), an aircraft (certain weight).

According to Kruger *et al.* (2001:53), investments, financial products, remuneration and profits that are excluded are the following:
- lump sums from local or foreign retirement funds;
- long-term insurance policies where the person entitled to the proceeds is the original owner, his or her spouse, dependent or beneficiary, or where the policy has been ceded;

- business insurance policies on the life of another (provided the other person did not pay any premiums, i.e. buy-and-sell policies);
- pension fund policies;
- provident fund policies;
- retirement annuity fund policies;
- any compensation paid to a natural person/beneficiary/special trust for injuries or illness;
- money from legal gambling or competitions;
- profits from the conversion of foreign currency;
- proceeds from a short-term insurance policy;
- donations to public benefit organisations; and
- capital gains exempted by the Income Tax Act.

It is, furthermore, important to note the time stipulated by the Act for the disposal or deemed disposal of an asset (e.g. an option, donation, expropriation, etc.). Also remember the three methods for determining the base cost of an asset in order to calculate the capital gain:

- the market value method;
- the time-apportionment method; and
- the 20% rule.

The market value method

The market value will be used in the following situations:
- Proceeds are greater than expenses (before and after 1 October 2001).
- Expenditure cannot be determined.

The time-apportionment method

This method will be used in the following situations:
- Proceeds are greater than expenditure (before and after 1 October 2001).
- Proceeds are less than expenditure (before and after 1 October 2001) and the owner (seller) did not determine the market value on 1 October 2001.

The 20% rule

This method will be used in the following situations:
- Proceeds are greater than expenditure (before and after 1 October 2001).
- Expenditure cannot be determined.

Note that when the proceeds are less than expenditure (before and after 01 October 2001) both the market value and the time apportionment methods must be used. The lower of the two values will be used to determine the base cost of the asset.

The next step is to effect certain allowable deductions from the valuation amount. If someone wants to use the market value method, the valuation must have been made before 1 October 2001. Deductions may include the following: improvements made, valuation costs, costs of professionals involved, brokerage costs, transfer duty, stamp duty, conveyancing fees, advertising costs and legal costs regarding ownership. The following, for example, may not be claimed as deductions: financing costs, rates and taxes and maintenance costs.

If an asset is purchased/acquired after 1 October 2001, the basis cost is the purchase price plus costs as already indicated. The value of an interest in property, for example a usufruct, is determined by capitalising it over the beneficiary's lifetime at a rate of 12% per year (2002).

The market values of some financial products are calculated as follows on 1 October 2001 and also after 1 October 2001:
- Financial instruments listed on the Johannesburg Securities Exchange (average quoted price on five trading days before 1 October 2001).
- South African unit trusts and property unit trusts (average buying price on last trading day before 1 October 2001).
- Other financial instruments (market value on 1 October 2001).
- Foreign listed securities and unit trusts (last price quoted/purchased on last trading day before 1 October 2001).

Market value after 1 October 2001:
- Listed shares (purchase price of share).
- Unlisted shares (purchase price of share).
- Other financial instruments (purchase price).
- Second-hand insurance policies (purchase price).
- Unit trusts and property unit trusts (price paid for the units).

10.3.15 The global investment process

Kruger *et al.* (2001:101) point out the following steps an investor must follow in view of South African exchange controls:
- Complete and submit a 'Declaration of Good Standing'. (The person making the investment must sign the form. Without it, the investor is limited to asset swops or tank containers. This form must be completed and handed in to the bank. The form will be approved if the applicant has paid all income tax. If there are outstanding amounts, these must be paid before approval is given.)
- Complete the South African Reserve Bank form. (This form must be completed in duplicate, and shows, amongst others, the offshore investment amount, as well as amounts already invested there. The specific bank making the investment on behalf of the investor handles this form and must inform the Reserve Bank as soon as the investment has been made.)
- Complete form MP 1423. (This form must be completed by the investor in duplicate, and shows where the investment will be made, and in which bank account.)
- Complete the investment application forms. (A form is completed for the specific investment product, and for the fund concerned. A second form indicates the transfer from the investor's account to the offshore account. A third form indicates whether the investment accrues to a trust. The trust doing the investment, and the products, must also be indicated.)
- Hand in the documentation. (The representative for the products collects all the forms and the investor's cheque, unless an electronic transfer is effected. The authorised representative receives the Declaration of Good Standing, SARB forms, MP 1423s, the cheque/authorisation for the electronic transfer and a copy of the investor's ID.)

10.4 OFFSHORE INVESTMENT ALTERNATIVES

It is important to remember that the products considered below should be taken out in offshore financial centres (tax havens), rather than in foreign countries (foreign jurisdictions), the main reason being the tax and estate duty advantages.

10.4.1 Policies

It is possible to contribute to retirement annuities and endowment policies via offshore investments (e.g. an offshore share portfolio). The usual income tax deductions for annuities will apply. Consult a broker for information about the latest products. You will also be allowed to borrow against this type of endowment policy, or cede it.

Life policies
Both life and disability coverage can be obtained abroad. The risk is somewhat higher because the businesses that market these are registered in offshore financial centres in those countries, and not here. Monthly premiums are usually paid from a foreign currency bank account (local or offshore). A life policy can, as in South Africa, be used to pay debts and meet other obligations after your death. The proceeds can also be used to protect existing investments. The premiums of a life policy issued from an offshore financial centre (tax haven) will be lower and the return higher than a South African life policy – the main reason would be the taxability of the returns of the policy in the hands of insurance companies in South Africa.

Endowment policies
Most endowment policies you can invest in involve a lump sum rather than monthly contributions. Nevertheless, you should receive a higher return because of the lower or no income tax, and the capital gain. Such policies include the following:
- market-linked policies (return depends on the market value of the underlying assets at maturity);
- with-profit-guaranteed policies (remember that the higher the guarantee and the less the risk, the lower the profit); and
- geared guaranteed policies (make use of the derivative market and guarantee capital as well as growth).

10.4.2 Unit trusts (mutual funds)

At present, South Africans may invest in about 35 000 unit trusts all over the world. For the purposes of this discussion, it is important to be informed about the three categories from which the investor may choose.

Firstly, you may invest in South African unit trusts that are investing in South African shares. These unit trusts do not invest in overseas assets. They include the well-known general, specialist and income trusts (as well as other groups).

Secondly, you may invest in South African unit trusts that invest in offshore assets (shares). These international trusts offer so-called 'onshore' investments. They include:
- ABSA International;
- BOE Global;
- Coronation International Growth;
- Fedsure Global;
- Guardbank Global;
- Investec Worldwide;
- Old Mutual World Equity;
- Sage Global;
- Sanlam Global;
- Southern Global;
- Standard Bank International;
- Syfrets International; and
- Syfrets Universal Opportunities.

As an investor, you do not need any form of approval from the Reserve Bank to invest in these onshore unit trusts. The main reason is that these investments must be returned to South African and do not form part of the R750 000 you are allowed to take out of the country to invest permanently overseas. You may, for example, invest R1 million (or more) overseas in this way through onshore unit trusts.

Thirdly, you may invest directly in offshore unit trusts as part of the R750 000 per person that may be invested permanently overseas. You have to obtain the approval of the Reserve Bank for this type of unit trust investment. Investors will have to complete certain Reserve Bank forms and supply proof that they do not have any overdue tax liabilities. These unit trust investments are known as offshore investments, because the money does not have to be returned to South Africa and does not have to go through the Reserve Bank. An offshore unit trust investment may be made via Sanlam's Dublin Fund or Old Mutual's Guernsey Fund, for example.

Like all other investments, the choice in overseas countries is not as easy as it is in South Africa, which is familiar to investors. Research has shown that people who want to invest offshore regard the security, trustworthiness and return of a fund as the most important criteria. These aspects are of the utmost importance when offshore unit trusts are selected, but there is one more vital question: Who will be able to link these criteria for you, as an investor, to specific offshore unit trusts?

It is clear that a multi-management approach or a 'fund of funds' approach should be followed. This means that a very reliable overseas company that is a good performer will give your investment to various offshore fund managers in various sectors to manage. These fund managers are regarded as the best in their fields.

If you are a more cautious investor, index trusts will be the best unit trusts to invest in. The return is always good and the risk relatively low. It would be even better to invest in a group of different index trusts.

An analysis of offshore unit trusts shows that specialist trusts are at the top of the list. A specialist trust is a unit trust that invests in shares in a specific industry, for example computers or finance. As with South African specialist trusts, the risk is higher, but so are the returns.

There are various methods of investing in offshore unit trusts. Brokers, financial institutions and insurance companies can help you here, either with a local investment or an international one.

Stick to offshore financial centres in order to avoid various future financial disappointments in the form of tax. Also remember to make sure that the specific fund you choose has been registered with the Financial Services Board. If so, it will reduce your investment risk. As you know, unit trusts offer no guarantees, and are medium- to long-term investments. If you want to compare yields, it is advisable to measure them against indexes such as the FTSE 100 (the top 100 companies on the London Stock Exchange). Also compare different fund managers, fund manager companies as well as the costs of offshore investments.

10.4.3 Shares

It is possible to invest in shares overseas through South African shares listed on the Johannesburg Securities Exchange (JSE). This type of share earns income mainly through overseas business. Examples are Richmond, Minorco, Charter, Sasol and Fit. Another possibility is to invest in export shares (that earn an income from exports), for example gold and platinum shares.

One advantage of shares is that your investment is more flexible. You can buy and sell shares at any time. Disadvantages include lack of security for your capital and the restrictions placed by the South African market on diversification. Risks and returns are high.

You may invest directly in overseas shares via a broker, or invest in prime overseas shares with an insurance company. Part of these shares may be used to make contributions to retirement annuities, endowment policies, preservation funds and provident funds. You are allowed the usual income tax deductions, even though the contributions to the retirement annuity form part of your offshore investment. This type of overseas share fund requires a minimum lump sum investment of R10 000, for example, or a monthly investment of R100.

Like ordinary South African shares, these overseas share funds hold a higher risk than other types of investment. Your objectives – and the return on your investment – should always be kept in mind.

Remember that an investment of R750 000 in offshore shares does not provide a very large portfolio after conversion of the rand.

10.4.4 Tank containers

Containers must be one of the least-known investment instruments. The lease of containers originated in the sixties, and today it is one of the ways in which South Africans can invest offshore.

What is a container?
A container is made of steel and is used to transport all sorts of products: food, cars, motorbikes, beverages, liquids, chemicals and the like.

How does an investment in a container work?
An individual or a group of people buys a container and leases it overseas to earn an income. The container will be in a pool with other containers and an income is earned from the pool.

Who can invest in containers?
Anyone who can afford to invest R150 000 may invest in containers. An investor who has R30 000 may club together with others to invest in a container. This type of investment is meant for wealthy investors, particularly those who are about to retire (or have just retired) and need an income from an investment.

Is the investment legal?
The Commissioner of Inland Revenue and the Reserve Bank (exchange control) have both approved this type of investment.

What are the most important benefits?
- Tax savings.
- Investments are protected against inflation.
- Protection against a weak rand.

- The beneficiary of an estate may inherit in a foreign country.

Can this investment be combined with other investments?

Yes, an investment in containers can be combined with:
- annuities;
- unit trusts; and
- managed investment accounts.

What are the prospects for the container market?

At the moment, about 90 000 containers are in use worldwide. The demand for containers is expected to grow immensely because traditional methods of transport are being abolished. Giant multinational industries in the USA are mainly responsible for the demand.

How can I finance the purchase?

Use borrowed money (a loan) to finance part of the transaction. You may even borrow the full amount. Because the loan is made in order to earn an income, the interest is tax-deductible. The purchase price is also written off over five years (at 20% per year) in the form of depreciation.

What do I have to pay tax on?

The investor pays income tax on the income earned; it forms part of the investor's gross income. If there is a capital profit when a container is sold, tax is payable. When a container is sold there will be a tax refund on amounts received to the date of sale. VAT is payable when the container is bought but may be refunded within two months of being claimed.

What proof do I obtain of my investment?

The investor receives a copy of the certified certificate of ownership from the Reserve Bank (where the original is kept). Each container has three numbers:
- an identity number;
- a trade number; and
- an international number of certification

How do I receive my income?

Income is paid out quarterly in arrears.

May I sell the container?

Yes. The agent will handle the marketing and the documentation. The container may only be sold to South African investors, because this type of investment was created specially for South Africans.

Are there any other risks?

No. The pool of containers carries the risk. The investor may never be held responsible for anything regarding the use of the container.

Who will manage my investment?

In foreign countries, leasing agents will manage your investment. In South Africa, the investor will appoint an agent when the container is bought. This agent will enter into certain agreements with the leasing agent on behalf of the investor. The agent will also charge a management fee of 5% of the gross income earned by the container.

Where do I buy or invest?

Investments in containers are marketed by Ocean Container Investments, Seeff Container Investments, Investec Bank, International Tank Containers, Multistar Container Transport and Medite Containers. New products are being developed in co-operation with financial institutions, for example First National Bank and Southern Life's 'Combo-Link'. Analyse and compare these companies before you choose one for your investment.

What return can I expect?

The return is determined by the measure of occupation/usage (10%, 20% and 80%) of the container pool. If the containers are used 80% of the time, they will provide a higher income. Very low usage (10%) will mean that you do not receive any return on your investment.

For what term should I invest?

You should invest for five to ten years in containers to get the maximum tax benefit and protection for your rand.

What percentage should I invest in containers?

Preferably not more than 10% of your investment portfolio.

10.4.5 Yachts

You may also invest in yachts to protect your rands. Investments in yachts function in the same way as investments in containers, and investors receive a free week per year on the yacht. MASMAS (Marine Syndicate Management Systems) is an example of a yacht investment company. These investments are meant for investors with the same needs as those who invest in containers.

10.4.6 Krugerrands

Krugerrands are a good rand protector and can be bought in the primary market at the South African Mint and in the secondary market (where they are traded) from banks, brokers and the public. The South African Reserve Bank also buys Krugerrands if you want to sell yours. The lower the value of the rand exchange rate, the higher the value of your Krugerrands.

There are of course certain risks associated with Krugerrands, namely theft, no capital growth or income from interest for certain periods, and the cost of keeping the Krugerrands safe in a bank.

If you have sufficient funds, you may invest part of them in Krugerrands, but Krugerrands should never make up more than 5% of your investment portfolio.

10.4.7 Fixed property

You can invest in fixed property in foreign countries through a reliable South African estate agency. You can invest directly by buying property, or by investing in property trusts. Another possibility is to invest in a timeshare that can be exchanged internationally.

Do not assume that you will necessarily receive a higher return on property overseas, especially if you are an individual investor. A syndicated investment (where you are part of a group of investors) may be preferable, since a better property may be bought or a better investment made because of the larger amount involved. A syndicated investment may, therefore, spread (lower) the investment risk through diversification.

At this stage, it seems that it is a full-time job to speculate from South Africa (even if the property is renovated and sold at a profit). Anyone who has lived in Pretoria and has invested money in fixed property in Cape Town will be familiar with the feelings of frustration and helplessness. It will be much worse if you invest in fixed property overseas.

If you use the R750 000 that may remain in a foreign country to buy fixed property overseas, you may find after conversion that you only have enough for the deposit.

In view of the relaxation of exchange controls, offshore property investments have become considerably more desirable. Just as with any other offshore investment, the main reason for and greatest advantage of such an investment is the possible future use thereof. Amongst others, the property (and/or return) can be:
- reinvested;
- occupied by children/grandchildren in the future;

- used for retirement purposes;
- used for emigration purposes;
- rented; and
- used for vacations.

Make sure you have knowledge of the following before you invest directly in property:
- the investment amount required;
- how the currency will decrease your available amount;
- the deposit you need in the foreign country;
- how you are going to finance the balance of the purchase price;
- other cost-items involved when buying a house;
- the tax position of residents/non-residents with regard to the various types of tax (income tax, capital gains tax, estate tax); and
- a comparison with existing property in regard to location (especially the convenience and exposure network), resale value, repairs, etc.

10.4.8 Bonds

Consult your broker regarding investments in bonds abroad. Apart from the usual foreign exchange advantages, the primary goals should be income and guaranteed capital. However, remember that interest rates are far lower abroad than in South Africa.

10.4.9 Unlisted companies

Handle such investments with great care and get advice from only the most reputable investment companies/brokers.

10.4.10 An export business

If you choose to invest in a business, you should rather invest in an export business, because it will offer you an ideal opportunity to profit from the continuously falling rand. The main advantage is that you will receive your business income in a currency that is worth more than the rand. You will get so much more if you convert your income to rands.

Information about export opportunities (businesses) is readily available and you will even be able to find out which products or services are required in which countries. As part of a complete business plan, you will also need to obtain information on how to start your business and how it will function. Television programmes, magazines, and seminars that are advertised in the newspapers are further sources of information.

10.4.11 A business in a foreign country

Another possibility is to establish or buy a business in an overseas country. If you receive income from an overseas business that is making a trade profit, the profit will not be taxable in South Africa but in the other country. Offshore businesses that earn an income from investments are excluded: this income will be taxed in South Africa.

10.4.12 An offshore trust

The long-term benefits of South African trusts are under threat.

Through estate duty, the government has placed a huge financial burden on individuals' assets or estates. This has forced many people to use trusts when they do their estate planning.

At present, about 600 to 650 trusts are registered in Pretoria every month. A problem that people who establish trusts may have to face in the future is that the government may levy estate duty on trusts.

As early as 1987, the previous government tabled a White Paper in which estate duty on trusts was proposed: trusts would be taxed every 15 to 21 years, as if the owner of the trust had died. It may be assumed that the budget (and the small number of taxpayers) will soon 'force' the South African government to take this drastic step.

Why?
Why tax trusts? To finance the budget and provide for the never-ending needs of an ever-increasing population for education, housing and medical services.

The end of trusts?
Will this mean the end of trusts? No, definitely not. At the moment, there is no alternative to trusts as estate planning instruments. But it is important that individuals who want to establish trusts (as well as those who have already done so) realise that this is not the end of their estate planning and that they should continue planning.

Implications
What are the implications for trust assets? The way a trust is structured (e.g. farms, buildings only, or cash only) will have different implications for donors, income beneficiaries and capital beneficiaries.

Trusts will have to be liquid enough to make provision for estate duty or tax on capital growth, say every 20 years. The implication of this is that donors who have only fixed assets in the trust (little

An offshore trust offers protection.

Soon we will have to pay estate duty on trusts.

cash liquidity) will have to donate cash to the trust (or convert assets into cash, inside or outside the trust) to meet these financial liabilities.

Suppose a man establishes a trust for his two-year-old son. In terms of existing legislation, the capital growth of trust assets does not incur estate duty. If estate duty on trusts is introduced, it would mean that in the next 63 years, the trust (with the son as beneficiary of the trust) will have to pay estate duty three times. If the father passes his assets to his son by inheritance or donates or sells them to the son without establishing a trust, the son would not pay any estate duty, even when he is 63 years older.

Higher tax? (CGT)
Will the rate of estate duty be increased first? The rate will definitely be increased (at the moment it is 20% on an estate that exceeds R1.5 million). The rate of 20% will be increased and the rebate of R1.5 million will be reduced. We expect that adjustments in the rate of estate duty and the rebate will be made before estate duty on trusts is introduced.

Interest-free loans?
What about interest-free loans? We expect that in future, loans to a trust will no longer be tax-free when assets are sold to the trust. If this occurs, it will have different financial implications for different estates.

South African investors seem to invest internationally not only for investment planning but also for estate planning, in order to protect their assets for their offspring. Some form of offshore trust in a country that is investment- and tax-friendly is particularly suited to this.

What is a trust?
A trust is an independent entity (legal entity) that is used for estate planning, in particular. The person who establishes the trust places assets in the trust to limit (or stop) their capital growth in his or her own estate. Estate duty is saved in this way. The founder of the trust (the donor) retains control over the assets but loses the right of ownership to the trust. There are also tax benefits.

What is an offshore trust?
An offshore trust is one that is registered in one of the 'tax-friendly' countries ('tax havens') of the world, such as Jersey, the Isle of Man, Guernsey, Luxembourg, Monaco, Liechtenstein and the Bahamas.

Advantages of an offshore trust

- An offshore trust is a substitute for drawing up an offshore will. In a will (local and international), the testator's assets are actually made known to everybody. In offshore trusts, the assets are not revealed to third parties. Confidentiality is of the utmost importance.
- Your assets are protected against local legal and political developments as they belong to an offshore trust and, thus, cannot be affected directly. New legislation, therefore, will not have any effect on your assets.
- Assets in offshore trusts are protected against current estate duty as well as an increase in the rate (in 2002, 20% on amounts above R1 500 000) and/or a reduction of the rebate (R1 500 000).
- If overseas assets are in an offshore trust, the beneficiaries will find it easy to trace them.
- It is easy to divide assets among capital beneficiaries.
- International tax benefits are obtained in tax-friendly countries.
- International fund managers are in an ideal position to manage these assets by investing and reinvesting. These fund managers have more freedom than their counterparts in South Africa.
- Assets in an offshore trust are protected against the sequestration of the person who established the trust. The same is true of future liabilities.
- Income tax benefits are obtained in these 'friendly' countries (this is really what they are, because they protect investors).

If you want to take your R750 000 overseas, you should seriously consider the benefits of an offshore trust.

Should amnesty be granted in the future to people who have money and assets in overseas countries illegally, they may also use the protection of an offshore trust.

10.4.13 A business trust

Establish a business trust if you want to:
- start a business in South Africa;
- start an export business;
- buy or establish a business in a foreign country; or
- manage overseas investments via a trust.

You should also look at tax havens and ask an expert to help you establish a business trust in a common-law country. When business trusts and companies are linked, there are many benefits for the person who establishes them. Some of the most important benefits are that you will save on income tax and estate duty. The other usual benefits of a trust will also apply.

10.4.14 An investment trust (asset protection trust)

A tax-friendly country or tax haven is the ideal place to establish an offshore investment trust. You can place investments in this trust by lending or selling them to the trust, depending on the nature of the investment (e.g. a lump sum of money or fixed property). An investment trust is particularly suited to people who already have capital overseas. Investments in further overseas countries may be made from the investment trust.

Once again, pay a lot of attention to the trust deed when you consult an expert. Take special note of the measure of control you will retain over the capital, for example by indicating that you, as the founder, are entitled to the income a well as the capital if you need it. Also note the political stability of the country in which you want to establish the investment trust. Ask a legal expert to explain the common-law or civil-law implications of that country for the establishment of an investment trust.

10.4.15 Banking overseas

A foreign currency bank account is particularly useful for making foreign payments. It saves a great deal of cost, for example, when converting one currency into another so as to apply the funds elsewhere. Such a bank account can be opened locally or abroad.

A local foreign exchange bank account

It is possible to invest internationally via a local bank account. The careful investor who wants to avoid all risks, no matter for what reason, usually chooses this option. You can invest your money either as call money or as a fixed deposit. The first step will be to decide in which overseas currency you want to keep your money. You may also decide to keep your money in different currencies. Note that this investment may only be made at an overseas bank and not in property or shares. Ascertain the minimum and/or maximum investment amounts, the interest rate and the costs involved. This kind of investment is particularly useful for small investors.

In the case of a local bank account, you will receive the same interest rate as the currency of the offshore bank. The greatest advantage comes when you want to convert the money back into rands (which depreciates). Every time you transfer money to the foreign country where your bank account is, you must first obtain tax clearance in South Africa.

A foreign exchange bank account in a foreign country

It is also possible to open a foreign exchange bank account in an overseas country to protect yourself against a falling rand. Unfortunately, the interest rates on these accounts are rather low. Even after the fall in the rand, they are unlikely to be higher than those of local banks. Compare the various banks and obtain all the necessary information. You may also use international banks that have branches in South Africa.

A foreign bank account in an offshore centre offers far greater confidentiality, as well as more income tax and estate planning advantages. These bank accounts offer many services, as well as debit card facilities (subject to certain requirements). The banks themselves decide which currencies are offered at their branches, so choose beforehand which currency your prefer, and check with the bank in the country concerned. If the bank account is in an offshore financial centre, you should not pay tax on interest (on your bank balance).

Rand denominated foreign investment

This is an offshore investment you can make in rands, and where you receive the returns on the investment in rands as well. It is possible to invest small amounts monthly with well-known local businesses specialising in such investments. Examples are unit trusts and endowment policies.

Foreign currency denominated investments

Since 2002 (February) South Africans can permanently invest R750 000 abroad. After tax clearance by the Reserve Bank, these funds can be applied abroad in any manner, namely in any currency, type of investment, spending or country. Investments usually require larger amounts, and not everyone can afford them. As a result, many South African investors prefer rand denominated investments.

Gough (1998:127) points out that offshore investors should not rely on confidentiality by foreign banks, even if they are situated in so-called tax havens. Similarly, Gough declares that banks find themselves in the grey area between politics and commerce: 'It should be plain by now that banks are not all the same! They vary from ultra-rich, ultra-conservative organisations with reputations to protect, to out-and-out crooks, with every shade and variety imaginable in between' (Gough 1998:129). According to Gough, the US, UK, German and Swiss banks offer the greatest stability and security. As with offshore trusts,

foreign bank accounts are not always worth it. They carry high costs. This is the reason why only very rich people make use of them on a large scale. Make sure that the bank you are contemplating can provide for your specific needs. If you do have sufficient financial means to open a foreign bank account, Gough (1998:131) suggests the following steps:

- Spread your business across various banks, countries and currencies.
- Do research about the stability of a bank, especially as regards new management (if applicable).
- Study the banking regulations of various countries and banks.
- Watch the media.
- Avoid unstable countries with undemocratic governments and nationalisation policies.

It is only logical that South Africans will largely have to make use of local bank managers and the Reserve Bank when judging and choosing foreign banks.

10.4.16 Offshore investor protection

The Financial Services Board (FSB) is perhaps the greatest protector of South Africans with regard to offshore investments. For example, the FSB requires the registration of all unit trust funds if they are marketed in South Africa. The protection of investors in foreign countries receives special attention. Find out from the FSB if they have any knowledge of the product you want to invest in, as far as the required local or foreign registration, history, risk, etc. is concerned. The protection must be the same as for local investment products. Of course, we could invest in products that are not registered here, for example hedge funds. Remember that the FSB does not protect you against all offshore products – it is still your responsibility to determine the pitfalls and risks.

10.5 YOUR ESTATE

The 'new' estate planning almost forces South Africans to include offshore activities where their money matters are concerned. After all, it is only logical that any investment decision (local or offshore) will influence all other personal financial planning areas, including your estate planning. Just as offshore investments are influenced by foreign income tax legislation, they are also influenced by foreign estate duty legislation. It is, therefore, very important to protect your assets by means of estate planning and to transfer them to your heirs in the most tax-efficient manner (or to keep and manage them on their behalf). If offshore investments are made, estate planning must be done beforehand with the help of an expert (on that foreign country or those countries).

For the purposes of estate planning, you may make an offshore investment in your own name, or that of a company or trust. Each of these methods has particular present and future financial implications for yourself and your heirs. Therefore, each method must be weighed and compared to determine what would be best in your situation, and would serve your goals the best. If you intend to realise the investments at a later stage, the best decision is probably to retain them in your own name. If they will go to your heirs at a later stage, either during your lifetime or after your death, it may be better to invest them in the name of a company or trust. You must also take account of capital gains tax. Make sure that you do not become liable for double estate duty after your death.

A company is mostly used for the purposes of perpetual succession, that is for continued trading. Where estate planning is concerned, a company is of particular value because it may be linked to a trust. You can, therefore, make investments in the name of a company which belongs to a trust (something you cannot do in the case of a close corporation). All legislation in the foreign country or countries that applies to companies and trusts should be studied carefully with expert aid. It is very important that 50% of the company should be in foreign ownership, or else the tax authorities will regard it as a controlled foreign entity managed from South Africa. This would result in your having to pay income tax in South Africa, which means the advantages offered by the company would disappear.

Trusts were discussed in Chapter 6 dealing with estate planning. Over many years, South Africans have placed money in offshore trusts. As in the case of a company, the specific legislation of the foreign country should be studied carefully so as to make sure that the trust is not regarded as a controlled foreign entity. Particularly note any legislation regarding the movement of assets to an offshore trust, and how this may be effected from within South Africa (or not). You will note that you may not grant interest-free loans to an offshore trust. Neither may you, as you may in South Africa, donate an annual amount of R30 000 to an offshore trust. In such cases, income tax, donations tax and interest income will be a factor.

It is fairly expensive to set up an offshore trust. Make sure that you structure the offshore trust, by means of a trust deed, in such a way that it satisfies your particular requirements. For example, if you know that you will be receiving an inheritance some time in the future, you could create an offshore trust with yourself as the beneficiary and ensure that your inheritance is left directly to the trust. The trust then, in effect, inherits, and you will receive the future benefits offshore.

In order to ensure that your offshore trust and your offshore assets/investments are not regarded as foreign controlled entities, you must ensure, amongst others, that:

- South Africans do not have a right to more than 50% of the trust benefits.
- South Africans do not control more than 50% of the trust by making up more than 50% of the trustees.
- South Africans are not entitled to more than 50% of the trust income.

Apart from income tax advantages (because no income tax is payable in certain offshore financial centres), an offshore trust offers estate protection of foreign assets and the same trust advantages as a South African trust. Furthermore, it offers protection from the slow administrative process in foreign countries known as probate, which is used to administer estate assets that do not form part of an offshore trust.

10.5.1 Types of offshore trust

At this stage you already know of the existence of the parties to a trust, namely the founder (or settlor), the beneficiaries and the trustees. In the case of an offshore trust, legislation in certain countries requires a protector. This protector ensures that the wishes of the founder are carried out. The protector also protects the trust fund and may even dismiss trustees at his or her discretion. The founder may appoint a friend or family member as protector.

As in South Africa, there are mainly two types of offshore trust: testamentary trusts and *inter vivos* trusts. The former type is established after a person's death, while the latter is established while a person (the founder) is still alive.

It is important to note that foreign countries permit trusts to exist for only limited periods. Do not, therefore, simply assume that you can create an offshore trust in perpetuity. Furthermore, you should make sure that you do not underestimate the costs (initial and annual) involved in an offshore trust, because these could erode the other financial advantages of the trust.

Many foreign countries accept the existence of trusts, but not all of them are tax havens. The taxability of a trust depends, amongst others, on the following:

- the legal jurisdiction of the trust;
- the legal jurisdiction of the country;
- the domicile of the settlor;
- the domicile of the trustees; and
- the domicile of the beneficiaries.

Gough (1998:18) points out that a trust is not worth it for a small investor, especially in view of the costs involved. He suggests that a person should rather move to a tax haven, study the local legislation and then decide whether it is essential to set up the trust. However, the arguments in favour of such a trust carry more weight if an heir is involved. Gough also warns against the temptations that offshore trustees are subjected to, amongst others applying money other than according to the wishes of the founder, in cases where the founder is no longer able to think for him- or herself (because of old age or illness). This is but one of many reasons why such a trust should not be set up without the help of competent lawyers.

10.5.2 The duration of a trust

Generally, only a special/charitable trust can exist or be created in perpetuity. Most countries have particular requirements regarding the duration of a trust. In England, for example, a trust can be set up for 80 years, or for a period that may extend for up to 21 years after the death of the last survivor of all the descendants who were alive when the trust was created – the 'royal lives period' (Gough 1998:105). Jersey and Guernsey allow a maximum of 100 years.

Gough (1998:105) points out that there are also restrictions in countries regarding the periods for which income may accumulate in trusts without being paid out to the beneficiaries. As soon as such a period has expired, the accumulated funds must be paid to the beneficiaries. England allows a maximum period of either 21 years or the term of the settlor's life. Jersey and Guernsey allow 100 years, while Ireland allows the royal lives period. All these aspects need to be taken into account when planning an offshore trust.

10.5.3 Choosing a jurisdiction

Various offshore financial centres allow you to choose the jurisdiction that applies to your trust or even to parts of it. This means that you may choose different jurisdictions for, amongst others, the following aspects of your trust (Gough 1998:111):
- the trust deed itself;
- the validity of the trust deed;
- how the trust is administered; and
- trust assets located in different countries.

Similarly, the settlor or the protector may be permitted to alter the jurisdictions applicable to various aspects of the trust in terms of the trust deed. However, the requirement is that there must be a court capable of imposing its jurisdiction so as to amend various aspects of the trust. There should also be a court that is capable of guiding the administration of the trust with regard to the following aspects, amongst others (Gough 1998:112):
- how the trustees can invest the trust's money;
- what happens when a trustee retires;
- how the trustees can delegate;
- the appointment of new trustees;
- how the trustees can be paid and claim expenses;
- the indemnity of trustees; and
- whether the court itself has the power to authorise particular acts or change the terms of the trust deed.

10.5.4 The protector

A protector offers great peace of mind if you are continents removed from your trust. According to Gough (1998:116) a protector may be afforded the power to, amongst others:
- approve the fees/expenses of trustees;
- change the trustees;
- change the jurisdiction of the trust;
- monitor the way the trust is being run;
- stop a proposed investment;
- stop the distribution of money to a beneficiary; and
- stop an addition of a beneficiary or the removal of one.

Consequently, it is very important that such a protector should know exactly what is happening to the trust, and when. If not, the role of the protector is undermined and becomes useless. Protectors, therefore, require hands-on information at all times in order to protect and carry out the wishes of the settlor.

10.5.5 Trusts in civil law countries

Civil law is based on Roman law, and has the following features, amongst others (Gough 1998:120):
- Ownership is an abstract concept.
- Ownership of property includes all ownership rights.
- Two people cannot be co-owners of the same property.
- The power to bequeath assets/belongings by the owner is more limited than in common law countries.

- The meaning of contract is much wider in civil law, and includes third parties.

A problem is that assets may be transferred to third parties who have not been declared beneficiaries. Similarly, probates may easily take place, or a trust may not be recognised. Do not, therefore, transfer assets to a civil law country. Stick to common law countries.

It should be clear by now that the creation of an offshore trust may involve various pitfalls, and is not suitable for smaller estates. Very few people know what they are letting themselves in for with regard to an offshore trust. Unless you know the field of personal finance in the foreign countries concerned very well (in particular, the legislation pertaining to the entire field), and already have the best foreign advisors on your side, you should not even contemplate an offshore investment or trust. Professional foreign trustees are of the utmost importance.

10.5.6 An offshore will

The purpose of any will is to help the executor of an estate to administer it after the death of the testator/testatrix. A South African with offshore assets should provide for the disposal thereof in a South African or an offshore will. Study the legislation of the foreign country or countries concerned to determine which situation would best satisfy your needs in regard to disposal, and at the lowest cost. Also consider the country or countries where your heirs are living or intend living. An offshore will for offshore heirs may be best if your advisor agrees.

Kruger *et al.* (2001:113) point out the following regarding an offshore will, which persons with offshore assets or investments should keep in mind:
- In the absence of an offshore will, the executor must first apply abroad to gain rights as a foreign executor.
- It may become even more difficult if the executor is confronted with a foreign language.
- This also creates higher costs and wastes time.
- There should be a separate will for each foreign jurisdiction.
- An offshore will makes it easier to trace the estate's assets and to administer the estate.
- The estate in each country needs to be administered in that country.
- A separate executor, therefore, needs to be appointed for each country, and each executor needs to be knowledgeable regarding local legislation and must be able to administer the estate without problems.
- It is important that the testator/testatrix should choose the legislation of the specific foreign country in his or her will for the purposes of administering the estate.
- South African legislation with regard to the administration of estates can be avoided in this way.
- Let an expert draw up your offshore will, and appoint a foreign executor and foreign trustees.

10.5.7 Estate duty

Kruger *et al.* (2001:115) discuss offshore estate planning in terms of the following guidelines:
- A South African's estate is made up of all of his or her assets/investments, no matter where in the world they are.
- However, the following assets are excluded:
  - assets that were acquired before a person became a South African citizen;
  - assets inherited from a foreign resident; and
  - assets donated by a foreign resident.
- Where no double taxation agreement exists, a person will first pay foreign estate duty and then be entitled to a rebate in South Africa.
- In the case of a double taxation agreement between the two countries, the specific agreement will determine which country is entitled to the estate duty.
- A non-resident does not pay estate duty in South Africa on assets in other countries.
- A non-resident does pay estate duty on assets in South Africa, subject to double taxation agreements.
- A non-resident does not pay donations tax on his or her South African assets, which means that estate duty is also avoided.

10.5.8 Donations

South Africans should be careful when they have to make decisions about donations tax and estate duty on offshore assets or investments. Consult an expert about international estate duty and donations tax, because otherwise you may make very expensive mistakes. Never assume that it will be possible to transfer certain assets or investments to, say, a trust at a later stage or after your death. Countries with a judicial system based on civil law may hold problems for your trust. You may have to pay donations tax or estate duty in two countries (South Africa will be one of them). An expert can help you to avoid paying donations tax or estate duty.

Specify the appropriate foreign legislation applicable to your offshore will.

Note that the beneficiaries of a trust and/or the trust may be held responsible for paying income tax. This depends on factors such as:

- the rights of the beneficiaries of the trust;
- the discretionary powers of the trustees;
- whether the income is divided among the trust, the beneficiaries of the trust and the trustees; and
- whether income is retained by the trust.

The taxability of income from overseas sources has been changed drastically by recent legislation (residence-based taxation):

- If capital donations or loans at low interest rates are made to a trust or a person who is not a South African resident, the donor will be responsible for paying tax on all income that may accrue.
- If more than 50% of the income from an offshore trust accrues to a South African resident, the income will be taxable even if it is received in the form of capital.

In the case of an offshore trust, do not:

- form an offshore trust via a donation or loan if you (as the donor) are also a beneficiary of the trust; or
- transfer trust income or trust capital to a South African resident unless there are other beneficiaries who are not resident in South Africa

10.6 SUMMARY

Offshore investment planning has become a part of the lives of all South African investors. There are thousands of offshore investment products and the South African investor will have to do a lot of homework before investing. Various specialists should be consulted about different subjects to help you master the information required. You should also consult the many sources of financial information that are readily available.

You will have to plan very carefully before you choose specific offshore investments, offshore fund managers, and particular countries and currencies. This will enable you to reap the benefits of investing offshore, while your rand is protected against depreciation and your risk is spread through diversification. You may also take advantage of the different economic cycles of the different countries to increase the long-term returns on your investments.

Use the various opportunities for investing offshore and do not keep all your financial eggs in the South African basket, particularly if you have children or grandchildren who may leave the country in the future.

It is recommend that investors who want to invest offshore make use of the services of fund managers. Choose the right fund manager and enjoy a higher investment return in the long term, as well as income tax and estate duty benefits. Do not even consider trying to make and manage an offshore investment on your own. If you are nervous of investing overseas, you should make less risky investments.

10.7 SELF-ASSESSMENT

- Explain the importance of offshore investments to South African investors.
- You are a South African who wants to invest offshore. Discuss the local research you should do before you actually make the investment.
- Explain the influence of offshore investments on your estate and estate planning.

BIBLIOGRAPHY

Gough, L. 1998. *Going offshore: How to boost your capital and protect your wealth.* 2nd edn. London: Pitman.

Kruger, N., De Kock, A. & **Roper, P.** 2001. *The practical guide to offshore investments: 2001 – 2002.* Sunnyside: The Offshore Investment Corporation.

Melton, P. 1996. *The investor's guide to going global with equities.* Melbourne: Pitman.

Swart, N.J. 1999. *Investing your package: All you need to know.* Pretoria: University of South Africa.

CHAPTER 11

PROTECTION PLANNING

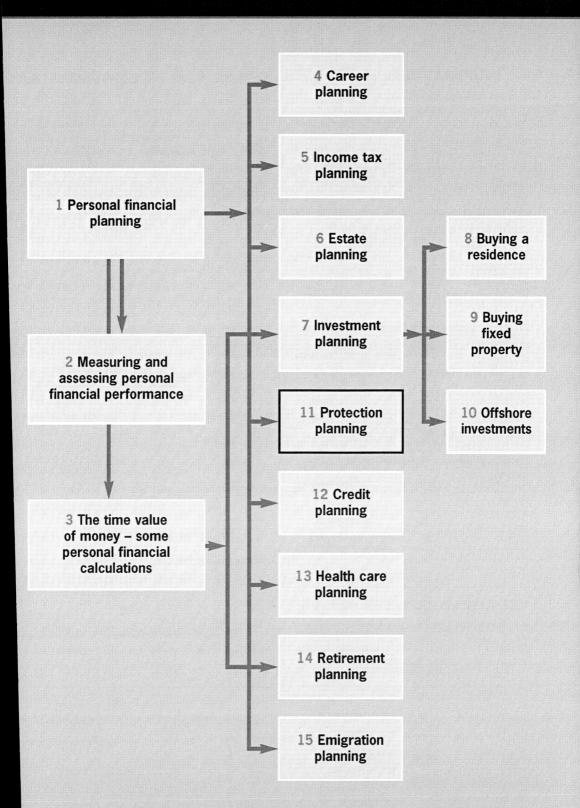

1 Personal financial planning

4 Career planning

5 Income tax planning

6 Estate planning

7 Investment planning

8 Buying a residence

9 Buying fixed property

10 Offshore investments

11 Protection planning

2 Measuring and assessing personal financial performance

3 The time value of money – some personal financial calculations

12 Credit planning

13 Health care planning

14 Retirement planning

15 Emigration planning

11.1 LEARNING OUTCOMES

After studying this chapter, you will be able to:

- Identify and quantify the various risks a house-hold is exposed to.
- Explain which financial products protect against which risks.
- Explain long-term, short-term, medical and business insurance.
- State the importance of protection planning.

11.2 INTRODUCTION

The process of personal financial planning is currently occurring in a very dynamic environment. Many amendments to legislation, as well as expected changes, leave individuals very uncertain when it comes to personal financial matters. Economic and political imperatives regarding widespread poverty, job-creation and a lack of international investment in South Africa contribute to this uncertainty.

Every individual and household is exposed to a great many financial risks. Perhaps the greatest risk is being or becoming unemployed, so each individual must continuously try to increase his or her employability. If you do have a job and receive a salary, the greatest risks are:

- a lack of knowledge of personal financial planning and management;
- too much debt and, consequently, too little cash flow for your livelihood and investments;
- children living with you, who fritter away both your life essentials and investments for retirement;
- receiving a retrenchment or retirement package and applying or investing it badly;
- children growing up with no knowledge of money matters; and
- domestic workers with no knowledge of money matters.

A basic human need is to protect ourselves and our possessions. The reason is that there is always a possibility of losing our possessions because of circumstances beyond our control, or even within our control. Uncertainty and risk have formed part of the human environment from the earliest times. To help us protect ourselves against all kinds of risk, financial institutions and insurance companies are prepared to carry part of the burden in return for a certain sum of money, paid in premiums.

You will note that risks create certain financial needs. Each individual must plan for him- or herself so as to meet these financial needs through financial and insurance products.

Buying affordable financial insurance products may result in high risk (because of inadequate financial protection), average risk (reasonable protection) or low risk (adequate protection). Many types of risk, or perhaps only the basic risks that will always be around, may remain.

The secret is to protect yourself in each of these various fields of financial planning. Below, you will be shown that there should currently be only one approach to financial planning, namely self-protection. Therefore, the protection planning perspective will be used.

As you will note, risks need to be planned for. We are, thus, also dealing with risk management as part of personal financial management.

11.3 HOUSEHOLD RISKS

Every household is unique, also regarding certain financial risks. Conversely, many risks will pertain to all individuals and households, and everyone should make provision for these.

Let us look at a list of possible financial risks that individuals and households may be exposed to. Identify the risks that apply to you in regard to each of the various personal financial planning areas:

Remember that you can provide for risks only if you are able to accommodate the associated expenses in your budget.

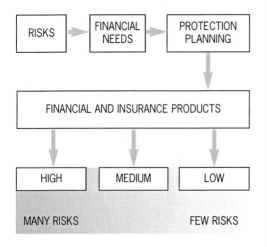

DIAGRAM 11.1 **Degrees of risk**

- career planning;
- income tax planning;
- estate planning;
- investment planning;
- protection planning;
- credit planning;
- productivity planning;
- health care planning;
- retirement planning;
- emigration planning; and
- business planning.

You should also consider the following specific risks:
- loss of income as a result of
  - death (a life policy, group insurance)
  - disease (medical insurance)
  - disability (disability insurance);
- loss of property
  - death/fire (mortgage, short-term insurance, life policy)
  - motor vehicle (short-term insurance)
  - contents of your house (short-term insurance);
- personal liability as a result of
  - home ownership (short-term insurance)
  - ownership of a motor vehicle (short-term insurance)
  - malpractices (insurance that covers liability);
- business risks (business insurance is discussed in Section 11.7.3);
- estate duty (life policy or trust with donations and loans);
- cost of winding up your estate (any investment);
- retirement (long-term investment with capital growth);
- too many debts because of 'living it up' (use borrowed money to provide for your needs and acquire assets that offer capital growth);
- inflation (investments with capital growth, adapt policies for inflation);
- income tax (use the legal instrument of tax avoidance where possible);
- frequent changes in legislation (be informed and consult a knowledgeable broker);
- interest rate changes – interest rates may drop but you are depending on your income from interest for your survival (invest for a fixed term of, say, two years);
- market risk – overseas markets may fluctuate and cause the prices of local unit trusts to drop (invest in money market funds);
- financial risks (do not finance your business with 95% borrowed money – the cost of interest is high and, therefore, your repayments will be very high);
- fluctuations in exchange rates – people who invest in foreign countries will be exposed to this risk, as will those who import or export (adapt your strategies to accommodate changes);
- national risks, for example investments in countries that are politically unstable; and
- health risks (health care planning is a prerequisite for retirement planning).

11.3.1 Needs and risks

The financial needs that arise from certain risks must be identified. After you have determined the extent of a specific risk, you must determine how often the risk may occur. As the risks increase and decrease, your financial needs will do the same. Financial needs are also determined by your goals for the future.

There are various types of financial need. All of them have their own characteristics, which will largely determine the type of financial product (investment) that should be bought (invested in) to satisfy each specific need. A single product could also satisfy a combination of financial needs.

Financial needs are made up mainly of income and capital needs. Income needs exist or develop during your lifetime, as well as in cases of unemployment, disability or disease. Capital needs exist or develop primarily after your death, in the form of mortgage debts, estate duty and the cost of winding up your estate. Your financial needs could be:
- temporary (three months, two years);
- permanent (estate duty);
- future (debts after your death);
- increasing (provision for retirement must beat inflation);
- decreasing (a mortgage bond which is decreasing); and
- constant (food, clothing).

Pay special attention to financial needs that may arise because of death, disability or retirement. Find out how you can combine provisions for these needs – ask a broker to help you. Remember, the better you know your own financial situation, the more your broker can help you.

11.4 TYPES OF RISK

There are various types of risk. Some are insurable, while others are not. Vaughan (1989:36) lists the following types of risk.

Financial and non-financial risks
In the insurance industry, the risks for which insurance is provided are restricted to financial losses. Such losses are called financial risks. A non-financial loss or risk is, for example, the emotional loss involved in the demise of a loved one (Du Toit &

Laas 1985:3). In turn, financial risks can be subdivided into speculative and pure risks.

Speculative risks
A speculative risk is one where either a profit or a loss may occur (Mowbray & Blanchard 1961:6–8). Investment in shares is an example of a speculative type of risk. The various insurance alternatives do not provide for speculative risks.

Pure risks
In the case of pure risks, there is no possibility of profit or benefit, only of loss (Mowbray & Blanchard 1961:6–8). A home destroyed by a fire is an example of pure risk, since the owner of the home would not normally derive any financial benefit from such an event.

Fundamental and specific risks
Fundamental risks have an impersonal source, such as a war (Insurance Institute of SA:3–4). These risks affect the community as a whole and it is generally accepted that the community should bear the burden of such risks. Specific risks, on the other hand, have a personal origin, and insurance provides protection against them.

11.5 CLASSIFICATION OF PURE RISKS – THE SUBJECT OF INSURANCE

We are all exposed to numerous risks. Armling & Droms (1986:237) and De Klerk (1978:39) provide the following categories of pure risk.

Personal risk
This type of risk is related to the loss of a life or an income as a result of one of the following events:
- untimely death;
- physical disability;
- age; or
- unemployment.

Property risk
Property risk is related to the possible loss of property. There are two types of such loss: direct loss and indirect loss. If your house burns down, the loss of the value of the house is a direct loss. Additional expenses involved, such as accommodation costs for six months, represent an indirect loss.

Liability risk
You may damage someone else's property unintentionally, or you may suffer injury as a result of another's negligence or unintentional action. In other words, there is a risk (called a liability risk) of being held liable for damage to another person or his or her property. The person held liable could lose assets or income as a result of a claim for damages instituted against him or her.

Insurance may be taken out against these risks, or funds may be invested with the objective of paying for such possible losses. However, sufficient funds may not be available for compensation in the event of fairly large losses. For that reason, it is essential to build up an insurance portfolio at an early stage (at a young age at a relatively low cost) in order to provide for risks resulting from unforeseen events/losses in the future.

Insurance is one method of providing cover for pure risks as part of a person's risk management. Risk management is our next point of discussion.

11.6 RISK MANAGEMENT

The purpose of risk management is to minimise the consequences of pure risks at the lowest possible cost. The following steps are distinguished (Du Toit & Laas 1985:6):
- the identification of risk;
- the evaluation of risk;
- the choice of a suitable method of handling risk; and
- the implementation of a suitable (chosen) risk programme, and periodic re-evaluation of the programme.

We will discuss these four steps briefly.

11.6.1 Step 1: The identification of risk

If you are not aware of a certain risk, you cannot take precautions against a possible loss. Table 11.1 indicates possible risks that may be identified, as well as the losses that may arise from these risks.

This table indicates risks to which individual people and small business enterprises are exposed (Athearn 1981:22). As an enterprise expands, its risk components and associated losses also increase. For the purpose of our discussion, we will concentrate on how an individual person identifies risks to his or her household.

TABLE 11.1 **The identification of risk**
(Source: Adapted from Athearn 1981:29)

Type	Risk	Possible loss
Personal		
Employee	Physical disability	Income, services, extra expenses
Employee	Death, illness, disability	Income, services, extra expenses
Property		
Industrial secrets	Theft	Income
Buildings	Damage or destruction	Assets, income, extra expenses
Equipment	Damage or destruction	Assets, income
Inventory	Damage or destruction	Assets, income
Liability		
Property (home)	Liability	Asset, extra expenses
Activities	Product liability	Asset, income, extra expenses
Activities	Pollution	Asset, extra expenses

11.6.2 Step 2: The evaluation of risk

Once the various risks have been identified, they must be expressed in financial terms. Financial implications and subsequent financial loss are determined for each type of risk. An evaluation of risk is conducted as follows (Du Toit & Laas 1985:8):

- the intensity or degree of a potential loss is calculated; and
- the frequency of a loss is determined.

Table 11.2 indicates a method of evaluating risk based on frequency and intensity (degree). Risk is classified as bearable, unbearable or unimportant.

TABLE 11.2 **The evaluation of risk**
(Source: Du Toit & Laas 1985:8)

Frequency	Intensity	Evaluation
High	High	Unbearable (1)
High	Low	Bearable (2)
Low	Low	Unimportant (3)
Low	High	Unbearable (4)

Risks that fall into group (1) should be avoided. It is possible to make your own provision for risks that fall into groups (2) and (3); it is not necessary to take out insurance for those risks. Risks falling into group (4) should be shifted to an insurance company. Whereas the risk premium would be too high for group (1), this would not be the case for group (4).

11.6.3 Step 3: Methods of handling risk

Dinsdale & McMurdie (1983:2–4) mention the following methods of handling risk:

- loss prevention and control;
- risk avoidance;
- retention; and
- transfer.

Table 11.3 gives an indication of the relationship between the various methods of handling risk.

TABLE 11.3 **Methods of handling risk**
(Source: Dorfman 1982:44)

		Frequency	
		Low	High
Intensity	High	Retention	Loss prevention
Degree	Low	Transfer	Avoidance

Loss prevention

Loss prevention or control is an activity aimed at limiting or lessening the intensity or degree of a loss. An example is the installation of a burglar alarm system in a home. In that way, thieves are deterred, which may limit the loss, for example by the arrival of the neighbours. A fire sprinkler system is another example of lessening the extent of fire damage.

Risk avoidance

Say, for example, the breadwinner of a household practises parachute jumping as a hobby. He also has a heart problem, which means that he cannot take out life insurance (he is uninsurable). Should he die or become disabled, his family would be left with a great amount of debt. In order to avoid the risk associated with the hobby, he should give it up.

Retention

Assume that a business carries stock valued at R100 000. Insurance against theft would amount to R10 000 per year (10% of turnover = 10% of the R100 000 in our example). Since the frequency of theft is low (or has been in the past), the owner may decide to carry the associated risk him- or herself. This would mean that the stock would be uninsured and the possible loss would be regarded as operating cost.

Transfer

In reality, risk cannot be shifted or transferred to someone else. However, the consequences of risk can be transferred, for example by taking out insurance against a specific risk (e.g. fire damage) with a financial institution. The risk remains with the owner of the property (for example, a home) that is insured.

11.6.4 Step 4: Implementation and re-evaluation

It is necessary to choose a programme (for example, a certain type of insurance such as a mortgage bond insurance) that will best meet your needs for protection against risk, and which is affordable.

Then, the programme must be implemented, for example by taking out insurance. The programmes or methods chosen and implemented must be re-evaluated from time to time to ensure that they are still able to prevent specific losses and to adapt to changing circumstances. Table 11.4 indicates possible products (insurance) or provisions to provide protection against risks.

11.7 NEEDS AND INSURANCE

It is important to choose the most suitable risk protection. A household is exposed to risks of all kinds. The needs arising from these risks should be addressed in order to provide the best cover possible.

It is essential to analyse the features of the different kinds of needs (see Table 11.5), since these features will determine the extent of the needs, as well as the type of product (for example, endowment insurance) best suited to the need for protection.

An income need relates to the monthly salary a person would require were he or she to become disabled and unable to work. A capital need, on the other hand, indicates the need for capital that would arise after a person's death in order to redeem his or her home mortgage bond.

A need is temporary when it is time-bound. A permanent need will arise after a person's death, when estate duty becomes payable. Although there is uncertainty about the period, there is certainty about the event (for example, death). In the case of a

TABLE 11.4 **Risk exposure**
(*Source: Amling & Droms 1986:237*)

Type of risk	Insurance
Personal risk	
• Loss of income – untimely death	Life insurance
• Loss of income – disability	Disability insurance
• Loss of income – illness or injury	Insurance with sick benefits
Property risks	
• Loss of or damage to vehicle	Vehicle insurance
• Loss of or damage to home and/or contents	Homeowner's insurance
• Loss of or damage to personal property	Personal property insurance
Liability risks	
• Liability as a result of home ownership	Homeowner's insurance
• Liability as a result of vehicle ownership	Vehicle insurance
• Liability as a result of negligence or malpractice	Comprehensive liability insurance
	Malpractice insurance

TABLE 11.5 **Features of needs**
(Source: Van der Walt 1990:11)

1. Category of needs	Income need Capital need	
2. Features of needs	Temporary need Permanent need Future need	Combination of 1, 2 and 3
3. Nature of needs	Increasing need Reducing need Consistent need	

future need, parents could, for example, begin saving to cover the cost of their children's future education.

The extent of a need could increase as a result of the declining purchasing power of money, in other words, inflation. The value of fixed property could rise, which would at the same time increase the need for capital to pay estate duty. A reducing need arises when, for example, the outstanding amount on a home loan (mortgage bond) decreases as monthly payments are made. A constant (level) need means that the financial obligation remains the same.

These needs can be dealt with separately or in combination. For example, a policy can be taken out for needs arising from someone's death, while needs arising from disability, could be avoided. These needs may also be combined, which would reduce administration costs and save money for the policyholder.

All these needs must be quantified to be of any use.

All the provisions made for needs after death must be available at the death of the person concerned.

Provision for needs must be taken into account in order to prevent unnecessary expenses. Information about existing provisions can be fairly readily obtained from insurance companies, employers and financial institutions.

The existing provisions are weighed up against the needs in order to determine shortfalls or surpluses. Shortfalls can be supplemented by acquiring a single- or a multi-insurance policy.

Various methods (or products) are available to meet the different kinds of need. The most suitable product(s) for each kind of need must be chosen within the constraints of your cash flow (personal budget). It is particularly important to compare the features of a specific product with your specific needs. In the paragraphs that follow, we will discuss some of the available insurance products.

11.7.1 Long-term insurance

By definition long-term insurance means insurance for a period of longer than a year. Long-term insurance provides for insurance:

- as an investment; and
- as protection against risks as a result of death or disability.

In the discussion below we will briefly look at the following types of long-term insurance:

- endowment policies;
- single premium policies;
- second-hand policies;
- life assurance;
- term insurance;
- universal policies;
- credit/debt life assurance;
- disability assurance;
- new generation products;
- funeral assurance; and
- medical assurance.

Insurance as a long-term investment instrument was developed with the following goals in mind:

- to provide policyholders with different kinds of indemnity; and
- to provide members with a savings plan aimed at retirement.

The broad categories of need individuals experience are the following:

- income in the case of death before retirement;
- income in the case of disability before retirement;
- income at retirement;
- capital in the case of death before retirement;
- capital in the case of disability before retirement; and
- capital at retirement.

Insurance products could serve all these needs. That is why insurance products should be included in all investment portfolios.

Insurance quotations

Policyholders (of endowment and life policies) currently receive two quotations on their policy documents, at a rate of 6% and of 12% (previously 12% and 15%). These amounts have been calculated by the Life Offices Association (LOA) and are based on future expectations of inflation and returns. The expected future values at 6% and 12% are called illustrative values. These are mere estimations and are not guarantees that policyholders will actually receive these amounts. In the case of retirement annuities, these values may be quoted at rates of 11% and 14%.

There is also a guaranteed growth rate for the investment, and sometimes a growth rate for the specific fund. Any unrealistic quotation (too high values or growth rates) should be investigated or reported to the LOA.

Let us suppose an investor takes out an endowment policy for an amount of R100 000. In the case of the policyholder's death (even after one day, week or year), an amount of R100 000 will be paid to the policyholder's beneficiary or estate. Should the policy mature, the policyholder will receive the R100 000 plus bonuses (if applicable). The R100 000 is, thus, a guaranteed amount should payments be maintained.

It is important to warn potential investors about a common error made in estimating growth rates of return when it comes to insurance quotations. Do not think that a monthly premium of R100, for example, would result in a return of a specific sum of money after a certain number of years. The return cannot simply be compared with the R100 per month to calculate a rate of return on the policyholder's money. The reason for this is the escalation clause that increases the monthly premium (initially R100) on an annual basis.

Signing your policy document

It is very important to know the composition of a policy, but even more important to check the details on your application form. Insurers sometimes examine the validity of a policy only on the date when they have to pay out the proceeds (after a claim). Applicants should be aware of what they declare and what not (e.g. diseases or surgery). It is not worth trying to omit some aspects of your life that might jeopardise the eventual payment to you of the proceeds of the policy.

Here are a few guidelines regarding the application form:
- Check all personal information before you sign.

- Ask the insurance broker to interpret the meaning and implications of questions and answers.
- If you see any errors on your application, rectify them immediately.
- Make sure that you understand what product you are buying (endowment, annuity, life, term policy), the implications of an escalation rate, medical check-ups, etc.
- Make sure that you really need the specific type of policy based on your requirements as an investor.

11.7.1.1 Endowment policies

Endowment insurance is probably the most common long-term investment vehicle. Many people have one or more endowment insurance policies. Although several uses for endowment insurance exist, probably the best uses are to provide capital at retirement and to supplement the provision for retirement. Pay special attention to the taxability of the proceeds of an endowment policy, the cession of a policy as well as the surrender value of a policy after three and five years respectively.

Endowment insurance is a very popular, traditional investment instrument. Investors contribute on a monthly basis to this investment and receive the lump sum (or income) tax-free after five years. Life cover could be added to an endowment policy. If life cover is excluded, the entire monthly premium, except for a small administration fee, is invested in an investment account.

The investor chooses a specific investment portfolio. There are three types of portfolio:
- a more stable (conservative) portfolio;
- a market related portfolio; and
- a share linked (risky) portfolio.

The first two portfolios guarantee the safety of the capital amount (total of premiums plus 4% interest). The share linked portfolio offers no guarantees but provides a much higher return on the capital invested.

Nowadays, it is possible for legal entities to invest in endowment policies (sinking funds), whereas previously only natural persons could invest in endowment policies. The fund for legal entities is taxed at 40%.

Investors tend to think about insurance products as investments on a monthly basis, for example in endowment policies and retirement annuities. It is also possible for potential investors to invest lump sums in insurance products, such as:
- single premium endowment policies;
- second-hand policies; and
- retirement annuities.

The needs that are addressed by an endowment policy are set out in Table 11.6.

Features	Needs
1. Temporary cover is provided.	1. Needs must be temporary.
2. The cover under the insurance may be constant or increasing.	2. Needs must be constant or increasing.
3. At death, disability or end of term.	3. Cash not required during the period.
4. Provides for cash/loans.	4. Need arises at death, disability and end of term.

11.7.1.2 Single-premium endowment policies

The scrapping of the Sixth Schedule to the Income Tax Act in 1993 made it possible to invest a single premium (lump sum) in an endowment policy on condition that, to be tax-free, such an investment may not be surrendered for a period of at least five years. During the term of investment, it has a very low surrender value. After the five year period, monthly cash withdrawals (from the amount left with the insurance company) are tax-free.

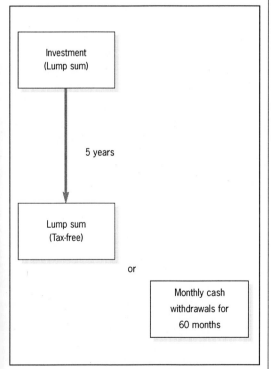

FIGURE 11.1 **Single-premium endowment policy benefits**

It is also possible to invest the lump sum and receive a monthly income (tax-free) from it.

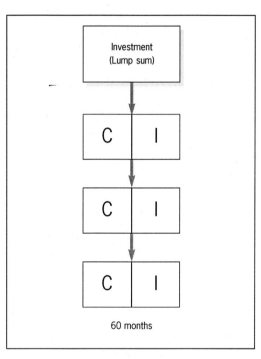

FIGURE 11.2 **Monthly income from a single-premium endowment policy**

In the case of monthly cash withdrawals, the following will happen:

- Interest (I) for the five-year period will be added to the capital (C) amount (lump sum).
- Interest and capital are divided into equal amounts (annuities) over a period of five years.
- Payments received have to be declared on the investor's income tax form, because the interest component is taxable.
- The capital portion of the payment is tax-free.
- After five years the lump sum (if it has been taken) will be tax-free.
- Income received after five years will also be tax-free.
- Capital growth is, thus, tax-free (the insurance company pays tax).

- Income received after five years does not have to appear on the investor's income tax form.

11.7.1.3 Second-hand policies

Policyholders often borrow against their policies in order to fulfil needs and desires or to handle debt crises. These loans are interest-free. Whatever the reason, in many policyholders lives their comes a day when they have borrowed as much as the policy is worth, with the result that the surrender value is either nil or very low after five years. The holder would like to get rid of these policies, preferably by selling them at a profit. Let us call this the supply side.

On the other hand, many potential investors would like to invest in an insurance policy, but do not want to wait five years for tax-free returns. This is the demand for the product. This product is known as a second-hand policy.

A potential investor could invest a lump sum in a second-hand policy. The investor would buy the policy from the insurance company and the price would be the following:
- the gross value of the policy after the five year period; plus
- 3% to 7% ('profit') on the value of the policy.

Advantages to the investor

There are quite a few important advantages to the investor, namely:
- The surrender value of the policy is tax-free at any time of the investment period.
- All income from the policy is tax-free.
- The investor receives tax-free cash bonuses or income per month.
- An increase in income is possible.
- The term of the policy can be increased or decreased.
- It is a relatively safe investment.
- A tax saving of up to 40% is possible.
- It is the ideal investment for investors in a high tax bracket.

Disadvantages to the investor
- Second-hand policies are not readily available.
- The cost of obtaining such an investment is relatively high (up to 7%).

It is important to remember that cost should never be seen in isolation. The tax savings and other advantages of second-hand policies justify such an investment.

11.7.1.4 Life assurance

The different uses of a life policy

Many individuals regard a life policy as something that is forced upon them at some stage of their lives by a 'policy hawker'. This is probably the most unin-formed view that any person could have about having a life policy. As this section will show, there is no investment that can provide more for human needs and goals than precisely such a policy. A life policy is an asset, just like a house or a block of flats. Besides the policy contract, a life policy is, at the same time, an intangible investment that enables a person to transfer his or her greatest financial risks to an insurance company. Besides peace of mind, the policyholder receives a very high return on his or her investment with a very low risk as compensation for monthly premiums.

The primary goal of every individual's personal financial affairs is to achieve financial independence after retirement. A life policy (even two or three) can help achieve this goal as no other investment can. Having a life policy, consequently, has far-reaching financial implications for the policyholder, his or her family and/or next of kin, in the case of the policyholder's death. Personal financial planning involves various planning areas. The role of a life policy in some of these planning areas will be indicated briefly.

Career planning

A life policy may be used to make provision for a child who might have university expenses in 18 years time. This can be done by having the policy paid out after 18 years. Any life policy has a surrender value after three years and this endowment value is tax-free after five years. Although a person could use an endowment policy, a life policy can also be used out of sheer necessity, for example to purchase a car.

The latter is not recommended. What about your own career, though? At any stage during your working years, or even after retirement, you may need or want to pursue another career. When this happens, you can borrow against or surrender your policy, unless you have an alternative.

People who are involved in a business should protect themselves against business risks. The closure of a business (for whatever reason) can have serious financial consequences for the owner, partner or shareholder. A private household may even be bankrupted as a result of one or more of the following (in the absence of the necessary business insurance or, rather, life policies):
- the untimely death of a key person who cannot be replaced in a partnership or company (profit turns into a loss);
- debts that a partner may incur on behalf of the partnership without the knowledge of the other partners;
- an owner, a partner or a director becoming disabled and unable to work; or
- key persons retiring.

Businesspeople can resort to the use of a variety of business insurance policies as part of their business management. Protection planning that involves taking out one, or more than one, life policy is not only advisable for employees working for an employer, but also for people who work for themselves.

Credit planning

In the case of debt, an event such as death could lead to an individual's assets having to be liquidated if he or she did not have a policy with life cover linked to that debt. Here, you could think of the debt associated with a car and especially a housing bond. If the policyholder survives paying off the car and/or house, the life policy could be used for estate duty and even as a legacy. A life policy can also serve as security for borrowing money, with the result that a car, vacant stand or house need not be offered as security. Parents often offer a life policy as security for student loans for their children. In case of an emergency, a life policy can be redeemed. In such a case, however, the policyholder loses a great deal of the investment.

Investment planning

A life policy represents the first investment that a person (with a job) ought to make. It is also the first investment that a young couple ought to make for their children. In an individual's middle age and even after retirement, a further life policy is an ideal no-risk investment. It would be well worth the potential investor's while to take the trouble to compare a life policy with other investment alternatives. The various investment criteria can be used for this purpose. In Table 11.7, a life policy is tested against these criteria.

Retirement planning

A life policy can be used to make provision for retirement. An individual can ask for the policy to pay out. Such a strategy should only be followed in the case of an emergency or where no alternative provision has been made for retirement. The same can be done in cases where the individual's estate is relatively small and/or there is no heir. The hedge against inflation and the capital growth that a life policy can offer serve to make it particularly suitable as a possible provision for retirement.

Protection planning

It is especially in the area of protection against possible risk and future events that an investment in a life policy has no equal. A basic need of every individual is to protect him- or herself and his or her possessions. From the earliest times, uncertainty and risk have formed part of the human environment. To be rid of this burden, the risks are transferred to an insurance company that is willing to carry it for a fixed remuneration. These risks are considered in Table 11.8.

TABLE 11.7 **Investment planning**

Investment criteria	Life policy
Risk	Low
Return	Acceptable
Amount invested	Very low (per month)/age factor
Term	3 years for surrender value. After 3 years it can be 'made' into an endowment policy
Ease of management	It is left to an insurance company
Knowledge required	None, an agent can inform you
Safety of capital	100% safe – it is guaranteed
Capital growth	Very good capital growth
Liquidity	Very liquid after 3 years. May be redeemed after 2 years
Taxability	Return is tax-free after 5 years
Flexibility	Very flexible – content can be adjusted
Transaction costs	Relatively low
Time calculation	Does not play a role – the best time is always to take out a policy immediately, while enjoying good health
Diversification	The risk of a portfolio may be lowered by taking out a policy
Protection against inflation	Premiums may be increased by up to 20% annually to make provision for inflation

TABLE 11.8 **Protection planning**

Type of risk	Insurance
1. Personal risk Loss of income as a result of death, disability, malpractices, sickness	Life policy
2. Property risk House with a bond, car-loan, liability	Life policy

3. Business risk
(a) Buying and selling contracts / agreements
(b) Partnership insurance
(c) Proprietary limited company - insurance
(d) Close corporation
(e) Professional incorporated company
(f) Policies favouring the employer
    (i) Key person insurance
    (ii) Overdrawn bank account
    (iii) To cover a personal guarantee
    (iv) To cover a shareholder's loan account
    (v) To cover a mortgage loan
    (vi) To provide a cash reserve
(g) Policies favouring the employee
    (i) Deferred remuneration scheme
	Life policy
	Individual life policy
	Joint life policy
	Policy on another's life
	Life policy
	Life policy
	
	Life policy
	Life policy
	Life policy
	Life policy
	Life policy
	Life policy
	Life policy
	Life policy

4. Responsibility for estate duty/capital gains tax	Life policy
5. Estate administration costs (a) Executor's fees (b) Transfer costs (c) Charges for selling assets	 Life policy Life policy Life policy
6. Transfer duty	Life policy

All the risks indicated in Table 11.8 can be covered with the help of a life policy.

Estate planning
A life policy can be used to good advantage to pay estate duty and all other estate administration costs. This can be done by using policy proceeds to pay for estate liabilities and debts, including the transfer costs (transfer duty, stamp duty and conveyancing fees) when property is transferred to beneficiaries (natural or legal persons).

Sometimes people consider the transfer of property to a trust *inter vivos*. Unfortunately, the cost involved in such a transfer is prohibitive. The only alternative is to make provision for a testamentary trust in a will, accompanied by a life policy to accommodate the higher estate duty because of the individual's larger estate. Only a life policy can provide R1 000 000 after a month (if, for example, one insurance payment of R1 000 is made once) in order to pay the estate's liabilities if the owner of the estate dies within a month after taking out the policy. No other investment of R1 000 can provide R1 000 000 after one month in the event of your death.

A spouse and children can benefit in the event of your death. If you do not have sufficient life cover, take out a life policy before you experience ill heath, in which case your monthly premium will be very high, provided of course that you can still obtain a life policy.

Remember that life insurance can also be included in your endowment policy or retirement annuity.

Whole-life assurance
Whole-life assurance can be taken out to protect you against the financial consequences of death or disability.

This type of insurance stretches over the whole life of the insured. The insured pays premiums until death, after which the benefits go into the estate or to the beneficiary/beneficiaries. Whole-life insurance does not have loan or surrender value and pays out only at death or disability. Table 11.9 shows for which needs this kind of life insurance is suitable.

TABLE 11.9 Features and needs of whole-life assurance
(Source: Van der Walt 1990:26)

Features	Needs
1. Cover is provided permanently	1. The need must be permanent
2. Cover under the insurance may be constant or increasing	2. It must be constant or increasing
3. Only required at death or disability	3. Cash not required during the period
4. Provides cash/loans	4. Need only arises at death or disability

11.7.1.5 Term insurance

As with whole-life assurance, you can take out term insurance to protect against the financial consequences of death or disability. It often happens that someone requires the coverage/protection only for a specific period, for example the 20 years required for paying off a mortgage bond.

The policyholder's mortgage will, therefore, be paid if he or she dies during this period. The coverage offered by the policy will also decrease as the outstanding amount on the mortgage decreases. In year 21, there be no more coverage. If the house or policy owner is still alive, the following will pertain:

- the mortgage bond remains paid up;
- there is no more life or disability cover; and
- no premiums need be paid.

Term insurance does not have loan or surrender value. Table 11.10 shows for which needs term insurance is suitable.

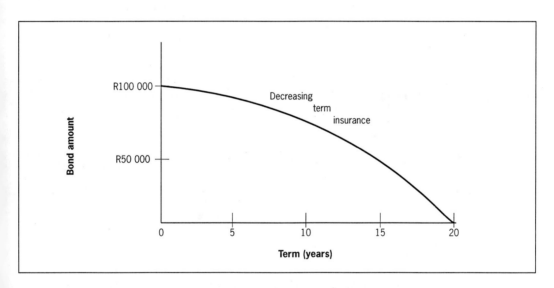

FIGURE 11.3 Term insurance and bond amount

TABLE 11.10: Feature and needs of term insurance
(Source: Van der Walt 1990:24)

Features	Needs
1. Cover is provided for a fixed term	1. The need must be temporary
2. The cover may be constant or reducing	2. It must be constant or increasing
3. Only required at death or disability	3. Cash not required during the period
4. Does not provide cash	4. Need only arises at death or disability

11.7.1.6 Universal policies

In the case of a universal policy, an endowment policy is combined with both life and disability cover. It has the same characteristics as an endowment policy and a life policy, with basically the same application possibilities, and therefore provides:

Investment + life insurance + disability insurance.

For example, a parent may take out a universal policy to pay for a child's studies in ten years' time. If the parent dies, the money is available, thanks to the life cover on the parent's life. If the parent is still alive when the ten-year period ends, the policy pays out, and the total amount is available.

11.7.1.7 Credit/debt life assurance

This type of life insurance offers coverage for present debts. If a person dies after incurring certain debts, the debts are repaid with the amount provided by the credit life assurance. Credit life assurance includes both life and disability coverage. It is also called decreasing-term life assurance, because the coverage amount decreases with the debt period. Decreasing-term life assurance is much cheaper (lower premiums) than term assurance.

As with any other type of debt financing, it is important that the debt term should be the same as the term of the debt coverage (i.e. the term of the policy). Always make sure whether you have an existing policy that could rather be ceded to pay the debt, unless you have written proof that the debt excess (after paying off the debt after death) of the policy will go to the policy beneficiaries or your estate (as you wished, and as indicated in your will).

11.7.1.8 Disability assurance

This kind of insurance can be taken out to provide for loss of income, and does not include medical expenses or medical cover. Disability insurance protects the family from loss of income if the breadwinner suffers a prolonged period of illness or becomes occupationally disabled. In the case of occupational disability, the need for an income is usually much greater than in the case of the breadwinner's death. Medical expenses are high in the case of a person who is unable to work or earn an income.

For this reason, it is possible to invest money to provide for occupational disability. However, the problem is that the investment has a slow growth rate and would be insufficient after a few years if a person becomes occupationally disabled. Another possibility is to purchase disability insurance. Penson et al. (1982:186) mention three considerations when purchasing disability insurance:

- Determine the level (amount) of income that will be received in the event of occupational disability. Most policies pay between one-half and two-thirds of a person's normal income. If more than this were paid out, it would encourage people to stay at home rather than return to work. The other half or third (the loss of income) will still have to be supplemented from investments (which may not even exist).
- Determine under which circumstances the policy will pay out. Before taking out a policy, you should ask yourself or the insurance agent or broker the following questions, in order to establish whether you have made adequate provision:
  - When is a person regarded as occupationally disabled?
  - Are benefits paid out if you are unable to do any work at all or only if you cannot do your present (previous) work?
  - Are both partial and total disability included in the policy?
  - For how long does the policyholder have to be disabled before he or she begins to receive benefits?
  - Is there a limit (cash amount) attached to the total benefits which will be received during the policyholder's lifetime?
  - Are benefits paid to the surviving spouse in the event of the policyholder's death?
  - Does the policy offer insurance/cover in the event of illnesses and accidents?
- Determine the costs of the policy. It may be impossible to pay the monthly premiums, unless you adjust your personal budget. Normally, the extent of the cover determines the premium amount. Occupational disability usually only lasts for a short period. Your choice will be influenced by this factor if you cannot afford the (extensive) cover.

If two policies offer the same total cover, it is better to choose the one with the higher cover over a shorter period. Remember to take into account the sick leave per annum allowed by your medical aid fund.

In Table 11.11, Mittra (1990:123) mentions further key questions and recommendations to be taken into account when purchasing disability insurance.

Disability insurance can be taken out for particular periods and amounts. It is also important to know about the various types of disability, because this influences the payment (or not) of disability benefits. The practical definition of disability mainly acknowledges the following types of disability:

- if you can no longer do your present work;
- if you can no longer do work similar to your present work; or
- if you can do no work at all.

TABLE 11.11 Features of a good disability policy
(Source: Mittra 1990:123)

1. How does the policy define disability?	Select the policy that covers partial disability, not the one that specifies benefits only for total disability.
2. What job definition does the company use?	Select the company which uses the 'your occupation' definition, not the 'any job' definition.
3. Is the policy non-cancellable and guaranteed renewable?	Choose a policy that guarantees that the policy will be renewed at the rates guaranteed in the policy up to the age specified (usually 65).
4. Does this policy cover disability resulting from both accident and illness?	Select the company that covers both forms of disability.
5. For what period of time will the policy pay?	Select the policy that covers at least until age 65.
6. How much will the policy pay?	Select the company which pays at least 60% of take-home pay at the time of the accident or illness.
7. How long is the waiting period?	A three-month waiting period is preferable.
8. Does the company offer cost-of-living adjustments?	The basic benefit should rise automatically by a set percentage or in step with inflation.
9. Does the policy offer standard-of-living adjustments?	After a policy has been in force, the insured should be able to boost the monthly benefit by a certain amount at standard rates without a medical examination.

As with life cover (a life policy), every person should have disability cover. Most employed people enjoy disability cover through their employers' group cover. You can get further cover from an insurance company. The type of work you do (dangerous or not) and the state of your health will be the main determinants of the premium you pay for this type of cover. Furthermore, make sure that you understand the maximum benefits you can get from all your disability benefits.

11.7.1.9 New generation products
Insurance companies currently offer not only products that will cover you in the case of financial risks as a result of death or disability, but also investment products that are known as new generation products. These products may be combined for maximum returns or capital growth, or for spreading local or international risks (total risks). In this case, we are thinking particularly of a product such as a fund of funds or a wrap fund.

11.7.1.10 Funeral assurance
A funeral policy is taken out to cover or help to cover funeral costs. No person can escape the costs involved in a funeral, because we will all die at some stage. Funeral expenses are, therefore, inevitable and require timely financial planning and provision.

Before a funeral policy pays out, an identity document, death certificate and form filled in by the next of kin (or executor or beneficiary) should be presented.

The costs involved in the funeral policy will vary on the basis of:
- the insured's age;
- the number of insured persons (e.g. the entire family); and
- the type of policy required.

Typical cost-items involved in a funeral include the following, depending on the insured's culture or prosperity:
- the coffin (R1 000–R20 000);
- a hearse (R500–R1 000);
- the undertaker (R1 000–R1 500);
- a mortuary fee (R500–R800);
- a higher municipal fee for a grave for someone living, for example, on a farm but wishing to be buried in town;
- a higher municipal fee for a grave in another residential area;
- catering costs for guests; and
- a gravestone (R1 200–R20 000 or higher).

Thus, a funeral may cost between R5 000 and R50 000, depending on your needs. Furthermore, funeral costs are constantly rising.

Funeral costs may be covered in various ways, for example:
- from existing investments;
- a life policy;
- a funeral policy (from a funeral insurance company); or
- through your group benefits.

Make sure that you know what your funeral policy contract stipulates. You should know what your cover involves, and review your requirements every year.

What about cremation?
Your will should clearly state whether you wish to be buried or cremated, and whether you wish to donate your organs. As an alternative, cremation involves the following cost-items:
- the cremation process itself (R300–R500);
- the cremation coffin (R200–R300);
- a place in a memorial wall (R500–R700);
- a small grave in a cemetery for the ashes (R1 100–R1 400);
- if a farm dweller wants such a facilities in the town's cemetery, it could cost up to three time as much as for someone living in town; and
- the usual funeral costs (catering, etc.).

11.7.1.11 Medical insurance
The financial risks involved in medical expenses may be handled in various ways. The costs and risks may partially or totally be:
- carried personally by paying for them in cash;
- 'covered' by public health care;
- transferred onto a financial institution or insurance company; or
- transferred onto a medical aid scheme.

A combination of one or more of these strategies is another possibility that is sure to be followed in most cases.

In this discussion, 'medical insurance' refers to something known in practice as additional cover or top-up cover. The reason for this is that the cover is taken out in addition to a medical aid fund, and is meant to help cover additional medical and related costs. Medical insurance is, therefore, not a medical aid fund, and involves a contract that includes an insurance policy. The benefits may be used as you wish, and the amount is paid directly to the policyholder. Specific cover is offered, and benefits are paid only in specific cases.

A hospital policy requires that members pay a monthly premium. The benefits received are based on the size of the monthly premium and not on the specific amount in medical expenses. The content of a hospital policy differs among different insurers, as in the case of medical aid funds. Nevertheless, there are some common features:
- Irrespective of the amount paid out by the policyholder's medical aid fund, the hospital policy pays out a cash sum. (This cash sum can be used in any way, according to Sanlam's hospital policy.)

- Amounts received from a hospital policy are tax-free.
- A basic policy consists of a hospital benefit and a recovery benefit.
- The whole family can be covered.
- Optional operation benefits may exist.
- Larger benefits are paid for more serious operations.
- In certain cases, an endowment amount is linked to a hospital policy (for example, Old Mutual's Flexicare).
- There is no limitation on the number of times a member (or family members, if they are covered by the policy) can be admitted to hospital.
- The premium is determined by the age of the person, as well as by the number of family members included in the policy.
- Benefits can be protected against inflation.

Guidelines when purchasing medical insurance
It is suggested that the following aspects of medical insurance be examined before purchasing such insurance:
- Most medical policies (for example, a hospital policy) offer a period of ten to 14 days to decide whether the policy is acceptable or not. This period should be used to examine the policy contract thoroughly.
- Note the policy's renewability, directions concerning cancellation, the waiting period, as well as which medical conditions are excluded. It is no use taking out a policy that excludes your particular kind of medical condition.
- Make sure that the policy will cover you worldwide. A traveller through various countries may require medical cover, irrespective of where he or she is. The same applies to people who only travel occasionally.
- Find out whether the policy will still be available to other members of the family at a lower tariff after your death.
- Not all policies cover children once they have achieved independence. A specified age (for example six to 18 years) is often established during which the dependants of a policyholder (excluding a spouse) still receive medical cover.
- Find out whether the policy covers medical conditions existing at the time of the policy date of commencement.
- Make sure that medical expenses will be covered every time they occur, irrespective of the number of times a year. Cover should, therefore, apply to every medical condition, irrespective of the frequency of the condition.
- Avoid a situation where various policies exist,

with each covering a single medical condition. Rather purchase a policy offering comprehensive cover. This eliminates the possibility of paying twice or more for the same cover (medical condition).

- It is usually in the policy applicant's interest to purchase a policy through a professional agent.
- Never allow an agent or a broker to exert pressure on you to purchase a certain policy. First make sure that you can afford the premiums from your domestic budget.

Top-up medical cover

As in the case of a hospital policy, top-up cover can be taken in addition to your medical aid fund. Top-up cover is a type of insurance and not a medical aid fund. As with a hospital policy, top-up only covers specific medical costs. You should, therefore, ensure that you know exactly what cost-items are involved or not involved.

Medical schemes

Most working individuals belong to their employers' medical aid funds. However, it is possible to belong to a medical aid fund if you do not belong to such a fund through your work relationship. In practice, such a medical aid fund is called an open-market medical scheme. Members of such a scheme pay a higher premium, because it is not subsidised by an employer.

Some concepts relating to medical aid schemes are now briefly explained:

- The Medical Association of South Africa (MASA) is a professional body to which doctors belong and which issues guidelines regarding medical fees.
- The Board of Healthcare Funders (BHF) is a body to which medical aid funds belong.
- Scale of Benefits (SOB) are BHF rates, that is medical fees.
- 'Contracted in' means that a doctor charges SOB fees, and your account is sent to the medical aid fund on your behalf.
- 'Contracted out' means that a doctor charges you higher than SOB fees, and then presents you with the invoice and you must pay it (you can then send the invoice and your receipt to your medical aid fund to recover the cost or a part thereof).

Managed care

Managed care means that medical aid schemes try to arrange their relationships with hospitals, doctors and pharmacists in such a way as to keep medical costs as low as possible. Members of the medical aid scheme are, therefore, encouraged by incentives (e.g. medical savings accounts) to limit medical 'claims'

to a minimum in order to keep costs down. Furthermore, they are encouraged to apply health care planning (see Chapter 13) in order to ensure the financial life of the medical aid scheme in the long run. Medical savings accounts mean that fund members who rarely visit a doctor have an investment they can use at a later stage, even if they are no longer with the same employer or medical aid scheme.

Life Offices Association (LOA)

This association represents the (long-term) insurance industry and attempts to protect its interests. The LOA also distributes information in the industry concerning people whose risk is too high and who should, consequently, not be allowed life insurance. This includes people who have experienced heart attacks or who have certain medical conditions and are, therefore, uninsurable.

The names of people at high risk are entered into a computer and no insurer will give them insurance. For this reason, it is important to obtain the necessary life insurance as early as possible, before some medical condition or accident makes this impossible. Sometimes, a person's name is given to the LOA by mistake and he or she would subsequently have to appeal to the courts to have his or her name removed in order to obtain insurance.

If your name has been given to the LOA by a medical practitioner, usually you cannot take out any insurance from any insurer for a period of eight years. However, if you pass the necessary medical tests, you may possibly be able to obtain a small amount of insurance. The monthly premium would be higher, however, because the insurer would load the policy.

Those who cannot obtain life insurance at all should apply for a pure endowment policy. The proceeds from such a policy are taxable within the first five years, however. Legislation does allow the taking out of a relatively small endowment policy on which the proceeds will be tax-free. The monthly premiums (per debit order) may not exceed R123 and must be kept up for a period of ten years.

One solution is to invest any available money every month for emergencies (sickness, medical expenses). In other words, uninsurable people should do everything in their power to place money in some scheme or another that promises a good return.

An alternative is to apply for membership of a medical aid scheme. People with AIDS will not be able to obtain life insurance or medical insurance anywhere, unless they are due to receive benefits from a policy that they have owned over a long period, or from a policy that includes AIDS cover.

The same applies to people who have tested HIV-positive during a medical examination after an application for an insurance policy.

11.7.2 Short-term insurance

As the name indicates, short-term insurance is insurance taken out to meet short-term needs, i.e. for periods of less than a year. This does not mean that the risk requirement disappears after a year. In this discussion, we will briefly look at the following types of short-term insurance:
- home owner's insurance;
- household insurance;
- motor vehicle insurance;
- travel insurance; and
- self-insurance.

11.7.2.1 Home owner's insurance

This type of insurance protects a house or building against risks like damage or destruction by fire. If a financial institution grants a mortgage bond, it usually insists that life cover be taken for the amount of the bond, so as to protect its interest in the property. As a property owner, you are also covered against personal liabilities in terms of such a policy.

You will notice that a house is not covered for political unrest, for example, in such a home owner's insurance policy. Extra cover will have to be taken for this as part of the short-term insurance under household contents insurance.

11.7.2.2 Household insurance

This type of insurance covers the contents of a dwelling (movable property), such as furniture and other personal belongings, against various types of damage. You must insure the contents for the full replacement value, or else the averaging method will be applied when you lodge a claim. This means you will be compensated in the same proportion (of the actual replacement value) as your underinsurance.

11.7.2.3 Motor vehicle insurance

You may insure your car in one of the following three ways:
- comprehensive insurance (covers your own car and another car in case of an accident, covers you against fire, theft and damage);
- third party (theft and fire) insurance (covers you against damage to another car and for theft/fire damage to your own vehicle); and
- third party insurance only (covers you against damage to another vehicle).

You should try to take out comprehensive motor vehicle insurance. You should also know that in case of an accident in which you sustain injuries, you may claim from both your short-term insurance company and the Road Accident Fund.

11.7.2.4 Travel insurance

Travel insurance is a must for travellers, be they in South Africa or abroad. This type of insurance offers cover against the following, amongst others:
- loss of luggage;
- costs of a delayed flight;
- medical costs; and
- legal costs.

This is particularly important because medical aid funds do not always cover your medical costs abroad. Make sure your broker is able to help you in an emergency, and that you know exactly the extent of the accident and medical benefits your travel insurance contract offers you. You must also always know for what period you will be requiring the travel insurance.

11.7.2.5 Self-insurance

Although monthly short-term insurance premiums are regarded as part of the household budget, many people do not accept these payments without protest. It upsets people to see how their premiums are increased every year, whether they have made claims or not.

People also find it difficult to be forced to increase their short-term insurance cover every year. If they do not, they become underinsured and will be entitled only to part of a claim. In addition, policyholders' monthly premiums are increased when they have submitted claims.

Before a motor vehicle is insured, the engine number must be stamped permanently on all the windows, and an alarm and/or a gear lock must be installed. A house must have burglar bars, an alarm system linked to a reaction unit, as well as safety gates and fences. All of these requirements cost people a lot of money before they can successfully submit an application for short-term insurance and later a possible claim for loss.

Why do we have to spend such a lot of money on short-term insurance when we do not get any return on our money? Could this money not be invested in unit trusts or kept in savings accounts?

Concerns and questions like these are often raised in the hope that somebody will be able to answer them. Is an emergency fund a solution?

What is an emergency fund?

When you establish an emergency fund, money is invested so that the accumulated amount will be available in a crisis situation. The owner of the emergency fund must be disciplined and deposit a premium in the fund every month. He or she has full control over the utilisation of the fund. The aim of such a fund is to make your own provision for possible future losses.

Assumptions for a successful emergency fund:
- A financial disaster such as car theft or a car accident will never occur to you, and your house will not burn down.
- When such a disaster does occur, the fund will be large enough to cover the damage.
- It is unlikely that more than one disaster will occur within a short period.
- No disaster will occur in the first ten years. This will allow the fund sufficient time to grow because of compound interest.
- You will pay many small claims yourself and will not use the money in the fund.

Why establish an emergency fund?

There are various reasons why people establish emergency funds to self-insure their houses, contents of their homes and cars:
- They do not receive any returns on their insurance premiums.
- They are 'throwing away' their money.
- They are under economic pressure.
- The household budget does not balance.
- They have an overdraft to repay.
- The premiums are too high.
- They personally never submit claims.
- As soon as a claim is submitted, the premiums are increased.
- They are unemployed.
- The premium covers all the furniture but thieves steal only TVs, video recorders, technical equipment, firearms and jewellery.
- Premiums are increased every year.

Types of emergency fund

- People could cancel all their short-term insurance and deposit the premiums in an emergency fund (savings account).
- They could self-insure part of their property but leave fire insurance and/or limited motor vehicle insurance in the hands of the short-term insurer. Limited motor vehicle insurance means, for example, that the person only has insurance against damage to somebody else's car.
- It is possible to establish a mutual fund with friends or family. Each year, joint premiums and compound interest will increase the amount in the fund. The members of the fund should draw up a written document with special conditions for the payment of claims. It would be advisable to consult an attorney before you establish such a fund.

Disadvantages of an emergency fund

There are many disadvantages:
- The interest is taxable.
- The value of the fund is eroded by inflation (depending on the type of investment).
- After-tax interest in the emergency fund will prevent rapid growth.
- Should a house be destroyed by fire within the first year, you may be sequestrated but still have to pay the mortgage bond.
- You will have to save for almost a decade to replace the furniture of an average household.
- You may be involved in an accident with a luxury car and, as a result, lose all your possessions.
- Two or three accidents (risk situations) can occur in the same year.
- It will take a lifetime to save enough money to replace a house that has burned down (should this be accompanied by various car accidents and thefts, you will die impoverished and unable to leave anything to your heirs).
- Possessions accumulated over 30 or 40 years could be lost at any time.
- This kind of fund causes stress, and you will not have peace of mind when you go on holiday.
- The risks of an emergency fund are higher than those of even the most risky share.
- Monthly payments into the emergency fund must be increased every year to keep up with inflation.
- Within a day of being established, the emergency fund will have to be large enough to cover the loss of a house, furniture and a car.
- Friends or family members may die and this may cause problems among fund members.
- Members of the fund may be sequestrated.
- People may get divorced and one of the spouses may make a claim against the emergency fund. The other spouse may also refuse to make further payments because he or she does not want to continue to insure the other's assets.
- If people also have business property, this will be even more risky to insure because of the higher risk of fire, for example.
- Making provision for your own insurance is just as risky as paying the premiums of your medical aid scheme into an emergency fund to cover medical expenses (on your own or with friends or family).

11.7.3 Business insurance

Protection planning is not only for employees working for an employer, but also for people who work for themselves. Anyone who is involved in a business in one way or another should protect him-

or herself against business risks. The closure of a business holds serious financial implications for the owner, partner or shareholder. A private household may even be liquidated as a result thereof.

Insurance affords protection against business risks. It is necessary to plan in order to avoid or eliminate these and other risks which may have far-reaching implications. Amling & Droms (1986:231) use the term *risk management* for this process of addressing needs that may arise in the future of a business enterprise. Businesspeople may use a variety of business insurance policies as part of their risk management. These polices are briefly discussed.

11.7.3.1 Buy-and-sell agreements
The purpose of this kind of insurance is:
- to ensure the continuity of the business; and
- to build up a reserve fund for unforeseen circumstances.

With this type of policy, all the partners and shareholders of the business enter into a buy-and-sell agreement. This agreement obliges them to sell their share in the business enterprise to the remaining partners or shareholders in the event of their death. The remaining partners or shareholders are also obliged to buy the deceased's share. The method to be used for the assessment of the deceased's share is also stipulated in the agreement.

This agreement means that the remaining partners and shareholders are at greater risk and must have sufficient funds available to buy the deceased's interest in the business. Partners and shareholders rarely have sufficient funds available. Besides, their assets are usually fixed in the business, while their profits have also been reinvested in the business.

A life policy on the lives of all partners, directors and shareholders (of a large business) would be the solution. In that way, a cash reserve would be built up with which the surviving partners (who take out the policy in the deceased's name) could buy the deceased's share. A separate life policy may be taken out on the lives of all the partners. After a partner's death, a new life policy would have to be taken out on the lives of the remaining partners or directors.

According to Jordaan (1988:60), a buy-and-sell agreement based on a life policy, has the following advantages:
- It ensures that the business can continue doing business.
- No goodwill is lost.
- It ensures the continuation of creditworthiness.
- It is not necessary to discharge (retrench) employees.
- The surviving partners do not suffer financial damage.

11.7.3.2 Partnership insurance
The primary purpose of this type of insurance is to provide sufficient capital to the other partners to enable them to buy the deceased's share in the partnership in the event of the death of one partner. The deceased's estate must be compensated for his or her portion of the partnership's assets.

The surviving partners usually do not have the necessary capital to buy the deceased's share in the business. The loss of specialised knowledge or special skills could force the partners to employ someone else with the necessary expertise. This would make further inroads into the capital available. Partnership insurance covers such risks, and the needs that may arise from them, by providing the necessary capital to the surviving partners.

The proceeds from the policy would eliminate the need for the surviving partners to take out loans, to sell their interests or other assets or to employ unacceptable partners (for their expertise) because of a lack of funds. Various types of partnership insurance policy will now be briefly discussed.

Joint insurance policy
This policy is taken out on the lives of two partners (rarely more than two). The costs involved are lower than they would be for two separate policies. The policy pays up and, therefore, ends at the death of the first of the two partners. After that, a new policy must be taken out.

Single life policy
A partner may take out a policy on his or her own life and cede it to the other partners. The agreement between the partners will state that this policy must be used to buy the deceased's share in the partnership. The surviving partners will have to pay the premiums of the life policy, however. In this way, the proceeds of the policy will be regarded as capital and the policyholders will not be liable for income tax. Obviously, these premiums are not deductible for income tax purposes.

Life-of-another policy
This type of policy is used where three partners (A, B and C) are in partnership. Partners A and B take out a life policy on the life of C. B and C take out a policy on the life of A. A and C take out a policy on the life of B. For the rest, the functions of the policy are similar to the previous two types of policy. For more information on this type of policy, consult Miller & Irwin (1990).

11.7.3.3 Proprietary limited company insurance

A company is a legal entity (body corporate) and exists separately from its shareholders. A proprietary limited company may even have only one shareholder. The shareholder owns shares in the company, may vote at general meetings and may also elect the board of directors (Miller & Irwin 1990:J8). The shareholders of a proprietary limited company are often family members or a group closely involved in running the business. When one shareholder dies or retires, the shareholders usually agree to a share selling transaction. If a shareholder in a proprietary limited company dies, the business usually continues as before and the deceased's shares go to his or her heirs and the surviving shareholders.

Conflict may arise between the surviving shareholders and the heirs for the following reasons (Miller & Irwin 1990:J9):

- The shareholders wish to see future growth, while the heirs want an immediate income.
- To the shareholders, salaries are of primary importance and dividends are secondary, while the heirs want high dividends.
- An heir may sell his or her shares to a stranger, even a competitor.

The above situations could interrupt business activities and have a negative effect on creditworthiness and profitability. The only possible solution to prevent all these negative consequences may be to buy the deceased's shares through a buy-and-sell agreement, supported by a life insurance policy (Miller & Irwin 1990:J9). The purpose of this business insurance policy is to provide sufficient funds at the time of a shareholder's death to enable the survivors to buy his or her shares. The directors should take out a life-of-another policy on each other's lives. Provision must be made to ensure that the proceeds of such a policy are payable to the directors and not to the company.

11.7.3.4 Close corporations

A close corporation is a legal entity (body corporate) that exists independently from its members. A close corporation may take out insurance policies on the lives of its members who have an interest in the corporation, in order to buy a member's interest at his or her death or disability at a later stage (Miller & Irwin 1990:J15). Because of the taxability of the proceeds, it is not recommended that a close corporation takes out policies on its members' lives to finance buy-and-sell agreements. Members should rather take out separate policies on each other's lives (Miller & Irwin 1990:J16).

11.7.3.5 Professional incorporated companies

Certain professional practises are also allowed to act as companies, provided that the directors accept liability jointly and separately and that they are properly qualified natural persons (Jordaan 1988:63). The shareholders of a professional incorporated company may also take out insurance policies, for example pensions and provident funds, on the same basis as shareholders of a proprietary limited company. Professional people normally do not have the right to pass their shares to their heirs. The shares have to be sold to the surviving shareholders or a qualified outsider. This problem could be solved by a buy-and-sell agreement, supported by life insurance policies (Jordaan 1988:63).

11.7.3.6 Policies on the lives of employees

Policies are usually taken out on the life of an employee or even a company director for one of the following reasons (Miller & Irwin 1990:C1):

- to provide a benefit for the employer or the company; or
- to provide a benefit for both employer and employee.

Policies in favour of the employer
Key person insurance
A business enterprise often has an employee or employees who contribute greatly towards profitability. The untimely death of such a key person could cause great financial loss, owing to the loss of his or her expertise, experience and training. An employer may protect him- or herself against such loss, however, by taking out key person insurance, thereby utilising bridging (hedging) funds from the key person insurance policy in order to:

- ensure the business enterprise's continuity;
- cover losses over the adjustment period;
- pay for the recruitment and training of a substitute;
- ensure continuous creditworthiness; and
- guarantee continued dividends (Jordaan 1988:61).

Insurance to cover a specific liability
To insure a bank overdraft. The untimely death of a director could seriously affect the creditworthiness of a business. For that reason, insurance policies are often taken out on the life of a key director in order to consolidate the loan capital of the business enterprise.

To cover a personal guarantee. A company director may wish to insure a personal guarantee which he or she may have provided (for example, to another company). In order to prevent a situation where the director's personal assets have to be used at the time of his or her death to honour the guarantee, he or she may transfer the burden to an insurance company by having the company take out a policy on his or her life (Miller & Irwin 1990:C11).

To cover a shareholder's loan account. Companies with a liquidity problem may not be in a position to redeem a shareholder's credit loan account at the time of his or her death. To prevent this problem from arising, a low-cost term policy may be taken out on the shareholder's life for twice the required amount (Miller & Irwin 1990:C13).

To cover a mortgage loan. A company with a mortgage loan on a property may insure the managing director's life for the outstanding amount, so that the property is unburdened should the director die unexpectedly. The company may take out a reducing term policy, whereby the covered amount reduces as the company's debt reduces (Miller & Irwin 1990:C14).

To provide a cash reserve. If a company should find it necessary to build up a cash reserve for future events, it may take out a policy on the life of a key director. A life or an endowment policy may be taken out. Such an insurance policy would enable the company to build up a cash reserve that would become available at the untimely death of the director or when the policy term expires (Miller & Irwin 1990:C14).

Policies in favour of the employee
Deferred compensation
Deferred compensation is normally used when a highly paid employee will not benefit from a salary increase because of the tax implications. Such employees often agree to the company taking out an endowment policy on their lives in lieu of a salary increase. An agreement is made that the company will pay the proceeds of the policy to the employee at retirement, or to his or her heirs in the event of an untimely death (Miller & Irwin 1990:C14).

The main objective of this insurance policy (or the deferred compensation) is to offer additional incentive schemes to key employees and to retain their services until they retire (Jordaan 1988:62). Consequently, continuity of management personnel and a stable worker corps is ensured. Many varieties of this compensation scheme are possible in terms of an agreement between the employer and the employee. Jordaan (1988:62) states that deferred compensation has the following advantages:
- additional tax benefits to the employee at his or her retirement;
- the employer may deduct a certain percentage of the premiums from his or her taxable income;
- employees' conditions of employment are improved and their loyalty retained; and
- it affords the employee's dependants and the business enterprise additional financial protection in the event of his or her untimely death.

Policies in favour of both employee and employer
Employers may take out a life or an endowment policy on the life of an employee for two reasons:
- to obtain the benefit for the company, should the employee die before his or her retirement; and
- to provide the employee with a benefit, should he or she live until retirement.

In these circumstances, a service contract, in which the two purposes of the policy are set out, would be entered into with the employee (Miller & Irwin 1991:C26).

11.7.3.7 Short-term insurance policies
To supplement long-term insurance policies, there is also a wide range of short-term insurance policies to cover the businessperson's exposure to risk. In return for the payment of premiums, the insurer undertakes to compensate the insured for certain events described in the policy.

As the name implies, short-term business insurance policies provide cover over the short term. Most short-term insurance companies provide for:
- fire insurance, against damage to a property owing to fire, lightning, explosions or other associated hazards;
- building insurance, against loss or damage to buildings and outbuildings, equipment and electricity and water mains;
- business interruptions, against loss suffered as a result of the described events;
- accounts receivable, where the relevant account books are damaged and outstanding debt balances cannot be determined;
- theft, where the contents of a building are lost as a result of breaking and entering;
- money lost or damaged;
- glass, both internal and external, as well as signage;
- dishonesty, where the insured loses money or property as a result of theft or fraud by an employee;
- goods damaged or lost in transit from transport vehicles;
- all-risk, for loss or damage of property anywhere in the world by any events which are not specifically excluded;
- public liability, against claims for damage for which the insured is held legally liable, as described in the policy; and
- employer liability, against claims by employees or next of kin in the event of sickness, injury or death.

Businesspeople may avoid risks in their environment by taking out insurance against these risks.

This insurance can be taken out on a long- or short-term basis. Long-term insurance is taken on the life of the employer or employee in favour of one or both parties. The main purpose of insurance is to avoid financial loss as a result of someone's death. The purpose of short-term insurance is to afford the businessperson protection against a wide variety of specifically defined risks.

11.8 SUMMARY

In summary, it may be said that everyone should protect him- or herself by means of protection planning. By identifying the risks a household is exposed to, specific needs may be addressed. Once these needs (risks) have been quantified, they may be addressed by buying the most suitable product or products.

There are many financial and insurance products that individuals should know about. Efficient protection planning can take place only after the risks, needs and particular products have been harmonised. In this way, you can protect your belongings in times of great uncertainty and change. You should seek this protection for every planning area.

11.9 SELF-ASSESSMENT

- Explain the importance of protection planning.
- Discuss the various financial risks to which South African households are exposed, as well as possible measures that can be taken against these risks.
- Explain medical insurance.
- Motivate the importance of business insurance.

BIBLIOGRAPHY

Amling, E.A. & Droms, W.G. 1986. *Personal financial management.* 2nd edn. Homewood: Irwin.

Athearn, J.L. 1981. *Risk and insurance.* 4th edn. New York: West.

De Klerk, G.J. 1978. *Versekeringswese: 'n Historiese oorsig en enkele bedryfsekonomiese aspekte met speciale verwysing na groepversekering.* D.Com. thesis. Potchefstroom University for Christian Higher Education.

Dinsdale, W.A. & McMurdie, D.C. 1983. *Elements of insurance.* 5th edn. London: Pitman.

Du Toit, G.S. & Laas, A.O. 1985. *Versekeringswese 1. Study guide 1 for BEC207-X.* Pretoria: Unisa.

Dorfman, M.S. 1982. *Introduction to insurance.* Englewood Cliffs: Prentice-Hall.

Insurance Institute of South Africa. *Grondbeginsels van versekering (Suid-Afrika).* (Course 551). Johannesburg.

Jordaan, J.H. 1988. *Boedel en finansiële beplanning: 'n Praktiese gids.* Cape Town: Old Mutual.

Miller, R.J. & Irwin, W. 1990. *Tax advantages of life insurance.* 15th edn. Johannesburg: MDR.

Mittra, S. 1990. *Practising financial planning.* Englewood Cliffs: Prentice-Hall.

Mowbray, A.H. & Blanchard, R.H. 1961. *Insurance.* 5th edn. New York: McGraw-Hill.

Penson, J.B., Levi, D.R. & Nixon, C.J. 1982. *Personal finance.* Englewood Cliffs: Prentice-Hall.

Van der Walt, P.J. 1990. *Lewensversekering en uittredingsannuïteite: 'n Besluitnemingsmodel.* Research project for B.Com. (Hons.) Pretoria: Unisa.

Vaughan. E.J. 1989. *Fundamentals of risk and insurance.* 5th edn. New York: John Wiley & Sons.

CHAPTER 12

CREDIT PLANNING

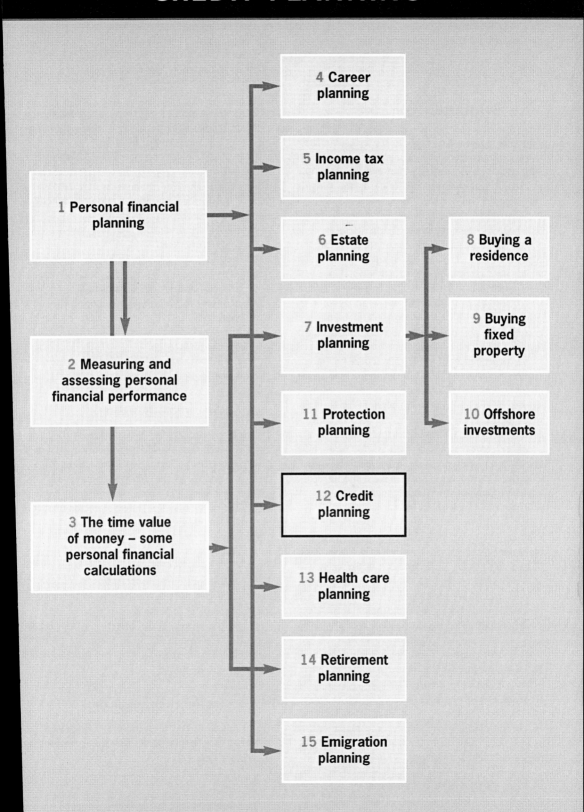

12.1 LEARNING OUTCOMES

After studying this chapter, you will be able to:
- Explain the importance of credit planning.
- Identify the problems that arise from making use of excessive credit.
- Explain the application for credit.
- Identify steps to handle a debt crisis.
- Apply debt self-management.
- Assess banking services.
- Explain the functioning of credit instruments.
- Examine a credit agreement more critically.
- Define micro-lenders and the role of the MFRC.
- Ensure that your name never appears on a credit information bureau's blacklist.

12.2 INTRODUCTION

Everyone makes use of credit at some stage in their lives. Without credit it is simply not possible to address all your needs. Today, however, many people desire far more than their basic needs and for this they acquire more credit than they are able to handle, which often results in huge financial problems with far-reaching financial consequences.

A personal budget should make provision for the repayment of credit. This will ensure that you know when you can afford to make further purchases and how much you can afford. Clearly, people should plan before they incur debt or use credit facilities. In other words, it is vitally important to maintain a planning programme before making use of credit facilities.

The consequences of utilising credit are profound, and everybody should be fully aware of how credit affects a household. In the discussion that follows, we will briefly examine credit planning and credit instruments. These instruments are used to address certain needs. It is crucial to understand how a credit agreement works, as well as how important good credit references are over the long term. Effective credit planning can prevent the unpleasantness of having your name appear on the credit information bureau's blacklist.

Most countries have large amounts of debt that they cannot repay, unless their repayments take place over centuries. This culture of debt has been passed on to us, as we finance our entire existence with debt. We, too, find it impossible to escape from this debt spiral; we get deeper into debt to finance the payment of existing debt. We then become 'debt slaves' without the financial freedom to live quality lives. In fact, we have so much debt that we can sustain great emotional and psychological damage. Still, each person has the power to decide whether he or she wants to keep on struggling as a 'debt slave' for ever, or whether to escape from the 'debt jail' once and for all.

Debt must be properly planned and managed. To escape from debt and stay out of debt requires purposeful debt self-defence. We are solely responsible for this aspect of our lives, which can have a profound positive or negative influence on our quality of life and financial freedom.

Unless debt is planned and managed very well, it is nobody's friend, certainly not in the long term. Most people who find themselves in a debt crisis (not to mention debt administration or sequestration) have done one of the following:
- continued accumulating debt without realising the long-term effects;
- ignored the use of a personal or household budget;
- begun to live tomorrow's dreams today;
- stood surety for the debt of someone else, or a business;
- lost his or her job;
- married or divorced; or
- continued with an undisciplined lifestyle where more was spent than was received.

12.2.1 Conceptual framework

Credit: The word 'credit' is derived from the Latin '*credere*', which means to charge someone with something or entrust someone with something. Today, credit is described as 'the ability to obtain goods and services immediately at a promised future cash repayment'. The buyer, therefore, offers a portion of his or her creditworthiness to the seller. The seller, on the other hand, accepts this credit offered by the buyer. In other words, the buyer makes use of the credit provided by the seller (Lovemore 1991:1).

Debtors: Debtors buy goods and/or services and promise to pay for them in future in terms of a mutual agreement of some kind.

Creditors: Creditors allow buyers to buy goods and/or services on credit from them (in terms of some kind of agreement) and to pay for the goods or services in the future.

12.2.2 The functions of credit

Credit has three specific functions, which all take effect at a separate level in the community (Lovemore 1991:11):

- the economic function (at macro-level trade and industry);
- the social function (at consumer level); and
- at management level (at micro-enterprise level).

For the purposes of personal financial management, the social function of credit is important. Individual consumers can make use of credit and obtain the immediate benefits of purchased goods and/or services while paying for them in the future. This means that a consumer does not have to save the required amount in cash before making a purchase. Credit enables consumers to improve their standard of living immediately.

12.2.3 The importance of credit

The importance of credit cannot be overemphasised. A prerequisite for effective credit management is an understanding of how credit works, an awareness of certain factors associated with credit and a sound knowledge of your own personal financial position. Only then is it possible to plan the utilisation of credit according to the objectives you have set for yourself.

If you do not make use of credit, it means that you have to pay cash for all your purchases. In other words, you would first have to save enough money before entering into any transaction. Since the prices of goods and services are continuously rising, whatever purchases you have in mind would have to be deferred indefinitely. Most people's standard of living would drastically decline and it may even result a return to the old bartering system!

12.2.4 Why people incur debt

There are countless reasons why people buy goods and/or services on credit at some stage of their lives. You should ask yourself why you are spending money you do not have. Buying on credit means that you are prepared to pay more (interest) for goods and/or services than they actually cost (the cash price). Different people have different motivations for buying on credit. Whittaker *et al.* (1990:83) list the good as well as the wrong reasons for incurring debt.

Good reasons
- A good bargain may be available today which would most likely cost double the price at a later stage.
- The cost of an article may be rising so rapidly that it would be impossible to save for it.
- An old motor car may require repairs every second month and it would be more economical to replace it.
- To finance an income-generating asset (e.g. fixed property).

The wrong reasons
- Being taken in by a clever salesperson.
- Credit encourages the buying of unnecessary gifts for friends and colleagues.
- Credit allows people to have large and expensive birthday parties.
- Credit encourages the purchase of expensive clothing to keep up with fashions.
- It is easy to purchase items such as a new car because a colleague has done so (he or she may have received a promotion and can afford it, while you cannot).
- Your neighbour's child is given a car to drive to university and you feel pressurised into buying one for your child too.
- To feel good about your material surroundings.
- To create the impression of being rich.
- Thinking that life is about material possessions.
- A financial power display to impress others.
- You feel you 'owe' it to yourself (especially when you feel emotionally weak or unstable).
- You want it all now (and are not prepared to wait until you can afford it, both financially and emotionally).
- Everybody else seems to use debt and to finance their lifestyles with debt.
- To invest in 'get-rich-quick-schemes' or over-optimistic projects or businesses (the problem here is that you keep on throwing good money after bad money).
- To live the life other people (colleagues, friends, admirers) expect of you.
- To lift your spirit when you suffer from low self-esteem.
- To use up all your credit facilities because you are creditworthy (this will erode your financial freedom).
- To impress your spouse or spouse to be.
- To feel successful and to portray a picture of success in life.
- To see debt as the only way to accumulate possessions.

Whittaker *et al.* (1990:84) point out that the right reasons are based on logical decisions, such as buying on credit in order to save, whereas the wrong reasons are based on emotional decisions. Emotional buying decisions are very often made in the absence of personal or household budgets. People who do not have a budget are often inclined to buy on credit without being aware of what they are letting themselves in for. The result is that when unexpected expenses or events crop up, there is no money to pay for them. The end result is a decline in standard of living.

12.2.5 Responsible conduct

Many people do not know how to use credit or when they should refrain from incurring any further debt. It is necessary to have a responsible attitude towards using credit facilities. Irresponsibility may well result in having to face the awful consequences of a sale in execution (liquidation).

A responsible person always endeavours to prepare him- or herself for unforeseen circumstances and events. This applies to financial matters as well. Everybody should live within their means, in order to protect their possessions. A person who makes excessive use of credit is living beyond his or her means and is in danger of losing all his or her possessions.

These days, the public is exposed to a great deal of clever advertising in the media, which encourages them to buy on easy terms. For those who are already struggling to meet their current financial obligations, 'easy terms' are misleading. They should avoid incurring any further debts.

All the members of a household should be aware of their responsibility in this respect, including the children. It is essential to make the whole family aware of the family's current financial situation and to elicit their co-operation in avoiding unnecessary credit.

12.2.6 Inexpensive credit

Credit is seldom, if ever, inexpensive. Usually the price of credit (interest) is high. Some employees receive a large enough allowance from their employers to make the purchase of a motor car less onerous. Bank managers, for example, receive home loans from their banks at such a low interest rate that you could call it inexpensive credit. Allowances and subsidies do make credit less expensive under certain circumstances.

Individuals pay hundreds of thousands or even millions of rand in interest on debt during their lifetimes. When interest rates rise or are at a high level, these interest payment amounts become even larger. Let us use a simple illustration to show someone's annual interest payments.

An amount of R71 800 is, therefore, paid annually in respect of interest on debt. It should be quite clear that debt is not cheap, and could put you in the 'debt jail' for a long period of time. For a 20-year period, the interest alone amounts to more than a million rand.

12.2.7 The cost of credit

The price paid for credit is called interest. It is important to know the difference between nominal and effective interest rates attached to an agreement. This aspect has been explained earlier.

The longer the term of a credit agreement, the lower the interest rate levied. A housing loan is a good example. Credit over a longer term, however, results in higher total interest than over a shorter term. When a motor vehicle is paid for in instalments or in terms of a leasing agreement, the interest rate is considerably higher (for example, 24%). A shorter term, not exceeding five years, means that the total interest paid is much less than over a longer term.

The costs of credit are called transaction financing costs. Loan rates vary according to the risk the applicant (potential buyer) holds for the creditor. People who hold a lower risk can borrow money at a lower rate than those who hold a higher financial risk. Potential buyers (applicants for credit) should compare effective interest rates (actual interest rates) before they decide to buy on credit

However, interest is not always the only cost item in a credit transaction. The applicant is often required to take out life as well as disability insurance. Creditors usually receive a commission for an insurance policy sold to a customer. The premiums for such a policy are frequently unnecessarily high. Potential buyers should be wary of purchase schemes that demand that a certain policy be taken out with a specific insurance company.

EXAMPLE

Type of debt	Debt amount (R)	Annual interest rate	Annual interest
Bond on house	R200 000	17%	R34 000
Car financing	R100 000	24%	R24 000
Bank overdraft	R50 000	18%	R9 000
Credit Card	R20 000	24%	R4 800
TOTAL	R370 000	–	R71 800

12.2.8 Linking the credit term to the term of need

You should match the term for which you borrow money with the term for which you are going to use the money. It is not advisable to take out a housing bond in order to buy a new lounge suite, since the interest would have to be paid over a fairly long period (for example 20 to 30 years), which would make the lounge suite very expensive.

It is also not advisable to use a bank overdraft to buy a home. A bank loan may be called up after one year, and the total loan amount would become payable. A short-term loan should, therefore, not be taken in order to meet a long-term need.

12.2.9 Need versus desire

It would be very nice if we could all buy whatever our hearts desired. However, lack of the necessary funds and/or creditworthiness makes this impossible. Good marketing often results in people feeling frustrated, because they are unable to buy goods and/or services they see advertised. This frustration motivates and encourages people to buy things whether or not they can afford them.

People should buy only those things they are capable of paying off. It is most unwise to incur a large amount of debt and then to lie awake worrying about how you are going to pay it off. Debt can also lead to many financial and psychological problems, particularly if you are forced to sell all your possessions in order to repay your debt. You should not try to fly higher than your wings allow.

It is important to make a distinction between needs and desires. A need refers to what a person really needs, whereas a desire refers to those things a person would like to own, chiefly because of their beauty or status value.

People should learn to withstand the temptation to acquire things they cannot afford. Competition with others for material welfare or status should be avoided. People who appear wealthy are often battling to pay off large amounts of debt. Do not be tempted to get into debt because you have confused apparent wealth (as a result of large debts) with the real thing.

12.2.10 Credit and savings

The more debt you incur, the less money you can save because you have to use most of your financial resources to repay the debt. If you were to save more, you would have more money to make cash purchases or to pay off your debts. People who save their money do not need to buy on credit. A house-

hold budget allows for a comparison of amounts available for savings and for repaying debts. It is essential to budget for both.

12.2.11 Credit and the household budget

If a household does not have a budget, the household often does not understand why it is so difficult to pay off their debts. Not only is it important to know how much money is coming in, but also how much money is going out. The household's income, as well as its expenditure, must be included in the budget. A budget enforces discipline and helps people to settle their debts. It also prevents them from incurring further debts, since a budget indicates when it is not possible or advisable to incur further debt and pay it off in instalments.

12.2.12 Advantages of credit

- It enables the buyer to maintain a higher standard of living.
- Goods and/or services may be bought at a lower price than in two or three years' time because of inflation.
- A person may purchase goods and/or services that he or she would not normally be able to afford, or would only be able to purchase years later.
- Debt may enable a person to earn a higher rate of return (for example, 15%) on borrowed money than the cost of the borrowed money (for example, 12%).
- Credit allows people to buy goods on a sale at a large discount (for example, half price).
- A credit facility protects people against unforeseen events, such as a motor car accident.

12.2.13 Disadvantages of credit

- Credit encourages people to buy things they cannot afford.
- Interest must be paid on the borrowed money.
- Should you lose your job and, consequently, your income, you would not be able to pay off the debt.
- Excessive credit often results in liquidation.
- Credit leads to impulsive buying.
- Security is necessary to obtain credit.
- Credit is usually accompanied by additional costs, such as life and disability insurance.

- People do not always accept the responsibility attached to obtaining credit.
- It is invariably more expensive to buy on credit than to pay cash.
- Debt erodes a person's security.
- People often buy things they do not really need.
- Even investments (insurance or shares) are often bought with borrowed money.
- Debt can put people in the 'debt jail' and keep them there for the rest of their lives.

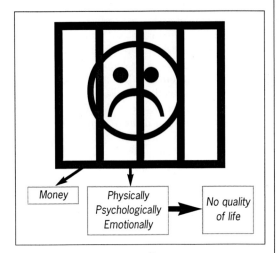

FIGURE 12.1 'Debt jail'

12.3 THE APPLICATION FOR CREDIT

When someone applies for credit, the creditor assesses the following aspects concerning the applicant before extending the credit (Swart 1992:27):
- gross annual income;
- marital status;
- number of dependants;
- life and endowment insurance policies;
- period at present address;
- career;
- references;
- ownership of a bank account;
- existing or new client;
- ownership of fixed property;
- possession of a home telephone;
- age of applicant;
- term of contract;
- applicant's credit record;
- employer;
- period employed by present employer;
- total annual expenses; and
- total amount of bonds and other debt.

These aspects of the credit applicant are called credit standards. Once the applicant has been assessed on the basis of these standards, the institution providing the credit determines how much credit can be allowed. This information concerning the applicant is kept for long periods.

Credit institutions are concerned about an applicant's stability as far as credit standards are concerned. People with unstable lifestyles (for example, frequent changes of address and accounts only paid every second or third month) will experience difficulty in obtaining credit, and their credit lines are usually lower than would normally be the case.

It has been found that applicants who have paid their debts regularly in the past will continue to do so in the future. People who do not pay their debts regularly seldom change their repayment behaviour. Creditors obviously do not like going to the trouble of collecting their money (by sending letters of demand or making personal visits). Think how you would feel if you have given someone a loan and have to incur costs in order to get your money back.

Creditors today normally contact the credit information bureau to find out about applicants' creditworthiness. People with an honest lifestyle have nothing to fear from this practice.

12.3.1 Credit policy

A seller's credit policy consists of guidelines that determine whether credit should be granted to an applicant. Normally, a credit policy consists of the following:
- the stipulation of conditions for extending credit;
- deciding on an acceptable degree of risk (which the applicant may hold);
- the gathering of information about the credit applicant in order to establish whether he or she meets the institution's credit standards;
- an analysis of the client's creditworthiness (his or her ability to incur debt and to pay it off); and
- the acceptance or refusal of the credit application.

The following aspects regarding the gathering of credit information should be stressed (Unisa 2001:141):
- establishing an applicant's legal capacity to enter a credit transaction;
- assessing the ability to repay the credit;
- checking the attitude of the person towards credit, and towards the payment of creditors in the past, by obtaining different references; and
- checking the person's stability with regard to residence (area), employment, contactability and income in relation to number of dependants.

It is important that the information below is supplied in the application form (Unisa 2001:142):

Biographical information
- full names;
- date of birth and age;
- title;
- identity number;
- marital status;
- number of dependants;
- language preference; and
- type of occupation.

Demographic information
- residential address;
- postal address;
- telephone numbers;
- employment address; and
- home ownership and type of home.

Income and ability to pay
- gross income;
- spouse's income;
- other sources;
- accounts; and
- other liabilities.

Stability factors
- period of residence;
- telephone at home;
- home ownership;
- political stability in area of residence;
- period of employment;
- industry employed in;
- position or status of employment;
- how well qualified for position held; and
- political stability in area of employment.

Contactability factors
- contactability by mail or telegram; and
- whether a legal process can be served on the debtor either at home or at work.

When someone has supplied the required information in the application form, the supplier of the credit will evaluate it. Points are awarded according to the information, and the amount of credit the person may be granted is determined on those grounds.

The seven Cs of credit

A person or institution is generally granted credit after the seven Cs have been thoroughly investigated, namely:
- character of the applicant (honest);
- collateral offered as security;
- capacity (being able to pay/repay);
- capital (the assets of the person);
- conditions in the market and country;
- credit history (payment obligations); and
- common sense.

12.3.2 Credit conditions

An institution's credit conditions specify the repayment conditions that are required of all credit clients. The amount of the instalments and the term of repayment are included in these conditions. These aspects of obtaining and granting credit are important when you apply for credit and when you need to evaluate a credit application (as employee or employer).

12.4 HANDLING A DEBT CRISIS

Many people run into trouble paying their monthly expenses at some stage. In the absence of a domestic budget, such problems may be encountered frequently. Even those who keep to a budget and exercise self-discipline may experience the following problems:
- a vehicle breaking down;
- a vehicle that has to be replaced;
- arrear tax that has to be paid; and
- an unexpected operation accompanied by high medical costs.

Careful personal financial planning, with provision for such unexpected events in a budget, will help prevent a shortage of funds. A crisis, however, is altogether another matter. It indicates long-term problems that urgently demand attention, after which action plans should be implemented meticulously.

A crisis often arises as a result of excessive debt. This occurs because a person has exhausted his or her creditworthiness and is simply no longer capable of fulfilling his or her financial obligations. For example, he or she may be unable to repay an overdrawn credit card or shop account or to repay a loan from a friend. The debts and the interest are just too much to cope with.

It is important that people or a household who run into financial trouble should understand that undisciplined buying habits and mismanagement of money have caused their predicament and that they have adopted a lifestyle that could bring about their financial downfall, unless they can find a solution to the crisis. In the event of the breadwinner losing his or her job and remaining unemployed, it would be virtually impossible to recover. Liquidation would be the result.

Firstly, the household should decide to change its lifestyle once and for all and never to revert to a situation of overspending. Unless they make this decision, they will suffer another financial crisis.

Communication with creditors is a second point of importance. The creditors should be approached and the situation explained to them. There may be another way of paying off the debt. Perhaps the creditor will accept a vehicle or will allow the debtor to do a job for him or her in repayment of the debt.

It may be possible to get a loan from the bank to cover all the debt. A new arrangement may then be made with the bank manager for repaying the loan over a longer term. This new agreement should be strictly adhered to, or the household may lose everything they own.

Finally, you may be declared insolvent. This would mean converting all your assets into cash (if possible) to pay your debtors. Thereafter, you will be known as an unrehabilitated insolvent for a specific period. You will not be allowed to enter into any business transactions within this period, with the exception of daily transactions with money earned in the form of a salary. You will be able to buy bread and clothing, for example.

Your name will inevitably appear on the credit information bureau's blacklist, which will deny you any further credit. After a certain period (stipulated by the court) you will become a rehabilitated insolvent, after which you may conclude transactions again in your own name. The problem would resurface if you required credit in the future.

In a financial crisis situation it is essential to draw up a new budget. In this way, you will know when you are spending too much. You must decide to eliminate all unnecessary spending and simply keep to basic everyday needs. A household finding itself in financial trouble may have to consider some of the following measures:

- sell the television set;
- allow the television service contract to lapse;
- give up a pay-to-view contract;
- sell or give away pets;
- use one car for driving the family to work and school;
- use the bus to get to work;
- never eat out;
- buy less meat;
- do the housework themselves;
- wash the family car themselves;
- remove certain electric lightbulbs;
- make fewer telephone calls;
- cut down on socialising; and
- stop entertaining.

Another option would be to work overtime or take a second, part-time job.

People often make use of their insurance products to escape from a debt crisis. We will now briefly consider:

- surrendering a policy;
- borrowing against a policy; and
- ceding a policy.

Surrendering a policy

When an investor surrenders a policy, it means that he or she decides to:

- stop paying premiums on a policy; and
- ask the insurance company to repay the invested payments to him or her.

Unfortunately such an investor would lose a substantial amount of money, as follows:

- In the first year of paying premiums, basically all the investor's contributions will be used to pay the commission accrued to the insurance broker.
- The return on investment will either be very low or negative.
- The insurance policy will no longer serve as an investment for retirement.
- The investor's financial discipline may deteriorate, with the result that more than one policy may be surrendered.

The main reasons for surrendering a policy are the following:

- The investor may be faced with a debt crisis.
- The investor may be without a job.
- A vacation may be needed.
- A non-investment like a car may be envisaged as a replacement for the insurance policy (an investment).
- The monthly premiums may be too high as a result of a 20% (for example) escalation clause.
- The investor may be unable to afford the monthly premiums, because the policy was bought injudiciously under sales pressure from an insurance broker.

Think twice before you surrender a policy. Although the reason(s) for surrendering a policy may be valid, policyholders should consider the following actions instead of surrendering the policy:

- Decrease or remove the escalation clause/rate.
- Stop the monthly premium payments and make the policy paid up.
- Secure the surrender value of the policy from the insurance company and sell the policy in the second-hand market.
- Take a loan against the second-hand market policy (see borrowing against a policy).

- Make use of another investment or non-investment (e.g. sell a car) to alleviate or solve your problem.

Borrowing against a policy

When in need of money, many people borrow money against their insurance policies. This is costly to the policyholder, more costly if the policy is paid up, and very costly where life cover is included. The premiums for life cover have to be paid, even if the policy is paid up. Where this occurs, it has an eroding effect on the amount of capital invested in the paid-up policy. It may be a cheaper option to obtain money by using the policy (even a paid-up policy) as collateral.

Where money has been borrowed against the policy, it is important to repay the loan if the investor wants to maintain the investment. Otherwise, the investor loses the value of the investment (as at the date of the loan) within a few years due to interest charges and (where applicable) life cover premiums.

The amount that may be borrowed against a policy may normally not exceed 90% of the current value of the policy. Certain loans require interest to be paid at a rate between 1% and 3%. Another type is interest free, but the policyholder loses the growth potential (for example, an investment in shares) of the borrowed money.

Ceding a policy

To cede a policy means that the policyholder passes the rights to the policy proceeds to a natural or legal person (a bank, for example). The cession may be temporary where the policyholder cedes a policy to a bank in order to obtain a loan. When the loan is repaid, the bank cancels the ceded policy and hands it back to the policyholder.

In the case of the death of the policyholder (who ceded the policy), the proceeds of the policy are paid to the bank. If this amount is larger than the debt, the remaining funds are paid back into the policyholder's estate.

It is also possible to cede a policy permanently as:
- a gift to a child, spouse, grandchild or friend;
- part of an antenuptial contract where one spouse cedes a policy for whatever reason to the other spouse (the policyholder normally undertakes to pay the premiums for the term or life); and
- part of a divorce settlement.

Policyholders should bear in mind that it is not possible to cede a policy within two years prior to:
- liquidation;
- insolvency; or
- sequestration.

According to Section 44 of the Insurance Act, such a ceded policy belongs to the curator of the insolvent estate. The practical implications are devastating from a financial viewpoint for the institution or person who supplied money in the case of a loan in return for the ceded policy.

12.5 DEBT SELF-MANAGEMENT

Debt must be managed. Unfortunately no one is going to manage your debt for you (unless it is the result of debt administration and insolvency or sequestration), so you must do it yourself. Furthermore, we must manage ourselves in regard to incurring debt, and the actual reasons for it (often emotional or psychological). This is the origin of the concept of debt self-management.
- Debt planning refers to the judicious and purposeful incurring of debt for needs and goals.
- Debt control means watching your cash inflows and cash outflows.

Debt self-management =
lifestyle management + lifestyle discipline + financial discipline

Of course debt management means that you must know:
- who is responsible for paying all your debt obligations, namely yourself;
- who incurred the debt in your life, namely yourself;
- who the only person in your life is who put you in the 'debt jail', namely yourself; and
- whose lifestyle will have to be changed once and for all in order to escape from the 'debt jail', namely your own.

Furthermore, it is important to know which factors in your life caused your debt, and whether you can control them or not.

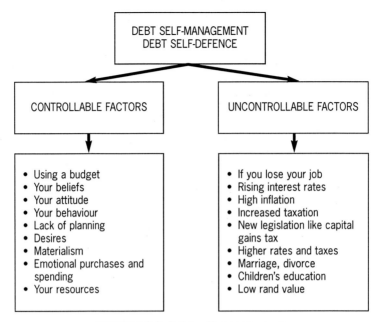

FIGURE 12.2 **Debt self-management**

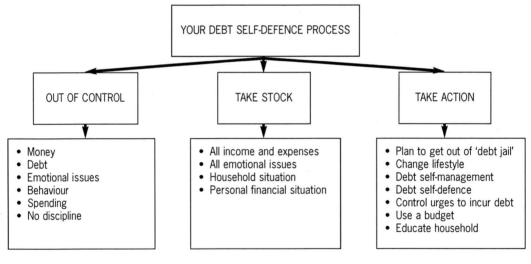

FIGURE 12.3 **Debt self-defence**

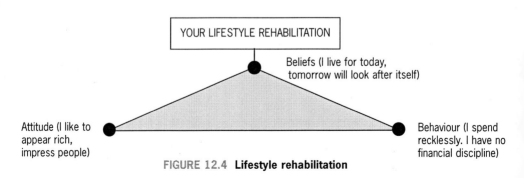

FIGURE 12.4 **Lifestyle rehabilitation**

A person can change his or her lifestyle in order to escape from the 'debt jail'. However, this involves a sustained process of debt rehabilitation over a long period of time. A lifestyle is not acquired overnight, and will not be changed or unlearned overnight. You should persevere in your efforts to change your debt situation for the better, forever.

Debt warning signs

Vorster (1996:63) offers the following debt quiz to determine whether there are danger signs on the debt horizon:

TABLE 12.1 **Warning signs quiz**

Question	Yes	No
Are you spending too much time worrying and thinking about your financial affairs, and debts in particular? Do you feel trapped?		
Are you always feeling guilty about your debt situation? About the risks you are taking?		
Do you only pay the minimum amount on your credit cards each month?		
Do you have to borrow money to help you out until the next pay-day?		
Do you have to borrow money every time when some unexpected expense (like unforeseen house or car repairs) crops up?		
Are you avoiding opening the mail?		
Have you ever lied to anyone about your finances?		
Have you considered changing you job because you can earn an extra R200 per month with the new employer?		
Have you recently tried to shift credit by paying the instalment on one credit card with another, or by increasing or taking up a bank overdraft?		
Do you borrow money to pay for holidays?		
Do your cheques sometimes bounce?		
Are you always behind with paying bills, or pay them just in the nick of time?		
Do you receive letters threatening legal action?		
Have you received a summons from a creditor during the last three months?		
Have you borrowed any money from your parents or relatives lately?		
Do you owe your parents or relatives for monies borrowed from them previously?		
Have you had the necessity to negotiate with any creditor, including the bank, to grant you a moratorium or accept smaller monthly instalments than they called for?		
Is your bank account permanently overdrawn to its limit?		
Have you used up the maximum credit allowed on your credit and retail credit cards?		
Do you have to use the budget option to pay for purchases financed through your credit card?		
Have you lately told some creditor that the cheque is in the mail, and you knew it was not true?		
Have you recently avoided answering the telephone or told your spouse not to answer it during the daytime or pretended you were someone else, for fear that some overdue creditor is looking for his or her money?		
Are you hiding some information about your debt situation from your spouse or partner?		
Do you jump at the opportunity when some retailer issues a new retail credit card?		
Have you issued a personal cheque without knowing if you have funds in your banking account, hoping that it will be honoured?		
Do you buy everything (including your food) on credit?		
Have you used up your credit limit in respect of your clothing accounts?		
Do you avoid balancing your cheque book?		
Have you seriously thought of being sequestrated (declared insolvent) lately?		
Have you contemplated (even in passing) to commit suicide because of your financial situation and debt problem?		
Have you considered misappropriating/embezzling money to square your debts?		
Do you have a budget?		
Do you know how much you owe your creditors?		
Do you know how much you are short each month?		

Vorster (1996:66) points out that apart from the final three questions, the answer to all the others should be 'no'. This warning signs quiz should be filled in regularly, unless you are living entirely without debt, which is Vorster's suggestion for financial freedom.

12.6 DEBT AND LEGAL REMEDIES

We have already mentioned the debt and debt crisis so many people find themselves in. We have also touched on some aspects of debt self-management to escape from the 'debt jail'. However, if you find it impossible to escape from this debt crisis by yourself, even after having applied the required debt self-management, there are still a few things you can do. These steps range from paying your debt to sequestration.

According to Theys (1993:26) the following legal remedies exist that could be used to escape from a debt crisis:
- offer of settlement;
- selecting certain creditors above others;
- voluntary distribution;
- administration order; and
- friendly or voluntary sequestration.

The discussion below will briefly touch on each of these aspects. Another option is compulsory sequestration, when the court orders you to pay your creditors. Let us first look at what you can do yourself to escape from your debt crisis without being summonsed by others.

12.6.1 Offer of settlement

There are unconditional and conditional offers of settlement.

Unconditional offer of settlement
Theys (1993:27) points out that you may offer your creditors any amount of money, either as a lump sum or in instalments. Of course, any of your creditors could use such a settlement offer against you as an 'act of insolvency'. This means that you admit that you are legally bankrupt and that your creditors may apply for your sequestration. Such an offer of settlement is made in the form of a letter. The creditor must react in writing.

Conditional offer of settlement
According to Theys (1993:28) the condition means that the offer is made for the 'full and final settlement of all claims against you'. The creditor is advised that if the attached cheque is cashed, you

will take it that all your debts have been paid and your conditions have been accepted.

Always dispatch such an offer by registered mail, keep a copy and remember to indicate who will pay the legal costs if the creditor has already issued a summons. Theys (1993:29) emphasises the importance of sticking to this offer, and making sure that you can afford it. According to him, a settlement is the best method to reduce the creditor's risk of non-payment.

12.6.2 Selecting certain creditors above others

Another 'act of insolvency' you may commit is to pick certain creditors above others and to pay them first. The other creditors then have to wait their turn until you decide to pay them. Some will be furious, and others will simply accept it; therefore, give priority to urgent debt, as opposed to less urgent debt. Urgent debt refers to creditors who can no longer wait.

12.6.3 Voluntary distribution

Theys (1993:30) defines voluntary distribution as a settlement agreement with all your creditors. This means you choose a trustworthy person to undertake the distribution amongst creditors on your behalf. You pay a monthly amount to this person, who may be, for example, your lawyer. It is important that your creditors should accept this person. You must indicate how much you will pay each creditor per month. The distribution is normally done on a *pro rata* basis according to the amount available for payment. Post the list of payments to all creditors by registered post. Voluntary distribution is also an act of insolvency.

12.6.4 Administration order

An administration order is a court order, according to Theys (1993:32), and is available to a debtor with less than R50 000 in debts (who is not able to pay these debts). An application for an administration order is lodged in the Magistrate's Court in the area in which the applicant (the debtor) lives. A great deal of information is required on the application form, which you can buy at any stationers that sell legal documents.

Feel free to consult a lawyer to help you complete the application for administration. The lawyer can also help you to send a copy of the application for administration to every creditor. Your application is then considered in court. Even though you may appoint anybody as your administrator, it is advisable to pick a lawyer who will be able to help you with the legal aspects.

Theys (1993:38) specifies the twin influences of an administration order:

- it protects you against creditors, who may take no further legal action against you; and
- you may contract no further debt.

12.6.5 Friendly or voluntary sequestration

Sequestration applies to persons with debts of more than R50 000 (2001). Such a sequestration is of a voluntary nature or is initiated by a 'friendly' creditor. A 'friendly' creditor is requested to lodge an application for sequestration in his or her name (or that of a business). As in the case of voluntary sequestration, where you bring an application for sequestration yourself, the following must be proven, amongst others:

- that you do owe money;
- that you are insolvent or have committed an 'act of insolvency'; and
- that creditors will get back a proportion of their money.

In all cases where you are 'addressed' by the court regarding your debt, it is recommended that you immediately approach a lawyer for the necessary legal advice.

Sequestration: Voluntary versus compulsory

Sometimes people allow themselves to get into so much debt that it is simply no longer possible to pay off their debts. This situation is aggravated where the person concerned is no longer able to borrow money from financial institutions, family members or friends. What do they do then? There are only two options:

- to allow your creditors to have you declared insolvent; or
- to have yourself declared insolvent voluntarily, an act which is also referred to as voluntary sequestration.

Sequestration and liquidation

Is there a difference between sequestration and liquidation? If a person, a partnership or a trust is declared insolvent (bankrupt), such act is referred to as sequestration. Where, however, this occurs in the case of a close corporation or a company, the act concerned is referred to as liquidation.

If your creditors have you sequestrated, this is known as compulsory sequestration. If, however, you decide to have yourself declared insolvent, such act is referred to as voluntary sequestration or the surrender of your estate.

Should I allow creditors to have me declared insolvent?

The answer to this question is 'no'. Rather do it yourself. In the majority of cases, people are too afraid to take such a step because, amongst others, it will cost more money.

However, should you not do it yourself but wait for your creditors to take the necessary action, there is the possibility that they will not succeed in their application for a court order (for compulsory sequestration). It may no longer be in their interest, on account of the fact that your assets are already worth too little to them (for example, creditors will receive only three cents for every R1 of debt).

In the absence of compulsory sequestration, your debt simply increases further (as a result of interest), and your financial suffering is aggravated and endures for longer.

Why must I have myself sequestrated voluntarily?

Simply because this is the only and last way of finally resolving your debt crisis. Advice regarding voluntary sequestration can cost between R500 and R3 000. What such form of sequestration amounts to, is that your assets are converted into money so that, as far as possible, your creditors can be paid.

Unfortunately, many people believe that voluntary sequestration means the end of their lives and is a tremendous disgrace. In reality, however, it means exactly the opposite, for the following reasons:

- it enables you to conclude an undesirable financial and personal episode; and
- it allows you to begin a new, disciplined life as far as personal money matters are concerned.

The application

- An application for voluntary sequestration (or the surrender of an estate) is made to the High Court. You can make such application yourself, or you can appoint a representative to do so.
- As the applicant (person seeking to be sequestrated or declared insolvent), you must disclose certain financial information in your application in order to enable your creditors to decide whether or not to oppose the application.
- A notice regarding the surrender of the estate must be placed by the applicant in the Government Gazette as well as in a local district newspaper. Such notice must indicate the date of the application for the surrender of the estate and must set out financial information (i.e. the financial posi-

tion) pertaining to the applicant. Furthermore, the application must be supported by affidavits.

- The court will grant the application for the surrender of the estate if the correct steps have been followed, if the estate is in fact insolvent, if the cost of sequestration can be covered and if sequestration will benefit the creditors.

What are the consequences?

Sequestration has numerous consequences and affects, amongst others, the following: the insolvent, the spouse of the insolvent, judgements and lawsuits, incomplete contracts (e.g. contracts of purchase and sale, leases and employment contracts) and specific voidable legal acts.

Proprietary legal consequences

The possessions of a person who is declared insolvent vest in the Master and, thereafter, in the curator of the insolvent estate. The curator occupies a position of trust with regard to both creditors and the insolvent. After the curator has gathered together the assets of the person, has liquidated such assets (i.e. converted them into money) and has paid the relevant creditors, he or she is discharged from his or her position as curator.

Up to the stage that the curator is thus discharged, the person who has been sequestrated is known as an unrehabilitated insolvent. However, once the curator is discharged of his or her duties, the insolvent is referred to as a rehabilitated insolvent (see below).

The insolvent (bankrupt) estate comprises all assets belonging to the person concerned (the insolvent) as at the date of sequestration, as well as certain other items which are acquired during the period of insolvency. Money that is received as a result of carrying on a profession or working may, however, be retained by the person (i.e. kept out of the insolvent estate) for the purpose of the subsistence of such person and his or her dependants. The following are also excluded from the insolvent estate:

- Policies taken out more than three year prior to the insolvency (up to an amount of R30 000).
- Policies in respect of the life of a spouse taken out prior to the marriage, unless the other spouse (the insolvent spouse) has paid the premiums.
- Policies taken out by a spouse (on his or her own life), which have been ceded to the other spouse (up to an amount of R30 000).
- Policies taken out by a spouse (on his or her own life) in favour of the other spouse (up to an amount of R30 000).
- Where the husband is insolvent, all policies taken out or ceded in terms of an antenuptial contract concluded more than two years prior to the sequestration are excluded from the insolvent estate.
- Should there be no antenuptial contract, any amount above R30 000 falls into the insolvent estate.

Where spouses are married in community of property, the assets of both spouses fall into the joint estate which is insolvent and has been placed under sequestration. Both spouses are, therefore, regarded as insolvent.

Section 21 of the Insolvency Act governs sequestration in the case of a marriage out of community of property. Where, for instance, the husband is sequestrated, it often happens that the wife claims that she possesses virtually everything. In such cases, the Act now requires her to prove which assets belong to her, and why. The wife (and this also applies to an unmarried couple) must prove that certain assets:

- were her property before the marriage;
- were acquired in terms of an antenuptial contract;
- were acquired during the marriage, but enjoy preference by law against the claims of creditors; or
- were acquired from the yield of the aforementioned three types of asset.

Personal consequences

The law presently 'protects' society against 'dishonest debtors' who are guilty of committing specific offences. Among other things, it provides that such debtors cannot occupy specific positions. In addition, the unrehabilitated insolvent's name will of necessity appear in the blacklists of credit information bureaux, which means that he or she will no longer be able to run up debts.

Even if the person concerned has been rehabilitated, his or her name will remain on such lists, with the result that obtaining credit will remain a long-term problem.

Rehabilitation does not occur automatically. An application for rehabilitation, either by the unrehabilitated insolvent or by someone else on his or her behalf, must be made to the same court that sequestrated the estate. The period of time which must elapse before such an application can be made is determined, amongst others, by the following factors:

- Whether creditors have already received 50 cents in the rand.
- Whether creditors have received security for such a payment.
- Whether 12 months have elapsed in the case of a first sequestration and no offences have been committed.

- Whether three years have elapsed in the case of multiple sequestrations and no offences have been committed.
- Whether five years have elapsed in the case where offences have been committed.
- Whether ten years have elapsed, in which case the insolvent is automatically rehabilitated without it being necessary to make an application for rehabilitation.

12.7 BANKING SERVICES

Banks offer many services of which people are unaware, until they need them some day. The most common services banks have been offering for years are fixed deposits and cheque accounts. Other services and products offered by banks include the following:
- autobank machines;
- autobank cards;
- customer contact (service) centres;
- autocheques;
- e-banking facilities;
- Internet banking;
- telephone banking;
- debit cards;
- credit cards;
- student loans;
- funeral cover;
- retirement annuity plans;
- life insurance;
- short-term insurance;
- loan protection plans;
- unit trusts;
- travel services;
- investment accounts;
- global investments;
- home loans;
- garage cards;
- term loans;
- overdraft facilities;
- estate planning;
- financial planning;
- income tax planning;
- completion of tax returns, provisional tax forms;
- negotiations with the SARS;
- comparisons of banking costs, for example
  - cash withdrawals
  - account payments
  - statements
  - transfers
  - balance enquiries
  - deposits
  - credit card fees
  - stop order fees/debit order fees
  - administration fees

- internet banking
- telephone banking
- cheque accounts
- travellers cheques sold;
- foreign exchange trading;
- business advice;
- working capital finance;
- asset finance;
- home loan protection plan;
- motor insurance;
- small and medium enterprise cards;
- retirement planning;
- disability cover;
- endowment policies;
- derivatives;
- travel cards;
- medical cards; and
- garage cards.

Let us now look at fixed deposits, saving accounts and cheque accounts.

12.7.1 Fixed deposits

Savings accounts and fixed deposits are well-known and very basic investment vehicles. Savings are prerequisites for investments. Especially note that a R6 000 (2002) tax-free amount of interest may be received annually by an individual. Both spouses may receive this tax-free amount. Inflation erodes the purchasing power of money in a fixed deposit or savings account. Interest rates on fixed deposits are published to enable investors to compare the rates of return (interest rates on fixed deposits) on investments in both the money and capital markets.

Fixed deposits are money market instruments, because the demand for and supply of these instruments function over the short- and medium-term. This neglected financial instrument, especially by the media and brokers, is offered by banks and building societies. Fixed deposits form part of the investment portfolios of many investors. The investor's needs, objectives and especially his or her stage in the life cycle (age bracket) largely determine the investor's attitude towards fixed deposits as an investment instrument.

Functioning
When an investor invests money in a fixed deposit, it is tied up for a specific (selected) period of between one and 60 months (five years). The investor's money is available only at the end of the selected period or after a specific notice period. This notice period may be as long as three months and may cause a problem if the investor is in urgent need of the money tied up in the investment.

Interest rates on fixed deposits vary between financial institutions and are fixed for the investment period. The interest rate is usually determined on the day the investment is made. The period or term of the fixed deposit determines the interest rate offered.

The minimum investment required is normally R100. Fixed deposits cannot be traded like shares on the JSE.

Advantages
A fixed deposit provides the investor with the following advantages:
- Relatively small amounts may be invested.
- The fixed deposit can be used as collateral for a deposit towards buying a house.
- The investor should be able to raise a loan from the institution where the deposit is held.
- Money is less tied up (in the case of short-term deposits) than in the case of an endowment policy.
- The safety of the capital amount (amount invested) is guaranteed by the institution.
- It provides income that is tax-free up to an annual amount of R6 000 per annum per individual (to both spouses individually).
- The investor can plan more accurately, knowing exactly when the investment amount will be paid/returned.
- The control of the capital amount invested is not entirely out of the investor's hands.
- No commission is paid by the investor on the amount invested, unlike in the case of unit trusts or shares.
- Interest is paid on the full amount invested.
- It can serve as an emergency fund where the term is very short.

Disadvantages
Although a fixed deposit offers numerous advantages, there are a few disadvantages as well:
- It does not offer an investor a hedge against inflation.
- Inflation erodes the purchasing power of a fixed deposit.
- A fixed interest rate may hamper an investor's return on investment when interest rates are rising.
- An investor may experience a negative return on investment in real terms (after tax and inflation).

Taxability
The interest an investor receives is taxable and forms part of an investor's taxable income. Bear in mind that an amount of R6 000 (interest) is tax-free for every investor. The capital amount or fixed deposit, will be tax-free at the end of the term of investment or when it is called up (after a notification period) by the investor.

12.7.2 Savings accounts

A savings account is a very basic form of 'investment'. It is more in the nature of an emergency fund than, for example, unit trusts (which are not really emergency funds in the short term). It offers a simple way of earning some income on your money, and guaranteeing the safety of your capital at the same time. All people in all age groups can use a savings account – from the young (particularly as a means of education) to the old. Money may also be placed in a savings account temporarily before it is invested. It can also accumulate in a savings account until the amount is large enough for a particular investment or in order to buy something with it (e.g. a deposit, holiday, furniture). You can, therefore, reach certain goals with the help of a savings account, and it can protect you against unforeseen events.

Functioning
A savings account is opened at a bank, and then money is deposited into it, and the required withdrawals are made. The interest on the account is calculated daily. As the investment amount increases, the interest you earn on the money also increases. The money you earn daily is paid into the account monthly, and then becomes part of the capital of your account. Where interest is calculated on interest, we talk of compound interest. You should already be able to do these calculations after studying the time value of money. If you leave the money in a savings account for some years without using it, the bank will transfer it to a suspense account (also in your name).

Customers are usually required to have a minimum amount in a savings account. A savings account is also opened with a minimum amount, for example R500. Certain banks allow the charges to fall away if a certain amount of money is left in the account. It is far cheaper to conduct transactions via an ATM machine. If someone wants to effect many transactions from a savings account (e.g. account payments), it is better to open a transmission account. Individuals, clubs, partnerships and bodies corporate may open savings accounts. Young persons usually do not pay transaction costs and administration costs. Children may open a savings account with as little as R10.

Advantages
- It provides a balance to your investment and protection planning portfolio.
- It serves as an emergency fund.

- You can systematically build up a nest egg to invest or spend at a later stage.
- You can save money for a specific goal.
- You can carry out certain simple banking transactions.
- You have access to your account and can withdraw within certain limits.
- You can transfer money electronically.
- You can withdraw as frequently as you like.
- You can make enquiries via telephone, the Internet, self-service terminals and electronic centres.

Disadvantages
- There is no capital growth.
- It is not a long-term investment.
- Inflation erodes the purchasing power of your money.

12.7.3 A current account (cheque account)

A current account holder can effect all transactions from this account. The account holder receives a cheque-book and an ATM card. The ATM card can be used for various types of transaction. There are costs involved in all types of transaction. The trick is to manage the cheque-book in such a way as to keep the bank costs to a minimum. Bank costs will also vary from bank to bank, depending on the cheque-book holder's situation, the number of transactions, the amounts involved and the specific bank package.

Interest is paid on money in your cheque account, either on your daily balance or on the minimum monthly balance. Interest is paid into your account monthly. The converse also applies. If you arrange for an overdraft facility on your account (i.e. a debit balance), you will be debited for the interest on this monthly. The interest rate you pay is determined by the prime interest rate. You usually pay a higher interest rate than the prime rate. Remember to make sure of the balance in your account before you write out another cheque. Each cheque you write costs you money.

Some banks offer you the following choices regarding the costs involved in a cheque account: costs per transaction, costs based on minimum balance or a monthly management fee. Feel free to speak to your bank manager to help you choose a particular cheque account package that will suit your needs and lifestyle.

An overdraft
An overdraft is a short-term borrowing option. It is normally linked to a cheque account. You can overdraw your account to an agreed (pre-arranged) limit. Criteria for an overdraft are:
- a cheque account;
- period as client;
- credit record;
- record with credit bureau; and
- repayment capacity.

Banks sometimes need some collateral like:
- deposits;
- counter investments;
- insurance policies; and
- someone who will guarantee payments.

Advantages
- Money is instantly available.
- Interest is only charged on amounts used.
- You can repay borrowed funds at any time.
- An overdraft amount can be increased, decreased, renewed or cancelled (by arrangement).

Disadvantages
- You can run into a permanent debt crisis.
- You can get used to debt.
- Debt can rise drastically because of rising interest rates.

Signing and completing a cheque
The Bills of Exchange Amendment Act changed the way to complete cheques (since 1 March 2001). The most important change is about non-transferable cheques. A non-transferable cheque can be paid only to the person to whom it is made out (the payee). It may not be transferred to any other person. A cheque should be marked 'non-transferable' or 'not-transferable'. These words must be clearly written or stamped on the front of the cheque. A 'crossed' cheque protects you against theft and nobody has a claim against you. You can still stop the stolen cheque. When you write these words on the cheque between crossed lines, the cheque is payable into a bank account only. Therefore, you cannot use a 'non/not-transferable' cheque to pay a person without a bank account.

Remember that electronic payments are much safer than cheques and are cheaper too.

Any person may cash a cash cheque, because it is not made out to anybody specific. This is why people rather use electronic banking services. This also means they do not have to carry large amounts of cash with them.

12.8 CREDIT INSTRUMENTS

Credit is obtained in a variety of ways. People sometimes use credit without realising that it is a form of credit. Everyone should have a basic knowledge of how credit works. For this reason, it is essential that we discuss this aspect of credit planning. Credit instruments consist of (Swart 1992:27):

- services credit accounts;
- open accounts;
- revolving credit;
- deferred payment;
- instalment sale agreements;
- lease transactions;
- personal loans;
- credit cards;
- petrol cards;
- mortgage bond loans;
- home-improvement loans;
- student loans;
- lay-bys;
- pawn shops;
- debit cards; and
- *stokvels*.

All these financing options should be thoroughly investigated before entering into any credit agreement. The following aspects should be investigated:

- the costs involved;
- whether available or not;
- security required;
- the instalment amount;
- the term of repayment;
- when ownership rights are transferred; and
- the entire risk involved in the financing.

12.8.1 Services credit accounts

Services credit refers to the kind of credit associated with the use of a telephone, water and electricity, and rates and taxes. These services are used during the month and the account is paid at the end of the month. This also applies to dental, medical and clothing accounts. No costs are involved in this kind of credit; in other words, no interest is charged.

12.8.2 Open accounts

This kind of account is arranged between a dealer and a customer. The customer is debited in the dealer's books with the sum of the sale. Accounts are payable over a certain period, usually not exceeding six months. No interest is charged, although the customer may forfeit a cash discount if the account is not paid within 30 days.

A customer's creditworthiness is assessed, but no security is required. Property rights are transferred to the customer when he or she takes possession of the goods. This form of credit usually serves as a good reference if you pay your debt regularly; the opposite applies equally.

12.8.3 Revolving credit

With revolving credit, a customer is granted an open account with a maximum credit limit and a fixed monthly payment. Once an instalment has been paid, the customer may make another purchase for the same amount. Otherwise, revolving credit functions in the same way as an open account.

12.8.4 Deferred payment

Deferred payment means that the customer pays for goods or services over a period of three to six months. No interest is charged, although the customer accepts the fact that prices are higher than they would be if paid for in cash. Credit limits are negotiated between dealer and customer.

12.8.5 Instalment sale agreements (ISAs)

Until 1 March 1981, an instalment sale agreement was called a hire-purchase transaction. This amendment was made in terms of the Credit Agreements Act 75 of 1980. An instalment sale agreement is used when a consumer requires financing to purchase goods such as a vehicle or furniture.

Financing is granted by a banking institution over a term of between three and 54 months. A deposit of 10% is required. Such financing may be direct (from a bank) or indirect (from a seller who, in turn, concludes an agreement with the bank). In the case of a direct transaction, the agreement is concluded on the bank's premises. With an indirect transaction, it is concluded on the premises of the seller, who refers it to the bank for evaluation over the telephone, by telex or in person.

The buyer takes possession of the vehicle (for example) immediately, although the seller retains property rights until the last instalment has been paid. In this way, the vehicle serves as security in the event of the buyer neglecting to pay the instalments.

The longer the term, the more interest the buyer pays. Krüger (1992:37) explains that people usually want to improve their cash flow and, therefore, accept a longer term and a slightly lower monthly instalment. Sellers are inclined to concentrate on the lower monthly instalments, but seldom mention the thousands of rands paid in interest.

It is also important to pay the largest deposit possible. This reduces the outstanding debt and the buyer saves on interest charges.

Badenhorst (1990:21) stresses that, for the consumer, the most important aspect to consider is the interest rate. The consumer should decide whether the interest rate should be fixed or varying. The financing rate should be linked to the prime loan rate; in other words, it should be varying. The customer's creditworthiness will determine the interest rate he or she has to pay. A customer with good creditworthiness, for example, would pay a prime rate plus two percentage points.

Laurie (1990:46) points out that financing by means of a bank overdraft is invariably cheaper than an instalment sale agreement, since interest is paid only on the outstanding amount. Money could be paid into the bank account regularly, in order to reduce the balance. A consumer could even have a credit balance in his or her bank account. With an instalment sale agreement, the terms are fixed, with the result that the outstanding debt can only be reduced by means of fixed monthly instalments.

Laurie (1990:46) recommends that money could be borrowed against an insurance policy or by enlarging a housing bond. However, he warns against incurring long-term debt to purchase an asset with a limited (short) life. It would be possible, however, to reduce the increased bond amount by means of regular payments, otherwise excessive interest would have to be paid over a long period.

It is a good idea to discuss the financing with the bank beforehand, in order to eliminate the commission the seller (trader/dealer) would otherwise receive. Specialists could also be consulted in this regard.

Credit life insurance should be included in the instalment sale agreement. This means that a vehicle, for example, would be fully paid off in the event of the buyer's death. Wear and tear and depreciation could be written off for income tax purposes.

Legislation prohibits a seller from selling a vehicle 'voetstoots' in an instalment sale agreement. This protects buyers against any latent (silent or invisible) defects the vehicle may have. After all, it is impossible to discover defective vehicle parts with the naked eye. If the buyer discovers a month later that the vehicle has serious defects, which it was impossible to detect with the naked eye, the seller has to repair the defects at his or her own cost in terms of the instalment sale agreement.

12.8.6 Lease transactions

A vehicle may be leased in terms of a lease agreement, instead of buying it in terms of an instalment sale agreement. No deposit is required and the vehicle remains the property of the lessor. The lessee may buy the vehicle at the end of the leasing period (five years) at its current value, or return it to the lessor.

Only certain people qualify for a lease transaction in terms of income tax legislation. A person who intends using the vehicle mainly for business purposes would qualify. When the lessee buys the vehicle after five years, its value has to be entered into the person's balance statement. Professionals, such as doctors, advocates, directors and architects often use lease transactions.

A lease transaction may also be concluded directly or indirectly, and the procedures are very similar to an instalment sale agreement. This method is particularly useful for people who wish to replace their vehicle after two or three years. Maximum benefit is derived in the form of income tax advantages, as the instalments are written off for income tax purposes (they are tax-deductible).

12.8.7 Personal loans

A personal loan involves an amount that may be borrowed over a specified term and at a specified rate. These loans may be granted by a family member, a friend, employers or financial institutions.

The procedures for a personal loan from a bank are more formal than a loan from a family member. More paperwork and negotiation are required for the former. A bank would be concerned mostly with the borrower's ability to repay the loan. The borrower would also have to provide the bank with security to protect the bank from non-payment. The following are forms of security:

- policies with surrender value;
- unit trusts;
- listed shares;
- fixed deposits and savings accounts;
- a motor car;
- a vacant plot; and
- a house.

A bank would accept any of the above as security for a personal loan. If the conditions of the loan are not adhered to, the bank could use the security at its discretion. It is advisable to keep to the loan agreement.

12.8.8 Credit cards

Credit cards are a form of financing that banks offer their clients. Cards are issued to clients, who may use them to buy goods and services. Cash facilities are offered together with this form of financing by means of terminals linked to a mainframe computer at the bank. Applications for credit cards are carefully evaluated, because the risks involved in credit cards are fairly high.

There are two kinds of credit card: those issued by financial institutions and those used in the retail trade. The latter merely facilitate the functioning of open accounts.

It is essential that credit card holders exercise self-discipline and restraint in their spending. In this way, the numerous advantages associated with credit cards can be enjoyed. A credit limit is usually attached to each credit card, which prevents excessive spending. Coetzee (1991:42) lists the following advantages and disadvantages of credit cards:

Advantages
- There is no need to carry cash and run the risk of being robbed.
- Credit card insurance, at a minimal fee, ensures that the credit card holder will not suffer a loss if the card is stolen.
- Even without insurance, the card holder is not liable for any transactions from the moment the theft of his or her card is reported.
- A budget account may be linked to a credit card, allowing the card holder to buy an expensive item over a longer period.
- The card holder receives a full statement of all purchases every month, which could serve as proof of purchases if the article has to be returned (if it is defective) to the seller.
- Most shops in South Africa accept credit cards.
- Uniform service is offered at a relatively low cost.
- Card holders receive 25 days' interest-free credit on purchases.
- A credit card account earns interest on a credit balance.

Disadvantages
- Credit cards may encourage people to incur debt.
- There is a levy for a lost card, but not when it is stolen.
- If the total monthly balance is not paid in full, interest is charged on the total balance (even if the balance is only R1).

Types of credit card
The most common credit cards used in South Africa are the MasterCard and the Visa Card. They are issued by banks as well as building societies. There are also the so-called prestige cards such as American Express and Diners Club.

Both MasterCard and Visa Card offer interest-free periods. The Diners Club Card differs in that purchases are debited to the card holder's account immediately. It does not offer an interest-free period. Diners Club Cards have no credit limit and are only offered to clients with very good creditworthiness. This service is not readily accessible to the person in the street (Whittaker *et al.* 1990:98).

Types of account
Van der Watt (1991:57) refers to two types of account that may be used for credit card purchases:
- a straight account; and
- a budget account.

When a consumer buys with a credit card, he or she must tell the seller what kind of account to use. A straight account is payable within the first three weeks of the next month. Thereafter, interest is payable on the outstanding balance. A budget account is paid over several months, because the purchases are bigger. Interest is charged, regardless of when payment occurs.

12.8.9 Petrol cards

Petrol and garage cards are issued to successful applicants. Petrol cards are credit cards that may be used to buy petrol at petrol stations. These cards are associated with fairly high costs for the consumer, because petrol (in terms of legislation) may not be sold on credit. Interest is charged from the first day of purchase. Van der Watt (1991:58) points out that these interest payments could be avoided by retaining a credit balance on the petrol card account.

You should note that there are both debit petrol cards and credit petrol cards. Make sure you know the difference between a debit and a credit card. With the former, purchases are immediately debited to your account. With a credit card the amount is payable after a specific period (55 days, for example) depending on the type of card (the period is even longer with a budget account).

12.8.10 Mortgage bond loans

Mortgage bond loans were dealt with in Chapter 8 on purchasing a home (home financing) and will not be discussed here.

12.8.11 Home improvement loans
Home owners sometimes require additional funds to build a swimming pool, an extra room, a garage or a fence. An additional loan or a bank overdraft may be used to pay for it. The larger the amount, the greater the advantage of a loan over an overdrawn bank account.

12.8.12 Student loans

Banks offer a special kind of loan to students. Usually, a policy is ceded to the bank as security. A student cheque account is also opened. During the life of the loan, the interest rate charged is considerably lower than for a normal loan. The student commences repaying the loan as soon as he or she has completed his or her studies and receives a monthly salary.

12.8.13 Lay-by

'Lay-by' means that a consumer buys an article and leaves it in the possession of the seller, because he or she does not have sufficient money to pay the whole amount. Regular payments are made to the seller until the full amount has been paid off, when the consumer takes possession of the article.

12.8.14 Pawn shops

Pawn shops take possession of goods as security for a loan. Once the loan has been paid off, the goods are returned. Goods are also bought at low prices from people who need money. Unemployment often results in the need for this kind of credit.

12.8.15 Debit cards

In contrast to a credit card, purchases (or payments) made by means of a debit card are debited to your bank account immediately. A debit card, therefore, gives you greater control over your expenses, because you are aware of the expenses you have incurred much sooner, and you also know how much money (or credit) there is left in your bank account. In general, you will be able to avoid a debt crisis more easily by using a debit card than would be the case with a credit card.

You need not carry around large amounts of cash, and the transactions are far cheaper than using a cheque, for example. Some debit cards can be PIN-coded to give you access to ATM machines and electronic banking services. The greatest advantage is that you know exactly what is happening in your bank account, because there are no pending credit card expenses that have to be processed at a later stage. A garage card is an example of such a debit card, and can be used to pay for fuel and oil, spares and repairs, vehicle maintenance, tollgate charges and vehicle accessories.

12.8.16 *Stokvels*

Join a local *stokvel* (or savings group) and start saving each month to attain your own goals.

Functioning
- You and a group of people will pay an amount each month to the *stokvel*.
- Say there are six people in the group and each of you pays R100 to the *stokvel* each month.
- Each month the *stokvel* receives R600 from the group.
- The six of you will each have a turn to receive the R600.
- This will help you to receive one large amount of money once in the six-month period.
- You can also borrow money from the *stokvel* if you make your payments each month.
- You will not receive interest on your money.
- You can use your large amount of money to pay your debts or to start a business.
- Remember that there are sometimes disagreements among members of a *stokvel*.
- Members sometimes walk away with your money.

12.9 THE CREDIT CONTRACT

A contract must satisfy many requirements before it is considered valid and legally enforceable. The same goes for credit contracts. You should remember the general requirements for establishing a valid contract, namely:
- There must be consensus between the parties (both must have the same purpose in mind when entering the contract).
- The parties must be legally competent (old enough, marital property regime, mentally competent, etc.).
- It must be physically possible to honour the contract (for example, it must be possible to borrow money and repay it.)
- The contract must be legally enforceable.
- The required legal formalities must be met.

12.10 BUYING AND SELLING A CAR

For a school leaver or young couple, a car is no investment. In fact, it is not even an investment in middle age. For at least the first 15 to 20 years after you have left school, you should invest as little money as possible in a car. Many young people, and older people, spend too much money on various vehicles throughout their lives. This is a drain on investment and retirement money.

Why do so many young people have such expensive cars? This is no mystery; a flashy new car makes you look good, especially in an affluent neighbourhood. People often buy four-wheel-drive vehicles as second vehicles to further impress and improve their 'competitive edge'.

Many people think you are what you drive. Nothing could be further from the truth. Rather invest your money as soon as possible in property (a house or second home) and pay off your bond as quickly as possible. The person down the road may be buying one beautiful car after another, but ten to 15 years from now, you will be buying one property after another in just as quick succession. For 20 or 30 years, what you drive will be less impressive, but the value of your property and other investments will more than make up for it. After many years, your properties/investments will start to look after you and allow you to buy expensive vehicles, because you can afford them and your financial future is already assured.

In the discussion below, we will briefly look at the following aspects regarding buying and selling a car:
- talk to various people;
- a new or used car;
- buying through a dealer;
- a private sale;
- buying at an auction;
- hints for buyers;
- hints for sellers;
- further help and information;
- how to finance the sale;
- buy, instalment sale or lease;
- car insurance; and
- what car to buy.

12.10.1 Talk to various people

When buying a car, you should talk to various people and interested parties, amongst others:
- those who own a car;
- those who own the make of car you want (if you know what you want);
- more than one new car dealer;
- people regarding buying a used versus a new car;
- suppliers of car financing; and
- buyers and dealers regarding car prices.

This will give you the information required to help you make a more informed purchasing decision. Also consult car magazines, for example *Auto Trader*. It is very useful to compare the prices of similar car models and odometer readings.

12.10.2 A new or used car

Someone buying a new car loses his or her money quickest, because the value of a new car drops far faster than in the case of a used car. As soon as a new car is driven out of the showroom, it becomes a used car. The best value for money remains a well-maintained car of about one to three years old, with a low odometer reading. Many used cars are virtually brand new even after five or ten years, because of their low odometer readings. Of course, the motor plan has usually expired because of the high age, even though it has done few kilometres. In the case of a three to five year-old used car, you will be able to buy a far 'larger' car with a more powerful engine at the same price as a smaller, less powerful new car.

12.10.3 Buying through a dealer

According to *Auto Trader* (2001:4), buying a car from a dealer offers the buyer the maximum protection, if:
- it is a reliable, well-established dealer (business); and
- the dealer subscribes to the code of conduct of the Motor Industries Federation (MIF).

The MIF looks after the interests of both buyers and sellers, and may be contacted to find out whether the dealer does indeed subscribe to the MIF code. Also ask the dealer for a detailed test in the case of a used car. The Automobile Association (AA) can help in this regard.

Furthermore, remember that you, as a buyer, have the right to:
- a car of a satisfactory quality (the average person test with regard to appearance, safety and durability);
- a vehicle without obvious defects (except those pointed out by the seller); and
- the vehicle as described (for example, no previous accidents).

12.10.4 A private sale

A private sale can save you a great deal of money, as long as you know the owner very well (reliability, history, etc.). Alternatively, such a 'cheaper' car can cost and lose you a lot of money, for one or more of the following reasons, amongst others (*Auto Trader* 2001:4):
- The car does not belong to the seller (it is stolen, borrowed, donated in terms of an antenuptial contract, or donated in terms of a settlement agreement during a divorce).

- It may be serving as security for a loan and actually belong to the lender of the money.
- It has never been serviced (has no service record).
- It has been involved in an accident.
- The seller can give no guarantees.
- The buyer enjoys fewer rights by law.

It is also possible that a dealer may create the impression of being a private seller. The reason is often a defective car or one with a selling price that is too high. Watch out for a dealer who, posing as a private seller, insists on bringing the car to your house.

12.10.5 Buying at an auction

You can pick up bargains at an auction, as long as you know all about the specific vehicle, the auction, the conditions of sale and the prices of similar cars. There are many risks if you do not have such knowledge, due to the short period prior to the auction, which leaves the potential buyer with little time to acquire such knowledge.

Auto Trader (2001:5) also points out the following:
- You may test drive the vehicle prior to the auction.
- The car's history appears on the form on the windscreen.
- Stick to your bid limit and do not allow other bidders to panic you into exceeding this limit.
- Beware when a vehicle is sold 'voetstoots', because this limits your rights as a buyer.
- The sale price does not include VAT (14%) or the buyer's commission (usually 10% of the sale price).

12.10.6 Hints for buyers

Swart & Coetzee (2000:28) offer potential buyers the following broad guidelines.

Step 1: Have a good look around and talk to a lot of people
- Make sure you know what you want.
- Beware of dishonest dealers.
- Decide on whether you want to buy a new or a second-hand car.
- Is it a private purchase or do you want to buy from a dealer?
- Compare prices (shop around).
- Take the second-hand car for an AA inspection (ask about the cost).
- Take the car for a roadworthy test if the AA inspection is too expensive.
- Make sure that all the promises made by the car dealer are in writing.

Step 2: Study your contract and papers
- Ask about your rights.
- Ask about an instalment sale agreement.
- Ask whether the sale includes a warranty.
- Ask about the amount of insurance you will need.
- Ask if a maintenance or service deal is included.

Step 3: Know the cost and plan where you will get the money
- Know how much you can afford.
- Know if you can get financing from a family member or friend.
- Know if you can get a loan from a bank.
- Know how to use an instalment sale agreement (you can get it directly from the bank, or the seller can help you to get one from the bank).
- Know that you will have to plan to get a 10% deposit, in the case of an instalment sale agreement.
- Know the different options of monthly payments; you can pay up to 54 monthly payments.

Auto Trader (2001:5, 6) offers some more hints:

- Test the vehicle in daylight, with the help of an expert.
- You enjoy greater legal protection if you buy the vehicle through a dealer, even if it is a stolen vehicle.
- The AA's 'Autocheck' service can check the legitimacy of a vehicle's engine number, chassis number and identification number.
- Make sure you get the vehicle's registration papers from the seller.
- Have the AA's 'Autocheck' service check whether the vehicle belongs to the person or a financial institution.
- Make sure that the 'low' odometer reading fits the car (e.g. interior scratches, worn carpets, damaged interior door handles).
- You can check the odometer reading through previous roadworthy certificates and service documentation (or by contacting the previous owner).
- Buy within your budget.
- Never do a deal over the telephone (first examine and drive the vehicle).
- Always negotiate regarding the selling price.
- Obtain a receipt that shows that the car is not a surety for a debt, and has been fully paid.
- Sign the change of ownership document and keep a copy.
- Ask a legal expert to help with the interpretation and assessment of possible guarantees.

12.10.7 Hints for sellers

Auto Trader (2001:7) has valuable hints for sellers; amongst others:

- Market the car in such a way (for example, by pointing out extras) that will make the car seem to be 'value for money'.
- Let *Auto Trader* help you determine a realistic price.
- Remember that potential hijackers may phone you to view the car somewhere; be prepared.
- Do not simply hand the registration papers to potential buyers (or hijackers).
- You will probably recover the cost of a valet service in the selling price.
- Always negotiate in a civilised manner.
- Keep the car's service record at hand.
- Also keep at hand any proof of recent repairs or improvements.
- The seller must inform the licensing authorities that the vehicle has been sold.
- Always keep the keys in your (as owner/seller) possession.
- Make sure that the car (and buyer) are insured, if you allow the other person (buyer) to test drive the vehicle
- Never cancel the insurance before the sales transaction has been completed.
- Accompany the buyer to the bank to deposit the sale price.
- Let the bank help you to guarantee the deposit of the amount in a particular account.
- Make sure that cheques have the required bank clearance.
- Only then should you hand over the car to the buyer.

12.10.8 Further help and information

Important telephone numbers (*Auto Trader* 2001:4):
- AA Autocheck: 0861 601 601
- Motor Industries Federation (MIF): (011) 789 2542
- Insurance Ombudsman: (011) 337 6525
- AA Technical Centres:
  Pretoria: (012) 335 3850
  Midrand: (011) 315 2296
  Boksburg: (011) 826 4386
  Randburg: (011) 781 0366/7
  Roodepoort: (011) 768 0642
  Cape Town: (021) 462 4426
  Parow: (021) 930 2550/112
  East London: (043) 743 9880
  Port Elizabeth: (041) 585 9307
  Bloemfontein: (051) 448 3279
  Durban: (031) 332 9212

> For the average person, buying a car is the second-largest 'investment' that person will make during his or her lifetime – after a house.

12.10.9 How to finance the sale

Of course you should only buy a car if you can afford one. You should also buy only the car that you can afford. Very few people can pay cash for a car, so some kind of financing is normally used. A car instalment is not a trivial matter.

This is why it is important to make use of the best type of financing for your specific situation. You should know the following, amongst others (after having done your homework):

- the interest rate(s) on the various options;
- whether you are entitled to a subsidy or allowance, or do not receive either;
- the tax implications of your buying decision;
- the best after-tax financing plan;
- whether your company can structure your salary package around this buying decision;
- the influence of your matrimonial property regime on your buying decision;
- whether you will require a deposit or not;
- what the monthly premiums will be;
- what your car insurance premium will cost;
- what you may possibly get for your present car as a trade-in, which will mean a lower price for the new car;
- whether you will have to offer security (for example, an investment or ceding a policy) to obtain financing;
- if you are buying the car for business purposes, you may make use of a lease to save tax;
- the bank will not offer financing for a private transaction in the form of an instalment sale transaction (if you offer security, the bank will grant a cash loan);
- remember that as soon as you sell the car, you must first pay the outstanding balance on your vehicle debt (always make sure that you ask the bank's permission before you conclude the sale);
- you must negotiate with the bank about the financing rate (lending rate) in order to get as close to the prime lending rate as possible (or lower if you are a very good and creditworthy client); and
- BMW, for example, offers approved used cars at a rate of 5% below the prime rate (of course, the selling price is somewhat higher than for a private sale, but a private sale holds greater risks).

Ways of financing
Own finance
There are those who can use their own funds (investments) to buy a car. No money is borrowed,

and the proceeds of a policy or units trusts are used. This is fine, unless you get a subsidy or car allowance, in which case it is cheaper to borrow the money to finance the car.

Family
Some may get help from their parents or spouse. They may give (or lend) a cash amount, cede a policy or offer collateral such as a fixed deposit to obtain a loan. You may also borrow money (with the necessary consent, of course) against your parents' mortgage bond, provided the monthly instalments are repaid at the current interest rate. Family can, therefore, help in various ways. Always remember to honour to the letter any agreement you may have concluded with your family.

Bank overdraft
You may approach a bank for an overdraft facility to finance the sale. Normally, you will need to offer some sort of security/collateral for this loan amount. You could possibly request this overdraft facility if you have a paid-up or partly paid-up mortgage bond. The bank knows you, and may use your collateral for both debts.

An instalment sale agreement
You may ask the bank or car dealer for an instalment sale agreement. It is a more expensive method of financing, but could be your only hope if you have no funds of your own. According to this method you, the buyer, pay a 10% deposit, after which you pay off the car over a period of up to 54 months. An instalment sale agreement is financed either directly (by the bank) or indirectly through the seller of the vehicle (the seller, in turn, enters into an agreement with the bank). With a direct transaction the agreement is concluded at the bank's premises. With an indirect transaction the agreement is concluded at the seller's premises. He or she then refers it to the bank by telephone, telex, fax or personally for assessment.

The buyer takes immediate possession of the car, but the seller retains the right of ownership until the last instalment has been paid. The car, therefore, remains the seller's security should the buyer fail to meet his or her obligations. Always include credit life insurance in your instalment sale agreement so that the car debt will be paid in full in the event of your death. Remember that a seller may never sell you a car 'as is' with such an agreement.

A lease
In the case of a lease, you pay for the car over a period of 60 months. However, you do not own the car, and at the end of this term, you have the option of buying the car at a residual value or of leasing it for a further period.

Rental
Rental is similar to leasing, except that VAT is not capitalised at inception, but is levied on each monthly rental amount.

12.10.10 Buy, instalment sale or lease

Schussler (2000:9) points out that someone without enough cash to buy a car should agree to an instalment sale agreement or lease. He comes to the following conclusions:
- For individuals, buying on an instalment sale agreement is cheaper than leasing.
- For businesses, leasing is cheaper than buying or an instalment sale agreement.

Of course, the type of business and the specific application of the car will also determine whether it should be bought with an instalment sale agreement or leased.

Furthermore, Van Tonder (2000:9) points out the following with regard to used cars that were previously leased with a residual value:
- The cars can be bought from dealers at a good price (where the dealer has decided to sell it after the lessee has decided not to buy it at the residual value, or does not wish to continue with the lease).
- If the initial residual value and valuation (which the dealer must calculate 30 days before the expiry date) are more or less R20 000, the dealer may not sell the car for more than R20 000 (in terms of the Usury Act).
- If you want to buy such a car, you must find out the real residual value and pay that amount.
- You must, therefore, pay the same as the price the dealer quoted the previous lessee (and no higher).

Apart from instalment sale, lease and rental agreements, NedCredit provides the following additional services:
- *Integrated vehicle-buying service.* Apply directly to Nedbank, either online or by telephone, to find the vehicle of your choice at the best available discount, with trade-in facilities, test drives, registration and licensing, plus free delivery to your doorstep.
- *Online car price search.* Search for new car prices according to various criteria, such as make, price, engine capacity and monthly repayments.
- *Online loan calculators.* User-friendly graphics allow you to:

- calculate the monthly repayments on your chosen car;
- calculate the interest you can save by using NedCredit;
- calculate how you can reduce your repayment term using NedCredit; and
- calculate the tax payable on your car allowance or company car.

12.10.11 Car insurance

The supplier of you car financing (e.g. bank) will insist that you insure the car (which belongs to the bank at this stage). This must be comprehensive insurance. As mentioned in our discussion of protection planning in Chapter 11, car insurance forms part of your household insurance policy (i.e. short-term insurance).

12.10.12 What car to buy

The best car is the one that suits your needs, requirements and pocket the best. For example, a single person could buy a sports car, but a family needs a family car. Air conditioning could, for example, be necessary even in a small and cheaper car. You will find that a new car offers you a greater choice. For example, it may not always be possible to find a 2001 model of a specific colour at a specific price at a particular time. I recommend that you wait patiently for a used car while studying *Auto Trader* weekly, to get yourself up to date with the market.

12.10.13 What about a guarantee?

Most new cars come with a three-year/100 000km guarantee. In the case of a used car, there may be a guarantee, depending on the car's age, odometer reading and price.

Forster (2000:71) points out that any guarantee excludes normal wear and tear. Beware of a car that is being sold 'voetstoots', without any guarantee.

Think carefully before buying an extended warranty on an old car or for too long a period (e.g. 40 000 kilometres) if the car could be a stolen one.

12.10.14 Maintenance and servicing

A new or recent model will still have a service plan for the car. This means services will cost less than without it, as is the case with older models. Normally, such a service plan will require you to take the car to specific dealers for the service. Of course, such dealers will be reliable.

In the case of some models you may buy a service plan for a ten-year period, for example. In South Africa, so many cars are stolen that it is not worth the effort and money to buy a service plan (if you have a choice) for 40 or 50 years, for example.

12.10.15 What to keep in your car

Forster (2000:70) points out that a motorist should keep the following in his or her car:
- a correctly inflated spare wheel, jack and wheel spanner;
- a small toolkit;
- spare radiator hoses, fan belts, fuses and globes;
- a torch with batteries; and
- a basic first-aid kit and rubber gloves.

12.11 E-SHOPPING

Virtually anything can be bought on the Internet nowadays. Bloemhof (2000:71) points out that people easily become Internet junkies and that their human relationships may suffer as a result.

Brown & Paul (2001:118) point out that E-shopping or E-banking is only possible if you have a computer, the correct software, and knowledge of how to link to the Internet.

McKenzie (2001:34), furthermore, suggests that people should also have an Internet account (get it through a local Internet Service Provider, or ISP) and a credit card (to pay for your purchases).

E-shopping does not only revolve around price, but in particular around the following, according to McKenzie (2001:35):
- you buy when you have the time;
- the convenience of the purchases (from your home);
- help from support personnel;
- the absence of people who hassle you at the shopping centre;
- availability of products;
- no queues or rush-hour traffic;
- the availability of international products; and
- delivery at your doorstep (at a price).

It is also important to know that you should keep in mind certain costs and risks:

Costs
- product price (credit card);
- Telkom (your telephone account);
- ISP costs;
- delivery charges (sometimes in dollars/pounds); and
- import duties.

Risks

- 'safe' delivery;
- excessive prices; and
- dishonest businesses (try About.com for reviews of the site).

Just as purchases can be made, it is also possible to sell things via the Internet. McKenzie (2001:36) points out the bargains that one can get at auctions, amongst others on the following websites:

- Aucor (www.aucor.co.za);
- Auxion (www.auxion.co.za);
- Bid or Buy (www.bidorbuy.co.za); and
- The Lot (www.thelot.co.za).

If you want to sell something, you do the following:

- Choose a website.
- Offer your item for sale.
- Choose the auction period and your minimum or reserve price.
- A prospective buyer will send you an e-mail and you will then have to conclude the deal yourself.

Consult the following websites for more information:

- jobs.mweb.co.za
- women24.com
- M-Web search (http://search.mweb.co.za)
- Yahoo! (Www.yahoo.com)
- Alta Vista (www.altavista.com)
- Infoseek (www.infoseek.com)
- Lycos (www.lycos.com)
- Excite (www.excite.com)
- Ananzi (www.ananzi.com)
- Aardvark (www.aardvark.co.za)
- http://afrikaans.mweb.co.za
- For the latest news: www.news24.com
- Ticket bookings (movies, theatre, concerts or festivals):
  www.computicket.com; www.sterkinekor.com
- For computer problems and information: http://computing.mweb.co.za
- Holiday planning: www.parks-sa.co.za (for information on and bookings at national parks); www.computravel.com; www.hotelogue.com; www.infoafrica.co.za

McKenzie (2001:38) names the following further sites:

Clothing
Polo Clothing: www.polo-sa.co.za
Swear Shoes: www.swear.co.za
Edgars: www.edgars.co.za
MegaShopper: www.megashopper.co.za
Truworths: www.truworths.co.za

E-shopping is much more than just price!

Food
Woolworths: www.inthebag.co.za
MegaGroceries: www.megagroceries.co.za

Jewellery
Jenna Clifford: www.jennaclifford.co.za
Arthur Kaplan: www.arthurkaplan.co.za

Books
Amazon: www.amazon.com – www.amazon.co.uk
Kalahari.net: www.kalahari.net
The Shopping Matrix: www.tsm.co.za

CDs
CD Zone: www.cdzone.co.za
Musica: www.musica.co.za

DVDs
DVD Zone: www.dvdzone.co.za
DVD Universe: www.dvduniverse.co.za

Flowers
Netflorist: www.netflorist.co.za
Virtual Florist: www.virtualflorist.co.za
Megaflorist: www.megaflorist.co.za

Toys
Reggies: www.reggies.co.za
Toys-R-Us: www.toysrus.co.za

Cellular
African Cellular: www.africancellular.co.za
MTN: www.mtn.co.za
Vodacom: www.vodacom.co.za

Electronics
The Brandshop: www.brandshop.co.za
Digital Sound and Vision: www.dsvhome.co.za
Digital World: www.digitalworld.co.za

Property
Property.co.za: www.property.co.za
MortgageSA: www.mortgagesa.com

Cars
AA Auto Finance: www.aaaf.co.za
Autonet: www.autonet.co.za
Autotrader: www.autotrader.co.za

Furniture
Bed Zone: www.bedzone.co.za

Computer hardware and software
Etenga: www.etenga.co.za

Legal documents
Doclegal.con: www.doclegal.com

General shopping
M-Web: www.mweb.co.za
Icon Club: www.iconclub.co.za
Tutuka.com: www.tutuka.com

12.12 E-BANKING

E-shopping may be more expensive than normal shopping, but E-banking is cheaper than doing your banking otherwise. Banks save a lot of money in this way, and all offer similar facilities.

Nedbank (2001) points out that E-banking is:
- time-saving (bank without visiting a branch);
- accessible (enjoy access at the touch of a button);
- convenient (pay accounts and transfer funds without queuing or writing out cheques);
- secure (choose your own PIN, preventing unauthorised access to your accounts); and
- safe (no need to carry around large amounts of cash).

At Nedbank, for example, clients can do their E-banking in the following ways (Nedbank 2001):
- by telephone (landline and cellular);
- via the Internet;
- through self-service terminals at the branch; and
- by cash point card (payment of accounts – link Nedbank accounts to third party accounts as well as accounts at other institutions).

Nedbank telephone banking
People with a cheque account, savings account or credit card (from Nedbank) can do their banking via any telephone. A 24-hour help desk is available (0860 115 060).
Services:
- Pay third-party accounts.
- Transfer money between linked accounts.
- Order a new cheque book.
- Change your PIN.
- Request mini-statements and balances.
- Ask for information about payments made.
- Enquire about exchange rates.

Nedbank: Internet banking
Full service banking via the Internet is possible. If you want to find how to link to the Internet, or what software and hardware you need, you may dial the help desk number above.

Services:
- Ask for statements and balances.
- Transfer funds between linked accounts.
- Pay linked third-party accounts (telephone, electricity).
- Order a new cheque book.
- Change your PIN.
- Request exchange rates.

Nedassist self-service terminals
Once again, a cheque or savings account (with Nedbank) is required.
Services:
- Pay third parties, including regular monthly bills.
- Make payments to accounts at other banks.
- Transfer money between linked accounts.
- Order a new cheque book.
- Obtain balances and statements.
- Request a statement search according to different criteria.
- Request PIN changes.

Cash point card
Nedbank Cash Point cards can be used at Cash Point ATMs.
Services:
- Draw cash, make deposits and obtain balances.
- Carry out counter transactions without completing forms.
- Order a cheque book.
- Transfer funds.

Nedbank electronic centres
Nedbank's electronic centres offer the following, amongst others:
- house cashpoint ATMs;
- house Nedassist self-service terminals; and
- a demonstration of Nedbank telephone banking.

These centres are mostly situated in large shopping centres and are available 24 hours per day.

The E-banking services above serve only as examples for 2002.

12.13 THE USURY ACT

According to the Department of Trade and Industry (DTI), all lenders using exemption from the Usury Act of 1968 after 15 September 1999 had to register with the Micro Finance Regulatory Council (MFRC). These lenders had to comply with the rules of the MFRC and the Exemption Notice. Those who did not register would be acting illegally. Micro-lenders who are not registered with the MFRC fall under the Usury Act. The maximum

interest rates that may be charged according to the Usury Act are:
- 26% for loans under R10 000; and
- 23% for loans above R10 000.

12.14 THE MICRO-LENDING INDUSTRY (MLI)

The micro-lending industry owes its existence to a need to offer credit to the millions of South Africans without access to the required credit facilities, and who, consequently, cannot open accounts or obtain loans from large financial institutions.

The poorer and low-income groups in South Africa (for example, those earning between R800 and R3 500 per month) were mainly those who had to live without credit. A large portion of the South African community now has access to credit through the micro-lending industry. This industry is very dynamic and currently supplies loans to approximately five million South Africans.

In the beginning (1992 especially), these micro-lending businesses lent money to individuals at excessive interest rates (for example, 300% or 500% per year). Many borrowers (completely uniformed about money matters and the usage of debt) fell into the debt trap ('debt jail') because of continuous borrowing. Individuals entered into loan agreements with several micro-lending businesses. As the MLI grew, various associations came into being, for example:
- the MLA (Micro Lenders Association);
- the AMLAC (Association for Micro Lenders And Consumers); and
- the MFRC (Micro Finance Regulatory Council).

Reputable micro-lenders became members of these organisations and became regulated by the MFRC. The industry was and is trying to get rid of so-called 'loan sharks', who are not regulated and who charge excessive interest rates.

Loans are made for both the short- (1 month) and medium-term (2–36 months). Those with a very low income may apply for such loans from a reputable micro-lender. The section below offers further practical information about how to obtain such a loan, or micro-loan.
- If you earn enough money to pay back a loan, you can go to a micro-lender to borrow money.
- Micro-lenders normally lend money to people who do not get large salaries or wages.
- You must tell the micro-lender how much money you need to borrow, what you want to buy, and how much money you can pay back over a period of time.

- The micro-lender will ask you for your payslips for the past three months, as well as your identity document. Take these with you to the micro-lender.
- If you have a monthly income, you will have a better chance of getting a loan. It will tell the micro-lender that you are earning money and that you will be able to pay back the loan.
- Give the micro-lender a copy of your budget. It will be easier to get a loan if you have a budget, because the micro-lender can see how much money you have left to pay back the loan over the agreed period of time.

The government has made specific rules that micro-lenders and banks must follow. They must give you a copy of the loan agreement. The loan agreement will tell you all you need to know about the rules and conditions of the loan.

12.14.1 The loan agreement

The loan agreement must tell you the following:

The amount you have borrowed
- This amount will include the insurance premiums you have to pay (an insurance premium is the monthly payment for your insurance).
- The amount will also include the amount of interest you have to pay on the money you have borrowed.

Money you want to borrow		R_____
Insurance premium	+	R_____
Interest, which includes administrative costs	+	R_____
TOTAL	R	
Amount to be paid back	=	R_____

The term of payment
The period of time (the term) over which you have to pay back the loan. You choose this period of time (or term), not the micro-lender.

The instalment
The amount you have to pay back each month is called the instalment.

$$\frac{\text{Total amount you have to pay back}}{\text{Period of time to pay back loan}}$$

= Monthly payment (instalment)

Failure to repay the loan

The loan agreement must tell you what will happen if you do not pay back the loan. You will then have to pay more interest.

The signing of the agreement

When you sign the agreement you tell the micro-lender that you agree with the rules and conditions for borrowing the money.

12.14.2 Which micro-lender is the right one to borrow from?

You must know the loan amount that you can afford

- Firstly, analyse how much you can pay back per month (draw up a budget).
- You need to go to a few micro-lenders to find out what interest rates they charge.
- Remember, if the interest rate goes up, your payment will also increase.

You cannot borrow the same amount from all micro-lenders

- Some only give loans of R10 000. They will not lend you R100 or R900.
- Choose the lender with the right amount for you.

How do you pay the loan back?

- Remember, some micro-lenders want their money back in three months.
- Choose one that is right for you.

Find out which micro-lender charges the lowest interest rate

- Go to a few micro-lenders and find out about their interest rates.
- Some micro-lenders give interest rates per month, other give interest rates per year.

Compare interest rates

- Ask someone to help you compare the interest rate per month and the interest rate per year.

- Change the monthly interest rate to interest rate per year.

Ask the Micro-lender to explain all the rules and conditions of your loan agreement. The law requires that micro-lenders should educate their clients.

Contact the Micro Finance Regulatory Council (MFRC) if you need more information.

12.14.3 What is the Micro Finance Regulatory Council (MFRC)?

The MFRC was established by the government to protect the clients of micro-lenders, particularly against very high interest rates.

Before you borrow money from a micro-lender, ask the micro-lender for proof of registration with the MFRC. Beware of a micro-lender that is not registered with the MFRC and charges you an interest rate higher than the maximum rate that the law allows. Contact the MFRC (Tel: 0860 100 406):

- To find out what maximum interest rate is allowed by the law.
- If you are unhappy with a micro-lender.
- If a micro-lender charges an interest rate higher than the maximum rate allowed.
- If the terms of your loan are not clear.
- If you are forced to sign a blank document (do not sign a blank document).
- If you are forced to give your bank card and secret pin number to the micro-lender (this is illegal).

12.15 CREDIT INFORMATION BUREAUX

Various credit information bureaux are found in South Africa. These bureaux store information on liquidations, and list the names of people who are incapable of paying their debts. People who regularly receive letters of demand, because they miss payments, appear on these lists. Once your name appears on such a list, it will be extremely difficult to obtain credit in the future.

As soon as someone applies for credit, a credit information bureau is contacted for more information about the applicant. No supplier of funds will extend credit to someone who does not regularly pay his or her debts. If it is found that the applicant has not paid debts in the past, he or she will definitely not be given a loan.

A good credit record is, therefore, an asset, even if it never appears on a person's balance statement. It is worth it over the long term to pay your debts according to the relevant agreements and to pay all your accounts regularly. In that way, you can prevent having your name appear on a credit information bureau's blacklist.

12.16 SUMMARY

In this discussion we have explained that credit should not be used at random. It requires thorough planning beforehand, based on knowledge and information. Credit should be used effectively within the constraints of the household budget. Mismanagement of credit has far-reaching consequences for many people. Think of the numerous daily liquidations and never forget the following saying that: 'borrowed money is a good servant but a bad master'.

12.17 SELF-ASSESSMENT

- Explain the importance of debt/credit planning.
- Explain the concept 'debt self-management'.
- Discuss how you would handle a debt crisis.
- Briefly explain the functioning of three credit instruments.
- Describe how you would go about applying for a micro-loan.
- List the functions of the MFRC.

BIBLIOGRAPHY

Auto Trader. 2001. *Helping hand: buyers/sellers guide*: 5, col. 1–3, Jan 21.

Badenhorst, P. 1990. Maak so met bruikhuur- of huurkoopkoerse. *Finansies & Tegniek*: 21, col. 1–2, Aug. 10.

Badenhorst, P. 1991. Wat jy moet weet as jy 'n tjekboek het. *Finansies & Tegniek*: 39, col 1–3, Aug. 16.

Bloemhof, F. 2000. PasopNet, hoor! *Sariehumor*: 71, col. 1–3, Nov 1.

Booyens, J. 2000. Gebruikte voertuie bied baie goeie waarde aan kopers. *Geld-Rapport*: 12, col. 1–5, Apr. 30.

Brown, A. & Paul, D. 2001. The busy woman's guide to the Internet. *Shape*: 118, col. 1–3, Jan./Feb.

Coetzee, J. 1991. Bestuur jou kredietkaart so. *Finansies & Tegniek*: 42, col. 1–3, July 12.

Forster, G. 2000. Wheel dreams. *Bona*: 66, col. 1–3, May.

Heystek, M. 1991. *Allied world of money*. Cape Town: Cream.

Krüger, A. 1992. Wees versigtig vir langer huurkooptermyn. *Finansies & Tegniek*: 37, col. 1–3 March 27.

Laurie, H de G. 1990. Die finansies van motorkoop. *Finansies & Tegniek*: 46, col. 1–3, June 22.

Lovemore, F.C.H. 1991. *Only study guide for CREDIT-3 (Credit Management)*. Revised edn. Pretoria: Unisa.

McKenzie, F. 2001. Net value. *Style*: 32, col. 1–2. Feb.

Nedbank. 2001. *Electronic banking*. Bank brochure.

Nedbank. 2001. *Vehicle finance*. Bank brochure.

Nieuwoudt, U. 2000. Die internet: jou lekegits. *Sarie Internet*: 65, col. 1–3, Nov. 1.

Schussler, M. 2000. Is koop, huur of huurkoop beste? *Rapport*: 9, col. 4–5, Febr. 20.

Seymour, M.L. 2000. *The Micro Lending Industry: a South African perspective*. For the partial fulfilment of the degree of Master of Business Administration. Oxford Brookes University. Project Supervisor: Professor Zak Nel.

South African National Consumer Union. 1991. *Buy right: Consumer guide for South Africa*. Cape Town: Tafelberg.

Standard Bank. 2001. *Financing options*. Bank Brochure.

Standard Bank. 2001. *Motor insurance*. Bank Brochure.

Standard Bank. 2001. *Pricing guide*. Bank Brochure.

Standard Bank. 2001. *Stannic asset finance*. Bank Brochure.

Swart, N.J. 1997. *How to plan your money matters after school and university*. Pretoria: Unisa.

Swart, N.J. 1992. *Only study guide for PERFIN-M (Personal Fiancial Management)*. Revised edn. Pretoria: Unisa.

Swart, N.J. & Coetzee, M. 2000. *My money matters: Six golden rules for planning your personal finances and using debt wisely*. Johannesburg: Creda.

Unisa. 2001. *Credit management principles (PBM108 – N)*. Programme in business management. Centre for Business Management.

Van der Watt, T. 1991. *The beginner's money manual*. Cape Town: Human & Rousseau.

Van Tonder, J. 2000. Betaal minder vir gebruikte motor. *Rapport*: 9, col. 4–7, Feb. 20.

CHAPTER 13

HEALTH CARE PLANNING

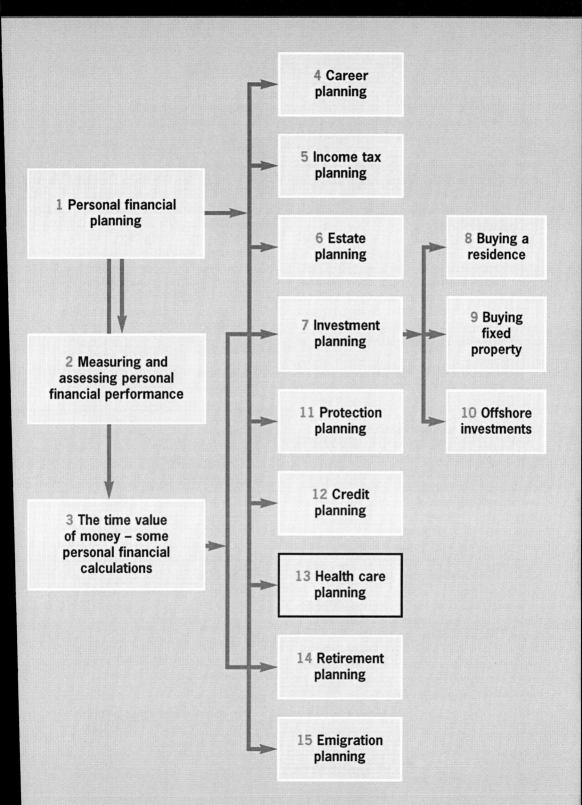

- 1 Personal financial planning
- 2 Measuring and assessing personal financial performance
- 3 The time value of money – some personal financial calculations
- 4 Career planning
- 5 Income tax planning
- 6 Estate planning
- 7 Investment planning
- 8 Buying a residence
- 9 Buying fixed property
- 10 Offshore investments
- 11 Protection planning
- 12 Credit planning
- 13 Health care planning
- 14 Retirement planning
- 15 Emigration planning

13.1 LEARNING OUTCOMES

After studying this chapter, you will be able to:
- Realise the importance of health care planning early in your life.
- Recognise health planning as the best long-term investment.
- Identify medical costs.
- Identify methods and products to provide for medical expenses.
- Differentiate between medical schemes and medical insurance.
- Identify alternative methods of health care.
- Explain the relationship between health care and retirement.

13.2 INTRODUCTION

Our health is probably our greatest asset. How long we are going to live, and, most important of all, the quality of life we are going to enjoy, depend on our health. If you were given the choice of living until the age of 70 without any serious health problems, or until the age of 80, but with your last 20 years dogged by ill-health and pain, you would probably choose the former.

Most people neglect their health while they are young, with the result that the quality of their lives after retirement leaves much to be desired. Your health is surely important enough to warrant doing everything in your power to protect and safeguard it. This does not imply that you have total control over your life and health. It is true, however, that you can arrange your affairs throughout your life so that your health does not suffer.

We all want to protect our assets, as indeed we should, and what could be more precious than our health? As with our other assets, we have to plan how to protect this asset over the long term, and health care planning is what this chapter is about.

Health care planning is not free and has to be included in a household budget (for example, the costs involved in recreational activities, an exercise bicycle, a policy, a medical aid scheme). Health planning affects other areas of planning, such as estate planning and retirement planning. Someone who is permanently ill will not be capable of building up a large estate, since a sick person cannot work to his or her full potential. Retirement planning will not be of much use if all you have to look forward to is ill health and pain.

Unfortunately, most people do not realise the benefits of good health before it is too late. We tend to think that an accident or a disease (especially a dreaded disease) will never happen to us. However, this is a mistake, since these things do happen to millions of people. Tables are available that set out life expectancy based on the following:
- age;
- gender;
- career;
- hobbies;
- family history;
- medical history;
- eating and drinking habits;
- fitness; and
- many other factors.

In Table 13.1, Boone & Kurtz (1989:646) illustrate the many factors that have an impact on our life expectancy. Health planning covers a much larger area than is generally thought. It is possible to assess how your health is affected by certain factors. It is possible to calculate more or less how long you are likely to live, taking into consideration certain factors.

TABLE 13.1 **Life expectancy table**
(Source: Boone & Kurtz 1989:646)

Start with number 72	
Personal facts	
– If you are male, subtract 3.	
– If you are female, add 4.	
– If you live in an urban area with a population over 2 million, subtract 2.	
– If you live in a town of under 10 000 or on a farm, add 2.	
– If any grandparents lived to 85, add 2.	
– If all four grandparents lived to 80, add 6.	
– If either parent died of a stroke or heart attack before the age of 50, subtract 4.	
– If any parent, brother or sister under 50 has (or had) cancer or a heart condition, or has had diabetes since childhood, subtract 3.	
– Do you earn over R150 000 a year? Subtract 2.	
– If you are 65 or over and still working, add 3.	
– If you live with a spouse or friend, add 5. If not, subtract 1 for every ten years alone since age 25.	
Lifestyle status	
– If you work behind a desk, subtract 3.	
– If your work requires regular, heavy physical labour, add 3.	

– If you exercise strenuously (tennis, running, swimming, etc.) five times a week for at least half an hour, add 4. Two or three times a week, add 2.	
– Do you sleep more than 10 hours each night? Subtract 4.	
– Are you intense, aggressive, easily angered? Subtract 3.	
– Are you easygoing and relaxed? Add 3.	
– Are you happy? Add 1. Unhappy? Subtract 2.	
– Have you had a speeding ticket in the past year? Subtract 1.	
– Do you smoke more than two packs a day? Subtract 8. One or two packs? Subtract 6. One-half to one? Subtract 3.	
– Are you overweight by 25kg or more? Subtract 8. By 15 to 25kg? Subtract 4. By 5kg to 15kg? Subtract 2.	
– If you are a man over 40 and have annual check-ups, add 2.	
– If you are a woman and see a gynaecologist once a year, add 2.	
Running total	
Age adjustment	
– If you are between 30 and 40, add 2.	
– If you are between 40 and 50, add 3.	
– If you are between 50 and 70, add 4.	
– If you are over 70, add 5.	
Add up your score to get your life expectancy.	

13.3 THE BEST INVESTMENT

Many personal financial advisers have been faced with trying to explain to clients which specific investments are the best at which time. This is never a simple task, and advice varies according to the current political and economic situation. However, one investment has proved itself through the ages, and the growth or return rate of this investment is not influenced by the economy, politics, inflation, personal tax rate, the size of your estate or the value of the rand. Yet, this type of investment influences your productivity, career, estate and especially retirement. Yes, there is such an investment instrument – your health!

Unfortunately people accept their health as a given, and do not realise that each person has been issued with only one set of health conditions. This determines not only how long you are going to live but, more importantly, the quality of life you are going to enjoy. Individuals need to order their affairs throughout their lives so as to make sure that their health does not suffer. Your lifestyle has to support a good quality of life until after retirement.

We may, therefore, speak of health planning, because individuals need to make different plans to protect their health in the long term (70 to 100 years). Estate planning and retirement planning are largely influenced by health care planning.

An ill person is far less productive than one who is in the pink of health. For people who believe that wealth and promotion do not come by themselves, this is obvious. A sick person's planning is regularly interrupted by some or other condition, and his or her use of time is far poorer; he or she can also not become involved in challenging and exhausting work. A career is influenced by this to a large extent, especially in the long term.

Estate planning consists mainly of acquiring assets, protecting them and passing them on to your heirs or other legal entity after your death. Due to poorer and less work, a sick person cannot acquire so many assets. Fewer additional investments are consequently made with a view to retirement.

The size of a sick person's estate is determined after his or her death. A sick person's estate will be smaller than that of a healthy person's, due to a smaller income to finance the acquisition of assets. Some people who do try to accumulate a sizeable estate, despite a particular condition, are often stopped in their tracks by a stroke, heart attack or early death.

A person's retirement, and especially its quality (in pain or not), is mainly influenced by his or her health and early planning in that regard.

Many factors influence your health. You should identify these factors and ensure that your health is positively influenced by them. It usually requires an adaptation to your lifestyle to prevent deteriorating health. Factors that may influence your health are, amongst others: history, exercise, smoking, drinking, stress, depression, religion and gender.

Stress is probably the most common 'illness' of our times. Only a few individuals do not suffer from it in one way or another, or at some time. It is really about too much tension, which means the body starts to suffer. Individuals become overtired, pessimistic, depressed, sleepless, unfriendly, unproductive, fearful and frustrated, and can no longer keep up with all the demands of their environment.

Amongst others, the following factors cause stress: The present and/or potential political situation of a country, your own financial matters, relationships with other individuals or family members, tension within a household, job security, unemployment, your future as a worker in or citizen of a country, your children's future, pressure from an employer, political pressure, pressure by trade unions, the pressure of competing with other employees (of the same employer), tax pressure, inflation (constantly rising prices) or an illness.

The following danger signs may warn an individual to give more attention to his or her level of stress: organic reactions (stomach ulcer, spastic colon, heart attack), psychological reactions (sleep disorders, heart palpitations), emotional reactions (a feeling of helplessness, guilt feelings, a feeling of being 'in jail'), cognitive reactions (memory loss, remembering stressful past events) and behavioural patterns (impulsiveness, smoking too much, drinking too much coffee, driving too fast, moodiness).

You should relax as much as possible. This changes your thought patterns and reduces the stress level. Creative work also helps. People often experience psychosomatic illness because of bitterness about a traumatic experience in their lives. The symptoms of such illnesses are, amongst others, head and chest pains.

Health care planning may be one of the most important planning areas in an individual's personal financial planning process. Unfortunately, this is exactly what is neglected most often. People do not realise that there can be no contented retirement, including financial independence, if there is no early and efficient health care planning.

Each individual must, therefore, identify the factors that will have an influence on his or her health now and in the future. People who neglect health planning, or who do not make the required financial provision, stand a far greater risk. This risk has nothing to do with any financial return, but rather with financial loss. Health planning is a must for any individual who is involved in personal financial planning.

13.4 THE NATURE AND IMPORTANCE OF MEDICAL COSTS

The annual rise of medical costs exceeds the rate at which other consumer goods rise. In other words, contributions towards medical costs and/or a medical aid fund are steadily increasing. It is generally accepted that medical expenses are the fifth largest item in the average household budget. More important expenses (in terms of monetary value) are usually food, housing, clothing and transport.

Furthermore, medical costs are unpredictable. A person can be healthy one moment and dead, sick or disabled the next. Although medical costs (such as contributions towards a medical aid fund) form part of a household budget, it is impossible to budget for unforeseen events such as death, a dreaded disease or occupational disability. An unex-

pected heart bypass operation could cost more than R50 000. If you do not have cover for such an operation, you will have to sell some of your assets. You could even face liquidation as a result of not being able to pay medical costs of one kind or another (such as for an operation or prolonged illness).

Most people take out medical and/or disability insurance to make provision for unforeseen medical expenses. A person could lose his or her source of income as a result of illness or occupational disability. A household could suffer a great financial loss (an unrecoverable loss) if the breadwinner loses his or her income.

So-called dreaded diseases, such as AIDS, are causing medical costs to rise and will continue to do so in future. This means that healthy people will have to pay to help cover sick people's medical costs. Tax money will also have to be used to fight these diseases. Medical care is becoming more and more expensive, as is medical equipment. Medical costs are constantly rising as a result of the following:

- a growing demand for medical services;
- population growth (especially in Africa);
- rising per capita income;
- medical research;
- higher educational levels;
- growing awareness of medical services available; and
- longer life expectancy (more 'old' people in the population).

It should be clear at this point that those who neglect to do health planning and to make the necessary financial provision, are running a great financial risk. Unlike certain investments, this kind of risk is not associated with some kind of financial return. On the contrary, if you do not protect yourself against this risk, you could face financial disaster. Health planning, therefore, is an essential part of everybody's personal financial planning.

Many people are in the dark about exactly what it means to belong to a medical aid fund or to have medical insurance. They do not know which medical costs and which treatments are covered, or what their dependants are entitled to.

As medical costs are constantly increasing, people lose their jobs and medical aid funds become increasingly exhausted financially, it is clear that health planning, as part of personal financial planning, is becoming more and more important. This is also because of the influence of health planning on investment and retirement planning, in particular. It is essential that individuals and households reconsider their medical product requirements (be it a medical aid fund or medical insurance). These requirements should be compared with the existing provision, in order to determine the shortage of medical provision.

Of course, such additional medical cover can only be taken if it can be accommodated in the household budget. During the discussion of protection planning (Chapter 11), some methods for cutting medical costs were pointed out. Here are some more hints:

- Do not see the doctor for every minor complaint.
- Do not rely on medication to keep you healthy if a change in lifestyle could do the same at no cost.
- Find information about medical matters on the Internet.
- Carefully check your medical and hospital accounts and ensure that you have received what you have paid for.
- Do not stay in a hospital unnecessarily (and expensively); rather sleep in your own bed if your condition permits it.

It is expected that medical costs will keep on rising in future, due to the following factors:

- The large number of medical claims due to AIDS and AIDS-related illnesses.
- The large number of older patients who may now join funds in terms of the new Medical Schemes Act.
- The small contributions being made to private medical aid funds by a small number of young people.
- The many people who no longer wish to make use of public health care, due to poor service and conditions.

We all have medical expenses at some stage of our lives. Medical expenses are unavoidable. These costs occur at times of birth, death, accident, sickness, operations, dental treatment, eye treatments and use of specialists, to mention only a few.

The extent of these costs will depend on the following:

- age;
- the type of medical condition (from flu to terminal cancer);
- the duration of the condition;
- whether the condition requires an operation;
- whether the person belongs to a medical aid fund;
- whether it is a 'deathbed operation' (which is tax-deductible) or another kind of operation;
- whether the person possesses a hospital policy; and
- the person's income level (the poor cannot pay and are subsidised).

Medical costs are rising at a faster rate than the current rate of inflation. On the other hand, incomes (salaries) are increasing at a slower rate than the rate of inflation. Consequently, medical costs are a problem. Medical inflation means that health planning is absolutely essential. This is the only way these costs can be accommodated.

Although medical costs differ from person to person, the following are common:

- loss of income (an accident or medical condition could result in occupational disability and the loss of both income and job);
- medical consultations (visits and injections);
- operations;
- hospitalisation (accommodation in general wards, intensive care units, theatre, medicine, physiotherapy, anaesthetist);
- maternity costs (general practitioner, gynaecologist, hospital ante- and postnatal classes);
- special costs (radiologists, blood transfusions, dieticians, clinical psychologists);
- dental treatment;
- medicine;
- eye treatment (consultation with ophthalmologist or optician, purchasing spectacles or contact lenses);
- private nursing (prescribed by doctor and offered by registered nurse);
- transplants (hip, knee-cap, arteries);
- orthopaedic aids (cervical collar, wheelchair, hearing aid, crutches, orthopaedic shoes or leg supports);
- homeopaths (registered) and others;
- ambulance services;
- cardiac pacemakers; and
- funeral costs.

It is essential to try to reduce the risk of such cost items by means of effective health planning. This can be done by making the necessary financial provision (which will be briefly discussed in the next section). Laurie (1991:28) suggests the following steps to keep medical costs as low as possible (particularly where people do not have any or sufficient provision):

- Consult a pharmacist instead of a doctor if the medical condition does not appear to be serious.
- Choose a doctor who charges reasonable 'scale of benefits' tariffs.
- Ask your doctor or pharmacist to suggest cheaper medicine (the cheapest possible).
- Go to a cheaper hospital.

Laurie (1991) also discusses the care of very old or terminally ill patients. Excessive medical costs are frequently incurred, which do not help these patients at all. Such expenses should be avoided where possible.

13.4.1 Medical tariffs

According to the Medical Association of South Africa (MASA) a doctor should in 2001 receive an amount of R99 for each 15 minutes of an examination. An hour in a consulting room will therefore cost R396. Medical aid funds currently want to pay only R80,10, so the patient has to pay the difference, unless additional medical provision has been made for this.

On the other hand, a dentist asks R57 for a consultation of 15 to 30 minutes (in 2001). In addition, a patient pays for each specific treatment, for example:

- dental hygiene (R89);
- fluoride treatment (R48); and
- fillings (R87 – R166).

Where doctors are paid for the type of service offered, dentists are paid for specific procedures.

In the figure below Gore (1997:24) points out the rising medical costs in a ten-year period. It should be quite clear that you need to make provision for medical costs (inflation) in time by topping-up a medical aid fund with additional cover and a hospital policy (long-term). It would be fatal to wait until retirement before making medical provision, or before having to pay for a serious operation at great medical cost.

13.4.2 Private versus public hospitals

In a survey about private and public hospitals by *Finance Week* (2000:2) the following came to light:

- Tariffs of private hospitals are much higher than those for public hospitals regarding: cost per day in wards; in intensive care.
- The payment of a deposit and the settlement of the account (some hospitals) is only applicable to private hospitals.
- Not all pensioners can afford private hospitals.
- People from overseas come to South Africa for 'cheap' private hospitals based on the cost of the rand).
- Ambulance services of private hospitals (contrary to those of public hospitals) are well equipped, staffed and maintained. The response time is also much faster. (People die because of the latter in the case of public hospitals.)

13.5 NEW HEALTH CARE LEGISLATION

The new Medical Schemes Act came into operation on 1 January 2000. This has changed the medical industry considerably and has relieved the pressure on public health care with its limited resources. On the other hand, more pressure has been placed on

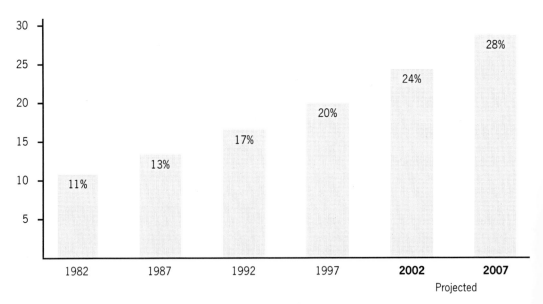

AVERAGE MEDICAL SCHEME CONTRIBUTIONS AS A % OF SALARY

FIGURE 13.1 **Rising medical scheme costs**
(Source: Gore 1997:24)

individuals to make use of private health care. Perhaps the greatest single influence on the medical industry has been the admission of AIDS sufferers to medical aid funds, as well as older people who could not belong to a medical aid fund before. Funds may not discriminate against people on the grounds of health or age in future. This means that healthy working people will be subsidising others who do not (or cannot) contribute to the fund, and this will mean an increase in premiums.

In addition, medical aid funds must now keep in reserve 25% of the annual premiums they receive. This protects members of the fund against the possibility that the fund could go under financially and, thus, that members could lose their benefits.

Many factors gave rise to the new legislation – amongst others:
- unnecessary/superfluous services being offered by doctors in order to increase their income;
- medical funds being in financial crisis, sometimes due to poor management;
- misuse of fund benefits by members who also insist on the best care;
- the heavy financial burden that public health must carry because younger people do not join medical aid funds and mainly make use of the former;
- the large numbers of unemployed persons who previously belonged to a medical aid fund but no longer contribute;
- emigration causing a reduction in the medical fund contributions; and
- medical aid funds encouraging members to become or stay healthy.

The Medical Schemes Act can briefly be summed up as follows:
- No person may be prohibited from becoming a member of a medical aid fund on the grounds of medical condition or age (however, certain provisos are applied to some medical conditions).
- As a member of the fund, the person is required to pay premiums.
- Someone with an own business may join any open fund in the medical industry.
- An employee who is not forced to belong to his or her employer's medical aid fund may join any other medical aid fund in the market (open fund).
- An individual's medical fund premium is determined by income and/or number of dependants.
- In terms of the income rating, all ages with the same income pay the same premium.

- In terms of the dependants rating, all persons with the same number of dependants pay the same premium.
- Medical aid schemes must offer all members a specific minimum coverage.
- There are certain penalties for persons who join a medical aid fund at a late stage (after the age of 30).
- In the case of divorce, the spouse not working for the employer concerned still remains a member of the fund (by continuing to pay the premiums of a closed fund).
- A medical scheme must also retain a reserve of 25% of members' annual premiums (smaller percentages apply until 1 January 2004).
- Members who retire from employment may remain members of their funds.
- The spouse of a deceased member of a fund may remain with the fund, subject to certain conditions.

13.6 PROVISION FOR MEDICAL EXPENSES

Considering the many uncertainties surrounding our health and the medical expenses that may arise in the future, it is clear that financial provision is essential. It is extremely risky not to make provision for medical expenses, for the following reasons:
- medical and health expenses crop up constantly; and
- the possibility of an unexpected accident or operation exists, which could destroy you financially.

Of course, you could provide for medical expenses in various ways, for example by making use of an existing investment. However, this is the wrong way, because you can transfer these risks to a medical aid fund and/or an insurance company. Furthermore, investments should be used for short-, medium- and long-term goals (e.g. retirement planning).

The financially correct method to provide for medical expenses is:
- a medical aid fund;
- top-up medical coverage (from an insurance company); and
- a hospital plan (short- and/or long-term).

In the discussion below, each of the above-mentioned methods is assessed as a means of providing for mainly three groups of expenses:
- small daily expenses (seeing a doctor for flu);
- larger daily expenses (for cancer or AIDS); and
- large medical expenses (operations).

13.7 MEDICAL SCHEMES

Not all medical aid funds are financially sound, and many have insuperable financial problems. There are many reasons for this, amongst others:

- poor management;
- too many medical claims (for many reasons); and
- doctors 'loading' medical prescriptions unnecessarily.

It is important to belong to a medical aid fund that will survive in the long term. If you belong to a medical aid fund that is suffering from insuperable financial problems, you will be held personally liable for all medical costs (accounts) by the suppliers of medical services (doctors, dentists, etc.). You will, furthermore, have to pay for expensive operations yourself, and this will have serious negative financial implications.

You could argue that you should simply be able to join a new fund immediately. Even if this were possible, there are waiting periods within which funds will not pay your medical claims.

13.7.1 How to evaluate a fund

It is not so easy for the layperson to evaluate a medical aid fund's future financial position. You can get help in this regard by looking at, for example, the credit rating that Duff & Phelps give specific funds. This credit rating refers to the financial creditworthiness of a particular fund. If you can get hold of the list of the most recent credit ratings, you should choose a fund with an acceptable rating. Over and above this rating, you must also look at the fund that offers you the most suitable benefits for a specific premium (which you can afford).

The different credit ratings are:

- AAA (highest claims paying ability);
- AA (very high claims paying ability);
- A (high claims paying ability);
- BBB (acceptable claims paying ability);
- BB (risky claims paying ability); and
- CCC (the scheme is likely to face liquidation).

Different funds

There will always be a few people who think they can establish their own medical aid fund at home, for example by investing money against the day that they will need to pay medical costs. As in the case of short-term insurance, self-insurance in this case is very risky personal financial planning. Avoid it at all times and join a legally registered medical aid fund.

Medical aid funds are provided mainly by:

Medical schemes:

- traditional schemes (employer schemes);
- new generation schemes (which divide medical costs to create a separate savings account for members); and
- any medical scheme and top-up cover (from an insurance company).

Insurance companies:

- private schemes (including both new generation schemes and health insurance); and
- private schemes and top-up cover (for medical shortfalls).

You will remember that during our discussion of protection planning in Chapter 11, we referred to 'closed' and 'open' schemes. In the case of a 'closed' scheme, membership is compulsory, and employers subsidise their employees' contributions. Only the employees may, therefore, belong to the employer's medical aid fund.

In the case of 'open' schemes, any person may belong. The premiums paid by members of the fund are higher, because they are not subsidised by an employer (unless your employer pays you a medical allowance). Persons who work for themselves will of necessity join an 'open scheme' at the higher (non-subsidised) cost.

There have also been references to doctors who are contracted in or contracted out of medical schemes. Where a doctor is contracted in, you pay SAMA (South African Medical Association) and BHF (Board of Health Care Funders) medical rates. If a doctor is contracted out, you will pay a higher tariff. SAMA determines doctors' medical tariffs, while BHF determines a SOB (scale of benefits) tariff for the industry. This tariff is lower than that of SAMA.

13.7.2 Managed care

Managed care refers to the purposeful management of the activities of all parties concerned with medical aid funds, in order to:

- control the costs of medical expenses; and
- ensure quality service.

It sounds as if medical aid funds should have done this from the very beginning, but unfortunately it is not that easy. Table 13.2 compares the management style of traditional medical aid funds and managed care.

13.8 MEDICAL INSURANCE

Someone belonging to a medical aid fund may take out additional medical cover in the form of medical

TABLE 13.2 **Traditional medical aid funds versus managed care**

Traditional medical fund	Managed care
1. You can choose any doctor	1. You choose from a group of doctors
2. No financial relationship between all/any parties	2. A financial relationship between all parties
3. No strict cost control	3. Strict cost control
4. No balancing of cost and quality of service	4. Balancing of cost and quality of service
5. Incentives to doctors to supply more services than necessary	5. Incentives to supply just the required services
6. Medical scheme carries all the risk	6. Medical service providers (doctors) carry the risk
7. Incentives to fund members to misuse medical benefits (visits to doctors, claims, etc.)	7. Incentives to fund members to use benefits in a just manner (own savings account, no unnecessary doctor visits/claims)
8. No reward for members	8. Reward for members
9. No protection for long-term existence of scheme	9. Protection for scheme's long-term existence
10. Members get all the treatment they want	10. Members get only the treatment they need

insurance products. Medical insurance can be used as an extra to supplement a medical aid fund in order to:

- cover a specific medical condition (an operation or organ transplant for which a specific amount, for example R20 000, will have to be paid) by taking out long-term medical insurance (top-up cover) or a long-term hospital plan; or
- cover a particular daily cost (for example, a three-day stay in hospital, in which case a daily amount of R500 is paid out) by taking out short-term medical insurance or a short-term hospital plan.

There are both long-term and short-term hospital plans that cover diverse medical needs. Equally, there are two types of long-term hospital plans, namely medical aid fund hospital plans and insurance hospital plans (i.e. short- and long-term). Make sure that you buy the correct product. The role of medical insurance, to supplement a medical aid fund in the form of top-up cover, has already been discussed.

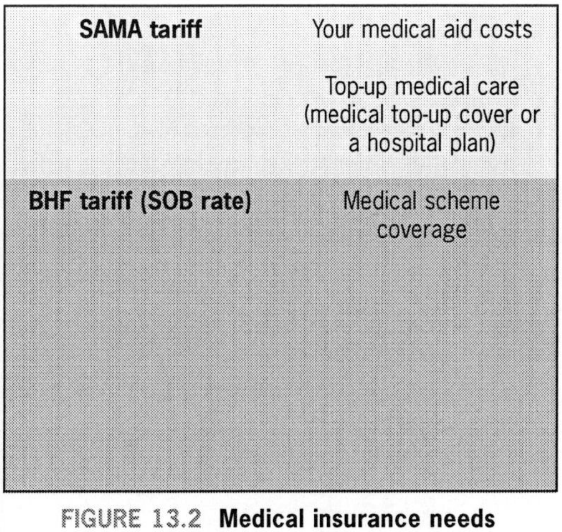

SAMA tariff	Your medical aid costs
	Top-up medical care (medical top-up cover or a hospital plan)
BHF tariff (SOB rate)	Medical scheme coverage

FIGURE 13.2 **Medical insurance needs**

Make sure that you understand the illustration, so that you can determine your own medical needs and satisfy them.

13.9 HEALTH CARE PRODUCTS – WHERE SHOULD I START?

This question brings us back to the personal financial planning process. You once again need to follow the various steps to determine whether particular medical expenses (funds and/or products) can be accommodated in your household budget. Only then will you be able to provide for medical needs, unless you are able to make alternative income and expenditure plans. The following procedure is recommended:

- Analyse your current financial situation. Do this as set out in Chapter 1, and specifically note the provisions you have already made for short- and long-term medical needs.
- Determine your short-, medium- and long-term goals. In particular, look at the medical coverage you would like to have. However, be realistic and remember your financial resources. For example, you may want the following products:
  - a short-term hospital plan; and
  - medical top-up cover (which will pay out R50 000 for a particular type of operation).
- Always remember your limitations. A spouse may lose his or her work, or you may not really have the money to afford additional medical products at present. In this case, you would have to determine priorities for your household and abandon certain activities. Always remember your medical needs.
- Choose certain products. Speak to a medical consultant accredited by the Association of Health Benefits Advisers (AHBA) or the

Financial Planning Institute of South Africa (formerly ILPA). This person will explain and market the required products (either a medical aid fund and/or insurance) to you.

- Draw up a household budget. If the budget balances, or if you can make use of alternative financing, you can buy the medical products. If not, you need to draw up new plans, which may imply cheaper products and lower medical coverage.
- Evaluate and revise. Medical provision must be re-evaluated constantly to identify new needs and to plan for them.

Go to your medical broker properly prepared so as to be in a position to ask the right questions.

13.9.1 Your medical broker

Just as when buying any financial product (or fixed property), a broker is used when buying medical products. The same criteria that are used to choose any other broker, are used in the case of a medical broker. Furthermore, it is important that such a broker should be accredited by:

- the Medical Schemes Council;
- the Association of Health Benefits Advisers (AHBA); or
- the Financial Planning Institute of South Africa (formerly ILPA).

If you need a quotation for particular products, you may consult two or three brokers and compare their rates. If you do not know how, you may always get an expert opinion and pay for it. For example, the Medical Schemes Act regulates who may market a medical scheme. Accreditation by the Medical Schemes Council does allow a broker to do this, and accreditation is reviewed every two years.

Also make sure that a broker has written permission to market a medical aid fund. Commission must be revealed – in 2002 this was 3% of the annual premiums. A broker must have at least a Grade 12 education and two years' appropriate experience. Feel free to evaluate the broker who is offering you a service, or you may not have the required protection in terms of the Medical Schemes Act.

13.9.2 Tax and your medical expenses

Medical costs may be recovered from income tax as follows (2002):

- persons younger than 65 years – an amount which exceeds 5% of taxable income;
- persons older than 65 years – all medical expenses that cannot be recovered from a medical aid fund;

- persons receiving a medical allowance – fringe benefit tax must be paid on any amounts you receive exceeding two-thirds of your own contributions;
- persons who sell medical insurance products – no tax advantages or deductions; and
- persons with physically or mentally handicapped children – all medical expenses are tax deductible for the entire household except for an amount of R500.

13.9.3 Legal insurance for medical protection

Say someone wants to sue a doctor following an operation. However, the legal costs would be so high that it would not be worth it. According to Van der Merwe (2001:58) a civil action costs between R80 000 and R100 000. The opinion of an independent expert could cost up to R3 000 in court. The problem arises when you lose a case and the lawyer has taken the case on a 'contingency' basis. If you lose, you must pay the other party's legal costs.

If you have no legal insurance, this may have negative financial implications for you as plaintiff.

Remember to consult a lawyer who specialises in medical law. Also remember that you need to follow certain procedures if you are injured while on duty. Ask your personnel department and lawyer about the correct procedure.

13.10 ALTERNATIVE METHODS OF HEALTH CARE

There are various alternative health care methods in South Africa, amongst others:

- homeopathy (sometimes covered by medical aid);
- reflexology and acupuncture;
- chiropractic;
- speech therapy (covered by medical aid);
- dietetics (covered by medical aid);
- home nursing services (covered by medical aid);
- occupational therapy (covered by medical aid);
- physiotherapy (covered by medical aid); and
- traditional healing (will be covered in future).

Before running up costs in regard to any of the above, you should make sure whether it is covered by your medical aid fund or not. Currently, the position in South Africa is that medical aid funds do not permit deductions if the method used does not enjoy strict medical control.

13.11 HEALTH CARE FOR YOUR RETIREMENT

The prerequisite of health planning for retirement planning has already been pointed out. The new Medical Schemes Act has made provision for employees (members of funds) who retire and receive a pension from the employer's retirement fund to stay on as members of the employer's medical aid fund. Where the employer no longer subsidises the retiree's medical aid fund contributions, that person will pay a higher premium. Your membership may continue until your death. Make sure that you know which medical benefits you will continue to receive, and at what cost (your premiums). In retirement you, therefore, need to speak to both your broker and your employer's representative for the medical aid fund.

People who work for themselves must make their own provision for medical care now and after retirement. Take the necessary medical cover (medical aid fund, top-up cover, hospital plans, etc.) and do not rely on your retirement investments for medical expenses. However, always determine your needs carefully and stay in touch with a good medical broker. Remember that you should already be building up your own medical savings account for unpredictable future medical events.

13.12 FURTHER INFORMATION

Make use of the following sources of medical information:
- Registar of Medical Schemes;
- Medical Schemes Council;
- Association of Health Benefits Advisors (AHBA);
- Financial Planning Institute of South Africa (formerly ILPA);
- South African Medical Association (SAMA);
- Board of Health Care Funders (BHF);
- The Hospital Association of South Africa;
- the list of Medical Schemes in South Africa with their credit ratings;
- the Long-term Insurance Ombudsman;
- the Short-term Insurance Ombudsman; and
- the Dental Ombudsman.

13.13 SUMMARY

Health planning is probably the most important aspect of personal financial planning. Unfortunately, it is frequently precisely this aspect that people tend to neglect. They do not realise that a happy retirement with financial independence is impossible without timely and effective health planning.

Everyone should, therefore, consider their present state of health and identify the factors most likely to affect their health in the future. Medical expenses are virtually inevitable, and most people have to cope with them almost daily, whether for headache tablets or hospitalisation. It is essential to make provision for medical expenses as early as possible. Timely provision will prevent the possibility of becoming uninsurable at a later stage.

Regular visits to a dentist and a doctor (at least once a year) are recommended. Timely and constant health planning inevitably reminds us of the saying: 'You cannot determine the years of your life but you can determine the life of your years.'

13.14 SELF-ASSESSMENT

- List advantages of timeous health planning.
- Briefly discuss a medical scheme, medical insurance and methods to provide for medical expenses.
- Identify different alternative methods of health care.
- Briefly explain the relationship between health planning and retirement planning.

BIBLIOGRAPHY

Albrecht, K. 1979. *Stress and the manager: Making it work for you.* Englewood Cliffs: Prentice-Hall.

Basson, D. 1990. Groter realisme oor Vigs. *Finansies & Tegniek*: 70, col. 1–3, Nov. 23.

Block, S.B., Peavy III, J.W. & Thornton, J.H. 1988. *Personal financial management.* New York: Harper & Row.

Boone, L.E. & Kurtz, D.L. 1989. *Personal financial management.* Homewood: Irwin.

Buchanan, R. 2001. Why (hic) you really ought to go slow. *Shape*: 59, col. 1, January/February.

Butler, G. & Hope, T. 1997. *Manage your mind: The mental fitness guide.* New York: Oxford.

Coetzee, J. 1991. Stres: Dis jou keuse! *Finansies & Tegniek*: 48, 50, col. 1–3, June 21.

Colino, S. 2001. 7 Health sins of your past. *Shape*: 50, col. 1–2, Jan/Feb.

Dasnois, A. 2001. Medical check-up. *Personal Finance*: 65, col. 1, January.

Glusac, E. 2001. Why you really should get more sleep. *Shape*: 56, col. 1–2, January/February.

Finance Week. 2000. Ambulance services under pressure. *Finance Week Supplement*: 31, col. 1, March 17.

Finance Week. 2000. Health care undergoes radical reform. *Finance Week Supplement*: 2, col. 1–2, March 17.

Finance Week. 2000. Private ambulance services indispensable. *Finance Week Supplement*: 31, col. 1–2, March 17.

Finance Week. 2000. SA institutions draw foreigners. *Finance Week Supplement*: 28, col. 1–2, March 17.

Gore, A. 1997. Provide for rising medical costs in your retirement plan. *Saturday Star*: 24, col. 1–5, April 19.

Jordaan, J.H. 1990. *Retirement planning: Your key to a happy retirement*. Cape Town: Don Nelson.

Labuschagne, Z. 2001. When sleep is never enough. *Weigh-less*: 30, col. 1–3, March.

Laurie, H. de G. 1991. Hou op kwel en begin leef! *Finansies & Tegniek*: 40, col.1, Sept. 20.

Laurie, H. de G. 1991. Hou mediese koste binne perke. *Finansies & Tegniek*: 40, col. 1, Sept. 20.

Mittra, S. 1990. *Practising financial planning*. Englewood Clifs: Prentice-Hall.

Old Mutual. 1990. Hoe Vigs die ekonomie kan raak. *Finansies & Tegniek*: 12, col. 1–3, May 18.

Penson, J.B., Levi, D.R. & Nixon, C.J. 1982. *Personal finance*. Englewood Cliffs: Prentice-Hall.

Robbins, A. 1991. *Awaken the giant within*. New York: Simon & Schuster.

Schlosberg, S. 2001. The cheat's guide to losing weight. *Shape*: 102, col. 2, 3, January/February.

Spratt, K. 2000. 20 ways to weigh less. *Weigh-less*: 29, col. 1–2, November/December.

Spratt, K. 2001. Making time for exercise. *Weigh-less*: 52, col. 1–2, March.

Van der Merwe, L. 2001. Jou dokter en jou regte. *Sarie: Medies*: 58, col. 1, March 21.

Van der Walt, P.J. 1990. *Lewensversekering en uittredingsannuïteite: 'n Besluitnemingsmodel*. Research project for B.Comm.Hons. Pretoria. Unisa.

Wyatt, T. 2001. Space-age your body for the 21st century. *Shape*: 76, col. 1–3, January/February.

CHAPTER 14

RETIREMENT PLANNING

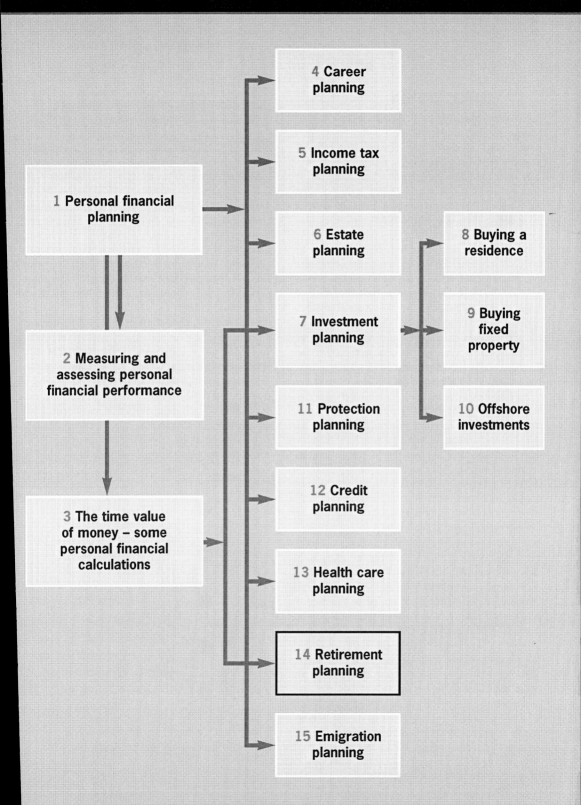

4 Career planning

5 Income tax planning

1 Personal financial planning

6 Estate planning

8 Buying a residence

7 Investment planning

9 Buying fixed property

2 Measuring and assessing personal financial performance

11 Protection planning

10 Offshore investments

12 Credit planning

3 The time value of money – some personal financial calculations

13 Health care planning

14 Retirement planning

15 Emigration planning

14.1 LEARNING OUTCOMES

After studying this chapter, you will be able to:

- Explain the importance of timely retirement planning.
- Identify the different methods that can be used to provide for retirement.
- Explain the functioning, problems, advantages and disadvantages of the different methods.
- Identify many other very important retirement issues.
- List the many questions that people have to ask themselves when they consider retiring.

14.2 INTRODUCTION

Retirement planning is primarily a product of advanced communities. Boone & Kurtz (1989:645) state that so-called primitive communities have no need for retirement planning.

In 1875 the American Express Company introduced one of the first retirement schemes. The wording of the scheme was: 'A pension will be provided to worn-out or disabled employees who have been in employment for twenty years.'

Many people do not plan for their retirement at an early stage, preferring to wait until they are in the last phase of their life cycle. Most people are so involved in their daily activities that they cannot spare the time to plan for the 'distant future'. Because of the great strides in medical care today, the average person can live another 20 years after retirement. This is a long time and warrants careful planning, since it is impossible to guarantee financial security and independence.

The ever-increasing rate of inflation is probably the main reason for the declining purchasing power of money over time. The time value of money implies that a certain amount of money is worth more today than the same amount will be in the future. If, because of inflation, the purchasing power of money is halved every six years, today's R100 000 will buy only R50 000 worth of goods in six years' time.

For these reasons, it is essential to start planning for your retirement as soon as possible. Once you have developed health problems you may no longer be eligible for a policy for retirement purposes. Occupational disability is a very real problem. For example, you may intend retiring at 60 years of age but become occupationally disabled at 45 years of age. Even if you do have an insurance policy, you may be forced to surrender it, which could leave you without an income after retirement.

A younger person will start off such retirement planning with a investment in one or more investment alternatives, for example an annuity, an endowment policy, unit trusts and a life policy. These four investment types are the ones most young people should concentrate on, over and above their employer's retirement fund, and buying a house.

> Retirement planning will vary from individual to individual because of different financial situations and, particularly, phases in the human life cycle.

As you become older, reaching your middle years (40 to 50), you already have a fairly good idea of your particular lifestyle, that is what you enjoy and would like to do with your life and belongings, and how you would like to apply these in your old age. From this stage onwards, your retirement planning decisions should be specifically based on your lifestyle, because you should already have some certainty about your financial situation, both current and future.

You should follow the same lifestyle approach when receiving your retirement package at a later stage (55 to 65 years). It is very important that your retirement package should serve your lifestyle. Someone who likes the quiet life and abhors a frenetic and tense lifestyle, should, for example, not invest in a risky holiday resort or restaurant. Such an investment does not suit such a person's lifestyle or path through life. The same argument applies to retirement planning throughout your life.

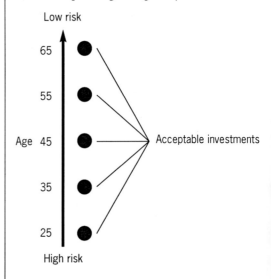

FIGURE 14.1 **Path through life**

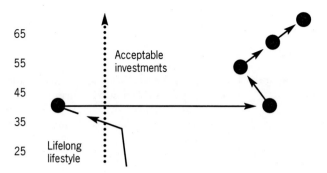

65

55

45

35

25

Acceptable
investments

Lifelong
lifestyle

- Unacceptable investments
  creating a stressful life for
  household with negative
  financial consequences
- Unacceptable investments not
  serving lifestyle and
  retirement goals
- Unacceptable investments
  leading to ill health and
  depletion of financial and
  retirement resources

FIGURE 14.2 **Path of life**

14.3 THE IMPORTANCE OF RETIREMENT PLANNING

The importance of retirement planning can hardly be overemphasised. The ultimate aim of personal financial planning is precisely to enable you to be financially independent after retirement. By financial independence we mean the ability and freedom to make financial decisions. Unfortunately, only 6% of all retired people are able to make independent financial decisions.

Figure 14.3 illustrates that 47% of all retired people are financially dependent on their relatives. The state has to provide pensions to 16% of the population, while 31% are obliged to continue working (irrespective of the state of their health).

Just as every person is unique, so every household is unique, with the result that there are numerous reasons why only 6% of the population are able to retire with financial independence. The main reasons are:

> Retirement planning does not mean exploiting the unknown.

- lack of knowledge about the importance of early personal financial and retirement planning;
- the absence of investments which lead to capital growth in the long term;
- the tendency some people have to spend all their money because they want certain possessions immediately and do not have enough money left to provide for retirement;
- the tendency to borrow money for non-essential possessions, which decrease in value, such as an extra motor car;
- the absence of planning according to objectives that have to be achieved sometime in the future;
- the erroneous impression that you can earn a good living for the rest of your working life, which will ensure a good standard of living after retirement;

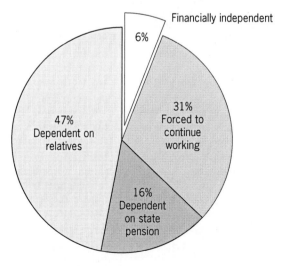

Financially independent

6%

47%
Dependent on
relatives

31%
Forced to
continue
working

16%
Dependent
on state
pension

FIGURE 14.3 **The financial position of retired people**
(Source: Adapted from Old Mutual 1992:7)

- the uncertainty of the future causes people with a negative attitude to be wary of investing their money – they believe it is better to enjoy their money while they can; and
- people regard retirement planning as an event to be tackled after retirement, not before.

A multitude of other factors affect your standard of living after retirement, such as:
- the number of homes possessed and lived in over the years, for which transfer duty costs had to be paid each time;
- the number of times estate agent's commission had to be paid for the same reason;
- the number of job or career changes, associated with loss of pension benefits, whether as a result of a loss of contributions by employers or because of the taxability of the lump sum;
- the number of children at school or university, as well as the cost of weddings for these children;
- the number of years during which a person has contributed towards a pension fund;
- the amount contributed towards a pension fund;
- the amount set aside for other retirement provisions; and
- whether both husband and wife contributed towards some kind of provision for retirement.

There are various factors that threaten your retirement. Unemployed children, who nowadays are forced to stay with their parents for a few years after leaving school or university, are the latest of these. The longer the period the parents have to carry this burden, the more disastrous the consequences are for retirement.

Parents could find themselves paying for food, clothing, transport, a deposit on a car, car maintenance and insurance, studies, a wedding, grandchildren, a deposit on their children's homes and possibly a divorce. This financial pressure on the household budget creates tension and stress in the parental home.

The personal financial education and empowerment of children and young people has become one of the best investments South African parents can make. Thousands of young people leave school without proper knowledge of financial matters. Because of our culture and educational system, parents probably were not taught personal financial planning either.

To solve this problem, parents and children should be taught to manage their personal finances, for the following reasons:
- It will have a positive effect on the financial conduct of young people.

- Young people will strive for financial independence and will receive the guidance they need.
- Young people will assume responsibility for their own finances.
- They will know more about financial matters.
- They will be able to survive financially.
- Financial winners will be created.
- Parents will be financially independent when they retire.
- Parents will realise that their financial future could be threatened by children who are not properly educated about financial matters.

Which young people should be taught about personal finances?

Students in Grades 10, 11 and 12, all young people (employed or unemployed), young people who want to get married, young married couples with or without children, young people who are living together and potential entrepreneurs should learn about personal finance. If you have children, you should help your children to become educated in this field, and help yourself at the same time.

What do young people need to know?

Young people should be educated about personal financial matters in such a way that they are empowered to take responsibility for their own financial future. Being able to take care of your own finances is one of the most important life skills you can have. This is even more important for young people, because timely and informed personal financial planning may have a positive effect on the rest of their lives.

A major problem nowadays is that neither South African parents nor their children have ever been taught to manage their personal finances. All of them have to rely on information that they get from the media. However, because of sensationalism and a total lack of educational structure, the myriad articles that are published resemble a jigsaw puzzle that can never be completed.

Young people should know about the uncertain financial future that awaits them. Figures (positive and negative) should be used to illustrate this reality. A lifetime (which to them seems so long) should be explained in terms of the life cycle and the planning required in the different life stages. Career choices and investments that need to be made should be pointed out. The importance of early planning should be stressed. Information should be given about the importance of further studies and about choosing a career as an employee or an entrepreneur.

If parents are sufficiently interested in their children and their financial future, they (and the educational system) can have a lasting, positive influence on their children's ability to handle financial affairs.

What is the most important life skill and investment you could have when you retire?

There are numerous opinions about the best life skill that South Africans should be taught these days. With the income that we earn, we accumulate assets, we protect these assets against various risks and, after our death, these assets go to our heirs.

If we want to live tranquil and purposeful lives, it is important to know how to manage our assets and income. We call this personal financial management, which is much more than knowledge about the stock market or insurance. It covers a vast field and includes all the aspects of our lives that we can express in monetary or financial terms.

Whether you have a lot of possessions or only a few, whether you are young or old, you should know how to handle your financial affairs. You should know which factors or events in your life will have a positive or negative effect on your financial affairs. This will help you to plan in order to obtain or avoid certain financial results. Financial planning affects many areas of your life, because you are 'linked' via money, amongst others, to your family and the people and institutions around you.

Today, millions of South Africans have to be taught how to work with money – not only those who have jobs, but also those who have their own businesses or want to start a business. It is not much use when you earn money but do not know what to do with it or how to use it. Everybody should also be informed about what is going to happen to their possessions after their death.

People should be aware of the financial consequences that an antenuptial contract may have on their future (in the event of death or divorce). All of us are going to die, and about one in every two people will be divorced. Many people are unaware that they or their children may suffer financial consequences when they live together.

Let us take this argument further. People who are knowledgeable in the field of personal finances (financially empowered) often find that more work opportunities are open to them. They may become brokers, or may be employed by financial institutions. They will also be more successful if they start their own businesses.

So, knowledge about personal finance is the most important life skill we have to learn. It should be included in the educational system, so that young people will be motivated and have self-confidence, a positive self-image and a positive attitude toward their financial future.

Let us make sure that our children are among this group of young people. Give them a chance to believe in their financial future because they are financially empowered.

14.4 THE INCOME GAP AFTER RETIREMENT

Figures 14.4 to 14.7 demonstrate the decline in income after retirement. Figure 14.4 shows the annual income of people during their life cycle. It is apparent that a person earns a positive annual income only after school and university. Income increases over the person's life cycle up to and at retirement; after that, it declines and a shortfall

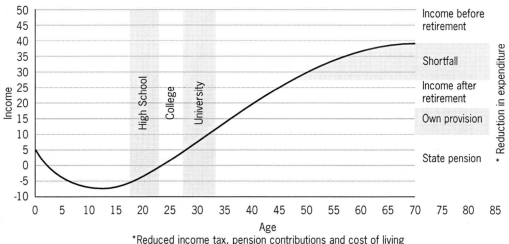

*Reduced income tax, pension contributions and cost of living

FIGURE 14.4 **Shortfall in income during retirement**
(Source: Adapted from Amling & Droms 1986:506)

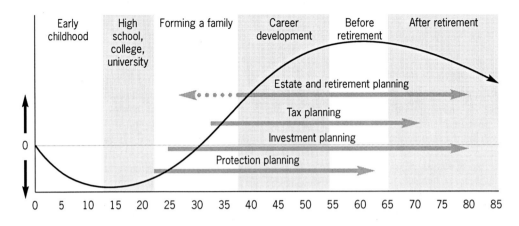

FIGURE 14.5 The personal financial planning cycle over a person's lifetime
(Source: Adapted from Gitman & Joehnk 1987:12)

arises. This shortfall must be replenished by means of effective retirement planning in the form of investments, if the person wishes to maintain the same standard of living after retirement as he or she did before retirement.

Figure 14.5 also shows the declining income of a person after retirement. Timely investments, with the necessary capital growth, can prevent this income from declining. Such investments should be started between the ages of 20 and 30 years.

Figure 14.6 shows gross income before and after retirement. The main expenditure deducted from gross income is listed. It is clear that, although the deductions decline after retirement, the net income (B_3) also declines. It is assumed that the person receives a pension. This results from the lower gross income (B_1). The net income can be increased, however, from B_3 to B_2 by means of an investment in a retirement annuity, an endowment policy, a provident fund, a fixed deposit or a mortgage

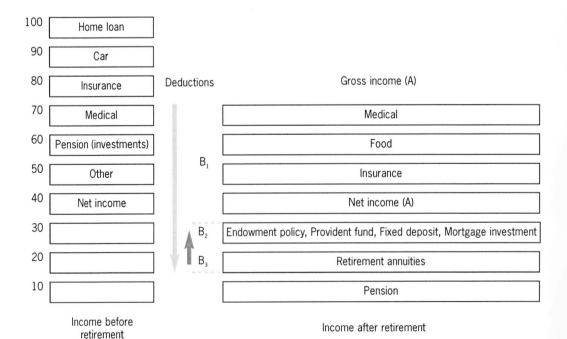

FIGURE 14.6 Income before and after retirement
(Source: Adapted from Amling & Droms 1986: 509)

investment. These investments are only examples used to make the net income before retirement equal to the net income after retirement.

Figure 14.7 illustrates the importance of planning and making provision for retirement at an early age. The earlier you start providing for retirement, the smaller the gap after retirement. For example, someone who contributes to a pension fund for 15 years will experience a much larger gap or shortfall (70%) than someone who contributes for a period of 30 years (40%).

Jordaan (1990:82) points out that an employee should work for the same employer for about 45 years in order to retire on 90% of his or her final salary (if the pension is calculated on the basis of 2% of the final salary for every year of service). If the 45 years is multiplied by the 2%, it amounts to 90% of the final salary. Every time an employee changes jobs, he or she forfeits a portion of his or her potential pension benefits (especially if the years of fund membership are very short – 5 years, for example).

Table 14.1 illustrates additional savings you need in order to supplement your pension. If you have 20 years of fund membership you will retire at 40% (20 years × 2%) of your final salary. Should you wish to retire at 90% of your current income, you need to save an additional 15% of your current income if you have 17 years before retirement (17 years to retirement: 49.71% [± 50% : 90% – 40%] is the income gap; 15% of the current income is needed to supplement retirement provision).

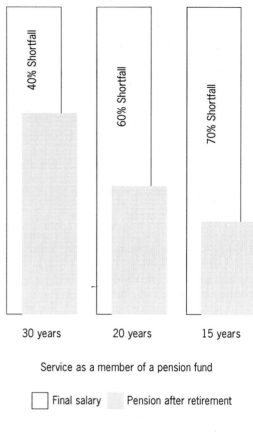

FIGURE 14.7 **Income gap at retirement**
(Source: Adapted from Old Mutual 1992:64)

TABLE 14.1 **Percentage additional savings of income needed to supplement retirement provision**
(Source: Van Tonder 2000:7; Adapted from Swart 1996:582)

Number of years to retirement	Percentage of existing income to be invested to maintain your standard of living after retirement								
	8.0%	9.0%	10.0%	11.0%	12.0%	13.0%	14.0%	15.0%	16.0%
10	13.63	15.58	17.45	19.50	21.46	23.41	25.97	27.33	29.29
11	15.41	17.32	19.49	21.67	23.84	25.01	28.19	30.38	32.53
12	16.69	19.08	21.48	23.87	26.26	28.66	31.05	33.44	35.84
13	18.26	20.88	23.50	26.11	28.73	31.35	33.96	36.58	39.20
14	19.86	22.71	25.55	28.40	31.24	34.09	36.93	39.78	42.62
15	21.49	24.57	27.65	30.72	33.80	36.88	39.95	43.03	46.11
16	23.15	26.46	29.78	33.09	36.40	39.72	43.03	46.34	49.65
17	24.84	29.23	31.94	35.50	39.05	42.61	46.16	49.71	53.27
18	26.55	30.35	34.15	37.95	41.75	45.55	49.35	53.14	56.94
19	28.30	32.35	36.40	40.45	44.50	48.54	52.59	58.84	60.69
20	30.08	34.39	38.69	42.99	47.29	51.59	55.89	60.20	64.50
21	31.90	36.46	41.02	45.58	50.14	54.70	59.26	63.82	68.38
22	33.74	38.56	43.39	48.21	53.03	57.86	62.68	67.51	72.33
23	35.62	40.71	45.80	50.89	55.98	61.08	66.17	71.28	76.34
24	37.53	42.89	48.26	53.62	58.99	64.35	69.72	75.08	80.45
25	39.48	45.12	50.76	56.40	62.05	67.69	73.33	78.97	84.61

14.4.1 The retirement planning process

Figure 14.8 illustrates the steps to be taken during retirement planning and gives an overview of the process of retirement planning. The first step involves setting objectives, which may include the following:

- to maintain the same standard of living as before retirement;
- to buy a holiday home;
- to make a mortgage investment valued at R1 million;
- to pay off all mortgage bonds; and
- to buy an expensive boat or motor car.

These objectives have to be placed in order of priority. Each objective should be accompanied by a time horizon, for example for 3, 5, 10, 20 and 30 years. If necessary, these objectives will have to be revised and altered from time to time.

The second step involves determining how much money will be required to achieve each objective. At least one page will be required in order to make these calculations. All household income and expenses during retirement must be determined and the difference calculated. It is important to work in terms of the current value of money, and to take the annual inflation rate into account.

EXAMPLE

	R
1 Retirement income required	
Monthly expenditure × 12 (R4 500 × 12)	
OR percentage of salary (R72 000 × 75%)	54 000
2 Subtract income available at retirement	
Pension e.g. years of service × percentage × last salary	
Self: 30 years × 2% × R72 000	43 200
Spouse _____ × _____ × _____	0
Other income (such as rent)	0
3 Income: surplus/shortfall	10 800
4 Conversion of income shortfall to capital	
Information required:	
Inflation rate 14%	
Interest rate on investment 15%	
Period until retirement: 10 years	
Shortfall × factor = Capital required to produce income R10 800 × 12.7756	137 976
5 Subtract present value of future capital amounts	
(a) Endowment policy R150 000 × 0.269744	-40 461
(b) Annuity R ×	
(c) ......R ×	
(d) Unit trusts	-30 000
Capital surplus/shortfall	-67 515
6 Monthly investment needed to eliminate shortfall after retirement	
Shortfall ÷ years to retirement ÷12 months	
R67 515 ÷10 years ÷12 months	562
MINUS: Any existing contributions	-250
Additional monthly investment to eliminate shortfall	312

(Source: Adapted from Hamp-Adams & Middleton 1992:190)

The shortfall that occurred in step two is financed in step three. Now we need to determine how to eliminate the shortfall (through investments). Here we are discussing investment planning. Investment objectives are, therefore, the same as the objectives set in step one.

In order to achieve investment objectives, various investment avenues are compared on the basis of investment criteria. Then we have to choose from available investment avenues. You will have to decide whether your budget can accommodate these investments. If not, you will have to set new objectives or discard certain investments.

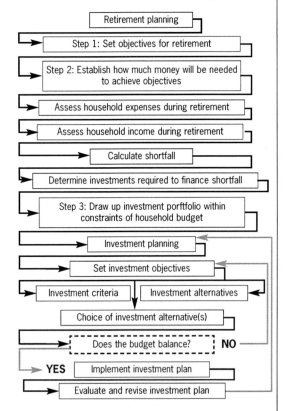

FIGURE 14.8 **Steps to be taken in retirement planning**

> Retirement planning, like personal financial planning, is an ongoing planning process. Although it only stops when you die, you should not plan yourself to death.

> Financial discipline is the key word.

Various investment avenues for retirement purposes are discussed in Section 14.5. These avenues are evaluated and compared on the basis of the following investment criteria:

- income;
- capital growth;
- safety of the investment;
- flexibility;
- liquidity;
- taxability;
- ease of management;
- risk;
- return;
- investment amount;
- investment term;
- investor's tax position/status;
- transaction costs;
- timing;
- diversity of investor's portfolio;
- control;
- knowledge or management requirements;
- protection against inflation; and
- investor's objectives.

14.5 METHODS OF PROVIDING FOR RETIREMENT

There are many methods of providing for retirement. Any combination of methods may be used to enable you to retire with financial independence. The important thing is that you should invest with a view to capital growth in the long term. In this way you are using the financial principle of compounding. This means you are earning interest on interest and on capital growth.

Unfortunately, investments must also constantly be used to make provision for household financial risks and taxes that will have to be paid after your death, for example estate duty, income tax and capital gains tax (CGT).

Investments made for retirement must be protected. They must last until your death and that of your spouse, and hopefully leave something for your heirs. These investments should not simply be spent on any and every desire. Leave your retirement investments alone!

You must, therefore, invest for capital growth, protect and save your investments and continue making investments for your retirement. Of course,

it is difficult to compare different people, because their financial status will determine whether they can provide for retirement, which investments they will choose and why. Unemployed persons, who are thinking and planning from a survival point of view, will not be able to invest funds for retirement. Their daily survival will be their only priority. If they do get a job at a later stage, for example, having a savings account may be the closest they will ever be to providing for retirement.

What one person may regard as an income method, with a view to providing for retirement, another may regard as a 'capital growth method', particularly in South Africa's neglected communities and rural areas. Financially speaking, however, one should distinguish between income and capital growth methods.

The following are ways of supplementing income over and above your employer's retirement fund, before, during and after retirement:

- retirement annuities;
- a money market fund;
- linked products;
- umbrella products;
- a lump sum endowment policy;
- a lump sum annuity (voluntary annuity);
- second-hand policies;
- rental income from immovable property;
- shares;
- fixed-interest-bearing securities (gilt-edged stocks, bonds and preference shares);
- participation bonds;
- unlisted companies;
- hard assets;
- a savings account;
- fixed deposits;
- 32 days notification deposits;
- income trusts (unit trusts);
- property unit trusts; and
- property loan stock.

The following are ways of achieving capital growth over and above your employer's retirement fund, before, during and after retirement:

- retirement annuities;
- unit trusts;
- linked products;
- umbrella products;
- immovable property;
- shares;
- investment trusts;
- unlisted companies; and
- hard assets.

14.5.1 A defined benefit pension fund

The Pension Fund Act 24 of 1956 regulates pension funds in South Africa. The goals of the Act are as follows:

- the provision of annuities for employees and previous employees at retirement;
- the provision of annuities for the dependants of these employees; and
- other benefits to the above-mentioned persons.

Types of pension plan

There are two broad categories of pension plan, namely:

- insured plans; and
- self-administered funds.

> Every employee should contribute to a pension or a provident fund. A self-employed person would have to invest in insurance products, shares and/or unit trusts.

Insured plans

According to an insured plan, a pension fund and an insurer reach an agreement whereby the insurer pays out all the benefits in the case of retirement, disability or death. These benefits are covered by an insurance contract (policy). The insurer undertakes the entire administration of this type of pension plan (fund).

Self-administered funds

The employer administers this type of fund. In the case of a self-administered fund, investments are made over the entire range of investment products, not only insurance (or insurance from the same company, as in the case of an insured plan).

For our purposes, it is important to distinguish between a *defined contribution pension fund*, which will be discussed in Section 14.5.2, and a *defined benefit pension fund*, the characteristics of which are discussed now:

- In order to be effective, the fund must have a large number of members.
- It is ideal for large organisations and businesses.
- The size of the fund is determined by the age of the employees, their salaries and years of membership.
- It is ideal for the remaining members where staff turnover is high.
- Monthly contributions by employees are tax deductible (the larger of R1 750 or 7.5% of remuneration from retirement funding services).
- Years of service may be bought.

- Where additional years of service have been bought, the outstanding amounts, up to R1 800 per year per person, can be deducted from income tax.
- It is wise to make additional contributions.
- There is no flexible retirement and estate planning.
- A married person will do better because there will be dependants who will need a monthly pension after the death of the member.
- The younger the spouse of a person who is a member, the more beneficial it will be.
- In the case where annual salary increases are high, the defined benefit fund will be better, because benefits are calculated on the basis of final salary. (There are problems with benefits for government and semi-government departments because of the absence of any real salary increases – except when inflation is lower than the rate of the increase over many years.)
- The primary objective of a pension fund is to provide a pension at retirement.
- Trustees are free to increase retirement benefits after retirement, based on the performance of the insurers.
- In the event of the death of a member after retirement, a pension is paid to the spouse and/or children. Pension increases are also paid out to the spouse and/or children.
- If you already receive a pension, it will be very difficult to qualify for a further state pension.
- Contributions to the fund are paid from pre-tax money and, therefore, your taxable income will be lower.
- Pension is taxed at the PAYE/SITE rate. Therefore, tax is deducted at your marginal rate.
- Except for the tax-free part of the lump sum (the larger of R120 000 and R4 500 × number of years of membership) the rest of the lump sum will be taxed at you average rate
- In the event of death, the tax-free part of the lump sum will be the larger of R60 000 or twice your annual salary (maximum R120 000). After this, tax is calculated at your average rate.
- Should you leave the fund before retirement the first R1 800 of your benefits will be tax-free. The balance will be taxed at your average rate.

Ceding your pension

It is not possible for a member of a pension fund to cede or pledge any pension fund benefits. If a member tries to do so, the fund in question may withhold or terminate the benefits. It is, however, possible for a creditor to claim these benefits while the member is still contributing to the fund.

Insolvency

If a member has already received the lump sum part of the pension benefits, this amount will form part of the member's insolvent estate. The pension payable (monthly) to the member or the member's dependants cannot form part of an insolvent estate.

It is important to remember that an employer may deduct the following from a member's benefits:

- amounts payable to the employer with regard to a home loan (for example, the deposit in the case of a 100% housing subsidy scheme);
- warranties with regard to a home loan in favour of other persons (employees, family, friends);
- any amount payable to an employer as a result of fraud and/or theft; and
- arrear contributions to a medical fund.

Estate duty

Estate duty is payable on the lump sum as it forms part of the members estate. No pension (or annuities) will ever from part of a person's estate for purposes of estate duty, unless it ceases to exist after the person's death. Although estate duty is saved, income tax is payable on the pension.

Group life benefits

Pension funds normally offer life cover to members by means of group life schemes. In the case of a member's death, the group life benefits are regarded as pension benefits. Life cover is provided to members without any proof of health. At retirement age or at withdrawal/resignation, a member may take out a life policy (at the standard rates applicable elsewhere) for the same cover as that provided by his or her group life scheme, provided this is done within one month of retirement/withdrawal/resignation.

Disability cover is also included in the group life scheme, while dreaded disease cover is excluded. Estate duty is payable on group life benefits as they are classified as normal insurance benefits.

Functioning

- Members' contributions form a fixed percentage of remuneration for the retirement funding service.
- The employer's contribution varies according to actuarial advice. The employer's contribution covers costs as well as death and disability benefits. The employer is responsible for members' benefits. The employer contributes more for older members than for younger ones.
- Benefits are promised and defined according to a formula based on the member's years of service and average final salary.

- Monthly pension equals 2.22% of the average final salary × years of service ÷ 12.
- Years of membership plus salary at retirement, therefore, determine retirement benefits.
- Investment performance does not have such a significant effect on retirement benefits. The employer must pay in the difference to make provision for the promised retirement benefits.
- The investment risk, therefore, rests with the employer.
- Members do not get back their contributions to the fund.
- At retirement, the member receives one third of the retirement benefit as a lump sum.
- The relation between the lump sum (one-third) and the pension (two-thirds) is fixed.
- The cost of administration is higher because of more actuarial calculations (salary adjustments, years of service, highest salary per period, etc.).

Advantages: Pension fund members

- Monthly contributions are tax deductible.
- The pension is protected against the insolvency of the member (while still contributing, as well as the pension part after retirement).
- Life and disability cover are included at low cost.
- The lump sum is tax-free up to an amount of R120 000 or R4 500 × years of membership (whichever is the greater).
- It is an important part of retirement provision.
- The investment risk is not yours, because your employer still has to pay you your pension, irrespective of the investment return.
- Even if you take early retirement because of ill health, you will receive a pension calculated on what you should have received at retirement age.

Disadvantages: Pension fund members

- Employees lose the employer's contributions as well as growth when they resign.
- Two-thirds of retirement benefits must be taken in the form of an inflexible pension (irrespective of good fund performance).
- Employees are not protected against their own indiscretions, because they can take their pension lump sum and squander it before retirement age (in the case of resignation).
- Monthly pensions do not keep up with inflation.

Similarities between defined benefit pension funds, defined contribution pension funds and defined contribution provident funds

- Membership requires an employer-employee relationship.
- Benefits cannot be ceded.

- With insolvency, benefits are dealt with in the same way.
- They all form an important part of provision for retirement.
- Estate duty is payable on the lump sum after the death of the member.
- In the case of a divorce, benefits are handled in the same way.
- Pension benefits (monthly) do not form part of an estate for the purposes of estate duty.
- Life and disability benefits are included in the membership at a low cost.
- Members are not protected against themselves, and may use the lump sum as soon as they have received it.
- Estate duty is paid on group benefits, because they form part of the member's estate.
- Life cover is provided by means of group benefits.
- It is very expensive to borrow from the fund, because of the cost of interest, loss of capital growth and the taxability of repayments made to the fund.

14.5.2 A defined contribution pension fund

A defined contribution pension fund clearly emphasises contribution. This is the major difference between it and a defined benefit pension fund. The difference lies in the fixed contributions that you and your employer make to the fund every month. The fixed amounts are predetermined on the grounds of a percentage of your salary.

The second great difference is the fact that the employer does not guarantee the amount of your retirement pension. Even though you will receive it some day:

- The amount you will receive depends on the contributions made to the fund, plus growth.
- Up to one-third of the retirement amount may be taken as a lump sum.
- More than two-thirds may be used to buy a pension (compulsory annuity).

EXAMPLE

	Lump sum	Pension
Defined benefit pension	$\frac{1}{3}$	$\frac{2}{3}$
Defined contribution pension	$0 - \frac{1}{3}$	$\frac{2}{3} - 100\%$

Advantages
- If the fund does well, you get the benefits.
- It is possible to receive more than in the case of a fixed benefit pension fund.

- There is a greater choice of funds in which to invest, because you have a say and may choose your portion yourself (this is riskier in a market-linked fund and less risky in a smoothed bonus fund – try to switch from the latter to the former shortly before retirement).
- Contributions are tax-deductible.

Disadvantages
- If the fund does badly, you will lose. You may even receive far less on retirement than the amount you expected, depending on the:
  - timing of your retirement (the stock market may be very low); and
  - the performance of the investment.
- Should you be forced to retire early because of poor health, you do not receive a pension on the basis of what you would have received at retirement age (as with a defined benefit pension fund) but only what has accumulated in your fund (on the basis of your contributions).

14.5.3 A defined contribution provident fund

An employer-employee relationship is a prerequisite for provident fund membership. A self-employed person cannot invest in a provident fund, but should make investments in insurance products, shares and/or unit trusts (as with a pension fund).

Investors nowadays want to be in control of their retirement money as far as possible. This is why provident funds have become so popular as investment instruments for retirement.

The Pension Fund Act regulates provident funds. The purpose of the Act is to provide lump sum and other benefits to employees and their dependants at retirement.

Types of provident fund
Like pension funds, provident funds fall in the classes of:
- insured plans; and
- self-administered funds.

Comparison with a defined benefit pension fund
Let us look at Table 14.2 and the differences between a defined benefit pension fund and a defined contribution provident fund.

TABLE 14.2 Defined benefit pension fund versus defined contribution provident fund

Defined benefit pension fund	Defined contribution provident fund
1. Retirement benefits based on final salary and membership years	1. Retirement benefits based on total contributions made by member plus growth
2. Employer bears the risk	2. Employee bears the risk
3. Favours older fund members	3. Favours younger fund members
4. Members do not get back what they invested in the fund	4. Members get back what they invested
5. Retiree receives one-third as lump sum	5. Retiree receives 100% of benefits as lump sum (or less if member prefers)
6. Relation (ratio) between lump sum and pension is fixed (one-third: two-thirds)	6. Member receives lump sum only
7. Higher administration costs because of more actuarial calculations	7. Lower administration costs (no salary changes, years of service, highest salary per period)
8. To be efficient the fund requires a large number of members	8. The fund requires a relatively small membership
9. Ideal for large organisations	9. Small and new organisations or businesses can use this fund
10. The size/strength of the fund is determined by the age of the employees and their salaries	10. The size of the fund is determined by monthly contributions
11. Ideal for remaining members where the staff turnover is high	11. Staff turnover does not influence the benefits of remaining members

Comparison with a defined contribution pension fund

The greatest differences between a defined contribution pension fund and a defined contribution provident fund appear in Table 14.3.

TABLE 14.3 Defined contribution pension fund versus defined contribution provident fund

Defined contribution pension fund	Defined contribution provident fund
1. Limited tax deductibility of monthly contributions	1. Contributions not tax-deductible
2. At retirement you should take at least $\frac{2}{3}$ of your benefits in the form of a pension	2. At retirement you can take 100% of your benefits in the form of a lump sum – you do not have to take any part thereof in the form of a pension

Characteristics and functioning of a defined contribution provident fund

- Monthly contributions to the fund are fixed, are determined as soon as you start work and are calculated as a percentage of your salary.
- Retirement benefits are based on the total contribution a member has made to the fund, plus growth.
- Employees bear the risk.
- Younger members of the fund benefit more.
- Members get back their contributions to the fund.

- At retirement, a member takes 100% of the total retirement benefit as a lump sum.
- There are low administration costs because of fewer actuarial calculations.
- The fund requires only a limited number of members.
- Small or new organisations and businesses may use the fund.
- The size of the fund is determined by the monthly contributions made by members.
- Staff turnover does not have an effect on the benefits of the remaining members.

- Monthly contributions by employees are not tax-deductible.
- Employers' contributions are tax-deductible.
- Lump sums of up to R120 000 or R4 500 × number of years of service (the larger of the two amounts) are tax-free.
- It is wise to make additional contributions.
- Because the member has control over benefits, very flexible retirement and estate planning is possible.
- It is not possible to buy years of service.
- A single person will do better, because there will be no dependants who need a monthly pension after the death of the member.
- A spouse's age is only relevant where a pension is chosen instead of a lump sum and the member dies soon after retirement.
- With relatively low real salary increases (or no increase at all) a defined contribution fund is effective, because benefits are not calculated on the final salary.
- The primary objective of a provident fund is to provide a lump sum at retirement.
- After the member has received the lump sum, the member has nothing to do with the fund.
- No member will receive death benefits if he or she dies after retirement, because the person is no longer a member of the fund. Death benefits will depend on arrangements the member has made with the insurer.
- Where benefits have been taken in the form of a lump sum, it is still possible to qualify for a state pension.
- Contributions to the fund are paid on a salary sacrifice basis or a non-contributory basis (the latter is more advantageous to members).
- Should you buy a pension in the form of a voluntary annuity with your lump sum, the pension will be only partly taxable.
- Should you leave the fund before retirement the first R1 800 of your contributions will be tax-free. The balance will be taxed at your average rate.

Advantages of provident funds
- A member can take all relevant benefits in the form of a single lump sum.
- Members are in control of the entire amount of their benefits (this can also be a disadvantage).
- Flexible retirement and estate planning is possible.
- Members can make additional contributions in order to increase their retirement provision.
- Investment performance has a direct effect on retirement benefits. If benefits are taken during an economic boom, or when the stock exchange is strong (a bull market), the member may receive high retirement benefits.

Disadvantages of provident funds
- Of all three funds, the risk is the highest in this case.
- Lump sum benefits may be squandered or invested in the 'wrong' investments.
- The rules of the fund do not allow members to buy back years of service.
- Contributions made by members are not tax-deductible.
- Lump sums received are taxable in total in any event (death, retirement, withdrawal, resignation).
- If the member retires during an economic downswing (a bear market), the member may receive low retirement benefits.
- The investment risk rests with the employee or member.
- It is possible to get far less after retirement than in the case of a defined benefit/contribution pension fund.
- As a member, you will always wonder how the fund is doing, and whether you will have enough money for your retirement.

14.5.4 Retirement annuities

Invest in a retirement annuity and enjoy the tax benefits allowed by law. An annuity is a series of payments or investments that are made in equal instalments.

A retirement annuity is a tax-friendly way of making provision for retirement. For each R100 invested in a retirement annuity, R40 (40%) is received back from the Receiver of Revenue. The investor, therefore, only pays R60 for each investment of R100 (if his or her marginal tax rate is 40%).

If you have an approved four-year post-matriculation qualification you may take out a PPS annuity. (PPS stands for the Professional Provident Society of South Africa.) The return on this annuity is higher than that of other annuities because of the lower risk of the members. A PPS annuity is an ordinary retirement annuity and functions in much the same way as other annuities. The only difference is that extra tax-free dividends are paid out for each share you own.

The retirement annuity's option must be exercised when you are between 55 and 70 years old:
- The investor must take one-third of his or her total investment as a lump sum and reinvest it.
- The remaining two-thirds must be used to buy a compulsory annuity.

The compulsory annuity may be a traditional annuity or a modern, flexible annuity. A traditional annuity may be taken out on the life of a single person or on the lives of both spouses. At the death of a single person, all further benefits will lapse. In the event of death in the case of a joint annuity, the surviving spouse will receive an income until he or she dies. Where both people are still alive (after exercising the option), there are different income combinations to choose from. For example, older people (as well as those who smoke) will receive a higher income because of their shorter life expectancy, while women will receive a lower income because of their longer life expectancy.

Two-thirds of the compulsory annuity may be invested in a living/flexible annuity. The investor is allowed to choose his or her own level of income, based on his or her current needs, for example between 5% and 20% of the two-thirds capital amount. This option is preferable when there are heirs. After the death of the surviving spouse (in a joint annuity) the heirs may receive the remaining funds over a period of five years, or continue with the annuity in the same way as the initial investor(s).

Investing the lump sum (one-third)

The lump sum should be used, in the first place, to pay off a current bond (on a dwelling, not income-producing property) or other debt if interest rates are high. A voluntary annuity (linked to an endowment policy or unit trusts) may be purchased if a secure income is required. Income trusts can also provide income for retirement, and unit trusts can provide a security fund for emergencies if no 'access' type bond exists. For the purposes of capital growth, an endowment policy, unit trusts or a share portfolio may be chosen, based on the investor's risk profile.

Annuities and emigration

The living annuity offers an opportunity to increase the amount of money that can be transferred out of the country. Interest to the amount of 20% of the investment (two-thirds compulsory annuity) can be transferred out, if the initial investment is part of a well-planned retirement scheme.

Uses of retirement annuities for different categories of investor

The main purpose of retirement annuities is additional provision for retirement. Quite a few other uses exist, however, for different categories of investor, namely:

- young investors;
- the middle-aged;
- businesspeople;
- pension and provident fund members;
- retirees; and
- recipients of lump sums.

Young investors

An investment in a retirement annuity would help young investors to entrench financial discipline. Due to the tax-deductibility of retirement annuity contributions, a considerable tax saving would be realised and a large amount would be invested over a lifetime for retirement purposes.

The middle-aged

The middle-aged are normally at the fullest extent of their potential income level and investment capacity. Tax advantages from retirement annuity contributions are relatively high for such people.

Businesspeople

The self-employed are in need of retirement annuity contributions for the purposes of retirement, mainly because they are not pension of provident fund members.

Pension and provident fund members

Members of these funds could use retirement annuity contributions for tax benefits and for additional retirement provision.

Retirees

Retirement annuity contributions should be extended until the age of 69 years and 11 months by retirees, if it is financially possible.

Recipients of lump sums

A lump sum could be invested in an annuity for tax purposes. The investment in this case is called a voluntary annuity.

Retirement annuities and insolvency

Retirement annuities do not form part of a person's estate and are, therefore, protected against the claims of creditors. If an investor has already received a lump sum, it forms part of the estate and would also form part of an insolvent estate.

Retirement annuities and estate duty

Income (annuities) received from a retirement annuity (after the annuitant's death) does not form part of the investor's estate and is, therefore, exempt from estate duty.

Beneficiaries

A contributor to a retirement annuity may appoint a beneficiary (other than a spouse and/or children) to whom the proceeds or the annuity must be paid. On the date of death, the trustees of the fund transfer the benefits to the surviving spouse and children (dependants). If there are no dependants, the trustees are obliged to pay the benefits to the appointed beneficiary. If there are neither dependants nor appointed beneficiaries, the benefits are paid into the deceased estate.

Employers and retirement annuities

Only the individual member may take out a retirement annuity. An employer may not hold or take out a retirement annuity on behalf of an employee. The following applies if an employer increases the employee's salary on condition that such an annuity be bought:

- the increase forms part of the employee's normal income; and
- the employee is entitled to claim tax deductions for contributing to the annuity.

Retirement annuities and divorce settlements

The applicable matrimonial regime of the spouses determines whether retirement annuities (that is, contributions plus interest) form part of a divorce settlement or not. They are included (form part of a spouse's assets – existing not prospective) in divorce settlements where spouses are married:

- in community of property; and
- out of community of property with inclusion of the accrual system.

Retirement annuities would be excluded from divorce settlements where spouses are married out of community of property with exclusion of the accrual system.

Retirement annuities and life coverage

Life cover may be added to a retirement annuity, in which case the annuity contributions remain tax deductible. A major disadvantage is the fact that the life cover influences the maximum tax-free amount of R120 000.

Compulsory versus voluntary annuities

When the purchase of an annuity is required by law (like the two-thirds you receive from a retirement annuity), it is called a compulsory annuity. The purchase of an annuity need not always come from the proceeds (two-thirds) of a retirement fund. An investor may inherit R50 000 and decide to invest in an annuity. Such an annuity is called a voluntary annuity.

An important difference between a compulsory and a voluntary annuity is in the tax assessment. The income from a compulsory annuity (two-thirds of the annuity) is taxed in full. In the case of a voluntary annuity, the income is divided into income and capital. Tax is payable on the income portion and not on the capital.

14.5.5 Preservation funds

A preservation fund is a type of retirement fund in which retirement benefits from a pension or provident fund are kept. Insurance companies have preservation funds.

With a lump sum annuity, you may not touch the benefits in the fund until you reach the age of 55. This is not the case with a preservation fund. Access to the benefits is, therefore, an important criterion that should be considered before you make a decision.

With a preservation fund, money may be withdrawn only once before retirement. It will, of course, be possible to withdraw the total amount from the fund with this single withdrawal. You must be careful and discipline yourself not to spend this money that you saved for retirement. The access facility may be a disadvantage for undisciplined people.

For the purposes of preservation funds, the retirement age is described as the age at which you leave the services of an employer, and which may not be before the age of 55 or after 70. Similarly, an unemployed person who deposits money in the fund may not retire from the fund before 55 or after 70.

The transfer of a retirement package from a pension fund or a provident fund to a preservation fund is tax-free. If money is transferred from a pension fund to a preservation provident fund (instead of a preservation pension fund), there are tax implications, however.

An advantage of a preservation fund is that the employee's years of membership of the employer's fund can be transferred to the preservation fund. The years of membership are still taken into account when the tax-free lump sum is calculated.

The flexibility (control) and transferability of the investment are important criteria. When you have little or no financial discipline, your retirement package should rather be transferred to a lump sum annuity for self-protection, in other words to protect your retirement benefits (even though you will have to pay commission on your investment).

14.5.6 Deferred compensation schemes

These schemes or plans are not available to everybody. Companies offer such a plan to benefit senior or selected staff. The purpose is to reduce their tax liability on an annual basis and, at the same time, to purchase an endowment policy for them (Goldman 1983:72).

TABLE 14.4 Provident fund versus deferred compensation plan
(Source: Goldman 1983:70,71)

Provident fund	Deferred compensation plan
1. Tax-free lump sum forms part of the maximum tax-free amount	1. A specified tax-free portion of the lump sum does not form part of the maximum tax-free amount; the balance of the lump sum is taxed at an advantageous tax rate and can be spread over three years
2. Both employee and employer contribute towards the fund	2. Only the employee contributes towards the fund by sacrificing a portion of his or her salary
3. Benefits at death are limited to contributions and interest	3. Life cover is enforced by law, over and above the return on contributions

The policy belongs to the employer. An agreement is entered into between the employer and employee, in which the policy is ceded to the employee under certain conditions. The employee receives a lump sum when he or she resigns or retires, of which a certain portion is tax-free. The advantage is that this tax-free portion does not form part of the maximum tax-free benefits stipulated by law for purposes of retirement.

The policy has life cover as well as maturity value. Benefits in terms of this scheme cannot be utilised before the age of 50 years in the case of a woman or 55 years in the case of a man. The lump sum forms part of your estate after your death.

Table 14.4 provides a comparison between a provident fund and a deferred compensation plan.

Advantages of a deferred compensation scheme

- *Income tax advantages.* The employee enjoys tax advantages after retirement, in the sense that the return on benefits is taxed separately from all other returns or policies.
- *Additional provision.* Because of the tax benefits, the employee has more money for retirement. He or she can, therefore, make better provision for retirement.
- *Improved working conditions.* Employees who conclude such a contract with their employers are more loyal and perform better. They are compensated for this extra performance, which further increases their income after retirement.
- *Protection for dependants.* Should the employee die before his or her retirement, the scheme can be used to benefit his or her dependants.
- *Flexible contributions.* The contributions the employee makes towards the scheme can be increased or reduced to suit his or her pocket or to beat inflation.

Perks tax

Deferred compensation is not subject to perks taxation (although it is actually a perk), because it provides retirement benefits to employees. In order to qualify for deferred compensation tax benefits at retirement, there has to be an employer-employee relationship. This requirement renders people in the following categories ineligible for such tax benefits:

- partners;
- sole owners of businesses;
- shareholders; and
- inactive members of a close corporation.

The agreement between employer and employee

An employer takes out a policy on the life of an employee. At the same time an agreement is concluded between the employer and the employee that makes provision for the following:

- payment of the proceeds of the policy at a certain age or at the employee's death, resignation, termination of employment or disability;
- cession of the policy to the employee;
- the rights of the employee in case the employer is declared insolvent; and
- payment of annuities instead of a lump sum (the employee should have a choice).

Death: Lump sums and annuities

In the case of the employee's death, the lump sum accrues to his or her estate and, unless it accrues directly to dependants or beneficiaries, the employer becomes liable for income tax payments on the lump sum.

Where the employer pays the premiums on the policy in the form of purchased annuities (not a voluntary annuity), the employer will have to pay double taxation. In order to prevent this, it is better to pay out the policy proceeds in the form of payments to the employee.

Estate duty
The policy proceeds accrue to the employee's estate in the case of his or her death. Estate duty is, therefore, payable unless the policy proceeds accrue directly to a dependant according to the agreement.

Cession of the policy
It is possible for an employer to cede a policy to an employee before the actual date of maturity (according to the agreement). The cession takes place at the discounted value of future proceeds and offers the employee a lower taxable amount (the amount that will be at issue when the income tax payment falls due at a future date). The discounted value forms part of the employee's taxable income.

It is also possible for the employer to pay a gratuity to the employee and allow the employee to use the gratuity to buy the policy from the employer. As in the case of the discounted value, the gratuity forms part of the employee's taxable income.

Tax implications for employees
The proceeds of the policy are exempt from income tax up to and including an amount or R30 000. Both spouses may deduct this amount if both receive deferred compensation. This amount is allowed apart from any other minimum or maximum amount (as prescribed by the Income Tax Act) received from a pension fund, a provident fund and/or a retirement annuity.

Insolvency
The insolvency of the employee will have no influence on the validity or value of the policy. Policy proceeds will still be payable to the employee (even by the curator of the insolvent estate). The policy is the property of the employer. However, a problem exists in the case of the employer being declared insolvent. Employees have no protection and will lose their expected proceeds in this event, unless alternative arrangements have been made.

14.5.7 Unit trusts

Unit trusts offer high capital growth (a high tax-free return) and may be realised quickly because they are very liquid. These unit trusts may be used as a deposit for a home if you do not already own one.

Unit trusts allow the relatively small investor to invest indirectly on the Johannesburg Securities Exchange. Money is invested in the shares of different companies. You may invest in unit trusts on a monthly basis.

Unit trusts can be divided into three general categories:
- general trusts;
- specialist trusts; and
- income trusts.

General trusts and specialist trusts are aimed at capital growth, while income trusts provide a regular income for investors such as retirees. Young people should invest in the first two types, never in income funds. The risk factor varies considerably among unit trusts. Young people should invest in risky unit trusts with a view to long-term capital growth, for example in the unit trusts of new, developing companies. It is also possible to invest in unit trusts with international interests, in other words, a type of international trust.

Money market funds (one of the latest types of unit trust) provide an income for investors, while their capital is protected. At present, money market funds have the lowest risk of all unit trusts.

Buying unit trusts requires a small initial deposit, for example R200 for certain trusts. Subsequently, even smaller amounts may be invested every month. Various methods may be used to buy unit trusts:
- completing application forms supplied by a broker or an institution;
- filling in newspaper and magazine advertisements;
- e-mail;
- websites on the Internet; and
- dialling the toll-free numbers of customer care services.

Unit trusts offer high capital growth, particularly when the investment is kept for more than three years (as long as 30 to 50 years, for effective capital growth).

They also protect the investor against inflation. Unit trusts are very liquid. The total investment may be called up within ten days, if the investor needs the money urgently.

For information about unit trusts and their returns or results over different periods consult books, newspapers, brokers, banks, insurance companies and the Internet. Here are a few useful Internet addresses:
- Bureau for Financial Analysis (UP) – www.bfa-net.com
- Brantom – www.brantom.co.za
- Stones – www.infostones.co.za
- Easyinfo – www.investment.co.za
- TMA – www.tma.co.za
- Guardbank – www.guardbank.com
- Norwich – www.norwich.co.za
- Plexus – www.plexus.co.za
- Old Mutual – www.oldmutual.com

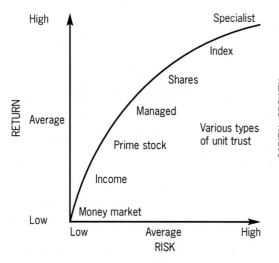

FIGURE 14.9 **Unit trusts: Risk versus return**

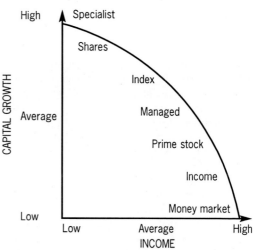

FIGURE 14.10 **Unit trusts: Capital growth versus income**

- Business Day – www.bday.co.za
- Financial Mail – www.atd.co.za/fm
- Finance Week – africa.com/mags/finweek
- Business Times – www.btimes.co.za

It is also possible to link an investment in unit trusts with a life policy, an endowment policy or a retirement annuity. Such a product or investment is called a unit trust-linked investment.

Your view of risk or risk profile (whether you are willing to take risks or anxious to avoid risks) will largely determine which unit trusts you will invest in.

Figures 14.9 and 14.10 illustrate some characteristics of unit trusts from the point of view of risk, return, capital growth, income, short-term needs, medium-term needs, long-term needs, knowledge required, age and taxability.

Short term versus long term
Different types of unit trust are suited to different periods of investment:
- Short term: Money market
  Income
- Medium term: Prime stock
  Specialist
- Long term: Managed
  Shares

Knowledge required
If you have relatively little knowledge of unit trusts, you should either not be involved at all in managing your unit trust portfolio, or your involvement should be very limited. If you have sufficient knowledge of unit trusts you can become actively involved in their management.

Options for unit trust investments at specific ages
- 20–40 years: Invest in high-risk unit trusts such as specialist trusts.
- 40–60 years: Invest in unit trusts with an average risk, for example managed trusts and index trusts.
- 60 years and older: Invest in low-risk unit trusts such as income trusts.

Taxability
Tax is paid on the income received from income trusts and money market funds. (For more information about unit trusts consult Oldert *et al.* 1998.)

Knowing your risk profile
Investors ought to know the different investment criteria before they invest in any product, including unit trusts, as investment instruments. Knowing your own tolerance for risk (risk averse/avoider, risk indifferent, risk-taker) is certainly very important to all investors. An investor's risk profile will determine the 'right' fund for the investor's situation.
- Risk averse investors should invest in low-risk unit trusts (or no unit trusts at all).
- Risk indifferent (neutral) investors should invest in medium-risk unit trusts.
- Risk-takers (seekers) should invest in high-risk unit trusts (or shares).

How to choose a unit trust
Apart from the investor's financial situation and risk profile, various other important factors require consideration in order to choose a unit trust or make up a selection of unit trusts. It is important (especially for the uninformed investor) to consult a

financial adviser or manager regarding investment in unit trusts. Investing in several unit trust funds will enable the investor to gain higher returns from the different strategies adopted by the various fund managers, in order to take advantage of cyclical movements in share prices.

Compounding (interest on interest added to the amount invested, i.e. the capital) will turn even a small difference in return between funds into a major difference over time (10 or 15 years). Choosing the best fund is, therefore, very important.

Potential investors normally evaluate the past performance of a fund to predict its future potential. Past performance cannot be bought, but unfortunately that is exactly what is being sold. According to Lambrechts (1996:60), historical performance is only useful to a limited extent, but investors have little else to use as a criterion. Information on the following relating to the fund manager's competence is also crucial to the potential investor:
- decision-making strategies;
- whether research has been done;
- whether decision-making is a disciplined process;
- the experience of the fund manager; and
- the type of companies and sectors invested in.

The objectives of the investor will always be of paramount importance. It may be advantageous to combine an investment in a unit trust with an insurance product.

An investment technique

De Lange (1996:50) discusses an investment technique according to which investors should divide unit trusts into four categories, in view of the different reactions of shares in these categories to market conditions.

The four categories are:
- cash and capital market funds;
- value funds;
- growth funds; and
- special opportunity funds.

Cash and capital market funds are very sensitive to changes in interest rate. These funds invest in money market instruments and offer a low risk to investors. Value funds concentrate on the prime shares of the Johannesburg Securities Exchange. Growth funds invest in smaller prime shares. Special opportunity funds offer high-risk investments in unit trusts.

Unit trust switches

Investors often want to switch between unit trusts. Unless the initial investment was based on a completely wrong decision, this is hardly ever to the advantage of the investor, especially over the long term. Switching may sound easy to the investor, but it is expensive and requires a very professional approach.

Guidelines on switching between unit trusts:
- Timing is of the utmost importance.
- Losses may be incurred.
- Switching entails the selling of units from one fund and then buying units from another.
- The new cost (in the case of in-house switching) will vary from between 0% and 1%.
- The real cost is determined by looking at the market value of the unit trusts before and after the switch.

Lambrechts (1996:57) says the following about market timing when switching between unit trusts:
- Keep your money in equity unit trusts when the stock market is surging.
- Switch to high-income funds (money market funds) when the stock market peaks.
- Past performance is used to predict future performance.
- Serious investors choose a buy-and-hold strategy (buy low and sell high).
- The volatility of the unit trust industry is the cause for market-timing services.
- Market timing combines the fundamental and the technical approaches.
- Academic studies (research) contradict the efficiency of the market-timing approach.
- It is almost impossible to predict the turning points in share prices over the medium and long term.
- Rand-cost averaging (diversification over time) is one way of solving the timing problem.
- In the case of rand-cost averaging (e.g. investing R100 a month in unit trusts) the average cost of the units will always be lower than the average market price.
- Investors are advised to take a long-term view (not buying and selling, i.e. not switching) for the entire economic cycle.

Money market funds

South Africa is somewhat behind several other countries when it comes to money market funds as investment instruments. The first money market funds were established in the USA in 1971 and ten years later in France, to counteract restrictive financial legislation. In South Africa, the small investor could never invest in the money market directly, because of the minimum amount (R100 000) that had to be invested. Money market funds now offer investors an opportunity to earn a high return on joint investments according to the *stokvel* principle.

What is a money market fund?

A money market fund is a unit trust that serves as a short-term investment instrument. The objective is to provide a current income to investors. A money market fund invests the joint investment of a large number of investors in the money market. The capital is safe (low risk), because it is invested in government and other public securities, treasury bills, debentures, bank deposits and other permissible money market instruments with a term of no longer than 12 months.

For what situations is it suitable?

- When you have a minimum of R2 000 to invest (the amount differs from institution to institution).
- If you want a monthly income from your investment.
- If you are looking for a risk-free investment.
- If you want to invest a rather large amount for a short period.
- If you want to create an emergency fund in which the money will be available within a day.
- When you have to invest money from an estate temporarily.
- When churches or schools need a continuous income.
- If you require total liquidity.
- When trust money can earn a relatively high interest.

What is the minimum amount that may be invested?

Institutions may vary considerably. The minimum initial investment is R2 000. After that, the minimum additional investment is R2 000, or R200 per month if money is invested by debit order.

What are the costs?

- Initial levy: 1.5% on R2 000 – R99 999; 1.0% on R100 000 – R999 999; and 0.6% on R1 000 000 or more.
- Service fee: 0.6% (already included in daily quoted rate).

Money market funds versus other unit trusts

Although certain unit trusts (such as income trusts) offer an income, capital growth is the primary objective of others. Money market funds are aimed at protecting capital and offering a high income at the same time. Unit trusts invest in the shares of listed companies, whereas money market funds invest in money market instruments. The risk involved in money market funds is much lower than in unit trusts. For unit trusts, the term is supposed to be more than three years, while for money market funds it may be from one day to 12 months. The income from both is fully taxable. Interest is paid every six months in unit trusts and every month in money market funds. Both are very liquid.

Money market funds versus fixed deposits

The interest rates of money market funds fluctuate, whereas those of fixed deposits do not. In money market funds, the investment (excluding the minimum balance) may be obtained within a day. The money in fixed deposits may be withdrawn only after a fixed term. Money market funds are, therefore, more liquid. In both cases, the interest or income is fully taxable. The interest rates of money market funds are higher than those of fixed deposits. The risk is lower in money market funds than in fixed deposits.

Benefits of money market funds

- Small investors may invest in them.
- Investments are very liquid.
- They yield a higher return than other short-term investments that offer an income.
- They are more diversified then other, similar investments.
- The competition they generate will lead to better service.
- The investor's capital is very safe.
- They are suitable for people who want to avoid risks.
- They provide a high return in inflationary conditions.
- No commission is payable.

Disadvantages of money market funds

- No fixed returns are guaranteed.
- Potential investors do not have the benefit of a South African track record.
- Fund managers are still 'inexperienced'.

How to choose a money market fund

As there will probably be relatively little difference in the returns of the various money market funds, you will not be able to base your choice on return only. The size of the fund also plays a role. Larger funds should pay higher interest rates, because of lower administration costs. The shorter the investment period of the instruments in which the money market funds invest, the safer the funds.

14.5.8 Unit trust-linked products

Unit trust-linked products are those in which unit trusts are linked to retirement annuities, living annuities, preservation funds, guaranteed income plans and guaranteed capital plans, for example. These products allow the investor to switch from one unit trust to another. You may invest monthly in unit trust-linked products, or invest a lump sum (or part of it) in unit trusts.

At present, unit trusts are the product used by most South African investors for long-term capital growth. If unit trusts are linked to other products, the investor obtains the benefits of both; for example, the capital growth of unit trusts plus the tax benefits of a retirement annuity.

Businesses that sell unit trust-linked products (through a broker) are known as 'product factories'. When retiring or investing, you should distinguish between the following unit trust-linked products:

- retirement annuities (the retirement annuity functions as usual but is linked to a unit trust);
- living annuities;
- preservation funds (the preservation fund is linked to a unit trust and functions as usual);
- guaranteed plans (part of the investment guarantees your income/capital and the rest is used for more risky investments); and
- unit trust exchanges (with unit trust-linked products it is cheaper to switch from one unit trust to another than with ordinary unit trust investments).

Advantages

- These products are particularly suitable for investing a lump sum package.
- They offer the benefits of unit trusts plus the benefits of other products.
- It is cheaper to switch between unit trusts.
- The investor's needs concerning risk and return are better satisfied, particularly in changing market conditions.
- Relatively small amounts may be invested (R1 000 per month or R10 000 as a lump sum).
- An investment may be gradually phased in to lower the risk.
- Information about your investment is easily obtained and all aspects of your investment (such as costs) are transparent.
- Your money is kept safely in a trust.
- Administration during the investment process is very simple for the investor.
- A computer system provides immediate information about your investment.

Disadvantages

- It may be to your disadvantage if you switch from one unit trust to another at the wrong time, for instance when you sell at a low price (in a weak market) and reinvest at a high price (and lose capital).
- If your needs change, you will not be able to cancel the unit trust link free of charge and reinvest the money in another product (which is not linked to unit trusts).
- If you choose the wrong unit trust portfolio, the average return of your linked investment may be considerably lower.
- Even though you will not be charged for switching between unit trusts, there are other compulsory charges that are not always mentioned by the broker.
- You may choose a company whose computer system is not up to standard, with the result that market disasters, such as very high sales volumes, cannot always be dealt with promptly and investors lose money.
- Investors do not always want to hold their offshore investments in the same product as their local investments.
- Linked-product companies charge annual management fees, which will increase your total costs.
- Linked-product companies need not pay back your investment at, or within, a specific time (e.g. on request). An annuity will only pay out when you are 55.

Umbrella products (split investments)

Cameron & Dasnois (2000:97–106) point out the following umbrella products: linked products, wrap funds, fund-of-funds and multi-manager. The main purpose of split investments is to offer you, as the investor, the greatest possible choice and freedom. People with a relatively large lump sum, for example after retirement, should invest in these. In the case of split investments, computer programs are mainly used to switch between the underlying investments.

We will now briefly look at the functioning of each of these types of umbrella product.

Linked products

In this case the investments are mainly in unit trusts. The umbrella products (or split investments) may be, amongst others, retirement annuities, living annuities and preservation funds. The costs of switching from one linked product to another are far less than where unit trusts are managed by various companies. The actual costs of the investment will largely depend on both the umbrella product and the size of your investment (management fees as well). The initial cost is between 2.5% and 6%, and the annual cost is 2%+ per year. However, the total costs are higher than for a normal direct investment in a unit trust, for example.

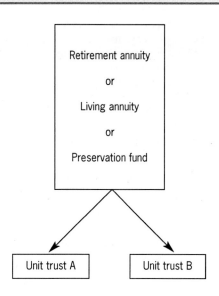

FIGURE 14.11 **Your choice of product**

Wrap funds

Cameron & Dasnois (2000:101) point to the various 'bundled' investments that make up wrap funds. Wrap funds provide large-scale diversification (spreading the investment risks) by investing in various sectors (or industries). In the same way, wrap funds offer many options, for example fund-of-funds and umbrella products offered by linked product companies. Even small investors can invest in these. The investment period varies with the type of product, for example endowment insurance (five years) or a retirement annuity (at least until 55 years of age). The minimum investment amount is R5 000 as a lump sum, or R500 per month.

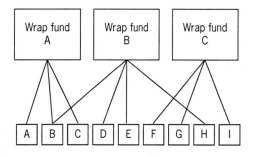

FIGURE 14.12 **Your choice of wrap fund**

As you can see, various wrap fund investments in various industries will have an effect on both your return and the risk that you face as an investor.

Fund-of-funds

In the case of a fund-of-funds, a unit trust invests in a number of other unit trusts.

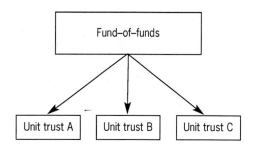

FIGURE 14.13 **A fund-of-funds**

Cameron & Dasnois (2000:103) point out that a fund-of-funds:
- should not have too many underlying unit trusts, because then you may as well invest in an index fund;
- which is international is very useful because you can invest in specific countries;
- makes your choice easier, because you do not have to pick the funds yourself;
- are not only for wealthy investors;
- give you access to a wide spread of investments;
- offer you greater diversification, even though you are investing in a single fund;
- may present you with over-diversification;
- do not have a fixed investment period;
- may have initial charges of up to 7%; and
- may have annual charges of up to 2%.

Multi-manager

This is actually an investment strategy where a 'multiple-manager' does the following on behalf of the investor (Cameron & Dasnois, 2000:105):
- decides how much should be invested in different asset classes;
- decides how much should be invested in the different sectors of an asset class;
- selects asset managers/management companies;
- monitors the performance of the asset class and sector; and

- monitors the specific instructions given to the asset manager.

The investment period depends on the specific product. The minimum investment is either R500 per month or a lump sum of R10 000. The costs will depend on the specific product.

14.5.9 Insurance products

Insurance as a long-term investment instrument was developed with the following goals in mind:
- to provide policyholders with different kinds of indemnity; and
- to provide members with a savings plan aimed at retirement.

The broad categories of need individuals experience are the following:
- income in the case of death before retirement;
- income in the case of disability before retirement;
- income at retirement;
- capital in the case of death before retirement;
- capital in the case of disability before retirement; and
- capital at retirement.

Insurance products could serve all of these needs. That is why insurance products should be included in all investment portfolios.

Endowment policies
Endowment insurance can be used to supplement pension benefits. If you are not a member of a pension scheme, an endowment policy is essential, particularly if you tend to avoid risk and are not interested in growth shares. Your attitude towards risk plays an important role in this respect.

In the case of endowment insurance, the insured amount is payable in the following cases:
- at the end of the specified term;
- at early death; or
- at a specified age.

This kind of policy is a combination of life insurance and investment, and has several applications:
- to provide capital at retirement;
- to buy a pension;
- to supplement a pension; and
- to provide cover for dependants during the policy term.

Advantages of endowment policies
- *Income tax advantages*. If the premiums are paid over a period of at least five years, the return is tax-free.

- *Cession*. An endowment policy may be ceded to someone else (spouse or financial institution). This lowers estate costs.
- *Surrender value*. An endowment policy can be surrendered (converted to cash) after three years. Within the first five years the return will be taxed, however. In an emergency, this is a good alternative or relief measure.
- *Flexibility*. Life cover can be added to an endowment policy. This means that the life cover can be increased or decreased. As soon as the need arises to decrease the life cover at a later stage, the life cover can be lowered, resulting in higher maturity value.

Lump sum investments in insurance products
Investors tend to think about insurance products as investments on a monthly basis, for example in endowment policies and retirement annuities. It is also possible for potential investors to invest lump sums in insurance products, namely:
- lump sum endowment policies;
- second-hand policies; and
- retirement annuities.

A lump sum endowment policy
You could also invest a lump sum (e.g. part of your retirement package) in a policy. One of the following investment options should be chosen when you take out a lump sum endowment policy:
- The amount may be invested for five years (without any withdrawals), after which cash withdrawals are made every month. These withdrawals are tax-free.
- Another option is to invest the lump sum for five years but to make monthly withdrawals for 60 months. The amount of the monthly withdrawal is divided equally between capital and income. The income is taxable, while the capital is tax-free. With monthly withdrawals the following will happen:
  - Interest received during the five-year period is added to the capital (investment amount).
  - The income should be indicated on the investor's income tax return, because it is taxable.
  - If the capital or income is taken only after five years, it will be tax-free.
  - Income received after five years does not have to be indicated on the investor's tax return.

Second-hand policies
Policyholders often borrow money against a policy to satisfy certain needs. These loans are interest-free. However, people sometimes borrow so much that their policies become worthless, and they want to

get rid of the burden (the loan against the policy). The value of the policy can even be equal to the loan, and the policyholder may want to sell the policy.

Some investors who want to invest in a policy are not willing to wait five years for it. They are interested in buying a second-hand policy from a policyholder. The purchase price usually amounts to the gross value of the policy at that stage, plus a 3% to 7% profit for the policyholder on the value of the policy

Of course, you should weigh up the cost against your tax savings and the numerous other benefits.

A lump sum retirement annuity (voluntary annuity)
See the discussion on retirement annuities and make sure that you know the difference between a compulsory annuity and a voluntary annuity. Note that the income and capital of a voluntary annuity are handled in the same way as the second option of a lump sum endowment policy (see above). The amount (your income) is divided between income and capital. Income is taxable, while capital is tax-free.

14.5.10 Immovable property

See Chapter 9 (Buying fixed property).

14.5.11 The securities exchange

For more information, consult Section 7.9 in Chapter 7 (Investment planning).

Shares
You can invest in shares via a stockbroker. If you do not have the knowledge or time, this is the best option. You should give the broker certain powers (or not) to make decisions about buying and selling shares on your behalf. A bank may also assist you with investing in shares. It is best to use a full-service broker (one who has a team of researchers and who offers all the necessary services).

Information about investing in shares can be obtained from the following sources:
- the Johannesburg Securities Exchange (JSE);
- full-service brokers;
- the Investment Analyst Society of Southern Africa (IAS);
- financial publications (e.g. *Business Day, Financial Mail, Finance Week* and *Finansies & Tegniek*);
- suppliers of electronic financial information (e.g. Reuters, Intelligent Network (I-Net), Dow Jones Telerate Southern Africa, Bureau for Financial Analysis (BFA) and McGregor Information Services);
- South African professional journals (e.g. *Investment Analyst Journal*);
- South African sources of information (e.g. the South African Reserve Bank (SARB) and Statistics South Africa); and
- other sources (e.g. banks and the Internet).

You may speculate with shares in the short term or make a long-term investment (more than five years). Insurance companies may also invest directly in shares on your behalf. This is accompanied by a guarantee scheme that lowers your risk and is also suitable for older investors.

You can, thus, supplement your income and/or capital by buying a computer and a share program to speculate with shares. Technical analyses (the historical analyses of share prices) are used to determine when shares should be bought or sold. Your timing must be right. Various programs are available, for example 'Sharefriend' and 'Compushare'. Via your computer package, you will receive information about developments at the Johannesburg Securities Exchange every day.

What are shares?
As a company grows, shares are issued to the public. You, therefore, invest money in the company and this money enables the company to grow. A certificate is issued as proof of the number of shares you own. These shares may be sold at a profit when the price has increased.

What is a unit trust?
A unit trust is an open trust (or fund) in which you may buy units and later sell these units back to the trust. A unit consists of securities and shares. To reduce the risk there are usually more than 20 securities and shares in a unit trust. Securities are financial assets issued by the government, state-aided institutions such as Eskom and Iscor, and larger municipalities and companies. You can also invest small amounts in unit trusts. Your capital grows and you also receive dividends (a share of the profit) and interest. In 2002 there were 369 unit trusts in South Africa and more than 35 000 worldwide.

Are shares more risky than unit trusts?
Yes, but shares offer a higher return. Investments in most unit trusts are spread over more than 20 shares, so the chance of losing money is much smaller. Different unit trusts also mean higher or lower risks for the investor, depending on the companies in whose shares the trust has invested.

How can I invest in shares?

You may invest either directly or indirectly. A direct investment means that you buy shares that are listed on the securities exchange. A unit trust is an indirect investment (money is invested in the shares of other companies). You or a broker (stockbroker, insurance broker/agent) may make direct investments as well as indirect ones.

Why invest in shares?

- You can make a relatively large profit (e.g. 30% or 50%) in a relatively short period
- You can sell your shares after a relatively short period if you want cash in your pocket.
- The value of most shares grows over the long term, so the return on your investment will be higher than the inflation rate.
- You receive income in the form of dividends.
- At present no tax is payable on dividends.
- If you are interested in capital growth, you may request that the dividends be reinvested. The company will keep the dividends and invest them somewhere else.
- A positive growth rate can be obtained over the long term (20 to 30 years).
- You can invest in companies that earn their income in foreign exchange. This will allow you to protect your rand against a depreciation in value (this is known as rand hedging).
- Capital may be increased (and lost!) quickly.

How much money do I need?

If you want to speculate, you can buy shares for a few hundred rand every now and then. You can also invest about R500 or R1 000 (or more) per month in shares. In this way, shares are obtained in the cheapest way over a long period. Remember, however, that a broker will take more trouble with an investment of R100 000 and more, because it will be possible to spread the risk of the portfolio.

What is the difference between an investment and speculation?

It depends on whether you are buying shares as an investment or to speculate.

- *An investment.* Shares are bought as a long-term investment. The investor keeps the shares for a long period (e.g. 10 or 50 years). You do not buy and sell shares all the time. The purpose is long-term capital growth.
- *Speculation.* The shares are bought and sold to make a profit. The speculator invests his or her money in the short term and is not interested in capital growth. A share may be bought today and sold after two weeks. (The period may be shorter or longer.) Speculators buy shares when they

think they are undervalued, and sell them when they think the shares are overvalued, or when the price has risen sharply.

Can people invest in shares on their own?

Yes, but it requires knowledge, time (one or two hours per day), motivation and discipline. You may follow a course, buy a computer and speculate with shares. Examples of such courses are 'WEN Software', 'Progressive Systems', 'Richard Cluver Investments' and 'Equitrac CC'. They cost anything between R2 000 and R6 000. Information about the securities exchange is supplied regularly.

Do I have to use the services of a broker?

If you do not want to speculate on your own, a broker is the answer. Choose a company that has its own research team that can provide a full range of services. You may decide yourself whether the company has to make all the investment decisions (buying or selling) on your behalf and whether you want to be consulted. You have to trust your broker with large amounts of money, so it is important that you both feel the same about risks. Discuss this beforehand.

How do share transactions take place?

Previously, shares were traded on the stock exchange floor, and there was total confusion, with everybody shouting. However, in 1997 the JET (Johannesburg Equities Trading) system was introduced. Dealers are linked to the JET system and share transactions are done by computer.

Are there any extra costs involved?

Costs are involved in most investments, including shares. Fees are payable when purchasing as well as selling shares. If you are buying, you have to pay broker's fees (1.5% of the value of the transaction, calculated according to a sliding scale – the more you buy, the lower the cost) and marketable securities tax (0.25%). When you are selling, you only have to pay broker's fees.

How do shares react to the economy?

This depends on the type of company in which you have invested. Not all industries are affected in the same way by a recession. Growth industries, such as the computer industry, would do well even in a recession. Defensive industries, such as the food and beverage industries, are least affected by the economy – people have to eat and drink. Cyclical industries (e.g. durable goods such as cars and furniture) may even do better than the economy in good times. In bad times, people will keep their old cars and furniture. Industries that are sensitive to interest rate fluctuations include financial services, the banking industry and the property industry.

What investment approach should I follow?

Shares are bought when they are undervalued and sold when they are overvalued. The value of an undervalued share is higher than the price perceived by people in the market. You, therefore, buy the share because you believe that it is worth more than the owner (shareholder) thinks. The owner believes that the share is worth less than the value you attach to it and, therefore, will sell it to you. There are two approaches to determining the value of shares:

- The *fundamental approach* consists of three steps: first a macro-economic analysis that determines and explains the course of the general economy, then the selection of an industry (e.g. electronics), and finally an analysis of the individual business in a specific branch of the industry.
- The *technical approach* analyses the historical movement of share prices.

Specific patterns and tendencies are taken into account. This gives an indication of the future course of share prices. The point of departure is that the actions of buyers and sellers will be similar in the same market conditions.

When should I invest?

First obtain information from the Johannesburg Securities Exchange, brokers and financial publications. If you are an older person you must never invest all your money in the hope of becoming rich overnight. Never invest the money you have saved for retirement, or your retirement package, in shares until you have made provision for your short-, medium- and long-term needs. Never borrow money to invest in shares. Shares should already be part of you investment portfolio (especially in your middle years). Begin investing in shares while you are young; first in unit trusts and then in shares.

What is the future of shares?

As in the past, many short- and long-term investors will either make money or lose money. Even if share prices drop, they will rise again. There is always an upward tendency. You can make a lot of money. You may also lose a lot of money, if you buy and sell shares indiscriminately and without expert advice.

How should you 'read' it?

What is the meaning of those fine-print share columns in newspapers?

- *H*: Highest price (in cents) of a share the previous day.
- *L*: Lowest price the previous day.

- *Co*: Company name (usually abbreviated).
- *Last*: Closing price the previous day (price at which the last transactions were closed).
- *Buy*: Price at which the buyers wanted to buy (how many cents buyers were prepared to pay for the share).
- *Sell*: The price at which the sellers wanted to sell (how many cents sellers were prepared to accept for the share).
- *DY*: Dividend yield.
- *Earnings per share*: Total net profit of the company divided by the total number of shares issued by the company.
- *PE*: Price-earnings ratio – this is calculated by dividing the price of the share by the earnings per share. Suppose the earnings are 20c and the share price is R1,20. The share is, therefore, sold at six times its yield (120c divided by 20c). The PE is therefore 6, which means that the present share price includes six years' earnings. If the PE was 20, it would mean that the earnings of 20 years have been included. Therefore, the higher the PE, the higher the expectation that the specific share will perform for many years to come.
- *±*: The movement of the day (the rise or fall of the daily selling price).
- *DV*: Day's volume (in hundreds or thousands – the number of shares that have been traded).

And what about those 'strange' terms?

Here are the meanings of some terms we often hear:

- *Money market*: Market for short-term funds.
- *Capital market*: Market for long-term funds.
- *Bank acceptance rate*: The interest rate banks pay for bank acceptances.
- *Bank acceptance*: A short-term investment instrument in which individuals and companies may invest. They are bought from a bank that guarantees a certain interest rate or rate of return; the amounts are very large (they amount to millions of rand).
- *Consumer price index*: The inflation rate (or average rise in the price of consumer goods).
- *Blue chips*: Blue chips are shares in the strongest companies with the best performance record.
- *Black chips*: Companies under 'black control' on the JSE.
- *Bull market*: A buying phase during which the prices of shares are continuously rising.
- *Bear market*: A tendency for share prices to fall.
- *Sentiment*: The sentiments of dealers in expectation of or following certain events or announcements concerning, for example, interest rates.
- *Gold index*: The total movement (or average price) of selected gold shares.

- *Industrial index*: The total movement (or average price) of selected industrial shares.
- *Dow Jones industrial index*: The industrial index of the American Stock Exchange.
- *Nikkei*: The total index of the Japanese Stock Exchange.

Derivatives: Options

For more information, consult Section 7.6.2.7 in Chapter 7 (Investment planning).

Derivatives: Futures

For more information, consult Section 7.6.2.8 in Chapter 7 (Investment planning).

14.5.12 Investment trusts

Laurie (1990a:109) explains how closed investment trusts work. An investment trust is a company that invests in the shares of other companies. Investment trusts have investments in both listed and unlisted companies, as well as in mines. Laurie refers to the unpopularity of investment trusts in South Africa, because of the low prices at which shares are traded. Investors invest directly in these shares in order to trade in them. Small investors, however, prefer unit trusts, because of the guaranteed buy-back prices and greater liquidity.

14.5.13 Fixed-interest-bearing securities

Securities are various financial vehicles that the state, state-aided bodies and municipalities use to obtain capital over the long term (Brümmer & Rademeyer 1982:310). With fixed-interest-bearing securities, investors are promised a given, predetermined return. There are various kinds of fixed-interest-bearing securities:
- *Gilt-edged stocks ('gilts')*: stocks issued by the state.
- *Semi-gilt-edged stocks*: debentures (IOUs) issued by state-aided bodies, such as Eskom, as well as the larger municipalities.
- *Debentures*: debentures issued by companies, consisting of:
  - debentures with or without cover of assets as security;
  - guaranteed debentures;
  - profit-sharing debentures; and
  - convertible debentures.

Preference shares are also fixed-interest-bearing securities and are a mixture of ordinary shares and debt. Preference shares are shares bearing a fixed annual rate of dividend, with a prior right over all ordinary shares in the distribution of dividends from annual profits.

Mortgage bonds (participation bond schemes) are another investment vehicle. Like the ones mentioned above, the investment amount is guaranteed at a given date in the future, and continuous interest payments are made to the participating bondholder (investor). We will not go into this type of security further, except to mention that fixed-interest-bearing securities are usually listed on the Johannesburg Securities Exchange. Listing means that securities appear on the official list of shares and can be traded on the securities exchange (Brümmer & Rademeyer 1982:10).

14.5.14 Unlisted companies

It is very risky to trade in unlisted shares. This does not imply that listed companies are not risky. The reason is primarily because an investment in unlisted companies is not protected by the Companies Act. All share investments are and always will be risky, hence the higher return.

Investments in unlisted companies are potentially catastrophic for the private investor, in the event of the unlisted company being liquidated. People who cannot afford such a risk are advised to avoid this kind of investment. Basson (1991:30,31) explains how the person in the street can identify such schemes if he or she is approached by a salesperson trying to sell them.

Basson states that salespersons tend to have very impressive, glossy brochures that could tempt anyone. Some even offer to appoint the investor to the board of directors of the unlisted company if the investment amount is large enough. Others offer the opportunity to invest in a gold mine. Investors should avoid any investments that are not in shares. Retired people should, in any event, never invest their hard-earned money in unlisted companies.

It is advisable to ask for the prospectus of any shares issue. The Companies Act requires that every prospectus should give details of the unlisted company (in this case). If the salesperson cannot provide the prospectus, his or her offer should be turned down. If a prospectus can be provided, the potential investor should ask an accountant to examine it. Where an unlisted company does have audited financial statements available, which the accountant finds acceptable, Basson (1991:31) recommends that the investor should not invest more than 5% of his or her investment portfolio in such a company.

14.5.15 Hard assets

Hard assets have intrinsic value (monetary value) as well as aesthetic value. Aesthetic value refers to the collector's value that the asset has for the owner; in other words, he or she also regards the investment as a hobby.

Some people prefer hard assets because they grow at a higher rate than the inflation rate. The returns on such investments (capital growth) are taxed (capital gains tax).

Examples of hard assets in which you can invest are:

- diamonds;
- postage stamps;
- works of art;
- gold;
- antiques;
- old coins; and
- silver.

Each of these kinds of hard asset is briefly discussed below.

Diamonds

For many people, their first experience with diamonds is when they buy an engagement or a wedding ring. It is important to obtain a valuation certificate on which the value of the ring is indicated. Many people are under the impression that they will be able to sell the ring for a large amount of money at a later stage. However, this is far from the truth.

Any property that is traded is sold at market value. By market value we mean the price a willing buyer on an open market is prepared to pay a willing seller at any given period. People who need money in a hurry could, consequently, receive a fairly low price for their diamond rings.

Purchasing diamonds for investment purposes (one carat or more) is not much different. Laurie (1990b:40) states that virtually no secondary market exists for investment diamonds. Jewellers normally do not stock such large stones and, if a client were to ask for a large stone, the jeweller would have to buy it from a supplier (diamond cutter).

Speculation in diamonds is not recommended for the average person. You need specialist knowledge about diamonds. According to Laurie (1990c:37), dealers in investment diamonds only trade with the more expensive stones. Such stones are studied in laboratories and a certificate is issued indicating their grading. At present there are a few such laboratories:

- where stones are graded according to the prescriptions of the International Association of Diamond Manufacturers; and
- where the prescriptions of the Gemological Institute of America (GIA) are followed.

Laurie (1990c:37) lists the five requirements for assessing stones:

- flawlessness (whether grey stripes and specks are present);
- colour (the less colour, the more valuable);
- size (the larger, the more valuable);
- finish (quality of cutting); and
- cut (relationships of design).

He also believes that ordinary, good quality jewellery is the best investment for the average person.

Postage stamps

Collecting postage stamps, in other words, buying and selling stamps, is both an investment and a hobby. For retirement purposes, it is suggested that stamp collecting be regarded as a hobby, unless you are extremely wealthy and literally have millions of rands to invest.

Stamp-collecting (philately) holds capital appreciation possibilities for the owner. Apart from the increase in value, the profit made when selling the stamps (or the entire collection) is tax-free.

Laurie (1990d:32) provides the following reasons for the increase in the value of postage stamps:

- there are always new collectors who are willing to pay in order to start or add to their collection;
- valuable stamps are usually fairly old; and
- the stamps contained in collections will never be produced again.

Laurie (1990d:32) provides some pointers for beginning a stamp-collection:

- Read as much as possible about stamps, the subject of philately and collectors.
- Consult collectors and make friends with them.
- Young people with minimum funds should buy one stamp at a time.
- Older people with lots of money should try to start by buying an existing collection.
- Join a stamp-collecting club.
- Build up your collection by regularly buying better stamps and selling those of lesser value.
- Be on the look-out for stamp-collections offered at auctions.
- Stick to a specific theme, such as the two best ones – stamps before the First World War or stamps about the postal service.
- Beware of fakes by always consulting experts first.
- Buy from members of the Philatelic Foundation of Southern Africa.

Works of art

In the following discussion, we refer to paintings when considering works of art as an investment.

Buying a painting is a method of combining an investment with the pleasure you derive from it. The more rare a painting and the more famous the painter, the higher the value or price will be. The value of such paintings will also increase faster than in the case of other paintings.

Not all paintings should or can be regarded as an investment. For the layperson any pretty painting with a relatively high price (measured in terms of the size of his or her pocket) may appear to be a good investment. However, this is not necessarily the case. It is advisable to consult an art expert. This will prevent an unnecessary waste of money.

De Lange (1990:35) lists the following basic guidelines when buying works of art (paintings):

- Because paintings comprise a long-term investment, they should not be bought with the intention of making a short-term capital profit.
- Famous works hold the lowest risk.
- The risk is higher when buying paintings by relatively unknown artists.
- If you buy a painting by an unknown artist, share the purchase with two or more people to spread or reduce the risk.
- Only consider promising young artists.
- Works of art should be kept for at least five years before selling them, unless the (famous) artist dies during this period.
- The costs involved in selling works of art are high (art galleries claim 40% commission and auctioneers usually 20%).
- It is not easy to sell a work of art immediately at a realistic price.
- Valuable works of art should be insured.
- Valuable works of art should be cared for and, in the case of old works, restored.
- The best methods should be used in the event of restoration.
- Paintings should be carefully hung in the right place (away from soot, damp air or sharp sunlight).
- Be careful with trendy or protest art, in other words art that is only popular in its own time and not for long afterwards.
- Try to recognise true artists in the progress and development of their work.
- Do not labour under the impression that all of Pierneef's work, for example, is expensive and then pay an exorbitant sum for one of his less successful works.

Gold

Even the most primitive civilisations used gold as a currency. From the earliest times, value has been attached to this yellow metal. Today, gold is synonymous with wealth throughout the world and it offers an excellent hedge against inflation.

Gold can be obtained in the form of jewellery, coins and gold shares in mining companies. The value of gold lies in its aesthetic appeal and in its purity. The purity of gold is measured in carats. The purest gold is 24 carats. Pure gold is soft and is often mixed with other metals to strengthen it. This reduces the purity to, for example, 12, 14 or 18 carats.

Gold is usually bought in a form that is valuable and easily traded. Boone & Kurtz (1989:610) emphasise political stability or uncertainty in a country as an important motivator for buying gold. The South African krugerrand can easily be traded in developed countries. Changes in government, the devaluation in the country's monetary unit and a change in the political power of a country are factors that make this kind of investment popular.

Antiques

Rare and attractive antiques will always be regarded as valuable. Antique furniture is very valuable but, again, requires the investor to have a certain amount of knowledge. Research should first be done about an antique before it is bought. Specialised knowledge is essential, or an investment in antiques could turn out to be a waste of money.

Old coins

Old coins enable you to spend money and still have money in your pocket. For the layperson, the same risks apply as in the case of buying works of art or stamps. People with the necessary knowledge should always be consulted first.

Those who wish to collect old coins should read the section on stamps. Similar steps can be followed. A layperson, who wishes to collect old coins, may easily buy 30 cheaper coins rather than two, which would ensure a better capital growth at the same price. A potential investor should first decide how much he or she wishes to invest. To ensure capital growth, the investment (coin) with the highest quality should be chosen.

Silver

Like gold, silver is subject to price fluctuations as a result of inflation, interest rates and political changes. A dealer once said: 'When gold catches a cold, silver catches pneumonia.' (Boone & Kurtz 1989:613) Because price fluctuations can be considerable, investors are advised to invest with the help of a professional. Once again, consult a specialist.

Other hard assets

There are many other hard assets with investment potential, such as wine, lamps from the East, first edition books and vintage cars or aeroplanes. Whether a person about to retire, or who has already retired, should decide to invest in hard assets would depend on his or her financial position and attitude towards risk, or whether he or she would rather just enjoy a hobby. A retired person should invest only a small portion (about 5%) of his or her investment portfolio in hard assets.

Advantages of hard assets
- *Aesthetic value*: Apart from the intrinsic value of these assets, they hold aesthetic value (collector's value) for the owner.
- *Transportation*: Hard assets can easily be transported, because they are light and do not take up much space.
- *Acceptability*: These assets are accepted internationally. Their value is, therefore, retained over international boundaries.

Disadvantages of hard assets
- *Theft*: These assets can easily be stolen. In 1991 a house in Krugersdorp was broken into and the owner was robbed of R2 million worth of krugerrands.
- *Loss*: It is very easy to lose one diamond or stamp.
- *Costs of insurance*: It is very expensive to insure these assets.
- *Specialist advice*: The services of specialists are required for purchasing hard assets, which could mean further expenditure. The person in the street seldom has sufficient specialist knowledge to invest in valuable paintings, for example.
- *Possibilities for selling*: It is not always possible to sell these assets within a short period of time. Although more liquid than fixed assets, capital losses are often suffered over the long term if money is required urgently.

14.5.16 A lifestyle approach towards retirement

Invest in your specific lifestyle, both before and after your retirement. However, self-knowledge is a prerequisite. Make sure that you know exactly what you like and who you are, and then make your investments to serve your lifestyle, in order to get the maximum advantage from your investments. We can call these lifestyle investments that are required to serve your goals in life. If you like photography, you can invest in this throughout your life, and even use your retirement package to serve this lifestyle one last time – this is something far different and far more than simply a return – it is all about life itself.

14.5.17 Financial discipline

Do things that force you to pay attention to personal financial planning. Amongst others you can do the following:
- Put aside one week per year when you can thoroughly investigate your personal financial situation.
- Discuss your finances with an expert (or more than one expert) twice a year.
- Keep open one day per month for personal financial planning.
- Attend four money-matters seminars per year.
- Join an investment club that will give you information about financial developments, and the opportunity to discuss and evaluate them.
- Buy new books on personal financial management every year, and study them well.

14.6 OTHER RETIREMENT PLANNING ISSUES

Retirement planning involves a great many decisions that need to be made in the course of a few years. These decisions can, unfortunately, not be set aside or be taken on your behalf, even though you may and should call in expert help. You must be involved yourself, and decide what would be the best in your life. This will ensure peace of mind before, during and after retirement. The secret is to do your homework as thoroughly as possible – this will save you a great deal of money.

14.6.1 Changing jobs

When you change jobs, you must ask the following questions, amongst others:
- Do you want to leave your retirement funds with your current employer?
- Do you want to invest your package in your new employer's retirement fund?
- Would you rather take out an annuity?
- Are you still uncertain about where you should invest your package?
- Have you considered a preservation fund?

Before blindly transferring money to some fund or other, you must find answers to these questions with the help of experts. Make sure that you get the necessary tax advice in order to avoid paying unnecessary tax, or to defer tax, and to prevent money that you have just received tax-free from becoming taxable again.

Furthermore, remember that your money may only be transferred from a pension fund to a pension preservation fund, and from a provident fund to a provident preservation fund. Make sure that you never draw the R1 800 tax-free portion, because this will be regarded as your single withdrawal from the preservation fund (up to the age of 55). If you make any further withdrawals from the preservation fund, you will be taxed on them.

The greatest advantages of a preservation fund are that you get the opportunity to think about what you want to do with your life and money, and that service years are transferred from your retirement fund. The latter means that you may get more than the tax-free lump sum amount of R120 000 during your retirement. In the case of an annuity, you would not be able to transfer the service years or to touch the money before the age of 55.

In the case of a preservation fund, you may make a single taxable withdrawal. This taxable withdrawal may be the entire amount in the preservation fund. If the entire amount is not withdrawn, but only a part, the rest has to stay there until retirement age. As in the case of an annuity, a member of a preservation fund may use the money (retire with it) before the age of 70 years. Furthermore, the proportion (one-third and two-thirds, as opposed to the lump sum) is the same for both the preservation pension fund and the preservation provident fund.

14.6.2 Your group life benefits

A soon as you retire, you lose all group life benefits, consisting of both life and disability cover. You must, therefore, try to take out disability cover or to increase it with your annuity, if you are leaving an employer but still have many years' work ahead of you. Of course, if you remain a member of your employer's group life scheme, either before or after retirement, you must do this. The reason is the much lower premiums you will have to pay in comparison with the same coverage elsewhere.

14.6.3 Taxation

It would be foolish to retire and then unwisely (without planning and informed decisions) pay a large part of your retirement money in income tax. In Chapter 5, dealing with income tax planning, income tax traps were discussed. As you know, there are various tax rules that apply to people before and after retirement. After retirement, the rebates are greater, with medical deductions for those who do not belong to a medical aid fund.

During the discussion of retirement planning, you should pay particular attention to the tax implications during retirement. This is very important, because someone who is retiring is receiving the sum total of a life's work, and should invest and apply this as intelligently as possible for the rest of his or her life.

It is important to know how to calculate the maximum single amount that may be received from retirement funds tax-free. These funds may involve fixed benefit funds, fixed contribution funds, fixed contribution provident funds and retirement annuities.

14.6.3.1 Tax-free amount of lump sums for pension, provident and retirement annuity funds

The following formula can be used to calculate the overall maximum tax-free lump sum from the three funds:

$$Z = Y + E - D$$

where:

Z = the tax-free amount
E = disallowed contributions to approved funds
D = any tax-free lump sums received in previous years

$$Y = \frac{N}{10} \times HAAS$$

where:

Y = amount to be determined
N = number of completed years of membership of the fund (N may not exceed 50 years, unless past years of service were purchased back within the rules of the fund)
$HAAS$ = Highest average annual salary (not exceeding R60 000)

Similarly, Hamp-Adams & Middleton (1992:122) suggest the following steps for the calculation of the maximum tax-free lump sum from a pension fund:

Calculate the value of Y for the $Y = \frac{N}{10} \times HAAS$

Apply this formula: $Z = Y + E - D$

Y is limited to the greater of R120 000 or R4 500 × N

Check the value of Y to determine maximum value $Y = Rx$

Apply maximum Y $Z = Y$

Add any disallowed deduction (E) that you made in previous years	$Z = Y + E$
Deduct any tax-free lump sums that you received in previous tax years (D)	$Z = Y + E - D$
The answer is the overall maximum tax-free lump sum for the pension fund	$Z = Rx$

The same steps may be followed in the case of a provident fund with the following exception. Y is limited to the greater of R120 000 or R4 500 × N and a minimum of R24 000. The minimum tax-free amount a member of a provident fund may receive is R24 000.

Membership of more than one pension and/or provident fund is treated in a different way. Firstly, the tax-free amounts of the lump sums from the different funds are calculated (Y = Rx). Then the combined maximum tax-free amount from pension, provident and retirement annuity funds is calculated (Z = Rx). When lump sums are received at retirement from both pension and provident funds, it is important to determine the years of simultaneous membership and apply this figure in the formula. The common period of, for example, five years may only be applied in the calculation of one of the funds. In the calculation of Y (greatest of R120 000 or R4 500 × N), the highest N value (including the common period of five years) will be used (Hamp-Adams & Middleton 1992:127–129).

It is also possible to retire from a pension and a provident fund at different dates. The application of the common period of membership to the fund with the higher average salary (for the employee) seems to be a wise decision, in order to increase the tax-free lump sum. When an employee retires from the first fund, SARS should be notified about which fund he or she has chosen to apply the common period to (otherwise SARS will choose the fund).

14.6.3.2 Tax treatment of a monthly pension
Where a pension is received from a pension, provident or retirement annuity fund, the pension is taxable like any other income. The tax payable will depend on the amount of the total taxable income, because the latter will determine the marginal tax rate.

14.6.3.3 Some tax avoidance guidelines
Keep in mind the following during your planning:
• If you have contributed more towards your retirement annuities than may be deducted annually by law, you may claim these amounts from future income.
• You can also bring these excessive contributions into account when calculating your taxable lump sum on retirement.
• Remember the R30 000 tax-free amount from a deferred compensation scheme.
• If you have enough retirement funds, you must take the greatest lump sum you are entitled to.
• No matter what your matrimonial property regime, both spouses may receive the same tax-free lump sum (so please do top up each other's pension benefits).
• Always protect the (maximum) number of years you have contributed towards a retirement fund (and in future investments), so as to receive the maximum tax-free lump sum.

14.6.4 Capital gains tax (CGT)

CGT was discussed in Chapter 5 on income tax planning and in Chapter 10 on offshore investments.

However, it is important that you should always keep the required documentation of everything that CGT may apply to. In this regard, think of your heirs. Therefore, keep a full CGT record for yourself and your heirs.

14.6.5 Investing your retirement package

For more information, see Section 7.14 in Chapter 7 on investment planning, or Swart (1999).

14.6.6 Medical cover

Consult Chapter 13 on health care planning.

14.6.7 Psychological preparation for retirement

As we progress through the different phases of our lives, we have to make certain psychological adjustments, the last of which occurs after retirement. We are all going to be old one day and none of us necessarily likes the idea. Nevertheless, it is inevitable, and we all have to prepare ourselves psychologically.

As we grow older and move through the last phases of life, we grow more aware of others around us who are retiring – the boss at the office, a colleague in the section where we work, our neighbour or a relative. This inevitably forces us to think of our own retirement.

Find new anchors

Before retirement, we still have various anchors that give structure to our lives, such as the post we fill, our status and our large and expensive company car. After retirement, most of these anchors disappear and we can feel that we have lost our identity. We no longer have those systems or anchors to support us.

Jordaan (1990:51) suggests that when you retire you should find new systems or anchors to give your life structure. Because your existing support systems have fallen away, you have to replace them. This does not happen automatically – it requires sound planning.

Older people should still pursue dreams for the future. You can join clubs or societies and perform community services. Hobbies can now be given all your attention. It is important to think about these things before you retire. This will prepare you psychologically for the event.

Adapt to changes

One of the characteristics of human beings is an inherent resistance to change. This resistance becomes even greater once you turn 60 or 65. After becoming an adult (say at 20 years of age) you start acquiring habits – a process lasting 40 to 45 years. You have fixed ideas about most matters, be it work, church or politics. Most retired people are not prepared to accept new ideas or ways of doing things.

Jordaan (1990:53) emphasises that a retired person's mental health depends largely on a willingness to accept changes. According to him, retired people should not respond reactively towards everything that is new or done differently. He suggests that retired people should stimulate themselves intellectually in order to ensure mental health. This will prevent them becoming isolated from the world around them, and help them to retain an understanding and perspective on reality. Without a healthy perspective on the world, emotional and mental confusion occurs.

In order to retain emotional and mental health, and to prevent mental confusion, Jordaan (1990:54–58) suggests the following:

- remain intellectually active, positive and rational;
- keep in contact with the active world;
- keep control over personal affairs that ensure an income;
- remain flexible;
- be prepared to change;
- retain membership of societies;
- go on holiday or travel regularly;
- relax sufficiently and have different activities every day;
- be as creative as possible;
- take up a neglected hobby;
- meet as may people as possible;
- be as independent as possible;
- prepare yourself for living in a home for senior citizens if this is inevitable;
- avoid stressful situations;
- stay away from your previous job – it belongs to the past;
- start taking up small or new jobs;
- avoid a fixed daily routine;
- maintain contact with sport and cultural events;
- help others where you can;
- pay attention to your personal appearance;
- do not become a slave to self-pity;
- speak positively – it stimulates your health;
- do not dwell on thoughts of depression, loneliness, hardship, bitterness and fear;
- organise your life from the beginning again;
- set objectives that have to be attained – avoid exhaustion;
- try to maintain your lifestyle;
- do not continue blaming yourself for mistakes you made during your life;
- retain your self-confidence; and
- do not give all your attention to others – think of yourself also.

Another problem retired people have is where to live. The question arises whether to remain in your own house, live with your children, in a retirement village or in the nearest senior citizens' home. These aspects are briefly discussed below.

14.6.8 Where to live after retirement

In your own home

By the time you have retired, your home bond should be paid off. If not, it will mean a lower standard of living, because of the lower income after retirement. If the home bond instalments cannot be paid, the house may have to be sold to redeem the bond. The family will have to move to a smaller house, a town house or even a home for senior citizens.

If your own house has been paid off, it is not too large and the maintenance of the house and garden is not too much to handle, you could continue living in your own home. People who find the housework physically demanding should consider moving.

Your own home has the advantage that its value increases at more or less the same rate as inflation. Consequently, it is a hedge against inflation. Another advantage is that it can always be sold at a later date at a capital profit. Money can also be borrowed with the house as security. In view of these advantages, you could use a certain amount of your pension to pay off the outstanding amount of the home loan.

The return on such an investment is even higher than the return on the most risky investment in shares. Besides, the return on such an investment is tax-free. Depending on current interest rates (borrowing rates), as well as a person's marginal tax rate, after-tax returns of between 18% and 40% can be achieved.

Before moving to a town house, a flat, a smaller house, retirement village or home for senior citizens, a retired couple should first ask themselves certain questions. Jordaan (1990:63–65) provides the following list of questions:

- Should we live in this house, or should we move to a smaller house?
- Should we remain in the same town or city, or should we move to the seaside or the country?
- What about a 'granny flat' with one of the children?
- Should we move to a retirement village or a home for senior citizens, and when will be the best time to go?
- Is the new home close to transport facilities?
- Is the house close to a place of worship, a doctor, a chemist, shops and recreational facilities?
- Is the place close to relatives, the children or friends?
- How safe is the new home (alarm, caretaker, burglar bars, in a built-up or isolated area)?
- Will the home be large enough when friends come to visit?
- Is the climate pleasant?
- Is there a large garden that has to be maintained or is it tended by others?
- Are there many stairs to climb or is the building on one level?
- Will it be possible to practice existing hobbies there?
- Do we have sufficient funds to allow us to live in our present house or intended house until our death?
- What will it cost to move house?
- Will our existing furniture or a motor car have to be sold?

A town house

Town houses are controlled and marketed in terms of the Sectional Titles Act 95 of 1986. People who consider moving to a town house should study the Act to gain insight into the rights and obligations of an investor in a sectional title unit. The following factors are important to keep in mind when buying a sectional title unit:

- exactly what you are buying (the property itself and a lock-up garage);
- all expenses apart from the purchase sum;
- all payments for the period in which the unit is occupied (levy);
- what privileges are included in the purchase sum (such as the use of a swimming pool or Jacuzzi);
- exclusive areas of use (those areas of the sectional title scheme which may be used only by the owner of a specific unit);
- whether the unit being bought (town house or flat forming part of the sectional title scheme) may be sold, and under what conditions;
- how the sectional title scheme is going to be managed, and by whom;
- who the trustees of the scheme are;
- the rights and obligations of the owner of a unit; and
- the liability of an owner for the debts of the legal entity (the group of trustees managing the scheme).

The same aspects must be checked where a scheme is sold in accordance with the Share Blocks Control Act 59 of 1980.

A retirement scheme

Sectional title and share-block schemes are often built in the form of retirement villages or retirement schemes. Certain schemes allow retired couples to buy a lifelong interest in a unit. After the person's death the unit is passed back to the scheme and can be sold again.

Advantages

- It is easy to make friends, as everybody lives in similar circumstances.
- Emphasis is placed on security.
- There are no maintenance costs.
- There is more time for yourself, because the gardens are maintained by the management.

Disadvantages

- Poor management of the scheme can cause investors to lose their money (investment).
- Monthly levies can be high.
- Levies are often low to begin with, but are then increased drastically.
- There may be a lack of medical facilities.
- Pets are not allowed.
- Parking is limited.
- There is practically no privacy.

Laurie (1990e:37) mentions some further aspects to be taken into account during or before the purchase of a unit in a retirement village. Potential buyers do not always realise that such a unit often costs more than they will obtain from the sale of their previous house. Sometimes, they have to secure an additional loan in order to buy.

You should never buy in haste. Visit several retirement villages and weigh them up against each other. Do not move out of your existing house too soon. Always keep a back door open, in the event of the scheme failing and not being completed. Buyers should not pay before the unit has been registered in their name; many people have lost money in this way. Rather buy under sectional title than otherwise.

Potential investors in such a scheme should consult a lawyer, in order to find out everything about the legal and financial aspects of the scheme. This will prevent a possible financial catastrophe.

In the country or by the sea
An investment in the country or by the sea has the advantages and disadvantages below, according to Jordaan (1990:67).

Advantages
- The purchase price of the house is lower (normally).
- Municipal costs (rates and taxes) are lower.
- Maintenance costs are lower (cheaper labour).
- Usually the climate is more pleasant.

Disadvantages
- Medical facilities are not always readily available.
- The absence of sports facilities, public transport, shopping centres, library, theatre and cultural activities.
- The area may even have no television reception, or perhaps only one channel can be received.
- The risk of theft and even attacks on your life is greater.
- Loneliness can be overpowering at a later stage if there are no relatives or friends close by.
- Incompatibility could also make one's retirement unpleasant.

Living with your children
Many retired couples decide to live with their children after their retirement. Sometimes they live in a granny flat and sometimes in the same house. People who take this step must realise that two different households are being combined – that of the children and that of the recently retired parents. Each household represents a set of rules, interests, values, customs and even ideas on bringing up children.

An explosive situation could therefore arise in and around the house, especially if the parents act as if they are in control of the household and pre-empt decisions. Retired parents must realise that they are no longer in control of their children. They have had their turn to run a household and now it is the children's turn.

It is possible for retired parents to live in peace and harmony with their children if they are prepared to allow their children to live their lives as they please. Parents should not interfere with domestic matters or get involved in arguments – this could even lead to the break-up of their children's marriage. They should make a positive contribution to the household, in order to lighten the trials and tribulations of everyday life (emotional, physical and financial, if applicable).

For example, parents should be very sensitive about the household budget and never interfere with the way their grandchildren are being brought up. Many grandparents are disturbed when they witness their children's strict disciplinary methods, and tend to interfere when the grandchildren are scolded. This can lead to a lot of unhappiness in the home. Under these conditions, it may just happen that a son- or daughter-in-law decides to pack up and leave.

Retired couples (parents in this case) should realise that, just as they want to retire happily and lead a peaceful life, their children also want to be happy with a minimum of marital strife during their economically active years. Parents should ask themselves the following questions to make sure that this alternative will work (Jordaan 1990:68):
- Is your relationship with your child and his or her partner of such a nature that arguments and tension may well arise, or is this unlikely?
- Will you be able to adapt to their lifestyle and routine?
- Would you be happy to look after the grandchildren frequently, while their parents pursue their social activities?
- Are you on the same wavelength as far as religious and political considerations are concerned, and on how to spend leisure time?
- What will happen if the children are forced to move house because of work obligations?
- Are your children happily married or are they considering a divorce?
- Are you happily married or are you considering a divorce?

It would be far better for all if the retired couple could live in a separate building, although on the same plot. It is never easy to live in the same house, since people sometimes simply want to rest or be alone.

If a retired couple does decide that they want to live with their children, they should approach them with the idea. They could offer to have a separate section built onto the house, over which they would have a life usufruct. They could even offer (if they are in a financial position to do so) to pay the outstanding amount on their children's home loan and agree to pay half of the rates and taxes, water and electricity, groceries and short-term insurance. Or they could cede a life or endowment policy to their children.

Home for senior citizens or frail-care centre
Those who are about to retire or have already retired, and no longer want to or are unable to care for themselves, could consider living in a home for senior citizens or a frail-care centre. These places provide occupants with the following: accommodation at a fairly low cost, inexpensive meals, medical care, recreational facilities and spiritual counselling. Frail-care centres also provide physical aid and support to those who can no longer walk, bath themselves and so on.

There is a big demand for such places and the waiting lists are usually long. It is necessary to apply at an early stage. The fact that there is such a demand does not necessarily increase the costs of the accommodation offered. Nevertheless, potential applicants should compare the costs involved in this option with their own financial means. Jordaan (1990:69) also points out that people who wish to live in such homes must realise that the independence they have become accustomed to will be restricted.

14.6.9 A job after retirement

Most people have to retire, whether they like it or not. The normal retirement age is 60 or 65, at which age employees are forced to leave their place of work. However, only about 6% of employees can actually afford to retire, and the rest are forced to carry on working to survive financially. The fortunate few who do retire financially independent have the choice of whether to work or pursue a hobby instead.

You may want to continue working because you are bored and miss the positive aspects of your job, such as status and recognition, a company car, job satisfaction, colleagues, relationships and self-fulfilment. Most retirees, however, simply need the money.

If you are toying with this idea, it is important to be very aware of why you want to carry on working and what you would like (and are able) to do. Jobs are increasingly hard to come by, and there are important considerations you should take into account before making your decision.

Clarify you motives
Ask yourself the following questions before starting a job:
- Do I have a choice or will it not be possible to survive financially without a job?
- Do I know my strong and weak points?
- How much money do I need?
- How much time do I have available?

- Do I want to work as an employee or as an employer?

An employee or employer who retires financially independent certainly has a choice as to whether he or she would like to carry on working or not. If this is the case, you must be clear in your motives for continuing to work. Consider your potential, your needs, desires and overall health. It is equally important that you try to limit your frustrations and stress levels after retirement, so positive aspects of a job, as well as self-fulfilment, should be pursued.

If you are not financially independent, or if you have no relatives to support you, you will probably have no other choice but to carry on working, irrespective of whether or not you would prefer to spend your retirement years in a more leisurely manner.

Either way, it is important that you consider your personal strengths and weaknesses before starting a new job.

Test your potential
Carefully evaluate your level of education, training, work experience, interests, skills and knowledge.

This 'personal situation analyses' will help give a clearer idea of your potential as a worker or as an applicant for a specific job. For example, you need to decide whether you prefer:
- working with people (or alone);
- risks – post-retirement is not the time to put yourself in a risky position;
- structured or unstructured work;
- working in an office situation or driving around in a car;
- working with people, figures or machinery; and
- high or low levels of responsibility.

You should then compare the results of this self-analysis with the nature of a specific job, for example:
- work activities (machinery, sales, writing);
- location (in an office, outside in nature, warm, cold, abroad);
- remuneration (salary, commission, car, allowances);
- job requirements (long hours, driving long distances, shifts);
- employment requirements (a degree, experience, language skills);
- standard of living (time for family, hobbies); and
- job satisfaction (challenges, promotion, motivation).

The nature of a job will determine whether you want it or not (if you have a choice). Remember, time is precious and the wrong job could mean many hours wasted that you might have spent doing something far more fulfilling.

How much money do I need?

Your primary objective in working should not be to get rich, but rather to supplement your retirement income. A pension is seldom enough to provide for your retirement needs, mainly as a result of inflation. It is, therefore, important that you calculate your retirement income deficit (RID), that is your financial requirements less your retirement income, in order to know how much money you are going to need from your new job.

Remember that upon retirement certain expenses such as bond payments, clothing and furniture will probably decrease, while others such as security and medical fees will increase.

A summary of all your costs, from average weekly purchases to monthly bills and other expenses, should be drawn up and totalled on a monthly calendar. These monthly totals should then be compared with your monthly income (your pension plus any other retirement provisions you may have made).

The difference between the two calculations is the retirement income deficit. The money you earn from a post-retirement job should, after tax, be sufficient to cover this gap.

Any additional income ought to be invested in a relatively low-risk investment like unit trusts, a life and endowment policy or retirement annuity. In this way, you provide for other future needs like estate duty, medical costs or physical disablement.

Keep your priorities straight

Time management and planning is very important after retirement. The idea is not to join the same rat race as before, with the same frustrations and stresses; so you need to decide how much time you would like to devote to your job, your family and hobbies.

Depending on what you did previously (working as an employee or employer), you might consider doing exactly the opposite. The decision is never an easy one, and you should give special attention to the advantages and disadvantages of each alternative.

Employee versus employer

The advantages of working as an employee include aspects such as job security, less risk, less stress and responsibility, and receiving pay while ill.

The disadvantages of being an employee include an oversupply of labour and, therefore, difficulty in finding a job, fierce competition from younger people within the job market, and often, as a result, less status, acknowledgement, admiration and benefits than before.

Finding a new job also means falling back on your knowledge of the personal interview (for employment) and the strength of your curriculum vitae.

These are your final opportunities to market yourself to a possible employer, so think back on all those hints and tips you followed in your early years of job-hunting:

- Be prepared to answer employer-related questions in your interview.
- The job application form should be completed neatly and legibly.
- Take special note of any news reports about the company, and find out as much as you can about its operations, target markets, position within the industry (anything you think might help you in your interview).
- Be punctual.
- Neat clothing always helps to create a good first impression.
- Answer questions clearly and simply, do not elaborate too much.
- Attach an updated CV to your application form.
- Ask questions about the job, not only about the expected salary.
- Be prepared to prove previous achievements.

If you intend to work as an employer, you have the advantage of being able to pursue real interests, with the flexibility to do what you feel like, when you feel like it, as well as being able to involve your whole family.

Disadvantages include the risk of losing all your assets, higher stress levels, which could cause a deterioration in health, and the greater effort that is required to earn a living from your own business.

Time management and planning are essential.

Buying a business

If you choose to buy an existing business instead of starting a new one, be aware of possible hidden pitfalls and costs. It is always advisable to see a business consultant before you put your retirement money into what may be an unprofitable venture.

Before you buy, give special attention to the following aspects of the business:

- market and financial viability;
- competitive position;
- the administration;
- the stock (which may be old, damaged or out of style);
- whether staff are properly trained;
- whether the lease of the building is transferable;
- the real reason(s) for selling;
- the selling price.

Whether you buy an existing business, start up a new one, or take on a job with someone else, be shrewd in your decision-making.

Be clear in your reasons for working, and spend time planning your course of action. Working after retirement is no easy decision, and the sooner you start thinking about it, the easier it will be.

There are different reasons for wanting to take on a job after retirement. Some do it for the intellectual stimulation, while others have job-related motives. Many retirees, however, have no choice but to do it for financial reasons.

14.6.10 Financial strategies at and after retirement

When to retire

Besides the decision on where to retire, it is also important to decide when to retire. By this we mean the following:
- at what age; and
- in which month of the financial year.

The longer the period (in years) over which your pension remains with your employer, the greater the benefits you will receive after retirement. In other words, it is best to retire as late as possible. The greater benefits you receive could relieve you of the need to find other work for the same or another employer if you have made inadequate provision for your retirement.

It is also important that any pension benefits, provident fund, retirement annuity and deferred compensation scheme should be received on different dates. The purpose is to keep tax liability as low as possible. If the benefits or lump sums and/or instalments are received simultaneously, the tax liability will be much bigger than if these bene-fits are received one to five years apart.

Exactly when to retire will also depend on aspects such as health, present financial means, work skills and opportunities available to you. Retirement can be deferred as long as possible or it can be combined with part-time or full-time work.

Assume that a person has about 20 years to live and considers retiring. The question that arises is whether he or she has sufficient income for the period of about 20 years. Laurie (1991:36) mentions the role of infla-tion in answering this question. Inflation halves the purchasing power of money every five to ten years (depending on the inflation rate). You would, there-fore, have to earn two to four times as much money after retirement than before retirement in order to be able to maintain the same standard of living as at present (again, depending on the inflation rate).

Laurie emphasises the fact that a person who retires at the age of 65 years receives almost double the amount of pension that he or she would have received retiring at 60 years of age. If further contri-butions are made that are large enough, the pension amount could be almost three times as much as at 60 years of age.

In what month of the year should you retire? Experts are of the opinion that March is the best month. Your income will generally always be at its peak about two to three years before retirement. If you retire in March, your income for the rest of the year will be lower than in the years before retire-ment that ended in February.

Tax-free investments

The purpose of tax-free investments is to lower your tax liability. A recently retired person, or someone who intends retiring within a year or two, may realise that his or her marginal tax rate or tax liability is or will be too high. It is possible to convert existing taxable investments to tax-free investments in order to save on tax.

We have already mentioned that a home mortgage bond represents a tax-free investment. Someone who is able to maintain his or her previous standard of living quite easily (in other words, who has made adequate provision), could buy a residential plot in a growth area with the proceeds of an investment. However, you should guard against accepting too high a risk or taking on a large bond amount (when buying fixed property) that may be difficult to repay.

Increase your pension

If you see that your pension is not going to be adequate (for example, if you have only been working for your employer for 15 years), there are two strategies open to you:
- to buy back years of service from your employer's pension fund; and/or
- to make voluntary additional monthly or annual contributions to your pension.

In the case of buying back pension from an employer, you increase your years of service and, consequently, also your pension benefits after retirement. In the case of making additional contributions, you increase your investment in the pension fund and, conse-quently, your ultimate pension benefits (the return on your investment).

If you resign from your job for whatever reason, you lose almost half of your pension in the form of tax. If you find yourself in this situation, make sure that your pension benefits are transferred to another scheme as soon as possible, if this is allowed. In this way, you will not have to pay tax and you will not lose almost half of your pension bene-fits. Not all schemes allow this, however.

Pay off your debts

It is dangerous to have large amounts of debt after retirement. Retired people could develop health problems as a result of the stress of having to continue working in order to pay off debt. There is also the fear that your estate will not be large enough to redeem the debt, which will leave next-of-kin not provided for. People who make adequate provision for estate duty liability will not have this problem.

Sufficient liquidity

It is important for retired people to possess sufficient funds, especially for emergencies. People who are obliged to make frequent loans from their children or relatives might feel that they are failures. It would be better to find light work in order to secure the necessary cash.

Buy annuities

If you have a tax problem, buy more annuities in order to reduce your tax liability.

Invest in the short term

Some people may decide, because of their attitude towards risk, rather to invest their money for a relatively short period (one to three years). Risk-avoiders regard a longer period as too risky.

Participation bonds

This kind of investment is particularly suitable for retired people. Their money is invested in fixed savings for five years, but the safety of the investment is guaranteed. At the same time, the investment produces a return.

Diversified investments

'Diversified' means that risk is spread. Retired people, in particular, should spread their risk, for example by investing in fixed property, insurance, equities and participation bonds. If a particular investment performs poorly, the investor will not lose everything. In other words, one investment compensates for another.

TABLE 14.5 **Projected cash flow after retirement**
(Source: Adapted from Boone & Kurtz 1989:650)

Income from	Husband R	Wife R	Combined R
State pension	_____	_____	_____
Pension fund	_____	_____	_____
Annuities	_____	_____	_____
Interest	_____	_____	_____
Dividends	_____	_____	_____
Policies	_____	_____	_____
Provident fund	_____	_____	_____
Deferred compensation scheme	_____	_____	_____
TOTAL INCOME	_____	_____	_____
MINUS EXPENDITURE	_____	_____	_____
Food	_____	_____	_____
Clothing	_____	_____	_____
Transport	_____	_____	_____
House maintenance	_____	_____	_____
Interest on bond	_____	_____	_____
Rates & Taxes	_____	_____	_____
Water & electricity	_____	_____	_____
Interest on overdraft	_____	_____	_____
Entertainment	_____	_____	_____
Medical	_____	_____	_____
Insurance premiums	_____	_____	_____
Personal	_____	_____	_____
Other	_____	_____	_____
Income tax	_____	_____	_____
Instalment sale payments	_____	_____	_____
TOTAL EXPENDITURE	_____	_____	_____
NET CASH FLOW	_____	_____	_____

Establish needs and requirements for retirement

It is essential to calculate (make a projection of) your cash flow after retirement with the help of a specialist (financial adviser). Such a cash flow statement will show your income (provision), expenditure and also your shortfall or surplus of funds.

Laure (1991:36) has the following suggestions for someone who has made inadequate provision for retirement:

- Consider a monthly investment in a unit trust (preferably a general fund).
- Invest in ten to 30 krugerrands and keep the investment for a fairly long period (20 years if possible).
- Invest in participation bonds.

14.6.11 Civil servants

According to Cameron & Heystek (2000:141), retirement planning for civil servants differs somewhat from that of other people. Even the calculation of the tax formula to determine the taxable lump sum has been adapted for civil servants. Therefore, make sure that you know how this amount is calculated in your case. They, furthermore, point out that you should not place retirement funds in a preservation fund, because tax-exempt benefits will be lost. Preservation funds do not accept member contributions, but only transfer benefits. Civil servants' benefits are considered to be member contributions for tax purposes, and not transfer benefits.

Cameron & Heystek (2000:147) also point out the following options for civil servants: below the age of 55 years; 55 years and older, with at least ten years' pensionable service; those between 50 and 55, with at least ten years' pensionable service; people younger or older than 55 with less than ten years' pensionable service. Let us briefly look at their guidelines:

Younger than 55 years in general

- Take the package if you have better investment opportunities.
- You can take the severance package, which will mean more money, with the normal one-third to two-thirds options.
- You can take early retirement on the Government Employees Pension Fund and retain the medical aid fund benefits. The amount will be less than for the severance package, your spouse will receive 50% of your pension when you die and you will be penalised for the years that you retire early.
- You can take the lump sum tax-free.
- The entire package may be transferred to another employer's fund

Older than 55 years, with at least ten years of pensionable service

- You receive a lump sum gratuity and a monthly pension package based on the greater of your final year's salary or your average salary over the last two years.

Those between 50 and 55, with at least ten years of pensionable service

- Gratuity and pension are calculated as above, except that the package is reduced by 3% per month for the early retirement up to and including the age of 55.

People younger or older than 55, with less than ten years of pensionable service

- You only receive a lump sum, and do not remain a member of either the pension or the medical fund.

14.6.12 Investor protection

If you have problems with you investments, due to incorrect information or fraud by your broker, you can consult the following sources of information, amongst others (Cameron & Heystek 2000):

South African Council for the Aged
PO Box 2335
Cape Town 8000
Tel: (021) 418-2145
Fax: (021) 419-5831
Black Pensioners' Organisation
Ny 53-9
Gugulethu
Association of Retired Persons and Pensioners
PO Box 403
Howard Place 7450
Tel: (021) 531-1758
Fax: (021) 531-5891
Pretoria
Tel: (012) 664-4288
Focus on Elder Abuse
5 Tussendal Ave
Bergvliet
Cape Town
Tel: (021) 712-5754
Fax: (021) 715-3344
Financial Services Board
PO Box 35655
Menlo Park
Pretoria
0102
Chief Executive Officer of FSB & Deputy Registrar of Pensions
Mr Rick Cottrell

PO Box 35655
Menlo Park 0102
Tel: (012) 428-8000
Fax: (012) 428-0221
**Deputy Executive Officer of FSB & Deputy
Registrar of Pensions**
Mr Andre Swanepoel
PO Box 35655
Menlo Park 0102
Tel: (012) 428-8000
Fax: (012) 347-0221
Ombudsman for Short-term Insurance
Mr Michael Bennett
PO Box 30619
Braamfontein 2017
Tel: (011) 339-6525
Fax: (011) 339-7063
Ombudsman for Life Assurance
Judge Jan Steyn
PO Box 4967
Cape Town 8000
Tel: (021) 674-0330
Fax: (021) 674-0902
Ombudsman for Banking
Mr Charl Cilliers
PO Box 5728
Johannesburg 2000
Tel: (011) 838-0035
Fax: (011) 838-0043
Pension Fund Adjudicator
Professor John Murphy
PO Box 23005
Claremont 7735
Cape Town 8000
Tel: (021) 674-0209
Fax: (021) 674-0185
Life Offices Association of SA
Executive Director:
Mr Gerhard Joubert
PO Box 5023
Cape Town 8000
Tel: (021) 423-2233
Fax: (021) 423-0222
Senior Citizens Employment Agency
Mr Wayne le Grange
PO Box 2107
Houghton 2041
Tel: (011) 482-4450
Fax: (011) 482-6052

14.6.13 Retirement planning for domestic workers

Unfortunately, where retirement is concerned, domestic workers are often not even aware of the following:

- the existence of a period 'after retirement';
- that they will have even less money (income) 'after retirement' than before;
- that living will be increasingly expensive; and
- that they will have to keep on working (even in old age and/or bad health) if they have not made provision for retirement.

With modern medicine, people are living much longer than before. In most families, children are no longer in a financial position (due to unemployment, for example) to support their retired parents. The government pays an old-age pension to South African citizens over a certain age (retirement age) and earning less than a certain amount of money. This is to prevent them from becoming impoverished; but, due to inflation, they will become indigent if they live long enough. As a result, domestic workers keep on working after reaching retirement age, because they cannot afford to retire.

Currently, there is no legal obligation on the employer of a domestic worker to provide for the latter's retirement. A responsible and caring employer, however, would be interested in the domestic worker's financial well-being after retirement. Retirement should be discussed with the domestic worker, and the following points should be raised:

- whether relatives or a spouse will provide financial assistance in retirement;
- whether a spouse belongs to a retirement fund;
- what would happen if a spouse should die;
- whether any savings exist for retirement and funeral costs;
- disability in the case of an employed spouse; and
- disability of the worker him- or herself.

If no savings exist, the employer may assist the domestic worker in one or more of the following ways:

- Take out an affordable insurance policy for the worker, in the worker's name. You can share in the payment of the premiums, or the full cost of the premiums can be borne by either the employer or the worker. Premiums can be as low as R30 for an insurance policy or R10 for a funeral policy.
- Open a savings account at a bank.
- Invest in unit trusts on a monthly basis. The minimum monthly premium is R50. On retirement, these unit trusts can be sold or converted

into income trusts to supply the necessary monthly income.

- A life policy can be taken out on the life of the employer. Cede this policy to the worker or relatives in the case of the worker's death. Disability cover should be included in such a policy.
- An annuity is another possibility.
- An amount could be bequeathed to the domestic worker by means of a will.

It is important that the chosen investment should provide a hedge against inflation. It should also provide capital growth.

The least any employer of a domestic worker can do is:

- inform such worker about the importance of saving for retirement;
- ask somebody else to do the informing;
- ask an insurance agent to explain how a savings plan works; and
- assist in planning such an investment.

14.7 SUMMARY

It is essential to start planning for retirement at an early stage. One or more of the methods described above should be used to make provision for retirement. It is necessary to invest in order to achieve financial independence after retirement. This is, in fact, the primary objective of personal financial management. Investments should be made constantly in view of retirement and it is essential to be familiar with the functioning, problems, advantages and disadvantages of each method (investment vehicle).

Furthermore, it is important to consider when to retire and to prepare yourself psychologically for the many changes that accompany retirement. A number of questions have to be asked and answered before taking this important step. The financial strategy followed at and after retirement must be aimed at the following:

- maintaining assets and income collected during a lifetime;
- maintaining an acceptable standard of living; and
- avoiding any situation that may hamper financial independence.

14.8 SELF-ASSESSMENT

Discuss retirement planning with specific reference to the following:

- Primary objectives.
- Retirement planning pitfalls (mistakes).
- Two methods of providing for retirement.

BIBLIOGRAPHY

Amling, F. & Droms, W.G. 1986. *Personal financial management.* 2nd edn. Homewood: Irwin.

Basson, D. 1991. Ongenoteerde beleggings hoogs riskant. *Finansies & Tegniek*: 30–31, March 8.

Block, S.B., Peavy, J.W. & Thornton, J.H. 1988. *Personal financial management.* New York: Harper & Row.

Boone, L.E. & Kurtz, D.L. 1989. *Personal financial management.* Homewood: Irwin.

Brümmer, L.M. & Rademeyer, W.F. eds. 1982. *Beleggingsbestuur.* 1st edn. Pretoria: Van Schaik.

Cameron, B. & Dasnois, A. 2000. *Personal finance: The scrapbook series.* Johannesburg: Worth.

Cameron, B. & Heystek, M. 2000. *Retirement: The amazing & scary truth.* Dainfern: Worth.

De Lange, L. 1996. Waar om te belê. *Finansies & Tegniek*: 11, col. 2, July 19.

De Lange, L. 1996. Nuwe tegniek lok belangstelling. *Finansies & Tegniek*: 50, col. 1, Aug. 23.

De Lange, N. 1990. So moet 'n maatskappy in kuns belê. *Finansies & Tegniek*: 35, col. 103, Nov. 2.

Gitman, L.J. & Joehnk, M.D. 1987. *Personal financial planning.* 4th edn. New York: Dryden.

Goldman, P.L. 1983. *A wealth optimisation model for personal financial decisions.* (M.B.A. script, Faculty of Business Administration, University of the Witwatersrand.)

Hamp-Adams, P. & Middleton, I. 1992. *Retirement and estate planning made simple.* Cape Town: Struik.

Jordaan, J.H. 1990. *Retirement planning: Your key to a happy retirement.* Cape Town: Don Nelson.

Lambrechts, H. 1996. *Unit trusts handbook.* 2nd edn. Johannesburg: Profile.

Laurie, H. de G. 1990a. *Sukses met beleggings.* 1st edn. Goodwood: Nasionale.

Laurie, H. de G. 1990b. Diamante is 'n belegging. *Finansies & Tegniek*: 40, col. 2–3, Aug. 10.

Laurie, H. de G. 1990c. Diamante is vir kenners. *Finansies & Tegniek*: 40, col. 2–3, Feb. 2.

Laurie, H. de G. 1990d. Posseëls is 'n plesier en belegging. *Finansies & Tegniek*: 32, col. 1–3, Dec. 7.

Laurie, H. de G. 1990e. Wees versigtig vir aftreedorpe. *Finansies & Tegniek*: 40, col. 1–3, May 25.

Laurie, H. de G. 1991. Wanneer om af te tree. *Finansies & Tegniek*: 36, col. 1–3, Feb. 8.

McGowan, D.A. 1981. *Contemporary personal finance.* Boston: Houghton Mifflin.

Old Mutual. 1992. In Hamp-Adams, P. & Middleton, I. *Retirement and estate planning made simple!* Cape Town: Struik.

Oldert, N. Lambrechts, H. & Still, L. 1998. *Unit trusts handbook.* Johannesburg: Profile.

Personal Finance. 1996. Personal finance to give a new view on your investments. *Pretoria News Weekend – Personal Finance*: 14, col. 4, Nov. 23.

Personal Finance 1996a. Surfing the Internet for your investment needs. *Pretoria News Weekend – Personal Finance*: 14, col. 3, Sept. 7.

Sake-Rapport. 1996. Kyk na jou rand met die beleggings. *Rapport: Sake-Rapport*: 4, col. 1, Apr. 28.

Swart, N.J. 1996. *Personal financial management.* 1st edn. Cape Town: Juta.

Swart, N.J. 1999. *Investing your package: All you need to know.* Pretoria: University of South Africa.

South Africa (Republic). 1980. Acts of the Republic of South Africa – Land (Act 59 of 1980.) Pretoria: Government Printer. (Share Blocks Control Act.)

South Africa (Republic). 1986. Acts of the Republic of South Africa – Land (Act 59 of 1986) Pretoria: Government Printer. (Sectional Titles Act.)

Sunday Times. 1996. Keeping track of every move. *Sunday Times – Business Times*: 10, col. 5. May, 12.

Trace, A.P. 1985. *The bond book.* Honeydew: Laymans Guide.

Van Tonder, J. 2000. Begin betyds geld belê vir jou oudag. *Geld Rapport*: 1, col. 3–4.

CHAPTER 15

EMIGRATION PLANNING

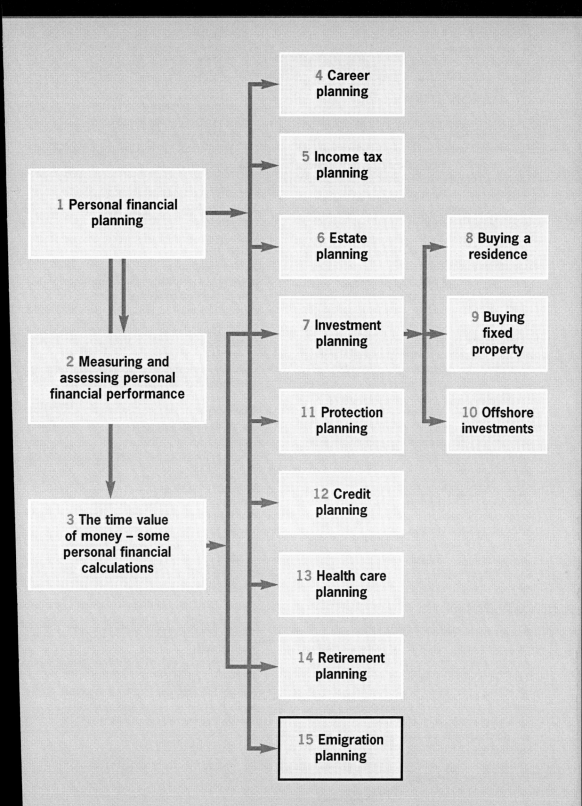

1 Personal financial planning

2 Measuring and assessing personal financial performance

3 The time value of money – some personal financial calculations

4 Career planning

5 Income tax planning

6 Estate planning

7 Investment planning

8 Buying a residence

9 Buying fixed property

10 Offshore investments

11 Protection planning

12 Credit planning

13 Health care planning

14 Retirement planning

15 Emigration planning

15.1 LEARNING OUTCOMES

After studying this chapter, you will be able to:

- List the many questions you have to answer when you consider emigrating.
- Identify the research that should be done before you can emigrate.
- Explain what will happen to your South African assets.
- Identify which financial factors to consider about South Africa.
- Identify which financial factors to consider about the foreign country.
- Evaluate the pros and cons of emigration.

15.2 INTRODUCTION

In the past decade, a few hundred thousand people have emigrated from South Africa. It is only logical that you do not simply pack your bags one day and wake up in another country the next. Unfortunately, it is not that simple. You need to make countless calculations before emigrating. There are many reasons for this; amongst others, it is about determining whether a person or family will be able to survive financially in the foreign country. Normally, such people also have a severance or retirement package from an employer.

If you receive such a package and you have already decided to emigrate, the package should be invested in such a way that it will facilitate your emigration. However, it is important to study and answer the questions below before you do so. Do not invest your funds before you have obtained all the information about the emigration process and the costs involved. You could save unnecessary investment costs and avoid making the wrong investment.

The decision to emigrate is by far the most dramatic decision any South African can make. Usually it is a well-planned decision, because you feel you can no longer live with:

- increasing violence;
- a lack of freedom to travel safely;
- continuous supervision of children after school or in other places;
- fear of travelling at night because of hijackings and rape;
- numerous murders of old people;
- farm killings;
- the very high AIDS risk;
- the lack of investor confidence;
- the depreciation of the value of the rand against the currencies of developed countries;
- the never-ending needs of the masses, for whom the same group of taxpayers must pay;
- the millions of illegal immigrants;
- the misuse of resources because of poor management;
- fewer employment opportunities;
- the deterioration of the educational system because of dwindling funds;
- the lowering of standards;
- the high cost of private health care;
- the enormous tax burden; and
- increasing financial pressure to lower existing standards of living.

However, do not forget the positive aspects:

- family members who will be left behind;
- many friends;
- the support offered by these people;
- a mild climate;
- familiar conditions;
- your current status and reputation;
- your history and education;
- the convenience of having domestic help and a gardener;
- a large house and more than one car (where applicable);
- a familiar work and financial environment; and
- a more familiar environment to retire in.

It is not the aim to encourage people to leave South Africa, but to provide those who are considering emigration with the financial information they require. We, therefore, need to find answers to the following questions:

- Can I afford to emigrate?
- To which country should I emigrate?
- Which and how many assets or how much capital may I take with me?
- What is going to happen to the assets I leave behind?
- May I transfer income from the assets I leave behind to a foreign country?
- Should I place my South African assets in a trust?
- How much does it cost to emigrate?
- Which financial aspects should I consider about South Africa?
- Which financial aspects should I consider about the foreign country?
- What is the exchange rate and the value of the rand?
- How do I go about emigrating?

Far away – oh far away –
We seek a world o'er the ocean spray!
We seek a land across the sea
Where bread is plenty and men are free,
The sails are set, the breezes swell –
England, our country, farewell! Farewell!

(*The Illustrated London News*, 6 July 1850)

You should certainly make emigration planning part of personal financial planning, because your quality and standard of life in the foreign/new country is so important.

It may sound as if you are gladly leaving a country, but it involves many emotions. The moment you depart by ship or plane, you remember the good times, all the while hoping for even better times in the new country.

Particularly in America, a country made up of immigrants from all over the world, a great deal of emphasis is placed on the official immigration policy. The same is true of other countries. Many articles have been written and many debates held among politicians to determine the desirability or otherwise of immigration. The greatest advantage is probably the skills a country gains. The greatest disadvantage is competition for jobs, particularly where (as in South Africa) there is a shortage of jobs. Unskilled immigrants exacerbate the latter situation and contribute to a country's socio-economic problems.

Matloff (1996) also points to the fact that (particularly in America) the downside of immigration falls on the poor minority groups. Even in South Africa, poor unemployed people raise their voices against illegal immigrants (with or without skills). Countries look askance at those who simply want to come and eat, sleep and drink. Oberlink (1995) poses the following questions: 'Does our nation need more workers competing for a limited number of jobs? Do our overburdened and overcrowded schools need more students crammed into the classrooms? Will our scenic parks be more enjoyable when shared with additional multitudes? Does precious wildlife habitat become easier to save in the face of additional human encroachment?'

Of course, such questions need to be asked by a country, whether it draws immigrants or not. We are thinking particularly of overcrowding, education and learning skills, especially in South Africa and Africa. Echoing Oberlink (1995): 'It is hard to believe that we need more workers, skilled or unskilled. If we do, let us train them, not import them.'

You, therefore, need to supply proof of the skills and resources you are able to take to the new country. It is an advantage if a new business can be established there, or jobs created (apart from new products and/or services). You should not create the impression of someone who is looking for welfare or will be burdening the state. Prove that you can make a positive contribution.

It will also be to a country's advantage if you can offer a product or service for which there is a strong demand; similarly, if there is a shortage of workers or businesses in a particular industry, and the country is in a growth phase.

Remember that the workers of the 'new country' will prefer unskilled immigrants, while companies, and the government, will prefer skilled immigrants. Skilled immigrants earn more, will pay more taxes and will make less use of social and welfare services.

Kennedy (1996) points out the economic theory that suggests that immigrants are an advantage to a country. The countries they came from trained these immigrants (to give them access to the work-force) and carried the costs involved. Such countries are, therefore, subsidising the countries to which the immigrants go. Of course, we are talking about skilled workers in this case.

15.3 CAN I AFFORD TO EMIGRATE?

Most people want to emigrate to countries such as the USA, Canada, the Unites Kingdom, Australia and New Zealand. Unfortunately, before these countries will accept you as an immigrant, you have to meet certain requirements, such as close links with them through birth or ancestry. Certain countries also have capital and income requirements. You may find that if you have to take R1 000 000 in capital to a country, yet earn only a few thousand rand in income, the result will be that you cannot afford to emigrate. Personal wealth is a prerequisite for emigration. Find out what a country's financial and other emigration requirements are before you try to emigrate to that country.

It is easier for highly skilled (professional and graduated) young people to emigrate than it is for others (few or no skills, much older, etc.). The latter group will find it difficult to become settled in any country. Spring (1998:18) provides the following information for various countries, based on those countries' unique immigration requirements:

Britain

Britain is probably the most difficult country to emigrate to or get work in. Even people with a British passport may not be able to live in Britain permanently. If your parents (father or mother) were born in Britain, British citizenship must be registered prior to your 18th birthday. If your grandfather was born in the UK, if you were born between May 1962 and December 1982 and your birth was registered within 12 months, you are entitled to British citizenship. A person with parents or grandparents who were born in the UK may work in Britain for four years. Such a person can then apply for permanent resident status, and later for British citizenship.

If it is not possible to emigrate to a country on the grounds of family ties, Spring points out that family association is a possibility. You can, therefore, marry a British citizen. If someone marries simply to gain citizenship rights, however, the British authorities will not grant residence rights.

Ireland

It is much easier to gain access to Ireland, where access is based on blood rights. If either of your parents was born in Ireland, you may apply for Irish citizenship. However, you need the original of your parent's Irish birth certificate, marriage certificate and/or death certificate. The same applies in the case of Irish grandparents.

Germany

It is relatively easy to emigrate to Germany, if you can prove German ancestry, and are able to speak German.

United States of America

You can gain US citizenship by marrying a US citizen who is older than 21 years, has not been found guilty of a serious offence, and does not have an infectious disease. This means you can gain a temporary 'green card', which is valid for two years. After two years you are questioned again, before a permanent 'green card' is issued.

Australia

Australian citizenship can also be obtained by means of association. An Australian can sponsor an immigrant. Amongst others, this sponsor may be:

- a spouse;
- an unmarried child;
- a parent (where all children are in Australia);
- a dependent relative;
- the only living brother/sister or non-dependent child; or

- a relative who provides for your needs (as a disabled person).

New Zealand

A New Zealand citizen can sponsor you as well. In New Zealand the concept of 'spouse' is interpreted more loosely, and may include a partner. The requirement is a stable relationship of two years for heterosexuals and four years for homosexuals.

15.4 TO WHICH COUNTRY SHOULD I EMIGRATE?

In addition to your financial position and ancestry there are further factors to consider, such as: finding a job, whether you have family in the new country to help you, the standard or quality of life you will be able to maintain, whether that country has an immigration programme to attract certain immigrants, whether that country has entered into a tax agreement with South Africa to avoid double taxation, and the exchange rate between the currencies of that country and South Africa.

15.5 WHICH ASSETS AND HOW MANY (HOW MUCH CAPITAL) MAY I TAKE WITH ME?

Reserve Bank exchange control regulations allow certain banks (authorised dealers) to deal in foreign exchange. You are allowed to take the following items out of the country, subject to certain financial limits (December 2002):

TABLE 15.1 **How much may I take?**

Item	Limit (R)
Household and personal belongings	1 000 000
Settling-in allowance, single person	200 000
Settling-in allowance per family	400 000
Travel allowance per adult per year	140 000
Travel allowance per child under the age of 12 per year	45 000
Study allowance per student per year	140 000
Study allowance per student accompanied by a spouse per year	280 000
Travel allowance per student per year	45 000
Travel allowance per student accompanied by a spouse per year	90 000

All capital brought into South Africa by natural persons after 1 July 1997 may be taken out of the country at any time. Note that a widower or widow and his or her dependants are regarded as family. Note that krugerrands require additional or special export permission.

Cameron & Heystek (2000:291) point out the following in regard to your foreign investment allowance:

- If you have already made use of the R750 000 foreign investment allowance, it will be deducted from your emigration allowance.
- If both you and your spouse have made use of the R750 000 (each), only the husband's allowance is used in the calculation, which still leaves the household with an additional R750 000.
- If the emigration allowance is not adequate to allow you to settle in the foreign country, you may apply to the Reserve Bank for an increased allowance.

15.6 WHAT WILL HAPPEN TO ASSETS THAT ARE LEFT BEHIND?

Assets that have been left behind are called blocked funds. They may be used, amongst others, as follows:

- daily allowance when visiting South Africa;
- the cost of travelling to and from South Africa;
- investments in listed shares in South Africa;
- the reinvestment of unit trusts in other trusts;
- the payment of overdue income tax;
- the payment of school fees and the costs of tertiary education for children who remain behind;
- the payment of property rates;
- membership fees of South African clubs and associations;
- the payment of insurance premiums;
- the payment of maintenance after a divorce;
- the remuneration of accounting officers and attorneys who are handling assets in South Africa;
- the payment of expenses for subsistence during visits to South Africa (R75 000 per family per year, R3 000 per day per adult and R1 500 per day per child under the age of 12);
- the payment of hospital, medical and dental fees during visits to South Africa;
- mortgage payments on South African property; and
- donations and support to third parties in South Africa to a maximum of R100 000 per year.

If, for example, you have a maturing annuity, you should rather not withdraw the one-third as a lump sum. Rather buy an annuity for the full amount. This means the one-third is not left behind in South Africa as blocked funds. As you will have gathered from reading Chapter 10 on local considerations, you will only be able to go abroad (and invest there permanently) if you have received tax clearance from the Receiver of Revenue (and, therefore, the Reserve Bank).

Spring (1999:15), furthermore, points out the following regarding a retirement annuity when emigrating:

- A retirement annuity (or other insurance policy) is not simply transferable to a foreign country.
- The only thing that can always be transferred is your insurability.
- If there is an insurer associated with your present insurer, it will offer you the same amount of life cover benefits as you are currently enjoying (no matter your present medical situation, and without a medical examination).
- You are given time to conclude the same contract as in South Africa with your new insurer, and to be placed on risk.
- However, the investment value of the policy is not transferred concurrently.
- Because term insurance and income protection policies have no investment value, they may be transferred.
- The investment value of a policy may be transferred only as part of the settling-in allowance.
- Before people go abroad, they may, amongst others:
  - surrender their policies. (The policy cash value is, therefore, requested. The policy may also be bought as a second-hand policy in the second-hand market. The cash may be left in South Africa as blocked funds, or used as part of the settling-in allowance.)
  - make them paid up. (The payment of premiums, therefore, ceases. As soon as the policy reaches the maturity date, the proceeds become part of your blocked funds.)
  - continue paying premiums from blocked funds, or from abroad.
- Consolidate your policies to save costs, and pay your policy annually.
- The income is subject to exchange control, as is the one-third if you wanted to take it out (it becomes part of the settling-in allowance).
- If you bought a voluntary annuity, the interest would be transferable, and the capital would become part of your blocked funds.

- This is why it is usually better to buy a compulsory annuity with the whole amount, and not take the one-third.
- Try to maintain the retirement annuity if you are older than 55 years – contributions may be paid from blocked funds.
- After your retirement, the entire pension will be fully transferable.
- However, remember that you need to have made contributions to a retirement annuity for some time, or exchange control will regard the sudden taking out of an annuity as suspicious and act accordingly.
- If you are much younger than 55 years, make the retirement annuity fully paid up.

Persons who do not really emigrate cannot receive their pension payments abroad. People often spend a great deal of the year abroad for many years in succession. It would, therefore, be very convenient for them to receive their pension abroad, but unfortunately exchange control does not allow this. This applies to both a pension and an annuity.

It is different for those who have emigrated. Annuities may be received abroad if the annuity was taken out more than five years previously. If the annuity was taken out in the past five years, the interest/income portion will be paid out abroad, but the capital portion will remain behind as blocked funds. In the case of a provident fund, the whole amount may be invested in an annuity, for example. The interest portion of this annuity may be paid out abroad, while the capital portion becomes part of your blocked funds (Horrocks 1998:14).

The lump sums of annuities and pension funds will always be treated as blocked funds.

15.7 MAY I TRANSFER INCOME FROM MY REMAINING ASSETS TO A FOREIGN COUNTRY?

You are allowed to earn income from another country (South Africa) in the form of interest, profits, dividends, the distribution of income by close corporations, director's fees, pension from a registered pension scheme or fund, cash bonuses from insurance policies, income from a trust *mortis causa* (testamentary trust), income from a property trust, income from letting fixed property, and pension for retirement because of disability or poor health.

The net income earned on South African assets may be transferred to a foreign country via the normal bank channels. You should, therefore, convert as many assets as possible into cash or income-producing investments before you emigrate. This is particularly important if you think that you might not have sufficient income to live on in your new country of residence.

15.8 SHOULD I PLACE MY SOUTH AFRICAN ASSETS IN A TRUST?

If you place your South African assets in a trust while you are still alive (a trust *inter vivos*) you will have to pay very high transfer duty and conveyancing fees on fixed property. Transfer duty alone could cause cash-flow problems.

A trust (such as a testamentary trust) could help the next generations to save on estate duty and capital gains tax. Remember that a trust does not offer any income tax benefits for non-residents.

15.9 WHAT WILL IT COST TO EMIGRATE?

Shipping your household appliances and car(s) are direct costs that may amount to as much as R80 000 for the average household. An unemployed South African emigrant (without a two-year work contract or permanent residence) may also be required to pay a deposit at customs.

15.10 WHICH FINANCIAL FACTORS SHOULD I CONSIDER ABOUT SOUTH AFRICA?

The most important factors probably have to do with your retirement. Find out whether your pension fund or provident fund will allow you to withdraw capital when you emigrate. In your new country, you may have to wait for this capital until you have reached the normal retirement age. Also find out whether you will still receive cover from your group benefit.

Remember that you will have to wait until the age of 55 for your retirement annuities and that you may lose a part of, or all, the tax benefits when you are in a foreign country. Your needs and objectives will, therefore, determine whether you will stop your premiums or keep on paying them over the long term. You may, however, use your living annuity for emigration purposes.

Try to sell loose assets while the market is good (in a seller's market), or keep your assets for visits to South Africa. Ask an estate agent to manage your property (or properties) in your absence.

If you keep a business in South Africa, it will be advisable to appoint somebody with the necessary authority to make decisions. Also appoint an accountant who has knowledge of international tax.

Buy timeshare (RCI-affiliated) and exchange it later for overseas timeshare to obtain more capital/assets in a foreign country.

15.11 WHICH FINANCIAL ASPECTS SHOULD I CONSIDER ABOUT THE FOREIGN COUNTRY?

Make sure that you know how the tax system of your new country operates. Find out whether your South African investments and income will be taxable. Choose the country with the lowest tax rate and pay your taxes there.

15.12 WHAT ABOUT THE EXCHANGE RATE AND THE VALUE OF THE RAND?

If you emigrate to a country with a stronger economy, you will soon find out how little your South African rand, and the money you have saved for your retirement, is worth. Make sure that you are aware of the effect of the exchange rate and the poor buying power of the rand on your financial future, before you emigrate.

15.13 HOW DO I GO ABOUT EMIGRATING?

- Consult with your bank and find out as much as possible about emigration and how it will affect you.
- Obtain the necessary forms from the Reserve Bank (www.resbank.co.za).
- Consult financial experts about emigration and international financial planning.
- Get tax clearance.
- Appoint an accountant, an attorney, a bank manager and a business manager to perform your duties on your behalf.

Spring (1998:16) gives the following practical guidelines that should be followed by every person who is emigrating:

Always keep financial independence after retirement in mind when you plan or prepare to emigrate.

- As regards furniture, it is important to remember that the 'new' house abroad will usually be smaller than the 'old' one in South Africa.
- The choice of a moving company is made after having asked for a few quotations (get the addresses in the Yellow Pages).
- The moving company will help with the required paperwork (forms).
- Make sure the power supply in the new country is the same as in South Africa. If not, leave all electrical equipment behind (sell/give away).
- Make sure the television will work (South African sets usually work in the United Kingdom, but not in Europe).
- Make sure there is no import ban on ivory or furs.
- Special export documents are required for cars, motorbikes, animals, firearms and wines (there are import regulations for cars to the United States of America, carpets to Australia and firearms to Great Britain).
- Take your own car, because buying one abroad will reduce your foreign settlement allowance considerably.
- Contact the Automobile Association to find out about the availability of spare parts in a particular country.
- The moving company's representative should be able to give you advice about which property you should take to a particular foreign country, and which you should leave.
- Ainslie (1998:16), furthermore, points out the contents of the written quotation you should receive from the representative:
  - all services on a 'residence to residence' basis;
  - packing at home and into the container;
  - clearance from South Africa, shipping, customs clearances in the destination country and unpacking at the new home;
  - storing goods if you request this;
  - the insurance required;
  - a complete list of everything that is shipped;
  - the foreign exchange rate on which the quotation is based; and
  - do not accept a quotation on 'volume', unless you know exactly what you want to ship.
- Your goods will be transported in a 6-metre or 12-metre container.
- The larger container should also be able to take your car.

- It takes several months to ship goods abroad – if you need something urgently, you should send it by air freight (as 'unaccompanied baggage').
- Make sure that insurance claims will be paid out in the currency of the country you are emigrating to.
- Beware of any type of underinsurance (see the averaging principle in Chapter 11 on protection planning).
- Some countries have strict quarantine regulations, if you want to take your pets, while other countries require only a letter from your vet to indicate that your animals have had the required vaccinations.
- Various companies handle the transporting of pets.
- Find out as much as possible about the regulations in the city and region you are going to.

15.14 OFFSHORE INVESTMENTS

Of course, prospective emigrants need to gather information about the various types of offshore investment. Some investments will be made while you are still in South Africa, and others as a citizen of the new country. You will make use of a broker, and all the sources of information in the new country for the latter.

Study Chapter 10, which deals with global investments. When you have studied the various types of foreign investment, you should particularly note the local and foreign considerations. This will help you to avoid possible pitfalls in this regard.

15.15 SUMMARY

It should be clear from this brief chapter that emigration planning could positively or negatively affect the rest of your life in a foreign country. It is, therefore, important that people contemplating this great and dynamic step should have enough information in order to take informed decisions about their future and new lives. Remember the important role played by money and other resources in determining a particular quality and standard of life, both now and in the future.

15.16 SELF-ASSESSMENT

- You are thinking of emigrating. Discuss the main local and foreign financial factors that might influence your decision.

BIBLIOGRAPHY

Ainslie, T. 1998. In Spring, M. Plan properly to take the heartache out of emigrating. *Sunday Times Business Times*: 16, col. 3, July 26.

Cameron, B. & Heystek, M. 2000. *Retirement: The amazing and scary truth*. Randburg: Paarl.

Horrocks, P. 1998. No pension payments overseas for part-emigrating. *Sunday Times Business Times*: 14, col. 1–7, Sept. 13.

Illustrated London News. 1850. The tide of emigration to the United States and to the British colonies. *The Illustrated London News*, col. 1, July 6.

Kennedy, D.M. 1996. Can we still afford to be a nation of immigrants? *The Atlantic Monthly*: 11, col. 1, Nov.

Matloff, N. 1996. *How immigration harms minorities.* Summer 1996. Web site: ftp://heather.cs.ucdavis.edu/imm.html

Oberlink, R. 1995. The case for shutting the door. *Los Angeles Times*, col. 1, Nov. 3.

Spring, M. 1998. How to emigrate if you don't have the right skills. *Sunday Times Business Times*: 18, col. 7–8, Oct. 18.

Spring, M. 1998. Plan properly to take the heartache out of emigrating. *Sunday Times Business Times*: 16, col. 1–5, July 26.

Spring, M. 1999. What to do about your RA should you emigrate. *Sunday Times Business Times*: 15, col. 8–9, July 25.

Swart, N.J. 1999. *Investing your package: All you need to know*. Pretoria: Unisa.

Swart, N.J. 1999. *Hoe moet ek my pakket belê*. Pretoria: Unisa.

Index